SMITHSONIAN
HANDBOOKS

BIRDS

OF THE WORLD

SMITHSONIAN HANDBOOKS

BIRDS
OF THE WORLD

COLIN HARRISON AND
ALAN GREENSMITH

MARK ROBBINS
Editorial Consultant

LONDON, NEW YORK, MUNICH,
MELBOURNE, and DELHI

Note on Classification
The arrangement of bird families in this book is based on the recently published work of
Richard Howard and Michael Moore. For the names of genera and species, the authors
have drawn on the work of Charles G. Sibley and Burt Monroe.

Editor Edward Bunting
Art Editor Chris Walker
Editorial Assistant Jeanette Cossar
Design Assistant Christina Betts
Production Caroline Webber
Picture Research Catherine O'Rourke
US Editor Charles A. Wills
US Consultant Mark Robbins, Department of Ornithology,
Academy of Natural Sciences of Philadelphia

First American Edition, 1993
Reprinted in 2000
Second American Edition, 2002
2 4 6 8 10 9 7 5 3 1

Published in the United States by
Dorling Kindersley, Inc.
375 Hudson Street
New York, New York 10014

ISBN 0-7894-9390-X

Computer page makeup by
The Cooling Brown Partnership, Great Britain
Text film output by P4 Graphics Limited, Great Britain
Reproduced by Colourscan, Singapore
Printed and bound in Singapore by Kyodo Printing Co.

See our complete product line at
www.dk.com

CONTENTS

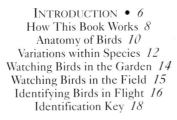

INTRODUCTION

Why have birds so captured the human imagination? Sixty million Americans watch birds. Some treat it as a quiet pastime, observing and perhaps photographing backyard species that frequent feeders and birdbaths. Others treat it as a sport, traveling widely in search of new species, or competing in "birdathons" to raise money for conservation organizations.

IN FACT, THE MONEY spent on watching birds (on equipment, travel, books, and art) is staggering. Surveys show that birding brings millions of dollars each year to places like Cape May in New Jersey, Point Pelee in Ontario, and southeastern Arizona. Birding in the USA alone is a $20 billion a year industry.

adjustable nose cone can be raised for streamlining at high speed

broad wings help provide lift during slower flight

ibises use their curved bills to probe mud for food

STRENGTH VERSUS SKILL
Aircraft are vastly superior to birds in power, speed, and range, but birds are much more maneuverable. Birds, for instance, do not need a runway to take off or land.

broad wings enable the ibis to maneuver skillfully at low speeds

THE AGE OF THE QUILL
One indispensable contribution birds have made to our civilization was to provide quills (*right*) for writing. The central quill of a large feather, usually from a goose, was trimmed with a penknife and the point sharpened and split to form a nib. The hollow quill is ideally suited for holding the ink.

trimmed shaft of feather

ORNAMENTAL HEADGEAR
An ostrich provided the plume for this cavalry helmet (*below right*), while the whole design bears a striking resemblance to the head plumage of a bird, such as the Royal Flycatcher (*below*). In the flycatcher, however, the crest is aligned sideways, rather than front to back.

Symbols of Honor and Wealth

German Army
Badge from
World War I

US Army
Distinguished
Service Medal and Cross

US Army Cap Badge
with Eagle

Congressional
Medal of Honor

Singapore $500 Note with
Symbolic Golden Oriole

Canadian $1 Coin with
Common Loon

New Zealand $20 Note
with New Zealand Pigeon

Birds in Many Cultures

For many cultures, birds are an integral part of the social fabric, playing a part in folklore, art, and religion. In South America, for example, feathers are an essential feature of ritual garments; they show membership and status in social groups and provide a sense of spiritual identity and protection.

Economic and Social Value

Birds also supply our most basic needs: food, tools, and clothing. Domesticated birds (and their eggs) are the basis of our poultry industry. We have used bird feathers for quill pens and fletched arrows and as insulation in goose-down coats and comforters. Birds have also catalyzed scientific discovery: their study has helped us to understand the physics of flight. The canary in the coal mine has a new equivalent – birds are indicators of the health of our environment. The decline of our migratory songbirds increased efforts to protect habitat in their breeding, stopover, and wintering areas.

Birdkeeping for Pleasure

Many people keep birds as pets. Parrots, Cockatiels, and other unusual species provide bird lovers with colorful and vocal companionship at home. The ancient art of falconry remains popular, and falconers' knowledge of the rearing of birds of prey has assisted in the reintroduction of threatened and endangered species into natural habitats. Birds bring us wonder, mystery, and pleasure. In their limitless variety of color, song, and behavior, birds embody a magic that we may celebrate, but only they can possess.

Peregrine Falcon on the hand

leg leashes are known as "jesses"

David S. Wiedner
Research Associate, Department of Ornithology, Academy of Natural Sciences of Philadelphia.

HOW THIS BOOK WORKS

THIS BOOK is arranged according to the major groups of birds: non-passerines, which include the largest birds, and passerines, which include the songbirds. Each entry describes a separate species or kind of bird. The entries are arranged in order of their scientific classification. Birds that belong to the same family are grouped together. Within each family, closely related birds are placed near each other. Readers can find a bird by its habitat and behavior in the Identification Key on pages 18–37, or by its scientific or common name in the Index. Each entry covers appearance, habitat, food, nest, and distribution, thus giving the most basic identification features. In many entries, additional details, such as song, calls, or behavior, are provided.

PLUMAGE ILLUSTRATIONS

Except when stated otherwise, the photograph in each entry shows the adult male. Many birds also have other plumages (*see pp. 12–13*), and the most important of these are illustrated beside the photograph.

SUBSPECIES   FEMALE   JUVENILE   MALE CREST

SUBSPECIES   FEMALE   JUVENILE   WING PATCH   MALE TAIL

DISTRIBUTION MAPS

These show where the bird is likely to be seen, either all year round or at certain times. For example, Purple Martins breed in North America and winter in Brazil; the map also shows the area through which they migrate. By contrast, in the western part of their range, European Robins stay all year, but in the east they are migrants. The Australian Brush-Turkey is a non-migrant, remaining in the same area all year round.

PURPLE MARTIN

EUROPEAN ROBIN

BRUSH-TURKEY

SCALE SILHOUETTES

These show the bird next to a copy of this book. For reasons of space, birds above 20 in (50 cm) long are shown in a smaller scale, so that the book appears in two different sizes. All birds are measured fully stretched out, from beak to tail tip. In species in which male and female look different, the male is illustrated.

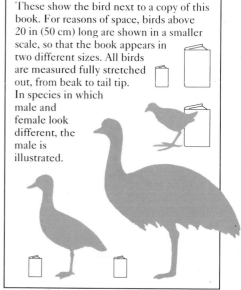

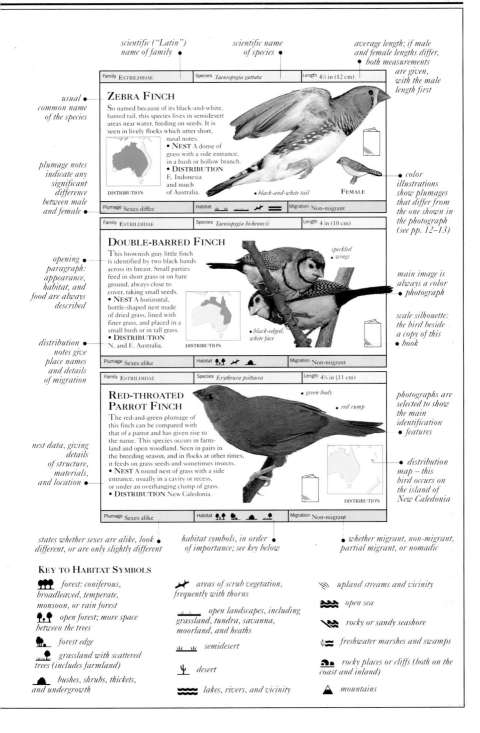

scientific ("Latin") name of family •

scientific name of species •

average length; if male and female lengths differ, both measurements are given, with the male length first

usual • common name of the species

Family ESTRILDIDAE | Species *Taeniopygia guttata* | Length 4¾ in (12 cm)

ZEBRA FINCH

So named because of its black-and-white, barred tail, this species lives in semidesert areas near water, feeding on seeds. It is seen in lively flocks which utter short, nasal notes.
• **NEST** A dome of grass with a side entrance, in a bush or hollow branch.
• **DISTRIBUTION** E. Indonesia and much of Australia.

DISTRIBUTION

plumage notes indicate any significant difference between male and female

• *black-and-white tail*   **FEMALE**

color illustrations show plumages that differ from the one shown in the photograph (see pp. 12–13)

Plumage Sexes differ | Habitat ⚬⚬ | Migration Non-migrant

Family ESTRILDIDAE | Species *Taeniopygia bichenovii* | Length 4 in (10 cm)

DOUBLE-BARRED FINCH

opening • paragraph: appearance, habitat, and food are always described

This brownish gray little finch is identified by two black bands across its breast. Small parties feed in short grass or on bare ground, always close to cover, taking small seeds.
• **NEST** A horizontal, bottle-shaped nest made of dried grass, lined with finer grass, and placed in a small bush or in tall grass.
• **DISTRIBUTION** N. and E. Australia.

DISTRIBUTION

speckled wings

main image is always a color photograph

scale silhouette: the bird beside a copy of this book

distribution • notes give place names and details of migration

• *black-edged, white face*

Plumage Sexes alike | Habitat 🌳 ✕ 🔺 | Migration Non-migrant

Family ESTRILDIDAE | Species *Erythrura psittacea* | Length 4¼ in (11 cm)

RED-THROATED PARROT FINCH

The red-and-green plumage of this finch can be compared with that of a parrot and has given rise to the name. This species occurs in farmland and open woodland. Seen in pairs in the breeding season, and in flocks at other times, it feeds on grass seeds and sometimes insects.
• **NEST** A round nest of grass with a side entrance, usually in a cavity or recess, or under an overhanging clump of grass.
• **DISTRIBUTION** New Caledonia.

DISTRIBUTION

• *green body*

• *red rump*

nest data, giving details of structure, materials, and location •

photographs are selected to show the main identification features

distribution map – this bird occurs on the island of New Caledonia

Plumage Sexes alike | Habitat 🌳 🔺 🔺 | Migration Non-migrant

states whether sexes are alike, look different, or are only slightly different

habitat symbols, in order of importance; see key below

whether migrant, non-migrant, partial migrant, or nomadic

KEY TO HABITAT SYMBOLS

🌳🌳 *forest: coniferous, broadleaved, temperate, monsoon, or rain forest*

🌳🌳 *open forest; more space between the trees*

🌳🌳 *forest edge*

🌳🌳 *grassland with scattered trees (includes farmland)*

🌳 *bushes, shrubs, thickets, and undergrowth*

✕ *areas of scrub vegetation, frequently with thorns*

▬▬▬ *open landscapes, including grassland, tundra, savanna, moorland, and heaths*

🌾 *semidesert*

🌿 *desert*

≈≈ *lakes, rivers, and vicinity*

≋ *upland streams and vicinity*

≈≈ *open sea*

≈≈ *rocky or sandy seashore*

≈≈ *freshwater marshes and swamps*

🪨 *rocky places or cliffs (both on the coast and inland)*

▲ *mountains*

ANATOMY OF BIRDS

BIRDS ARE ANIMALS that can fly, and virtually every feature of a bird shows that it is highly adapted to this purpose. The body is short, strong, and compact, the internal organs being protected by the breastbone and the pelvis. The breastbone is broad and flattened to carry large flight muscles. The legs are strong and springy and are muscular at the point where they join the body. They must provide the push

for takeoff and cushion the shock on landing. Anatomically, a bird's wings correspond to human hands, but most of the "finger" bones are absent in birds. The wings carry the large fans of feathers used in flight but folded away when at rest. Since a bird has no hands, its bill must be adapted for all feeding. The tail has evolved into a short row of bones carrying the large, adjustable fan of tail feathers.

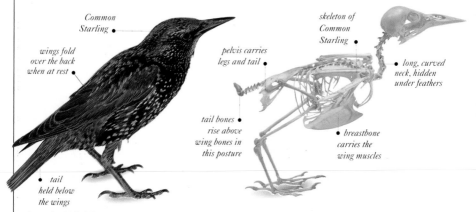

Common Starling

wings fold over the back when at rest

pelvis carries legs and tail

skeleton of Common Starling

long, curved neck, hidden under feathers

tail bones rise above wing bones in this posture

breastbone carries the wing muscles

tail held below the wings

A typical bird has a neat, streamlined shape, formed with its feather-covered body and wings; its bill is covered by a hard sheath, and it has bare, scale-covered legs and feet.

The skeleton has a thinner structure and is lightly made to aid flight. The bill lacks the smooth sheath of the living bird, and the wings and tail look short and bony.

FOUR FEATHER TYPES

Contour feathers are small and cover the body, while down feathers form a layer underneath providing extra insulation. Flight feathers are long and stiff. There are two types: tail feathers, which are often symmetrical, and wing feathers, which are unevenly shaped. The feathers on this page are not to scale – many birds have wing feathers, for instance, that would be taller than this book.

CONTOUR   DOWN   TAIL   WING

SHAPE AND MOVEMENT

The shape of a bird and of its various parts are clues to the way in which it lives. The bill, for instance, is always very precisely adapted to a bird's particular method of feeding. Similarly, a bird's way of flying, standing, or moving on the ground – for instance, whether it hops or walks – are related to its way of life. The way a bird clings to its perch is always closely adapted to its habitat or to the type of vegetation in which it normally lives. People who watch birds learn to take an interest in shape and movement, as they help indicate the overall category in which to place the bird being watched. This can be combined with other information to help identify the bird.

CORMORANT: SHARP BILL OF A FISH-EATER

SUNBIRD: DOWNCURVED BILL FOR PROBING FLOWERS FOR NECTAR

HERON: A STRONG, DAGGER-LIKE BILL FOR STABBING AND SEIZING

WARBLER: A SLENDER, INSECT-EATING BILL

GOLDFINCH: CRACKS SEEDS WITH ITS STRONG BILL

TOUCAN'S LONG BILL REACHES OUT FOR FRUIT

DUCK'S BILL FILTERS FOOD FROM WATER

FLESH-EATER'S SHARP, HOOKED BILL

Look carefully at flight silhouettes: forest raptors (a) have rounded wings; martins (b) have narrow, tapering wings.

The tapering wings and narrow tail of a falcon (c) contrast with the broad, splayed wings and broad tail of an eagle (d).

Terns (e) have long, elegant wings; albatross wings (f) are very long, with an extended inner section.

Look, too, at posture and gait. Some birds like the Reed Warbler (g) cling to vertical stems. Pipits (h) always walk; pittas (i) travel by hops and leaps along the ground.

Many birds, including most finches, perch upright (j) on a level branch. Wagtails (k) run after insects on the ground, using their tails as rudders or brakes when turning.

Look for birds that clamber up trees, using sharp claws, like this treecreeper (l). The Water Rail (m) has long legs and a narrow body for squeezing through marsh vegetation.

VARIATIONS WITHIN SPECIES

A SPECIES is a kind of bird, a number of related individuals that can interbreed and produce fertile young. However, there are many species in which the birds do not all look alike. Male and female adults are often differently colored. Young birds look different from adults, which may give them better camouflage or may prevent unnecessary fighting for territory. This page shows how "family members" (male, female, and juvenile) can look different; the page opposite shows other ways in which a species can vary: it may have subspecies (local forms) or two or more color phases.

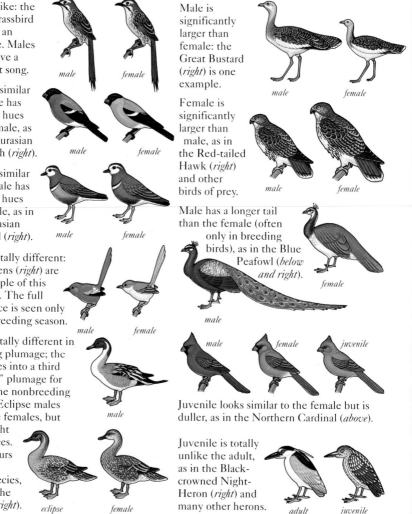

Sexes alike: the Cape Grassbird (*right*) is an example. Males often have a different song.

male *female*

Pattern similar but male has brighter hues than female, as in the Eurasian Bullfinch (*right*).

male *female*

Pattern similar but female has brighter hues than male, as in the Eurasian Dotterel (*right*).

male *female*

Sexes totally different: fairy-wrens (*right*) are an example of this category. The full difference is seen only in the breeding season.

male *female*

Sexes totally different in breeding plumage; the male goes into a third "eclipse" plumage for part of the nonbreeding season. Eclipse males look like females, but with slight differences. This occurs in many duck species, such as the Pintail (*right*).

male

eclipse *female*

Male is significantly larger than female: the Great Bustard (*right*) is one example.

male *female*

Female is significantly larger than male, as in the Red-tailed Hawk (*right*) and other birds of prey.

male *female*

Male has a longer tail than the female (often only in breeding birds), as in the Blue Peafowl (*below and right*).

female

male

male *female* *juvenile*

Juvenile looks similar to the female but is duller, as in the Northern Cardinal (*above*).

Juvenile is totally unlike the adult, as in the Black-crowned Night-Heron (*right*) and many other herons.

adult *juvenile*

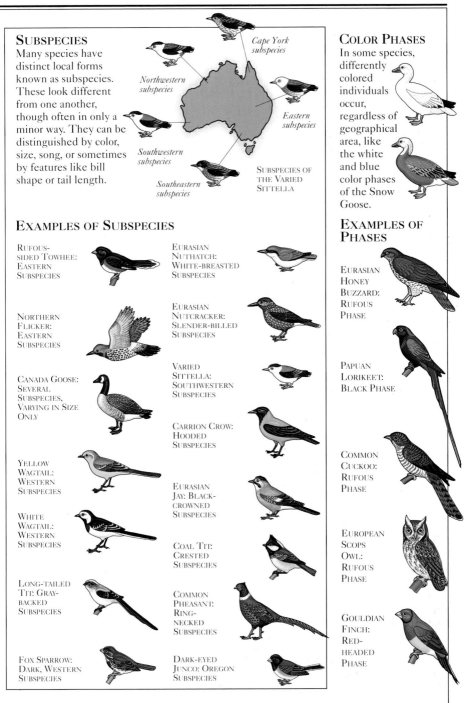

SUBSPECIES

Many species have distinct local forms known as subspecies. These look different from one another, though often in only a minor way. They can be distinguished by color, size, song, or sometimes by features like bill shape or tail length.

Cape York subspecies

Northwestern subspecies

Eastern subspecies

Southwestern subspecies

SUBSPECIES OF THE VARIED SITTELLA

Southeastern subspecies

COLOR PHASES

In some species, differently colored individuals occur, regardless of geographical area, like the white and blue color phases of the Snow Goose.

EXAMPLES OF SUBSPECIES

RUFOUS-SIDED TOWHEE: EASTERN SUBSPECIES

NORTHERN FLICKER: EASTERN SUBSPECIES

CANADA GOOSE: SEVERAL SUBSPECIES, VARYING IN SIZE ONLY

YELLOW WAGTAIL: WESTERN SUBSPECIES

WHITE WAGTAIL: WESTERN SUBSPECIES

LONG-TAILED TIT: GRAY-BACKED SUBSPECIES

FOX SPARROW: DARK, WESTERN SUBSPECIES

EURASIAN NUTHATCH: WHITE-BREASTED SUBSPECIES

EURASIAN NUTCRACKER: SLENDER-BILLED SUBSPECIES

VARIED SITTELLA: SOUTHWESTERN SUBSPECIES

CARRION CROW: HOODED SUBSPECIES

EURASIAN JAY: BLACK-CROWNED SUBSPECIES

COAL TIT: CRESTED SUBSPECIES

COMMON PHEASANT: RING-NECKED SUBSPECIES

DARK-EYED JUNCO: OREGON SUBSPECIES

EXAMPLES OF PHASES

EURASIAN HONEY BUZZARD: RUFOUS PHASE

PAPUAN LORIKEET: BLACK PHASE

COMMON CUCKOO: RUFOUS PHASE

EUROPEAN SCOPS OWL: RUFOUS PHASE

GOULDIAN FINCH: RED-HEADED PHASE

WATCHING BIRDS IN THE GARDEN

BIRD WATCHING, OR BIRDING, usually begins at home. In any garden or yard, there are bound to be a number of birds that are already present; it doesn't take much work to adapt a garden so that it offers the best for birds and brings in more than the usual handful of species. Some things are particularly likely to attract birds: water, both for drinking and bathing; maximum variety in the habitats available; providing possible nest sites; and offering food, at the appropriate time and in the appropriate way.

NEST BOXES

Birds that use nest boxes range in size from passerines, like chickadees, robins, and nuthatches, to some ducks and birds of prey. Boxes shown here are for small passerines; other species need boxes of different sizes and designs.

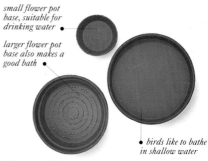

small flower pot base, suitable for drinking water •

larger flower pot base also makes a good bath •

• *birds like to bathe in shallow water*

WATER CONTAINERS

Many passerines like water to be provided in a raised site, such as a bird table. Other birds prefer to drink from a shallow pool on the ground, with good all-round visibility.

BIRD TABLES

In colder climates, many people build food tables to feed birds in winter. This prevents food from being lost in the snow or taken by scavengers. Shown here are two views of a simple table that can be made at home.

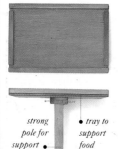

strong pole for support •

• *tray to support food*

Some food should be suspended; some placed flat on a raised site; some scattered on the ground

coconut for small birds

peanut dispenser

bread is less nutritious for birds, but a useful stopgap in winter

"bird pudding"

mixed loose seeds

fat and seed ball

WATCHING BIRDS IN THE FIELD

THE THOUGHT OF learning how to find and identify birds out in the wild seems a daunting one, but once you have been there to look for them, perhaps with someone who knows the birds of the area, your skill will develop rapidly. You will very soon get used to looking carefully at the shapes and colors of birds and to watching their actions. The type of habitat in which the birds occur, their location (such as whether high or low in the trees, or down on the ground), and any vocalizations they make are all useful clues.

BINOCULARS

Lightweight types are the most practical, with magnifications of 7 to 10. With higher powers, you may spend too long aiming and focusing.

well balanced, lightweight model

BIRD PHOTOGRAPHY

The most suitable type of camera for photographing birds is a 35 mm SLR model. Practice on garden birds first, to acquire the skills of judging distance, focusing in the time available, and steadying the camera for the shot.

short lens for normal use

WATCHING FROM A BLIND

Birds are often alarmed at the sight of people, but if you hide behind or within a simple structure they will soon forget your presence and go about their business. A temporary, movable blind can be made by camouflaging a simple tent with branches and leaves (*above left*). A parked car (*left*) is a very effective blind, as the birds usually fail to realize that it contains humans.

NOTEBOOK

Make notes of what you see, or even a fast sketch; there is no better way to train your eye for detail. A notebook also provides a record of the birds you have seen and forms a log of activities, which will help in planning future trips.

LONG LENSES

To photograph small or distant birds, you will need a high-powered lens (200 mm focal length or more) and, for best results, a tripod to keep it steady.

PERMANENT BIRD BLINDS

Large blinds, often seen in nature reserves for wildfowl, can accommodate many visitors.

BIRD PROTECTION IN THE BREEDING SEASON

Remember that birds breeding are birds sensitive to disturbance. Nothing should be done that frightens them or alters the surroundings of their nests. Once frightened, they may abandon the nest, which could set their breeding back a whole year.

IDENTIFYING BIRDS IN FLIGHT

FLIGHT IS A helpful identification feature for many birds. Some whole groups of species can be recognized by their flight patterns. During courtship, many birds perform special display flights, and these, too, can help in identification. As soon as a bird takes off or opens its wings, the markings it reveals may provide crucial clues as to what species you are looking at.

Steady flight with regular wingbeats, along a direct path, is typical of a very large number of species. These range from crows (*above*) to geese, pigeons, and many smaller birds.

Some small birds, such as finches (*above*), conserve energy by rising on a wingbeat, then closing the wings to the body, and swooping until the next wingbeat.

Some larger birds (*above*) often soar and glide without flapping their wings, rising a little each time they turn into the wind.

Woodpeckers (*above*) have an undulating flight style. They ascend with several wingbeats, then swoop down on closed wings like finches.

Some large birds (*right*) have an energy-saving style of flight in which bursts of strong wingbeats alternate with long, level glides.

DISPLAY FLIGHTS

Birds that are breeding often perform aerobatic display flights to attract a mate or show their presence to rivals. This is especially common in open-country birds.

Flying from the treetops, the Common Wood-Pigeon (*below*) rises steeply, often with loud, clapping wingbeats, then glides down.

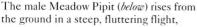

The Northern Lapwing (*above*) has an erratic, tumbling display, with wild calls.

Some eagles (*right*) perform swoops and dives high in the air. They close their wings to dive, turn up again briefly, and then continue the plunge before finally leveling out.

The male Meadow Pipit (*below*) rises from the ground in a steep, fluttering flight, during which he utters weak "tip" calls. Then he parachutes down again, uttering one long trill.

"Pendulum" displays (*right*) are seen in some birds of prey and some hummingbird species.

MARKINGS ON THE WINGS

The moment a bird takes to the air, it is likely to display vivid markings on the spread wings and tail. These include white or colored patches, bars, or stripes, that are hidden while the bird is perched. Other birds feeding nearby, often in a mixed-species flock, notice the change in appearance and interpret it as a warning of danger and the need to fly. The pattern also enables each bird to recognize members of its own species, which it will then follow to safety. We, too, are able to use the pattern, together with details like song or behavior, to identify the species.

ALARM SIGNAL On taking off, the male Chaffinch reveals a vivid pattern (*above*).

WING PATCHES

Look for the flash of wing patches. These are panels of a conspicuous, vivid color, as seen on the female Evening Grosbeak (*right*).

WING STRIPES

These are bands of a bright, contrasting color that show along the extended wing when the bird is seen in flight, as in the Eurasian Goldfinch (*right*).

WINGS OF WADERS AND DUCKS

| GREATER YELLOWLEGS | COMMON REDSHANK | EURASIAN OYSTERCATCHER | RUDDY TURNSTONE | BEACH THICK-KNEE | PIED AVOCET |

In shorebirds, also known as waders (*above*), most species have their own characteristic patterns of white on the wing. These marks become visible only when the birds fly.

As well as having patterns of white stripes on the wing, some ducks (*below*) also have a speculum – a white or vividly colored panel located on the inner flight feathers.

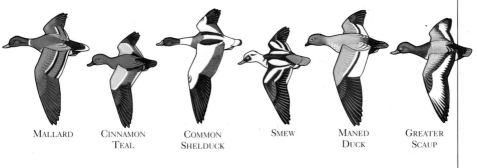

| MALLARD | CINNAMON TEAL | COMMON SHELDUCK | SMEW | MANED DUCK | GREATER SCAUP |

IDENTIFICATION KEY

THE FAMILIES to which birds belong are not always useful as guides to how they will look when seen in the field. A good number of families include birds that are very unlike one another in vital respects, such as color, shape, habitat, or behavior. This key solves the problem by setting up categories that are not based on family but on habitat and feeding manner. Bear in mind that categories like this cannot be watertight – birds are living creatures and can rarely be tied down to a single habitat or style of behavior. This means that in some cases you may find it helpful to try alternative ways through the key. Stage 1 (*opposite*) divides all birds into five basic types. Choose the relevant one and follow its symbol into Stage 2, where the basic types are divided into helpful categories. Silhouette images lead from here into Stage 3 (*pp. 22–37*), giving possible identifications.

STAGE 2: WALKING AND WADING BIRDS

LARGE FLIGHTLESS BIRDS
Very big birds, some taller than humans, mostly with long legs and necks. Some live in open country and survive by their ability to walk or run long distances.

SMALLER FLIGHTLESS BIRDS
Birds from pigeon- to chicken-size that live on the ground and hide in vegetation or in burrows; some are nocturnal.

STAGE 2: WATERBIRDS

WATERBIRDS SWIMMING WITH WEBBED FEET
Birds mostly feeding at the surface; some reach beneath the surface, and some dive to pursue fish or other prey.

WATERBIRDS SWIMMING WITHOUT WEBBED FEET
Mostly surface feeders, though some dive. Some have lobes on their toes as swimming aids.

STAGE 1

This part of the key groups birds into basic types. Most birds fit into one of the first four categories, enabling you to move on immediately to Stage 2. A few belong to the category of Specialized Feeders. To understand this group, turn to the relevant parts of Stage 2 (*bottom of pp. 20–21*) and then look at the examples shown in Stage 3 (*pp. 36–37*); this will make it clear which birds belong to this category.

WALKING
AND WADING
BIRDS

WATERBIRDS

FRUIT-EATERS,
NECTAR-FEEDERS,
AND SEED-EATERS

HUNTERS ON
LAND AND IN
TREES

SPECIALIZED
FEEDERS

SMALLER RUNNERS WITH SHORT BILLS

Ranging from pigeon- to chicken-size, these are birds that spend most or all of their time on the ground, often feeding on seeds but that can fly when necessary.

SMALLER RUNNERS WITH LONG BILLS

Pigeon- to chicken-size birds with slender bills for probing the ground and feeding on insects. Most of them can fly when necessary.

MEDIUM-SIZE RUNNERS

These are turkey-size birds that spend most of their time on the ground, though all are able to fly. A number of them nest and roost in the branches of large trees.

LARGE, LONG-LEGGED WADING BIRDS

Nearly all these birds wade in shallow water or marshes – the rest feed in grassland. All can fly. Most have long necks for reaching down to feed.

WATERBIRDS THAT SNATCH FROM THE AIR

Birds that locate their prey by flying over water, then snatch it from the surface or just below, without swimming.

WATERBIRDS THAT PLUNGE-DIVE FROM THE AIR

Birds that generally spot prey while flying over water, then plunge beneath the surface to seize it or chase after it.

WATERBIRDS THAT DIVE FROM THE SURFACE

Surface-swimmers that submerge to hunt. Most swim with their feet, some with their wings.

WATERBIRDS THAT ALIGHT ON THE SURFACE

Birds that settle from the air to take food from the surface; some make a shallow dive.

STAGE 2: FRUIT-EATERS, NECTAR-FEEDERS, AND SEED-EATERS

FRUIT-EATERS
This category consists mainly of tree-dwelling birds. Most eat the fruit where it grows on the branch, some without plucking it. Some birds merely remove the flesh from the inside of large, soft fruits. Fruit-eating bills are adapted in various ways. Some are very long, enabling the bird to reach fruit without having to walk on thin twigs; others are shorter and stouter and are useful for cutting or grasping fruit.

STAGE 2: HUNTERS ON LAND AND IN TREES

ACTIVE HUNTERS
Birds of this category seek out their prey and pounce on it in a sudden, aggressive attack, pursuing it if necessary. Some are seen patrolling in flight, watching with keen eyes for any movement. Some watch from a perch before swooping down on prey. This group includes many nocturnal hunters.

GROUND FEEDERS
These are flying birds that take food from the surface of the ground or just below.

TREE TRUNK AND BRANCH FORAGERS
These birds hunt insects that are hidden in cracks in the bark of tree trunks or branches or rest on the bark. Some also chisel out grubs of insects that bore into rotten wood.

STAGE 2: SPECIALIZED FEEDERS

CARRION-EATERS
Birds of this category feed on dead animals that they have not killed. Some soar high overhead and scan the ground with their keen eyes to locate carcasses.

AERIAL FEEDERS
Smaller members of this group feed by catching flying insects. Larger members, such as the frigatebirds, piratically rob other birds of their prey in mid-flight.

NECTAR-FEEDERS

A number of birds feed by inserting their bills into flowers and sucking out nectar. Some of these, such as the lorikeets, are also capable of eating fruit. Many also eat pollen and have brush-tipped tongues for this purpose. Others are more specialized for nectar-feeding and have tubular tongues. Most nectar-feeders also eat small insects that they find in or beside the flowers.

SEED-EATERS

Included in this category are the seed-eaters known to cage and aviary bird enthusiasts – the finches, waxbills, weavers, sparrows, and buntings. Seeds are taken both from vegetation and from the ground. There are many pigeons, parrots, larks, and members of the crow family that also take seed. Acorns and nuts are large seeds, and birds that feed on them, such as jays and nutcrackers, also appear here.

INVERTEBRATE PROBERS

A rich supply of insects and other invertebrates is found in the soil, especially beneath the turf in grassland. Birds in this category exploit this resource, probing the ground with their long, strongly made bills. All birds in this category can fly.

SIT-AND-WAIT HUNTERS

A very large number of species adopt the policy of sitting at some vantage point and watching, ready to swoop to the ground or to fly out after prey when they see it.

INSECT GLEANERS

Birds of this category feed by moving through tree foliage, undergrowth, or low-growing plants and taking small creatures from twigs and leaves at random. Any insect that happens to be resting on a leaf or clinging underneath is seized as soon as it is noticed. These birds often hunt in flocks.

INSECT PURSUERS

A number of passerines are small equivalents of the Active Hunters, moving around in search of insects and pouncing on them or chasing them on sight.

SPECIALIZED EXPLOITERS OF ANIMALS

A number of birds rely on other animals to provide their food. Herds of animals attract parasites and disturb ground insects on which birds can feed. Army ants cause small creatures to flee in panic. The honeyguides rely on any animal, including humans, that will break open bees' nests.

OPPORTUNISTS

Some species do not restrict themselves to a particular type of food or method of finding it. They are able to eat many different types of food and quickly take advantage of any food supply as soon as the opportunity occurs. They may be seen feeding, like other birds, on insects, fruit, or seeds; they may hunt small animals or eat carrion, or they may scavenge at garbage dumps.

STAGE 3

This part of the key brings you closer to identifying the bird you are considering. The categories from Stage 2 are broken down, either to a precise species or to a small group that may contain it. Numbers after the names refer to the pages, or parts of pages, on which the birds appear. This handbook contains descriptions of 819 species, out of some 9,600 known to exist – in other words, one in 11 of the world's birds. Bird species have been specially selected, so that the book covers

WALKING AND WADING BIRDS

LARGE
FLIGHTLESS
BIRDS

Ostrich **39**

Rheas **38**

Emperor Penguin **44**

SMALLER FLIGHTLESS
BIRDS

Kiwis **42t**

Mesites **118t**

Smaller Penguins **45–46t**

SMALLER RUNNERS
WITH
SHORT
BILLS

Quails **109b–110, 113t**

Stone-Curlews **134b–135t**

Tinamous **42b–43**

Grouse **108b–109t**

Button-Quails **118b**

Plains Wanderer **119t**

the full range of diversity. In many cases, Stage 3 offers a precise identification, as in the case of the Emu or the Kakapo below. In other cases, Stage 3 refers you to a group of species, such as Pheasants at the bottom of this page. This means that your bird is one of the pheasants illustrated in the book (on pages 113–115 or on 117) or a similar pheasant that is not included in the book. In a group reference of this kind, the name of the type of bird is given in the plural.

Cassowaries 40

Emu 41

ABBREVIATIONS
Page references use abbreviations to indicate the part of the page to which they apply:

t = top of the page
m = middle
b = bottom

Kagu
128b

Takahe
127t

Kakapo
185b

Weka
124t

Guans
106b–107t

Sheathbills
146b

Partridges
111–112

Coursers
135b–136t

Sandgrouse
158

Pheasants
113b–115,
117t

Guineafowl
117b

Seedsnipes
146t

STAGE 3

WALKING AND WADING BIRDS *(continued)*

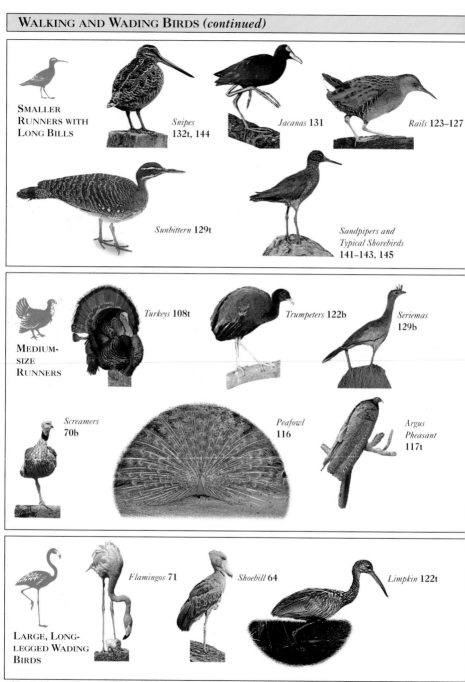

SMALLER RUNNERS WITH LONG BILLS

Snipes **132t, 144**

Jacanas **131**

Rails **123–127**

Sunbittern **129t**

Sandpipers and Typical Shorebirds **141–143, 145**

MEDIUM-SIZE RUNNERS

Turkeys **108t**

Trumpeters **122b**

Seriemas **129b**

Screamers **70b**

Peafowl **116**

Argus Pheasant **117t**

LARGE, LONG-LEGGED WADING BIRDS

Flamingos **71**

Shoebill **64**

Limpkin **122t**

Hoopoe **228b**

Crab-Plover **132b**

Avocets and Stilts
133b–134t

Plovers
137b–140

Oystercatchers
133t

Megapodes
105b–106t

Ground-
Hornbills **231b**

Secretary Bird
100

Curassows
107b

Crowned
Pigeon **166t**

Bustards
130

Storks **65b–68t**

Ibises **68b–69t**

Spoonbills **69b–70t**

STAGE 3

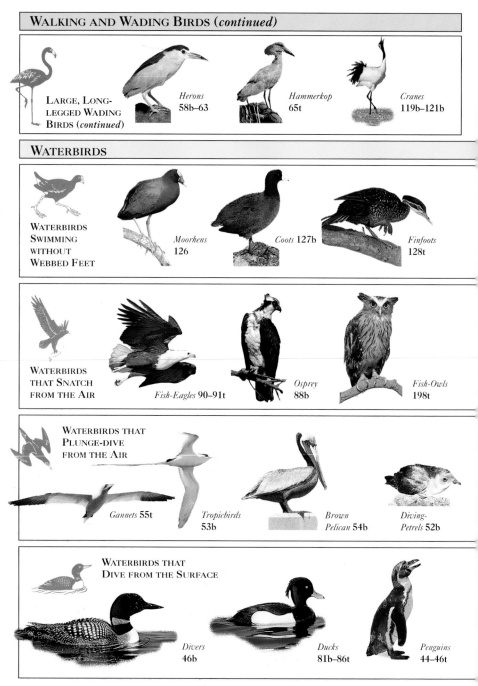

WALKING AND WADING BIRDS (*continued*)

LARGE, LONG-
LEGGED WADING
BIRDS (*continued*)

Herons
58b–63

Hammerkop
65t

Cranes
119b–121b

WATERBIRDS

WATERBIRDS
SWIMMING
WITHOUT
WEBBED FEET

Moorhens
126

Coots 127b

Finfoots
128t

WATERBIRDS
THAT SNATCH
FROM THE AIR

Fish-Eagles 90–91t

Osprey
88b

Fish-Owls
198t

WATERBIRDS THAT
PLUNGE-DIVE
FROM THE AIR

Gannets 55t

Tropicbirds
53b

*Brown
Pelican* 54b

*Diving-
Petrels* 52b

WATERBIRDS THAT
DIVE FROM THE SURFACE

Divers
46b

Ducks
81b–86t

Penguins
44–46t

WATERBIRDS

WATERBIRDS SWIMMING WITH WEBBED FEET

Swans 73

Ducks 76–86t

Geese 72t, 74t–75

Pelicans 54

Dippers 280m

Phalaropes 143m

Storm-Petrels 52t–52m

Frigatebirds 58t

Skimmers 155b

Terns 152t, 154–155t

Kingfishers 219b–222

Boobies 55b

Sea-Terns 152b–153

Cormorants 56t–57t

Auks 156–157

Darters 57b

Grebes 47

STAGE 3

WATERBIRDS (*continued*)

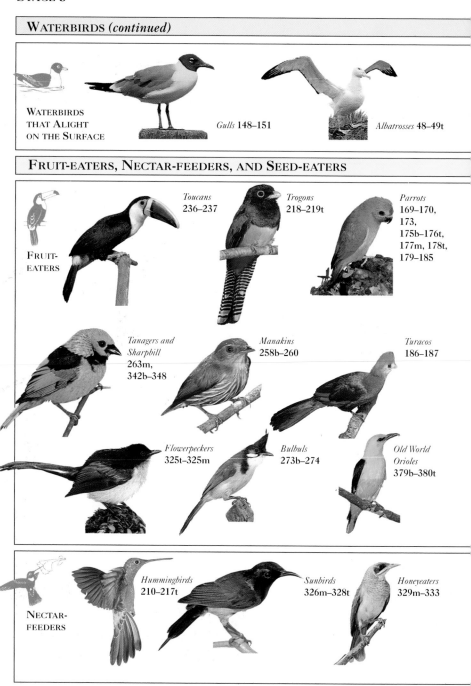

WATERBIRDS THAT ALIGHT ON THE SURFACE

Gulls 148–151

Albatrosses 48–49t

FRUIT-EATERS, NECTAR-FEEDERS, AND SEED-EATERS

FRUIT-EATERS

Toucans 236–237

Trogons 218–219t

Parrots 169–170, 173, 175b–176t, 177m, 178t, 179–185

Tanagers and Sharpbill 263m, 342b–348

Manakins 258b–260

Turacos 186–187

Flowerpeckers 325t–325m

Bulbuls 273b–274

Old World Orioles 379b–380t

NECTAR-FEEDERS

Hummingbirds 210–217t

Sunbirds 326m–328t

Honeyeaters 329m–333

STAGE 3

FRUIT-EATERS, NECTAR-FEEDERS, AND SEED-EATERS (*continued*)

SEED-
EATERS

Finches
360–365m

Waxbills
365b–369

Pigeons
159–164

Larks 267–268

*Jays, Magpies, and
Nutcrackers* 388b–392

HUNTERS ON LAND AND IN TREES

ACTIVE
HUNTERS

Owls 194–203t

Typical Birds of Prey
88b–90t, 91–99

Falcons
101b–105t

GROUND
FEEDERS

*Wagtails
and Pipits*
270b–272t

Dunnocks
283m–283b

Crows
393–395

Pittas
264–265t

Larks
267–268

Kea
185t

Tapaculos
251m

Buntings
334–338,
339m, 341t

Parrots
171–173t,
174–185

Cardinals 339t,
339b–340,
341b–342m

Sparrows
370t–370m

Bobolink
356b

Weavers
370b–373

Shrikes 276–278

Skuas 147

Australian
Ground Feeders
266b,
294b–295t,
314t, 382

Hoopoe
228b

Ground-
Rollers 227b

Cuckoos
191–193t

Pigeons
159–164

Lyrebirds
266t

Starlings
374–377

STAGE 3

HUNTERS ON LAND AND IN TREES (continued)

TREE TRUNK AND BRANCH FORAGERS

Woodpeckers
238–243

Woodcreepers
245

Pearled Treerunner
247t

INVERTEBRATE PROBERS

Common Starling
375m

Sunbird-Asity
265b

Wrynecks
238t

Saddleback
381b

SIT-AND-WAIT HUNTERS

Puffbirds
232b–233t

Bee-eaters
224–225

Jacamars
232t

Owlet-Nightjars
205t

Frogmouths and Potoos
204

Rollers
226–227t, 228t

Wood-
Hoopoes
229

Nuthatches
323t–323m

Sittellas
323b

Treecreepers
324

Wrens
280b–283t

New World Blackbirds
355m–358

Thrashers
285

Choughs
393t

Motmots
223b

Drongos
380b–381t

Trogons
218–219t

Todies 223t

Kingfishers
219b–222b

Tyrant Flycatchers
251b–258m

Flycatchers
308b–309, 314b

STAGE 3

HUNTERS ON LAND AND IN TREES (*continued*)

INSECT GLEANERS

Cuckoos 188–191t

Ovenbirds 246–247

Hornbills 230–231t

Thornbills 312–313

Broadbills 244

Flowerpeckers 325–326t

Spiderhunters 328m

Mockingbirds 284–285

White-eyes 328b–329t

Ioras and Leafbirds 275

New World Blackbirds 355m–359

Fairy-Wrens 310m–311

Monarchs and Batis 310t, 315

Bulbuls 273b–274

INSECT PURSUERS

Antbirds 248–250

Shrikes 276–278

Whistlers
318–319t

Starlings
374–378

Australian Robins
316b–317

Cuckoo-Shrikes
and Minivets
272m–273t

New World
Warblers
349–352m

Old World
Warblers
301–308m

Chats and
Thrushes
286–294t

Gnatcatchers
and Gnateaters
251t, 300b

Babblers
295–300m

Fantails
316t–316m

Tyrant
Flycatchers
251b–258m

Tits
319m–
322

Jays and
Magpies
388–392t

Vireos
353b–355t

Vangas 279t

Butcherbirds
383b–384t

Currawongs 384b

STAGE 3

SPECIALIZED FEEDERS

CARRION-EATERS

New World Vultures **86b–88t**

Kites **89b**

Giant Petrels **49b**

Crows and Magpies **391, 394–395**

AERIAL FEEDERS

Swifts **208–209**

Frigatebirds **58t**

Oilbird **203b**

Pratincoles **136b–137t**

Nightjars **205m–207b**

SPECIALIZED EXPLOITERS OF ANIMALS

Cattle Egret **61b**

Honeyguides **233b**

Oxpeckers **379t**

Antbirds **249m–250**

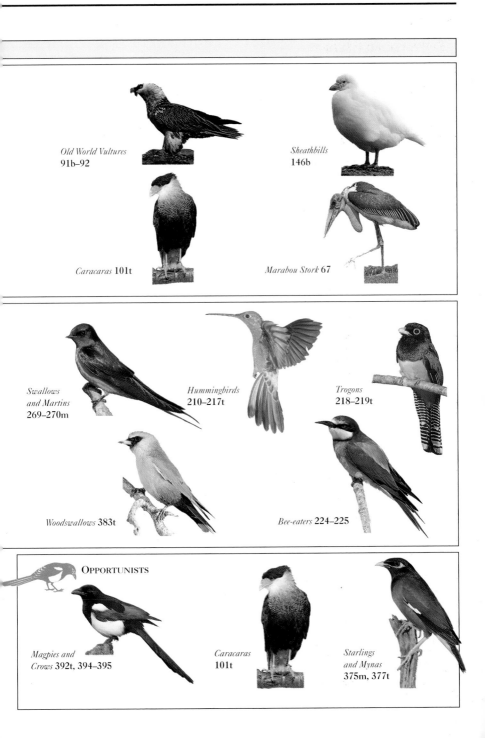

Old World Vultures
91b–92

Sheathbills
146b

Caracaras **101t**

Marabou Stork **67**

*Swallows
and Martins*
269–270m

Hummingbirds
210–217t

Trogons
218–219t

Woodswallows **383t**

Bee-eaters **224–225**

OPPORTUNISTS

*Magpies and
Crows* **392t, 394–395**

Caracaras
101t

*Starlings
and Mynas*
375m, 377t

NON-PASSERINES

N EARLY HALF THE BIRD species in the world, including all the larger ones, belong to the 98 non-passerine families. The non-passerines occupy a varied range of habitats and include birds of fresh water and the sea, birds that are almost permanently airborne, flightless birds, species that dwell on the ground, and some that are adapted to perching in trees or bushes.

Non-passerines often build very simple nests, or the eggs may be laid on bare ground or rock. The young are helpless in some species, but in others they are downcovered, active chicks that can run and feed themselves almost from hatching. Non-passerines vary in voice, but few produce the complicated and musical songs typical of many passerine birds.

Family RHEIDAE	Species *Rhea americana*	Length 51 in (130 cm)

GREATER RHEA

This large, flightless bird lives on open plains, particularly where grass is tall and bushes are plentiful. Here it feeds on the leaves, roots, and seeds of plants, together with insects and other small animals. Although it never flies, the Greater Rhea comes nearest to doing so when it races over the open grassland, holding its wings up to gain a very slight lift. It can also swim, and flocks visit lakes or rivers to drink and to bathe. This species is always sociable, except that some older males live alone. In the breeding season, rival males fight, mainly by kicking with their powerful legs. Males also display, either to deter rivals or to attract females, ruffling their wings and uttering low, roaring calls. A male normally mates with several females, which he then leads to his nest. Up to a dozen females will visit the same nest, normally producing 15 to 30 eggs, sometimes more than 60. The male incubates the eggs alone, covering as many as he can, and cares for the downy young.

• **NEST** A shallow hollow in the ground, sparsely lined with grass.

• **DISTRIBUTION** South America in open country from Brazil south of the Amazon to C. Argentina.

feathers on head, face, and neck

loose, shaggy wing feathers

strong legs

short, thick toes

DISTRIBUTION

Plumage Sexes alike	Habitat	Migration Non-migrant

Family STRUTHIONIDAE	Species *Struthio camelus*	L. 98 in (250 cm)/79 in (200 cm)

OSTRICH

The world's largest and tallest bird species, the Ostrich stands at an average height of 8 ft 2 in (2.5 m). It is flightless, with drooping, loose-textured feathers on its wings and tail. Large, strong legs enable it to walk about with easy strides and to run fast, with a top speed of some 40 mph (64 km/h). The Ostrich inhabits open landscapes such as desert, semi-desert, and grassland, living by its keen sight and its ability to cover long distances to reach safety or a food supply. It feeds on the leaves, stems, flowers, and seeds of plants, plucked with its blunt-tipped and proportionally small bill. Breeding males are seen squatting in their sexual display posture, waving their wings and necks. A male that has successfully defended his territory pairs with a female, which lays her eggs in a shallow nest. The male Ostrich may also mate with as many as five subordinate females, which add their eggs to the clutch. As many as 40 eggs may accumulate, but the dominant female pushes out all but 20, which include her own. She incubates these with the help of the male. The downy young are tended by both parents, sometimes later merging with other broods.

bristles on head and face

FEMALE

• **NEST** A hollow, some 9 ft 10 in (3 m) across, scraped with the feet and formed by body pressure in sandy soil.
• **DISTRIBUTION** Africa from Senegal to Ethiopia and south to Tanzania; population in southern Africa.
• **REMARK** The Ostrich is farmed in southern Africa for its wing and tail plumes. The former wild population in the Arabian Peninsula is now extinct.

• *fine, downy wing plumes*

• *no feathers on the upper leg*

two large toes on • *each foot*

DISTRIBUTION

Plumage Sexes differ	Habitat	Migration Non-migrant

Family CASUARIIDAE	Species *Casuarius casuarius*	Length 72 in (183 cm)

SOUTHERN CASSOWARY

This sturdily built, heavy, flightless bird lives in rain forests among thick, tropical vegetation. Its feathers are coarse in texture, and some end in long, hairlike filaments. The wings are tiny, and in place of flight feathers they carry only a few quills. The bare skin on the head and neck, and the wattles that hang from the neck, are colored red and blue in a pattern that varies with age. On top of the head there is a hornlike casque that may give protection when the birds dash with lowered heads through dense vegetation, as they frequently do when alarmed. The bill is narrow and is normally used for feeding on fallen fruit, and sometimes on green plants, seeds, and some small animals. This species utters a variety of calls, including deep booms, roars, hisses, and low, rumbling sounds. Individuals live alone much of the time. The female is slightly larger than the male, with brighter head and neck colors and a slightly taller casque. When breeding, a female sometimes pairs with more than one male, laying a clutch of eggs for each. The downy chicks are boldly striped and are cared for by the male for the first nine months of life.

- **NEST** A shallow hollow in the leafy floor of the forest, sometimes sparsely lined with grass and fallen leaves.
- **DISTRIBUTION** Rain forests in New Guinea and N.E. Australia.
- **REMARK** The large, bladelike claw on the outer toe is used in aggressive fights.

• *bony casque*

ear • opening

ornamental • neck wattles

• *wing feathers reduced to quills*

• *scaly skin on leg*

DISTRIBUTION

JUVENILE

Plumage Sexes differ slightly	Habitat 🌳 🌿	Migration Non-migrant

Family DROMAIIDAE	Species *Dromaius novaehollandiae*	Length 83 in (210 cm)

EMU

A large, flightless bird, the Emu lives in a variety of open-country habitats, ranging from semidesert to grassland and open woodland. Its wings are very small and are usually hidden in its long, loose, shaggy feathers. Females are slightly larger than males and have stronger blue coloration on the bare skin of the head and neck. The Emu can run at up to 30 mph (48 km/h), though it normally walks. Pairs or small parties feed on plants including grasses, also taking insects. The call is low and booming. Males incubate the eggs and care for the striped, downy chicks.

• **NEST** A slight hollow in the ground, either bare or lined with trampled-down vegetation.

• **DISTRIBUTION** Australia, except for the wetter coastal areas and thick forests.

FEMALE

• *bare skin on neck*

• *sparse feathering on the neck*

• *much reduced wing*

coarse, • *drooping feathers*

• *long, scaly legs*

strong, heavy feet •

DISTRIBUTION

Plumage Sexes differ slightly	Habitat	Migration Non-migrant

Family APTERYGIDAE	Species *Apteryx australis*	Length 28 in (70 cm)

BROWN KIWI

This flightless, forest-dwelling bird is nocturnal, hiding by day in a burrow
or cavity and feeding at night. Its eyesight is poor, but it has a good sense of
smell, and its nostrils are placed at the tip of the bill. Sensory bristles at the
base of the bill also help locate food. The Kiwi probes the soil for
worms and other invertebrates, also eating some seeds and berries.
It can run fast but is always unobtrusive. The call is a high,
whistling sound. The female lays one or two large eggs,
each about one-fifth of her body weight.
The male incubates these, hatching
out the feathered, active young.
• **NEST** A bare hollow in a burrow
in the ground, in a hole among
tree roots, or in a hollow log.
• **DISTRIBUTION** Thinly
distributed in New Zealand.

coarse, hairy plumage •

nostrils located • at tip of bill

strong, thick legs •

DISTRIBUTION

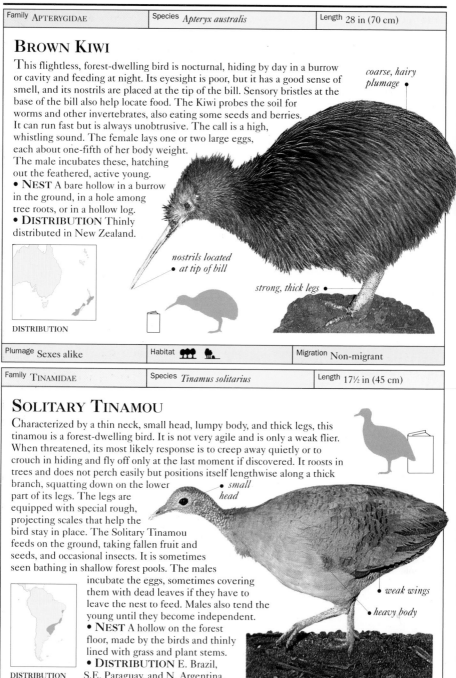

Plumage Sexes alike	Habitat 🌳 🪨	Migration Non-migrant

Family TINAMIDAE	Species *Tinamus solitarius*	Length 17½ in (45 cm)

SOLITARY TINAMOU

Characterized by a thin neck, small head, lumpy body, and thick legs, this
tinamou is a forest-dwelling bird. It is not very agile and is only a weak flier.
When threatened, its most likely response is to creep away quietly or to
crouch in hiding and fly off only at the last moment if discovered. It roosts in
trees and does not perch easily but positions itself lengthwise along a thick
branch, squatting down on the lower *• small*
part of its legs. The legs are *head*
equipped with special rough,
projecting scales that help the
bird stay in place. The Solitary Tinamou
feeds on the ground, taking fallen fruit and
seeds, and occasional insects. It is sometimes
seen bathing in shallow forest pools. The males
incubate the eggs, sometimes covering
them with dead leaves if they have to
leave the nest to feed. Males also tend the
young until they become independent.
• **NEST** A hollow on the forest
floor, made by the birds and thinly
lined with grass and plant stems.
• **DISTRIBUTION** E. Brazil,
S.E. Paraguay, and N. Argentina.

• weak wings

• heavy body

DISTRIBUTION

Plumage Sexes alike	Habitat 🌳	Migration Non-migrant

Family TINAMIDAE	Species *Eudromia elegans*	Length 16 in (40 cm)

ELEGANT TINAMOU

The slender, upward-curving crest helps identify this tinamou, which is adapted to living in open country, dry grassland, scrub, and woodland. It is capable of running fairly fast across open ground, but if alarmed it is more likely to crouch and hide, waiting until danger is past. If approached directly it makes a short, low flight on whirring wings as a last resort. At times the Elegant Tinamou is a solitary-living species, but after the breeding season it is seen in family parties, and these sometimes combine to form small flocks. The male incubates the eggs. The young are downcovered and can run and feed within minutes of hatching. They soon leave the nest, under the supervision of the male. The diet consists of seeds, fruit, and other parts of plants, as well as insects.
• **NEST** A hollow in the ground, made by the birds, often situated close to a low bush.
• **DISTRIBUTION** Much of Argentina; also scattered, small populations in E. Chile.

• thin crest

• slender neck

DISTRIBUTION

camouflage
• plumage

Plumage Sexes alike	Habitat	Migration Non-migrant

Family TINAMIDAE	Species *Crypturellus undulatus*	Length 12 in (30 cm)

UNDULATED TINAMOU

A common bird within its range, this tinamou occurs in forest, scrub, and secondary growth (where trees have regrown after forest clearance). It lives on the ground among low vegetation. Pairs and families maintain contact with whistling calls. The diet consists of seeds, berries, and insects. Studies suggest that the male may mate with several females, which move in a group from one male to another. Each male guards a single nest, in which he incubates eggs from all his partners.
• **NEST** A hollow in the ground, situated among grass and low vegetation.
• **DISTRIBUTION** Amazon Basin in Brazil and adjoining countries.

• wavy markings

• plump body

DISTRIBUTION

Plumage Sexes alike	Habitat	Migration Non-migrant

Family SPHENISCIDAE	Species *Aptenodytes forsteri*	Length 45 in (115 cm)

EMPEROR PENGUIN

This is the largest and most heavily built of all the penguins. It puts on a deep layer of fat all over its stout body during the times of year that it spends feeding in the sea. Propelled by flipperlike wings, the Emperor pursues fish and squid to depths as great as 870 ft (265 m). On ice or snow, it walks upright or drops on its belly and toboggans along, pushing with its flippers. Emperor Penguins breed in colonies on the Antarctic ice, each recognizing its mate or parents by individual variations in the nasal, trumpeting call. After pairing in early winter, the female lays an egg and leaves for coastal waters. The male incubates the egg for two months by standing upright and supporting it on his feet. Males huddle together for warmth through the blizzards of the polar winter. The female returns from the sea just as the young one hatches, and she feeds it with regurgitated food. The male, having lost almost half his original weight, then walks to the sea to feed for some weeks before returning to help rear the chick.
• **NEST** No nest. The single egg, and chick, rest on the feet behind a fold of feathered belly skin.
• **DISTRIBUTION** Antarctic coasts.

DISTRIBUTION

JUVENILE

• *well insulated body*

• *dense, furlike plumage*

protective fold • of skin

chick resting • on the feet

uptilted feet support the • chick

short, stiff tail •

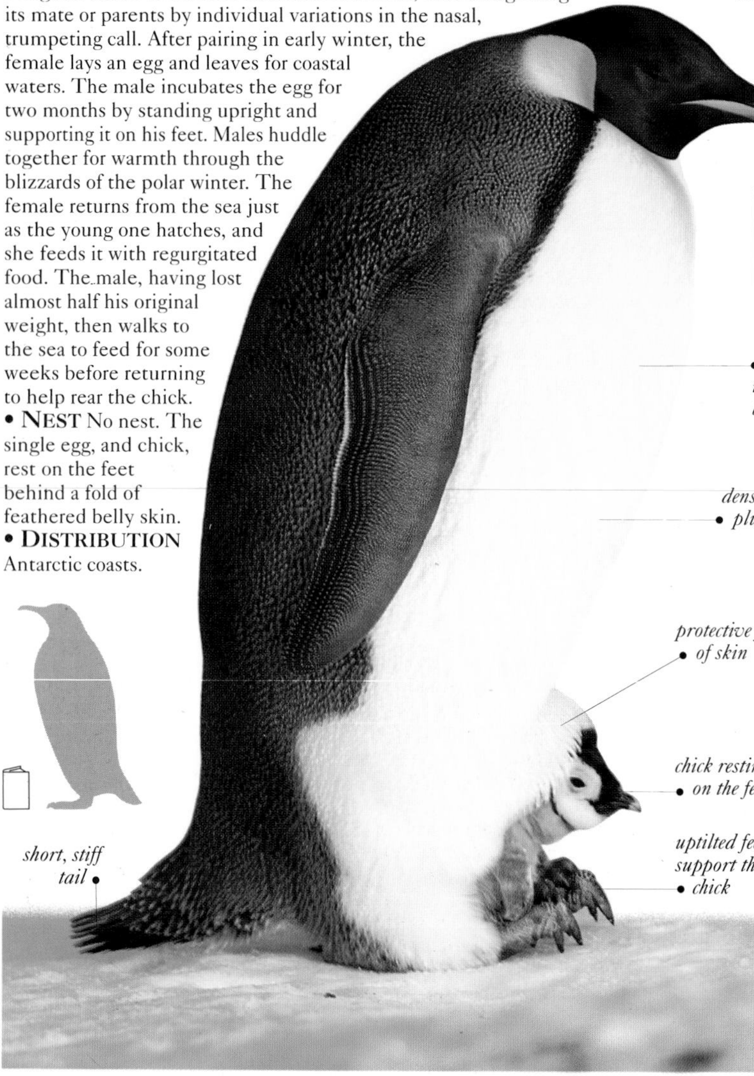

Plumage Sexes alike	Habitat	Migration Partial migrant

Family SPHENISCIDAE	Species *Pygoscelis adeliae*	Length 28 in (70 cm)

ADELIE PENGUIN

A thickset, heavily feathered little penguin, this bird is adapted for polar conditions. Its feathering is dense, short, and furlike. Feeding in the cold waters off the Antarctic coast, it hunts mostly for krill, a shrimplike creature, also taking small fish. Adelie Penguins usually nest in crowded colonies in the Antarctic summer. Each bird returns to the same nest site and the same mate. Pairs usually rear two young each year. During the season, juveniles that have grown large enough leave the nest and are seen gathering at the seashore to beg food from their returning parents.
• **NEST** A low heap of pebbles, collected by the male.
• **DISTRIBUTION** Breeds around much of the coast of Antarctica and on nearby islands. Winters out at sea.

JUVENILE

• *dense, waterproof plumage*

• *very short legs*

• *large, fleshy foot*

DISTRIBUTION

Plumage Sexes alike	Habitat	Migration Migrant

Family SPHENISCIDAE	Species *Eudyptula minor*	Length 16 in (40 cm)

LITTLE PENGUIN

When on land, this tiny penguin avoids predators by being nocturnal and by the camouflage afforded by its nondescript, plain plumage. The birds feed at sea, swimming underwater to catch fish. When not breeding or molting, Little Penguins normally rest by floating on the open water. Parties come ashore to their colonies after dark and leave again before dawn. The penguins typically use underground burrows for breeding and stay in the burrows afterward to molt their plumage. Noisy braying and yapping calls betray the presence of the penguins. Parents take turns of up to several days to incubate the eggs and guard the young.
• **NEST** A burrow in a colony on a sandy shore; sometimes in a cave or under thick vegetation beside the sea.
• **DISTRIBUTION** Breeds on coasts and islands of S. and S.E. Australia and New Zealand. Spends the winter out at sea.

• *plain, unpatterned head*

• *short, thick feathering*

DISTRIBUTION

Plumage Sexes alike	Habitat	Migration Partial migrant

Family SPHENISCIDAE	Species *Spheniscus humboldti*	Length 27 in (68 cm)

HUMBOLDT PENGUIN

With a banded pattern on its breast and face and a raucous, braying call, this bird is easily recognized as one of the "jackass" penguins that occur in South Africa, South America, and the Galapagos Islands. It feeds in the cold but fish-rich Humboldt Current, taking anchovies, pilchards, and other surface-schooling fish, as well as squid. The penguins hunt in groups or small flocks, diving simultaneously to chase and herd the fish underwater. Breeding success or failure is linked to the season's supply of fish. Humboldt Penguins nest in large colonies of burrows, using caves if they can find no suitable soil for burrowing. Like most nestling penguins, the two downy young grow and fatten until they look a little larger than their parents before molting into their first adult plumage.
• **NEST** A bare hollow in a burrow, cave, or rock crevice, situated close to the sea.
• **DISTRIBUTION** Peru and N. Chile.
• **REMARK** Commercial quarrying for fertilizer has destroyed many colonies of burrows and taken away the soil, forcing the birds to nest in caves or rock crevices.

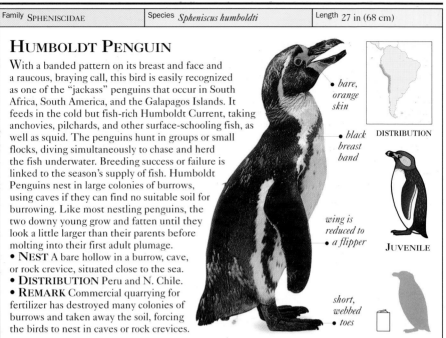

• *bare, orange skin*

DISTRIBUTION

• *black breast band*

wing is reduced to a flipper

JUVENILE

short, webbed toes

Plumage Sexes alike	Habitat 〜〜 〜〜	Migration Non-migrant

Family GAVIIDAE	Species *Gavia immer*	Length 36 in (91 cm)

COMMON LOON

This bird is easily detected in its northern breeding grounds, where its wailing, laughing calls echo across the freshwater lakes on whose shores and islands it nests. Head and body are streamlined for chasing fish underwater, but the bird walks clumsily when it comes ashore to nest.

WINTER

DISTRIBUTION

strong, dagger bill •

• **NEST** A low heap of plant materials by the water.
• **DISTRIBUTION** Breeds in N. North America, Greenland, and Iceland. Winters on coasts of N.W. Europe and North America.

striped neck patch •

Plumage Sexes alike	Habitat 〜〜 ⸺ 〜〜	Migration Migrant

Family PODICIPEDIDAE	Species *Podilymbus podiceps*	Length 15 in (38 cm)

PIED-BILLED GREBE

A small grebe with a stout bill, this bird is usually found on streams and ponds. In spring, it occurs in pairs or family parties, but in winter, larger groups gather on lakes and larger ponds. The birds swim rapidly underwater, catching fish and insects.
• **NEST** A heap of decayed plant material, lying in shallow water or floating among growing waterplants.
• **DISTRIBUTION** Breeds in much of the Americas. Populations in far north and south migrate to warmer areas in winter.

short, deep bill

long neck

plump, rounded body

DISTRIBUTION

WINTER

Plumage Sexes alike	Habitat	Migration Partial migrant

Family PODICIPEDIDAE	Species *Podiceps cristatus*	Length 19 in (48 cm)

GREAT CRESTED GREBE

Ornamented with crests on their crowns and chestnut "tippets" on the sides of their heads, pairs of this species display together on lakes and rivers. The birds hunt for fish, insects, and other aquatic animals underwater.
• **NEST** A heap of plant materials, floating in shallow water or among waterplants.
• **DISTRIBUTION** Breeds in much of Eurasia and in Africa and Australasia. Populations in the north of the Eurasian range winter as far south as the Mediterranean and N. India.

DISTRIBUTION

slim, dagger bill

WINTER

Plumage Sexes alike	Habitat	Migration Partial migrant

Family DIOMEDEIDAE	Species *Diomedea exulans*	Length 53 in (135 cm)

WANDERING ALBATROSS

This gigantic seabird has long, narrow wings with a span of
some 9 ft 9 in (3 m). It flies effortlessly over the southern oceans,
where strong winds and gales are usual. Saving energy by soaring
on the wind, it often travels for dozens, or even hundreds, of
miles while prospecting for a good food source. A typical feeding
site would be an area of water in which upward currents bring
nutrients to surface waters. The bird feeds mainly at night,

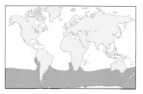

DISTRIBUTION

reaching down from the surface for prey, or on rare occasions making shallow
dives. Squid and other cephalopods are the main food. During the night, these
and other marine animals rise to the surface. The albatross stores food as an oily
liquid in its stomach, to be either digested later or regurgitated for its young.
Wandering Albatrosses nest in small colonies on the exposed tops and slopes
of small, oceanic islands from which they can easily launch themselves off
into the wind. Courting adults display to one another by spreading their
wings, waving their heads, and rapping their bills together, amid frequent,
braying calls. Pairs thus formed stay together for life. The single egg is incubated for
11 weeks by both parents in turn. The young bird is fed on fish and regurgitated oil
for up to ten months, before it flies. Breeding normally takes place
every two years. The young bird spends its first ten years at sea
until it is mature enough to breed. By then its plumage will have
changed gradually, through a series of molts, from chocolate brown
to mainly white. The birds live on average for about 30 years.
• **NEST** A large, drum-shaped mound scraped together out
of earth and plant materials, with a small hollow in the top.
• **DISTRIBUTION** Oceans and islands surrounding Antarctica,
and coasts of the southern continents.

JUVENILE

*snowy white plumage of
fully mature bird •*

*very long,
narrow
wing •*

Plumage Sexes alike	Habitat 〰〰 〰〰	Migration Migrant

Family DIOMEDEIDAE	Species *Phoebetria palpebrata*	Length 34 in (85 cm)

LIGHT-MANTLED SOOTY ALBATROSS

Three features identify this small albatross: its plumage is mostly dark, its back is pale gray, and, when seen in flight, its tail forms a perfect wedge shape. It glides for long distances with spread wings. To feed, it floats on the sea and catches fish, squid, and crustaceans. Courtship behavior includes paired flights and face-to-face ground displays in which the white eye crescent and bill stripe are shown off. The birds nest in scattered pairs on ledges of steep slopes on islands in the southern oceans.
• **NEST** A tall mound scraped together out of soil and plant materials, with a deep, cupped hollow on the top.
• **DISTRIBUTION** Oceans and islands around Antarctica and the southern coasts of South America, Australia, and New Zealand.

FLYING ADULT

DISTRIBUTION

ADULT IN GROUND DISPLAY

Plumage Sexes alike	Habitat	Migration Migrant

Family PROCELLARIIDAE	Species *Macronectes giganteus*	Length 37 in (95 cm)

SOUTHERN GIANT PETREL

A heavy, albatross-size petrel, this bird looks slightly humpbacked in flight. On land, it walks with far greater agility than other petrels, which creep on lowered legs. Southern Giant Petrels feed both at sea and on the shore. Birds are seen fighting over carrion, such as a beached whale, or killing smaller seabirds. Breeding colonies are situated on islands or on mainland shores.
• **NEST** A shallow depression in the ground, bordered by pebbles or dry vegetation.
• **DISTRIBUTION** Breeds on coasts and islands of Antarctica. Winters on the southern oceans.

NORMAL PHASE

• *drab, mottled plumage*

WHITE PHASE

webbed feet •

DISTRIBUTION

Plumage Sexes alike	Habitat	Migration Migrant

Family PROCELLARIIDAE	Species *Fulmarus glacialis*	Length 18½ in (47 cm)

NORTHERN FULMAR

A stout-bodied seabird with a rounded head and thick bill, this species occurs in color phases (*see p. 13*) from gray-and-white to dark blue-gray. It flies strongly, alternating a few quick wingbeats with a glide on stiffly spread wings. When feeding, it catches fish at the sea surface or dives to depths up to several feet, taking small animals drifting in the plankton. Flocks also gather around fishing boats for offal. Fulmars nest on coastal cliffs, singly or in noisy colonies.

• **NEST** Eggs are laid on a bare ledge on a cliff or crag.

• **DISTRIBUTION** Breeds on N. Atlantic and N. Pacific coasts. Disperses out to sea in winter.

DARK PHASE

wings held level for gliding

DISTRIBUTION

bird maneuvering in an updraft over nest site

legs lowered for landing

tubular nostrils on the bill

Plumage Sexes alike	Habitat	Migration Migrant

Family PROCELLARIIDAE	Species *Daption capense*	Length 15½ in (39 cm)

CAPE PETREL

With its checkered plumage, this seabird was likened to a pigeon by seamen aboard the whaling vessels around which it flocked: hence its traditional name, the Cape Pigeon. Its flight pattern consists of rapid wingbeats alternating with stiff-winged glides. To feed, it swims and reaches down or dives for small fish and other animals in the plankton. Cape Petrels breed in small groups or colonies on shores and islands.

• **NEST** A shallow depression in a layer of loose rock fragments, on a rocky ledge, or in a crevice.

• **DISTRIBUTION** Breeds on islands and coasts of southern continents. Winters on the southern oceans.

FLYING ADULT

DISTRIBUTION

checkered plumage

Plumage Sexes alike	Habitat	Migration Migrant

Family PROCELLARIIDAE	Species *Pterodroma cookii*	Length 13 in (33 cm)

COOK'S PETREL

Seen in fast, erratic flight over the ocean, this petrel is recognized by its bold wing markings. It floats on the sea to feed, snatching up small drifting animal life from the plankton. From a tiny breeding range, it journeys extensively over the ocean. When breeding, it comes ashore by night to avoid predators.

FLYING ADULT

• **NEST** A hollow in a burrow, usually high on a forested slope.
• **DISTRIBUTION** Breeds on two small islands at opposite ends of New Zealand. Winters at sea over much of the Pacific Ocean.

• *dark wing mark*

• *weak legs*

• *tubular nostrils on the bill*

DISTRIBUTION

Plumage Sexes alike	Habitat 〰️ 〰️	Migration Migrant

Family PROCELLARIIDAE	Species *Pachyptila turtur*	Length 10½ in (27 cm)

FAIRY PRION

This small petrel flies over the ocean for much of its life. It feeds in flocks by night, skimming the sea surface with its bill to scoop up small crustaceans, squid, and other animals. The bill is equipped with fine plates (lamellae) that filter these animals from the water. Fairy Prions land by night at their breeding colonies, which are always situated on small islands. Incoming birds utter soft, cooing calls as they arrive; if their breeding partners are in the burrow, they reply with similar calls. On land, they walk clumsily on weak legs, in a low, crouching gait.

FLYING ADULT

• **NEST** A burrow dug with the bill and feet in soil, often hidden among vegetation, or a hollow in a rock crevice.
• **DISTRIBUTION** Breeds on coasts of southern continents. Winters at sea.

weak legs

• *long wings*

DISTRIBUTION

Plumage Sexes alike	Habitat 〰️ 〰️	Migration Migrant

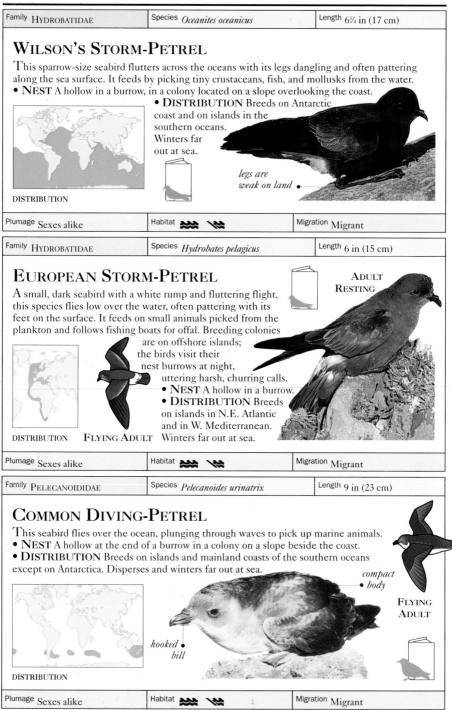

| Family HYDROBATIDAE | Species *Oceanites oceanicus* | Length 6¾ in (17 cm) |

WILSON'S STORM-PETREL

This sparrow-size seabird flutters across the oceans with its legs dangling and often pattering along the sea surface. It feeds by picking tiny crustaceans, fish, and mollusks from the water.
• NEST A hollow in a burrow, in a colony located on a slope overlooking the coast.

• DISTRIBUTION Breeds on Antarctic coast and on islands in the southern oceans. Winters far out at sea.

legs are weak on land

DISTRIBUTION

| Plumage Sexes alike | Habitat | Migration Migrant |

| Family HYDROBATIDAE | Species *Hydrobates pelagicus* | Length 6 in (15 cm) |

EUROPEAN STORM-PETREL

ADULT RESTING

A small, dark seabird with a white rump and fluttering flight, this species flies low over the water, often pattering with its feet on the surface. It feeds on small animals picked from the plankton and follows fishing boats for offal. Breeding colonies are on offshore islands; the birds visit their nest burrows at night, uttering harsh, churring calls.
• NEST A hollow in a burrow.
• DISTRIBUTION Breeds on islands in N.E. Atlantic and in W. Mediterranean. Winters far out at sea.

DISTRIBUTION   FLYING ADULT

| Plumage Sexes alike | Habitat | Migration Migrant |

| Family PELECANOIDIDAE | Species *Pelecanoides urinatrix* | Length 9 in (23 cm) |

COMMON DIVING-PETREL

This seabird flies over the ocean, plunging through waves to pick up marine animals.
• NEST A hollow at the end of a burrow in a colony on a slope beside the coast.
• DISTRIBUTION Breeds on islands and mainland coasts of the southern oceans except on Antarctica. Disperses and winters far out at sea.

compact body

FLYING ADULT

hooked bill

DISTRIBUTION

| Plumage Sexes alike | Habitat | Migration Migrant |

Family PROCELLARIIDAE	Species *Puffinus puffinus*	Length 13½ in (34 cm)

MANX SHEARWATER

A dark-backed seabird with a white underside, the Manx Shearwater flies low over the sea, making rapid, tilting glides alternating with quick wingbeats. The shearwater feeds at the surface or in shallow plunge-dives, taking small fish, squid, crustaceans, and offal from fishing boats. Nesting colonies are located on hilly offshore islands. Flocks are seen floating offshore, waiting to visit their nests after dark. They eventually go ashore, amid a chorus of crowing calls.
• **NEST** A hollow, sometimes lined with grass, in a burrow or occasionally in a rock crevice or cavity.
• **DISTRIBUTION** Breeds along coasts of N. Atlantic Ocean. Winters in mid-ocean, as far south as S. Atlantic Ocean.

narrow, tapering • wings

DISTRIBUTION

ADULT

Plumage Sexes alike	Habitat	Migration Migrant

Family PHAETHONTIDAE	Species *Phaethon lepturus*	Length 31 in (80 cm)

WHITE-TAILED TROPICBIRD

This beautiful seabird flies gracefully with its streamlined body, slender tail, and long wings. It feeds by plunge-diving into the sea for fish, squid, and crustaceans. Both sexes have long, white tail streamers, which they show off in acrobatic display flights over the nesting area.
• **NEST**
Eggs are laid in a crevice, on bare ground, or underneath overhanging rocks.
• **DISTRIBUTION** Breeds on islands in the Pacific, Atlantic, and Indian Oceans. Disperses out to sea.

strong dagger • bill

FLYING
ADULT

very • long wing

DISTRIBUTION

JUVENILE

Plumage Sexes alike	Habitat	Migration Migrant

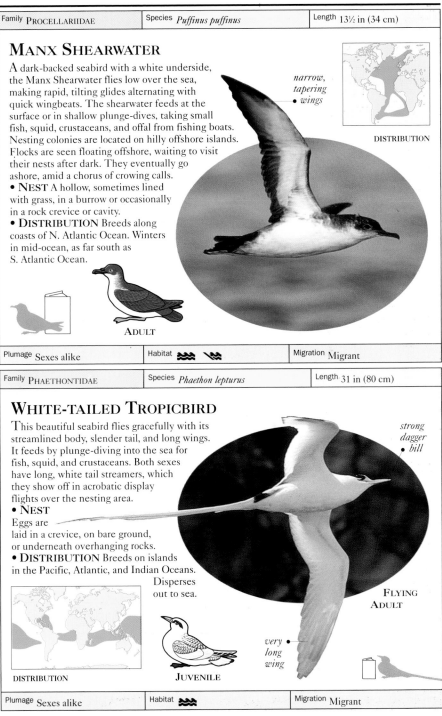

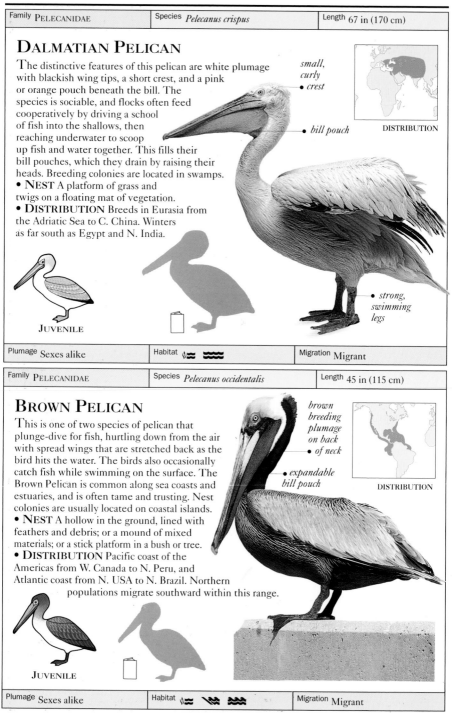

Family PELECANIDAE	Species *Pelecanus crispus*	Length 67 in (170 cm)

DALMATIAN PELICAN

The distinctive features of this pelican are white plumage with blackish wing tips, a short crest, and a pink or orange pouch beneath the bill. The species is sociable, and flocks often feed cooperatively by driving a school of fish into the shallows, then reaching underwater to scoop up fish and water together. This fills their bill pouches, which they drain by raising their heads. Breeding colonies are located in swamps.
• **NEST** A platform of grass and twigs on a floating mat of vegetation.
• **DISTRIBUTION** Breeds in Eurasia from the Adriatic Sea to C. China. Winters as far south as Egypt and N. India.

small, curly
• crest

• bill pouch

DISTRIBUTION

• strong, swimming legs

JUVENILE

Plumage Sexes alike	Habitat	Migration Migrant

Family PELECANIDAE	Species *Pelecanus occidentalis*	Length 45 in (115 cm)

BROWN PELICAN

This is one of two species of pelican that plunge-dive for fish, hurtling down from the air with spread wings that are stretched back as the bird hits the water. The birds also occasionally catch fish while swimming on the surface. The Brown Pelican is common along sea coasts and estuaries, and is often tame and trusting. Nest colonies are usually located on coastal islands.
• **NEST** A hollow in the ground, lined with feathers and debris; or a mound of mixed materials; or a stick platform in a bush or tree.
• **DISTRIBUTION** Pacific coast of the Americas from W. Canada to N. Peru, and Atlantic coast from N. USA to N. Brazil. Northern populations migrate southward within this range.

brown breeding plumage on back
• of neck

• expandable bill pouch

DISTRIBUTION

JUVENILE

Plumage Sexes alike	Habitat	Migration Migrant

Family SULIDAE	Species *Morus bassanus*	Length 31 in (80 cm)

NORTHERN GANNET

This powerful and highly streamlined seabird is adapted for plunge-diving for fish. Gannets sometimes drop vertically into the sea, from heights as great as 148 ft (45 m). They often feed in flocks and catch mainly schooling fish, such as herrings and mackerel. Gannets fly strongly, alternately flapping and gliding, often in groups in single file. They nest in gannetries (colonies) on raised slopes and cliff tops, or on broad cliff ledges. Gannets are aggressive and the nests are spaced by a distance corresponding to the bill reach of two sitting birds. Their calls are deep and harsh. Juveniles take five annual molts to attain adult plumage.
• **NEST** A mound of seaweed and debris, on the ground or on a ledge.
• **DISTRIBUTION** Breeds on the coasts of the N. Atlantic Ocean. Winters as far south as E. USA and W. Africa.

DISTRIBUTION

• *bare skin around eye*

JUVENILE

• *streamlined body for plunge-diving*

tapering tail •

Plumage Sexes alike	Habitat	Migration Partial migrant

Family SULIDAE	Species *Sula nebouxii*	Length 32 in (81 cm)

BLUE-FOOTED BOOBY

A coastal seabird that plunge-dives for fish, this bird resembles a gannet but is more lightly built and has a longer tail. These features enable it to dive into shallow water. Flocks sometimes plunge simultaneously from a height. The birds nest on offshore islands in small colonies. In courtship, they display their blue feet, which also provide warmth for incubation.
• **NEST** Eggs are placed on flat ground, usually with no nest materials.
• **DISTRIBUTION** E. Pacific on islands from N.W. Mexico to Galapagos and along the South American coast to N. Peru.

DISTRIBUTION

strong, tapering bill •

• *tapering tail*

long, narrow wings •

JUVENILE

Plumage Sexes alike	Habitat	Migration Partial migrant

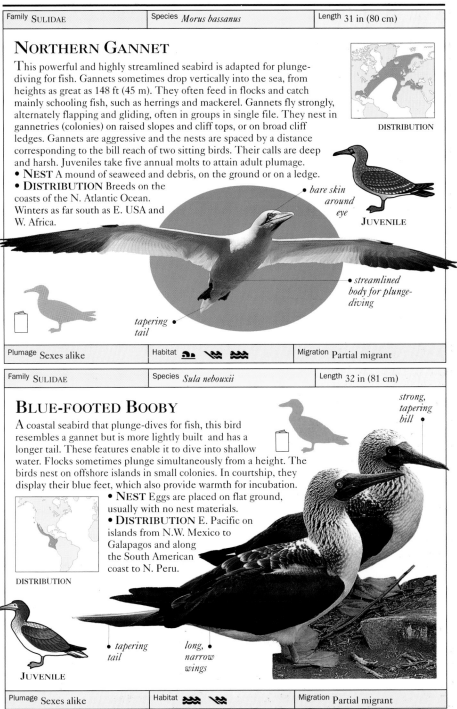

| Family PHALACROCORACIDAE | Species *Phalacrocorax auritus* | Length 31 in (80 cm) |

DOUBLE-CRESTED CORMORANT

The two crests crossing the head of this large, dark cormorant are normally barely visible, raised only for short periods when the birds display. The Double-crested Cormorant is found as often on rivers and freshwater lakes as on the coast. It swims characteristically low in the water and dives in pursuit of fish, propelling itself with its large, webbed feet. Nest colonies are found either on the coast or beside large inland waters.
• **NEST** A large platform of twigs, placed in a tree or on a rock ledge.
• **DISTRIBUTION** Breeds from S. Alaska and Newfoundland to C. Mexico and Cuba. Northern populations migrate south within this range.

DISTRIBUTION

slender • bill

wings spread for drying

strong legs for underwater swimming •

large, webbed • feet

JUVENILE

| Plumage Sexes alike | Habitat | Migration Partial migrant |

| Family PHALACROCORACIDAE | Species *Phalacrocorax carbo* | Length 36 in (91 cm) |

GREAT CORMORANT

This large cormorant is found on any large stretch of water in its worldwide distribution, including lakes, rivers, estuaries, and coastal waters. To feed, it swims low in the water, often peering under the surface to locate fish, and dives to pursue its prey. Fish are brought to the surface to be gulped down in the cormorant's wide gullet. Like other cormorants, this species has poorly waterproofed plumage and is often seen standing with its wings spread out to dry. In the air, it travels in steady, flapping flight with occasional glides. When breeding, birds have white patches on the flanks and head and a glossy sheen on the dark plumage.
• **NEST** A bulky, cup-shaped nest made of seaweed and debris, placed on a flat rock or cliff ledge; or a stick nest in a tree.
• **DISTRIBUTION** E. North America; much of Eurasia; parts of Africa; S. and S.E. Asia; parts of Australia.

bare • patch

"scaly" pattern on • the wings

white flank • patch

DISTRIBUTION

DARK-HEADED FORM

LIGHT-HEADED FORM

| Plumage Sexes alike | Habitat | Migration Partial migrant |

Family PHALACROCORACIDAE	Species *Phalacrocorax gaimardi*	Length 30 in (75 cm)

RED-LEGGED CORMORANT

This slender, narrow-billed cormorant has a star pattern around the eye and fine, white spotting on its back and wings. When swimming, however, its wet plumage makes the bird look black, except for the white patch on its neck. It can be identified by its bright red legs, which show as it arches its body to plunge underwater. The species occurs entirely on coastal waters. Although not strongly social with its own kind, it joins other cormorant species and boobies in mixed flocks that fish and rest communally. It feeds on fish, squid, and crustaceans. Red-legged Cormorants breed in pairs or in small colonies, developing white, hairlike plumes among their head feathers when in breeding condition.

JUVENILE

• slender bill

• patterned bare skin around eye

• **NEST** A low mound of seaweed, placed on a rock ledge, usually in the shelter of a sea cave.
• **DISTRIBUTION** Coast and islands of South America on Pacific side from Peru to S. Chile, around southern tip of South America to Atlantic coast of Argentina.

DISTRIBUTION

Plumage Sexes alike	Habitat	Migration Non-migrant

Family ANHINGIDAE	Species *Anhinga anhinga*	Length 35 in (90 cm)

ANHINGA

A small head with a straight bill and a slender neck are sometimes all that can be seen of this bird as it swims with body submerged. One of its other names, the Snakebird, reflects this appearance. Resembling a cormorant, it differs in having a longer neck and in lacking a hooked bill. It inhabits freshwater swamps and catches fish underwater, spearing them on its bill, then taking them to the surface to be swallowed. Like cormorants, Anhingas spread their wings to dry their plumage.

• sharp, dagger bill

• snake-like neck

• **NEST** A stick platform in a tree.
• **DISTRIBUTION** From S.E. USA to S. Brazil and N. Argentina.

white wing patch • of male

webbed • feet

DISTRIBUTION

FEMALE

Plumage Sexes differ	Habitat	Migration Partial migrant

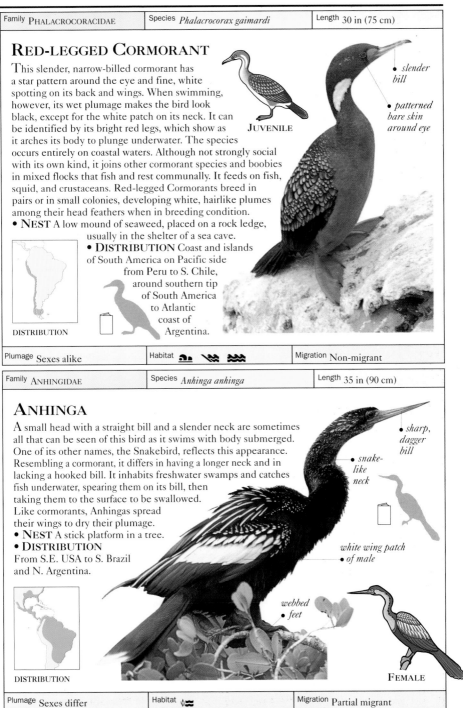

| Family FREGATIDAE | Species *Fregata minor* | Length 39 in (100 cm) |

GREAT FRIGATEBIRD

This bird is often seen soaring and gliding on the winds over coast
and sea, with long wings extended. It feeds in the air, either swooping
to snatch fish from the sea or piratically attacking other seabirds and
forcing them to drop or disgorge their food for its own consumption.
When breeding, male Great Frigatebirds inflate their red throat sacs in display.
• **NEST** A frail platform of twigs, placed in a low bush or tree, usually on an island.
• **DISTRIBUTION** Breeds along coastlines
of C. America, S. Brazil, E. Africa,
S.E. Asia, and N. Australia, and
on islands in the Pacific,
S. Atlantic, and
Indian Oceans.

*long,
hooked
• bill*

FEMALE

DISTRIBUTION

| Plumage Sexes differ | Habitat 〰️ 🏔️ | Migration Partial migrant |

| Family ARDEIDAE | Species *Ardea cinerea* | Length 38 in (97 cm) |

GRAY HERON

The large, gray figure of this heron, resting
with its head hunched on its shoulders or
standing alert, with neck outstretched, is a regular
sight beside lakes, ponds, rivers, or marshes. To feed,
it either stands still or wades slowly and watchfully, its
angled neck allowing the head to dart forward to seize
a fish or any small animal. The heron flies with slow beats
of its large, broad wings, its head tucked back on its
shoulders and its legs extended. It is usually
silent but occasionally utters a harsh call.
• **NEST** A platform of sticks, to which
more material is added each year.
• **DISTRIBUTION** Eurasia, Africa, and Asia.

• black, drooping crest

*• black
shoulder
patch*

*• long
legs*

JUVENILE

• long, thin toes

DISTRIBUTION

| Plumage Sexes alike | Habitat 🌿〰️ 〰️〰️ | Migration Partial migrant |

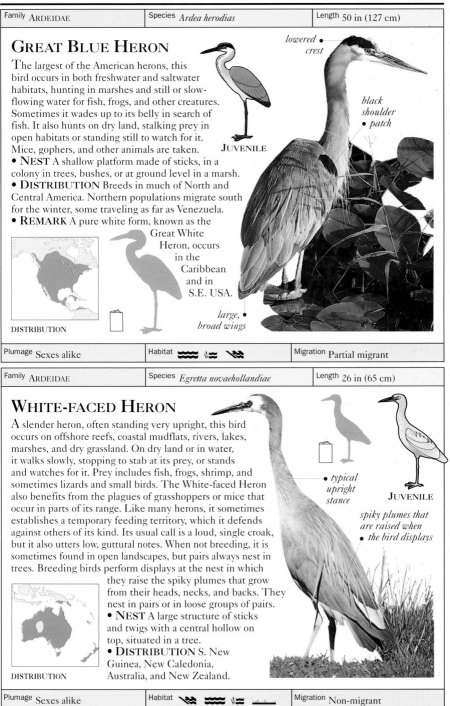

Family ARDEIDAE	Species *Ardea herodias*	Length 50 in (127 cm)

GREAT BLUE HERON

The largest of the American herons, this bird occurs in both freshwater and saltwater habitats, hunting in marshes and still or slow-flowing water for fish, frogs, and other creatures. Sometimes it wades up to its belly in search of fish. It also hunts on dry land, stalking prey in open habitats or standing still to watch for it. Mice, gophers, and other animals are taken.

• NEST A shallow platform made of sticks, in a colony in trees, bushes, or at ground level in a marsh.

• DISTRIBUTION Breeds in much of North and Central America. Northern populations migrate south for the winter, some traveling as far as Venezuela.

• REMARK A pure white form, known as the Great White Heron, occurs in the Caribbean and in S.E. USA.

lowered crest

black shoulder patch

JUVENILE

large, broad wings

DISTRIBUTION

Plumage Sexes alike	Habitat	Migration Partial migrant

Family ARDEIDAE	Species *Egretta novaehollandiae*	Length 26 in (65 cm)

WHITE-FACED HERON

A slender heron, often standing very upright, this bird occurs on offshore reefs, coastal mudflats, rivers, lakes, marshes, and dry grassland. On dry land or in water, it walks slowly, stopping to stab at its prey, or stands and watches for it. Prey includes fish, frogs, shrimp, and sometimes lizards and small birds. The White-faced Heron also benefits from the plagues of grasshoppers or mice that occur in parts of its range. Like many herons, it sometimes establishes a temporary feeding territory, which it defends against others of its kind. Its usual call is a loud, single croak, but it also utters low, guttural notes. When not breeding, it is sometimes found in open landscapes, but pairs always nest in trees. Breeding birds perform displays at the nest in which they raise the spiky plumes that grow from their heads, necks, and backs. They nest in pairs or in loose groups of pairs.

• NEST A large structure of sticks and twigs with a central hollow on top, situated in a tree.

• DISTRIBUTION S. New Guinea, New Caledonia, Australia, and New Zealand.

typical upright stance

JUVENILE

spiky plumes that are raised when the bird displays

DISTRIBUTION

Plumage Sexes alike	Habitat	Migration Non-migrant

Family ARDEIDAE	Species *Ardea goliath*	Length 59 in (150 cm)

GOLIATH HERON

This is the tallest and largest heron in the world. It occurs at the edges of large lakes and swamps, where it can wade deeper than other herons. Other habitats include mudflats, mangrove swamps, rivers, and papyrus swamps. When not breeding, birds are either solitary or live in pairs. A Goliath Heron tends to fish over the same areas daily. It often hunts among thickly crowded floating vegetation on tropical waters or wades up to its belly in open water, either stalking slowly or standing still to watch for prey. When about to strike, it lowers its body, head, and back-curved neck to crouch near water level. The neck has a kink that can suddenly straighten, shooting the head forward. Prey is mostly impaled on the sharp point of the bill or sometimes seized in the bill. Fish, frogs, small mammals, reptiles, and invertebrates are taken. Like other herons, the Goliath has special patches of downy feathers on its lower body. These constantly break down to a powder, which the heron works into its plumage with its bill as part of the preening process. The powder absorbs fish slime, and the heron cleans both off together with the comb-shaped claw of its front middle toe. The call of the Goliath is a deep, repeated, raucous note. Flight is slow and heavy, with the legs sagging slightly. Goliath Herons usually nest in pairs, sometimes at the edge of mixed colonies of birds of other species.

• **NEST** A platform of sticks and reed stems, placed on top of growing swamp vegetation, in a bush, in a low tree, or on the ground.

• **DISTRIBUTION** Parts of Africa, Arabian Peninsula, and the Indian subcontinent.

DISTRIBUTION

resting posture with • folded neck

• brown "shoulder" patch

• marbled pattern on the neck of mature bird

plumes • hanging from nape

• bird often rests with one leg raised

• long, wading leg

comblike claw on the middle front toe, • used in feather care

JUVENILE

Plumage Sexes alike	Habitat	Migration Non-migrant

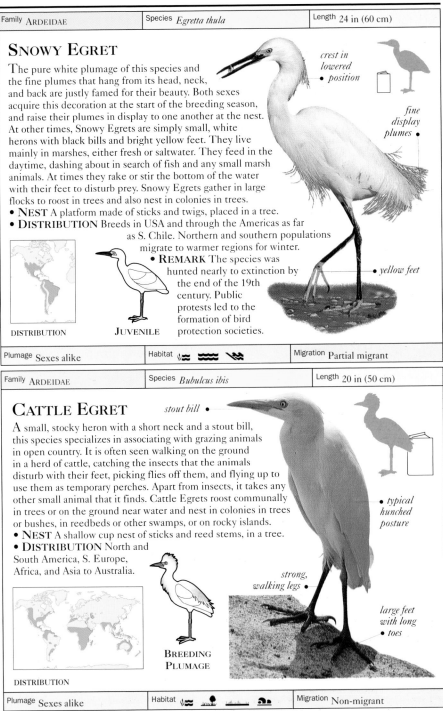

| Family ARDEIDAE | Species *Egretta thula* | Length 24 in (60 cm) |

SNOWY EGRET

The pure white plumage of this species and
the fine plumes that hang from its head, neck,
and back are justly famed for their beauty. Both sexes
acquire this decoration at the start of the breeding season,
and raise their plumes in display to one another at the nest.
At other times, Snowy Egrets are simply small, white
herons with black bills and bright yellow feet. They live
mainly in marshes, either fresh or saltwater. They feed in the
daytime, dashing about in search of fish and any small marsh
animals. At times they rake or stir the bottom of the water
with their feet to disturb prey. Snowy Egrets gather in large
flocks to roost in trees and also nest in colonies in trees.
• **NEST** A platform made of sticks and twigs, placed in a tree.
• **DISTRIBUTION** Breeds in USA and through the Americas as far
as S. Chile. Northern and southern populations
migrate to warmer regions for winter.
• **REMARK** The species was
hunted nearly to extinction by
the end of the 19th
century. Public
protests led to the
formation of bird
protection societies.

crest in lowered • position

fine display plumes •

• yellow feet

DISTRIBUTION   **JUVENILE**

| Plumage Sexes alike | Habitat | Migration Partial migrant |

| Family ARDEIDAE | Species *Bubulcus ibis* | Length 20 in (50 cm) |

CATTLE EGRET
stout bill •

A small, stocky heron with a short neck and a stout bill,
this species specializes in associating with grazing animals
in open country. It is often seen walking on the ground
in a herd of cattle, catching the insects that the animals
disturb with their feet, picking flies off them, and flying up to
use them as temporary perches. Apart from insects, it takes any
other small animal that it finds. Cattle Egrets roost communally
in trees or on the ground near water and nest in colonies in trees
or bushes, in reedbeds or other swamps, or on rocky islands.
• **NEST** A shallow cup nest of sticks and reed stems, in a tree.
• **DISTRIBUTION** North and
South America, S. Europe,
Africa, and Asia to Australia.

• typical hunched posture

strong, walking legs •

large feet with long • toes

**BREEDING
PLUMAGE**

DISTRIBUTION

| Plumage Sexes alike | Habitat | Migration Non-migrant |

Family ARDEIDAE	Species *Butorides virescens*	Length 18 in (46 cm)

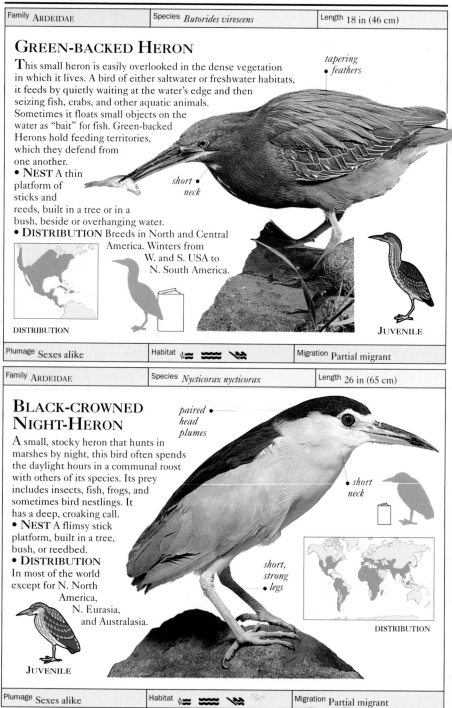

GREEN-BACKED HERON

This small heron is easily overlooked in the dense vegetation in which it lives. A bird of either saltwater or freshwater habitats, it feeds by quietly waiting at the water's edge and then seizing fish, crabs, and other aquatic animals. Sometimes it floats small objects on the water as "bait" for fish. Green-backed Herons hold feeding territories, which they defend from one another.

• **NEST** A thin platform of sticks and reeds, built in a tree or in a bush, beside or overhanging water.

• **DISTRIBUTION** Breeds in North and Central America. Winters from W. and S. USA to N. South America.

tapering
• feathers

short •
neck

DISTRIBUTION

JUVENILE

Plumage Sexes alike	Habitat	Migration Partial migrant

Family ARDEIDAE	Species *Nycticorax nycticorax*	Length 26 in (65 cm)

BLACK-CROWNED NIGHT-HERON

A small, stocky heron that hunts in marshes by night, this bird often spends the daylight hours in a communal roost with others of its species. Its prey includes insects, fish, frogs, and sometimes bird nestlings. It has a deep, croaking call.

• **NEST** A flimsy stick platform, built in a tree, bush, or reedbed.

• **DISTRIBUTION** In most of the world except for N. North America, N. Eurasia, and Australasia.

paired •
head
plumes

• short
neck

short,
strong
• legs

DISTRIBUTION

JUVENILE

Plumage Sexes alike	Habitat	Migration Partial migrant

Family ARDEIDAE	Species *Cochlearius cochlearius*	Length 20 in (50 cm)

BOAT-BILLED HERON

Looking like a night-heron except for its capacious bill, this bird is adapted for night hunting, even in total darkness. Its prey consists of small creatures such as fish, shrimp, and insects, and the Boat-bill is believed to be able to feel these in the dark with its bill, which is touch sensitive. As soon as contact is made the bill opens, drawing in a current of water and with it the prey. The Boatbill feeds at the edges of mangrove creeks, beside other tidal inlets, and in either fresh or partly saltwater lagoons, lakes, and marshes. It roosts and nests in trees or bushes, either in pairs or in small groups of pairs.

large eye for feeding at night

• **NEST** A frail platform made of twigs, placed in mangroves or other swamp trees.

• **DISTRIBUTION** From Mexico to N. Argentina.

JUVENILE

DISTRIBUTION

Plumage Sexes alike	Habitat	Migration Non-migrant

Family ARDEIDAE	Species *Tigrisoma lineatum*	Length 30 in (75 cm)

RUFESCENT TIGER-HERON

The strongly streaked, black-and-yellow plumage of juveniles, as well as the markings of the adults, give the tiger-herons their name. This shy heron is found in extensive tropical rain forest. It occurs beside slow-moving, marshy waters or lowland rivers, and also in swamps and mangroves. Rufescent Tiger-Herons hunt alone and mainly at night, prowling slowly or waiting motionless to catch shrimp and insects. When disturbed, birds usually freeze motionless to escape detection, but if forced to break cover, they take refuge in the trees.

stout bill

camouflage plumage

• **NEST** A frail platform of twigs and plant stems, usually built high in a tree.

• **DISTRIBUTION** From E. Honduras to Paraguay and N. Argentina.

long, green legs

JUVENILE

ADULT

DISTRIBUTION

Plumage Sexes alike	Habitat	Migration Non-migrant

Family BALAENICIPITIDAE	Species *Balaeniceps rex*	Length 47 in (120 cm)

SHOEBILL

This large, storklike bird, recognized by its enormous, hook-tipped bill, occurs only in the freshwater swamps of east and central Africa. Shoebills live singly or in pairs, remaining most of the time in a small area of marshland. They sometimes feed in wet grassland or shallow water, but their favored hunting grounds are deep marshes and rivers or lakes choked with vegetation. When hunting, a Shoebill walks slowly and deliberately, often climbing over floating waterplants, spreading its weight on long, straight toes. The bird pauses to watch the water for prey such as lungfish, catfish, frogs, water snakes, or small turtles. On sighting a victim, the Shoebill lunges forward and down, stretching its neck and whole body and spreading its wings. If it succeeds in making a catch, it usually also grabs a mass of waterweed together with the prey and has to separate out the food by turning it over in its bill. The flight of the Shoebill is slow but strong, with heavily beating wings and with the head resting back on the shoulders. The legs are extended behind. Shoebills are also seen circling and soaring on rising air currents to gain height. The species nests in isolated pairs among tall vegetation, usually over water. Parent birds are seen bringing water in their bills to pour over the small young in hot weather.

- **NEST** A bulky platform of rushes, grasses, and leaves, in thick vegetation, with the base usually in water.
- **DISTRIBUTION** In African freshwater marshes from S. Sudan to Zambia and S.E. Zaire.

• small tuft on the crown

FLYING ADULT

• large head

DISTRIBUTION

• typical upright posture

large, • broad wing

long toes for spreading weight •

Plumage Sexes alike	Habitat	Migration Non-migrant

| Family SCOPIDAE | Species *Scopus umbretta* | Length 20 in (50 cm) |

HAMERKOP

This waterside bird is recognized by the hammerhead shape made by its bill and crest. It feeds in shallow water at the edges of rivers, lakes, and marshes, taking amphibians, small fish, and other aquatic creatures. It occurs in pairs or small family groups that tend to stay within a restricted area, but sometimes roam further afield during dry seasons. Hamerkops fly with a mixture of flapping and gliding, their legs stretching out behind. The neck is drawn back when flapping and extended when gliding.
• **NEST** A huge, oven-shaped mass of sticks with a small front entrance, lined with mud and placed in a tree or on a cliff, usually sited near or over water.
• **DISTRIBUTION** Africa and Madagascar.

back-swept crest •

FLYING ADULT

large, broad • wings

DISTRIBUTION

| Plumage Sexes alike | Habitat | Migration Non-migrant |

| Family CICONIIDAE | Species *Mycteria americana* | Length 40 in (102 cm) |

WOOD STORK

A large stork resembling an ibis, this bird frequents wooded marshland, resting and nesting in the trees. It walks sedately and flies with slow, deliberate wingbeats. The Wood Stork hunts in muddy pools, marshes, and wet grassland, feeding on fish, crustaceans, mollusks, frogs, and insects. In muddy water, it can feel and catch its prey with its bill.
• **NEST** A thin platform of sticks in a treetop colony.
• **DISTRIBUTION** From S.E. USA and Mexico through Central and South America to N. Argentina.

bare head enables the Wood Stork to feed by dipping into muddy • waters – no feathers to spoil

• black wing tips

DISTRIBUTION   **JUVENILE**

| Plumage Sexes alike | Habitat | Migration Partial migrant |

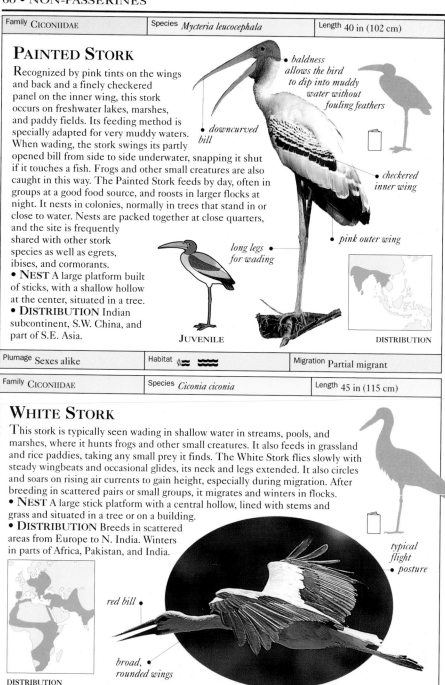

| Family CICONIIDAE | Species *Mycteria leucocephala* | Length 40 in (102 cm) |

PAINTED STORK

Recognized by pink tints on the wings and back and a finely checkered panel on the inner wing, this stork occurs on freshwater lakes, marshes, and paddy fields. Its feeding method is specially adapted for very muddy waters. When wading, the stork swings its partly opened bill from side to side underwater, snapping it shut if it touches a fish. Frogs and other small creatures are also caught in this way. The Painted Stork feeds by day, often in groups at a good food source, and roosts in larger flocks at night. It nests in colonies, normally in trees that stand in or close to water. Nests are packed together at close quarters, and the site is frequently shared with other stork species as well as egrets, ibises, and cormorants.
• NEST A large platform built of sticks, with a shallow hollow at the center, situated in a tree.
• DISTRIBUTION Indian subcontinent, S.W. China, and part of S.E. Asia.

baldness allows the bird to dip into muddy water without fouling feathers

• *downcurved bill*

• *checkered inner wing*

• *pink outer wing*

long legs for wading

JUVENILE

DISTRIBUTION

| Plumage Sexes alike | Habitat | Migration Partial migrant |

| Family CICONIIDAE | Species *Ciconia ciconia* | Length 45 in (115 cm) |

WHITE STORK

This stork is typically seen wading in shallow water in streams, pools, and marshes, where it hunts frogs and other small creatures. It also feeds in grassland and rice paddies, taking any small prey it finds. The White Stork flies slowly with steady wingbeats and occasional glides, its neck and legs extended. It also circles and soars on rising air currents to gain height, especially during migration. After breeding in scattered pairs or small groups, it migrates and winters in flocks.
• NEST A large stick platform with a central hollow, lined with stems and grass and situated in a tree or on a building.
• DISTRIBUTION Breeds in scattered areas from Europe to N. India. Winters in parts of Africa, Pakistan, and India.

typical flight posture

red bill •

broad, rounded wings

DISTRIBUTION

| Plumage Sexes alike | Habitat | Migration Migrant |

Family CICONIIDAE	Species *Leptoptilos crumeniferus*	Length 59 in (150 cm)

MARABOU STORK

A large, scavenging stork, this species lives in grassland and marshes, sometimes near human habitation. It feeds on animal carcasses of all sizes, sometimes competing with vultures, and also searches garbage dumps. Live prey is often taken, including insects, fish, rats, and small birds. Flamingo colonies are raided for eggs, young, and even adult birds. The Marabou's bald head enables it to eat messy foods such as carrion with minimal fouling of the feathers. Attached to the bare neck is a dangling, inflatable wattle, used in various forms of display behavior. The Marabou flies heavily on slowly beating wings, also soaring to considerable heights on rising air currents. It roosts in flocks and nests in large colonies. Courtship behavior includes a ritual slow raising and lowering of the head, with a variety of mooing, grunting, and whistling calls.

• **NEST** A large mass of sticks with a hollow at the center, which is lined with smaller twigs and green leaves. The nest is situated in a colony in a tree or on a cliff.

• **DISTRIBUTION** Much of Africa south of the Sahara.

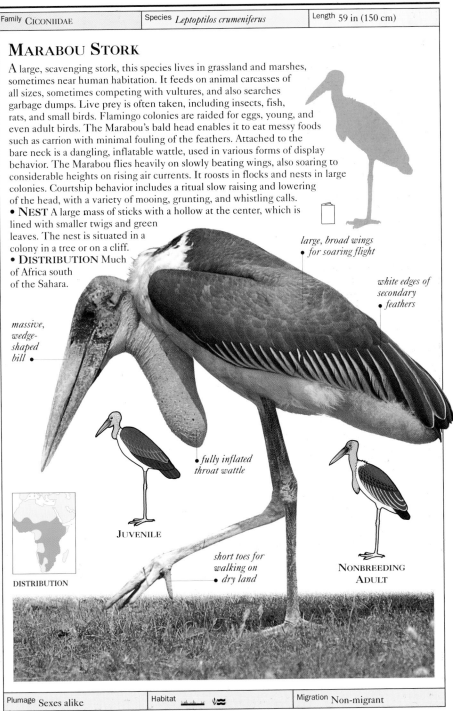

large, broad wings for soaring flight

white edges of secondary feathers

massive, wedge-shaped bill

fully inflated throat wattle

JUVENILE

short toes for walking on dry land

NONBREEDING ADULT

DISTRIBUTION

Plumage Sexes alike	Habitat	Migration Non-migrant

| Family CICONIIDAE | Species *Ephippiorhynchus senegalensis* | L.57 in (145 cm)/51 in (130 cm) |

SADDLE-BILLED STORK

Like other wading storks, this species is tall
and long-legged, with a long, thick bill and strong
colors. It occurs in any kind of water where it can
fish. The Saddlebill has several feeding methods.
It stands in water and stabs fish on sight; it walks
among waterplants and jabs at random; or it may
sweep its bill through muddy water to catch fish
by touch. Occasionally it stirs up the mud with
one foot to disturb fish. Saddlebills roost in
pairs in trees and nest in scattered pairs.
In courtship, they run with wings spread,
displaying their boldly marked plumage.
• **NEST** A platform of sticks, lined with
reeds, sedges, and earth, on a bush or
tree, usually near water.
• **DISTRIBUTION**
Much of Africa south
of the Sahara Desert.
• **REMARK**
Apart from the
difference in body
size, the female can be
recognized by her yellow iris.

distinctive, **FEMALE**
• red leg joints

*large bill
with yellow
• saddle*

DISTRIBUTION

| Plumage Sexes alike | Habitat | Migration Non-migrant |

| Family THRESKIORNITHIDAE | Species *Threskiornis aethiopicus* | Length 30 in (75 cm) |

SACRED IBIS

Birds with downcurved bills are mostly
specialized for probing in soil or mud for food,
but the Sacred Ibis is very much a general
feeder. It frequents marshy ground, the
edges of lakes or rivers, grassland (especially
after grass fires), cultivated fields, and even garbage dumps
at the edges of towns. It hunts any kind of small animal
as well as eggs and nestlings of other birds, and also eats
carrion and offal. The Sacred Ibis flies on broad, black-tipped
wings with neck extended, alternately flapping and gliding,
often in flocks in V formation. It feeds and roosts in large or
small flocks and nests in crowded colonies. Young birds lack the
long bill. They feed directly from the throat of the parent bird.
• **NEST** A platform made of twigs and sticks,
lined with grass and leaves, and placed
in a tree, in a bush, or on the ground.
• **DISTRIBUTION** Africa south of
the Sahara, N. Yemen, and S. Iraq.
• **REMARK** This bird
was held sacred
by the ancient
Egyptians.

*• bare, black
skin on head
and neck*

JUVENILE

*decorative
plumes on
• the back*

DISTRIBUTION

| Plumage Sexes alike | Habitat | Migration Migrant |

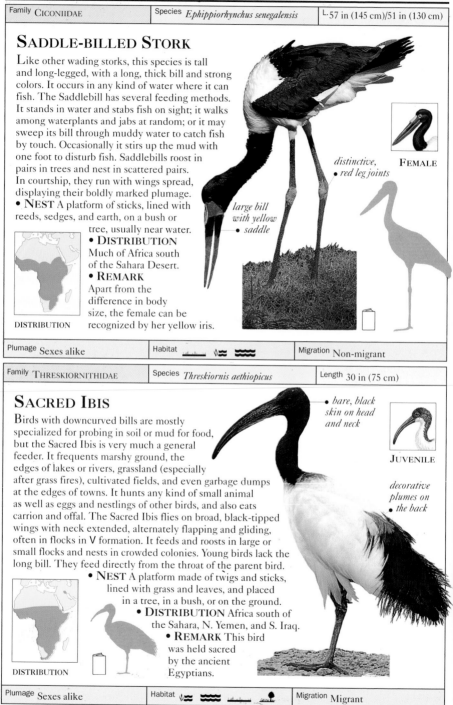

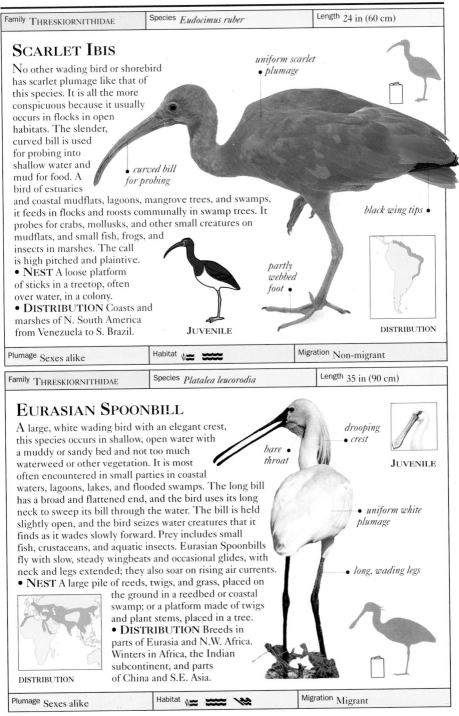

Family THRESKIORNITHIDAE	Species *Eudocimus ruber*	Length 24 in (60 cm)

SCARLET IBIS

No other wading bird or shorebird has scarlet plumage like that of this species. It is all the more conspicuous because it usually occurs in flocks in open habitats. The slender, curved bill is used for probing into shallow water and mud for food. A bird of estuaries and coastal mudflats, lagoons, mangrove trees, and swamps, it feeds in flocks and roosts communally in swamp trees. It probes for crabs, mollusks, and other small creatures on mudflats, and small fish, frogs, and insects in marshes. The call is high pitched and plaintive.

• **NEST** A loose platform of sticks in a treetop, often over water, in a colony.
• **DISTRIBUTION** Coasts and marshes of N. South America from Venezuela to S. Brazil.

uniform scarlet
• plumage

• *curved bill for probing*

black wing tips •

partly webbed foot •

JUVENILE

DISTRIBUTION

Plumage Sexes alike	Habitat	Migration Non-migrant

Family THRESKIORNITHIDAE	Species *Platalea leucorodia*	Length 35 in (90 cm)

EURASIAN SPOONBILL

A large, white wading bird with an elegant crest, this species occurs in shallow, open water with a muddy or sandy bed and not too much waterweed or other vegetation. It is most often encountered in small parties in coastal waters, lagoons, lakes, and flooded swamps. The long bill has a broad and flattened end, and the bird uses its long neck to sweep its bill through the water. The bill is held slightly open, and the bird seizes water creatures that it finds as it wades slowly forward. Prey includes small fish, crustaceans, and aquatic insects. Eurasian Spoonbills fly with slow, steady wingbeats and occasional glides, with neck and legs extended; they also soar on rising air currents.

• **NEST** A large pile of reeds, twigs, and grass, placed on the ground in a reedbed or coastal swamp; or a platform made of twigs and plant stems, placed in a tree.
• **DISTRIBUTION** Breeds in parts of Eurasia and N.W. Africa. Winters in Africa, the Indian subcontinent, and parts of China and S.E. Asia.

drooping
• crest

bare •
throat

JUVENILE

• *uniform white plumage*

• *long, wading legs*

DISTRIBUTION

Plumage Sexes alike	Habitat	Migration Migrant

Family THRESKIORNITHIDAE	Species *Ajaia ajaja*	Length 31 in (80 cm)

ROSEATE SPOONBILL

The elegance of this spoonbill's rose-colored plumage contrasts with its bizarre-looking, bare green head. The species often forms flocks that wade in shallow coastal waters, mangrove creeks, lagoons, flooded marshlands, and swamps. The birds fish by sweeping their broad-tipped bills from side to side through the water, seizing any small fish that they chance to contact.
• **NEST** An untidy structure of twigs and sticks, lined with leaves, in a colony in the treetops.
• **DISTRIBUTION** From S. USA to C. Argentina.

bare green skin on head

broad, flat bill tip

scarlet wing patch

JUVENILE

DISTRIBUTION

Plumage Sexes alike	Habitat	Migration Non-migrant

Family ANHIMIDAE	Species *Chauna torquata*	Length 36 in (91 cm)

SOUTHERN SCREAMER

A goose-size bird of marshland and wet grassland, the Southern Screamer looks strangely proportioned, with its small head and big feet. The small, hooked bill is used for feeding on leaves, buds, and other parts of green plants. The large, broad wings carry bony spurs that project forward from the leading edge; these are used as weapons in fights with rival birds or predators. The Southern Screamer flies strongly and circles and soars on rising air currents, sometimes attaining considerable heights. The species gets the name of "screamer" from its characteristic habit of uttering frequent, screaming calls, both during flight and also when walking on the ground.
• **NEST** A structure of sticks and reeds, placed on the ground near or in shallow water.
• **DISTRIBUTION** From S. Brazil to C. Argentina.

FLYING ADULT

small head with hooked bill

resting leg hidden under the feathers

square tail

large feet with long toes

DISTRIBUTION

Plumage Sexes alike	Habitat	Migration Non-migrant

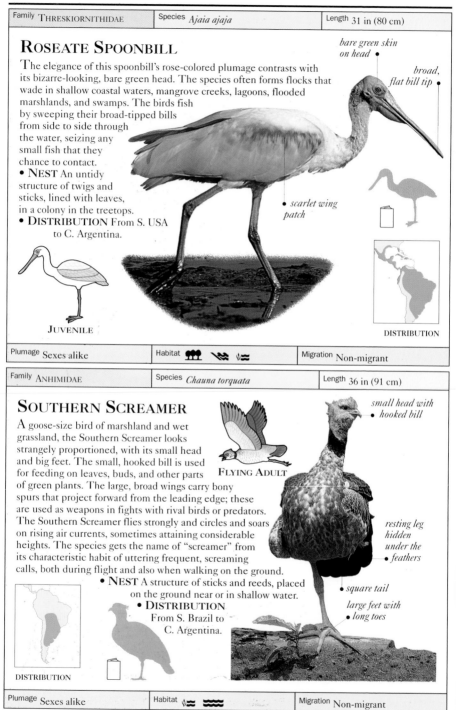

Family PHOENICOPTERIDAE	Species *Phoenicopterus ruber*	Length 57 in (145 cm)

GREATER FLAMINGO

This tall, slender bird is seen on shallow lakes and coastal waters. It specializes in feeding in lakes with a high concentration of either saline or alkaline salts. These waters contain sufficient food to feed a large number of birds, but the food is usually very small, consisting of insects, shrimp-like animals, and tiny plants including diatoms and algae. The Greater Flamingo wades in the shallow water, reaches down with its long neck, and sucks in the water through its upturned bill. Inside the bill, small animals are collected on a comblike arrangement of fine plates (lamellae) between which the water drains. Suitable lakes are few and far between, and the birds must travel long distances from one feeding site to another, often in large flocks.

• **NEST** A cone of mud with a hollow top, in a dense colony on a mudflat or salt lake.

• **DISTRIBUTION** Scattered locations in the Caribbean, Africa, S.W. Europe, and Asia.

DISTRIBUTION

elongated plumes used in display

folded wing

FLYING ADULT

JUVENILE

blunt, angled bill

chick is down-covered and has a straight bill

webbed feet

Plumage Sexes alike	Habitat	Migration Migrant

| Family ANATIDAE | Species *Anseranas semipalmata* | Length 34 in (85 cm) |

MAGPIE-GOOSE

This large, black-and-white goose inhabits tropical marshes, rivers, and lakes. It is distinctively tall, having unusually long legs for a goose as well as an upright posture. It is one of the few geese with only half-webbed feet. The bill is large and powerful with a strong tip for digging, and the crown of the male's head is raised in a domed shape. Magpie-Geese form flocks of several thousands after breeding. They feed by grazing in grassland and crops or by wading in water to eat roots and seeds of marsh plants. When alarmed, the geese fly up and perch in bare trees. Their normal flight is slow and steady, on broad wings.
• **NEST** A platform of trampled reed stems, lying in shallow water.
• **DISTRIBUTION** N. Australia and S. New Guinea.

• *high crown of male*

female has a flatter head than the male

• *long, flexible neck*

DISTRIBUTION

FULL VIEW OF ADULT

• *legs are either pink or yellow*

| Plumage Sexes alike | Habitat | Migration Partial migrant |

| Family ANATIDAE | Species *Dendrocygna eytoni* | Length 24 in (60 cm) |

PLUMED WHISTLING-DUCK

The slim, upright body, long neck, and long legs of this species are typical of whistling-ducks. In flight the head and neck are extended and droop slightly downward, giving the bird a humpbacked look. Plumed Whistling-Ducks are sociable birds, living in noisy flocks close to water, moving from area to area as wetlands dry out seasonally. Pairs stay together for life and nest on dry land, later leading the young back to the water. They also feed on land, eating leaves and seeds of grasses and low-growing plants. They visit marshes during drier periods to feed on sedges and rushes.
• **NEST** A hollow in the ground among vegetation, lined with grass and usually sheltered by a bush, hidden a little distance from water.
• **DISTRIBUTION** N. and E. Australia.
• **REMARK** The name is derived from the loud, whistling calls that ducks in a flock constantly utter to one another.

long neck typical of • *whistling-ducks*

DISTRIBUTION

• *decorative flank plumes*

| Plumage Sexes alike | Habitat | Migration Partial migrant |

Family ANATIDAE	Species *Cygnus olor*	Length 60 in (152 cm)

MUTE SWAN

This species occurs on freshwater lakes and rivers and is the largest and heaviest swimming bird in this habitat. It is identified by the red color of the bill in adult birds, contrasting with the gray bills of juveniles and with the yellow bills of adults of other swan species in its range. Its body is streamlined for swimming, and its legs are short and strong. The neck is long and flexible enough to reach underwater for aquatic plants and roots, which are the bird's main food. The diet also includes worms, shellfish, and other small animals. It leaves the water to graze but is slow and ungainly on dry land and never ventures far from water. The Mute Swan flies on tapering wings, with its neck stretched forward. Pairs stay together for life. When not breeding, the birds are sociable, forming flocks on lakes, rivers, and estuaries, but nesting pairs defend their territories vigorously against other swans. As its name implies, this species is silent, apart from hisses, grunts, and throaty noises.

DISTRIBUTION

• **NEST** A large mound of plant material placed in reeds, on a small island, on the shore of a lake, or beside a river or stream.
• **DISTRIBUTION** Scattered areas across Eurasia. Introduced in areas of North America, South Africa, Australia, and New Zealand.

black knob on bill

long, curved neck

large, powerful wing

long, boat-shaped body

JUVENILE

Plumage Sexes differ slightly	Habitat 〜〜 〜	Migration Non-migrant

| Family ANATIDAE | Species *Anser anser* | Length 35 in (90 cm) |

GREYLAG GOOSE

This goose is seen swimming on rivers, lakes, and marshes and walking or running in grassland and pasture. It is strongly built and has a short, stout bill that can demolish leaves and stems and dig up roots for food. Its flight is strong and direct, showing conspicuous, blue-gray wing coverts, and birds often travel in V formation. The Greylag is an alert, suspicious goose, raising the alarm at the slightest disturbance with loud, harsh calls.
• **NEST** A shallow, natural depression in the ground, lined with leaves and an inner cup of feather down.
• **DISTRIBUTION** Across Eurasia apart from N. Russia and N. Siberia. Winters as far south as N. Africa, Iran, India, and China.
• **REMARK** Farm geese (often white) are the domesticated form of the Greylag Goose.

EASTERN FORM

• *"ribbed" neck feathers*

WESTERN FORM

DISTRIBUTION

| Plumage Sexes alike | Habitat | Migration Partial migrant |

| Family ANATIDAE | Species *Anser caerulescens* | Length 28 in (70 cm) |

SNOW GOOSE

An Arctic goose breeding in marshy parts of the tundra, this species feeds by digging up roots and bulbs, and also grazes on buds and leaves. It is sociable, even in the breeding season, when pairs nest only a short distance apart. After breeding, the geese migrate in flocks, sometimes several thousand strong, to winter on marshes and coastal grassland. The call is a harsh cackle.
• **NEST** A natural hollow in the ground, lined with leaves and an inner down cup.
• **DISTRIBUTION** Breeds in Arctic zone of North America. Winters as far south as Mexico.
• **REMARK** There are two color phases (*p. 13*): white, and "blue" (gray, tinged blue in parts).

"BLUE" PHASE

short, strong bill •

• snowy white plumage

WHITE PHASE

DISTRIBUTION

| Plumage Sexes alike | Habitat | Migration Migrant |

Family ANATIDAE	Species *Anser canagicus*	Length 26 in (65 cm)

EMPEROR GOOSE

A dark goose with a white head, this species breeds near the coast in the Arctic tundra and winters in family parties on rocky shores and islands. It feeds on a mixed diet that includes green plants, seaweed, and shellfish.
• **NEST** A hollow lined with down and moss.
• **DISTRIBUTION** Breeds on coastal tundra of Alaska and N.E. Siberia. Winters as far south as W. USA and Kamchatka.
• **REMARK** The head and neck are sometimes stained orange by iron salts in the water in which the birds dip for food.

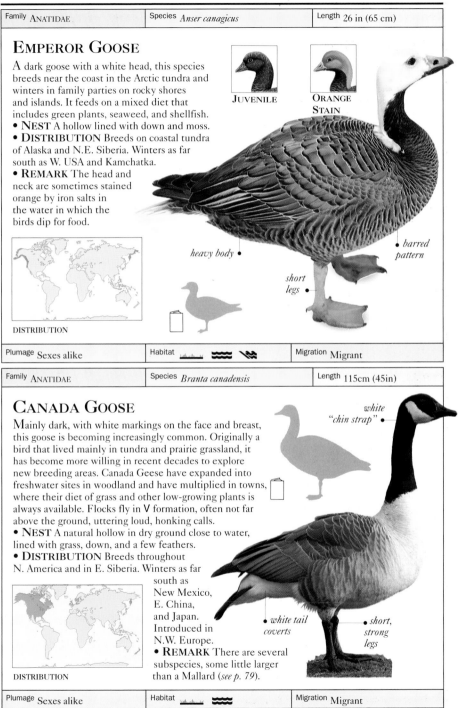

JUVENILE

ORANGE STAIN

heavy body •

• *barred pattern*

short legs •

DISTRIBUTION

Plumage Sexes alike	Habitat	Migration Migrant

Family ANATIDAE	Species *Branta canadensis*	Length 115cm (45in)

CANADA GOOSE

Mainly dark, with white markings on the face and breast, this goose is becoming increasingly common. Originally a bird that lived mainly in tundra and prairie grassland, it has become more willing in recent decades to explore new breeding areas. Canada Geese have expanded into freshwater sites in woodland and have multiplied in towns, where their diet of grass and other low-growing plants is always available. Flocks fly in V formation, often not far above the ground, uttering loud, honking calls.
• **NEST** A natural hollow in dry ground close to water, lined with grass, down, and a few feathers.
• **DISTRIBUTION** Breeds throughout N. America and in E. Siberia. Winters as far south as New Mexico, E. China, and Japan. Introduced in N.W. Europe.
• **REMARK** There are several subspecies, some little larger than a Mallard (*see p. 79*).

white "chin strap" •

• *white tail coverts*

• *short, strong legs*

DISTRIBUTION

Plumage Sexes alike	Habitat	Migration Migrant

| Family ANATIDAE | Species *Branta ruficollis* | Length 22 in (55 cm) |

RED-BREASTED GOOSE

This rare goose is a migrant to the Arctic, breeding on mountain tundra and feeding mainly on grasses and sedges. Other foods include broadleaved plants, roots, tubers, and, in winter, cultivated grain. Migrating birds fly in ragged groups or in slanting lines, rather than in the V formation well known in other species of geese. The frequent call is a harshly piercing, double note.

• **NEST** A hollow, lined with down and feathers, in the top of a raised piece of ground. Pairs often choose a site close to the nest of a Peregrine Falcon (*see p. 105*). Surprisingly, this relationship gives protection to the geese, as the falcon attacks or deters any predators that approach the nest intending to attack the geese or steal their young.

• **DISTRIBUTION** Breeds in Arctic Siberia. Winters near the Black, Caspian, and Aral Seas.

• **REMARK** Endangered, mainly because of being heavily hunted in its winter range.

flank feathers overlapping the wing

chestnut-colored breast

DISTRIBUTION

| Plumage Sexes alike | Habitat | Migration Migrant |

| Family ANATIDAE | Species *Alopochen aegyptiacus* | Length 30 in (75 cm) |

EGYPTIAN GOOSE

This bird lives in marshes, lakes, and rivers, where it sometimes swims and dives, but it is more usually seen on land. It grazes on grass, also eating leaves and seeds of plants including crops, and possibly occasional insects. The female can be distinguished by her trumpet-like quacking, in contrast with the male's soft, husky calls. Pairs mate for life, forming flocks after breeding that perch and roost in trees.

• **NEST** A hollow in the ground under vegetation, or a hole in a cliff, cave, or tree.

• **DISTRIBUTION** Upper Nile Valley and Africa south of the Sahara; introduced in England.

• **REMARK** Although it is called a goose, this bird is really a species of shelduck.

shaggy neck feathers

GRAY PHASE

glossy green patch (speculum) on hind edge of wing

DISTRIBUTION

| Plumage Sexes alike | Habitat | Migration Partial migrant |

| Family ANATIDAE | Species *Tadorna tadorna* | Length 27 in (68 cm) |

COMMON SHELDUCK

dark green
• head

Recognizable by its alternate panels of black, white, and chestnut brown, this bird is seen in winter flocks on estuaries and mudflats. Flocks also occur inland, for instance on salt lakes in semi-arid areas. Shelducks feed by dabbling with their bills, either on mud exposed by the tide or in shallow water. They take small shellfish, crustaceans, insect larvae, and waterweed. The birds nest inland and lead the young to the water as soon as they hatch. After breeding, adults migrate in large flocks for their annual molt, a process during which they are unable to fly. This takes place in safety from predators on vast offshore mudflats.
• **NEST** A cavity in a tree or bank, or a hollow under bushes, lined with down, some distance from the shore.
• **DISTRIBUTION** Breeds in N.W. Europe and from S. Europe through C. Asia and N. China to E. Siberia. Winters as far south as N.W. Africa, Pakistan, and S.W. China.

FEMALE

DISTRIBUTION

| Plumage Sexes differ | Habitat | Migration Partial migrant |

| Family ANATIDAE | Species *Nettapus auritus* | Length 13 in (33 cm) |

AFRICAN PYGMY GOOSE

Living on pools and lagoons, this species feeds mainly on water lily seeds. These, as well as other waterplants, insects, and fish, are taken either by dabbling at the surface or by diving. The bird spends most of its time on the water and uses its short legs for swimming and for perching on floating branches and trees, rather than for walking. In drier areas, birds travel nomadically in search of water.
• **NEST** A hole in a tree, termite mound, or cliff, lined with white down.
• **DISTRIBUTION** Africa south of the Sahara, and Madagascar.

• stout, seed-
eating bill

FEMALE

short,
broad
tail •

DISTRIBUTION

| Plumage Sexes differ | Habitat | Migration Partial migrant/nomadic |

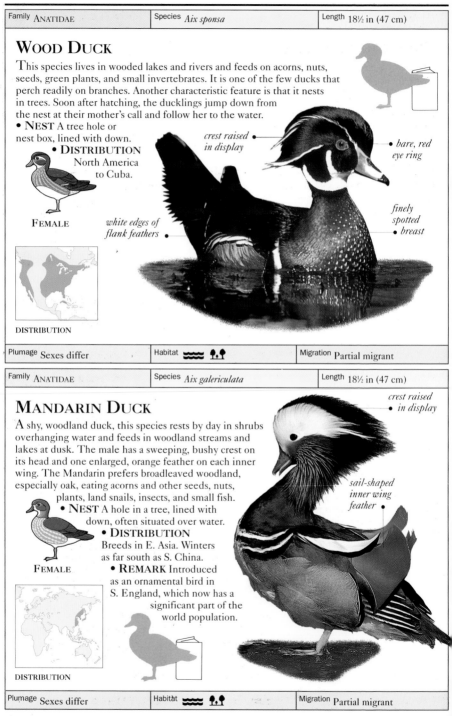

| Family ANATIDAE | Species *Aix sponsa* | Length 18½ in (47 cm) |

WOOD DUCK

This species lives in wooded lakes and rivers and feeds on acorns, nuts, seeds, green plants, and small invertebrates. It is one of the few ducks that perch readily on branches. Another characteristic feature is that it nests in trees. Soon after hatching, the ducklings jump down from the nest at their mother's call and follow her to the water.

• NEST A tree hole or nest box, lined with down.

• DISTRIBUTION North America to Cuba.

crest raised in display

bare, red eye ring

finely spotted breast

FEMALE

white edges of flank feathers

DISTRIBUTION

| Plumage Sexes differ | Habitat 〰️ 🌳🌱 | Migration Partial migrant |

| Family ANATIDAE | Species *Aix galericulata* | Length 18½ in (47 cm) |

MANDARIN DUCK

A shy, woodland duck, this species rests by day in shrubs overhanging water and feeds in woodland streams and lakes at dusk. The male has a sweeping, bushy crest on its head and one enlarged, orange feather on each inner wing. The Mandarin prefers broadleaved woodland, especially oak, eating acorns and other seeds, nuts, plants, land snails, insects, and small fish.

• NEST A hole in a tree, lined with down, often situated over water.

• DISTRIBUTION Breeds in E. Asia. Winters as far south as S. China.

• REMARK Introduced as an ornamental bird in S. England, which now has a significant part of the world population.

crest raised in display

sail-shaped inner wing feather

FEMALE

DISTRIBUTION

| Plumage Sexes differ | Habitat 〰️ 🌳🌱 | Migration Partial migrant |

| Family ANATIDAE | Species *Anas crecca* | Length 14½ in (37 cm) |

GREEN-WINGED TEAL

This small dabbling duck often swims inconspicuously in shallow pools where marsh vegetation provides partial cover. If disturbed, it rockets up from the water in rapid flight, revealing a green, white, and black wing patch (the speculum). It feeds on a wide range of plants and small animals, mainly eating seeds in winter and animal food in summer. As in other dabbling ducks, males utter whistling calls, but females quack.
• **NEST** A depression in dry grass, lined with down, among marsh plants.
• **DISTRIBUTION** Breeds in North America and Eurasia. Winters as far south as Central America, Africa, India, and S.E. Asia.

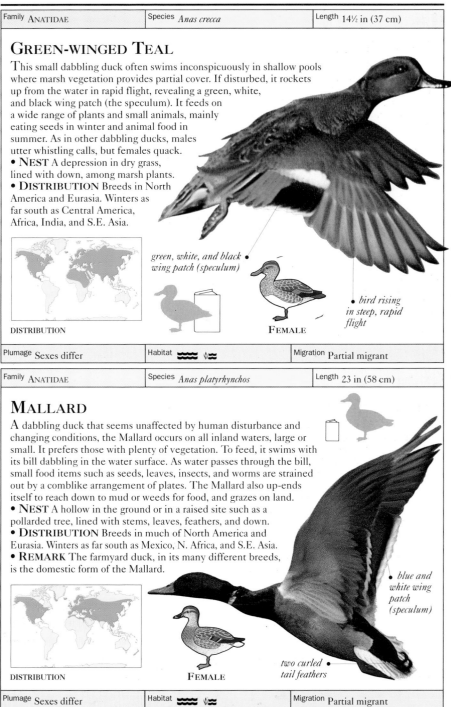

green, white, and black • wing patch (speculum)

• bird rising in steep, rapid flight

DISTRIBUTION

FEMALE

| Plumage Sexes differ | Habitat 〰〰 〰 | Migration Partial migrant |

| Family ANATIDAE | Species *Anas platyrhynchos* | Length 23 in (58 cm) |

MALLARD

A dabbling duck that seems unaffected by human disturbance and changing conditions, the Mallard occurs on all inland waters, large or small. It prefers those with plenty of vegetation. To feed, it swims with its bill dabbling in the water surface. As water passes through the bill, small food items such as seeds, leaves, insects, and worms are strained out by a comblike arrangement of plates. The Mallard also up-ends itself to reach down to mud or weeds for food, and grazes on land.
• **NEST** A hollow in the ground or in a raised site such as a pollarded tree, lined with stems, leaves, feathers, and down.
• **DISTRIBUTION** Breeds in much of North America and Eurasia. Winters as far south as Mexico, N. Africa, and S.E. Asia.
• **REMARK** The farmyard duck, in its many different breeds, is the domestic form of the Mallard.

blue and white wing patch (speculum)

DISTRIBUTION

FEMALE

two curled • tail feathers

| Plumage Sexes differ | Habitat 〰〰 〰 | Migration Partial migrant |

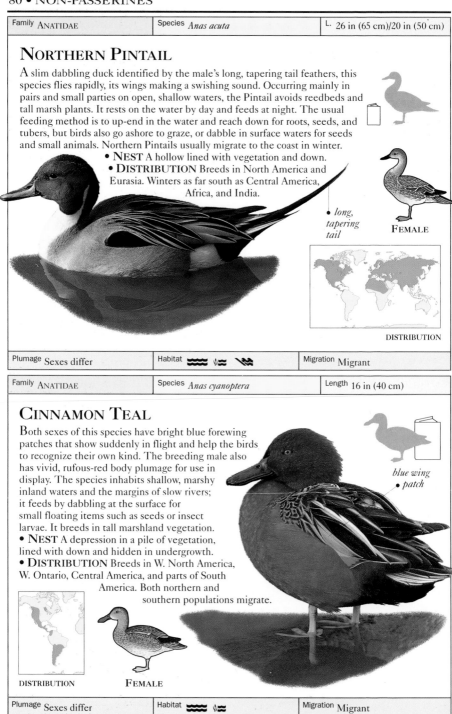

Family ANATIDAE	Species *Anas acuta*	L. 26 in (65 cm)/20 in (50 cm)

NORTHERN PINTAIL

A slim dabbling duck identified by the male's long, tapering tail feathers, this species flies rapidly, its wings making a swishing sound. Occurring mainly in pairs and small parties on open, shallow waters, the Pintail avoids reedbeds and tall marsh plants. It rests on the water by day and feeds at night. The usual feeding method is to up-end in the water and reach down for roots, seeds, and tubers, but birds also go ashore to graze, or dabble in surface waters for seeds and small animals. Northern Pintails usually migrate to the coast in winter.
- **NEST** A hollow lined with vegetation and down.
- **DISTRIBUTION** Breeds in North America and Eurasia. Winters as far south as Central America, Africa, and India.

• *long, tapering tail*

FEMALE

DISTRIBUTION

Plumage Sexes differ	Habitat 〰️ 〰️ 〰️	Migration Migrant

Family ANATIDAE	Species *Anas cyanoptera*	Length 16 in (40 cm)

CINNAMON TEAL

Both sexes of this species have bright blue forewing patches that show suddenly in flight and help the birds to recognize their own kind. The breeding male also has vivid, rufous-red body plumage for use in display. The species inhabits shallow, marshy inland waters and the margins of slow rivers; it feeds by dabbling at the surface for small floating items such as seeds or insect larvae. It breeds in tall marshland vegetation.
- **NEST** A depression in a pile of vegetation, lined with down and hidden in undergrowth.
- **DISTRIBUTION** Breeds in W. North America, W. Ontario, Central America, and parts of South America. Both northern and southern populations migrate.

blue wing • patch

DISTRIBUTION

FEMALE

Plumage Sexes differ	Habitat 〰️ 〰️	Migration Migrant

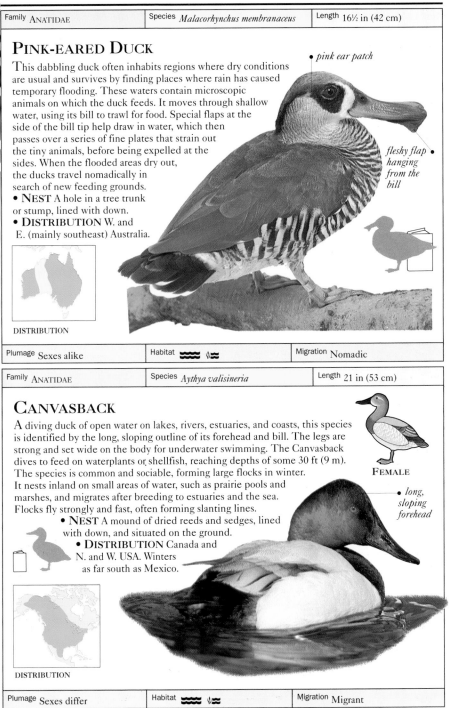

Family ANATIDAE	Species *Malacorhynchus membranaceus*	Length 16½ in (42 cm)

PINK-EARED DUCK

This dabbling duck often inhabits regions where dry conditions are usual and survives by finding places where rain has caused temporary flooding. These waters contain microscopic animals on which the duck feeds. It moves through shallow water, using its bill to trawl for food. Special flaps at the side of the bill tip help draw in water, which then passes over a series of fine plates that strain out the tiny animals, before being expelled at the sides. When the flooded areas dry out, the ducks travel nomadically in search of new feeding grounds.
• **NEST** A hole in a tree trunk or stump, lined with down.
• **DISTRIBUTION** W. and E. (mainly southeast) Australia.

pink ear patch

fleshy flap hanging from the bill

DISTRIBUTION

Plumage Sexes alike	Habitat	Migration Nomadic

Family ANATIDAE	Species *Aythya valisineria*	Length 21 in (53 cm)

CANVASBACK

A diving duck of open water on lakes, rivers, estuaries, and coasts, this species is identified by the long, sloping outline of its forehead and bill. The legs are strong and set wide on the body for underwater swimming. The Canvasback dives to feed on waterplants or shellfish, reaching depths of some 30 ft (9 m). The species is common and sociable, forming large flocks in winter. It nests inland on small areas of water, such as prairie pools and marshes, and migrates after breeding to estuaries and the sea. Flocks fly strongly and fast, often forming slanting lines.
• **NEST** A mound of dried reeds and sedges, lined with down, and situated on the ground.
• **DISTRIBUTION** Canada and N. and W. USA. Winters as far south as Mexico.

FEMALE

long, sloping forehead

DISTRIBUTION

Plumage Sexes differ	Habitat	Migration Migrant

| Family ANATIDAE | Species *Aythya fuligula* | Length 17 in (43 cm) |

TUFTED DUCK

A slender crest dangling over the nape identifies this diving duck. Naturally a bird of deep, open water on lakes and rivers, it has adapted itself to live in built-up areas. Of all the birds seen in an urban setting, the Tufted Duck is unique for two features: males have black plumage with white sides and bellies, and both sexes have yellow, button eyes. Tufted Ducks swim well underwater, sometimes to depths of 45 ft (14 m), and feed on a wide range of tiny aquatic animals and plants.
• **NEST** A hollow lined with grass and down, usually in vegetation close to water.
• **DISTRIBUTION** Breeds in Eurasia. Winters as far south as S. Sudan and N. India.

FEMALE

DISTRIBUTION

yellow iris

tail slopes down into the water

white flank patch

| Plumage Sexes differ | Habitat 〜〜 〜 | Migration Migrant |

| Family ANATIDAE | Species *Somateria spectabilis* | Length 22 in (55 cm) |

KING EIDER

This stout sea duck dives for shellfish in cold, coastal waters at all times of year. The feathering is dense, with a thick layer of down. Males have an unusual bulging forehead.
• **NEST** A hollow lined with down, that the birds pluck from their undersides.
• **DISTRIBUTION** Breeds in N. Alaska, Canada, and Eurasia. Winters as far south as S. Alaska, New England, and Kamchatka.

FEMALE

DISTRIBUTION

decorative, upward-curving feathers

forehead bulge

plumes drooping from the shoulder

| Plumage Sexes differ | Habitat 〜 〜〜 〜 | Migration Migrant |

Family ANATIDAE	Species *Histrionicus histrionicus*	Length 16½ in (42 cm)

HARLEQUIN DUCK

The brilliant, fragmented pattern of this duck's plumage is a subtle camouflage against clear, moving waters. The Harlequin breeds beside cold, fast-flowing streams and rivers, feeding on the aquatic insects that cling to rocks and shingle. It flies strongly and low, following watercourses. After breeding it migrates to the sea, where it dives for shellfish, crustaceans, and other food.
• **NEST** A hole in a tree or bank, lined with down.
• **DISTRIBUTION** Breeds in Alaska, Canada, Greenland, Iceland, E. Siberia. Winters on coasts.

FEMALE

DISTRIBUTION

short neck

tapering, short bill

strong, compact build for swimming in rough water

Plumage Sexes differ	Habitat 〰〰 〰 〰〰	Migration Migrant

Family ANATIDAE	Species *Melanitta nigra*	Length 19 in (48 cm)

BLACK SCOTER

The orange bill patch of the male and the pale cheeks of the female identify the Black Scoter. The species spends much of the year at sea. Large flocks float in shallow coastal waters or fly low over the water in straggling formations. Birds dive, often simultaneously, to feed on mussels and other marine animals.
• **NEST** A down-lined hollow on the ground.
• **DISTRIBUTION** Breeds in tundra of North America and Eurasia. Winters as far as California, N. Africa, and China.

FEMALE

DISTRIBUTION

stocky build of a sea-diving duck

stiff, tapering tail

orange patch on bill

Plumage Sexes differ	Habitat 〰〰 〰〰	Migration Migrant

Family ANATIDAE	Species *Bucephala clangula*	Length 20 in (50 cm)

COMMON GOLDENEYE

With its thick head feathering this diving duck looks big-headed but, when the head is raised, the neck looks narrow. Both sexes have golden-yellow eyes. The birds spend summer beside inland waters in the northern forests, nesting in tree holes. They winter on estuaries, coastal bays, and large inland lakes. The diet consists mainly of shellfish, crustaceans, and insects.

• NEST A hole in a tree, or a nest box, lined with down.

• DISTRIBUTION Breeds in North America, Eurasia. Winters as far as S. USA, Middle East, and China.

row of drooping, black-and-white shoulder feathers

FEMALE

DISTRIBUTION

Plumage Sexes differ	Habitat	Migration Migrant

Family ANATIDAE	Species *Mergellus albellus*	Length 17 in (43 cm)

SMEW

A small diving duck with a neat plumage pattern, the Smew is well adapted for fishing underwater. The mandibles of its bill carry rows of spikes resembling teeth, and the bill has a small, sharp hook at the tip which helps to grip slippery fish. The bird floats on the surface and peers into the water to locate prey, then dives underneath to give chase, using its feet for propulsion. Smew walk well on land and are fast and agile in flight. They breed beside freshwater lakes and rivers in the northern coniferous forest zone, where they feed mainly on aquatic insects.

• NEST A hole in a tree, lined with down.

• DISTRIBUTION Breeds N. Eurasia. Winters as far south as N. India and S.E. China.

FEMALE

bushy crest

narrow bill

tail slopes down into the water

DISTRIBUTION

Plumage Sexes differ	Habitat	Migration Migrant

Family ANATIDAE	Species *Mergus merganser*	Length 26 in (65 cm)

COMMON MERGANSER

This large, fish-eating duck is adapted for fast underwater swimming in pursuit of its prey. Its body is streamlined, and the bill is long and narrow. Each mandible carries a row of backward-pointing spikes on each side. These, and the hooked bill tip, help grip slippery fish. The birds fish in estuaries, lowland rivers, lakes, and the fast-flowing rivers and streams of the uplands. They fly fast and low, often following the course of a river. Young birds start by learning to hunt aquatic insects, then graduate to fish. Common Mergansers live in family parties or small flocks, often roosting in larger numbers on the ground or in trees.
• **NEST** A cavity in a tree, bank, rock crevice, or stone wall.
• **DISTRIBUTION** Breeds in N. North America and Eurasia. Winters as far south as S. USA and C. China.

DISTRIBUTION

• crest feathers lying sleeked down on nape

FEMALE

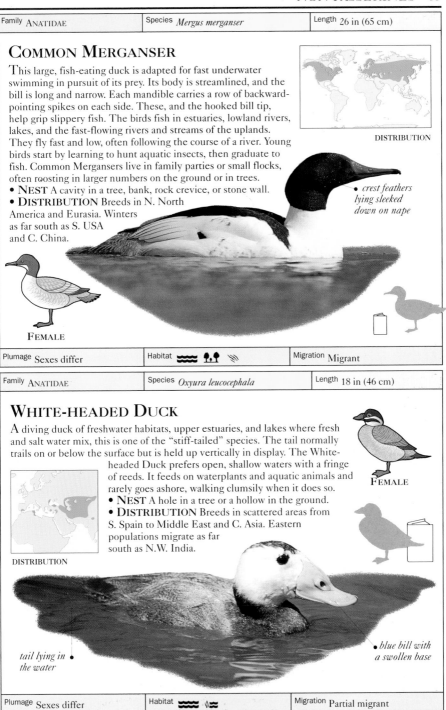

Plumage Sexes differ	Habitat 〰️ 🌲 〰️	Migration Migrant

Family ANATIDAE	Species *Oxyura leucocephala*	Length 18 in (46 cm)

WHITE-HEADED DUCK

A diving duck of freshwater habitats, upper estuaries, and lakes where fresh and salt water mix, this is one of the "stiff-tailed" species. The tail normally trails on or below the surface but is held up vertically in display. The White-headed Duck prefers open, shallow waters with a fringe of reeds. It feeds on waterplants and aquatic animals and rarely goes ashore, walking clumsily when it does so.
• **NEST** A hole in a tree or a hollow in the ground.
• **DISTRIBUTION** Breeds in scattered areas from S. Spain to Middle East and C. Asia. Eastern populations migrate as far south as N.W. India.

FEMALE

DISTRIBUTION

tail lying in the water •

• blue bill with a swollen base

Plumage Sexes differ	Habitat 〰️ 〰️	Migration Partial migrant

| Family ANATIDAE | Species *Biziura lobata* | L. 27 in (68 cm)/21 in (53 cm) |

MUSK DUCK

This large diving duck has a rounded back, a stout head, and a heavy bill from which an unusual, disk-shaped lobe is suspended. It gets its name from the musky scent of its plumage. The Musk Duck feeds mainly on small aquatic animals, ranging in size from insects to frogs. It rarely leaves the water, moving with difficulty on land.

• **NEST** A hollow among plants at the water's edge; occasionally a hollow in a fallen tree.

• **DISTRIBUTION** S. Australia.

• **REMARK** Males are much larger than females.

DISTRIBUTION

disk-shaped lobe for • display

FEMALE

tail lying • in the water

| Plumage Sexes differ | Habitat 〰️ 〰️ | Migration Non-migrant |

| Family CATHARTIDAE | Species *Cathartes aura* | Length 28 in (70 cm) |

TURKEY VULTURE

A common vulture often seen soaring and circling in search of food, this species feeds mainly on carrion. Like other vultures of the Americas, it uses its acute sense of smell to locate a dead animal. Besides eating carrion, it sometimes kills small animals such as lizards or steals the eggs or nestlings of birds.

• **NEST** A platform of sticks situated in a tree, cliff, or rocky place.

• **DISTRIBUTION** From S. Canada to S. South America and the Falklands.

JUVENILE   DISTRIBUTION

bird sunbathing • with spread wings

| Plumage Sexes alike | Habitat | Migration Partial migrant |

Family CATHARTIDAE	Species *Gymnogyps californianus*	Length 45 in (115 cm)

CALIFORNIA CONDOR

In its natural state this large, carrion-eating bird lives by cruising over a wide area to find food. It cannot gain the required height without calm, warm weather and rising air currents on which to soar and circle upward. On cold or very windy days, the Condor has to remain on the ground. When not foraging, it spends long periods idling or preening its feathers at a roost site.

• **NEST** A single egg is laid on the ground, on a rock ledge, or in a cave.
• **DISTRIBUTION** W. USA (but now mainly found in captivity).
• **REMARK** The California Condor was considered a threat to livestock and birds were killed to the point where the species was in danger of extinction. Prospects of recovery were restricted by the slow breeding rate of the Condor, which reproduces every two years and takes five to seven years to mature. Numbers continued to fall, with only 17 left in 1984. The remaining population was taken into captivity in the middle 1980s. Since then they have increased with captive breeding, and a few birds have been experimentally released into the wild.

DISTRIBUTION

bare head of a
• scavenging bird

inflated
throat
• pouch

• bare neck

JUVENILE

white wing
• mark

• feet are very large, with long toes and claws, but are too weak for hunting live prey

Plumage Sexes alike	Habitat	Migration Non-migrant

Family CATHARTIDAE	Species *Sarcoramphus papa*	Length 30 in (75 cm)

KING VULTURE

Living chiefly in rain forest, this vulture is recognized by pied plumage, a brightly colored head, broad wings, and a short tail. In calm weather, it flies low over the treetops or descends to the forest floor to feed. On warm days, it finds rising air currents (thermals) and circles to gain height. Foraging birds often leave the forest for tropical grassland, particularly in areas where cattle are ranched. Though not normally sociable, King Vultures sometimes gather at a large carcass. Here they take precedence over other species because of their greater size and strength. Within the forest, King Vultures are not easily observed, but are known to take stranded fish from sandbanks in forest rivers. They are also thought to kill small reptiles and young mammals.
• **NEST** Few data recorded; where observed, the single egg has been placed in a hollow in a forest tree stump.
• **DISTRIBUTION** Mexico to N. Argentina.

- colorful, bare head
- bulging crop stores recently eaten food

JUVENILE

large feet

DISTRIBUTION

Plumage Sexes alike	Habitat	Migration Non-migrant

Family PANDIONIDAE	Species *Pandion haliaetus*	L. 20 in (50 cm)/23 in (58 cm)

OSPREY

Often soaring over lakes, rivers, and coasts, the Osprey is a fish hawk, swooping down to take its prey from the water. It plunge-dives with feet first and wings raised, often submerging itself almost completely, to reappear with a fish and continue with its flight. The prey is usually carried head forward, held in both feet, to be eaten on a tree branch or on the nest.
• **NEST** A mass of sticks placed on a tree, a seashore, a crag, or an artificial nest platform.
• **DISTRIBUTION** Breeds in North America, Eurasia, Africa, and Australia. Winters in South America, Africa, and Asia.
• **REMARK** Females are larger than males.

- crest pushed up by the wind (normally lies flat)
- dark band through the eye and down to the nape

long claws for holding fish

JUVENILE

DISTRIBUTION

Plumage Sexes alike	Habitat	Migration Migrant

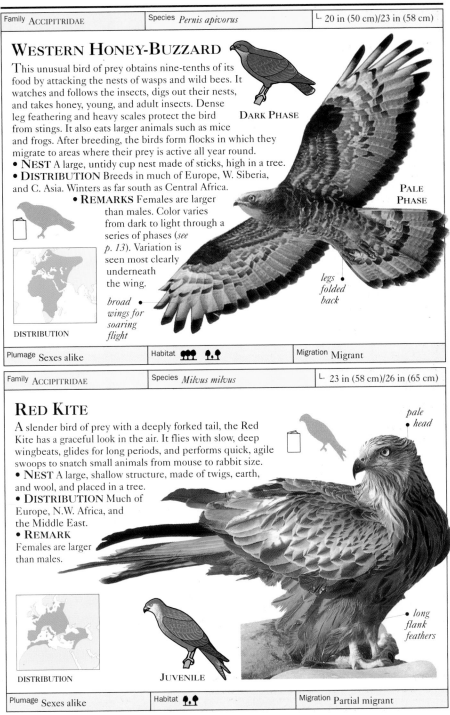

Family ACCIPITRIDAE	Species *Pernis apivorus*	L. 20 in (50 cm)/23 in (58 cm)

WESTERN HONEY-BUZZARD

This unusual bird of prey obtains nine-tenths of its food by attacking the nests of wasps and wild bees. It watches and follows the insects, digs out their nests, and takes honey, young, and adult insects. Dense leg feathering and heavy scales protect the bird from stings. It also eats larger animals such as mice and frogs. After breeding, the birds form flocks in which they migrate to areas where their prey is active all year round.
• NEST A large, untidy cup nest made of sticks, high in a tree.
• DISTRIBUTION Breeds in much of Europe, W. Siberia, and C. Asia. Winters as far south as Central Africa.
• REMARKS Females are larger than males. Color varies from dark to light through a series of phases (*see p. 13*). Variation is seen most clearly underneath the wing.

DARK PHASE

PALE PHASE

broad wings for soaring flight

legs folded back

DISTRIBUTION

Plumage Sexes alike	Habitat	Migration Migrant

Family ACCIPITRIDAE	Species *Milvus milvus*	L. 23 in (58 cm)/26 in (65 cm)

RED KITE

A slender bird of prey with a deeply forked tail, the Red Kite has a graceful look in the air. It flies with slow, deep wingbeats, glides for long periods, and performs quick, agile swoops to snatch small animals from mouse to rabbit size.
• NEST A large, shallow structure, made of twigs, earth, and wool, and placed in a tree.
• DISTRIBUTION Much of Europe, N.W. Africa, and the Middle East.
• REMARK Females are larger than males.

pale head

long flank feathers

DISTRIBUTION

JUVENILE

Plumage Sexes alike	Habitat	Migration Partial migrant

| Family ACCIPITRIDAE | Species *Haliaeetus vocifer* | L. 25 in (63 cm)/ 30 in (75 cm) |

AFRICAN FISH-EAGLE

Most often seen singly or in pairs on high branches in its waterside territory, this is a specialized, fish-eating eagle. Watching from a perch more often than hunting in flight, it swoops to snatch fish from just beneath the surface, using a backward swing of the feet. It also eats stranded fish and other carrion, as well as killing waterbirds. The species is well known for its yelping, four-note call.
• **NEST** A large pile of sticks with a central bowl, lined with grass and usually placed in a tree near water.
• **DISTRIBUTION** Africa south of the Sahara.
• **REMARK** Females are larger than males.

DISTRIBUTION

JUVENILE

bird launching itself into the air from a perch

| Plumage Sexes alike | Habitat 〰️ 〰️ | Migration Non-migrant |

| Family ACCIPITRIDAE | Species *Haliaeetus leucocephalus* | L. 30 in (75 cm)/43 in (110 cm) |

BALD EAGLE

This large eagle gets its food from a wide range of sources. Most of its victims are caught live, including ducks, gulls, other seabirds, fish from lakes or the sea, and salmon from rivers. Bald Eagles challenge Ospreys (*see p. 88*), forcing them to abandon their catch. They also feed on dead and dying fish as well as other carrion.
• **NEST** A large structure of sticks and twigs, situated in a tree close to water.
• **DISTRIBUTION** Breeds in much of North America. Northern populations winter in S. USA and parts of Mexico.
• **REMARK** Females larger than males.

pure white head and neck

strong, grasping feet

DISTRIBUTION

JUVENILE

white tail and rump

| Plumage Sexes alike | Habitat 〰️ 〰️ 〰️ | Migration Partial migrant |

| Family ACCIPITRIDAE | Species *Haliaeetus albicilla* | L. 28 in (70 cm)/36 in (91 cm) |

WHITE-TAILED EAGLE

A large, heavy eagle of rocky coasts, islands, estuaries, and inland lakes, this species is recognized by its repeated, yelping calls. It is adept at snatching fish and birds from lakes and the sea, and seeks carrion along the shore. Pairs stay permanently in their territories in areas where winters are sufficiently mild.
• **NEST** A large structure of sticks to which more material is added each year, with a hollow in the center, lined with twigs and sometimes wool, placed on a cliff, rock ledge, or tree.
• **DISTRIBUTION** Breeds in Greenland and N. Eurasia. Some northern and northeastern populations migrate as far south as the Middle East and C. China.
• **REMARK** Females are larger than males.

• *prominent brow shields eye from sunlight*

JUVENILE

white tail

DISTRIBUTION

| Plumage Sexes alike | Habitat | Migration Partial migrant |

| Family ACCIPITRIDAE | Species *Torgos tracheliotus* | Length 39 in (98 cm) |

LAPPET-FACED VULTURE

This large vulture takes first place at any animal carcass, dominating the smaller carrion-eating birds. Its heavy bill enables it to tear open the carcass, incidentally helping smaller species to feed and to consume tougher parts such as skin and ligaments for which there is less competition. The Lappet-face roosts solitarily or in pairs, and spends much of the day in soaring flight.
• **NEST** A platform of sticks with a central hollow, lined and placed on a flat-topped bush or tree.
• **DISTRIBUTION** Parts of Africa, Israel, S. and W. Arabian Peninsula.

bare head and neck of a scavenger

lappets (folds of bare skin)

broad wing for soaring flight

long legs for walking

JUVENILE

DISTRIBUTION

| Plumage Sexes alike | Habitat | Migration Non-migrant |

| Family ACCIPITRIDAE | Species *Neophron percnopterus* | L. 25 in (63 cm)/28 in (70 cm) |

EGYPTIAN VULTURE

A small vulture with a bare face and shaggy neck feathering, this species occurs in open plains and semidesert. It cannot compete with larger vultures at an animal carcass. On the other hand, being smaller, it is less dependent on rising currents of warm air to gain height and starts flying soon after dawn, so reaching the carrion first. It raids nesting colonies of birds, seizing chicks and carrying away eggs in its bill. When attacking an Ostrich nest, it lifts stones with its bill and throws them about until one of the eggs is cracked.
• **NEST** A small platform made of sticks, lined with dung, hair, and skin, and placed on a rock ledge.
• **DISTRIBUTION** S. Europe, Middle East, Africa, W. Asia, and the Indian subcontinent.
• **REMARK** Females are larger than males.

DISTRIBUTION

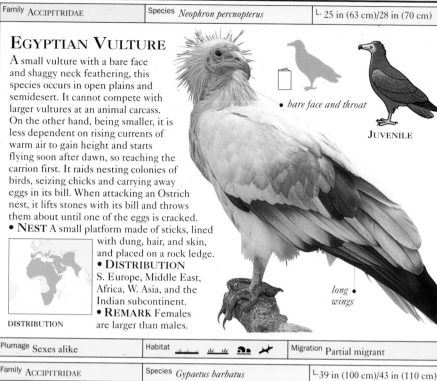

• *bare face and throat*

JUVENILE

long wings

| Plumage Sexes alike | Habitat | Migration Partial migrant |

| Family ACCIPITRIDAE | Species *Gypaetus barbatus* | L. 39 in (100 cm)/43 in (110 cm) |

LAMMERGEIER

A very large carrion-eating bird, thinly dispersed in its mountain habitat, the Lammergeier glides and soars for long periods on long, tapering wings and a wedge-shaped tail. It can eat parts of the carcass that other carrion-eaters cannot digest, including bones, which it smashes by dropping them onto rocks from the air.
• **NEST** A platform of twigs with a central hollow lined with grass, hair, skin, and bones, in a cave or on a cliff ledge.
• **DISTRIBUTION** Scattered areas in S. Europe, Africa, and through the Middle East to C. Asia.
• **REMARK** Females are larger than males.

JUVENILE

tuft of bristly, black feathers

thick covering of feathers on • *upper leg*

DISTRIBUTION

| Plumage Sexes alike | Habitat | Migration Non-migrant |

Family ACCIPITRIDAE	Species *Terathopius ecaudatus*	L. 22 in (55 cm)/28 in (70 cm)

BATELEUR

Beautifully adapted for prolonged and fast gliding and for agility in the air, this small eagle inhabits scrub, open woodland, and savanna (tropical and subtropical grassland) with scattered trees. It roosts in trees and is on the wing for most of the day, crisscrossing the same area in very fast, gliding flight as it searches for prey. The shortness of the tail gives the Bateleur an "all-wings" appearance in flight and causes the gliding bird to swerve first to one side, then to the other. The bird swoops on its prey, sometimes from a great height, intercepting birds in flight, and taking reptiles, small mammals, and large insects from the ground. Pairs in courtship perform spectacular aerial maneuvers, from which the name Bateleur (French for juggler or acrobat) is derived.

• **NEST** A cup nest made of twigs, lined with leaves, and placed in the canopy of a tree.
• **DISTRIBUTION** Africa south of the Sahara.
• **REMARK** Females are larger than males.

DISTRIBUTION

JUVENILE

very short tail hidden by wings

Plumage Sexes alike	Habitat	Migration Non-migrant

Family ACCIPITRIDAE	Species *Melierax canorus*	L. 20 in (50 cm)/23 in (58 cm)

PALE CHANTING-GOSHAWK

prominent brow

This is a large hawk with long wings and tail, inhabiting open landscapes such as arid thornbush and semidesert. It watches from a perch and swoops in rapid flight to take a small animal such as a lizard, bird, or mammal, or sometimes even a large insect. The bird follows through with its flight, eventually landing on a new perch or circling back to where it began. Adults generally live in pairs, and each pair occupies its own territory. Pale Chanting-Goshawks roost in trees by night, and rest in shady foliage during midday heat.

JUVENILE

• **NEST** A platform of sticks with a central hollow which is lined with hair, dung, grass, and skin, placed in the fork of a thorn tree just below the canopy.
• **DISTRIBUTION** Africa south of the Sahara.
• **REMARK** Females are larger than males.

long legs

long, narrow wings

DISTRIBUTION

Plumage Sexes alike	Habitat	Migration Non-migrant

| Family ACCIPITRIDAE | Species *Circus cyaneus* | L. 17 in (43 cm)/20 in (50 cm) |

NORTHERN HARRIER

This species is a typical harrier, hunting by searching the ground in low, fast, gliding flight. The wings are usually held in a shallow V shape. This method enables the bird to surprise small or disabled birds, small rodents, and even large insects. The species occurs in open landscapes such as moors, marshes, steppe grassland, and sand dunes.
• **NEST** A mound of small twigs, grass, and reeds, placed on the ground in dense cover.
• **DISTRIBUTION** Breeds in much of North America and Eurasia. Winters as far south as Central America, N. Africa, and S.E. Asia.
• **REMARK** Females larger than males.

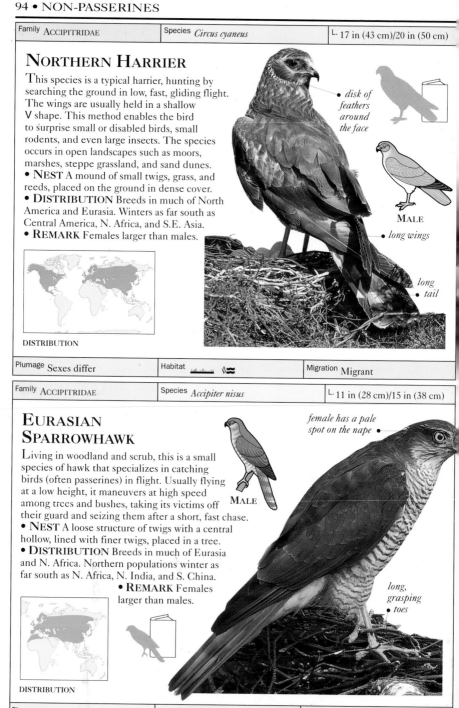

• disk of feathers around the face

MALE

• long wings

long • tail

DISTRIBUTION

| Plumage Sexes differ | Habitat | Migration Migrant |

| Family ACCIPITRIDAE | Species *Accipiter nisus* | L. 11 in (28 cm)/15 in (38 cm) |

EURASIAN SPARROWHAWK

Living in woodland and scrub, this is a small species of hawk that specializes in catching birds (often passerines) in flight. Usually flying at a low height, it maneuvers at high speed among trees and bushes, taking its victims off their guard and seizing them after a short, fast chase.
• **NEST** A loose structure of twigs with a central hollow, lined with finer twigs, placed in a tree.
• **DISTRIBUTION** Breeds in much of Eurasia and N. Africa. Northern populations winter as far south as N. Africa, N. India, and S. China.
• **REMARK** Females larger than males.

female has a pale spot on the nape •

MALE

long, grasping • toes

DISTRIBUTION

| Plumage Sexes differ | Habitat | Migration Partial migrant |

Family ACCIPITRIDAE	Species *Accipiter striatus*	L. 10½ in (27 cm)/13½ in (34 cm)

SHARP-SHINNED HAWK

This small, bird-hunting hawk has broad wings with narrow-tipped primary feathers that splay out like fingers when the bird soars. Its tail is long and broad. It is a woodland bird that hunts by maneuvering in low flight between trees and bushes, taking songbirds by surprise and capturing them in brief, sprinting chases. In higher and more open flight or on migration, it seems to lack power and travels slowly. As it passes, parties of small, fast-flying birds such as Common Starlings or Swallows (*see pp. 270, 375*) "mob" the Sharp-shinned Hawk, flocking round it with mock attacks.

• **NEST** A platform of sticks and twigs, lined with bark, smaller twigs, and feathers, and built in a tree.

• **DISTRIBUTION** Breeds in North America and Mexico. Northern and mountain populations winter in southern parts of this range.

• **REMARKS** Females are larger than males. Observations reveal that the two sexes reduce competition by taking slightly different sizes of prey, thus sharing the available food supply.

• large, keen eyes

DISTRIBUTION

JUVENILE

long, grasping • toes

Plumage Sexes differ slightly	Habitat	Migration Partial migrant

Family ACCIPITRIDAE	Species *Accipiter gentilis*	L. 19 in (48 cm)/23 in (58 cm)

NORTHERN GOSHAWK

A large relative of the Eurasian Sparrowhawk, this bird lives in mature, tall forest. It hunts in forests, at the forest edge, and in adjoining areas of open country. Its main prey are birds in flight. The Goshawk either flies low, taking a bird by surprise, or watches from a high perch in a tree and swoops on its victim. Prey includes crows, jays, pigeons, thrushes, grouse, pheasants, squirrels, and rabbits.

• **NEST** A platform of twigs and sticks, lined with bark, smaller twigs, and feathers, built in a tree.

• **DISTRIBUTION** Breeds in North America, Eurasia, and N. Africa. Northern populations migrate south.

• **REMARK** Females are larger than males.

• pale, prominent brow

broad, rounded wing shape revealed in • flight

• typical hunched resting posture

large • spots on breast of juvenile

long • tail

DISTRIBUTION

ADULT

JUVENILE

Plumage Sexes differ slightly	Habitat	Migration Partial migrant

| Family ACCIPITRIDAE | Species *Parabuteo unicinctus* | L. 17½ in (45 cm)/23 in (58 cm) |

HARRIS' HAWK

This is a heavily built hawk of the tropics and subtropics, living in dry regions including semi-desert, semi-arid woodland, and scrub. It is a fast-flying hunter that swoops from a perch to pursue desert rabbits, rats, snakes, lizards, and birds. Unlike other hawks, this species has a strong pattern of cooperative behavior, in which it is common for three birds to hunt together and share the kill. Larger family parties have been seen hunting in this way. Groups work together to catch prey that has taken cover, one bird approaching directly to drive it out, the others hanging back, ready to give chase. Often a nesting female is fed by two or more males, and in some cases she mates with two males. The whole group cares for the young.

chestnut wing patch

DISTRIBUTION

• **NEST** A neat structure of twigs, roots, and stalks, lined with leaves, grass, and bark, in a tree or on top of a tall yucca or cactus.
• **DISTRIBUTION** From USA south through Central America to Chile and Argentina.
• **REMARK** Females are considerably larger than males.

JUVENILE

| Plumage Sexes alike | Habitat | Migration Partial migrant |

| Family ACCIPITRIDAE | Species *Buteo jamaicensis* | L. 19 in (48 cm)/25 in (63 cm) |

RED-TAILED HAWK

A typical open-country bird of prey, this species commonly seeks out rising air currents (thermals) on which it circles and soars while looking for prey. Alternatively, it often perches high in a tree to watch for its prey. Any animal that moves is taken, whether mammal, reptile, bird, or large insect. As well as occurring in open landscapes, the Red-tailed Hawk is found in mixed country with both fields and trees, and in semidesert, especially where there are scattered trees.

large, broad wings

ADULT

• **NEST** A bulky platform made of sticks, with a cup-shaped hollow lined with finer twigs and stalks, sited in a tree.
• **DISTRIBUTION** North and Central America and the Caribbean. Some populations migrate within this range.
• **REMARKS** Females larger than males. Color phases (*see p. 13*) are dark, rufous, and light. Subspecies include Harlan's Hawk, found in Alaska and W. Canada, which lacks the red tail.

powerful feet for holding prey

DISTRIBUTION

| Plumage Sexes alike | Habitat | Migration Partial migrant |

Family ACCIPITRIDAE	Species *Buteo buteo*	L. 20 in (50 cm)/22 in (55 cm)

COMMON BUZZARD

This stoutly built bird of prey with broad, bluntly rounded wings and a wide tail is seen over fields, hills, forest clearings, and forest edges. It soars for hours, slowly searching for prey, or watches from a perch such as a tree or post before swooping down to take any animal from beetle to rabbit size. Small carrion is also taken.
• **NEST** A bulky mass of twigs and roots, with a cup-shaped hollow, lined and sited on a tree or a cliff ledge.
• **DISTRIBUTION** Breeds in much of Eurasia. Winters as far south as South Africa, India, and S.E. Asia.
• **REMARKS** Females are larger than males. There are three color phases (*p. 13*): pale, dark, and rufous.

• rounded head
• large eye

DARK PHASE

large, broad • wings

DISTRIBUTION

RUFOUS PHASE

Plumage Sexes alike	Habitat	Migration Partial migrant

Family ACCIPITRIDAE	Species *Harpia harpyja*	L. 35 in (90 cm)/40 in (102 cm)

HARPY EAGLE

A huge eagle with powerful feet and talons, this is the dominant bird of prey in the rain forests of Central and South America. It flies among trees and branches with agility, taking forest animals such as monkeys, sloths, possums, and snakes.
• **NEST** A large structure of thick sticks with a cup-shaped hollow, high in the fork of a tall tree.
• **DISTRIBUTION** From Mexico to N. Argentina.
• **REMARK** Females are larger than males.

short, rounded • wings

JUVENILE

• deep bill

• massive feet

long • tail

DISTRIBUTION

Plumage Sexes alike	Habitat	Migration Non-migrant

| Family ACCIPITRIDAE | Species *Pithecophaga jefferyi* | L. 37 in (95 cm)/40 in (102 cm) |

PHILIPPINE EAGLE

One of the largest of the world's birds of prey, this rain forest eagle has the typical shape of a forest-dwelling raptor. The wings are large with broad, rounded tips, and the tail is long. This combination provides speed and agility when the bird maneuvers among the branches. At times the eagle is seen soaring over the forest, but it hunts mainly in the trees, moving from branch to branch and pausing to watch for prey. It takes forest animals such as monkeys, flying lemurs, and large birds up to hornbill size and is sometimes known as the Monkey-eating Eagle. The Philippine Eagle utters long, drawn-out whistles that seem weak for such a powerful bird. A single egg is laid, and the species probably nests only every second year.
• **NEST** A bulky structure of sticks and twigs, lined and placed in the fork of a large branch in a tree rising above the surrounding rain forest.
• **DISTRIBUTION** Philippine Islands.
• **REMARKS** Females are slightly larger than males. This species is rare and threatened, chiefly because of the felling of rain forests.

DISTRIBUTION

broad, rounded wings for maneuvering among • branches of forest trees

large, strong • feet

• long tail

| Plumage Sexes alike | Habitat 🌳🌳 | Migration Non-migrant |

| Family ACCIPITRIDAE | Species *Aquila chrysaetos* | L. 30 in (75 cm)/35 in (90 cm) |

GOLDEN EAGLE

Adapted for hunting in open landscapes at high altitudes, this eagle is a strong and skillful flier, often seeming to plunge and dive in turbulent winds for sheer pleasure. Its typical hunting method is to fly fast and low, closing in on prey with a slanting dive. The eagle grips its prey with outstretched feet. Mammals such as hares are the main prey, but grouse and many birds, as well as carrion in winter, are also taken. The Golden Eagle is usually silent, but occasionally utters a yelping call.
• **NEST** A large nest made of sticks, lined with finer materials, and placed on a cliff or in a tree.
• **DISTRIBUTION** Breeds in much of North America, Eurasia, N. Africa, and the Middle East. Populations in N., C., and E. Eurasia migrate, wintering as far south as the Himalayas and China.
• **REMARK** Females are larger than the males.

golden-bronze • tint

DISTRIBUTION

JUVENILE

| Plumage Sexes alike | Habitat 🔺 🐾 | Migration Partial migrant |

| Family ACCIPITRIDAE | Species *Hieraaetus morphnoides* | L. 18½ in (47 cm)/21 in (53 cm) |

LITTLE EAGLE

This is a small, compact eagle with a short crest and fully feathered legs. It frequents partly wooded country, soaring and gliding to watch for prey on the ground below, or hunting from a perch. Approaching in low flight, it takes young rabbits and other small mammals, birds, reptiles, and insects.

• **NEST** A large cup nest made of sticks, lined with green leaves and placed high in a tree.
• **DISTRIBUTION** Australia, New Guinea, and the Moluccan Islands in Indonesia.
• **REMARKS** Females are larger than males. There are two color phases: light and dark (*see p. 13*).

DISTRIBUTION

• *lowered crest feathers*

• *dark face*

DARK PHASE

LIGHT PHASE

| Plumage Sexes alike | Habitat | Migration Non-migrant |

| Family ACCIPITRIDAE | Species *Polemaetus bellicosus* | L. 31 in (80 cm)/33 in (83 cm) |

MARTIAL EAGLE

A large eagle of open country, with a shaggy crest and feathered legs, this bird watches for prey by soaring and gliding, occasionally waiting on a perch. It takes a wide range of animal prey, attacking in a slanting dive and striking with wings and tail spread.

• **NEST** A large basin of thick twigs, with a small, cup-shaped hollow, lined and placed in the fork of a large tree.
• **DISTRIBUTION** Much of Africa south of the Sahara.
• **REMARK** Females are marginally larger than the males.

lowered crest •

heavy, hooked bill •

strong, feathered legs

DISTRIBUTION

JUVENILE

| Plumage Sexes alike | Habitat | Migration Non-migrant |

Family SAGITTARIIDAE	Species *Sagittarius serpentarius*	Length 59 in (150 cm)

SECRETARY BIRD

This large species, inhabiting grassland and open spaces, is an unusual type of bird of prey that has adapted itself so fully to a life of hunting on the ground that it rarely flies. This has resulted in its unusual appearance, with a tall, slender build, long legs, small feet, and long neck. The long wings and tail are useful mainly for keeping balance when the bird is walking, running, hunting, or engaged in territorial fights, which always take place on the ground. Flight is mainly restricted to visiting trees to roost and nest. The name of this

FLYING ADULT

species dates from pre-industrial times, when secretaries were court officials who carried quill pens tucked behind their ears. The Secretary Bird walks with a steady stride, nodding its head forward with each step. It catches and kills prey on the ground, using its bill or stamping with its feet. When catching a snake, it holds out its wings to change its outline, which confuses the snake and prevents it from striking. Prey also includes insects, frogs, lizards, birds, and rodents.
• **NEST** A flat platform made of sticks and twigs, with a hollow in the center, lined with grass, dung, and pellets of the undigested remains of prey, and placed on top of a bush or tree.
• **DISTRIBUTION** Africa south of the Sahara.
• **REMARK** This is the African counterpart of the Red-legged Seriema, a grassland bird of South America (*p. 129*).

slim, athletic •
build for hunting
on the ground in
open country

long wings rarely •
used in flight

long tail feathers •
provide balance

strong legs for
walking and running
• in grassland

small feet cannot hold or
• seize prey but are used
to stamp it to death

DISTRIBUTION

Plumage Sexes alike	Habitat	Migration Non-migrant

Family FALCONIDAE	Species *Polyborus plancus*	L. 21 in (53 cm)/25 in (63 cm)

CRESTED CARACARA

Feeding on carrion as well as on live-caught prey, the Crested Caracara is a member of the falcon family that is adapted for walking and hunting on the ground. The legs are long and suited to walking and running in its grassland and scrub habitat. The feet, like those of a falcon, are versatile enough to grasp prey, hold food down, turn objects over, and scratch the ground. Flight is direct, with steady wingbeats, unlike the soaring flight of a falcon, and reveals white patches on the wings and tail. Besides eating carrion, the Crested Caracara catches insects, frogs, reptiles, and weak or injured birds. It also robs the nests of birds and turtles. Its name is derived from its harsh, cackling call.
• **NEST** A large, untidy structure made of twigs and sticks, and placed either in a tree or on the ground.
• **DISTRIBUTION** S. USA, and Central and South America to Cape Horn and the Falkland Islands.
• **REMARK** Females larger than males.

shaggy crest

long legs

long toes and claws

DISTRIBUTION

JUVENILE

Plumage Sexes alike	Habitat	Migration Non-migrant

Family FALCONIDAE	Species *Herpetotheres cachinnans*	L. 18 in (46 cm)/22 in (55 cm)

LAUGHING FALCON

A large and heavily built forest falcon, this bird is recognized by its stiff crown feathers that form a bushy crest above a dark face mask. Its name refers to the laughing call it utters when disturbed, although at other times its call is a single or double note repeated many times. A sluggish species, it spends most of the time perched in a tree watching the ground for prey. Snakes are its main food, and the falcon swoops down and pounces heavily on its victim, biting it behind the head or biting the head off. The snake is then carried to a perch, either in the feet or the bill, to be eaten. The Laughing Falcon also eats lizards, small mammals, and invertebrates. It flies infrequently, with rapid wing-flaps alternating with level glides, and rarely soars.
• **NEST** A tree hollow, or a disused bird nest.
• **DISTRIBUTION** Much of Central and South America.
• **REMARK** Females are larger than males.

deep bill

long tail

short wings

powerful feet for lifting and carrying prey

DISTRIBUTION

Plumage Sexes alike	Habitat	Migration Non-migrant

| Family FALCONIDAE | Species *Falco sparverius* | L. 11½ in (29 cm)/12½ in (32 cm) |

AMERICAN KESTREL

This small and beautifully patterned bird is one of the less powerful falcons, taking smaller and slower prey. It flies rapidly with quick downward wingbeats. When perched, it has a habit of wagging its tail up and down. When hunting, it often hovers and drops onto prey, less commonly watching from a perch. In summer, it feeds chiefly on large insects, while in winter it more often takes mice and small birds. It utters a repeated "klee" or "killy" call.
• NEST A bare hollow in a natural cavity or crevice. Pairs occasionally make use of nest boxes, or old nests of larger tree-nesting birds.
• DISTRIBUTION North, Central, and South America and Caribbean islands.
• REMARK Females are slightly larger than males.

• *pale cheek patch*

DISTRIBUTION

narrow • *wings*

FEMALE

| Plumage Sexes differ | Habitat | Migration Partial migrant |

| Family FALCONIDAE | Species *Falco tinnunculus* | L. 13 in (33 cm)/ 14½ in (37 cm) |

COMMON KESTREL

A bird of open country that has adapted to the town environment, this species is often seen searching the ground in flight, hovering until it sees prey, and dropping gradually before the final pounce. Prey includes voles, mice, and smaller creatures such as grasshoppers or beetles. In towns and suburbs, sparrows are often taken. Prey is carried to a perch, plucked if necessary, and eaten. For a resting place, the bird often selects a perch with a wide view. The Common Kestrel flies with small, rapid, downward wingbeats interspersed with glides. At times it soars on rising air currents. It is often mobbed by flocks of Common Starlings (*see p. 375*) or martins (*see pp. 269–270*).
• NEST A natural hollow on a ledge of a cliff or a building, a cavity in a tree trunk, or an old nest of a larger bird.
• DISTRIBUTION Eurasia and Africa. Northern and eastern populations winter as far south as South Africa, India, China, and Japan.
• REMARK Females are larger than males.

long, narrow • *wings*

DISTRIBUTION   FEMALE

| Plumage Sexes differ | Habitat | Migration Partial migrant |

Family FALCONIDAE	Species *Falco columbarius*	L. 10½ in (27 cm)/12½ in (32 cm)

MERLIN

This is a small, fierce falcon with fast flight and good hunting ability. It inhabits open places such as moorland, marshes, grassland, and low-lying coasts. The Merlin hunts in flight, often following an erratic course but always moving fast, and sprinting for the kill. It flies low above the ground, using trees and ridges as cover. Birds in flight are its most common prey, but it also swoops down for animals such as mice. It also catches dragonflies in flight.
• **NEST** A hollow made by the birds, often among heather. Old nests of larger birds, in trees or bushes, are sometimes used.
• **DISTRIBUTION** Breeds across much of North America and Eurasia. Winters as far south as N. South America, N. Africa, N. India, and S. Vietnam.
• **REMARK** Females are larger than males.

large eye

MALE

streaked breast

FEMALE

DISTRIBUTION

Plumage Sexes differ	Habitat	Migration Migrant

Family FALCONIDAE	Species *Falco berigora*	L. 17 in (43 cm)/20 in (50 cm)

BROWN FALCON

Although as big as the largest and fiercest falcons, including the Peregrine (*see p. 105*), this species is a less aggressive hunter and seeks smaller, slower-moving prey. It also differs from the typical falcons in having longer legs and broader wings. The Brown Falcon occupies a range of habitats but favors open landscapes. When hunting, it sits and watches from a high vantage point for long periods, swooping down to the ground to take small mammals, young or injured birds, reptiles, and insects. The call is a harsh, cackling sound.
• **NEST** Old nests of other large birds, such as crows, are used. Brown Falcons sometimes nest on termite mounds.
• **DISTRIBUTION** S. New Guinea and much of Australia.
• **REMARKS** Females are larger than males. Color phases (*see p. 13*) include light, rufous-breasted, and dark plumage.

large eye

RUFOUS-BREASTED PHASE

legs are longer than in most falcons

DISTRIBUTION

LIGHT PHASE

Plumage Sexes alike	Habitat	Migration Non-migrant

Family FALCONIDAE	Species *Falco subbuteo*	L. 12 in (30 cm)/14½ in (37 cm)

EURASIAN HOBBY

One of the small hunting falcons, the Eurasian Hobby is built for speed with narrow, tapering wings and a long tail. It is fast enough to catch swallows (*see p. 270*) and swifts (*see pp. 208–209*), moving very rapidly in level flight with bursts of fast wingbeats. Its vision is keen enough for it to hunt bats in poor light, and it also takes large insects such as dragonflies. These are often carried in the feet and eaten during flight.

• **NEST** An old nest of a large tree-nesting bird or a squirrel.
• **DISTRIBUTION** Breeds in much of Eurasia and in N.W. Africa. Winters as far south as South Africa, India, S. China, and S. Vietnam.
• **REMARK** Females are larger than males.

bird in molt, growing new feathers

chestnut thighs

JUVENILE

old tail feathers

narrow, tapering wings

DISTRIBUTION

Plumage Sexes differ slightly	Habitat	Migration Migrant

Family FALCONIDAE	Species *Falco biarmicus*	L. 13½ in (34 cm)/20 in (50 cm)

LANNER FALCON

A robust hunting falcon, the Lanner occurs in desert and savanna (tropical and subtropical grassland) with occasional rocky crags on which it perches and nests. The species also occurs in open woodland. Lanners hunt either by striking small birds in the air after a steep dive (stoop) or by seizing ground prey, which they approach in fast, low flight. Prey taken in flight includes fruit bats and winged termites as well as birds. Ground prey includes francolins (*see pp. 111–112*), guineafowl (*see p. 117*), and small bustards such as the Black Koorhaan (*see p. 130*). When birds are scarce, rats and large burrowing desert lizards are caught. Lanners are usually silent but nesting pairs utter shrill, screaming and chattering calls.

• **NEST** A hollow on a ledge on a cliff or building, or an old nest of a larger species.
• **DISTRIBUTION** S.E. Europe, Middle East, and much of Africa.
• **REMARK** Females are larger than males.

DISTRIBUTION

pale under-side of adult bird

JUVENILE

long, tapering wings

Plumage Sexes differ slightly	Habitat	Migration Partial migrant/nomadic

Family FALCONIDAE	Species *Falco peregrinus*	L. 15 in (38 cm)/19 in (48 cm)

PEREGRINE FALCON

PALE-BREASTED FORM

This fierce and very fast hunter catches birds in the air by flying high overhead and diving to take them by surprise. In the final stage of its dive (stoop), it is believed to attain speeds up to 250 mph (400 km/h). The falcon strikes its victim in passing with its feet, returning to catch the falling bird and carry it away.

• **NEST** Typically a bare place on a rock ledge.
• **DISTRIBUTION** Breeds in all continents except Antarctica. Some winter migration.
• **REMARKS** Females are larger than males. This is the main species used in falconry. Breast varies from pale to orange among the many subspecies and color phases (*see p. 13*) found within the wide distribution.

• *back color varies in darkness*

ORANGE-BREASTED PHASE

DISTRIBUTION

Plumage Sexes differ slightly	Habitat	Migration Migrant

Family MEGAPODIIDAE	Species *Leipoa ocellata*	Length 24 in (60 cm)

MALLEEFOWL

This is a mound-building bird of the Australian mallee (dry scrub of dwarf eucalyptus trees). Pairs live in territories, apparently mated for life. The male scratches twigs and leaves backwards to fill a hole, and after these have been moistened by rain he covers the material with soil to form a nest mound some 16½ ft (5 m) wide and 5 ft (1.5 m) high. He is then constantly occupied with tending the mound. He opens it, mixes the contents, and closes it to control the heat produced by the rotting plant material. The diet includes seeds (mainly acacia), buds, shoots, and some insects.

• **NEST** The female lays about 24 eggs each season, burying them individually in the mound, to be incubated by the warmth of the decaying materials.
• **DISTRIBUTION** S. Australia.

• *male digging mound*

DISTRIBUTION

Plumage Sexes alike	Habitat	Migration Non-migrant

Family MEGAPODIIDAE	Species *Alectura lathami*	Length 28 in (70 cm)

AUSTRALIAN BRUSH-TURKEY

This species resembles a lanky gamebird with a long, bare neck, from which folds of wrinkled skin ("neck wattles") hang down. It is a forest dweller, feeding on insects, fruit, and seeds. The male scratches the ground, kicking leaf litter and mold behind him to form a nest mound that may be several times his height. This material rots and becomes warm, and he tests it with his bill, keeping the temperature constant by adding or removing material.

• **NEST** The female digs holes in the mound, laying an egg in each one, to be incubated by the heat of decay. The downy chicks hatch, dig their own way out, and fend for themselves.

• **DISTRIBUTION** N.E. and E. Australia.

bare skin on head and neck

flat-sided tail

CAPE YORK RACE

yellow wattle of typical race

DISTRIBUTION

Plumage Sexes alike	Habitat 🌳 🌱 ✈	Migration Non-migrant

Family CRACIDAE	Species *Ortalis vetula*	Length 24 in (60 cm)

PLAIN CHACHALACA

Looking like a slender gamebird with long neck, legs, and tail, this species inhabits forest, scrub, and thickets, spending much of its time aboveground. It usually occurs in small parties, walking along branches and feeding on fruit, buds, and leaves. The name is a version of the birds' harsh call, which is uttered in chorus, mostly at dusk and dawn. The whole flock roosts together in thickets; and small young clamber and flutter up to roost with their parents, each under a wing.

• **NEST** A small platform made of twigs, placed in dense tree foliage at medium height.

• **DISTRIBUTION** S.E. Texas to Nicaragua.

MALE

short wings

feet adapted for grasping twigs

DISTRIBUTION

Plumage Sexes differ slightly	Habitat 🌱 ✈	Migration Non-migrant

Family CRACIDAE	Species *Pipile pipile*	Length 27 in (68 cm)

COMMON PIPING-GUAN

A forest species resembling a gamebird, the Common Piping-Guan has a slender build, long legs, and strong feet, all of which are adaptations for walking along tree branches. It lives mostly in the upper and middle levels of the forest, where it walks, jumps, and flies among branches. Its diet consists mainly of fruit, with some buds, leaves, and occasional small animals. Birds usually occur in groups and often perch in open view on a high branch. As the name indicates, they utter high pitched, whistling calls. Breeding birds perform a display flight from treetop to treetop, in which the flight feathers make a loud, whirring sound.

• **NEST** A scanty twig nest, placed high in the canopy.
• **DISTRIBUTION** South America, in the Amazon and Orinoco river basins.

slender head with small crest

long, slender neck

throat wattle

feet are adapted for walking on tree branches

long, slender tail

DISTRIBUTION

Plumage Sexes alike	Habitat	Migration Non-migrant

Family CRACIDAE	Species *Mitu mitu*	Length 35 in (90 cm)

RAZOR-BILLED CURASSOW

This stoutly built bird is capable of moving among the branches of trees, but it spends most of its time foraging on the forest floor. It takes to the trees if disturbed or alarmed and also roosts there. The short, curved-tipped bill is extended upward to form a prominent, thin ridge with flattened sides, forming the "razor" edge from which the name is derived. This feature seems to serve purely as a decoration. The species feeds mainly on fallen fruit, also taking buds, leaves, seeds, and occasional insects.

• **NEST** A saucer-shaped nest of leaves and stems, in foliage at low or medium height.
• **DISTRIBUTION** Amazon basin in C. Brazil, E. Peru, and N. Bolivia. The small population recorded in E. Brazil may be extinct.

heavy head with small crest

stocky build

strong legs for walking on branches

broad tail with a rounded end

DISTRIBUTION

Plumage Sexes alike	Habitat	Migration Non-migrant

| Family PHASIANIDAE | Species *Meleagris gallopavo* | L. 49 in (125 cm)/36 in (91 cm) |

WILD TURKEY

In the wild, turkeys are cautious and evasive birds of forest edges and clearings. They feed on the ground, taking berries, seeds, nuts, other parts of plants, and invertebrates. In winter, Wild Turkeys often live in flocks. Some flocks are segregated, containing birds of only one sex. In spring, the breeding male displays with his tail spread, attracting a small flock of females that nest individually after mating.
• **NEST** A shallow hollow in the ground, sparsely lined with leaves and stems, often in vegetation.
• **DISTRIBUTION** Patchily distributed in S. Canada, much of USA, and N. Mexico.

fully fanned • tail

FEMALE

DISTRIBUTION

| Plumage Sexes differ | Habitat | Migration Non-migrant |

| Family PHASIANIDAE | Species *Tetrao tetrix* | L. 22 in (55 cm)/17 in (43 cm) |

BLACK GROUSE

A gamebird of forest edges and scrub, this species is seen perching, and sometimes roosting, in trees. It feeds mainly on tree buds, also eating insects in summer. In spring, males display competitively on a piece of ground known as a "lek." They leap in the air with whirring wings and make excited, bubbling and sneezing calls. Females visit the lek, mate with a male, then nest alone.
• **NEST** A hollow in the ground, made by the birds and hidden among fairly tall vegetation.
• **DISTRIBUTION** Eurasia from British Isles to E. Siberia.

elongated • undertail feathers

upright display posture

tail feathers

short, thick legs

DISTRIBUTION

FEMALE

| Plumage Sexes differ | Habitat | Migration Non-migrant |

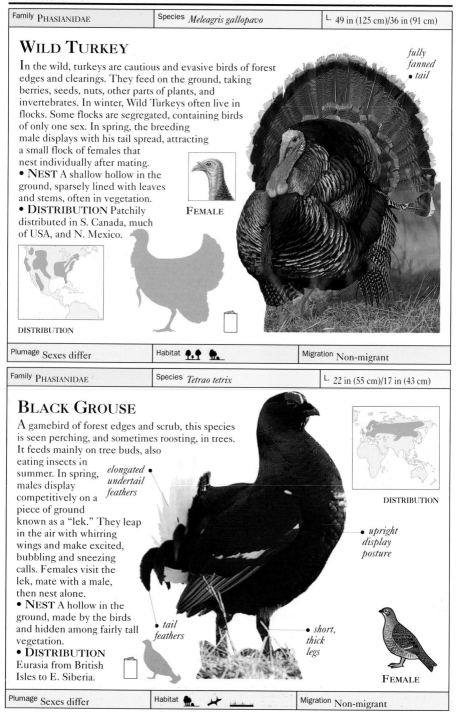

| Family PHASIANIDAE | Species *Centrocercus urophasianus* | L. 31 in (80 cm)/22 in (55 cm) |

SAGE GROUSE

Dwelling in extensive scrub formed by sage bushes, this species alternates between the plains in winter and the foothills in summer. It feeds on sage leaves and insects. In spring, groups of males advertise themselves to the females over a distance, spreading out their tails in a spiky fan, swelling out their necks, and repeatedly inflating the air sacs on their breasts. They utter deep, bubbling noises. Females select a mate and subsequently nest alone.
• **NEST** A hollow in the ground, often situated under a sage bush.
• **DISTRIBUTION** Interior of W. North America.

hairlike crest on the nape •

• *spiky tail feathers*

• *raised flight feathers*

DISTRIBUTION

FEMALE

| Plumage Sexes differ | Habitat | Migration Non-migrant |

| Family PHASIANIDAE | Species *Callipepla californica* | L. 11 in (28 cm)/10 in (25 cm) |

CALIFORNIA QUAIL

A small gamebird of open woodland, scrub, and farmland, the California Quail is often seen in flocks. Although it can fly well, it usually walks or runs. It perches and roosts (rests at night) in thick cover, on low branches. The diet consists of seeds, parts of green plants, and insects, taken from the ground.
• **NEST** A hollow in the ground, lined with plant stems plucked from close by, often sheltered by vegetation.
• **DISTRIBUTION** W. North America. Introduced in other countries, mainly for ornamental use in gardens and parks, with local populations of escaped birds.

both sexes have the forward-nodding crest •

streaked flank •

FEMALE

DISTRIBUTION

| Plumage Sexes differ | Habitat | Migration Non-migrant |

Family PHASIANIDAE	Species *Colinus virginianus*	Length 10 in (25 cm)

NORTHERN BOBWHITE

For most of the year, this small quail is fairly
unobtrusive, but in spring it makes its presence known
with its loud "bobwhite" call, given from a low perch
such as a stone or a tree stump. It is common in
thickets, in shrubby countryside, and in open
woodland. In spring, the birds feed in pairs or
family parties, gathering into small flocks later in
the year. They are seen walking or running on the
ground, often venturing into open fields. If
disturbed, they first crouch among bushes, then fly
low from one patch of cover to another on whirring
wings. They roost huddled together on the ground,
facing outward so that all can take off and scatter if
alarmed. They feed on seeds, shoots, leaves, and roots,
with some insects and other small invertebrates.
• **NEST** A shallow hollow in the ground,
lined with dead vegetation, often in a
relatively open site, such as a meadow.
• **DISTRIBUTION**
From E. USA to Mexico.
Introduced in other countries,
with relatively small local
populations of escaped birds.

DISTRIBUTION

• upright calling posture

white-flecked • underside

FEMALE

Plumage Sexes differ	Habitat	Migration Non-migrant

Family PHASIANIDAE	Species *Cyrtonyx montezumae*	Length 8½ in (22 cm)

MONTEZUMA QUAIL

Characterized by a bolder head pattern
than those of other quails, this is a bird
of woodlands in drier mountain areas. It is
found in canyons where oaks are interspersed
with grass and on hillsides with scattered
conifers. Very much a ground dweller, it
tends to crouch and hide among grasses
when alarmed. Both male and female look
big-headed because of the way in which
the crest curves back to enlarge the nape.
The male's sandy-colored crest may conceal
the vivid black-and-white pattern on the face
when he crouches. The birds nest in pairs
in the late summer and gather in small flocks
after breeding. They feed on seeds and some
insects and also scratch up the
ground for tubers and bulbs.
• **NEST** A hollow in
the ground, lined with
grass, and situated in grass.
• **DISTRIBUTION**
From S.W. USA to S. Mexico.

• heavy crest on nape

DISTRIBUTION

white spots • on breast and flanks

jet black • underside

strong, scratching • feet

FEMALE

Plumage Sexes differ	Habitat	Migration Non-migrant

| Family PHASIANIDAE | Species *Alectoris chukar* | Length 14 in (35 cm) |

CHUKAR

Camouflaged by soft colors, this shy partridge inhabits barren mountainsides, grassy slopes, and arid valleys. The name is derived from its call. In winter, Chukars form coveys (social groups) of five to 40 birds, feeding on seeds, shoots, and insects.
• **NEST** A shallow hollow scraped with the feet and shaped by body pressure, lined with grass, in an open situation among grass.
• **DISTRIBUTION** From S. Europe to China. Introduced in W. North America and elsewhere.

chestnut ear patch

bare, scarlet patch around the eye

black "necklace"

JUVENILE

short, rounded wings

strong feet for running

DISTRIBUTION

| Plumage Sexes alike | Habitat | Migration Non-migrant |

| Family PHASIANIDAE | Species *Francolinus francolinus* | L. 22 in (55 cm)/16½ in (42 cm) |

BLACK FRANCOLIN

Noticeable for the male's rich mixture of black, brown, chestnut, and white, this bird can also be detected by the harsh, far-carrying call note of both sexes. The Black Francolin is a type of partridge that occurs both in lowlands and at altitudes of up to 5,250 ft (1,600 m) in the mountains. It is popular with hunters and shooters as a gamebird. Its diet consists of the seeds, shoots, and buds of plants, supplemented with insects, worms, and other invertebrates.
• **NEST** A hollow in the ground, lined with grass, beneath a bush.
• **DISTRIBUTION** S. Eurasia, from Cyprus and Turkey east to Pakistan and N. India.
• **REMARK** Its past range extended west as far as Spain.

chestnut nape patch

DISTRIBUTION

finely barred back

spotted flank

streaked wing

FEMALE

| Plumage Sexes differ | Habitat | Migration Non-migrant |

Family PHASIANIDAE	Species *Francolinus afer*	Length 15 in (38 cm)

RED-NECKED FRANCOLIN

Identified by its red face and throat, this partridge lives in hot, dry countries. Throughout its wide range, it is a bird of the lowlands, living in scrub and open woodland, at the forest edge, and in wooded gorges. Red-necked Francolins live either in pairs or in family parties and will sometimes allow francolins of other species to feed alongside them in their territories. Their diet consists mainly of seeds, shoots, leaves, and berries, but they also scratch the ground for roots and bulbs and take insects and other invertebrates. They do not readily fly, preferring to escape danger by running.
• **NEST** A hollow formed by body pressure, lined with grass and roots, and surrounded by thick vegetation.
• **DISTRIBUTION** Africa from Gabon and Kenya south to the coastal strip of South Africa.

bare skin around the eye

bare throat patch

DISTRIBUTION

• strong feet for running and scratching

Plumage Sexes alike	Habitat	Migration Non-migrant

Family PHASIANIDAE	Species *Perdix perdix*	Length 12½ in (32 cm)

GRAY PARTRIDGE

This is one of the commonest gamebirds within its range; its populations are artificially maintained for the benefit of hunters and shooters. Gray Partridges usually live in pairs in spring, forming coveys (social groups) of up to 20 birds in autumn. The birds feed on the ground in farmland, taking seeds, insects, and grains. When alarmed, they crouch in the grass, passing for a clod of earth or a piece of dry turf. If a bird is approached directly, it bursts out of hiding in a rapid escape flight, low over the ground at first, making a sharply audible whistling sound with its wings.
• **NEST** A small hollow, often lined with dead plant materials, in an open situation in grass.
• **DISTRIBUTION** From Europe to W. China. Introduced in North America.

JUVENILE

alert posture typical of • male bird

MALE

FEMALE

DISTRIBUTION

Plumage Sexes differ slightly	Habitat	Migration Non-migrant

Family PHASIANIDAE	Species *Coturnix coturnix*	Length 7 in (18 cm)

COMMON QUAIL

This species is one of the smaller gamebirds of the world. Its distinctive call, consisting of three liquid notes, can be heard both day and night. It hides in dry grassland and among growing crops. If threatened, it prefers to escape danger by running rather than flying but will reluctantly make short, low flights. On its long-distance migratory journeys, however, it shows its ability to fly strongly. The Common Quail feeds on the ground, its diet consisting mainly of seeds, buds, shoots, and leaves.
• **NEST** A shallow hollow in the ground, scraped with the feet and shaped by body pressure, lined with dried grass and situated in thick cover.
• **DISTRIBUTION** Breeds from Europe to east C. Siberia and Mongolia, and in Iran, N. India, Africa, and Madagascar. Eurasian birds winter as far south as C. Africa and India.

streaked facial pattern

MALE

"dead grass" camouflage pattern

DISTRIBUTION

Plumage Sexes differ	Habitat	Migration Migrant

Family PHASIANIDAE	Species *Tragopan temminckii*	Length 25 in (63 cm)

TEMMINCK'S TRAGOPAN

A bird of evergreen or mixed forest in mountains, Temminck's Tragopan occurs at altitudes of up to 15,000 ft (4,600 m) and is normally solitary. Like other birds living in unpopulated regions, it is tame in human company. Its diet consists of plant matter, such as buds, shoots, and seeds, supplemented with insects. This species is remarkable for the male's colored throat wattle, which is inflated in display, expanding to cover his breast.
• **NEST** A platform made of twigs, gathered from the immediate surroundings, and placed in a bush or low tree.
• **DISTRIBUTION** Tibet, C. China, N.E. India, Burma, and N. Vietnam.

DISTRIBUTION

spotted plumage

FEMALE

Plumage Sexes differ	Habitat	Migration Non-migrant

| Family PHASIANIDAE | Species *Lophophorus impejanus* | L. 26 in (65 cm)/22 in (55 cm) |

IMPEYAN MONAL

The magical, iridescent colors of this species seem poorly suited to its ungainly shape. It is a short-tailed pheasant with stout legs and a large, eaglelike bill. At a distance, the male's velvet-black breast is the most conspicuous feature. This is a mountain species, living in open forest and among stands of rhododendron at altitudes of some 8,000–16,000 ft (2,500–5,000 m). Singly or in small groups of three or four, the birds root around, often in snow-covered soil. They feed on grass and flower seeds, tubers, bulbs, berries, and insects.
• **NEST** A shallow hollow scraped by the feet and formed by body pressure, under an overhanging rock or a fallen tree trunk, generally on a steep hillside, and often hidden among the grass.
• **DISTRIBUTION** Himalayas in Afghanistan, N. Pakistan, N. India, and S. Tibet.
• **REMARK** The male's crest is always erect, while the female's tends more to lie flat.

crest feathers broaden at the tip

DISTRIBUTION

rufous tail

velvet-black underside

FEMALE

| Plumage Sexes differ | Habitat | Migration Non-migrant |

| Family PHASIANIDAE | Species *Gallus gallus* | L. 22 in (55 cm)/17 in (43 cm) |

RED JUNGLEFOWL

Small, shy groups of this species live at the edge of rain forest and secondary growth (regrown after forest clearance), scratching for invertebrates and plant material. They can be detected by the crowing of the males.
• **NEST** A hollow formed by body pressure, lined with dry grass and bamboo leaves, and hidden in dense undergrowth.
• **DISTRIBUTION** From the E. Himalayas through S. China to the Malay Peninsula, Indonesia, and the Philippines.

FEMALE

male closely resembles its domesticated relative, the farm cockerel

DISTRIBUTION

| Plumage Sexes differ | Habitat | Migration Non-migrant |

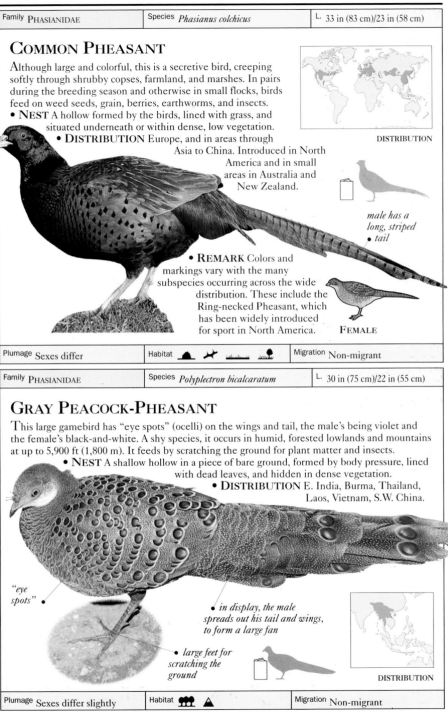

Family PHASIANIDAE	Species *Phasianus colchicus*	L. 33 in (83 cm)/23 in (58 cm)

COMMON PHEASANT

Although large and colorful, this is a secretive bird, creeping softly through shrubby copses, farmland, and marshes. In pairs during the breeding season but otherwise in small flocks, birds feed on weed seeds, grain, berries, earthworms, and insects.
• **NEST** A hollow formed by the birds, lined with grass, and situated underneath or within dense, low vegetation.
• **DISTRIBUTION** Europe, and in areas through Asia to China. Introduced in North America and in small areas in Australia and New Zealand.

DISTRIBUTION

male has a long, striped tail

• **REMARK** Colors and markings vary with the many subspecies occurring across the wide distribution. These include the Ring-necked Pheasant, which has been widely introduced for sport in North America.

FEMALE

Plumage Sexes differ	Habitat	Migration Non-migrant

Family PHASIANIDAE	Species *Polyplectron bicalcaratum*	L. 30 in (75 cm)/22 in (55 cm)

GRAY PEACOCK-PHEASANT

This large gamebird has "eye spots" (ocelli) on the wings and tail, the male's being violet and the female's black-and-white. A shy species, it occurs in humid, forested lowlands and mountains at up to 5,900 ft (1,800 m). It feeds by scratching the ground for plant matter and insects.
• **NEST** A shallow hollow in a piece of bare ground, formed by body pressure, lined with dead leaves, and hidden in dense vegetation.
• **DISTRIBUTION** E. India, Burma, Thailand, Laos, Vietnam, S.W. China.

"eye spots"

• *in display, the male spreads out his tail and wings, to form a large fan*

• *large feet for scratching the ground*

DISTRIBUTION

Plumage Sexes differ slightly	Habitat	Migration Non-migrant

| Family PHASIANIDAE | Species *Pavo cristatus* | L. 84 in (213 cm)/34 in (85 cm) |

COMMON PEAFOWL

As a wild bird, the Common Peafowl (commonly known as the Peacock) lives in deciduous tropical forests and feeds in open places such as clearings or cultivated fields. Its diet consists of seeds, fruit, and other parts of plants, as well as small animals ranging from insects to mice. The male's long and colorful train is not the bird's tail but an ornament, composed of some 150 large feathers growing from his lower back. The real tail is short and dull-colored, hidden underneath the train. The female lacks a train, as does the male in winter. Both sexes, and even the tiny young, possess little, fan-shaped crests on the crown of the head. In display, the male raises up his train in a symmetrical fan by lifting his tail. At the same time, he lowers and shakes his chestnut-colored wings, which he reveals when strutting and turning in front of the female. He also utters a loud, far-carrying call. A displaying male will soon attract, and then guard, a small flock of females. The flock remains with him for a few days, during which time he mates with each of them. Each female then departs to nest alone, without the help of the male. Both sexes are agile enough to fly up into the higher branches of trees to roost.

• **NEST** A shallow hollow made by the birds, bare or lined with sticks, leaves, and grass, and often concealed in thorny undergrowth.

• **DISTRIBUTION** Indian subcontinent, including Sri Lanka.

DISTRIBUTION

FEMALE

vivid eye spots •

train feathers raised in a • *half-circle*

| Plumage Sexes differ | Habitat 🐦🐦 🌳 | Migration Non-migrant |

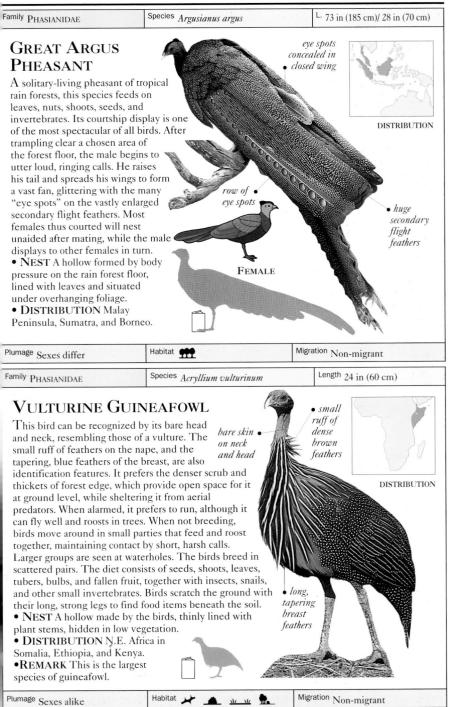

Family PHASIANIDAE	Species *Argusianus argus*	L. 73 in (185 cm)/ 28 in (70 cm)

GREAT ARGUS PHEASANT

A solitary-living pheasant of tropical rain forests, this species feeds on leaves, nuts, shoots, seeds, and invertebrates. Its courtship display is one of the most spectacular of all birds. After trampling clear a chosen area of the forest floor, the male begins to utter loud, ringing calls. He raises his tail and spreads his wings to form a vast fan, glittering with the many "eye spots" on the vastly enlarged secondary flight feathers. Most females thus courted will nest unaided after mating, while the male displays to other females in turn.
• NEST A hollow formed by body pressure on the rain forest floor, lined with leaves and situated under overhanging foliage.
• DISTRIBUTION Malay Peninsula, Sumatra, and Borneo.

eye spots concealed in closed wing

DISTRIBUTION

row of eye spots

• huge secondary flight feathers

FEMALE

Plumage Sexes differ	Habitat	Migration Non-migrant

Family PHASIANIDAE	Species *Acryllium vulturinum*	Length 24 in (60 cm)

VULTURINE GUINEAFOWL

This bird can be recognized by its bare head and neck, resembling those of a vulture. The small ruff of feathers on the nape, and the tapering, blue feathers of the breast, are also identification features. It prefers the denser scrub and thickets of forest edge, which provide open space for it at ground level, while sheltering it from aerial predators. When alarmed, it prefers to run, although it can fly well and roosts in trees. When not breeding, birds move around in small parties that feed and roost together, maintaining contact by short, harsh calls. Larger groups are seen at waterholes. The birds breed in scattered pairs. The diet consists of seeds, shoots, leaves, tubers, bulbs, and fallen fruit, together with insects, snails, and other small invertebrates. Birds scratch the ground with their long, strong legs to find food items beneath the soil.
• NEST A hollow made by the birds, thinly lined with plant stems, hidden in low vegetation.
• DISTRIBUTION N.E. Africa in Somalia, Ethiopia, and Kenya.
• REMARK This is the largest species of guineafowl.

bare skin on neck and head

• small ruff of dense brown feathers

DISTRIBUTION

• long, tapering breast feathers

Plumage Sexes alike	Habitat	Migration Non-migrant

| Family MESITORNITHIDAE | Species *Mesitornis unicolor* | Length 12 in (30 cm) |

BROWN MESITE

This rare bird lives in tropical rain forest, where it feeds on the ground, taking seeds, fruit, and small insects. Superficially, it looks like a largish passerine with a small, rounded head and a pointed bill. The body is rather heavy and ends in a surprisingly broad tail. The wings are short and rounded, and the bird is virtually flightless. On the other hand, this species has strong, agile legs, and it walks and runs easily on its lightly built feet. The Brown Mesite builds its nest in a tree, in a position that can be reached by walking up and down a sloping trunk or across branches.
• **NEST** A thin, concave platform made of twigs, sparsely lined with grass or leaves, and placed in a tree.
• **DISTRIBUTION** E. Madagascar.

large eye for finding food in poor light

short, round wings, hardly ever used for flight

large, broad tail

long legs of a ground-living bird

small, round head

lightly built feet

DISTRIBUTION

| Plumage Sexes alike | Habitat 🌳 | Migration Non-migrant |

| Family TURNICIDAE | Species *Turnix sylvatica* | Length 5 in (13 cm) |

SMALL BUTTON-QUAIL

A soft, booming call may be the only indication of the presence of this small and secretive species. A ground-dwelling bird of open woodland, scrub, and grassland, it resembles a quail in behavior and shape but has a more slender bill. Females are a little larger and more brightly colored than males; they take the dominant role in breeding, calling, and establishing territories. Males incubate the eggs and care for the downy young.
• **NEST** A shallow hollow lined with fine grasses, situated in grass. Grass stems and leaves are pulled over the nest to hide it.
• **DISTRIBUTION** Extreme S. Spain, parts of Africa, and from Pakistan and India to S.E. Asia, including the Philippines.

DISTRIBUTION

staring, pale iris

"dried-grass" pattern for camouflage

strong feet, lacking a hind toe

| Plumage Sexes differ slightly | Habitat ✈ 🎋 🌾 | Migration Non-migrant |

| Family PEDIONOMIDAE | Species *Pedionomus torquatus* | Length 6¾ in (17 cm) |

PLAINS WANDERER

This small, ground-dwelling bird of dry, open grassland has a compact body, strong legs and feet, staring eyes, and a slender bill. In all these respects, it is similar to the Small Button-Quail. However, it prefers more open habitats, moving cautiously and only occasionally standing on tiptoe to peer over the grass. It may be seen in fluttering, dipping flight, or perching on a fence post or mound. The diet consists of seeds and insects. The female is more brightly colored than the male and is the dominant partner. She may mate with several males, which act as the main carers for the eggs and young.

patterned neck

brown breast patch

• **NEST** A shallow hollow in the ground, lined with grass, and situated alongside a tussock or small shrub.

• **DISTRIBUTION** Interior of S.E. Australia.

DISTRIBUTION

MALE

FEMALE

| Plumage Sexes differ | Habitat | Migration Nomadic |

| Family GRUIDAE | Species *Grus canadensis* | Length 41 in (105 cm) |

SANDHILL CRANE

This small crane is mostly gray, apart from its red crown and white cheek. Some individuals are stained reddish with iron salts that are present in the water and are transferred to the plumage when the bird preens itself with a wet bill. A bird of open, marshy landscapes and grassland, the Sandhill Crane breeds in scattered pairs, but gathers in large and often noisy flocks for migration. It feeds on seeds including grain, and on buds, shoots, leaves, and small animals from insects to mice.

• *bare, red display patch*

DISTRIBUTION

• **NEST** A heap of plant material, large if on a wet site, with a central hollow.

• **DISTRIBUTION** Breeds in N.E. Siberia and much of N. North America, also Florida. Winters in North America, as far south as Mexico.

slender build of a small crane

upper leg feathering

• *drooping feathers from the lower back (can be raised in display)*

• *long stride of a grassland bird*

| Plumage Sexes alike | Habitat | Migration Migrant |

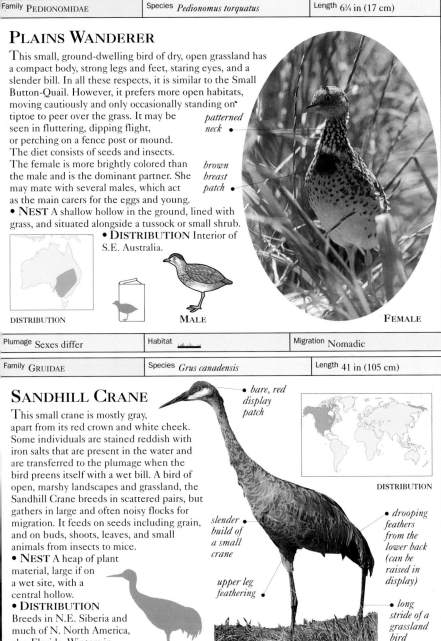

Family GRUIDAE	Species *Grus japonensis*	Length 55 in (140 cm)

JAPANESE CRANE

Of all the world's crane species, this rare and beautiful bird is among the tallest. It occurs in grassland in wide valleys with swampy areas, where its height is a natural advantage, giving a clear view of danger from a safe distance. The Japanese Crane walks with a deliberate, striding gait, pausing now and then to pick up food items, which may be relatively small. Mice, frogs, and large insects, seeds, buds, and leaves, form its diet. Flight is strong, with neck and legs extended, and with deliberate wingbeats, interspersed with gliding. Flocks usually fly in chevrons ("V shapes") or slanting lines. Migration to and from the winter feeding grounds tends to follow traditional routes. Pairs mate for life, and the bond between them appears to be strengthened by mutual displays.

Displaying birds stand side by side with raised heads, uttering loud, trumpet-like calls. They then begin to perform a wild dance, very different from their usual, placid behavior. Dancing birds wave their heads up and down, raise and flap their wings, and make clumsy-looking leaps into the air. They sometimes pick up sticks or pull up tufts of grass and throw these into the air. Although each nesting pair normally has two eggs, one chick usually dies at an early age. The survivor is often seen walking behind the parents, which feed it with small insects, offered one at a time. The young bird migrates with its parents and stays with them until the following season.

- **NEST** A large mound of plant stalks and grasses, gathered at the nest site and piled together on the ground, with a hollow in the top.
- **DISTRIBUTION** Breeds in Japan, E. Siberia, and N. China. Winters in Korea, N.E. China, and S. Japan.

• *head raised in mutual trumpeting posture*

drooping, decorative plumes, raised above the • *tail in display*

snowy white • *plumage*

wings partly raised from the • *body*

DISTRIBUTION

long, slender toes •

JUVENILE

Plumage Sexes alike	Habitat	Migration Migrant

| Family GRUIDAE | Species *Grus grus* | Length 44 in (112 cm) |

COMMON CRANE

For the most part a plain-looking crane of grassland and marshes, this bird's presence is given away by its bright head color and far-carrying calls. The calls are used as part of the pairing display and are also uttered in flight. The diet consists of insects, frogs, mice, seeds, and other parts of green plants. In winter, cranes visit drier habitats, such as farmland.
• **NEST** A mound of reeds, grass, and other vegetation, with a shallow hollow on top, often in a marsh and located near, or in, shallow water.
• **DISTRIBUTION** Breeds across Eurasia. Winters in S. Eurasia, N.W. and N.E. Africa, India, and China.
• **REMARK** Because it needs large, undisturbed areas of marshland, bogs, and grassland for breeding, the Common Crane has lost ground during the present century as a result of the spread of human settlement. It occurs in areas where this type of habitat remains, also spreading into birch scrub or woodland.

• *decorative patch of bare, red skin*

DISTRIBUTION

• *plumes droop from lower back (can be raised in display)*

JUVENILE

| Plumage Sexes alike | Habitat | Migration Migrant |

| Family GRUIDAE | Species *Balearica regulorum* | Length 41 in (105 cm) |

GRAY CROWNED-CRANE

The large, white wing patches on the gray plumage of this species are noticeable in flight and in display. This crane inhabits marshland, where it feeds on animals such as large insects, frogs, and toads, and on grain and other plant materials. It is seen in heavy flight, with neck and legs drooping slightly, or roosting in trees. Mated birds display to one another with a leaping dance and loud, two-note calls.
• **NEST** A large, flattened mound of reeds, rushes, and grass, screened by vegetation, in a marsh.
• **DISTRIBUTION** From Uganda and Kenya to South Africa.
• **REMARK** A closely related species, the Black Crowned-Crane, is found along the southern edge of the Sahara and in Sudan.

spiky crest •

red • throat wattle

DISTRIBUTION

• *long plumes on the neck and breast*

white • wing patch

JUVENILE

| Plumage Sexes alike | Habitat | Migration Non-migrant |

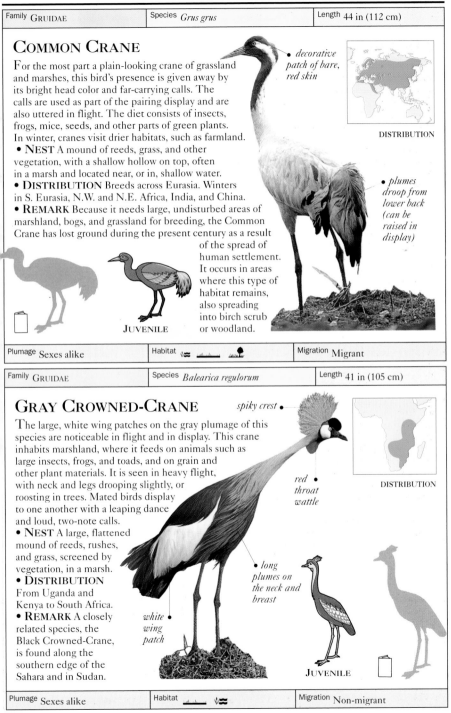

Family ARAMIDAE	Species *Aramus guarauna*	Length 26 in (65 cm)

LIMPKIN

The most noticeable characteristic of this marshland bird is the long, slender shape of its bill, neck, legs, and toes. The wings, however, are short and rounded in shape. Normally a wading bird of tropical and subtropical wooded swamps, it can swim well. It rests by day and becomes active at dusk and during the night, when it utters loud calls that can sound like clucking, wailing, or screaming. The diet consists mainly of large water snails; the Limpkin's vertically flattened bill is adapted for extracting these from their shells. Limpkins also feed on other mollusks and swamp creatures, from worms to crayfish and large reptiles.
• **NEST** A large structure of sticks and rushes, built on the ground or, in wet areas, in trees at low or medium height.
• **DISTRIBUTION** From Florida and the Caribbean to Argentina.

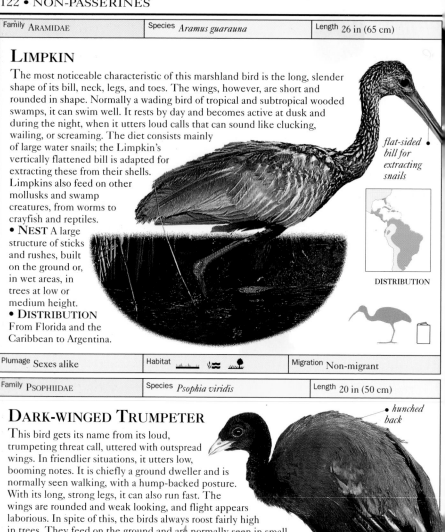

flat-sided bill for extracting snails

DISTRIBUTION

Plumage Sexes alike	Habitat	Migration Non-migrant

Family PSOPHIIDAE	Species *Psophia viridis*	Length 20 in (50 cm)

DARK-WINGED TRUMPETER

• hunched back

This bird gets its name from its loud, trumpeting threat call, uttered with outspread wings. In friendlier situations, it utters low, booming notes. It is chiefly a ground dweller and is normally seen walking, with a hump-backed posture. With its long, strong legs, it can also run fast. The wings are rounded and weak looking, and flight appears laborious. In spite of this, the birds always roost fairly high in trees. They feed on the ground and are normally seen in small social groups. The diet consists mainly of fallen fruit, nuts, and insects. Trumpeters rely on other tree-dwelling animals, such as parrots and monkeys, to knock these down while feeding, and will also take berries and some insects. Little is known of their breeding behavior.
• **NEST** A loose structure made of sticks and leaves and placed high in a tree, in a large tree hole, in an open cavity, or on a bare branch.
• **DISTRIBUTION** Middle and lower Amazon basin in C. Brazil.

• strong, walking legs

DISTRIBUTION

Plumage Sexes alike	Habitat	Migration Non-migrant

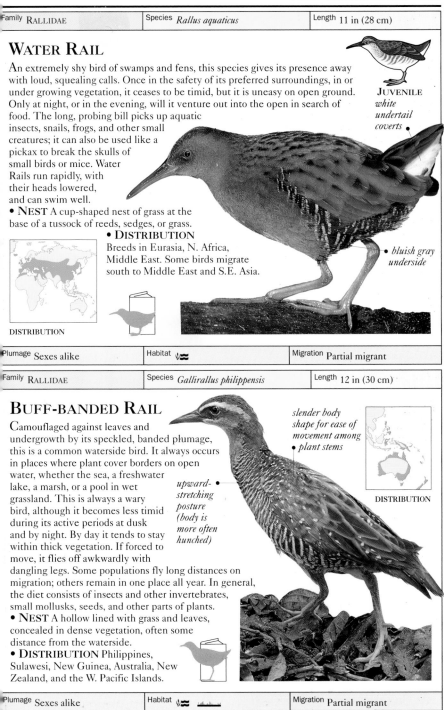

Family RALLIDAE	Species *Rallus aquaticus*	Length 11 in (28 cm)

WATER RAIL

An extremely shy bird of swamps and fens, this species gives its presence away with loud, squealing calls. Once in the safety of its preferred surroundings, in or under growing vegetation, it ceases to be timid, but it is uneasy on open ground. Only at night, or in the evening, will it venture out into the open in search of food. The long, probing bill picks up aquatic insects, snails, frogs, and other small creatures; it can also be used like a pickax to break the skulls of small birds or mice. Water Rails run rapidly, with their heads lowered, and can swim well.

JUVENILE
*white
undertail
coverts*

• **NEST** A cup-shaped nest of grass at the base of a tussock of reeds, sedges, or grass.

• **DISTRIBUTION** Breeds in Eurasia, N. Africa, Middle East. Some birds migrate south to Middle East and S.E. Asia.

*• bluish gray
underside*

DISTRIBUTION

Plumage Sexes alike	Habitat	Migration Partial migrant

Family RALLIDAE	Species *Gallirallus philippensis*	Length 12 in (30 cm)

BUFF-BANDED RAIL

Camouflaged against leaves and undergrowth by its speckled, banded plumage, this is a common waterside bird. It always occurs in places where plant cover borders on open water, whether the sea, a freshwater lake, a marsh, or a pool in wet grassland. This is always a wary bird, although it becomes less timid during its active periods at dusk and by night. By day it tends to stay within thick vegetation. If forced to move, it flies off awkwardly with dangling legs. Some populations fly long distances on migration; others remain in one place all year. In general, the diet consists of insects and other invertebrates, small mollusks, seeds, and other parts of plants.

*slender body
shape for ease of
movement among
• plant stems*

*upward-
stretching
posture
(body is
more often
hunched)*

DISTRIBUTION

• **NEST** A hollow lined with grass and leaves, concealed in dense vegetation, often some distance from the waterside.

• **DISTRIBUTION** Philippines, Sulawesi, New Guinea, Australia, New Zealand, and the W. Pacific Islands.

Plumage Sexes alike	Habitat	Migration Partial migrant

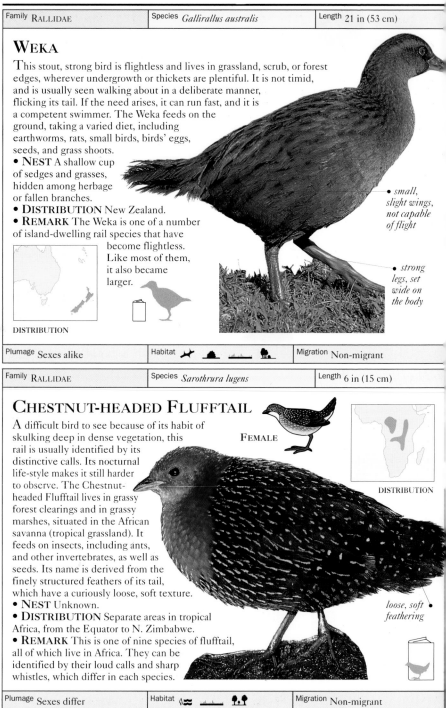

| Family RALLIDAE | Species *Gallirallus australis* | Length 21 in (53 cm) |

WEKA

This stout, strong bird is flightless and lives in grassland, scrub, or forest edges, wherever undergrowth or thickets are plentiful. It is not timid, and is usually seen walking about in a deliberate manner, flicking its tail. If the need arises, it can run fast, and it is a competent swimmer. The Weka feeds on the ground, taking a varied diet, including earthworms, rats, small birds, birds' eggs, seeds, and grass shoots.
• **NEST** A shallow cup of sedges and grasses, hidden among herbage or fallen branches.
• **DISTRIBUTION** New Zealand.
• **REMARK** The Weka is one of a number of island-dwelling rail species that have become flightless. Like most of them, it also became larger.

small, slight wings, not capable of flight

strong legs, set wide on the body

DISTRIBUTION

| Plumage Sexes alike | Habitat | Migration Non-migrant |

| Family RALLIDAE | Species *Sarothrura lugens* | Length 6 in (15 cm) |

CHESTNUT-HEADED FLUFFTAIL

A difficult bird to see because of its habit of skulking deep in dense vegetation, this rail is usually identified by its distinctive calls. Its nocturnal life-style makes it still harder to observe. The Chestnut-headed Flufftail lives in grassy forest clearings and in grassy marshes, situated in the African savanna (tropical grassland). It feeds on insects, including ants, and other invertebrates, as well as seeds. Its name is derived from the finely structured feathers of its tail, which have a curiously loose, soft texture.
• **NEST** Unknown.
• **DISTRIBUTION** Separate areas in tropical Africa, from the Equator to N. Zimbabwe.
• **REMARK** This is one of nine species of flufftail, all of which live in Africa. They can be identified by their loud calls and sharp whistles, which differ in each species.

FEMALE

DISTRIBUTION

loose, soft feathering

| Plumage Sexes differ | Habitat | Migration Non-migrant |

Family RALLIDAE	Species *Crex crex*	Length 11 in (28 cm)

CORNCRAKE

At first sight, this species might be mistaken for a gamebird such as a partridge, but its bright, chestnut wings, conspicuous in flight, identify it for certain. It is a spring migrant to grassland, fallow land, and fields of growing crops, strongly favoring regions in which farming is more traditional and hay is cut by hand. Males newly arrived from migration can be seen walking in the short grass, not yet high enough to hide them. They become still easier to see when they stand upright, raising their bills to utter rasping "crex-crex" calls to attract females. The birds soon form pairs and then nest in the fields. The diet consists of earthworms, insects, mollusks, frogs, seeds, and shoots.
• **NEST** A shallow cup nest lined with leaves and grasses, concealed in grass or in an isolated tussock.
• **DISTRIBUTION** Breeds in Europe and C. Asia. Winters in Mediterranean region and throughout Africa.
• **REMARK** Originally a bird of moist natural grassland, the Corncrake survived the spread of agriculture in past centuries by nesting in hay meadows. On modern farms, mechanized hay production destroys nests, eggs, and young of Corncrakes, so the bird has become rare.

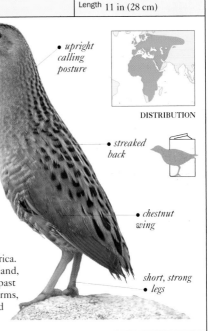

• *upright calling posture*

DISTRIBUTION

• *streaked back*

• *chestnut wing*

• *short, strong legs*

Plumage Sexes alike	Habitat	Migration Migrant

Family RALLIDAE	Species *Porzana carolina*	Length 8½ in (22 cm)

SORA

This secretive marsh bird usually hides among vegetation, but it may emerge at dusk. It also visits open water, walking on water lily leaves and occasionally swimming. It feeds on insects and other small creatures, also taking seeds.
• **NEST** A cup-shaped nest of dried rushes and leaves, in swampy vegetation, placed slightly above the water level.
• **DISTRIBUTION** Breeds in North America. Winters from S. USA south to N.W. South America.

streaked camouflage plumage •

white undertail coverts •

• *long legs for wading*

long toes •

JUVENILE

DISTRIBUTION

Plumage Sexes differ slightly	Habitat	Migration Migrant

| Family RALLIDAE | Species *Gallinula chloropus* | Length 13 in (33 cm) |

COMMON MOORHEN

A cautious, sharp-voiced bird of the waterside, this species has managed to exploit most stretches of fresh water, however small, and is common and sometimes tame on village and town ponds. It walks on land and swims with nodding head, feeding on insects and small water creatures, waterweeds, seeds, and berries.
• **NEST** A neat, bowl-shaped nest made of reeds and stems, concealed in growing plants at or above water level.
• **DISTRIBUTION** Parts of North and South America, Africa, Europe, Asia as far south as Java, and the W. Pacific.

DISTRIBUTION

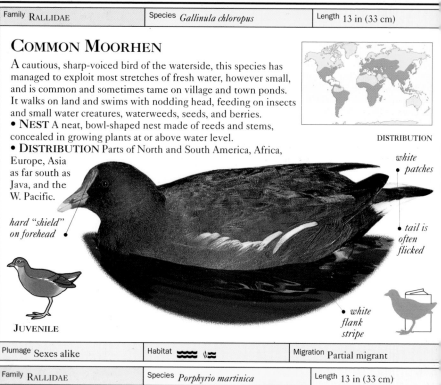

white patches

tail is often flicked

hard "shield" on forehead

JUVENILE

• *white flank stripe*

| Plumage Sexes alike | Habitat 〜〜 〜 | Migration Partial migrant |

| Family RALLIDAE | Species *Porphyrio martinica* | Length 13 in (33 cm) |

PURPLE GALLINULE

• *tough, blue "shield"*

At first sight, this bird resembles the Common Moorhen, but it is more brightly colored and has a more slender build, with longer neck and legs. In adults, the legs are bright yellow and the hard "shield" over the bill is bright blue. The Purple Gallinule occurs on lakes, pools, waterways, and wet marshes, where vegetation is tall and abundant, in regions where the climate is warm. It wades and walks easily over floating plants and water lilies with its long-toed feet. Although it will venture onto open ground to feed, it does not stray far from cover. It walks with an upward jerking tail and on shorter flights the legs dangle. Birds often climb up reeds, rice plants, bushes, and trees, in order to feed. The diet consists of invertebrates, frogs, waterplants, seeds, and berries.
• **NEST** A bulky cup nest made of fresh or dead stems and leaves of rushes and cattails, built in marshland and situated in plants in or near water, or in bushes above water level.
• **DISTRIBUTION** S.E. USA, Central America, West Indies, and South America to N. Argentina.

DISTRIBUTION

JUVENILE

• *long toes*

| Plumage Sexes alike | Habitat 〜〜 〜 | Migration Partial migrant |

Family RALLIDAE	Species *Porphyrio mantelli*	Length 25 in (63 cm)

TAKAHE

A heavy, flightless bird with a capacious bill and stout legs, the Takahe feeds on tussock grass. It consumes the seeds and the fleshy bases of the stems. To eat the stem bases, it holds down a tuft of grass with one foot and shears through it with its bill, removing the inedible upper stalks. The Takahe's small population lives in a few high-altitude valleys in mountains. In cold weather, the birds retreat into beech forests on lower slopes.
• **NEST** A hollow in the ground, lined with grass and leaves, and hidden between grass tussocks.
• **DISTRIBUTION** New Zealand on South Island.
• **REMARK** This species evolved after becoming isolated in New Zealand, where predators were absent. It became flightless and, no longer needing to be light, grew large and heavy. Man brought in predators such as cats, and grazing competitors such as deer. The Takahe was thought to be extinct until a relict population was discovered in 1948. Conservationists are trying to save this by breeding birds in captivity and releasing them in safer areas.

massive • bill for shearing grass

DISTRIBUTION

• solid, heavy build

Plumage Sexes alike	Habitat	Migration Non-migrant

Family RALLIDAE	Species *Fulica americana*	Length 15½ in (39 cm)

AMERICAN COOT

This is a bird of larger areas of open water. It is seen on lakes, large rivers, and flooded swamps; winter flocks sometimes settle on sheltered salt water areas such as estuaries. Coots feed on buds, leaves, and stems of water plants, as well as on seeds, insects, and other small creatures. They feed by foraging on the ground at the waterside or by diving in open water, taking waterweed from the bottom. They cannot take off easily and need to run along the surface to get airborne. Breeding pairs defend territories aggressively, both birds fighting intruders.
• **NEST** A bulky cup nest made of dead leaves and stems, placed among vegetation in or beside the water, or on low or submerged branches.
• **DISTRIBUTION** Breeds in North and Central America, in the Caribbean region, and in the Andes of Colombia. North American populations winter as far south as Colombia.

• very small "shield"

uniform, dark gray plumage •

DISTRIBUTION

• short tail

• lobed toes

Plumage Sexes alike	Habitat	Migration Partial migrant

Family HELIORNITHIDAE	Species *Podica senegalensis*	L. 23 in (58 cm)/20 in (50 cm)

AFRICAN FINFOOT

With its streamlined body, the African Finfoot is able to swim well, either fully on the surface or with its body submerged and the neck and head out of the water. The feet, with their wide, fleshy lobes, make very effective "paddles." The bill is slender and streamlined.
This secretive bird lives where trees and bushes overhang a river or lake. It spends as much of its time on land as on the water, feeding on insects and small aquatic life.

• **NEST** A large, flat nest of grass and stems, placed in dense vegetation at the waterside or on a partly submerged branch.
• **DISTRIBUTION** Africa south of the Sahara.
• **REMARK** The female is more brightly colored than the male and is thought to play the dominant role in breeding, while males look after the nest and young.

DISTRIBUTION

FEMALE

• *fleshy-lobed toes*

Plumage Sexes differ	Habitat 〰	Migration Non-migrant

Family RHYNOCHETIDAE	Species *Rhynochetos jubatus*	Length 22 in (55 cm)

KAGU

The squat body shape, strong legs, and powerful bill of the Kagu are adaptations to a ground-dwelling life. It inhabits forested mountainsides with undergrowth and small streams. The Kagu is virtually flightless but can glide down hill slopes. It normally walks, tapping the ground to detect the earthworms and other small creatures on which it feeds. In display, it erects its shaggy crest into a tall, vertical fan and sometimes spreads its wings, showing the black, chestnut, and white barring on the flight feathers. It feeds in loose flocks, but breeding birds live in pairs. Kagus utter noisy, rattling calls, and pairs maintain contact with melodious notes, heard especially before dawn.
• **NEST** A loose structure of sticks and leaves, placed on the ground.
• **DISTRIBUTION** New Caledonia in the S.W. Pacific.

DISTRIBUTION

• *weak, little-used wings*

RAISED CREST

Plumage Sexes alike	Habitat ▲ 🌳 ✈	Migration Non-migrant

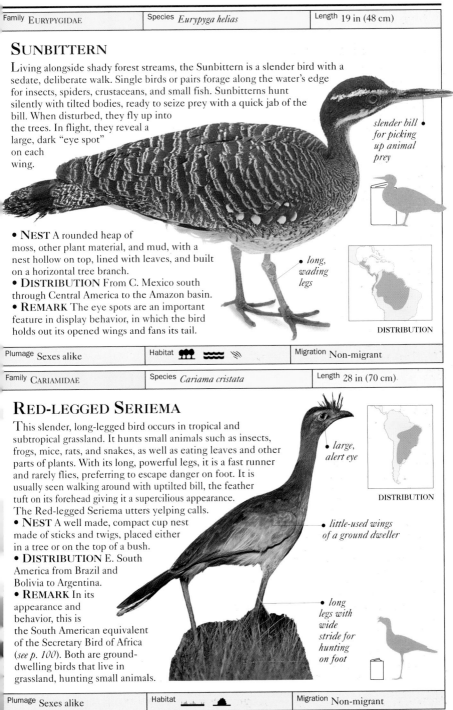

Family EURYPYGIDAE	Species *Eurypyga helias*	Length 19 in (48 cm)

SUNBITTERN

Living alongside shady forest streams, the Sunbittern is a slender bird with a sedate, deliberate walk. Single birds or pairs forage along the water's edge for insects, spiders, crustaceans, and small fish. Sunbitterns hunt silently with tilted bodies, ready to seize prey with a quick jab of the bill. When disturbed, they fly up into the trees. In flight, they reveal a large, dark "eye spot" on each wing.

slender bill for picking up animal prey

• **NEST** A rounded heap of moss, other plant material, and mud, with a nest hollow on top, lined with leaves, and built on a horizontal tree branch.
• **DISTRIBUTION** From C. Mexico south through Central America to the Amazon basin.
• **REMARK** The eye spots are an important feature in display behavior, in which the bird holds out its opened wings and fans its tail.

long, wading legs

DISTRIBUTION

Plumage Sexes alike	Habitat	Migration Non-migrant

Family CARIAMIDAE	Species *Cariama cristata*	Length 28 in (70 cm)

RED-LEGGED SERIEMA

This slender, long-legged bird occurs in tropical and subtropical grassland. It hunts small animals such as insects, frogs, mice, rats, and snakes, as well as eating leaves and other parts of plants. With its long, powerful legs, it is a fast runner and rarely flies, preferring to escape danger on foot. It is usually seen walking around with uptilted bill, the feather tuft on its forehead giving it a supercilious appearance. The Red-legged Seriema utters yelping calls.

large, alert eye

DISTRIBUTION

• **NEST** A well made, compact cup nest made of sticks and twigs, placed either in a tree or on the top of a bush.
• **DISTRIBUTION** E. South America from Brazil and Bolivia to Argentina.
• **REMARK** In its appearance and behavior, this is the South American equivalent of the Secretary Bird of Africa (*see p. 100*). Both are ground-dwelling birds that live in grassland, hunting small animals.

little-used wings of a ground dweller

long legs with wide stride for hunting on foot

Plumage Sexes alike	Habitat	Migration Non-migrant

Family OTIDIDAE	Species *Otis tarda*	L. 39 in (100 cm)/31 in (80 cm)

GREAT BUSTARD

The long neck and legs of the Great Bustard give it an unobstructed view in its open grassland habitat. Here it moves with a slow, deliberate walk, flying infrequently. In spring the males display to the females in a group, on a specially reserved display ground. Females then nest and raise the young unaided. The diet consists of plants, insects, and other small animals.
• NEST A hollow in the ground, often hidden in crops or high grass.
• DISTRIBUTION Breeds in parts of Spain, Morocco, E. Europe, and C. and E. Asia. Winters in the south of this range.

inflated throat pouch

wing twisted in display

DISTRIBUTION

MALE IN FULL DISPLAY

FEMALE

Plumage Sexes differ	Habitat	Migration Non-migrant

Family OTIDIDAE	Species *Eupodotis afra*	Length 21 in (53 cm)

BLACK BUSTARD

This is a sturdily built bird of grassland and other open landscapes. Both sexes have camouflaged upperparts to prevent detection by predators overhead. Males have a black neck and underside, which are conspicuous to other birds at ground level. Black Bustards live in pairs, each pair holding its own territory. The male utters a harsh, repetitive "cracker" call, either from a raised perch or in a display flight. Displaying males rise in flapping flight, then drop slowly with fluttering wings and dangling legs. The birds feed on the ground, pairs sometimes walking together with sedate steps and heads held high. They feed mainly on growing plants, also taking insects.
• NEST A slight hollow in the ground scraped by body pressure, among tufts of grass.
• DISTRIBUTION Parts of southern Africa.

camouflage pattern on the back

bold, black-and-white underside

long legs for constant walking

DISTRIBUTION

FEMALE

Plumage Sexes differ	Habitat	Migration Non-migrant

| Family JACANIDAE | Species *Hydrophasianus chirurgus* | Length 22 in (55 cm) |

PHEASANT-TAILED JACANA

This bird lives on lakes and swamps, its chief adaptations being long legs, toes, and claws. These enable it to spread its weight, so that it can walk on the floating leaves of waterplants. It feeds on invertebrates, frogs, and fish. A female may mate with up to ten males, each of these incubating a clutch and raising his own brood.

narrow, drooping tail •

both sexes have long tails during the breeding season •

WINTER

• *black wing tips*

• *white wings*

• **NEST** A thin layer of dried waterweeds and other plants, placed on floating leaves.
• **DISTRIBUTION** Indian subcontinent and from C. China through S.E. Asia as far as Java and the Philippines.
• **REMARK** Females are slightly larger than males, with similar but brighter colors.

long toes and • *claws*

DISTRIBUTION

| Plumage Sexes differ slightly | Habitat 〰〰 ↓〰 | Migration Partial migrant |

| Family JACANIDAE | Species *Jacana spinosa* | Length 9½ in (24 cm) |

NORTHERN JACANA

• *soft, fleshy wattle*

Long legs, toes, and claws enable this bird to walk on floating waterplants. It can swim, but does so reluctantly, and will occasionally fly, usually slowly with dangling legs. In more sustained flight, the legs are extended backward, with the long toes projecting. Both sexes display to one another by raising their wings to reveal vivid yellow patches underneath. They also hold the wings up after landing. The female is bigger than the male and, when breeding, holds a large territory that encompasses up to four male territories. Each male has his own nest, in which he incubates a clutch of her eggs and rears and feeds the young.

JUVENILE

long toes and claws •

• **NEST** A loose layer of dried water-weeds, on floating leaves.
• **DISTRIBUTION** Central America and the larger islands of the Caribbean.

DISTRIBUTION

| Plumage Sexes alike | Habitat 〰〰 ↓〰 | Migration Non-migrant |

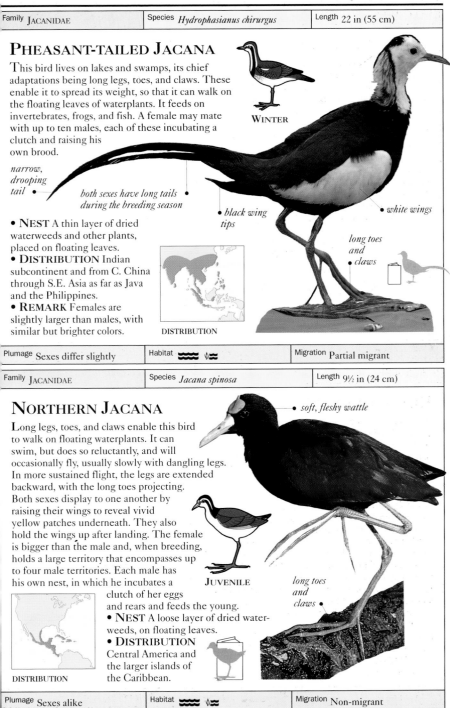

| Family ROSTRATULIDAE | Species *Rostratula benghalensis* | L. 10 in (25 cm)/ 11 in (28 cm) |

PAINTED SNIPE

A bird of shallow swamps, the
Painted Snipe hides among low
vegetation or reeds during the
day, where it is inconspicuous
despite its patterned plumage.
Birds are active from dusk until
dawn, probing the mud with their
bills. They feed on earthworms,
crustaceans, insects, and some plant
seeds. Early in the breeding season, the
female performs a display flight over her
territory with soft, hooting calls. She
may pair with several males, and each of
these will incubate a clutch of eggs and
also rear the young.

large eyes for night feeding

female has a darker, stronger pattern

long, wading legs

MALE

FEMALE

• **NEST** A pile of
plant materials amid
marsh vegetation.
• **DISTRIBUTION**
Scattered areas in Africa,
Asia, and N. and E. Australia.
• **REMARK** Females are larger
and more colorful than the males.

DISTRIBUTION

| Plumage Sexes differ | Habitat | Migration Non-migrant |

| Family DROMADIDAE | Species *Dromas ardeola* | Length 16 in (40 cm) |

CRAB PLOVER

Occurring on sandy seashores or tidal flats,
this species feeds like a plover, running
and making sudden jabs to catch prey
on the ground. It eats crabs, cracking
their shells with its powerful
bill. Crab Plovers are seen
in low, slow flight. They
often feed in groups and
roost in large flocks on the shore.
• **NEST** A burrow in sand, 6 ft
(1.5 m) or more in length. Nests are
packed closely together in colonies,
located on sandy islands or dunes.
• **DISTRIBUTION** Coastline of Indian Ocean,
Red Sea, and Persian
Gulf. Some birds winter
as far south as Madagascar
and Malay Peninsula.
• **REMARK** Of all the
shorebirds (220 species),
this is the only one that
nests in a burrow.

long legs extend beyond tail

JUVENILE

DISTRIBUTION

| Plumage Sexes alike | Habitat | Migration Partial migrant |

Family HAEMATOPODIDAE	Species *Haematopus ostralegus*	Length 17 in (43 cm)

EURASIAN OYSTERCATCHER

Bold, black-and-white plumage, a bright orange bill, and a piping "kleep" call make this a well known bird of shores and mudflats. In flight it reveals a large, white wing stripe and white rump. Winter flocks feed on open shores or estuaries. The bladelike bill tip is useful for smashing open shellfish and detaching limpets from rocks. The diet consists of shellfish, worms, and small fish. In display, males run side by side with lowered bills, trilling noisily, and also perform a flight with slowly flapping wings.
• **NEST** A hollow scraped by body pressure, in shingle, sand, or grass.
• **DISTRIBUTION** Breeds in N. Europe, C. Asia, and N.E. Asia. Winters to the south, as far as Africa, India, and S. China.

bill tip is vertically flattened, like a knife blade

white wing stripe, revealed in flight

JUVENILE

DISTRIBUTION

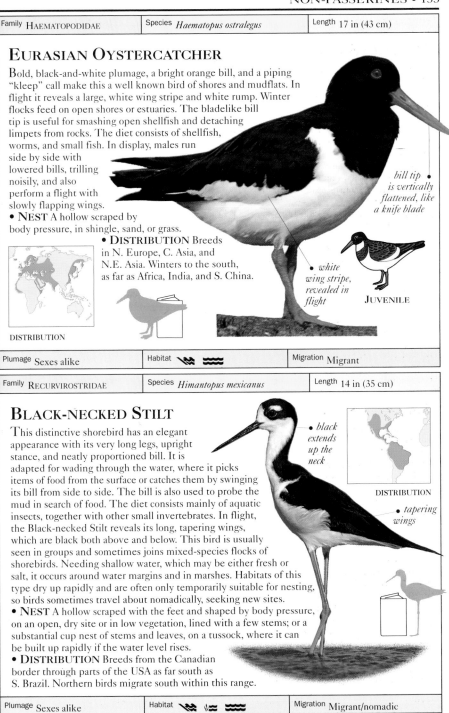

Plumage Sexes alike	Habitat	Migration Migrant

Family RECURVIROSTRIDAE	Species *Himantopus mexicanus*	Length 14 in (35 cm)

BLACK-NECKED STILT

This distinctive shorebird has an elegant appearance with its very long legs, upright stance, and neatly proportioned bill. It is adapted for wading through the water, where it picks items of food from the surface or catches them by swinging its bill from side to side. The bill is also used to probe the mud in search of food. The diet consists mainly of aquatic insects, together with other small invertebrates. In flight, the Black-necked Stilt reveals its long, tapering wings, which are black both above and below. This bird is usually seen in groups and sometimes joins mixed-species flocks of shorebirds. Needing shallow water, which may be either fresh or salt, it occurs around water margins and in marshes. Habitats of this type dry up rapidly and are often only temporarily suitable for nesting, so birds sometimes travel about nomadically, seeking new sites.
• **NEST** A hollow scraped with the feet and shaped by body pressure, on an open, dry site or in low vegetation, lined with a few stems; or a substantial cup nest of stems and leaves, on a tussock, where it can be built up rapidly if the water level rises.
• **DISTRIBUTION** Breeds from the Canadian border through parts of the USA as far south as S. Brazil. Northern birds migrate south within this range.

black extends up the neck

DISTRIBUTION

tapering wings

Plumage Sexes alike	Habitat	Migration Migrant/nomadic

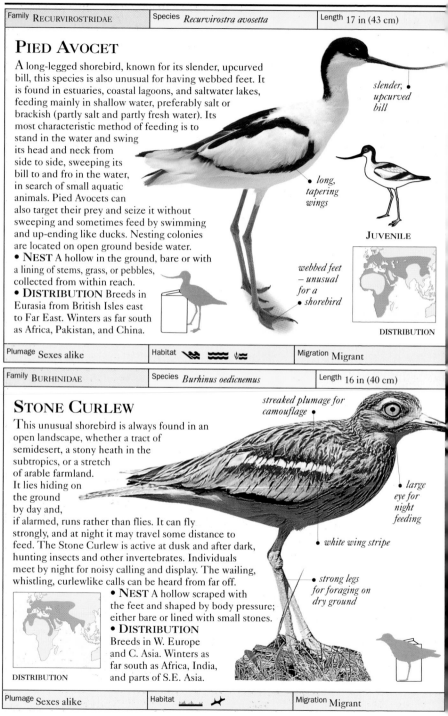

| Family RECURVIROSTRIDAE | Species *Recurvirostra avosetta* | Length 17 in (43 cm) |

PIED AVOCET

A long-legged shorebird, known for its slender, upcurved bill, this species is also unusual for having webbed feet. It is found in estuaries, coastal lagoons, and saltwater lakes, feeding mainly in shallow water, preferably salt or brackish (partly salt and partly fresh water). Its most characteristic method of feeding is to stand in the water and swing its head and neck from side to side, sweeping its bill to and fro in the water, in search of small aquatic animals. Pied Avocets can also target their prey and seize it without sweeping and sometimes feed by swimming and up-ending like ducks. Nesting colonies are located on open ground beside water.
• **NEST** A hollow in the ground, bare or with a lining of stems, grass, or pebbles, collected from within reach.
• **DISTRIBUTION** Breeds in Eurasia from British Isles east to Far East. Winters as far south as Africa, Pakistan, and China.

slender, upcurved bill

long, tapering wings

JUVENILE

webbed feet – unusual for a shorebird

DISTRIBUTION

| Plumage Sexes alike | Habitat | Migration Migrant |

| Family BURHINIDAE | Species *Burhinus oedicnemus* | Length 16 in (40 cm) |

STONE CURLEW

This unusual shorebird is always found in an open landscape, whether a tract of semidesert, a stony heath in the subtropics, or a stretch of arable farmland. It lies hiding on the ground by day and, if alarmed, runs rather than flies. It can fly strongly, and at night it may travel some distance to feed. The Stone Curlew is active at dusk and after dark, hunting insects and other invertebrates. Individuals meet by night for noisy calling and display. The wailing, whistling, curlewlike calls can be heard from far off.
• **NEST** A hollow scraped with the feet and shaped by body pressure; either bare or lined with small stones.
• **DISTRIBUTION** Breeds in W. Europe and C. Asia. Winters as far south as Africa, India, and parts of S.E. Asia.

streaked plumage for camouflage

large eye for night feeding

white wing stripe

strong legs for foraging on dry ground

DISTRIBUTION

| Plumage Sexes alike | Habitat | Migration Migrant |

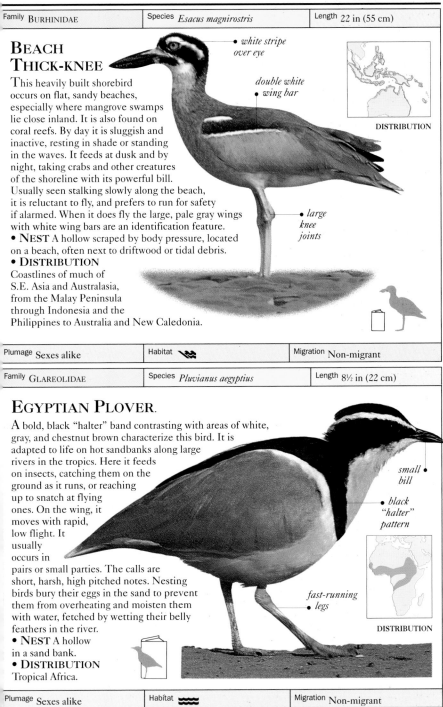

Family BURHINIDAE	Species *Esacus magnirostris*	Length 22 in (55 cm)

BEACH THICK-KNEE

• *white stripe over eye*

double white • *wing bar*

DISTRIBUTION

This heavily built shorebird occurs on flat, sandy beaches, especially where mangrove swamps lie close inland. It is also found on coral reefs. By day it is sluggish and inactive, resting in shade or standing in the waves. It feeds at dusk and by night, taking crabs and other creatures of the shoreline with its powerful bill. Usually seen stalking slowly along the beach, it is reluctant to fly, and prefers to run for safety if alarmed. When it does fly the large, pale gray wings with white wing bars are an identification feature.
• **NEST** A hollow scraped by body pressure, located on a beach, often next to driftwood or tidal debris.
• **DISTRIBUTION** Coastlines of much of S.E. Asia and Australasia, from the Malay Peninsula through Indonesia and the Philippines to Australia and New Caledonia.

• *large knee joints*

Plumage Sexes alike	Habitat	Migration Non-migrant

Family GLAREOLIDAE	Species *Pluvianus aegyptius*	Length 8½ in (22 cm)

EGYPTIAN PLOVER.

A bold, black "halter" band contrasting with areas of white, gray, and chestnut brown characterize this bird. It is adapted to life on hot sandbanks along large rivers in the tropics. Here it feeds on insects, catching them on the ground as it runs, or reaching up to snatch at flying ones. On the wing, it moves with rapid, low flight. It usually occurs in pairs or small parties. The calls are short, harsh, high pitched notes. Nesting birds bury their eggs in the sand to prevent them from overheating and moisten them with water, fetched by wetting their belly feathers in the river.
• **NEST** A hollow in a sand bank.
• **DISTRIBUTION** Tropical Africa.

small • *bill*

• *black "halter" pattern*

fast-running • *legs*

DISTRIBUTION

Plumage Sexes alike	Habitat	Migration Non-migrant

| Family GLAREOLIDAE | Species *Cursorius temminckii* | Length 8 in (20 cm) |

TEMMINCK'S COURSER

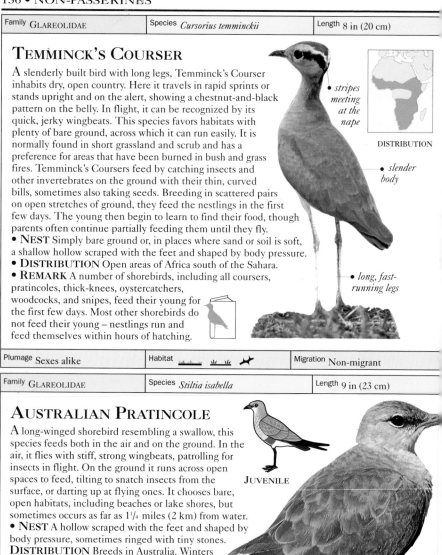

A slenderly built bird with long legs, Temminck's Courser inhabits dry, open country. Here it travels in rapid sprints or stands upright and on the alert, showing a chestnut-and-black pattern on the belly. In flight, it can be recognized by its quick, jerky wingbeats. This species favors habitats with plenty of bare ground, across which it can run easily. It is normally found in short grassland and scrub and has a preference for areas that have been burned in bush and grass fires. Temminck's Coursers feed by catching insects and other invertebrates on the ground with their thin, curved bills, sometimes also taking seeds. Breeding in scattered pairs on open stretches of ground, they feed the nestlings in the first few days. The young then begin to learn to find their food, though parents often continue partially feeding them until they fly.
• NEST Simply bare ground or, in places where sand or soil is soft, a shallow hollow scraped with the feet and shaped by body pressure.
• DISTRIBUTION Open areas of Africa south of the Sahara.
• REMARK A number of shorebirds, including all coursers, pratincoles, thick-knees, oystercatchers, woodcocks, and snipes, feed their young for the first few days. Most other shorebirds do not feed their young – nestlings run and feed themselves within hours of hatching.

• stripes meeting at the nape

DISTRIBUTION

• slender body

• long, fast-running legs

| Plumage Sexes alike | Habitat | Migration Non-migrant |

| Family GLAREOLIDAE | Species *Stiltia isabella* | Length 9 in (23 cm) |

AUSTRALIAN PRATINCOLE

A long-winged shorebird resembling a swallow, this species feeds both in the air and on the ground. In the air, it flies with stiff, strong wingbeats, patrolling for insects in flight. On the ground it runs across open spaces to feed, tilting to snatch insects from the surface, or darting up at flying ones. It chooses bare, open habitats, including beaches or lake shores, but sometimes occurs as far as 1¼ miles (2 km) from water.
• NEST A hollow scraped with the feet and shaped by body pressure, sometimes ringed with tiny stones.
DISTRIBUTION Breeds in Australia. Winters in N. Australia, New Guinea, Sulawesi, S.E. Borneo, and islands from Timor to Java.

JUVENILE

• dark belly pattern

• short tail

long • wings

DISTRIBUTION

| Plumage Sexes alike | Habitat | Migration Migrant |

Family GLAREOLIDAE	Species *Glareola nordmanni*	Length 10 in (25 cm)

BLACK-WINGED PRATINCOLE

This species is a typical pratincole, a shore-dwelling bird that has become adapted to feeding in the air like a swallow, catching insects. It has large eyes, a broad-based bill, long, narrow wings, and a forked tail. Equipped with fairly long legs, this bird will also chase insects on the ground. The black underwings become visible in flight, which is distinctively agile and rapid. The species is highly sociable, feeding in flocks, and is particularly active at dusk and dawn. In the breeding season, it flocks on the margins of steppe lakes and marshes with short vegetation or bare mud. It rests, and nests, on the ground, where its coloration makes it inconspicuous on mud or soil.
• **NEST** A shallow, bare depression, in sparse vegetation or on bare ground.
• **DISTRIBUTION** Breeds in C. Asia. Winters in Africa south of the Sahara.

long, slender wings

• white underside

DISTRIBUTION

WINTER PLUMAGE

Plumage Sexes alike	Habitat	Migration Migrant

Family CHARADRIIDAE	Species *Vanellus vanellus*	Length 12 in (30 cm)

NORTHERN LAPWING

A conspicuous bird of farmland and grazing marshes, the Lapwing is most noticeable in spring, when the male performs a tumbling display flight over the nest territory, uttering wild "peewit" calls. The species prefers to feed in short, grazed grass and hunts by sight, making short runs and sudden, forward-tilting pecks at the ground. The diet consists of earthworms, insects, and other small invertebrates. After nesting the birds begin forming into flocks. These migrate to moister, milder wintering areas, most often in the west.
• **NEST** A hollow, scraped with the feet and shaped by body pressure, on open ground or in grass, lined with plant stems and grass from within reach.
• **DISTRIBUTION** Breeds across Eurasia. Winters as far south as N. Africa and N.W. India but mainly in Europe.

• slender, black crest

SUMMER MALE

DISTRIBUTION

SUMMER FEMALE

female's throat and face are whiter than the male's in summer

WINTER (BOTH SEXES)

Plumage Sexes alike	Habitat	Migration Migrant

Family CHARADRIIDAE	Species *Vanellus armatus*	Length 12 in (30 cm)

BLACKSMITH PLOVER

A conspicuous but wary bird, the Blacksmith Plover gets its name from its loud, clinking alarm note. This is its most frequently heard call, although it is usually silent unless disturbed. It lives in open landscapes with moist, short grass or sparse bushes, close to lakes or large rivers. Most of the time birds are seen singly or in pairs, although they sometimes form flocks, particularly when not breeding. In flight, conspicuous features are broad wings, a flapping wingbeat, white underwings, and a white tail with a black tip. This assertive species has a sharp spur on the front angle of the wing, which is used when fighting. The diet consists of insects, worms, and mollusks.
• NEST A hollow scraped with the feet and shaped by body pressure in open soil, sparsely lined with small pebbles, dry fragments of dung, or plant stems.
• DISTRIBUTION Open country areas in Africa south of the Equator.

white nape patch

red eye

black frontal patch

fighting spur on wing, hidden in plumage

white belly

very long legs for a plover

DISTRIBUTION

JUVENILE

Plumage Sexes alike	Habitat	Migration Non-migrant

Family CHARADRIIDAE	Species *Pluvialis dominica*	Length 10 in (25 cm)

AMERICAN GOLDEN PLOVER

The combination of a gold-spangled back, a black underside, and a black face surrounded by a white border make this a spectacular plover. The back is camouflaged against tundra vegetation for safety from birds of prey, but the black underside is visible to other birds at ground level, especially in the display flight. This species breeds on drier areas of the Arctic tundra and winters on coasts, marshes, and sometimes grassland. It feeds in the typical manner of a plover, running rapidly and snatching prey from the ground, taking worms, insects, and other invertebrates. A long-distance migrant, it flies strongly on tapering wings.
• NEST A thinly lined hollow in the ground, in an exposed site with a wide view for safety.
• DISTRIBUTION Breeds in N. North America. Winters in S. Brazil, N. Argentina, Uruguay.

large eye

black display plumage on underside

DISTRIBUTION

WINTER

Plumage Sexes alike	Habitat	Migration Migrant

Family CHARADRIIDAE	Species *Pluvialis squatarola*	Length 11 in (28 cm)

BLACK-BELLIED PLOVER

A black-and-white plover of the bare tundra, this species has the tapering wings and strong flight of a long-distance migrant. In winter, it is mainly ash-gray and can be identified by the black "armpits" on its white underside and by its "thee-oo-wee" call. During winter, it feeds on mudflats whenever the tide is out. Feeding birds walk slowly forward, probing the mud for worms, small shellfish, crustaceans, and other invertebrates.
• **NEST** A shallow hollow in the ground, sparsely lined with moss and fragments of lichen, on a raised, dry site.
• **DISTRIBUTION** Breeds in tundra regions of N. North America and N. Eurasia. Winters on coasts in most of the world.

mottled gray crown

stout bill

black display plumage

WINTER

DISTRIBUTION

Plumage Sexes alike	Habitat	Migration Migrant

Family CHARADRIIDAE	Species *Eudromias morinellus*	Length 8½ in (22 cm)

EURASIAN DOTTEREL

This species of plover breeds on high mountains, where the summer is short. The female is slightly larger than the male, and her breeding plumage has stronger colors. She takes the dominant role in breeding and displays to attract a mate. After the eggs are laid, the male helps incubate them and tend the young. Sometimes the female mates with several males, who each incubate their own clutch of eggs and care for the young. This species is unaccustomed to disturbance and is often tame and trusting. After breeding, the birds gather into small flocks and migrate. Dotterel eat insects, spiders, and other invertebrates.
• **NEST** A hollow in the ground, scraped with the feet and shaped by body pressure, situated in the open.
• **DISTRIBUTION** Breeds in N. Eurasia. Winters in the Mediterranean region.

thin, white breast band

male in breeding plumage (female is more vivid)

DISTRIBUTION

blackish belly patch of breeding plumage

WINTER

Plumage Sexes differ slightly	Habitat	Migration Migrant

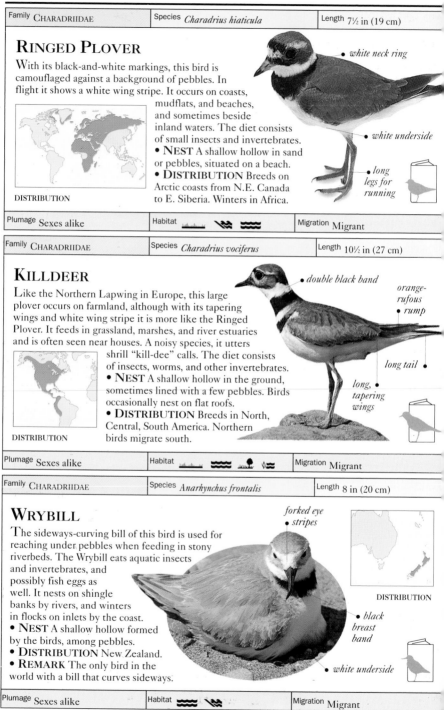

Family CHARADRIIDAE	Species *Charadrius hiaticula*	Length 7½ in (19 cm)

RINGED PLOVER

With its black-and-white markings, this bird is camouflaged against a background of pebbles. In flight it shows a white wing stripe. It occurs on coasts, mudflats, and beaches, and sometimes beside inland waters. The diet consists of small insects and invertebrates.
• **NEST** A shallow hollow in sand or pebbles, situated on a beach.
• **DISTRIBUTION** Breeds on Arctic coasts from N.E. Canada to E. Siberia. Winters in Africa.

DISTRIBUTION

• *white neck ring*

• *white underside*

• *long legs for running*

Plumage Sexes alike	Habitat	Migration Migrant

Family CHARADRIIDAE	Species *Charadrius vociferus*	Length 10½ in (27 cm)

KILLDEER

Like the Northern Lapwing in Europe, this large plover occurs on farmland, although with its tapering wings and white wing stripe it is more like the Ringed Plover. It feeds in grassland, marshes, and river estuaries and is often seen near houses. A noisy species, it utters shrill "kill-dee" calls. The diet consists of insects, worms, and other invertebrates.
• **NEST** A shallow hollow in the ground, sometimes lined with a few pebbles. Birds occasionally nest on flat roofs.
• **DISTRIBUTION** Breeds in North, Central, South America. Northern birds migrate south.

DISTRIBUTION

• *double black band*

orange-rufous • *rump*

long tail •

long, tapering wings

Plumage Sexes alike	Habitat	Migration Migrant

Family CHARADRIIDAE	Species *Anarhynchus frontalis*	Length 8 in (20 cm)

WRYBILL

The sideways-curving bill of this bird is used for reaching under pebbles when feeding in stony riverbeds. The Wrybill eats aquatic insects and invertebrates, and possibly fish eggs as well. It nests on shingle banks by rivers, and winters in flocks on inlets by the coast.
• **NEST** A shallow hollow formed by the birds, among pebbles.
• **DISTRIBUTION** New Zealand.
• **REMARK** The only bird in the world with a bill that curves sideways.

forked eye • *stripes*

DISTRIBUTION

• *black breast band*

• *white underside*

Plumage Sexes alike	Habitat	Migration Migrant

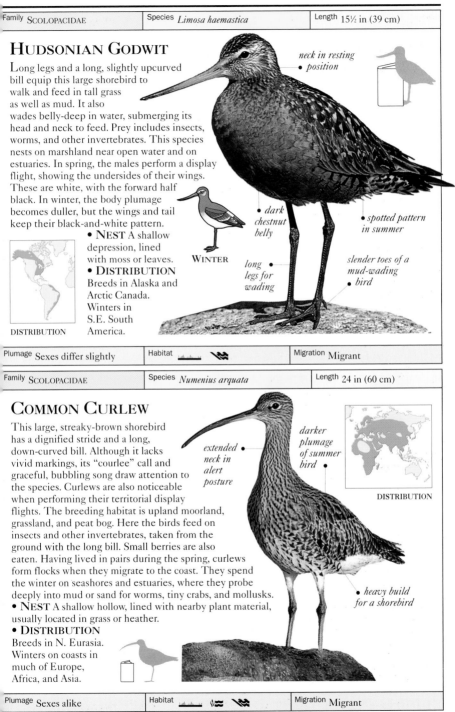

Family SCOLOPACIDAE	Species *Limosa haemastica*	Length 15½ in (39 cm)

HUDSONIAN GODWIT

Long legs and a long, slightly upcurved
bill equip this large shorebird to
walk and feed in tall grass
as well as mud. It also
wades belly-deep in water, submerging its
head and neck to feed. Prey includes insects,
worms, and other invertebrates. This species
nests on marshland near open water and on
estuaries. In spring, the males perform a display
flight, showing the undersides of their wings.
These are white, with the forward half
black. In winter, the body plumage
becomes duller, but the wings and tail
keep their black-and-white pattern.

• **NEST** A shallow
depression, lined
with moss or leaves.
• **DISTRIBUTION**
Breeds in Alaska and
Arctic Canada.
Winters in
S.E. South
America.

neck in resting position

WINTER

dark chestnut belly

long legs for wading

spotted pattern in summer

slender toes of a mud-wading bird

DISTRIBUTION

Plumage Sexes differ slightly	Habitat	Migration Migrant

Family SCOLOPACIDAE	Species *Numenius arquata*	Length 24 in (60 cm)

COMMON CURLEW

This large, streaky-brown shorebird
has a dignified stride and a long,
down-curved bill. Although it lacks
vivid markings, its "courlee" call and
graceful, bubbling song draw attention to
the species. Curlews are also noticeable
when performing their territorial display
flights. The breeding habitat is upland moorland,
grassland, and peat bog. Here the birds feed on
insects and other invertebrates, taken from the
ground with the long bill. Small berries are also
eaten. Having lived in pairs during the spring, curlews
form flocks when they migrate to the coast. They spend
the winter on seashores and estuaries, where they probe
deeply into mud or sand for worms, tiny crabs, and mollusks.
• **NEST** A shallow hollow, lined with nearby plant material,
usually located in grass or heather.
• **DISTRIBUTION**
Breeds in N. Eurasia.
Winters on coasts in
much of Europe,
Africa, and Asia.

extended neck in alert posture

darker plumage of summer bird

DISTRIBUTION

heavy build for a shorebird

Plumage Sexes alike	Habitat	Migration Migrant

Family SCOLOPACIDAE	Species *Tringa totanus*	Length 11 in (28 cm)

COMMON REDSHANK

Standing erect on its long legs, with head held high, this alert shorebird quickly notices any intruder in its surroundings. It utters piping alarm calls, which often alert all the other birds in the area. Apart from its red legs and bill, it is inconspicuous on the ground with its brown plumage. In flight, the white rump and hind edges of the wings help identify the species. In spring it lives in meadows, wet grasslands, and marshes. Here it raises its young, feeding on insects and other invertebrates, which it takes from vegetation, the ground surface, or from the marsh. It feeds with a nervous, jerky manner. In winter the Common Redshank is found on estuaries and mudflats, where it feeds on tiny shellfish, crustaceans, and other small creatures. These it either picks from the mud surface or finds by probing with its long, pointed bill.
• **NEST** A hollow scraped with the feet and shaped by body pressure, lined, and hidden in tall grass and plants.
• **DISTRIBUTION** Breeds in Iceland and across Eurasia from the British Isles to E. Asia. Winters on coastlines of much of Eurasia, Africa, India, and S.E. Asia.

slender • build

DISTRIBUTION

• white hind edge of wing revealed in flight

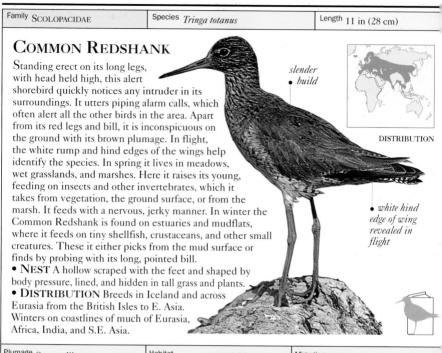

Plumage Sexes alike	Habitat	Migration Migrant

Family SCOLOPACIDAE	Species *Tringa melanoleuca*	Length 14 in (35 cm)

GREATER YELLOWLEGS

Typically seen wading in shallow water, this active shorebird can be recognized by its piping calls. In spring it lives in swamps and the edges of coniferous forests, and its plumage is black-and-white above and heavily spotted below. The Greater Yellowlegs winters on lake shores and coastal mudflats, molting into a grayer and paler plumage. It feeds by probing shallow water and mud for invertebrates.
• **NEST** A shallow hollow in moss or dry peat, with a scanty lining of plant materials, built in an open site, usually near water.
• **DISTRIBUTION** Breeds in North America. Winters from S. USA to S. South America.

long, slender bill

• barred tail

• pale colors of winter plumage

long, thin legs for wading in • shallow water

DISTRIBUTION

Plumage Sexes alike	Habitat	Migration Migrant

Family SCOLOPACIDAE	Species *Arenaria interpres*	Length 9½ in (24 cm)

RUDDY TURNSTONE

A stout and busily active shorebird, the Ruddy Turnstone thrusts its bill under stones or fronds of seaweed, flipping them over to get at the small animals hidden underneath. In flight, white patterns on the wings and back help identify this species.

- **NEST** A shallow hollow in the ground.
- **DISTRIBUTION** Breeds in the high Arctic. Winters on coasts throughout the world.

WINTER

striped crown

DISTRIBUTION

Plumage Sexes differ slightly	Habitat	Migration Migrant

Family SCOLOPACIDAE	Species *Phalaropus lobatus*	Length 8 in (20 cm)

RED-NECKED PHALAROPE

This dainty shorebird is a long-distance migrant. It feeds on aquatic life in tundra pools in spring and on sea plankton in winter.
- **NEST** A hollow lined with grass, hidden in grass.
- **DISTRIBUTION** Breeds in the high Arctic. Winters mid-ocean.

WINTER

pale, straw-colored stripes •

female is more brightly colored than male •

FEMALE

DISTRIBUTION

Plumage Sexes differ slightly	Habitat	Migration Migrant

Family SCOLOPACIDAE	Species *Calidris canutus*	Length 10½ in (27 cm)

RED KNOT

In summer, when few people see this bird, its plumage is a blend of chestnut, black, and white. In winter, it is pale gray, and flocks are seen on mudflats, feeding on invertebrates.
- **NEST** A shallow hollow in the ground, lined with lichens.
- **DISTRIBUTION** Breeds on tundra in the high Arctic. Winters on coastal sands and mudflats throughout much of the world.

rich pattern of summer • plumage

DISTRIBUTION

WINTER

Plumage Sexes alike	Habitat	Migration Migrant

Family SCOLOPACIDAE	Species *Scolopax rusticola*	Length 13½ in (34 cm)

EURASIAN WOODCOCK

The main habitat of this species, in winter and summer alike, is woodland. Active mainly after dark, it walks and probes for food in moist and marshy areas. Its long bill has a flexible, touch-sensitive tip that is useful for probing into mud or soft soil to locate invertebrates. In their display behavior, known as "roding," males fly slowly at treetop level over their territories, uttering piping and croaking calls, at dusk and dawn.

• **NEST** A hollow in mossy ground, lined with a layer of dead leaves.

• **DISTRIBUTION** Breeds across much of Eurasia. Winters as far south as N. Africa, India, and S.E. Asia, moving west as well as south.

very stout body

large eyes, set high on the head

DISTRIBUTION

Plumage Sexes alike	Habitat 🌳 🌲 〰	Migration Migrant

Family SCOLOPACIDAE	Species *Gallinago gallinago*	Length 10½ in (27 cm)

COMMON SNIPE

The straight bill of the Common Snipe is the longest, in proportion to its body, of all the shorebirds. The tip of the bill is flexible, enabling the bird to probe into soft mud, sensing and feeding on worms, small mollusks, and other creatures. The eyes are set high on either side of the head, allowing it to remain vigilant when resting and feeding. It rests in low marsh vegetation or grass, camouflaged by the striped plumage, rising in twisting flight when alarmed. Newly hatched chicks have short bills and have to be fed worms by the parents. The Common Snipe performs a "roller-coaster" display flight, in which the outer tail feathers produce a sound like bleating as the bird dives steeply.

• **NEST** A hollow, scraped with the feet and shaped by body pressure, and lined with grass.

• **DISTRIBUTION** Breeds in North America and Eurasia. Winters as far south as N. South America, and C. Africa.

streaked camouflage pattern

short tail

DISTRIBUTION

Plumage Sexes alike	Habitat 〰 ﹏	Migration Migrant

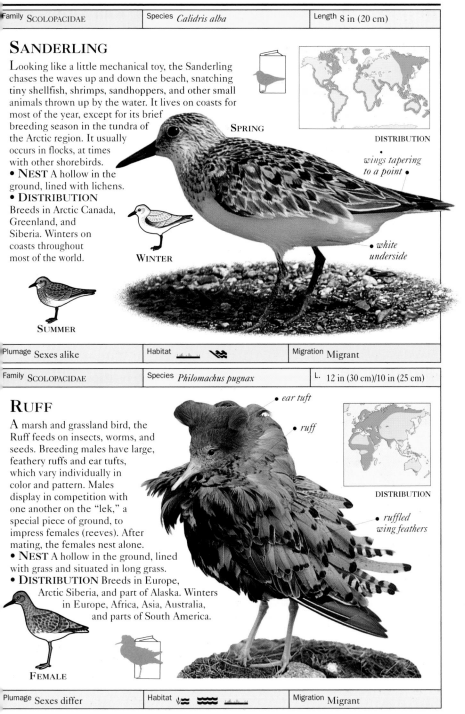

Family SCOLOPACIDAE	Species *Calidris alba*	Length 8 in (20 cm)

SANDERLING

Looking like a little mechanical toy, the Sanderling chases the waves up and down the beach, snatching tiny shellfish, shrimps, sandhoppers, and other small animals thrown up by the water. It lives on coasts for most of the year, except for its brief breeding season in the tundra of the Arctic region. It usually occurs in flocks, at times with other shorebirds.

SPRING

• **NEST** A hollow in the ground, lined with lichens.
• **DISTRIBUTION** Breeds in Arctic Canada, Greenland, and Siberia. Winters on coasts throughout most of the world.

DISTRIBUTION

• *wings tapering to a point* •

• *white underside*

WINTER

SUMMER

Plumage Sexes alike	Habitat	Migration Migrant

Family SCOLOPACIDAE	Species *Philomachus pugnax*	L. 12 in (30 cm)/10 in (25 cm)

RUFF

A marsh and grassland bird, the Ruff feeds on insects, worms, and seeds. Breeding males have large, feathery ruffs and ear tufts, which vary individually in color and pattern. Males display in competition with one another on the "lek," a special piece of ground, to impress females (reeves). After mating, the females nest alone.

• *ear tuft*

• *ruff*

DISTRIBUTION

• *ruffled wing feathers*

• **NEST** A hollow in the ground, lined with grass and situated in long grass.
• **DISTRIBUTION** Breeds in Europe, Arctic Siberia, and part of Alaska. Winters in Europe, Africa, Asia, Australia, and parts of South America.

FEMALE

Plumage Sexes differ	Habitat	Migration Migrant

Family THINOCORIDAE	Species *Thinocorus orbignyianus*	Length 8½ in (22 cm)

GRAY-BREASTED SEEDSNIPE

This hardy species lives on the high plateau of the southern Andes, only moving to lower altitudes during severe weather. It is a ground-dwelling bird with a round body and short legs, using its short, stubby bill to feed on seeds, berries, and other parts of plants. It walks and runs rapidly but, if alarmed, crouches and relies on camouflage. When forced to flee, it escapes in zig-zag flight, usually returning to cover after a short distance. Both sexes utter brief alarm or contact calls. Birds also perform a repetitive, cooing song, either from the top of a rock or in a low display flight.

• **NEST** A depression in an open site or among low vegetation, sparsely lined with plant fragments.

• **DISTRIBUTION** Southern Andes, and extreme south of South America.

• **REMARK** This bird evolved from the shorebirds, but in its ground-dwelling life-style and behavior it is more like a gamebird, such as a partridge.

short, stout, plant-eating bill

FEMALE

camouflage plumage on back

plump body

short legs

DISTRIBUTION

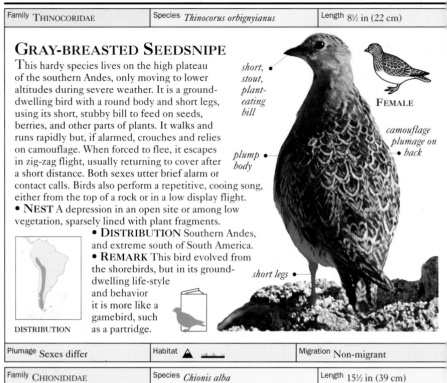

Plumage Sexes differ	Habitat ▲	Migration Non-migrant

Family CHIONIDIDAE	Species *Chionis alba*	Length 15½ in (39 cm)

SNOWY SHEATHBILL

This is a scavenging bird of rocky South Atlantic coasts, where it visits colonies of seals, penguins, cormorants, and of other seabirds. It feeds on eggs and any kind of carrion. Despite its squat shape it is a fast and agile runner. On short flights, it looks ungainly in the air, with its legs dangling, but it flies more strongly, with feet tucked up, when crossing open water.

• **NEST** An untidy construction of shells, pebbles, and stones, placed in a crevice in a cliff or rocky outcrop.

• **DISTRIBUTION** Breeds on coast of Antarctica and offshore islands. Winters in the Falkland Islands and S. Argentina.

• **REMARK** This species evolved from the shorebirds and became a scavenger. The sheathlike cover on its bill, and the bare skin on its face, enable it to eat messy food without harming the bill or feathers.

bare skin on face

DISTRIBUTION

dense, white plumage

squat, heavy build

Plumage Sexes alike	Habitat 〰	Migration Migrant

| Family STERCORARIIDAE | Species *Catharacta skua* | Length 23 in (58 cm) |

GREAT SKUA

Resembling a large, brown gull, this species is a powerful, predatory seabird that dominates others within its range. It feeds by catching fish, taking eggs and nestlings of seabirds, and killing adult birds, including gulls, ducks, and shorebirds. Although its flight is normally powerful and slow, it can chase birds with speed and agility. It forces them to disgorge fish that they have swallowed. When nesting, it shows off a large, white patch on each wing in "raised wing" displays and fiercely attacks all intruders.
• **NEST** A depression on the ground, lined with grass, moss, or heather. Birds nest in colonies at a few locations on islands in the ocean.
• **DISTRIBUTION** Breeds in N. Atlantic. Winters at sea, some birds reaching equatorial waters.

powerful, stocky build

DISTRIBUTION

short, blunt tail

strong legs

webbed feet

| Plumage Sexes alike | Habitat | Migration Migrant |

| Family STERCORARIIDAE | Species *Stercorarius longicaudus* | Length 22 in (55 cm) |

LONG-TAILED JAEGER

This small, lightly built seabird has long, narrow wings and, when fully grown, long central tail feathers. It flies with great agility, soaring upward, or hovering over the water looking for food. It picks fish from the sea surface, follows boats for discarded fish, and attacks gulls or terns to make them disgorge fish that they have caught and swallowed. On its Arctic breeding grounds, it hunts lemmings and other small animals, as well as eating berries.
• **NEST** A depression lined with mosses, lichens, or grass.
• **DISTRIBUTION** Breeds in N. Eurasia and N. North America. Winters in Southern Pacific and Atlantic oceans.

long, narrow wing

light, slender build

DISTRIBUTION

JUVENILE

| Plumage Sexes alike | Habitat | Migration Migrant |

Family LARIDAE	Species *Larus pacificus*	Length 25 in (63 cm)

PACIFIC GULL

This large gull with black back and wings has
the largest bill of all the gull family. It patrols the
shoreline, foraging for food, and makes shallow dives
after fish, squid, crabs, and other marine creatures.
Large shellfish are cracked open by dropping them
onto rocks. Also included in its diet are the eggs and
young of nesting seabirds, and even adults of smaller
bird species. The Pacific Gull occurs in small,
loose colonies or in scattered pairs on the coast
and is only occasionally seen inland.
• **NEST** A loose structure of grass
and plants, under a bush or rock.
• **DISTRIBUTION**
Restricted to coastal areas
of W. and S. Australia.

massive
head and
bill

JUVENILE

powerful,
sturdy build

long,
powerful
wings

black
back

DISTRIBUTION

Plumage Sexes alike	Habitat 〰️	Migration Non-migrant

Family LARIDAE	Species *Larus delawarensis*	Length 20 in (50 cm)

RING-BILLED GULL

This gull has a pearl-gray back and a black band toward the tip of its bill. It
nests in noisy colonies, usually beside a lake or reservoir, but in winter it is more
often seen on the coast. It looks for food wherever the opportunity arises,
catching fish, hunting invertebrates on the ground, or seeking out carrion.
• **NEST** An untidy nest, made of vegetation, situated on the ground.
• **DISTRIBUTION** Breeds N. North America. Winters
in North and Central America,
and in Bahamas and
N. Caribbean.

JUVENILE

legs tucked into
belly feathers

DISTRIBUTION

Plumage Sexes alike	Habitat 〰️ 〰️ 🌾	Migration Migrant

Family LARIDAE	Species *Larus canus*	Length 16 in (40 cm)

MEW GULL

Seen alongside other gulls, this
species has a relatively fine bill,
giving the head a neat, rounded
look. The Mew Gull often comes
inland and often feeds on the ground.
Typical food items are worms, insects, mice,
berries, and fallen grain on farmland. It also
forages in shallow waters. This species nests
in colonies, on the coast or inland, sometimes
on moors or grassland away from water.
• NEST A natural hollow in the ground, lined
with dried grass and other plant materials.
DISTRIBUTION Breeds in much of Eurasia,
N. Africa, W. and N. North America. Northern
populations migrate
south within breeding range.

• plain
white head

light gray
• back

slim
• build

• slender legs

DISTRIBUTION

JUVENILE

Plumage Sexes alike	Habitat	Migration Partial migrant

Family LARIDAE	Species *Larus argentatus*	Length 24 in (60 cm)

HERRING GULL

Well known for its presence in coastal towns, harbors, and
garbage dumps, this powerful gull, with its yodeling calls
and wails, typifies the seaside for many people. Always
ready to exploit any source of food, it has become an
urban scavenger, and also hunts small animals. It does
not venture far out to sea but is becoming more common
inland. Nesting colonies are located on dunes, cliffs, and buildings.
• NEST A shallow cup nest, made from any plant materials locally
available, and placed on the ground.
• DISTRIBUTION Breeds throughout most of the
Northern Hemisphere. Winters in the south of this
range, as far as Central America, N. and N.E.
Africa, India, and parts of S.E. Asia.

pale iris •

JUVENILE

• white tips of
secondary feathers

DISTRIBUTION

Plumage Sexes alike	Habitat	Migration Partial migrant

Family LARIDAE	Species *Larus atricilla*	Length 16½ in (42 cm)

LAUGHING GULL

Common in coastal areas of North America in summer, this gull is recognized by its very dark "hood." It is boldly inquisitive, feeding wherever the opportunity occurs: it follows the plough to pick worms from the soil, scavenges for whatever is washed up on the shoreline, and follows ships for refuse and food scraps. Breeding colonies are located in marshes, by seashores, and on offshore islands.
• **NEST** A cup nest made of plant material, located among tall plants or bushes.
• **DISTRIBUTION** Breeds in E. and S. USA and the Caribbean. Migrates as far south as Peru in winter.

• *broken ring around eye*

black primary flight feathers

white tips of inner secondary flight feathers

long, blackish gray legs •

WINTER

DISTRIBUTION

Plumage Sexes alike	Habitat	Migration Migrant

Family LARIDAE	Species *Larus ridibundus*	Length 16 in (41 cm)

COMMON BLACK-HEADED GULL

With its agile flight and nagging voice, this gull is familiar both on the coast and inland. It feeds according to opportunity, taking small animals, food scraps, and refuse. Birds breed in large colonies, on freshwater or salt marshes. In winter it visits suburbs and garbage dumps, and roosts on lakes and reservoirs.
• **NEST** A well made, open cup nest, made of available plant materials.
• **DISTRIBUTION** Breeds in Eurasia and E. North America. Siberian and N.E. European populations migrate south into Africa and Asia.

incomplete eye ring •

• *pure white triangle revealed in flight*

chocolate brown hood of breeding plumage •

WINTER

• *long, dark red legs*

DISTRIBUTION

Plumage Sexes alike	Habitat	Migration Migrant

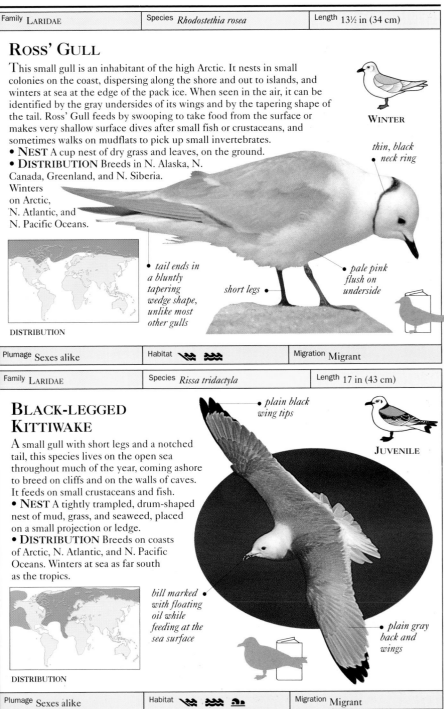

Family LARIDAE	Species *Rhodostethia rosea*	Length 13½ in (34 cm)

ROSS' GULL

This small gull is an inhabitant of the high Arctic. It nests in small colonies on the coast, dispersing along the shore and out to islands, and winters at sea at the edge of the pack ice. When seen in the air, it can be identified by the gray undersides of its wings and by the tapering shape of the tail. Ross' Gull feeds by swooping to take food from the surface or makes very shallow surface dives after small fish or crustaceans, and sometimes walks on mudflats to pick up small invertebrates.
• **NEST** A cup nest of dry grass and leaves, on the ground.
• **DISTRIBUTION** Breeds in N. Alaska, N. Canada, Greenland, and N. Siberia. Winters on Arctic, N. Atlantic, and N. Pacific Oceans.

WINTER

thin, black neck ring

tail ends in a bluntly tapering wedge shape, unlike most other gulls

short legs

pale pink flush on underside

DISTRIBUTION

Plumage Sexes alike	Habitat	Migration Migrant

Family LARIDAE	Species *Rissa tridactyla*	Length 17 in (43 cm)

BLACK-LEGGED KITTIWAKE

A small gull with short legs and a notched tail, this species lives on the open sea throughout much of the year, coming ashore to breed on cliffs and on the walls of caves. It feeds on small crustaceans and fish.
• **NEST** A tightly trampled, drum-shaped nest of mud, grass, and seaweed, placed on a small projection or ledge.
• **DISTRIBUTION** Breeds on coasts of Arctic, N. Atlantic, and N. Pacific Oceans. Winters at sea as far south as the tropics.

plain black wing tips

JUVENILE

bill marked with floating oil while feeding at the sea surface

plain gray back and wings

DISTRIBUTION

Plumage Sexes alike	Habitat	Migration Migrant

Family LARIDAE	Species *Chlidonias niger*	Length 10 in (25 cm)

BLACK TERN

Occurring inland in summer and by the sea in winter, this bird flies over water to feed. It dips down to pick insects and small fish from the surface, without diving. Breeding colonies are located on shallow lakes and flooded marshes.
• **NEST** An untidy heap of waterplants, lined with finer material, floating on the water, or situated at the water's edge.
• **DISTRIBUTION** Breeds across North America and Europe to mid-Siberia. Winters as far south as N.W. South America, and the Persian Gulf.

DISTRIBUTION

• *small, fine bill*

WINTER

long, slender • wings for agile flight while feeding from water surface

• *short legs*

Plumage Sexes alike	Habitat	Migration Migrant

Family LARIDAE	Species *Sterna caspia*	Length 21 in (53 cm)

CASPIAN TERN

This is the largest tern, with a heavy bill, slow flight, and loud raspy calls. It flies over water and plunge-dives to catch fish and shrimps. Sea coasts, islands, and large lakes are its chief habitats. It nests mainly in colonies, but sometimes in single pairs.
• **NEST** A hollow scraped by the feet and formed by body pressure, either bare or sparsely lined with plant materials.
• **DISTRIBUTION** Breeds in North America, Eurasia, Africa, and Australia. Winter range extends into N. South America and E. Asia.

WINTER

crossed • tips of folded wings

large, • heavy bill

• short, bluntly forked tail

AUTUMN

SUMMER

DISTRIBUTION

Plumage Sexes alike	Habitat	Migration Migrant

Family LARIDAE	Species *Sterna hirundo*	Length 14½ in (37 cm)

COMMON TERN

This bird spends much of its time in flight over water, normally at sea but sometimes over lakes. When feeding, it hovers and then plunge-dives, taking fish and crustaceans. It nests in colonies and migrates in flocks.
• **NEST** A hollow in the ground, sometimes lined.
• **DISTRIBUTION** Breeds all round the Northern Hemisphere. Winters as far south as coastal waters of the southern continents.

WINTER

sharp • bill of a plunge-diver

long, forked tail •

long, narrow wings •

short legs, not often used for running or walking •

DISTRIBUTION

Plumage Sexes alike	Habitat 〰〰〰	Migration Migrant

Family LARIDAE	Species *Sterna dougallii*	Length 15½ in (39 cm)

ROSEATE TERN

A graceful, seagoing tern with long tail streamers, this species develops a pink tinge on its mostly white plumage, when breeding. It feeds by plunge-diving for small fish. Nesting colonies are located on offshore islands or on banks of sand or shingle by the coast.
• **NEST** A shallow hollow in the ground.
• **DISTRIBUTION** Breeds on coasts in parts of all continents. Migrates within this range when not breeding.

JUVENILE

long, deeply forked tail •

very pale wings and back •

DISTRIBUTION

Plumage Sexes alike	Habitat 〰	Migration Migrant

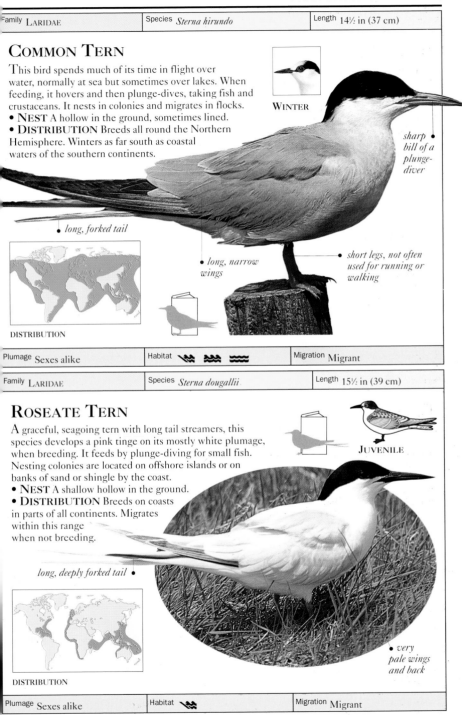

Family LARIDAE	Species *Larosterna inca*	Length 16½ in (42 cm)

INCA TERN

This dark gray tern has characteristic, outward-curling, white plumes in the shape of a mustache. It flies over the sea, keeping close to the coast. Agile in flight, it feeds by dipping to snatch small fish from the sea surface. When the opportunity arises, it preys on shoals of fish as they flee in panic from sea lions, whales, and flocks of cormorants. It is often seen in large flocks.

• *outward curling "mustache" plume*

• *heavy build*

• **NEST** A flat space in a crevice among rocks or in an old burrow of another seabird, such as a diving-petrel or penguin.
• **DISTRIBUTION** Breeds in South America on coasts of Peru and N. Chile. Winters from Ecuador south to C. Chile.

JUVENILE

• *migration study ring*

DISTRIBUTION

Plumage Sexes alike	Habitat 🌊 🏖	Migration Migrant

Family LARIDAE	Species *Anous stolidus*	Length 15½ in (39 cm)

BROWN NODDY

This species spends much of the time flying over the sea, either in coastal waters or in mid-ocean. It flies low over the sea surface, beating its wings rapidly. When feeding, it hovers and then dips to snatch food from the surface. The main prey items are fish and squids. To rest, it usually comes ashore to perch on a rock or tree, but it sometimes swims and even sleeps on the water. The name is derived from the courtship display, in which both sexes nod to show off their pale foreheads.

pale forehead patch
• *used in display*

• *long, sharp bill for snatching prey from sea surface*

• *dark brown plumage, typical of a noddy*

• **NEST** A mass of twigs and seaweed, placed in a tree, in a bush, or on the ground.
• **DISTRIBUTION** Tropical Pacific, Atlantic, and Indian Oceans.

DISTRIBUTION

Plumage Sexes alike	Habitat 🌊 🌊	Migration Partial migrant

| Family STERNIDAE | Species *Gygis alba* | Length 12½ in (32 cm) |

WHITE TERN

This is an elegant sea tern of tropical oceans, with a gentle, delicate appearance. In behavior it is unusually tame and will allow an observer to approach. It has a forked tail and a slender bill that appears to be tilted slightly upward. This is the only tern species that has all-white plumage. It spends much of the time flying over the sea, either in coastal waters or in mid-ocean. Its flight is light and buoyant, combining agility with graceful movement. The wings are broader and more rounded in flight than are those of other terns. When feeding at sea, it follows a rising, then falling, flight path, dipping to snatch fish and small squids from the surface. It also catches fish as they leap. The large eyes appear to be an adaptation for night feeding, its prey normally rising to surface waters after dark.
• **NEST** No nest is made, but the female lays her egg and balances it throughout incubation on a small space on a tree branch, in the fork of a twig, on a palm frond, or on a rock ledge.
• **DISTRIBUTION** Pacific, Atlantic, and Indian Oceans.

large eye for night feeding

DISTRIBUTION

long, slender wings

strongly forked tail

| Plumage Sexes alike | Habitat 〰🌊🌊 | Migration Partial migrant |

| Family RHYNCHOPIDAE | Species *Rhynchops niger* | Length 18 in (46 cm) |

BLACK SKIMMER

Seen on coasts, estuaries, and rivers, this bird has a distinctive bill in which the lower mandible is longer than the upper one and is flattened sideways like a vertical knife blade. When feeding, the Black Skimmer flies along the water surface and ploughs the lower mandible through the water, snapping the bill shut when it touches a fish. Skimmers live in flocks, breeding in colonies on beaches and sandbanks.
• **NEST** An unlined hollow in the sand, formed by feet and body pressure.

long wings

heavy head

long lower mandible

• **DISTRIBUTION** From E. USA to S. South America.

DISTRIBUTION

| Plumage Sexes alike | Habitat 〰🌊🌊 | Migration Partial migrant |

Family ALCIDAE	Species *Alle alle*	Length 8½ in (22 cm)

DOVEKIE

This black-and-white seabird has a dumpy outline and narrow wings, which give it a characteristic, whirring flight. It feeds at sea, diving from the surface to swim underwater, using its wings as flippers, and taking animal plankton (tiny, drifting marine life). Dovekies breed in swarming colonies on rocky screes in the far north, wintering on the open sea, and sometimes driven inland by storms.
• **NEST** Eggs are layed in an unlined rock crevice or in a burrow.
• **DISTRIBUTION** Breeds on coasts of the Arctic Ocean. Winters at sea in N. Atlantic Ocean.

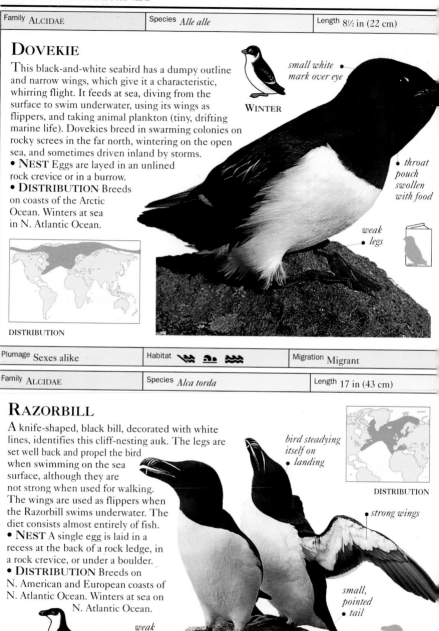

small white mark over eye

WINTER

throat pouch swollen with food

weak legs

DISTRIBUTION

Plumage Sexes alike	Habitat	Migration Migrant

Family ALCIDAE	Species *Alca torda*	Length 17 in (43 cm)

RAZORBILL

A knife-shaped, black bill, decorated with white lines, identifies this cliff-nesting auk. The legs are set well back and propel the bird when swimming on the sea surface, although they are not strong when used for walking. The wings are used as flippers when the Razorbill swims underwater. The diet consists almost entirely of fish.
• **NEST** A single egg is laid in a recess at the back of a rock ledge, in a rock crevice, or under a boulder.
• **DISTRIBUTION** Breeds on N. American and European coasts of N. Atlantic Ocean. Winters at sea on N. Atlantic Ocean.

bird steadying itself on landing

DISTRIBUTION

strong wings

small, pointed tail

weak legs

WINTER

Plumage Sexes alike	Habitat	Migration Partial migrant

| Family ALCIDAE | Species *Fratercula cirrhata* | Length 15 in (38 cm) |

TUFTED PUFFIN

This heavily built auk has head tufts that can be swept back and that do not impede underwater fishing. Bill and head decorations are used only for display. With its muscular body, the bird cannot take off from the water without a wing-flapping run. The birds breed in colonies on rocky islands, and spend the winter out in mid-ocean.
• **NEST** A burrow or a hollow in a rock crevice, lined with grass and feathers.
• **DISTRIBUTION** Breeds on W. and E. coasts of N. Pacific Ocean. Winters at sea in N. Pacific.

WINTER

• *display tuft*

• *sheath lost in winter*

• *short tail*

DISTRIBUTION

| Plumage Sexes alike | Habitat | Migration Migrant |

| Family ALCIDAE | Species *Fratercula arctica* | Length 12½ in (32 cm) |

ATLANTIC PUFFIN

A stout bird with a large head and a short tail, the Atlantic Puffin has a comical appearance, with its masked eyes and massive bill. In breeding birds, the bill is covered with a red sheath, with yellow stripes and a gray triangle at the base. Pairs perform face-to-face bill-rapping displays in spring. The Atlantic Puffin flies strongly on fast-beating wings and swims underwater, chasing fish, particularly sand eels. It packs these crosswise in its bill to carry them to its young. Breeding colonies are located on cliff tops on coasts and islands. In winter, birds stay out at sea.
• **NEST** A shallow hollow in an underground burrow, lined with grass and feathers.
• **DISTRIBUTION** Breeds on W. and E. coasts of N. Atlantic Ocean. Winters on N. Atlantic Ocean.

WINTER

orange display wattle (lost in winter)

DISTRIBUTION

• *upright posture*

short • *tail*

| Plumage Sexes alike | Habitat | Migration Migrant |

| Family PTEROCLIDAE | Species *Pterocles lichtensteinii* | Length 10 in (25 cm) |

LICHTENSTEIN'S SANDGROUSE

A semidesert species, this sandgrouse prefers rocky
and hilly country where some bushes occur. It feeds
chiefly on seeds and other parts of plants including
acacia trees and shrubs. During the hot midday hours,
it rests in the shade and is reluctant to move. It flies
to drink daily, late at dusk or before dawn, uttering
soft, two-note calls. The nest is often up to 19 miles
(30 km) from a water source, and the male brings
water for the young, carried in his belly feathers.
• NEST A slight hollow on
bare ground, without a lining.
• DISTRIBUTION Scattered
areas from Morocco through
Africa to Arabia and Pakistan.

FEMALE

long,
tapering wings

short
tail

short,
powerful
legs

narrow,
black breast
bands

DISTRIBUTION

| Plumage Sexes differ | Habitat | Migration Non-migrant |

| Family PTEROCLIDAE | Species *Pterocles alchata* | Length 11 in (28 cm) |

PIN-TAILED
SANDGROUSE

This is a sandgrouse of flat, dry country.
Its fine pattern of colors camouflages
it against sand, pebbles, and sparse
vegetation. This species normally
occurs in flocks and sometimes breeds
in loose colonies. Birds are seen
creeping or running on their rather
short legs and feeding on seeds,
shoots, and leaves. They fly
considerable distances to water
and, when drinking, sometimes float
on the surface. Males carry water for
the young in their soft breast feathers.
• NEST An unlined hollow on bare ground.
• DISTRIBUTION Breeds in Portugal, Spain,
S. France, N. Africa, Middle East,
and C. Asia. C. Asian
populations winter as
far south as Pakistan
and N.W. India.

thin, black
eye stripe

chestnut
breast band,
edged in gray

DISTRIBUTION

FEMALE

| Plumage Sexes differ | Habitat | Migration Partial migrant |

| Family COLUMBIDAE | Species *Columba livia* | Length 12½ in (32 cm) |

ROCK DOVE

This is the wild ancestor of all domestic pigeons, such as messenger and racing birds, and of the fancy pigeons that have been bred in many colors, including pure white, and in various patterns. Escapes have led to feral (semi-wild) populations, most of which live in towns as street pigeons. Truly wild Rock Doves nest in colonies, on ledges in caves, and in cliff crevices, feeding on seeds.
• **NEST** A scanty platform of twigs and feathers, on a rock ledge or a building.
• **DISTRIBUTION** W. Europe, N. Africa, and through the Middle East to India. Feral birds have established populations throughout the world.

• glossy neck pattern

• two black wing bars

• pink feet

TYPICAL STREET PIGEON

DISTRIBUTION

| Plumage Sexes alike | Habitat | Migration Non-migrant |

| Family COLUMBIDAE | Species *Columba guinea* | Length 13¼ in (33 cm) |

SPECKLED PIGEON

This pigeon resembles some street pigeons in general appearance, but has silvery-tipped neck feathers that are slightly forked. During mating displays, when the male inflates his neck, these stand out as a big, bristling ruff. The species is the natural African counterpart of the wild Rock Dove and has learned to live with humans and to use buildings as substitutes for the cliffs and gorges that it uses in the wild. Its natural diet consists of seeds including grain, and the leaves, shoots, and buds of green plants.
• **NEST** A flimsy platform made of twigs, sticks, and grass, situated on the ledge of a cave or cliff or on a building or bridge.
• **DISTRIBUTION** Two separate populations in nonforested parts of Africa south of the Sahara.

• bare skin around the eye

forked feathers • (raised in display)

DISTRIBUTION

triangular • wing spots

• long wings

| Plumage Sexes alike | Habitat | Migration Non-migrant |

| Family COLUMBIDAE | Species *Columba palumbus* | Length 16½ in (42 cm) |

COMMON WOOD-PIGEON

Originally a woodland bird, this pigeon has learned to take advantage of gardens and farmland. It frequently advertises its presence from within the trees with a deep, throaty, cooing call. When seen in the open, it can be identified by its white wing patches and white neck patches. Flight is usually swift and direct and, in its display, the bird mounts steeply, often with a series of loud wing claps, then glides downward. Frightened flocks, too, make noisy wingbeats. The species is highly sociable and forms flocks when not breeding. Birds feed mainly on seeds, but they also eat berries, buds, and leaves. The short legs assist in clambering after acorns.
• **NEST** A shallow saucer of thin twigs, placed inconspicuously in a leafy tree, fairly high up.
• **DISTRIBUTION** N. Europe, Africa, and through the Middle East to N. India.

iridescent patch

white neck patch

JUVENILE

DISTRIBUTION

short legs of a tree pigeon

| Plumage Sexes alike | Habitat | Migration Partial migrant |

| Family COLUMBIDAE | Species *Streptopelia turtur* | Length 11 in (28 cm) |

EUROPEAN TURTLE-DOVE

This is a small pigeon with a checkered pattern of bronze and black on the wing coverts. It flies rapidly with short, stiff wingbeats. European Turtle-Doves live in woodland, and on summer days fill the air with a soft, purring coo. They feed on the ground, where they search for small seeds; leaves and buds are also eaten.
• **NEST** A flimsy platform of twigs, situated in a low tree or bush.
• **DISTRIBUTION** Breeds Europe to C. Asia. Winters in Africa.

bare skin around the eye

black-and-white neck patch

bronze feather edges make a lattice pattern

white edge of tail

strong legs for foraging on the ground

DISTRIBUTION

| Plumage Sexes alike | Habitat | Migration Migrant |

| Family COLUMBIDAE | Species *Streptopelia decaocto* | Length 12 in (30 cm) |

EURASIAN COLLARED DOVE

A plain-colored pigeon with a narrow, black collar, this bird can be recognized by its monotonous, three-note call. The species occurs in open woodland, farmland, and suburban yards, eating wild seeds, grain, berries, and livestock feed. In its gliding display flight, it shows off the black-and-white pattern underneath its tail.
• **NEST** A flimsy platform of twigs, often in a conifer.
• **DISTRIBUTION** From Europe through the Middle East, S. and E. Asia, to China and Korea.
• **REMARK** This species has spread across most of Europe from the Balkan region since 1930.

narrow, black collar •

• *uniform, pale, sandy color*

DISTRIBUTION

• *long tail with black-and-white underside, shown in flight*

| Plumage Sexes alike | Habitat | Migration Non-migrant |

| Family COLUMBIDAE | Species *Reinwardtoena reinwardtsi* | Length 20 in (50 cm) |

GREAT CUCKOO-DOVE

This tree-dwelling dove with a very long tail is a bird of tropical forest. It shares the name "cuckoo-dove" with a number of smaller, brown, long-tailed doves, some of which have calls like those of the Common Cuckoo (*see p. 188*). This species has two different calls: a repeated, three-note phrase, and a rapid, laughing sound. It lives mainly in the middle to higher levels of the forest foliage, and at the forest edge, while birds are sometimes seen on the ground. Flight is strong, powerful, and graceful. Great Cuckoo-Doves tend to be solitary, although birds sometimes gather in a temporary flock at a plentiful food source, such as a fruiting tree. The diet consists of fruit, taken from trees or climbing plants.
• **NEST** A shallow, saucerlike structure of roots, moss, ferns, and sticks, built on a level branch in a tree or bush.
• **DISTRIBUTION** New Guinea and the Moluccan Islands.

• *small, slender head and neck*

pale blue-gray color extending from the head to the belly •

rounded wings • *of a forest bird for maneuvrable flight among branches*

DISTRIBUTION

JUVENILE

• *long, broad tail for fast, level flight*

| Plumage Sexes alike | Habitat | Migration Non-migrant |

Family COLUMBIDAE	Species *Oena capensis*	Length 10 in (25 cm)

NAMAQUA DOVE

A tiny, ground-feeding dove with a long, tapering tail, this bird is similar in size, shape, and life-style to the Budgerigar (*see p.177*). Only the male has a black face mask and bright bill. Both sexes have chestnut-orange on the wing feathers, revealed in flight. Namaqua Doves fly rapidly, with quick, irregular wingbeats. They occur in dry, open country, scrub, and farmland, and are seen singly, in pairs, or in parties. They feed on the ground, taking small seeds. In more arid regions, they travel about nomadically, soon colonizing places where food and water have become available.

• *black face and throat*

• *glossy dark wing spots*

• **NEST** A small, flimsy, saucer-shaped nest fashioned of rootlets, fine twigs, and grass stems, situated in a low bush.

• **DISTRIBUTION** Africa south of the Sahara, and parts of the Middle East and Arabian Peninsula.

DISTRIBUTION

FEMALE

Plumage Sexes differ	Habitat	Migration Partial migrant/nomadic

Family COLUMBIDAE	Species *Phaps elegans*	Length 11½ in (29 cm)

BRUSH BRONZEWING

This stoutly built pigeon favors areas of low, thick vegetation that conceal its colors, including the double bar of iridescent plumage on its wings. These sparkle in a range of colors, from purple to bronze, giving the bird its name. It usually occurs in pairs, living unobtrusively among dense bushes and low trees, particularly in coastal heathland, or in the undergrowth of open woodland. The birds feed on the ground, mainly taking seeds, and sometimes venture into fields adjoining their normal habitat to take grain. They are cautious when visiting water, coming to drink quietly after dusk and before dawn. Their call is a subdued, mournful cooing.

chestnut head
• *stripe*

DISTRIBUTION

• **NEST** A substantial platform of twigs and stems, located in a small tree, thick shrub, or occasionally on the ground in a sheltered site.

• **DISTRIBUTION** S.W. and S.E. Australia, including Tasmania.

FEMALE

• *bright, iridescent wing bars*

• *bluntly tapering tail*

Plumage Sexes differ	Habitat	Migration Non-migrant

| Family COLUMBIDAE | Species *Leucosarcia melanoleuca* | Length 14½ in (37 cm) |

WONGA PIGEON

A secretive bird in spite of its size and powerful build, the Wonga Pigeon lives on the ground in deciduous forest and rain forest. Here, it can often be detected by its penetrating call note. This sound is repeated continuously until the bird senses an approach, when it becomes silent. It normally avoids danger by walking, often covering considerable distances on the forest floor. Otherwise, it may take flight for a short distance, then watch from a perch. Wonga Pigeons are seen singly or in pairs or in larger numbers at a good food source. They eat fallen fruits, berries, and seeds.
• **NEST** A platform of fine twigs, placed on a horizontal fork, in a forest tree.
• **DISTRIBUTION** S.E. and E. Australia.

short, broad tail

short, rounded wings

large, plump body

small head

DISTRIBUTION

| Plumage Sexes alike | Habitat | Migration Non-migrant |

| Family COLUMBIDAE | Species *Zenaida macroura* | Length 12½ in (32 cm) |

MOURNING DOVE

Common in a wide variety of habitats, this bird is found in arid scrub, open woodland, farmland, gardens, and towns. It flies rapidly with whistling wingbeats and has a characteristic upward flip of the tail after landing. Mourning Doves are seen in pairs or small, loose groups. When not breeding, they are seen in larger groups at feeding sites or roosts. The call is a mournful-sounding series of coos. Birds feed on the ground, chiefly taking small seeds, and also grain and green shoots. The male's display flight consists of a noisy, flapping ascent followed by a downward glide. On the ground, displaying males bow to the females with puffed-up necks.
• **NEST** A scanty platform of thin twigs, sometimes lined with finer stems, usually in a tree or shrub.
• **DISTRIBUTION** From the US–Canadian border area as far south as Panama, the N. Caribbean and the Bahamas. Northern populations migrate south within this range.

dark spots on the wings

DISTRIBUTION

long, narrow wings

JUVENILE

| Plumage Sexes alike | Habitat | Migration Partial migrant |

Family COLUMBIDAE	Species *Petrophassa plumifera*	Length 8½ in (22 cm)

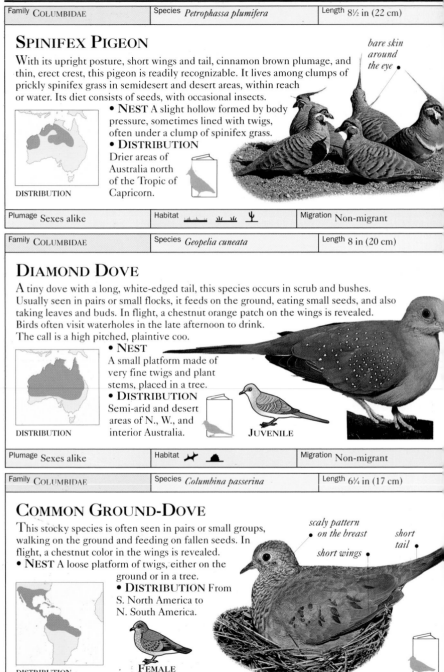

SPINIFEX PIGEON

With its upright posture, short wings and tail, cinnamon brown plumage, and thin, erect crest, this pigeon is readily recognizable. It lives among clumps of prickly spinifex grass in semidesert and desert areas, within reach or water. Its diet consists of seeds, with occasional insects.

bare skin around the eye

• **NEST** A slight hollow formed by body pressure, sometimes lined with twigs, often under a clump of spinifex grass.
• **DISTRIBUTION** Drier areas of Australia north of the Tropic of Capricorn.

DISTRIBUTION

Plumage Sexes alike	Habitat	Migration Non-migrant

Family COLUMBIDAE	Species *Geopelia cuneata*	Length 8 in (20 cm)

DIAMOND DOVE

A tiny dove with a long, white-edged tail, this species occurs in scrub and bushes. Usually seen in pairs or small flocks, it feeds on the ground, eating small seeds, and also taking leaves and buds. In flight, a chestnut orange patch on the wings is revealed. Birds often visit waterholes in the late afternoon to drink. The call is a high pitched, plaintive coo.

• **NEST** A small platform made of very fine twigs and plant stems, placed in a tree.
• **DISTRIBUTION** Semi-arid and desert areas of N., W., and interior Australia.

DISTRIBUTION

JUVENILE

Plumage Sexes alike	Habitat	Migration Non-migrant

Family COLUMBIDAE	Species *Columbina passerina*	Length 6¾ in (17 cm)

COMMON GROUND-DOVE

This stocky species is often seen in pairs or small groups, walking on the ground and feeding on fallen seeds. In flight, a chestnut color in the wings is revealed.

scaly pattern on the breast *short tail* *short wings*

• **NEST** A loose platform of twigs, either on the ground or in a tree.
• **DISTRIBUTION** From S. North America to N. South America.

DISTRIBUTION

FEMALE

Plumage Sexes differ	Habitat	Migration Non-migrant

Family COLUMBIDAE	Species *Caloenas nicobarica*	Length 13 in (33 cm)

NICOBAR PIGEON

An island-dwelling pigeon, this odd-looking species has a thin head and neck, an upright wattle on the bill, and long, spiky neck feathers that can be raised in a ruff. The tail is short and white. Nicobar Pigeons feed in the forest undergrowth, taking fruit and seeds. The birds fly nomadically from island to island in search of feeding sites. Nesting colonies are close packed and sometimes very large.
• **NEST** An untidy structure made of twigs, either in a bush or in a tree.
• **DISTRIBUTION** From the Nicobar Islands (in the Indian Ocean off Burma) through S.E. Asia to Indonesia, New Guinea, and the Solomon Islands.

ruff of elongated feathers

irregular wattle on the bill

large, strong feet

ring of an aviary bird

DISTRIBUTION

JUVENILE

Plumage Sexes alike	Habitat	Migration Nomadic

Family COLUMBIDAE	Species *Gallicolumba luzonica*	Length 11½ in (29 cm)

LUZON BLEEDING-HEART

The bloodlike breast markings of this species vary from one bird to another and must serve as recognition marks by which individuals can identify each other. This is necessary because they live in the permanent semi-darkness of the rain forest floor. Here they move quietly among low, shrubby vegetation in search of seeds and berries, and also taking grubs, snails, and other invertebrates.
• **NEST** A scanty nest of twigs, placed in a shrub or low tree.
• **DISTRIBUTION** N. Philippine Islands.

bright breast mark

DISTRIBUTION

Plumage Sexes alike	Habitat	Migration Non-migrant

| Family COLUMBIDAE | Species *Goura victoria* | Length 30 in (75 cm) |

VICTORIA CROWNED-PIGEON

The lacy crest of this enormous pigeon is made up of fan-shaped tufts and is permanently raised over the head. Displaying males utter soft, booming calls as they show off their crests and tails to the females. Both sexes perform threat or defense displays in which they wag their tails and hold out one or both wings, like banners. This ground-feeding species lives on the rain forest floor, walking around slowly and taking fallen fruits, seeds, and berries. It flies heavily, either to escape danger or to ascend into the branches of the trees, where it also roosts and nests.
• **NEST** A large, solid, platformlike mass of stems and twigs, in a tree.
• **DISTRIBUTION** N. New Guinea.

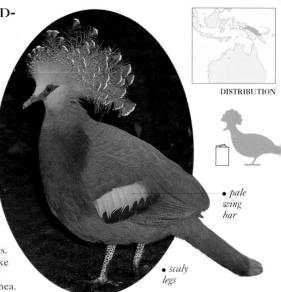

DISTRIBUTION

• *pale wing bar*

• *scaly legs*

| Plumage Sexes alike | Habitat 🌳 | Migration Non-migrant |

| Family COLUMBIDAE | Species *Treron bicincta* | Length 11½ in (29 cm) |

ORANGE-BREASTED GREEN-PIGEON

Strong legs and feet, useful for clambering in trees, and a stout bill for eating soft fruits, make this species a typical example of the fruit-pigeons. Flocks are usually seen in the lower branches of trees or in bushes, feeding on figs, wild dates, berries, and other fruits. Birds rarely visit the ground and when they do, for instance to drink, they walk clumsily, with their tails raised.
• **NEST** A flimsy platform of twigs in a small tree, close to open space.
• **DISTRIBUTION** India and parts of S.E. Asia.

FEMALE

strong feet grip • *perch firmly*

white • *tail tip*

DISTRIBUTION

| Plumage Sexes differ | Habitat 🌳 🌿 ⛰ | Migration Non-migrant |

| Family COLUMBIDAE | Species *Ptilinopus superbus* | Length 8½ in (22 cm) |

SUPERB FRUIT-DOVE

The vivid plumage of this species provides surprisingly good camouflage among the fruit and foliage of sun-dappled forests. It feeds in forest trees that produce small, oil-rich fruits. Birds live in pairs or alone, although large groups sometimes gather temporarily at a plentiful food source.
• **NEST** A platform of twigs, in a tree or vine tangle.
• **DISTRIBUTION** Australasian region from Sulawesi through New Guinea to the Solomon Islands, and in N.E. and E. Australia.

DISTRIBUTION

white belly and undertail coverts

green back with dark spots

FEMALE

| Plumage Sexes differ | Habitat | Migration Partial migrant |

| Family COLUMBIDAE | Species *Ducula pacifica* | Length 14 in (35 cm) |

PACIFIC-IMPERIAL PIGEON

This is a large and subtly colored fruit dove that inhabits small, wooded islands and atolls. Flocks wander between islands in search of fruit. They are capable of long sea crossings. The Pacific-Imperial Pigeon is an agile bird, clambering, hanging, and reaching for food among the higher foliage, taking fruit and berries. The call is a single, growling note from high in the tree canopy.
• **NEST** A platform made of bare twigs and placed high up in a large tree.
• **DISTRIBUTION** Islands from N.E. New Guinea through Tonga, Fiji, and New Caledonia to islands of S.W. Pacific.

fleshy wattle on the bill

long wings for distance flight

DISTRIBUTION

| Plumage Sexes alike | Habitat | Migration Partial migrant |

| Family COLUMBIDAE | Species *Lopholaimus antarcticus* | Length 17¼ in (43 cm) |

TOPKNOT PIGEON

long, drooping crest •

A large, gray, long-tailed pigeon, this tree-dwelling species has a swept-back, double crest that runs from forehead to nape. It is a sociable and nomadic bird that roams the treetops of rain forests in flocks, feeding on a wide variety of fruit. The short legs and strong feet are typical of a fruit-pigeon and enable the birds to cling acrobatically to the twigs when feeding, often hanging upside down with flapping wings to keep in place. Topknot Pigeons rarely come down to the ground even to drink, normally obtaining water from tree hollows or wet leaves or by hanging from a low twig over a stream or freshwater pool.
• **NEST** A flat platform made of twigs, and usually placed high in a tree.
• **DISTRIBUTION** E. Australia.

• blue-gray plumage

long • wings

• short legs and strong feet of a tree-living fruit-pigeon

JUVENILE

DISTRIBUTION

| Plumage Sexes alike | Habitat | Migration Nomadic |

| Family COLUMBIDAE | Species *Hemiphaga novaeseelandiae* | Length 20 in (51 cm) |

NEW ZEALAND PIGEON

The dull colors of this stout fruit-pigeon are broken up by sparkling, green and purple sheens. These help provide camouflage among foliage, but the bird can often be detected by the loud flapping of its wings as it steadies itself while clambering about in search of fruit. This species lives in forests, sometimes venturing into nearby gardens and farmland with trees. The diet includes fruit, berries, buds, flowers, and leaves from trees and shrubs. Birds also come down to the ground to feed from small plants. They are seen in pairs or small parties. The male's display flight consists of a rapid ascent, followed by a downward glide with spread wings and tail.
• **NEST** A flimsy structure of twigs, built on the branch of a tree.
• **DISTRIBUTION** New Zealand.

• dark plumage with a dull, green gloss

DISTRIBUTION

| Plumage Sexes alike | Habitat | Migration Non-migrant |

| Family PSITTACIDAE | Species *Chalcopsitta duivenbodei* | Length 12½ in (32 cm) |

BROWN LORY

One of the more soberly colored
lories, this parrot feeds mainly on
the flowers of forest trees. It visits
large heads of tree blossoms, from
which it laps nectar with its thin tongue.
On the tip of the tongue there are special
projections that gather up pollen. The pollen
is important to the birds, as it provides protein
in an otherwise sugary diet. Some fruit is also
included in the diet. Brown Lories are usually
seen in pairs, or in parties of six to eight birds,
in the treetops of lowland rain forest, and are
fairly common within their normal range. They
utter shrill screeches and short, harsh contact
calls as they move through the trees in search of
food. When feeding, the birds sometimes join
company with other blossom-feeding species,
especially other parrots such as Rainbow Lorikeets.
• **NEST** Unknown; however, birds have been seen
investigating holes high in trees during the breeding
season, which may suggest cavity nesting.
• **DISTRIBUTION** Forests of N. New Guinea.
• **REMARK** Also known as Duyvenbode's Lory.

*crest ruffled
in excitement*

DISTRIBUTION

*yellow
wing
patch*

*short legs
and strong
feet of a tree
dweller*

| Plumage Sexes alike | Habitat 🌳🌲 | Migration Non-migrant |

| Family PSITTACIDAE | Species *Trichoglossus haematodus* | Length 10½ in (26 cm) |

RAINBOW LORIKEET

A vividly colored and noisy bird, this species is often seen in chattering and
screeching flocks, feeding in flowering trees. It is common in lowland forests
and also in open woodland and parkland. Birds feed on pollen and nectar,
also eating blossoms, some seeds and fruit, and occasional insects.
• **NEST** In a cavity in a hollow limb or tree trunk.
• **DISTRIBUTION** Parts of E. Indonesia; New
Guinea; S.W. Pacific islands to New
Caledonia; N., E.,
and S. Australia.
• **REMARK**
Plumage varies
over the range; some
island forms lack the
blue and red coloring.

DISTRIBUTION

RED-
COLLARED
FORM

*yellow
underwing
patches*

| Plumage Sexes alike | Habitat 🌳🌲🌿 | Migration Non-migrant |

Family PSITTACIDAE	Species *Vini peruviana*	Length 7 in (18 cm)

TAHITIAN LORIKEET

This rarely seen parrot has deep blue plumage all over, except for a white triangle on the lower face and throat. The bill and feet are bright red. This simple arrangement makes the bird unusual among lorikeets, which are generally vivid birds with complex patterns. The Tahitian Lorikeet lives on remote tropical islands, where its main food is probably the nectar and pollen of the flowers of coconut palms.
• **NEST** A hollow in a tree or a broken-off coconut stump.
• **DISTRIBUTION** S. Pacific Ocean: in the Society Islands (but no longer occurring in Tahiti), and introduced in the Cook Islands.
• **REMARK** Endangered as a result of the raiding of nests by an introduced predator, the Black Rat.

DISTRIBUTION

• *uniform, deep blue plumage*

• *short legs and strong feet of a tree-dwelling bird*

• *short, tapering tail*

Plumage Sexes alike	Habitat	Migration Non-migrant

Family PSITTACIDAE	Species *Charmosyna papou*	Length 16½ in (42 cm)

PAPUAN LORIKEET

Living in tropical forests on mountainsides, this colorful parrot feeds in the trees on the flowers of epiphytes (independent plants that grow on the branches). It drinks the nectar and also eats pollen and the blossoms of the epiphytes, as well as taking berries and seeds. Its long, curving tail is an encumbrance as it hops jerkily through the twigs. Papuan Lorikeets occur in pairs or small parties and are seen in the upper branches of the forest. Their flight is direct but not fast, with the tail trailing behind. Birds fly among the branches, rather than over the top of the canopy. Their calls are soft and subdued.
• **NEST** Unknown.
• **DISTRIBUTION** Mountains of New Guinea.
• **REMARK** There is also a black phase (*see p. 13*) of this species, in which much of the red is replaced by black.

blue-and-black nape pattern •

• *red underside*

DISTRIBUTION

BLACK PHASE

• *two long central tail feathers*

Plumage Sexes alike	Habitat	Migration Non-migrant

Family PSITTACIDAE	Species *Calyptorhynchus funereus*	Length 27 in (68 cm)

YELLOW-TAILED BLACK COCKATOO

This large, forest-dwelling cockatoo has a massive bill that can destroy any unprotected wooden structure, whether it be a live tree or part of an aviary containing a captive specimen. In the forest, the cockatoo tears open branches to take out the large, wood-boring grubs of moths and beetles that form the greater part of its diet. It also eats seeds, nuts, berries, and blossoms. Yellow-tailed Black Cockatoos live mainly up in the trees, roosting and feeding in the branches. They descend to drink at dawn and in the late afternoons. In spite of their size, their slow, flapping flight is light and bouncy. The birds fly low over the trees in search of good feeding sites, maintaining contact with loud calls. Adults utter a drawn-out, high pitched yell, and juveniles a growling note. The yellow cheek and tail patches are conspicuous in flight.
• **NEST** A spacious hollow limb or a large cavity in the trunk of a tree, without any lining.
• **DISTRIBUTION** E. and S. Australia from S. Queensland as far as Eyre Peninsula and Tasmania.

yellow face patch

massive bill

long tail with yellow side panels

DISTRIBUTION

Plumage Sexes alike	Habitat	Migration Non-migrant

Family PSITTACIDAE	Species *Cacatua galerita*	Length 14 in (35 cm)

SULFUR-CRESTED COCKATOO

The snowy plumage of this beautiful cockatoo is often soiled, as the bird feeds on the ground in open locations, such as farmers' fields. Large flocks utter screeching calls as they feed on seeds, buds, leaves, and fruits of plants, also digging up roots, tubers, and bulbs with their bills. They visit trees to roost by night, and to rest in the midday heat.
• **NEST** An unlined hollow in a tree.
• **DISTRIBUTION** Parts of New Guinea and N., E., and S. Australia.

erect crest

powerful bill

pure white plumage

short legs with strong feet

short, rounded tail

DISTRIBUTION

Plumage Sexes alike	Habitat	Migration Non-migrant

Family PSITTACIDAE	Species *Eolophus roseicapillus*	Length 14 in (35 cm)

GALAH

A gray and pink
cockatoo with a folding
crest, the Galah is the commonest
species of parrot in Australia. Large flocks
maneuver in the air over open country
or feed on the ground, uttering screeching
contact calls. Their habitats also include
thinly wooded areas, as well as lines of
woodland alongside rivers. The Galah
feeds on grain and other seeds, leaf buds,
and insects. It also digs up roots, tubers,
and invertebrates with its bill. The species
thrives on cereal fields. Its numbers increased
enormously with the spread of wheat growing in
Australia. It has long since come to be considered an
agricultural pest. Galah pairs stay together for life, and
share the tasks of caring for the young. Fledgling
Galahs live together in flocks in the treetops, and
juveniles spend their first two or three years in large
flocks that roam about the country.
• **NEST** A hollow in a branch or trunk of
a tree, lined with a layer of eucalyptus leaves.
• **DISTRIBUTION** Australia, except for wetter coastal areas.

*eastern form •
has a slightly
pinker crest*

**WESTERN
FORM**

DISTRIBUTION

*• pink plumage
extends through
underside to the
belly*

Plumage Sexes alike	Habitat	Migration Non-migrant

Family PSITTACIDAE	Species *Nymphicus hollandicus*	Length 12½ in (32 cm)

COCKATIEL

A strong-flying parrot of arid country,
this species looks like a cockatoo but is
more agile and active in its behavior. The
Cockatiel occurs on open plains, sometimes
with light woodland. Pairs or small flocks are
seen feeding on the ground, camouflaged by
their colors. They pick up fallen seeds of
grasses, weeds, shrubs, and trees, as well as
eating berries and visiting harvested fields
to feed on leftovers of grain. If alarmed while
feeding, the birds fly up, often settling in a dead
tree, where they make themselves inconspicuous
by perching lengthwise on larger branches. Flight
is fast and direct, with strong, regular wingbeats, in
which the large, white wing patches are conspicuous.
Birds maintain contact during flight with a loud, warbled,
double note. In some parts of its range the Cockatiel leads
a nomadic life, traveling about in any direction in search
of areas where food is available. Other populations migrate
between summer and winter ranges.
• **NEST** A hollow in a tree, often near or standing in water.
• **DISTRIBUTION** Australia, except for wetter coastal areas.

*raised •
crest*

*light red
• cheek patch*

DISTRIBUTION

*• white
wing
patch*

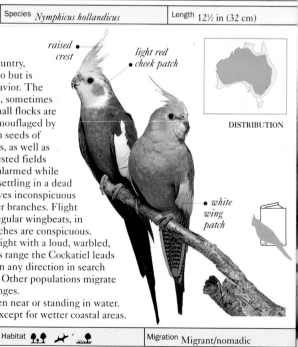

Plumage Sexes differ	Habitat	Migration Migrant/nomadic

Family PSITTACIDAE	Species *Eclectus roratus*	Length 14 in (35 cm)

ECLECTUS PARROT

FEMALE

MALE

There is a startling difference in color between the sexes in this stoutly built parrot species. It is seen mainly in lowland forest, also occurring in more open country where groups of tall trees are found. Birds occur in pairs and small parties, in which males are more in evidence than females. Flocks gather to feed where fruit is ripe, and larger flocks are seen roosting in trees. The diet consists mainly of fruit, but nuts, seeds, buds, blossom, and nectar are also eaten. The flight is strong but rather slow, with deliberate, downward wingbeats and frequent, short glides. During longer journeys, the Eclectus Parrot often flies high above the tree canopy. The call is a raucous, screeching sound.

• **NEST** A hole in the trunk of a tall tree, often situated close to the forest edge.
• **DISTRIBUTION** Islands of E. Indonesia, New Guinea, the Solomon Islands, and extreme N.E. tip of Australia.

DISTRIBUTION

Plumage Sexes differ	Habitat	Migration Non-migrant

Family PSITTACIDAE	Species *Psittrichas fulgidus*	Length 18 in (46 cm)

VULTURINE PARROT

Bald-headedness in birds is usually associated with eating messy foods, and this parrot has a bare face that may possibly be connected with its mainly fruit diet. It eats softer fruits, particularly figs, as well as blossoms and probably sips nectar from flowers. Living in mountain forest, it sits for long periods on high, bare branches that project above the forest foliage. It tends to jump from twig to twig with a quick wing-flick, rather than using the bill to climb about. Birds screech noisily during flight. They fly strongly but slowly, with rapid, shallow wingbeats and the occasional glide.

bare face

red underside

very broad tail

• **NEST** Unknown.
• **DISTRIBUTION** Highland forests of New Guinea.

DISTRIBUTION

Plumage Sexes alike	Habitat	Migration Non-migrant

Family PSITTACIDAE	Species *Polytelis alexandrae*	Length 17½ in (45 cm)

ALEXANDRA'S PARROT

FEMALE

The slender build of this parrot, and the long, narrow wings and tapering tail, are probably adaptations to its nomadic life in the deserts of Australia. Its flight is undulating, with irregular wingbeats, as it moves between the scattered trees of its arid habitat or follows the lines of eucalyptus trees that mark the presence of a creek. It is also seen in acacia scrub. Most of the day is spent at ground level, searching for the small seeds of grasses and other plants that form its diet. Alexandra's Parrot also eats tree blossoms and mistletoe berries. A quiet bird, it has a soft twitter of alarm and a harsher, rattling call. When alarmed, it flies up and perches lengthwise along a branch, making its outline less conspicuous.
• **NEST** An unlined cavity, either in a hollow branch or in the trunk of a tree.
• **DISTRIBUTION** Interior of W. and C. Australia.

slender build

MALE

long wings

tail feathers are graduated in length

long tail for distant flight

DISTRIBUTION

Plumage Sexes differ	Habitat	Migration Nomadic

Family PSITTACIDAE	Species *Platycercus eximius*	Length 12 in (30 cm)

EASTERN ROSELLA

With its bright plumage in the primary colors, and scalelike black markings on the back, this parrot is a well known inhabitant of the farmland and gardens within its range. Pairs or small groups search for a variety of food, including fruit, blossoms, nectar from trees, berries from shrubs, and seeds from the ground. Because it takes fruit from orchards, it is considered an agricultural pest. It also feeds on spilled grain in harvested fields. The Eastern Rosella's calls include loud metallic notes, screeches, and chattering. Its flight is undulating, usually close to the ground, with a final upward swoop to a perch. The male performs a swaggering display in which he walks on the ground, wagging his tail from side to side.
• **NEST** An unlined hollow in a living or dead tree.
• **DISTRIBUTION** S.E. Australia.

DISTRIBUTION

tail feathers are graduated in length

Plumage Sexes differ	Habitat	Migration Non-migrant

| Family PSITTACIDAE | Species *Psephotus chrysopterygius* | Length 10½ in (27 cm) |

GOLDEN-SHOULDERED PARROT

This parrot with its subdued but beautiful coloring occurs only in small areas of semi-arid tropical grassland with scattered trees. Here it feeds on the ground, eating mainly the seeds of native grasses, but also taking other seeds, and sometimes blossoms and buds. Birds take to the trees when alarmed and also rest in the branches in the hottest hours of the day. The Golden-shouldered Parrot has a rapid, undulating flight.
• **NEST** A tunnel and nest chamber are excavated in a tall termite mound on the ground, preferably standing in water. The termites then seal the inner walls.
• **DISTRIBUTION** Grassland areas of Cape York Peninsula in N.E. Australia.
• **REMARK** This species is now seriously endangered owing to the illegal collection of birds for the live bird trade. Numbers had already dwindled, probably because of the introduction of grazing cattle, which ate the native grasses.

golden shoulder patch

long tail with turquoise outer feathers **FEMALE**

DISTRIBUTION

| Plumage Sexes differ | Habitat | Migration Non-migrant |

| Family PSITTACIDAE | Species *Psittacus erithacus* | Length 13 in (33 cm) |

GRAY PARROT

bare skin round the eye

A stocky and short-tailed parrot, this bird occurs in lowland forest and mangroves, where it feeds on seeds, nuts, and oil palm fruits. It lives mainly in the trees, occasionally coming to the ground to feed on maize crops and to obtain grit, which it requires to digest grain. Flight is fast, direct, and high. Birds are noisy, with screeching and whistling calls.
• **NEST** An unlined hole high in a tree.
• **DISTRIBUTION** Tropical W. Africa, the Zaire basin, and N. Angola.
• **REMARK** Because these birds breed well in captivity and are easily taught to "talk," they are popular in the pet trade.

strong bill

stout build

bright red tail

powerful feet

DISTRIBUTION

| Plumage Sexes alike | Habitat | Migration Non-migrant |

| Family PSITTACIDAE | Species *Cyclopsitta diophthalma* | Length 5½ in (14 cm) |

DOUBLE-EYED FIG-PARROT

Despite its bright plumage, this little parrot
is easily overlooked as it feeds quietly in the rain
forest canopy. It forages in pairs or small flocks,
searching for figs and berries, seeds, nectar, and
the grubs of wood-boring insects.
Its flight is fast and direct
with short, shrill calls.
• **NEST** A hole bored by
the birds in a rotten tree.
• **DISTRIBUTION**
New Guinea and isolated
areas in N.E. Australia.

• *bright
face pattern
of male*

FEMALE

DISTRIBUTION

| Plumage Sexes differ | Habitat | Migration Non-migrant |

| Family PSITTACIDAE | Species *Neophema bourkii* | Length 7½ in (19 cm) |

BOURKE'S PARROT

This delicately colored parrot is rarely
seen in the wild. Pairs or small groups
forage nomadically through dry acacia scrub,
feeding on the seeds of grasses and herbaceous
plants. Bourke's Parrot has large eyes
that are adapted to poor light. It drinks at
waterholes after sunset or before dawn, when it is cooler
and there is less danger from predators. The male shows
off his blue underwings and flanks in a raised-wing display.
• **NEST** An unlined hole in a tree trunk.
• **DISTRIBUTION** Interior of Australia.
• **REMARK** This species breeds well in
captivity, and color varieties have been produced.

DISTRIBUTION

• *scaly pattern
on the wings*

FEMALE

| Plumage Sexes differ | Habitat | Migration Non-migrant/nomadic |

| Family PSITTACIDAE | Species *Neophema pulchella* | Length 8 in (20 cm) |

TURQUOISE PARROT

Small flocks of this beautiful species feed
quietly on the ground in grassy areas bordering
dry woodland, taking small seeds, buds, and
leaves. When alarmed, they fly into trees or
bushes. The birds fly swiftly but erratically,
uttering soft, two-note,
whistling calls.
• **NEST** A hollow
in a tree stump,
fencepost, or log
on the ground.
•**DISTRIBUTION**
E. Australia.

FEMALE

• *male
displaying to
the female*

DISTRIBUTION

| Plumage Sexes differ | Habitat | Migration Non-migrant |

| Family PSITTACIDAE | Species *Melopsittacus undulatus* | Length 7 in (18 cm) |

BUDGERIGAR

In the wild this familiar small parrot lives in nomadic flocks that search for seeding grasses and other vegetation in their arid habitat. Flight is strong and rapid. Flocks rarely stay long in one place, but the birds settle and breed in holes available during the brief period of plant growth that follows rain.
• **NEST** An unlined hole or hollow in a tree trunk, a rotten stump, or a fencepost.
• **DISTRIBUTION** Australia.
• **REMARK** Many color variations have been bred in captivity, but the wild bird is always green and yellow.

DISTRIBUTION

| Plumage Sexes alike | Habitat | Migration Partial migrant/nomadic |

| Family PSITTACIDAE | Species *Poicephalus rueppellii* | Length 9 in (23 cm) |

RUEPPELL'S PARROT

Uncommon and inconspicuous, this species betrays its presence with a short, sharp call note. Found in the large trees of dry forest, particularly along watercourses, it feeds at all levels. In addition to prizing insect grubs from rotten wood, it also feeds on berries, green shoots, seeds, and the pods of melon and acacia.
• **NEST** An unlined hole in a tree.
• **DISTRIBUTION** S.W. Africa.

• orange iris of female

DISTRIBUTION

• blue flank patch of female

MALE

| Plumage Sexes differ | Habitat | Migration Non-migrant |

| Family PSITTACIDAE | Species *Agapornis personatus* | Length 5¾ in (14.5 cm) |

MASKED LOVEBIRD

This short-tailed little parrot is usually seen in small flocks. It inhabits seasonally arid grassland with scattered trees and shrubs. Here it feeds mainly on seeds, which it extracts while clinging to plant stems, also taking berries, green buds, and leaves. Flight is fast and direct. Breeding in loose colonies, pairs form a strong bond, perching close together and preening one another (hence the name lovebird).
• **NEST** A bulky, domed nest of thin twigs and bark strips, in a hole in a tree or building.
• **DISTRIBUTION** Tanzanian Highlands. Introduced in coastal Tanzania and S. Kenya.

DISTRIBUTION

• blackish head with white eye ring

• short, rounded wings

| Plumage Sexes alike | Habitat | Migration Non-migrant |

Family PSITTACIDAE	Species *Loriculus galgulus*	Length 4¾ in (12 cm)

BLUE-CROWNED HANGING PARROT

This tiny parrot of open woodland occurs in small, fast-flying flocks. It uses its brush-tipped tongue to gather nectar and also eats flowers, fruit, and seeds, sometimes (though rarely) hanging upside down. Hanging parrots, like some lovebird species, carry nesting material tucked into their rump feathers.
• NEST Tree hole lined with leaves.
• DISTRIBUTION Malay Peninsula, Sumatra, Borneo.

DISTRIBUTION

FEMALE

female lacks red throat patch

Plumage Sexes differ	Habitat 🌳🌳	Migration Non-migrant

Family PSITTACIDAE	Species *Forpus coelestis*	Length 4¾ in (12 cm)

PACIFIC PARROTLET

Not easily seen among the foliage, this tiny, green-faced parrot inhabits secondary forest (regrown after felling) and scrub. Here it feeds mainly on small seeds taken from grasses and other low plants, and on berries from bushes. It usually occurs in flocks or family parties, uttering noisy, chattering calls. Its flight is fast and erratic.
• NEST An unlined hole in a branch, tree trunk, or post.
• DISTRIBUTION W. Ecuador and N.W. Peru.

blue stripe

FEMALE

DISTRIBUTION

short tail

Plumage Sexes differ	Habitat 🌳🌳 ✈	Migration Non-migrant

Family PSITTACIDAE	Species *Brotogeris chiriri*	Length 8½ in (22 cm)

YELLOW-CHEVRONED PARAKEET

This small parrot is hard to detect when resting in foliage. It is more easily noticeable when it moves about and calls shrilly in its forest habitat. It eats seeds, fruits, flowers, and shoots. At times, it forms large flocks, but pairs scatter to breed.
• NEST A hole in a tree trunk, hollow branch, or tree-termite nest.
• DISTRIBUTION From C. Brazil to N. Argentina and Paraguay.

yellow chevron is conspicuous in flight

DISTRIBUTION

tapering tail

outer toe turns backward

Plumage Sexes alike	Habitat 🌳🌳 🌳🌳🌳	Migration Non-migrant

| Family PSITTACIDAE | Species *Psittacula cyanocephala* | Length 13 in (33 cm) |

PLUM-HEADED PARAKEET

The glowing head plumage of
the male Plum-headed Parakeet is
unmistakable. This is an active species and
usually occurs in small flocks that move swiftly
over the treetops with rapid wingbeats, calling
with shrill, screeching notes. It lives in the lower,
warmer zones of hill woodland, and in lowland
forest, particularly where the trees border
cultivated areas. Though normally
wary of feeding at ground
level, it often feeds
on cultivated
grain and rice.
It also eats other
seeds, berries, and other fruits, particularly figs, and takes nectar from
blossoming trees. When not breeding, it gathers in large communal
roosts at night, but breeding pairs usually remain at the nest hole,
guarding it closely against possible takeover by other birds, such
as mynas. Its calls, though shrill, are fairly short and musical.
• **NEST** A cavity in a hollow branch, or an old woodpecker hole.
• **DISTRIBUTION** Much of the Indian subcontinent.

*purple
shoulder
• patch*

DISTRIBUTION

*yellow •
outer tail
feathers*

*long,
fine
• tail*

FEMALE

| Plumage Sexes differ | Habitat 🌳🌳🌳 🌳🌿 🌾 | Migration Non-migrant |

| Family PSITTACIDAE | Species *Psittacula columboides* | Length 15 in (38 cm) |

MALABAR PARAKEET

The subtle combination of hues in the plumage of
this long-tailed parakeet provide camouflage among
leaves and branches. It lives mainly in evergreen and
broadleaved hill woodland, but on the borders of its range
it is sometimes seen in the drier woodland of lower altitudes,
in the company of Plum-headed Parakeets. The Malabar
Parakeet usually travels in family parties or small flocks. Its
flight is rapid and level, with fast wingbeats. The species
gets most of its food from forest trees, taking buds,
nectar and pollen from tree blossoms, nuts, and fruits
such as figs and berries. Where the forest borders
on to farmland, Malabar Parakeets often take
the opportunity to feed on crops such as grain,
vetches, and orchard fruits. This is a noisy
species with a shrill,
harsh, two-syllable call.
  • **NEST** An unlined hole
in the trunk or branch of a
tall tree, situated high
above the ground.
    • **DISTRIBUTION**
S.W. India.

*• black and
turquoise
neck ring*

*long,
fine
• tail*

FEMALE

DISTRIBUTION

| Plumage Sexes differ | Habitat 🌳🌳🌳 🌳🌿 | Migration Non-migrant |

Family PSITTACIDAE	Species *Anodorhynchus hyacinthinus*	Length 39 in (100 cm)

HYACINTH MACAW

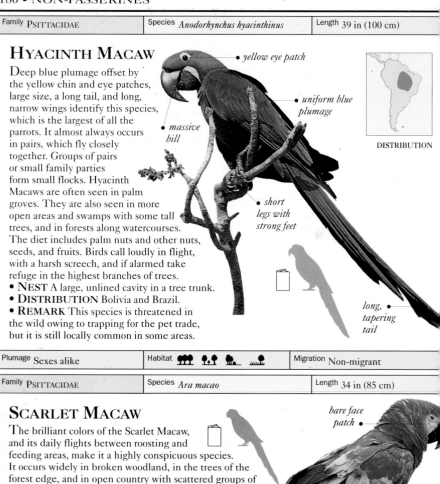

Deep blue plumage offset by the yellow chin and eye patches, large size, a long tail, and long, narrow wings identify this species, which is the largest of all the parrots. It almost always occurs in pairs, which fly closely together. Groups of pairs or small family parties form small flocks. Hyacinth Macaws are often seen in palm groves. They are also seen in more open areas and swamps with some tall trees, and in forests along watercourses. The diet includes palm nuts and other nuts, seeds, and fruits. Birds call loudly in flight, with a harsh screech, and if alarmed take refuge in the highest branches of trees.
• **NEST** A large, unlined cavity in a tree trunk.
• **DISTRIBUTION** Bolivia and Brazil.
• **REMARK** This species is threatened in the wild owing to trapping for the pet trade, but it is still locally common in some areas.

yellow eye patch

uniform blue plumage

massive bill

short legs with strong feet

DISTRIBUTION

long, tapering tail

Plumage Sexes alike	Habitat	Migration Non-migrant

Family PSITTACIDAE	Species *Ara macao*	Length 34 in (85 cm)

SCARLET MACAW

The brilliant colors of the Scarlet Macaw, and its daily flights between roosting and feeding areas, make it a highly conspicuous species. It occurs widely in broken woodland, in the trees of the forest edge, and in open country with scattered groups of tall trees. Pairs keep together, and flocks are composed of pairs or small parties. The diet consists of a variety of fruits, nuts, and seeds. In areas of human settlement, the Scarlet Macaw has become scarce because of trapping. The birds are usually silent when feeding, but utter harsh calls in flight and screech when alarmed.
• **NEST** A cavity in the trunk of a forest tree.
• **DISTRIBUTION** Mexico to Brazil and Bolivia.

bare face patch

yellow wing patch

DISTRIBUTION

long, tapering tail

Plumage Sexes alike	Habitat	Migration Non-migrant

Family PSITTACIDAE	Species *Aratinga solstitialis*	Length 12 in (30 cm)

SUN PARAKEET

With its vivid, golden-orange head and neck, green wings, and scarlet belly, the Sun Parakeet is the most eye-catching of the smaller South American parrots. Juveniles have more green in their plumage and stand out less among the tree foliage. This is a relatively uncommon species, numerous only in certain areas in hot, lowland country. Habitats include open forest, savanna (tropical grassland) with scattered trees, and palm groves. Sun Parakeets usually occur in small parties, but tend to congregate in larger numbers where food is abundant. The birds feed on larger fruits, particularly figs, and also on berries, nuts, seeds, and probably on tree blossoms. Feeding takes place almost entirely in the trees, where flocks are seen clambering among the twigs. The birds are made even more noticeable by their shrill, two-syllable shrieks, which they frequently utter either when they are in the trees or during flight. The flight is rapid and direct.
• **NEST** A hole in the trunk of a palm tree.
• **DISTRIBUTION** S.E. Venezuela, the Guianas, and N.E. Brazil.

• *bare eye ring*
• *golden-orange head and neck*

JUVENILE

• *green secondary feathers*

• *blue tips of flight feathers*

DISTRIBUTION

Plumage Sexes alike	Habitat	Migration Non-migrant

Family PSITTACIDAE	Species *Cyanoliseus patagonus*	Length 18 in (46 cm)

PATAGONIAN PARAKEET

This parrot has adapted successfully to life in open grassland. It is one of the very few parrots that nest in a burrow in the ground. Colonies of burrows are dug into cliff faces, often overlooking a river or the sea. Small parties feed on or near ground level, taking seeds and small fruits, roosting either in their burrows or aboveground on trees or telephone wires.
• **NEST** A burrow up to 10 ft (3 m) long with an unlined cavity at the end, dug by the birds in a bank or cliff face.
• **DISTRIBUTION** Breeds in Argentina and Chile. Irregularly winters as far north as N. Argentina and possibly Uruguay.

• *bare eye ring*

reversed
• *outer toe*

• *bronze sheen on the wings*

DISTRIBUTION

Plumage Sexes alike	Habitat	Migration Partial migrant

Family PSITTACIDAE	Species *Myiopsitta monachus*	Length 8½ in (22 cm)

MONK PARAKEET

A stout little parrot living in colonies in open woodland, the Monk
Parakeet is conspicuous for its lively, noisy behavior. Besides
breeding in their colony, the birds use it as a communal roosting
place, which makes it the permanent center for all their
activity. From here they disperse daily to feed, usually
on open ground near trees. They eat seeds, nuts, fruit,
buds, and blossoms and raid citrus orchards. Activity is
accompanied by constant, short shrieks and chattering.
• **NEST** An unlined, domed nest made of twigs,
preferably thorny, with a low, upward-slanting
entrance. Each pair builds its nest up against
the next, forming a large colony in a tree.
• **DISTRIBUTION** S.W. and S. Brazil,
and through Paraguay to N. Argentina
and Uruguay. Introduced
in E. North America,
the Bahamas, and
Puerto Rico.

*male
has a
scaly
breast
pattern*

*bluish •
flight
feathers*

FEMALE

DISTRIBUTION

Plumage Sexes differ slightly	Habitat	Migration Non-migrant

Family PSITTACIDAE	Species *Pionus menstruus*	Length 11 in (28 cm)

BLUE-HEADED PARROT

Large-headed, short-tailed, and solidly built, this is
a parrot of heavily forested areas, living mainly in
the treetops. It forms flocks when not breeding, and
roosts in large numbers in the trees. Birds often fly
for some distance daily to and from their roosting
places, usually traveling in strong, fast flight high
above the trees. In flight, they are
noisy, with loud, harsh screams and
high pitched, screeching calls. After
settling to feed in the trees, they
become silent. The diet consists
of fruit, seeds, and blossoms, mostly
taken from trees, but birds sometimes visit
farmland to take crops such
as corn or bananas.
• **NEST** A bare, natural
hollow, extended by the birds,
in a dead or living tree, often
high above ground level.
• **DISTRIBUTION**
From Costa Rica south as
far as Bolivia and S.E. Brazil.

*small,
black cheek
patch*

*red
undertail
coverts*

JUVENILE

DISTRIBUTION

Plumage Sexes alike	Habitat	Migration Non-migrant

| Family PSITTACIDAE | Species *Amazona oratrix* | Length 14 in (35 cm) |

YELLOW-HEADED PARROT

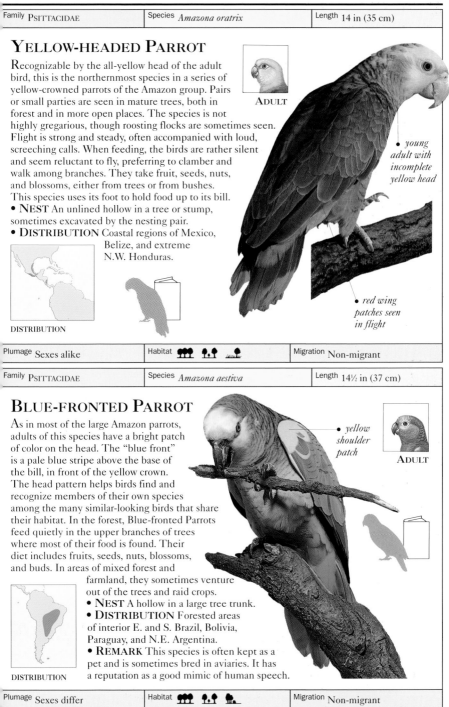

Recognizable by the all-yellow head of the adult bird, this is the northernmost species in a series of yellow-crowned parrots of the Amazon group. Pairs or small parties are seen in mature trees, both in forest and in more open places. The species is not highly gregarious, though roosting flocks are sometimes seen. Flight is strong and steady, often accompanied with loud, screeching calls. When feeding, the birds are rather silent and seem reluctant to fly, preferring to clamber and walk among branches. They take fruit, seeds, nuts, and blossoms, either from trees or from bushes. This species uses its foot to hold food up to its bill.
• **NEST** An unlined hollow in a tree or stump, sometimes excavated by the nesting pair.
• **DISTRIBUTION** Coastal regions of Mexico, Belize, and extreme N.W. Honduras.

ADULT

• *young adult with incomplete yellow head*

• *red wing patches seen in flight*

DISTRIBUTION

| Plumage Sexes alike | Habitat | Migration Non-migrant |

| Family PSITTACIDAE | Species *Amazona aestiva* | Length 14½ in (37 cm) |

BLUE-FRONTED PARROT

As in most of the large Amazon parrots, adults of this species have a bright patch of color on the head. The "blue front" is a pale blue stripe above the base of the bill, in front of the yellow crown. The head pattern helps birds find and recognize members of their own species among the many similar-looking birds that share their habitat. In the forest, Blue-fronted Parrots feed quietly in the upper branches of trees where most of their food is found. Their diet includes fruits, seeds, nuts, blossoms, and buds. In areas of mixed forest and farmland, they sometimes venture out of the trees and raid crops.
• **NEST** A hollow in a large tree trunk.
• **DISTRIBUTION** Forested areas of interior E. and S. Brazil, Bolivia, Paraguay, and N.E. Argentina.
• **REMARK** This species is often kept as a pet and is sometimes bred in aviaries. It has a reputation as a good mimic of human speech.

• *yellow shoulder patch*

ADULT

DISTRIBUTION

| Plumage Sexes differ | Habitat | Migration Non-migrant |

Family PSITTACIDAE	Species *Amazona guildingii*	Length 16 in (40 cm)

ST. VINCENT PARROT

This large and impressive island parrot occurs in two color phases (*see p. 13*). One phase is mainly green, the other bronze, and both have patches of blue, yellow, and orange. The species lives in rain forest growing on hill slopes, where it feeds in the treetops on fruits, seeds, and blossoms. Pairs and small families form small flocks. St. Vincent Parrots fly strongly and directly with rapid, jerky wingbeats, uttering loud, harsh, screeching cries.
• **NEST** A cavity in a large branch or tree trunk.
• **DISTRIBUTION**
The island of St. Vincent in the E. Caribbean.
• **REMARK** This is an endangered species with a very small population. Its survival depends on conservation of its rain forest habitat.

scaly-edged • nape feathers

DISTRIBUTION

GREEN PHASE

BRONZE PHASE

• yellow and orange wing patches are revealed in flight

• yellow tail tip

Plumage Sexes alike	Habitat 🌳🌳	Migration Non-migrant

Family PSITTACIDAE	Species *Deroptyus accipitrinus*	Length 14 in (35 cm)

RED-FAN PARROT

The shaggy, elongated crest feathers and broad tail of this parrot make it instantly identifiable, particularly when the bird is excited and spreads its crest into a broad fan framing the face. At other times the red feathers are sleeked back, giving the head a flat-crowned look. This, with its hooked bill and staring eye, explains why it is also known as the Hawk-headed Parrot. The species usually occurs in pairs or flocks. Its three main habitats are dense tropical forest, the more open type of forest that occurs on ridges of sandy ground, and savanna (tropical grassland) with scattered trees. Red-fan Parrots feed quietly among the foliage on fruit, seeds, and nuts, often flying between the trees with outspread tails. Individuals, and probably pairs and families, roost in tree holes. Calling birds utter wailing sounds, "chacking" notes, and shrieks.
• **NEST** An abandoned woodpecker hole in a tree.
• **DISTRIBUTION** From Colombia and Venezuela through N. Peru and the Guianas into Brazil.

crest raised • in a fan

blue-edged breast • feathers

long, broad • tail

DISTRIBUTION

Plumage Sexes alike	Habitat 🌳🌳 🌴 🌿	Migration Non-migrant

Family PSITTACIDAE	Species *Nestor notabilis*	Length 19 in (48 cm)

KEA

Large and heavily built with bright orange underwings and a long point on its bill, the Kea is a mountain parrot. It lives in alpine scrub, in grassland, and at the forest edge in areas with winter snows. The Kea spends most of its time foraging on the ground. It is bold and inquisitive in its behavior, prepared to look for new food sources and to explore around houses and farms. With its long bill, it probes the ground for insects and grubs and tears into carrion. Other foods are buds, leaves, fruits, seeds, nectar, and blossoms. Keas fly powerfully and wheel and circle in the strong mountain winds, calling with the raucous "kee-ah" that provides the name. Young birds form flocks, but adult males live in territories and are polygamous, with up to four mates.

• **NEST** A rock crevice or cavity under a rock, among tree roots, or in a log, lined with moss, lichen, leaves, twigs, and chewed wood.

• **DISTRIBUTION** Mountains on South Island of New Zealand.

dark feather • edges

DISTRIBUTION

• glossy green wings

strong legs of a • walking bird

Plumage Sexes alike	Habitat 🔺 🐾 🌳 ⚓	Migration Non-migrant

Family PSITTACIDAE	Species *Strigops habroptilus*	Length 25 in (63 cm)

KAKAPO

This creeping, nocturnal bird is unique among parrots. Camouflaged by its mottled plumage, it lives on the ground in groups, roosting by day in holes and emerging to feed at night. Walking slowly, it follows a network of paths and clambers into bushes and trees to find food. It eats pollen-bearing cones from conifer trees, flowers, fruits, and seeds, and also chews green plants for their juices. Although it is unable to fly, it can make short, downhill glides. Breeding males gather at mating grounds called "leks," each digging a hollow and advertising for females with a booming noise.

• **NEST** A cavity in a burrow, in a low or fallen tree trunk, or in a crevice.

• **DISTRIBUTION** New Zealand, in south of South Island, on Stewart and other islands.

• **REMARK** Threatened with extinction by introduced rats and stoats. Survivors have been transferred to predator-free islands.

• stout build

mottled camouflage plumage •

DISTRIBUTION

Plumage Sexes alike	Habitat 🌳🌳 🌲	Migration Non-migrant

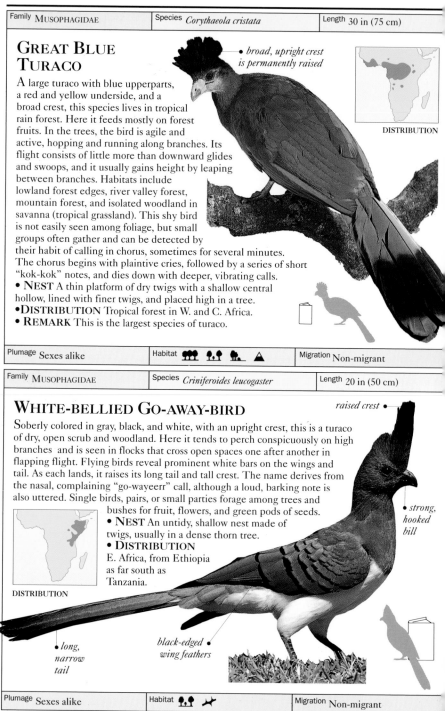

Family MUSOPHAGIDAE	Species *Corythaeola cristata*	Length 30 in (75 cm)

GREAT BLUE TURACO

• *broad, upright crest is permanently raised*

A large turaco with blue upperparts, a red and yellow underside, and a broad crest, this species lives in tropical rain forest. Here it feeds mostly on forest fruits. In the trees, the bird is agile and active, hopping and running along branches. Its flight consists of little more than downward glides and swoops, and it usually gains height by leaping between branches. Habitats include lowland forest edges, river valley forest, mountain forest, and isolated woodland in savanna (tropical grassland). This shy bird is not easily seen among foliage, but small groups often gather and can be detected by their habit of calling in chorus, sometimes for several minutes. The chorus begins with plaintive cries, followed by a series of short "kok-kok" notes, and dies down with deeper, vibrating calls.

• **NEST** A thin platform of dry twigs with a shallow central hollow, lined with finer twigs, and placed high in a tree.

• **DISTRIBUTION** Tropical forest in W. and C. Africa.

• **REMARK** This is the largest species of turaco.

DISTRIBUTION

Plumage Sexes alike	Habitat 🌳 🌿 🌿 ⛰	Migration Non-migrant

Family MUSOPHAGIDAE	Species *Criniferoides leucogaster*	Length 20 in (50 cm)

WHITE-BELLIED GO-AWAY-BIRD

raised crest •

Soberly colored in gray, black, and white, with an upright crest, this is a turaco of dry, open scrub and woodland. Here it tends to perch conspicuously on high branches and is seen in flocks that cross open spaces one after another in flapping flight. Flying birds reveal prominent white bars on the wings and tail. As each lands, it raises its long tail and tall crest. The name derives from the nasal, complaining "go-wayeerr" call, although a loud, barking note is also uttered. Single birds, pairs, or small parties forage among trees and bushes for fruit, flowers, and green pods of seeds.

• **NEST** An untidy, shallow nest made of twigs, usually in a dense thorn tree.

• **DISTRIBUTION** E. Africa, from Ethiopia as far south as Tanzania.

• *strong, hooked bill*

DISTRIBUTION

• *long, narrow tail*

black-edged • *wing feathers*

Plumage Sexes alike	Habitat 🌿 ✈	Migration Non-migrant

Family MUSOPHAGIDAE	Species *Tauraco erythrolophus*	Length 16 in (40 cm)

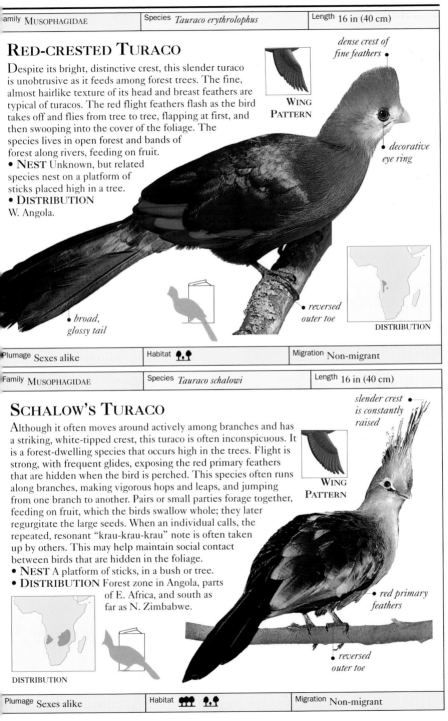

RED-CRESTED TURACO

Despite its bright, distinctive crest, this slender turaco is unobtrusive as it feeds among forest trees. The fine, almost hairlike texture of its head and breast feathers are typical of turacos. The red flight feathers flash as the bird takes off and flies from tree to tree, flapping at first, and then swooping into the cover of the foliage. The species lives in open forest and bands of forest along rivers, feeding on fruit.
• NEST Unknown, but related species nest on a platform of sticks placed high in a tree.
• DISTRIBUTION W. Angola.

dense crest of fine feathers •

WING PATTERN

• decorative eye ring

• reversed outer toe

• broad, glossy tail

DISTRIBUTION

Plumage Sexes alike	Habitat	Migration Non-migrant

Family MUSOPHAGIDAE	Species *Tauraco schalowi*	Length 16 in (40 cm)

SCHALOW'S TURACO

Although it often moves around actively among branches and has a striking, white-tipped crest, this turaco is often inconspicuous. It is a forest-dwelling species that occurs high in the trees. Flight is strong, with frequent glides, exposing the red primary feathers that are hidden when the bird is perched. This species often runs along branches, making vigorous hops and leaps, and jumping from one branch to another. Pairs or small parties forage together, feeding on fruit, which the birds swallow whole; they later regurgitate the large seeds. When an individual calls, the repeated, resonant "krau-krau-krau" note is often taken up by others. This may help maintain social contact between birds that are hidden in the foliage.
• NEST A platform of sticks, in a bush or tree.
• DISTRIBUTION Forest zone in Angola, parts of E. Africa, and south as far as N. Zimbabwe.

slender crest • is constantly raised

WING PATTERN

• red primary feathers

• reversed outer toe

DISTRIBUTION

Plumage Sexes alike	Habitat	Migration Non-migrant

Family CUCULIDAE	Species *Clamator glandarius*	Length 15 in (38 cm)

GREAT SPOTTED CUCKOO

Hunting in trees and bushes for its prey, this cuckoo eats hairy caterpillars that most other birds find distasteful. It also takes other insects, particularly grasshoppers and locusts, and other small creatures. Usually silent, it becomes noisy when breeding, with a song that is partly a harsh chatter and partly a gobbling sound. After hatching, the young cuckoo imitates the calls of the nestlings of the host species, begging for food from the parent. Before long it outgrows the other young birds, though it does not eject them from the nest.
• **NEST** This bird is a nest parasite. A single egg is laid in the nest of a magpie, crow, or (in South Africa) one of several species of starling.
• **DISTRIBUTION** Two populations: one breeds in S. Europe and winters in W. Africa; the other breeds in South Africa and winters in tropical Africa.

• *black head of juvenile*

ADULT

chestnut wing patch of juvenile

spotted plumage retained by adult birds

long tail with tapering tip

DISTRIBUTION

Plumage Sexes alike	Habitat	Migration Migrant

Family CUCULIDAE	Species *Cuculus canorus*	Length 13 in (33 cm)

COMMON CUCKOO

The loud "cuckoo" call of the male gives this species, and the family, its name. It feeds on large, hairy caterpillars and other small invertebrates. The female watches a pair of small birds building their nest; then, at an opportune moment, she visits it, removes and often eats an egg, and lays one of her own in its place.
• **NEST** This bird is a nest parasite. A single egg is laid in the nest of an insect-eating bird which rears the young cuckoo.
• **DISTRIBUTION** Breeds in Eurasia, east to E. Siberia and south to N. Africa. Winters in South Africa and Asia.

JUVENILE

broad tail with white spots

• *small feet*

DISTRIBUTION

Plumage Sexes alike	Habitat	Migration Migrant

Family CUCULIDAE	Species *Chrysococcyx caprius*	Length 7 in (18 cm)

DIDRIC CUCKOO

Common in a variety of habitats from open forest to savanna, this small, glossy green-and-white cuckoo feeds mainly on caterpillars. Its name refers to the plaintive "deea-deea-deedaric" call used by males when breeding. The male displays with shivering wings and spread tail, calling continuously.
• **NEST** A nest parasite; the female lays a single egg in the nest of a passerine bird, preferring those of weaver and sparrow species. The young cuckoo sometimes pushes the chicks of the host bird out of the nest.
• **DISTRIBUTION** Africa south of the Sahara; S.W. Arabian peninsula.

• *orange eye ring*

• *broken white stripe across the eye*

• *glossy bronze-green plumage*

• *barred flanks*

• *white bars on outer tail feathers revealed when spread*

FEMALE

DISTRIBUTION

Plumage Sexes differ slightly	Habitat	Migration Migrant

Family CUCULIDAE	Species *Scythrops novaehollandiae*	Length 26 in (65 cm)

CHANNEL-BILLED CUCKOO

With its huge, powerful bill, long wings, and long tail, in flight this cuckoo resembles a hornbill (*see pp. 230–231*). It is most active at dusk and dawn and sometimes flies at night. Loud, raucous calls are uttered in flight. This is a bird of the treetops, feeding mainly on fruit such as figs but also taking insects, and sometimes eggs and small nestlings.
• **NEST** Parasitizes nests of currawongs, butcherbirds, crows, and Australasian Magpies (*see pp. 383–384*).
• **DISTRIBUTION** Breeds in N. and E. Australia. Winters in New Guinea and the island of Sulawesi in Indonesia.

JUVENILE

DISTRIBUTION

• *dark-tipped wing feathers*

• *mottled pattern of sunlight and shadow from foliage*

• *white tail tip*

Plumage Sexes alike	Habitat	Migration Migrant

Family CUCULIDAE	Species *Coccyzus erythropthalmus*	Length 12 in (30 cm)

BLACK-BILLED CUCKOO

This is one of the many cuckoos that do not parasitize other species'
nests. Instead, pairs build their own nests and rear their own
young, with both parents sharing the task of feeding the
nestlings. A bird of tree foliage and streamside
thickets, it runs and leaps easily among the
branches. Caterpillars are an important part
of the diet for both adults and young.

• **NEST** A cup nest of twigs and
stems, lined with grasses and leaves,
placed low in a bush or tree.

• **DISTRIBUTION** E. USA
and S. Canada. Winters in
South America.

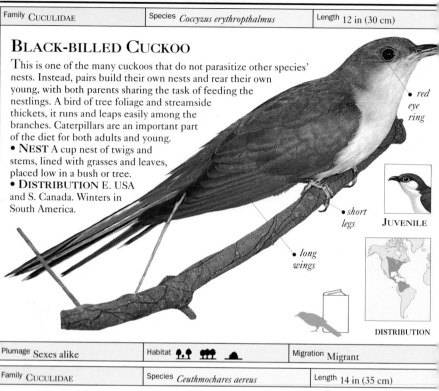

• *red eye ring*

• *short legs*   JUVENILE

• *long wings*

DISTRIBUTION

Plumage Sexes alike	Habitat	Migration Migrant

Family CUCULIDAE	Species *Ceuthmochares aereus*	Length 14 in (35 cm)

YELLOWBILL

Agile and active, this slender, long-tailed cuckoo hides in dense, leafy thickets and
lives in forest and clusters of scrubby vegetation in grassland. Often occurring in
pairs, it takes small animals such as insects,
slugs, and tree frogs. It sometimes joins
hunting flocks of mixed passerines.
Although it is evasive and rarely
seen it can be detected by its
harsh, low pitched "chaaa."

• **NEST** This cuckoo does
not parasitize nests of other
birds. A saucer of sticks is
built in a tree fork.

• **DISTRIBUTION**
Africa south of the Sahara.

DISTRIBUTION

Plumage Sexes alike	Habitat	Migration Non-migrant

Family CUCULIDAE	Species *Crotophaga ani*	Length 14½ in (37 cm)

SMOOTH-BILLED ANI

With a short, squat body and heavy head, this disheveled-looking bird does not resemble other cuckoos. It has a deep, blunt bill and a long, wedge-shaped tail that droops and wags as though loosely attached. Despite its ungainly appearance it walks and runs well, but its flight is poorly developed, consisting of a few rapid flaps interspersed with short glides. Feeding mainly on the ground, it takes grasshoppers and other insects, and follows cattle to catch the insects they disturb. The bird may also settle on the back of an animal and pick ticks off its skin. The species is highly sociable and feeds in small groups, communicating with a long, whining note. When resting, either on the ground or in bushes and small trees, the birds huddle together, sometimes preening each other. Breeding is loosely communal. Several pairs cooperate to build a nest, several females lay their eggs in it, and the whole group shares in incubation and in rearing the nestlings. The young often stay with the group and help to rear subsequent broods.
• **NEST** This bird does not parasitize the nests of other species. A cup nest of coarse twigs is made, with a lining, in a thorny tree.
• **DISTRIBUTION** From S. USA (C. Florida) south through Central and South America to W. Ecuador and N. Argentina. Also in the West Indies.

DISTRIBUTION

Plumage Sexes alike	Habitat	Migration Non-migrant

Family CUCULIDAE	Species *Guira guira*	Length 14½ in (37 cm)

GUIRA CUCKOO

Almost always encountered in small groups of 8–10 individuals, this is a highly sociable species. It lives on dry, grassy plains with widely scattered trees. At night it roosts in flocks that perch closely together on the branch of a tree. Resting in daytime in a similar fashion, the birds huddle in a tight knot, occasionally preening each other. Flight consists of a labored series of flaps and swoops on short, rounded wings, with a pronounced, dipping swoop when landing. Birds are seen flying one after another from bush to bush. Feeding occurs mostly on the ground, but occasionally groups of birds forage in trees. A variety of prey is taken, including worms, insects, small lizards, and mice, as well as eggs and nestlings. The Guira Cuckoo nests communally, with a number of pairs building the nest and several females laying their eggs in it. The group cooperates to incubate and rear the young.
• **NEST** This bird does not parasitize the nests of other species. A primitive structure of twigs is built in a tree.
• **DISTRIBUTION** South America in Bolivia, Paraguay, Brazil, and Argentina.

• *birds sun-bathing with back feathers fluffed*

• *loose, untidy plumage*

long • *tail*

DISTRIBUTION

Plumage Sexes alike	Habitat	Migration Non-migrant

| Family CUCULIDAE | Species *Geococcyx californianus* | Length 23 in (58 cm) |

GREATER ROADRUNNER

With its long legs and narrow tail, this ground-dwelling cuckoo is
famous for its ability to run swiftly. It lives in arid, sparsely vegetated
country and is often seen hurrying across open spaces, with head and
tail extended horizontally, either to snatch up prey or avoid enemies.
Although it can fly, it crouches or relies on its speed when alarmed.
Prey items include insects, lizards, scorpions, and young snakes. Pairs
hold permanent territories, calling with a series of cooing notes.
• **NEST** Not a nest parasite; a cup nest is made, lined
with debris, and placed in a cactus or thorn bush.
• **DISTRIBUTION** From S.W. USA
to C. Mexico.

• *shaggy crest*

• *bare blue stripe behind the eye*

• *long, narrow tail provides balance when running and maneuvering rapidly on the ground*

short, rounded, little-used wings

• *long legs for fast running*

DISTRIBUTION

| Plumage Sexes alike | Habitat | Migration Non-migrant |

| Family CUCULIDAE | Species *Carpococcyx renauldi* | Length 27 in (68 cm) |

CORAL-BILLED GROUND-CUCKOO

This long-legged, long-tailed bird, with its compact build, is adapted
for ground-dwelling in forest conditions. It lives in warm, moist forest,
secondary forest (areas where the trees have regrown after forest clearance),
and scrub, in lowlands and hills.

Within these habitats
it prefers areas of thick vegetation,
running fast to escape when danger
threatens. An evasive bird, it is difficult to
observe, and is thinly distributed across its range.
It eats a wide range of small creatures. Calls are used
to maintain contact between
individuals; pairs are heard "duetting"
with a harsh, deep, whistling note.
• **NEST** Not a nest parasite; a cup
nest of twigs and leaves is made, in
a tree or occasionally on the ground.
• **DISTRIBUTION** From
N.W. Thailand to S. Vietnam.

• *long legs of a ground dweller*

DISTRIBUTION

| Plumage Sexes alike | Habitat | Migration Non-migrant |

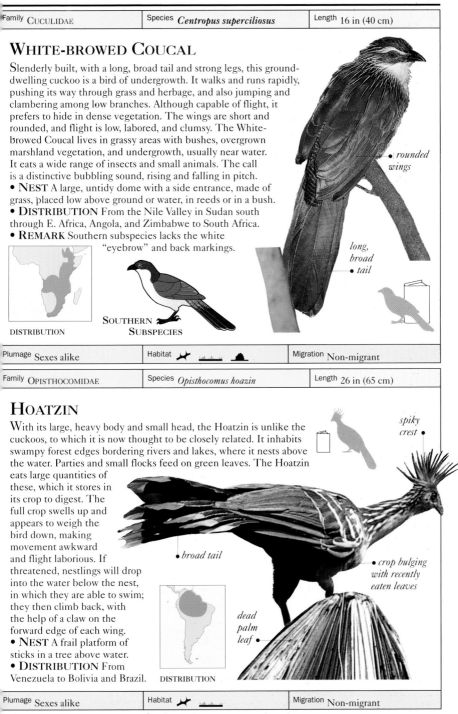

| Family CUCULIDAE | Species *Centropus superciliosus* | Length 16 in (40 cm) |

WHITE-BROWED COUCAL

Slenderly built, with a long, broad tail and strong legs, this ground-dwelling cuckoo is a bird of undergrowth. It walks and runs rapidly, pushing its way through grass and herbage, and also jumping and clambering among low branches. Although capable of flight, it prefers to hide in dense vegetation. The wings are short and rounded, and flight is low, labored, and clumsy. The White-browed Coucal lives in grassy areas with bushes, overgrown marshland vegetation, and undergrowth, usually near water. It eats a wide range of insects and small animals. The call is a distinctive bubbling sound, rising and falling in pitch.

• **NEST** A large, untidy dome with a side entrance, made of grass, placed low above ground or water, in reeds or in a bush.
• **DISTRIBUTION** From the Nile Valley in Sudan south through E. Africa, Angola, and Zimbabwe to South Africa.
• **REMARK** Southern subspecies lacks the white "eyebrow" and back markings.

rounded wings

long, broad tail

DISTRIBUTION

SOUTHERN SUBSPECIES

| Plumage Sexes alike | Habitat | Migration Non-migrant |

| Family OPISTHOCOMIDAE | Species *Opisthocomus hoazin* | Length 26 in (65 cm) |

HOATZIN

With its large, heavy body and small head, the Hoatzin is unlike the cuckoos, to which it is now thought to be closely related. It inhabits swampy forest edges bordering rivers and lakes, where it nests above the water. Parties and small flocks feed on green leaves. The Hoatzin eats large quantities of these, which it stores in its crop to digest. The full crop swells up and appears to weigh the bird down, making movement awkward and flight laborious. If threatened, nestlings will drop into the water below the nest, in which they are able to swim; they then climb back, with the help of a claw on the forward edge of each wing.

• **NEST** A frail platform of sticks in a tree above water.
• **DISTRIBUTION** From Venezuela to Bolivia and Brazil.

spiky crest

broad tail

crop bulging with recently eaten leaves

dead palm leaf

DISTRIBUTION

| Plumage Sexes alike | Habitat | Migration Non-migrant |

Family TYTONIDAE	Species *Tyto alba*	Length 16 in (40 cm)

BARN OWL

This bird can be recognized by the "heart shape" formed by the pair of facial disks around its eyes. It has an easy, drifting style of flight, and hunts by flying low over open ground, or by watching from a perch before swooping on silent wings to seize prey. The species can hunt in total darkness, locating prey by sound. Mice, rats, and any small animals that move are eaten. The best known call is a long, quavering screech uttered in flight, but nesting birds also make snoring, hissing calls.

• **NEST** An unlined scrape or cavity in a tree hole, or in a barn or other building.

• **DISTRIBUTION** Much of North and South America, Europe, Africa, and through S. and S.E. Asia to Australia.

• **REMARK** Color phases (*see p. 13*) range from light to dark.

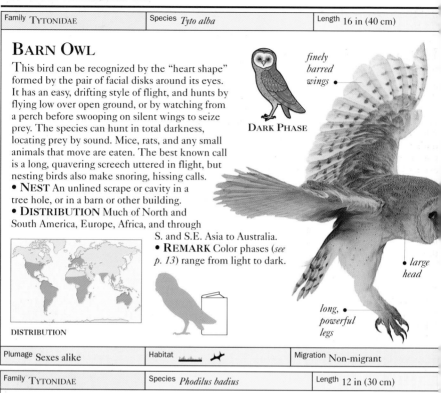

finely barred wings

DARK PHASE

large head

long, powerful legs

DISTRIBUTION

Plumage Sexes alike	Habitat	Migration Non-migrant

Family TYTONIDAE	Species *Phodilus badius*	Length 12 in (30 cm)

ORIENTAL BAY-OWL

A bird of thick forest, the Oriental Bay-Owl has a distinctive oval face but is difficult to observe as it hunts at night among dense branches and foliage. The facial disks are narrow, and the inner side of each disk projects forward from the head at the top. This results in two blunt projections of feathers at the upper end of the forehead, equivalent to the ear tufts of some "typical" owls (*see pp. 195–203*). The Oriental Bay-Owl occurs in dense forest and secondary forest (areas where trees have regrown after forest clearance). By day it roosts in a hole in a tree, becoming active at night, when it often relies on its hearing to hunt in complete darkness. The short, rounded wings and square tail enable it to maneuver through close-set young trees, and it uses its strong claws to cling to vertical stems, one foot gripping high above the other. A variety of prey is taken, including large insects, frogs, lizards, small birds, and mammals. The call is a rising phrase of musical whistles.

• **NEST** A cavity in the trunk or branch of a tree.

• **DISTRIBUTION** N. India, Sri Lanka, and through Asia to China, Borneo, and Java.

narrow facial disk

foot holds prey

DISTRIBUTION

Plumage Sexes alike	Habitat	Migration Non-migrant

Family STRIGIDAE	Species *Otus scops*	Length 8 in (20 cm)

EURASIAN SCOPS-OWL

The streaked plumage of this tiny owl provides camouflage as the bird roosts by day. If alarmed, the bird stands motionless and erects its ear tufts vertically, relying on its ability to blend into tree bark for protection. A bird of warm, dry climates, it hunts in open spaces, and rests in scattered trees during the day. Flight is rapid and level, with regular wingbeats. When hunting, the Scops-Owl swoops down from its perch to seize prey with its feet, sometimes landing beside it first, taking insects, earthworms, amphibians, lizards, and small birds. Sometimes it catches moths in midair. This species is predominantly a night hunter, but males also hunt during the day when the females are incubating eggs or tending the young. The call is a penetrating "tyu" note, the female's note being a little higher in pitch than the male's.
• **NEST** An unlined hole or cavity in a tree.
• **DISTRIBUTION** S. Europe east to Russia and W. China. Winters in N. and C. Africa and N. India.
• **REMARK** In this species there are two distinct color phases (*see p. 13*): gray and rufous brown.

DISTRIBUTION

RUFOUS PHASE

• *upright alarm posture, with feathers sleeked down*

Plumage Sexes alike	Habitat	Migration Migrant

Family STRIGIDAE	Species *Otus leucotis*	Length 11 in (28 cm)

WHITE-FACED SCOPS-OWL

ear tufts • not fully raised

This small owl can be identified by its white face with gray ear tufts and large, fiery-orange eyes. The plumage is mottled, providing camouflage against tree bark when the bird roosts. When alarmed, it freezes into an upright posture with sleeked-down feathers and erect ear tufts, resembling a broken-ended branch. If provoked into a reaction, it opens its eyes wide and snaps aggressively with its bill. The White-faced Scops-Owl is a bird of savanna (tropical and subtropical grassland) and thorn scrub, also inhabiting open forest. It is a nocturnal hunter, taking large insects, small rodents, and small birds caught while roosting. The male utters a two-note hoot; the female has a quavering trill.

large eyes with • orange irises

• **NEST** An unlined hole in a tree, or an old nest of various birds such as a turacos (*see pp. 186–187*), some sparrowhawks (*see p. 94*), or crows (*see pp 394–395*). Some pairs nest on the ground.
• **DISTRIBUTION** Africa south of the Sahara.

DISTRIBUTION

Plumage Sexes alike	Habitat	Migration Non-migrant

Family STRIGIDAE	Species *Otus asio*	Length 8½ in (22 cm)

EASTERN SCREECH-OWL

This small woodland owl roosts in tree cavities or thick foliage and hunts prey including insects, birds, and squirrels. Its calls are a descending series of quavering whistles, or the wailing sounds to which the name refers, or a long, sharp trill.
• **NEST** An unlined cavity in a tree.
• **DISTRIBUTION** From S. Canada through E., C., and S. USA to N.E. Mexico.
• **REMARKS** This species has two distinct color phases (*see p. 13*): rufous and gray. This is one of the many owls that possess earlike tufts, which can be raised or lowered; they express a bird's mood, e.g. whether excited or at rest.

• lowered ear tufts

GRAY PHASE

DISTRIBUTION

Plumage Sexes alike	Habitat	Migration Non-migrant

Family STRIGIDAE	Species *Pulsatrix perspicillata*	Length 18 in (46 cm)

SPECTACLED OWL

A large and roundheaded forest owl, this species has an unmistakable face pattern that accounts for its name. Even more striking is the white-bodied juvenile bird, with its black face-mask. The species lives in such habitats as thick rain forest, open woodland, and riverside bands of trees, but it is nocturnal and rarely seen. Its most typical call is a series of rapid, low pitched hoots. The Spectacled Owl roosts by day on a branch and hunts at night, being most active on moonlit nights. Prey includes insects, tree frogs, birds, mammals, and, in mangrove forest, crabs.
• **NEST** A large hole or cavity in a tree.
• **DISTRIBUTION** From Mexico south as far as N. Argentina, Paraguay, and S. Brazil.

JUVENILE

feet have two • toes forward, two toes back

DISTRIBUTION

Plumage Sexes alike	Habitat	Migration Non-migrant

| Family STRIGIDAE | Species *Bubo virginianus* | Length 22 in (55 cm) |

GREAT HORNED OWL

Largest and fiercest of the American owls, with large ear tufts and a finely barred breast, this species occurs in a range of habitats from rocky desert to broadleaved and coniferous forest. Usually hunting by night, it watches from a perch before swooping silently on its prey. It takes any prey from insect size to hares, geese, and turkeys. Its call is a series of deep, soft hoots.
• **NEST** An old nest of a large bird of prey, in a tree or on a cliff.
• **DISTRIBUTION** The Americas.
• **REMARK** Color phases (*p. 13*) from dark to pale.

powerful feet • hold prey

DISTRIBUTION

PALE PHASE

| Plumage Sexes alike | Habitat | Migration Non-migrant |

| Family STRIGIDAE | Species *Bubo bubo* | Length 28 in (70 cm) |

EURASIAN EAGLE-OWL

This powerfully built bird is the largest of the world's owls. It has prominent ear tufts and a boldly streaked breast. Most of the rest of the plumage, too, is mottled, giving camouflage when resting. The Eurasian Eagle-Owl is found in most types of country, although it favors rocky outcrops and forests. In parts of its range it is active by day as well as night. It relies on sharp sight when hunting, taking a range of prey from insects to hares, foxes, ducks, and large gamebirds. The call is a deep hoot.
• **NEST** A hollow on a rock ledge or in a cave, or an old nest of an eagle or buzzard (*see pp. 97–99*).
• **DISTRIBUTION** Much of Europe, east to Siberia and south to India and China.
• **REMARK** There is considerable variety of color, with phases and local subspecies (*see p. 13*) ranging from dark to light.

pupils reduced • in daylight

mottled • plumage

GRAY SUBSPECIES

DISTRIBUTION

| Plumage Sexes alike | Habitat | Migration Non-migrant |

Family STRIGIDAE	Species *Ketupa ketupa*	Length 16½ in (42 cm)

BUFFY FISH-OWL

Looking like an eagle-owl (*see p. 197*) in its general appearance, this is one of the fish-owls, in which a number of features are suited to their specialized diet. The legs are bare, the soles of the feet have sharp-edged, spiky scales, and the claws are long and curved for snatching fish from water. Fish-owls lack the silent flight of other owls, whose feathers have a fine surface layer of downy strands and a downy edge that muffle the sound of the flying bird. The wings of fish-owls make a slight noise in flight, presumably without impairing fishing ability. The Buffy Fish-Owl occurs in pairs alongside rivers, roosting in the thick foliage of trees beside water. Hunting at night, it watches from a bare branch and swoops to snatch fish from the water surface, also taking crabs, crayfish, amphibians, reptiles, birds, and some large insects. It has a soft, musical, two-note, hooting call.

• **NEST** An unlined cavity in a large tree, or an old nest of another large tree-nesting bird.
• **DISTRIBUTION** S.E. Asia from Burma and Borneo to Java.

bare legs of a fish • catcher

• long claws

DISTRIBUTION

Plumage Sexes alike	Habitat 🌳 〰️	Migration Non-migrant

Family STRIGIDAE	Species *Nyctea scandiaca*	Length 23 in (58 cm)

SNOWY OWL

With thick, white plumage that extends to the toes, the Snowy Owl is insulated from cold and camouflaged against snow. Living and nesting on Arctic tundra, it hunts by day as well as night. It feeds on lemmings for most of the time, occasionally taking larger prey such as hares, gulls, and ducks. The usual call is a single hoot, while barking, cackling calls are used at the nest site.
• **NEST** A shallow hollow in the ground, on a slightly raised site in open tundra.
• **DISTRIBUTION** Breeds in N. North America, Greenland, and N. Eurasia. Migrates beyond southern limits of this range in years of food shortage.

insulating plumage covers • nostrils

FEMALE

DISTRIBUTION

Plumage Sexes differ	Habitat	Migration Partial migrant

| Family STRIGIDAE | Species *Strix aluco* | Length 15 in (38 cm) |

TAWNY OWL

A bird of woodland and open areas with large trees, this stout, roundheaded owl roosts inconspicuously among branches or hidden in a hole. It has two calls: one is an advertisement call consisting of a short and a long hoot, while a sharp "ke-wick" call is also uttered for contact purposes. These are the sounds represented by the popular "to-whit to-whoo" imitation of an owl. The Tawny Owl is nocturnal and is able to hunt in complete darkness, using only its hearing to locate prey. The main foods are mice and voles.
• **NEST** A hollow in a tree or rock.
• **DISTRIBUTION** From Europe and N.W. Africa east to China and Korea.
• **REMARK** Three color phases (*see p. 13*): gray, rufous brown, and dark brown.

rich, rufous • plumage

downy • covering on legs and feet

GRAY PHASE

DISTRIBUTION

| Plumage Sexes alike | Habitat | Migration Non-migrant |

| Family STRIGIDAE | Species *Strix varia* | Length 21 in (53 cm) |

BARRED OWL

The large, dark eyes of this species adapt to the darkness and make use of the slightest amount of light. It is a typical owl of forest habitats, both coniferous and broadleaf, though it also hunts in more open country. It frequently occurs near water. By day it roosts in thick foliage. Like other owls, it is able to hunt in total darkness, provided the prey moves. This is made possible by the asymmetrical positioning of the owl's ear openings on either side of its head. One opening is set a little higher than the other, enabling the bird to pinpoint the source of a sound accurately and to pounce on it. Hunting in this way, the owl catches a wide variety of prey – mainly mice and voles, though other animals, from lizards and frogs to squirrels and hares, are taken. In swampy places, it catches crayfish and fish. The species advertises its presence with a rhythmic series of four or five deep hoots.
• **NEST** The eggs are laid in an unlined cavity in a tree.
• **DISTRIBUTION** North America, mostly east of the Rockies, and the Central Plateau of Mexico to Veracruz and Oaxaca.

DISTRIBUTION

• mottled back

• barred wings

| Plumage Sexes alike | Habitat | Migration Non-migrant |

Family STRIGIDAE	Species *Strix nebulosa*	Length 27 in (68 cm)

GREAT GRAY OWL

small, yellow eyes •

This owl inhabits the cold forests and birch scrub of the far north. It has a round head with very large feather disks on each side of its face. The tops of these stand like bold, questioning eyebrows over the small eyes. The Great Gray Owl looks sturdy but is in fact moderately sized and slender; its large appearance is created by a deep, dense layer of feathers extending to the toes and insulating it against cold weather. This species hunts both by day and by night, watching from a perch and swooping silently to seize prey. Sometimes it plunges through deep snow in pursuit of prey. It roosts in trees, perching close to the trunk. The diet consists mainly of small voles and mice, and also of shrews and small birds.
• **NEST** An old nest of another large bird in a tree,

• *large facial disk*

dense, soft • *plumage*

particularly a conifer; or a hollow in a large, broken tree stump.
• **DISTRIBUTION** Much of N. North America and across N. Eurasia. Some populations move south irregularly in winter.

DISTRIBUTION

• *large wings*

Plumage Sexes alike	Habitat 🌳🌳 🏔 ✈	Migration Partial migrant/nomadic

Family STRIGIDAE	Species *Surnia ulula*	Length 15 in (38 cm)

NORTHERN HAWK-OWL

With long, tapering wings, a long tail, and a low-crowned head, this species resembles a hawk or a falcon in outline. It is an active daytime hunter and often leans forward on a conspicuous perch to watch for prey. Flight is steady and direct, with short bursts of wingbeats alternating with glides, and quick turns of agility when catching small birds in the air. The Northern Hawk-Owl usually hunts from a perch, though it will sometimes patrol slowly overhead, hover, and then drop down onto prey. Voles are its main prey, but it also takes some larger mammals. Birds are taken, and are an important item in the diet in winter when other food is scarce. They are sometimes seized in flight. This species utters a deep, rolling hoot and sharp, yelping calls.
• **NEST** A hole in a tree, or the old nest of another bird.
• **DISTRIBUTION** Much of N. North America and across N. Eurasia. Some birds move south in winter within this range.

JUVENILE

• *typical lookout posture*

• *long tail*

DISTRIBUTION

Plumage Sexes alike	Habitat 🌳🌳 🏔	Migration Partial migrant/nomadic

Family STRIGIDAE	Species *Athene noctua*	Length 8½ in (22 cm)

LITTLE OWL

This small, compact owl has a broad head, round wings, a short tail, and feathered legs. The small, wide-set facial disks combined with the low forehead give the bird a scowling expression. An occupant of open places with some cover, it is found in a variety of habitats including farmland, parks, and stony plains. It is active by day as well as by night, and is able to walk, run, and hop. Alternating bursts of wingbeats and brief glides produce a distinctly undulating style of flight. The Little Owl hunts by sight, taking insects, small mammals including rats, and small birds.
• **NEST** A hole in a tree or rock face, a cranny in a barn or outbuilding, or a hollow in a rabbit burrow.
• **DISTRIBUTION** From Europe east to China and south into Africa.
• **REMARK** Color phases range from dark to light.

PALE DESERT FORM

small facial disks

feathered legs and feet

DISTRIBUTION

Plumage Sexes alike	Habitat	Migration Non-migrant

Family STRIGIDAE	Species *Speotyto cunicularia*	Length 9½ in (24 cm)

BURROWING OWL

Small but long-legged, this is a ground-dwelling owl of open, grassy plains. The facial disks are wide-set and the forehead is low, imparting a permanent frown. At all times of the year, this species frequents a burrow in the ground, which is used for breeding in the season and as a refuge at other times. Being mainly a night-time hunter, it is seen only in the vicinity of the burrow during the day, disappearing inside if alarmed. Flight is low and undulating, a series of rapid wingbeats alternating with brief glides. The Burrowing Owl hunts by swooping from a perch or from the air, or it may hover first, then drop down onto prey. It feeds mainly on insects, particularly grasshoppers and beetles, and sometimes takes lizards, snakes, mice, rats, and birds. It utters a cooing hoot and a clucking alarm note.
• **NEST** A chamber in the old burrow of a ground squirrel or other mammal, or a burrow dug by the pair, lined with stems or dry dung.
• **DISTRIBUTION** From S.W. Canada, W. USA, Florida, and Central America to S. South America.

DISTRIBUTION

short, rounded wings

long legs for running and walking

short tail

Plumage Sexes alike	Habitat	Migration Partial migrant

| Family STRIGIDAE | Species *Aegolius funereus* | Length 10 in (25 cm) |

BOREAL OWL

This small, tree-dwelling owl has large, high facial disks and close-set eyes, which combine to give it a surprised expression. It is always found in pine forest, both in densely grown tracts and in more openly spaced fringes and clearings. Its flight is level with rapid wingbeats and straight glides, maneuvering with great skill between trees and branches. The Boreal Owl roosts by day in thick foliage in trees, and is active at night; it also hunts by day when it has nestlings to feed. Its diet consists mainly of voles and some mice, shrews, and small birds. The call is a rapid series of musical, cooing notes.
• **NEST** An unlined hole in a tree, or a nest box.
• **DISTRIBUTION** Breeds across N. Eurasia and in N. North America, and from Wyoming to New Mexico. Some birds migrate south.

JUVENILE

• *short wings and tail*

DISTRIBUTION

| Plumage Sexes alike | Habitat | Migration Partial migrant |

| Family STRIGIDAE | Species *Ninox novaeseelandiae* | Length 14 in (35 cm) |

SOUTHERN BOOBOOK

With a rounded head, prominent bill, and poorly defined facial disks, this species is typical of Australasian hawk-owls. Birds live in pairs but roost singly in thick foliage. Like most nocturnal owls, it is mobbed by songbirds if they find it by day. Living in any areas with trees, including suburbs and even towns, it feeds at night, eating mainly insects, and also mice, small birds, and other creatures. Its name is derived from its "boobook" call.
• **NEST** In a hole in a tree.
• **DISTRIBUTION** Timor, S. New Guinea, Australia, and New Zealand.

• *large eyes*

GRAY PHASE

downcovered legs and feet •

DISTRIBUTION

| Plumage Sexes alike | Habitat | Migration Non-migrant |

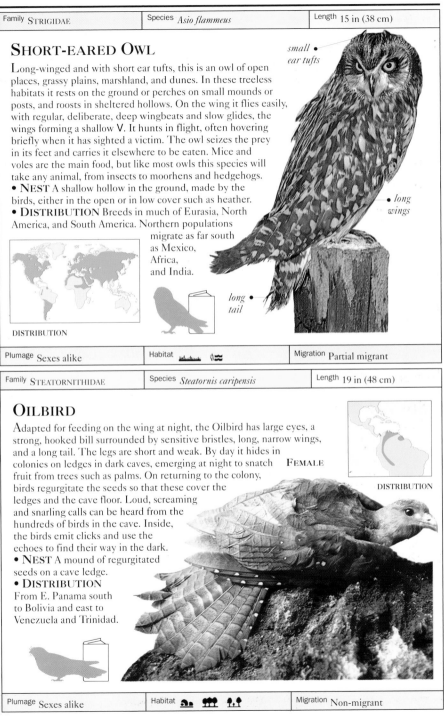

Family STRIGIDAE	Species *Asio flammeus*	Length 15 in (38 cm)

SHORT-EARED OWL

Long-winged and with short ear tufts, this is an owl of open places, grassy plains, marshland, and dunes. In these treeless habitats it rests on the ground or perches on small mounds or posts, and roosts in sheltered hollows. On the wing it flies easily, with regular, deliberate, deep wingbeats and slow glides, the wings forming a shallow **V**. It hunts in flight, often hovering briefly when it has sighted a victim. The owl seizes the prey in its feet and carries it elsewhere to be eaten. Mice and voles are the main food, but like most owls this species will take any animal, from insects to moorhens and hedgehogs.
• **NEST** A shallow hollow in the ground, made by the birds, either in the open or in low cover such as heather.
• **DISTRIBUTION** Breeds in much of Eurasia, North America, and South America. Northern populations migrate as far south as Mexico, Africa, and India.

small • ear tufts

• long wings

long • tail

DISTRIBUTION

Plumage Sexes alike	Habitat	Migration Partial migrant

Family STEATORNITHIDAE	Species *Steatornis caripensis*	Length 19 in (48 cm)

OILBIRD

Adapted for feeding on the wing at night, the Oilbird has large eyes, a strong, hooked bill surrounded by sensitive bristles, long, narrow wings, and a long tail. The legs are short and weak. By day it hides in colonies on ledges in dark caves, emerging at night to snatch fruit from trees such as palms. On returning to the colony, birds regurgitate the seeds so that these cover the ledges and the cave floor. Loud, screaming and snarling calls can be heard from the hundreds of birds in the cave. Inside, the birds emit clicks and use the echoes to find their way in the dark.
• **NEST** A mound of regurgitated seeds on a cave ledge.
• **DISTRIBUTION** From E. Panama south to Bolivia and east to Venezuela and Trinidad.

FEMALE

DISTRIBUTION

Plumage Sexes alike	Habitat	Migration Non-migrant

Family PODARGIDAE	Species *Podargus papuensis*	Length 20 in (50 cm)

PAPUAN FROGMOUTH

This is one of several nocturnal birds that hide during the day by imitating the appearance of a broken-ended branch. It has finely mottled plumage and rests on a tree branch or projecting snag with eyes closed and bill uptilted. Tail, body, head, and bill form a stiff, slanting shape like a piece of wood, and the ragged tuft on the forehead helps to break up the bird outline. The frogmouth sits motionless all day among forest foliage or on a more open perch, singly or in groups of up to four. At dusk it opens its large eyes and surveys the ground for prey. It swoops down and, instead of taking prey with its feet, opens its bill and mouth in a wide gape and scoops the prey from the ground. Insects are the main food, but frogs, lizards, mice, and birds are also eaten.
• **NEST** A small, flat nest made of twigs, and placed either in a tree fork or in a cavity on a large branch.
• **DISTRIBUTION** New Guinea and extreme N.E. Australia.
• **REMARK** This species has two distinct color phases, rufous and gray.

typical upright posture

small legs

camouflage plumage

GRAY PHASE

DISTRIBUTION

Plumage Sexes differ slightly	Habitat 🌳	Migration Non-migrant

Family NYCTIBIIDAE	Species *Nyctibius jamaicensis*	Length 16 in (40 cm)

COMMON POTOO

A nocturnal, forest-dwelling bird with camouflage plumage, this is one of the species that hides during the day by imitating the appearance of a broken-ended branch. Usually solitary, it perches upright on a sloping branch or the upper end of a vertical snag. It sits with head raised, eyes closed, and bill tilted upward, looking like an extension of the branch. The bill is short and slender with a downcurved tip, but when it is opened a gaping mouth is revealed that stretches across the width of the head. The Potoo becomes active at night. Opening its large eyes, it watches intently from its perch and darts out to catch insects in the air, before returning to the perch. Its calls are a guttural "ho-wow," and a hoarse "waark-cucu." When breeding, the Common Potoo incubates its egg in a similar upright posture to that used during its normal daytime rests.
• **NEST** A single egg is laid in a bare depression or knothole on a branch, at the top end of a broken branch, or on a broken stump.
• **DISTRIBUTION** Jamaica, Hispaniola; from Mexico to Costa Rica.

upright resting posture

DISTRIBUTION

Plumage Sexes alike	Habitat 🌳 🌳	Migration Non-migrant

| Family AEGOTHELIDAE | Species *Aegotheles insignis* | Length 12 in (30 cm) |

FELINE OWLET-NIGHTJAR

The long, bristling whiskers on the face of this bird resemble those of a cat, giving the species its name. A nocturnal bird of mountain forest, it roosts in tangles of vines or in tree cavities. It is thought to snatch insects from where they rest, in the foliage or branches.
• **NEST** Probably in a cavity in a tree.
• **DISTRIBUTION** New Guinea Highlands.

long, touch-sensitive bristles

BROWN PHASE

DISTRIBUTION

| Plumage Sexes alike | Habitat | Migration Non-migrant |

| Family CAPRIMULGIDAE | Species *Chordeiles minor* | Length 9½ in (24 cm) |

COMMON NIGHTHAWK

Gray plumage, long, tapering wings with a white patch, and a white throat band help to identify this nightjar. During the day it rests on the ground, on a post, or perched along a branch, but it begins to hunt flying insects in the late afternoon, continuing after dark. Males perform a display flight in which their vibrating wings make a roaring noise. The call is a low, nasal note.
• **NEST** Any bare, flat surface.
• **DISTRIBUTION** Breeds in North and Central America. Winters in South America to N. Argentina.

JUVENILE

small legs and feet

DISTRIBUTION

| Plumage Sexes alike | Habitat | Migration Migrant |

| Family CAPRIMULGIDAE | Species *Eurostopodus argus* | Length 12 in (30 cm) |

SPOTTED EARED-NIGHTJAR

The plumage of this species provides camouflage among dead leaves. It rests on the ground by day in open places, dry woodland, and scrub. At night it hunts in low flight, taking moths, beetles, and other insects. The call is a rising series of whistles.
• **NEST** A hollow in the ground.
• **DISTRIBUTION** Australia. Winters as far north as Aru Islands off New Guinea.

JUVENILE

tip of left wing

bird resting with wing tips crossed

tail feathers

DISTRIBUTION

| Plumage Sexes alike | Habitat | Migration Migrant |

Family CAPRIMULGIDAE	Species *Nyctidromus albicollis*	Length 11 in (28 cm)

PAURAQUE

This species lives in forest edges, secondary growth (regrown after clearance), and open scrub, nesting in more open areas. By day it rests on the ground or on a low branch, where, in typical nightjar fashion, it perches lengthwise, crouching so that its tapering outline looks like a projection on the branch. It hunts by night, in low, patrolling flight or by darting out from a perch, to seize flying insects such as beetles, moths, and fireflies. In flight, a white patch is revealed on each blunt-tipped wing. The Pauraque often rests on roads at night. The name of this bird imitates its "pur-wheee" call.

• **NEST** A natural, shallow hollow in the ground, close to low-growing plants.
• **DISTRIBUTION** From S. Texas and Mexico south to Bolivia, Brazil, and N.E. Argentina.

MALE TAIL   FEMALE TAIL

camouflage against • dead leaves

white tail stripe of male •

DISTRIBUTION

Plumage Sexes differ	Habitat 🌱🌿 ✈	Migration Non-migrant

Family CAPRIMULGIDAE	Species *Phalaenoptilus nuttallii*	Length 8 in (20 cm)

COMMON POORWILL

This small nightjar has a dumpy look, being short and rounded in both wings and tail. A two-syllable whistled "poor-will" call, with a barely audible third note, gives the bird its name. Being nocturnal, the Common Poorwill is more often heard than seen. By day it rests on the ground, in desert sagebrush, dry scrub, or open pinewood. At night it hunts flying insects, either cruising low above the ground or perching on the ground, on a rock, or a low branch, to watch and fly out to intercept its prey. When nesting, it relies on camouflage for protection.
• **NEST** A slight depression on the ground.
• **DISTRIBUTION** Breeds in W. Canada and USA. Winters as far south as C. Mexico.
• **REMARK** One bird was found, in several successive years, apparently hibernating in a rock crevice in S.W. USA.

camouflage plumage •

DISTRIBUTION

Plumage Sexes differ slightly	Habitat ✈	Migration Partial migrant

| Family CAPRIMULGIDAE | Species *Caprimulgus europaeus* | Length 11 in (28 cm) |

EURASIAN NIGHTJAR

Rarely seen except when startled from its daytime resting place, this well camouflaged bird is best known for the prolonged, churring note, on a rising or falling trend, that the breeding male utters at night. This sound is difficult to locate. The bird rests by day, on the ground or lying along a branch. By night it silently chases insects in quick, erratic flight. The species favors open sites close to trees where the ground is covered with leaves and twigs.
• **NEST** A piece of open ground, usually close to trees or bushes.
• **DISTRIBUTION** Eurasia and N. Africa, east to China. Winters as far as South Africa.

DISTRIBUTION

white wing patch of male

FEMALE

| Plumage Sexes differ | Habitat | Migration Migrant |

| Family CAPRIMULGIDAE | Species *Macrodipteryx longipennis* | Length 9 in (23 cm) |

STANDARD-WINGED NIGHTJAR

The breeding male of this species has one of the most startling forms of display plumage of all birds. Having evolved to fly in poor light at dusk and dawn, nightjars generally tend to display by flying erratically or by showing unusual white patches or shapes. In this case, a huge feather grows from the middle of each wing. Seen in flight, these appear as two long, slender shafts, each supporting a big, flaglike vane at the tip. In display, the male circles above the female with vibrating wingbeats, raising his two large feathers. These feathers are lost after the breeding season. The Standard-winged Nightjar occurs in dry, stony country with scattered bushes. By day it rests on the ground, where it lies unnoticed unless disturbed. At night it catches insects on the wing. It advertises its presence to females and rival males with a shrill, churring call.
• **NEST** A slight, natural hollow in a bare piece of open ground.
• **DISTRIBUTION** Africa south of the Sahara, from Senegal east to Ethiopia; isolated population in Uganda and W. Kenya.

FEMALE

flaglike feather vane

DISTRIBUTION

| Plumage Sexes differ | Habitat | Migration Migrant |

| Family APODIDAE | Species *Tachymarptis melba* | Length 8½ in (22 cm) |

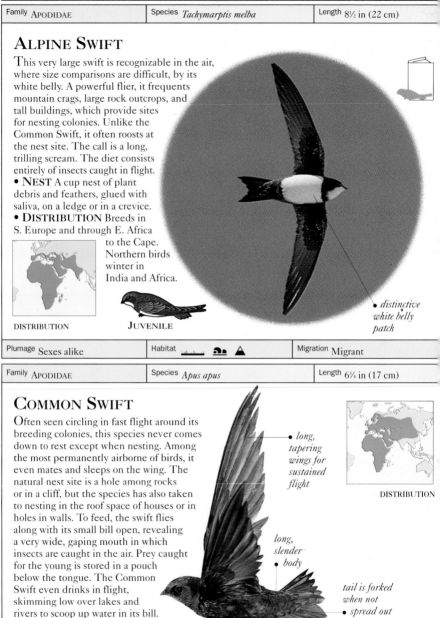

ALPINE SWIFT

This very large swift is recognizable in the air, where size comparisons are difficult, by its white belly. A powerful flier, it frequents mountain crags, large rock outcrops, and tall buildings, which provide sites for nesting colonies. Unlike the Common Swift, it often roosts at the nest site. The call is a long, trilling scream. The diet consists entirely of insects caught in flight.
• **NEST** A cup nest of plant debris and feathers, glued with saliva, on a ledge or in a crevice.
• **DISTRIBUTION** Breeds in S. Europe and through E. Africa to the Cape. Northern birds winter in India and Africa.

DISTRIBUTION

JUVENILE

• distinctive white belly patch

| Plumage Sexes alike | Habitat | Migration Migrant |

| Family APODIDAE | Species *Apus apus* | Length 6¾ in (17 cm) |

COMMON SWIFT

Often seen circling in fast flight around its breeding colonies, this species never comes down to rest except when nesting. Among the most permanently airborne of birds, it even mates and sleeps on the wing. The natural nest site is a hole among rocks or in a cliff, but the species has also taken to nesting in the roof space of houses or in holes in walls. To feed, the swift flies along with its small bill open, revealing a very wide, gaping mouth in which insects are caught in the air. Prey caught for the young is stored in a pouch below the tongue. The Common Swift even drinks in flight, skimming low over lakes and rivers to scoop up water in its bill.
• **NEST** A shallow cup nest of plant debris, and feathers caught drifting in the air, stuck together with saliva, and placed on a ledge or in a hole.
• **DISTRIBUTION** Much of Europe east to North India, Mongolia and China. Winters in tropical and southern Africa.

• long, tapering wings for sustained flight

DISTRIBUTION

long, slender • body

tail is forked when not • spread out

| Plumage Sexes alike | Habitat | Migration Migrant |

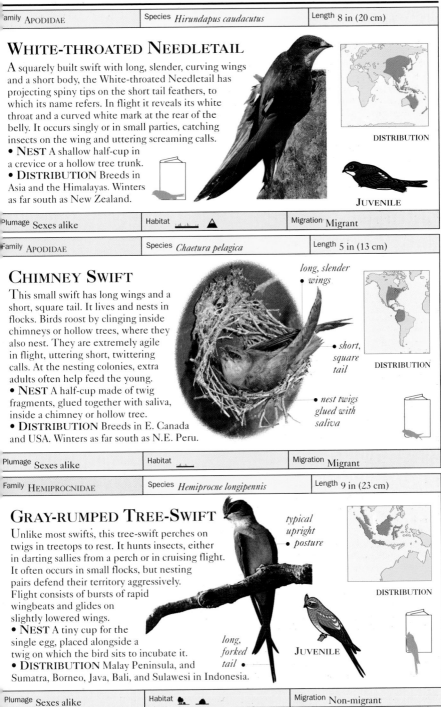

| Family APODIDAE | Species *Hirundapus caudacutus* | Length 8 in (20 cm) |

WHITE-THROATED NEEDLETAIL

A squarely built swift with long, slender, curving wings and a short body, the White-throated Needletail has projecting spiny tips on the short tail feathers, to which its name refers. In flight it reveals its white throat and a curved white mark at the rear of the belly. It occurs singly or in small parties, catching insects on the wing and uttering screaming calls.
• **NEST** A shallow half-cup in a crevice or a hollow tree trunk.
• **DISTRIBUTION** Breeds in Asia and the Himalayas. Winters as far south as New Zealand.

DISTRIBUTION

JUVENILE

| Plumage Sexes alike | Habitat | Migration Migrant |

| Family APODIDAE | Species *Chaetura pelagica* | Length 5 in (13 cm) |

CHIMNEY SWIFT

This small swift has long wings and a short, square tail. It lives and nests in flocks. Birds roost by clinging inside chimneys or hollow trees, where they also nest. They are extremely agile in flight, uttering short, twittering calls. At the nesting colonies, extra adults often help feed the young.
• **NEST** A half-cup made of twig fragments, glued together with saliva, inside a chimney or hollow tree.
• **DISTRIBUTION** Breeds in E. Canada and USA. Winters as far south as N.E. Peru.

long, slender • wings

• short, square tail

DISTRIBUTION

• nest twigs glued with saliva

| Plumage Sexes alike | Habitat | Migration Migrant |

| Family HEMIPROCNIDAE | Species *Hemiprocne longipennis* | Length 9 in (23 cm) |

GRAY-RUMPED TREE-SWIFT

Unlike most swifts, this tree-swift perches on twigs in treetops to rest. It hunts insects, either in darting sallies from a perch or in cruising flight. It often occurs in small flocks, but nesting pairs defend their territory aggressively. Flight consists of bursts of rapid wingbeats and glides on slightly lowered wings.
• **NEST** A tiny cup for the single egg, placed alongside a twig on which the bird sits to incubate it.
• **DISTRIBUTION** Malay Peninsula, and Sumatra, Borneo, Java, Bali, and Sulawesi in Indonesia.

typical upright • posture

DISTRIBUTION

long, forked tail •

JUVENILE

| Plumage Sexes alike | Habitat | Migration Non-migrant |

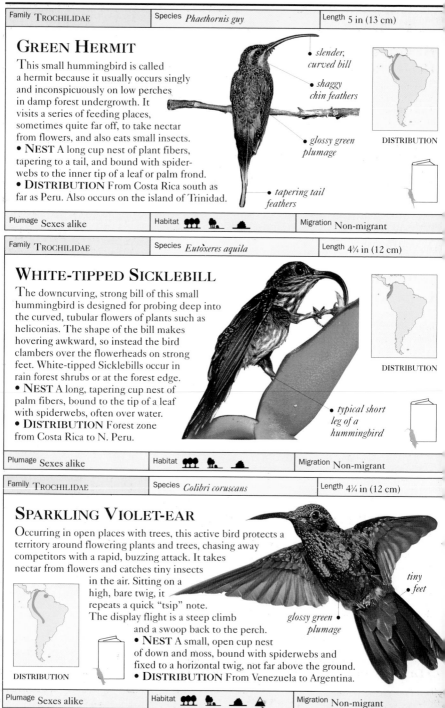

| Family TROCHILIDAE | Species *Phaethornis guy* | Length 5 in (13 cm) |

GREEN HERMIT

This small hummingbird is called a hermit because it usually occurs singly and inconspicuously on low perches in damp forest undergrowth. It visits a series of feeding places, sometimes quite far off, to take nectar from flowers, and also eats small insects.
• **NEST** A long cup nest of plant fibers, tapering to a tail, and bound with spiderwebs to the inner tip of a leaf or palm frond.
• **DISTRIBUTION** From Costa Rica south as far as Peru. Also occurs on the island of Trinidad.

• *slender, curved bill*

• *shaggy chin feathers*

• *glossy green plumage*

DISTRIBUTION

• *tapering tail feathers*

| Plumage Sexes alike | Habitat | Migration Non-migrant |

| Family TROCHILIDAE | Species *Eutoxeres aquila* | Length 4¾ in (12 cm) |

WHITE-TIPPED SICKLEBILL

The downcurving, strong bill of this small hummingbird is designed for probing deep into the curved, tubular flowers of plants such as heliconias. The shape of the bill makes hovering awkward, so instead the bird clambers over the flowerheads on strong feet. White-tipped Sicklebills occur in rain forest shrubs or at the forest edge.
• **NEST** A long, tapering cup nest of palm fibers, bound to the tip of a leaf with spiderwebs, often over water.
• **DISTRIBUTION** Forest zone from Costa Rica to N. Peru.

DISTRIBUTION

• *typical short leg of a hummingbird*

| Plumage Sexes alike | Habitat | Migration Non-migrant |

| Family TROCHILIDAE | Species *Colibri coruscans* | Length 4¾ in (12 cm) |

SPARKLING VIOLET-EAR

Occurring in open places with trees, this active bird protects a territory around flowering plants and trees, chasing away competitors with a rapid, buzzing attack. It takes nectar from flowers and catches tiny insects in the air. Sitting on a high, bare twig, it repeats a quick "tsip" note. The display flight is a steep climb and a swoop back to the perch.
• **NEST** A small, open cup nest of down and moss, bound with spiderwebs and fixed to a horizontal twig, not far above the ground.
• **DISTRIBUTION** From Venezuela to Argentina.

tiny
• *feet*

glossy green •
plumage

DISTRIBUTION

| Plumage Sexes alike | Habitat | Migration Non-migrant |

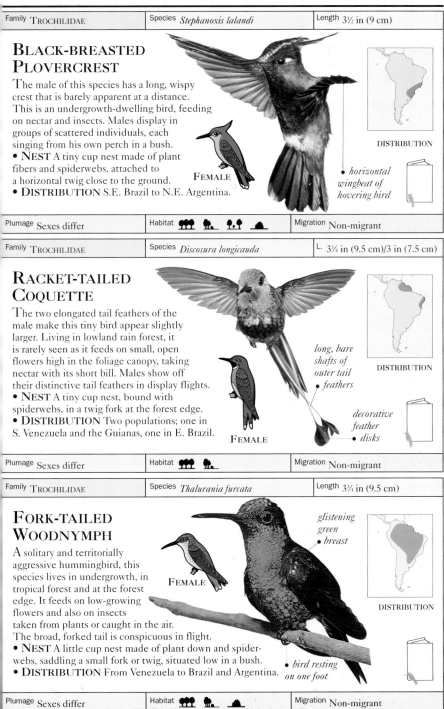

Family TROCHILIDAE	Species *Stephanoxis lalandi*	Length 3½ in (9 cm)

BLACK-BREASTED PLOVERCREST

The male of this species has a long, wispy crest that is barely apparent at a distance. This is an undergrowth-dwelling bird, feeding on nectar and insects. Males display in groups of scattered individuals, each singing from his own perch in a bush.
• **NEST** A tiny cup nest made of plant fibers and spiderwebs, attached to a horizontal twig close to the ground.
• **DISTRIBUTION** S.E. Brazil to N.E. Argentina.

FEMALE

DISTRIBUTION

• *horizontal wingbeat of hovering bird*

Plumage Sexes differ	Habitat	Migration Non-migrant

Family TROCHILIDAE	Species *Discosura longicauda*	L. 3¾ in (9.5 cm)/3 in (7.5 cm)

RACKET-TAILED COQUETTE

The two elongated tail feathers of the male make this tiny bird appear slightly larger. Living in lowland rain forest, it is rarely seen as it feeds on small, open flowers high in the foliage canopy, taking nectar with its short bill. Males show off their distinctive tail feathers in display flights.
• **NEST** A tiny cup nest, bound with spiderwebs, in a twig fork at the forest edge.
• **DISTRIBUTION** Two populations; one in S. Venezuela and the Guianas, one in E. Brazil.

long, bare shafts of outer tail • feathers

DISTRIBUTION

decorative feather • disks

FEMALE

Plumage Sexes differ	Habitat	Migration Non-migrant

Family TROCHILIDAE	Species *Thalurania furcata*	Length 3¾ in (9.5 cm)

FORK-TAILED WOODNYMPH

A solitary and territorially aggressive hummingbird, this species lives in undergrowth, in tropical forest and at the forest edge. It feeds on low-growing flowers and also on insects taken from plants or caught in the air. The broad, forked tail is conspicuous in flight.
• **NEST** A little cup nest made of plant down and spiderwebs, saddling a small fork or twig, situated low in a bush.
• **DISTRIBUTION** From Venezuela to Brazil and Argentina.

FEMALE

glistening green • breast

DISTRIBUTION

• *bird resting on one foot*

Plumage Sexes differ	Habitat	Migration Non-migrant

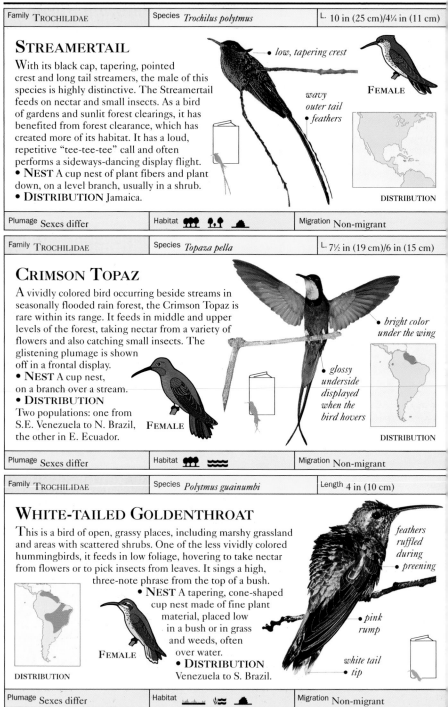

| Family TROCHILIDAE | Species *Trochilus polytmus* | L. 10 in (25 cm)/4¼ in (11 cm) |

STREAMERTAIL

With its black cap, tapering, pointed crest and long tail streamers, the male of this species is highly distinctive. The Streamertail feeds on nectar and small insects. As a bird of gardens and sunlit forest clearings, it has benefited from forest clearance, which has created more of its habitat. It has a loud, repetitive "tee-tee-tee" call and often performs a sideways-dancing display flight.
• NEST A cup nest of plant fibers and plant down, on a level branch, usually in a shrub.
• DISTRIBUTION Jamaica.

• *low, tapering crest*

wavy outer tail • feathers

FEMALE

DISTRIBUTION

| Plumage Sexes differ | Habitat | Migration Non-migrant |

| Family TROCHILIDAE | Species *Topaza pella* | L. 7½ in (19 cm)/6 in (15 cm) |

CRIMSON TOPAZ

A vividly colored bird occurring beside streams in seasonally flooded rain forest, the Crimson Topaz is rare within its range. It feeds in middle and upper levels of the forest, taking nectar from a variety of flowers and also catching small insects. The glistening plumage is shown off in a frontal display.
• NEST A cup nest, on a branch over a stream.
• DISTRIBUTION Two populations: one from S.E. Venezuela to N. Brazil, the other in E. Ecuador. FEMALE

• *bright color under the wing*

• *glossy underside displayed when the bird hovers*

DISTRIBUTION

| Plumage Sexes differ | Habitat | Migration Non-migrant |

| Family TROCHILIDAE | Species *Polytmus guainumbi* | Length 4 in (10 cm) |

WHITE-TAILED GOLDENTHROAT

This is a bird of open, grassy places, including marshy grassland and areas with scattered shrubs. One of the less vividly colored hummingbirds, it feeds in low foliage, hovering to take nectar from flowers or to pick insects from leaves. It sings a high, three-note phrase from the top of a bush.
• NEST A tapering, cone-shaped cup nest made of fine plant material, placed low in a bush or in grass and weeds, often over water.
• DISTRIBUTION Venezuela to S. Brazil.

feathers ruffled during • preening

• *pink rump*

white tail • tip

FEMALE

DISTRIBUTION

| Plumage Sexes differ | Habitat | Migration Non-migrant |

Family TROCHILIDAE	Species *Oreotrochilus estella*	Length 5½ in (14 cm)

ANDEAN HILLSTAR

A bird of high mountains, this species lives all year round in the sparse vegetation and grassland of the Puna Plateau in the Andes. On cold nights it becomes torpid (inactive, maintaining a reduced body temperature) to conserve energy, reviving and becoming active in warm sunlight. In open, windy places it uses its strong feet to cling to branches instead of hovering to feed. It takes nectar from flowers, also catching insects. Andean Hillstars are unusual for their territorial behavior. The females hold permanent territories where nesting takes place, and after nesting the males move out and live elsewhere, usually at higher altitude.
• **NEST** A thick-walled cup nest of moss, plant down, and lichens, suspended under a cliff overhang, in a cave, or under house eaves.
• **DISTRIBUTION** Andes from Peru to Argentina and Chile.

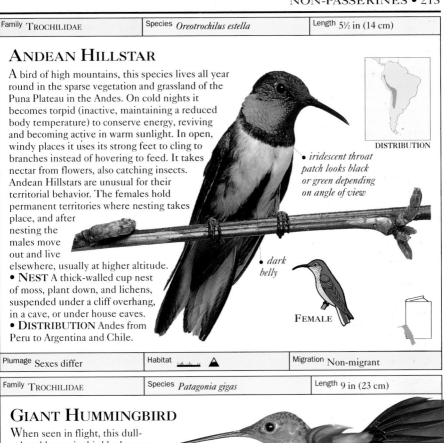

DISTRIBUTION

• *iridescent throat patch looks black or green depending on angle of view*

• *dark belly*

FEMALE

Plumage Sexes differ	Habitat	Migration Non-migrant

Family TROCHILIDAE	Species *Patagonia gigas*	Length 9 in (23 cm)

GIANT HUMMINGBIRD

When seen in flight, this dull-colored hummingbird looks more like a martin or a swift with a long bill. Its wingbeats are slower and more visible than those of other hummingbirds as it hovers, batlike, in front of a flower to take nectar. It often perches to feed. This is an aggressive bird that will chase other species away from its feeding sites. Like other hummingbird species, it also eats small insects. A bird of semi-open scrub in the more arid parts of the Andes, at altitudes where the climate is temperate, it also frequents cultivated areas. Its size helps it to withstand the low temperatures in the mountains; having less surface area relative to body size than the smaller hummingbirds, it is better able to conserve its body heat. During cold weather it moves down to lower altitudes.
• **NEST** A small cup nest made of moss and lichens, placed on top of a level branch or sometimes on a cactus stem. The nest appears too small for a bird of this size.
• **DISTRIBUTION** Andes from Ecuador to Chile, and in lowlands in W. Argentina.
• **REMARK** This is the hummingbird with the largest body size.

• *pale rump*

• *tiny feet*

DISTRIBUTION

Plumage Sexes differ	Habitat	Migration Non-migrant

| Family TROCHILIDAE | Species *Ensifera ensifera* | Length 10 in (25 cm) |

SWORD-BILLED HUMMINGBIRD

The long, slender bill of this species doubles its total length. When the bird perches to rest, it tilts back its head and slants the bill steeply upward, to balance its weight more easily. This is also the typical angle at which the bill is inserted into the large, hanging, trumpet-shaped flowers of *Datura* and similar plants. These provide the bird with nectar and pollen for food and are pollinated in return. The bird also manages to catch insects in its bill in flight.

iridescent breast and belly •

tiny feet extended for landing •

• *iridescent patch under the wing*

iridescent underside of • *tail feathers*

• **NEST** A small cup nest of moss, usually set on a twig in a tree at the forest edge, or sometimes suspended in root fibers exposed on a steep slope.
• **DISTRIBUTION** Andes from Venezuela south to Bolivia.

• *tail spread for landing*

DISTRIBUTION

| Plumage Sexes differ | Habitat 🔺 🌳 🌿 | Migration Non-migrant |

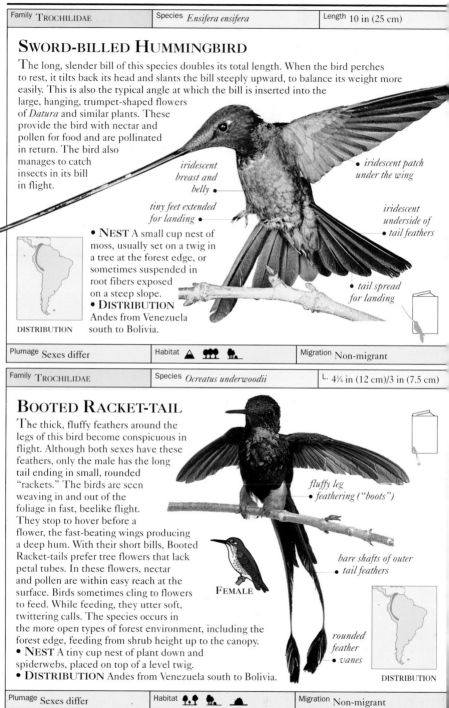

| Family TROCHILIDAE | Species *Ocreatus underwoodii* | L. 4¾ in (12 cm)/3 in (7.5 cm) |

BOOTED RACKET-TAIL

The thick, fluffy feathers around the legs of this bird become conspicuous in flight. Although both sexes have these feathers, only the male has the long tail ending in small, rounded "rackets." The birds are seen weaving in and out of the foliage in fast, beelike flight. They stop to hover before a flower, the fast-beating wings producing a deep hum. With their short bills, Booted Racket-tails prefer tree flowers that lack petal tubes. In these flowers, nectar and pollen are within easy reach at the surface. Birds sometimes cling to flowers to feed. While feeding, they utter soft, twittering calls. The species occurs in the more open types of forest environment, including the forest edge, feeding from shrub height up to the canopy.
• **NEST** A tiny cup nest of plant down and spiderwebs, placed on top of a level twig.
• **DISTRIBUTION** Andes from Venezuela south to Bolivia.

fluffy leg • *feathering ("boots")*

FEMALE

bare shafts of outer • *tail feathers*

rounded feather • *vanes*

DISTRIBUTION

| Plumage Sexes differ | Habitat 🌿 🌳 🏔 | Migration Non-migrant |

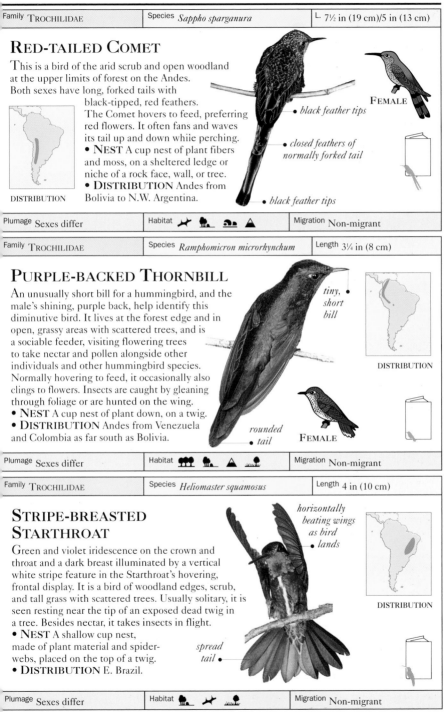

Family TROCHILIDAE	Species *Sappho sparganura*	L. 7½ in (19 cm)/5 in (13 cm)

RED-TAILED COMET

This is a bird of the arid scrub and open woodland
at the upper limits of forest on the Andes.
Both sexes have long, forked tails with
black-tipped, red feathers.
The Comet hovers to feed, preferring
red flowers. It often fans and waves
its tail up and down while perching.
• **NEST** A cup nest of plant fibers
and moss, on a sheltered ledge or
niche of a rock face, wall, or tree.
• **DISTRIBUTION** Andes from
Bolivia to N.W. Argentina.

FEMALE

• black feather tips

*• closed feathers of
normally forked tail*

DISTRIBUTION

• black feather tips

Plumage Sexes differ	Habitat	Migration Non-migrant

Family TROCHILIDAE	Species *Ramphomicron microrhynchum*	Length 3¼ in (8 cm)

PURPLE-BACKED THORNBILL

An unusually short bill for a hummingbird, and the
male's shining, purple back, help identify this
diminutive bird. It lives at the forest edge and in
open, grassy areas with scattered trees, and is
a sociable feeder, visiting flowering trees
to take nectar and pollen alongside other
individuals and other hummingbird species.
Normally hovering to feed, it occasionally also
clings to flowers. Insects are caught by gleaning
through foliage or are hunted on the wing.
• **NEST** A cup nest of plant down, on a twig.
• **DISTRIBUTION** Andes from Venezuela
and Colombia as far south as Bolivia.

*tiny, •
short
bill*

DISTRIBUTION

*rounded
• tail*

FEMALE

Plumage Sexes differ	Habitat	Migration Non-migrant

Family TROCHILIDAE	Species *Heliomaster squamosus*	Length 4 in (10 cm)

STRIPE-BREASTED
STARTHROAT

Green and violet iridescence on the crown and
throat and a dark breast illuminated by a vertical
white stripe feature in the Starthroat's hovering,
frontal display. It is a bird of woodland edges, scrub,
and tall grass with scattered trees. Usually solitary, it is
seen resting near the tip of an exposed dead twig in
a tree. Besides nectar, it takes insects in flight.
• **NEST** A shallow cup nest,
made of plant material and spiderwebs, placed on the top of a twig.
• **DISTRIBUTION** E. Brazil.

*horizontally
beating wings
as bird
• lands*

DISTRIBUTION

*spread
tail •*

Plumage Sexes differ	Habitat	Migration Non-migrant

Family TROCHILIDAE	Species *Archilochus colubris*	Length 3½ in (9 cm)

RUBY-THROATED HUMMINGBIRD

This migrant species visits birdfeeders
and garden flowers in summer. Besides its
main diet of nectar, it takes insects and spiders.
• **NEST** A small cup nest made of plant down,
bound with spiderwebs
and covered with lichen.
• **DISTRIBUTION** Breeds in
E. North America.
Winters in
S. Florida,
Central
America.

iridescent throat patch

bird holds position accurately in hovering flight

DISTRIBUTION

FEMALE

Plumage Sexes differ	Habitat	Migration Migrant

Family TROCHILIDAE	Species *Calypte anna*	Length 3¾ in (9.5 cm)

ANNA'S HUMMINGBIRD

Living in woodlands, gardens, and scrub,
this bird feeds on nectar and insects. Males
have a red head, females a red-flecked throat.
• **NEST** A cup nest of
stems, plant down, and
feathers, bound with spiderwebs, and placed on
a level twig.
• **DISTRIBUTION**
Breeds in W. USA.
Winters as far south as Mexico.

• iridescent ear patch

• iridescent throat patch

• inner flight feathers curve forward as bird hovers

DISTRIBUTION

FEMALE

Plumage Sexes differ	Habitat	Migration Partial migrant

Family TROCHILIDAE	Species *Stellula calliope*	Length 3¼ in (8 cm)

CALLIOPE HUMMINGBIRD

This is North America's smallest bird,
occurring by streams in canyons, upland
meadows, and conifer forest. It takes nectar,
mainly from red flowers.
• **NEST** A small, lichen-covered
cup on a twig in a bush or low tree.
• **DISTRIBUTION**
Breeds in W. USA.
Winters
in S.W.
Mexico.

light green crown and back •

• elongated, iridescent feathers

feet held under the belly in flight

DISTRIBUTION

FEMALE

Plumage Sexes differ	Habitat	Migration Migrant

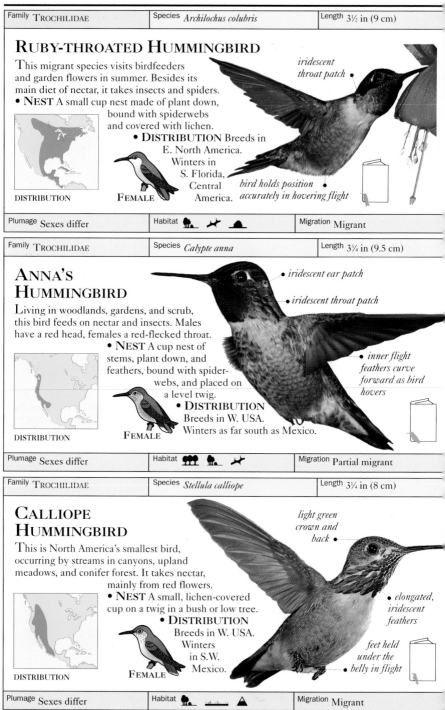

Family TROCHILIDAE	Species *Selasphorus rufus*	Length 4 in (10 cm)

RUFOUS HUMMINGBIRD

Bright, orange-rufous plumage on the head and body of this hummingbird is enhanced by a glittering throat patch. It is lively and aggressive, and feeds on nectar from the flowers of low plants and shrubs.

• **NEST** A tiny cup nest, decorated with lichens, on a twig fork in a bush or tree.

• **DISTRIBUTION** Breeds in N.W. North America. Winters on the gulf coast, in S. California, and in much of Mexico.

tongue extended for feeding

tip of bill

iridescent red throat patch

DISTRIBUTION

FEMALE

broad, notched tail

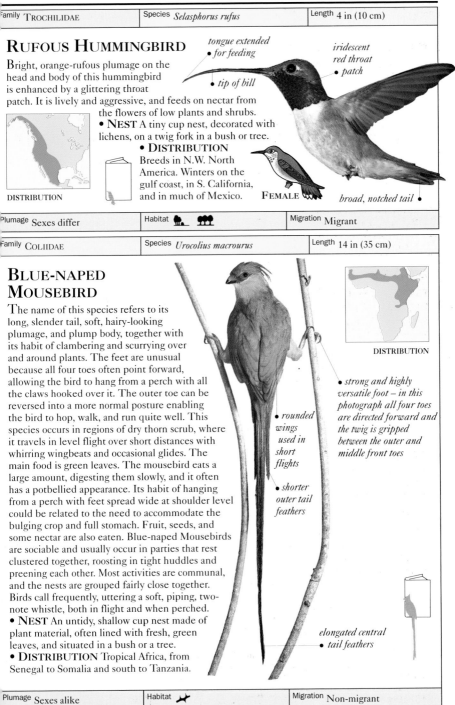

Plumage Sexes differ	Habitat	Migration Migrant

Family COLIIDAE	Species *Urocolius macrourus*	Length 14 in (35 cm)

BLUE-NAPED MOUSEBIRD

The name of this species refers to its long, slender tail, soft, hairy-looking plumage, and plump body, together with its habit of clambering and scurrying over and around plants. The feet are unusual because all four toes often point forward, allowing the bird to hang from a perch with all the claws hooked over it. The outer toe can be reversed into a more normal posture enabling the bird to hop, walk, and run quite well. This species occurs in regions of dry thorn scrub, where it travels in level flight over short distances with whirring wingbeats and occasional glides. The main food is green leaves. The mousebird eats a large amount, digesting them slowly, and it often has a potbellied appearance. Its habit of hanging from a perch with feet spread wide at shoulder level could be related to the need to accommodate the bulging crop and full stomach. Fruit, seeds, and some nectar are also eaten. Blue-naped Mousebirds are sociable and usually occur in parties that rest clustered together, roosting in tight huddles and preening each other. Most activities are communal, and the nests are grouped fairly close together. Birds call frequently, uttering a soft, piping, two-note whistle, both in flight and when perched.

• **NEST** An untidy, shallow cup nest made of plant material, often lined with fresh, green leaves, and situated in a bush or a tree.

• **DISTRIBUTION** Tropical Africa, from Senegal to Somalia and south to Tanzania.

DISTRIBUTION

strong and highly versatile foot – in this photograph all four toes are directed forward and the twig is gripped between the outer and middle front toes

rounded wings used in short flights

shorter outer tail feathers

elongated central tail feathers

Plumage Sexes alike	Habitat	Migration Non-migrant

Family TROGONIDAE	Species *Trogon curucui*	Length 9½ in (24 cm)

BLUE-CROWNED TROGON

In spite of its bright colors, this is an inconspicuous, forest-dwelling bird with soft, dense plumage, a stout bill, small, weak feet, and an upright, watchful posture. It is uncommon, living in lowland rain forest, and tall secondary growth (areas where the trees have regrown after forest clearance). Perching in the middle or lower levels of forest vegetation, it sits quietly for long periods. The diet consists of fruit and insects. The bird watches for an insect from a perch, then swoops out, hovers momentarily with a flutter of wings, snatches the insect, and takes it back to the perch. The song is a series of "kyou" notes, accelerating and then stopping abruptly. There is also a low, purring call.
• **NEST** A cavity in a tree, or a woodpecker hole, or a hole excavated by the bird in rotten wood or a tree-termite nest.
• **DISTRIBUTION** From Colombia and N.W. Brazil as far south as Peru, Bolivia, Paraguay, and N.E. Argentina.

DISTRIBUTION

barred outer tail feathers covering dark • inner feathers

FEMALE

Plumage Sexes differ	Habitat 🌳	Migration Non-migrant

Family TROGONIDAE	Species *Apaloderma narina*	Length 12½ in (32 cm)

NARINA TROGON

Sitting motionless for long periods on an open branch, this quiet bird is inconspicuous in the upper levels of forest. It is mainly a solitary bird, although pairs sometimes perch near each other. The diet consists of insects, particularly caterpillars. The bird flies out to seize an insect from foliage or a twig while hovering, afterward returning to its perch. Insects are also sometimes chased and caught in midair, and at times the bird creeps along branches in search of prey. Usually the flight is direct and heavy, but the bird is capable of fast, twisting movements when chasing insects in flight. The Narina Trogon sometimes joins the mixed-species flocks of birds that hunt insects through the forest. The male bird utters a soft, rapidly repeated, dovelike "coo," while flexing his tail up and down.
• **NEST** An unlined, natural cavity in a tree trunk, branch, or dead stump.
• **DISTRIBUTION** Forested regions of Africa south of the Sahara.

• pale markings on the face

• mottled gray wings

FEMALE

• white outer tail feathers

DISTRIBUTION

Plumage Sexes differ	Habitat 🌳 🌿	Migration Non-migrant

Family TROGONIDAE	Species *Harpactes diardii*	Length 12 in (30 cm)

DIARD'S TROGON

short, very broad bill •

A quiet and inconspicuous bird, Diard's Trogon is widely distributed but nowhere common in the forested lowlands where it lives. It has the rounded wings and long tail with square-tipped feathers that are typical of the trogons but, as in other Asiatic species, its back is rufous-brown instead of green. Usually occurring in pairs, it perches on bare branches in the middle and lower levels of forest foliage. Here the bird sits upright and motionless for long periods, except for slight, watchful movements of the head. When pursuing small insects such as beetles and moths, it moves in rapid and agile flight among branches and vines. The prey is grabbed with a quick movement and a loud flutter of wings before the bird returns to the perch. Diard's Trogon also snatches insects from leaves or twigs while it flies.

FEMALE

• **NEST** An unlined hole in a rotten tree stump, excavated by the nesting pair. Sometimes the birds enlarge an existing hole.
• **DISTRIBUTION** S.E. Asia from Sumatra and the Malay Peninsula to Borneo.

white outer tail feathers •

DISTRIBUTION

Plumage Sexes differ	Habitat 🌳🌳	Migration Non-migrant

Family ALCEDINIDAE	Species *Megaceryle alcyon*	Length 13 in (33 cm)

BELTED KINGFISHER

short, shaggy crest •

A big, shaggy-headed kingfisher with mainly blue-gray and white plumage, this is a conspicuous bird of rivers, ponds, and streams. It is seen in unsteady-looking flight along streams, or pausing to sit on a prominent perch. From here it watches the water below and when a fish or other moving creature is sighted, the bird plunge-dives to seize it, often first hovering briefly. Fish are carried to the perch, slapped against it, then swallowed head first.
• **NEST** An upward-slanting burrow in a bank beside water, up to 16½ ft (5 m) long.
• **DISTRIBUTION** Breeds in North America. Winters as far south as N. South America.

gray breast band •

barred outer tail feathers •

white spots on tips of covert feathers •

chestnut flanks of female •

DISTRIBUTION

MALE

Plumage Sexes differ	Habitat 〰〰	Migration Migrant

| Family ALCEDINIDAE | Species *Ceryle rudis* | Length 11 in (28 cm) |

PIED KINGFISHER

Boldly patterned in black and white, with a short, shaggy crest, this conspicuous plunge-diving bird frequents waters of many kinds, from coasts and rivers to inland marshes. It usually hunts in flight, pausing and hovering, with body almost vertical and head looking down, before plunging to catch a fish, crustacean, or large insect. This bird is noisy, with high pitched, squeaky calls.
• **NEST** A burrow in a sandy bank, with a layer of regurgitated fish scales and bones.
• **DISTRIBUTION** Much of Africa, Middle East, India, and S.E. Asia.

shaggy crest in partly raised position

long, tapering bill of a plunge-diver

incomplete breast band of male

FEMALE

uptilted tail

long wing used in hovering flight

DISTRIBUTION

| Plumage Sexes differ | Habitat 〜〜 〜 | Migration Non-migrant |

| Family ALCEDINIDAE | Species *Dacelo novaeguineae* | Length 17½ in (45 cm) |

LAUGHING KOOKABURRA

Largest of the kingfishers, this bird occurs in dry country, well away from water. It lives in open forest and woodland, where it swoops down from its perch to snatch insects, lizards, snakes, rodents, and small birds. Young birds stay with their parents for several years as "nest helpers." Pairs and their helpers utter cackling calls, with heads stretched up and tails raised, to advertise possession of their territory. The bird's name is an imitation of these calls.
• **NEST** An unlined cavity in a trunk or branch.
• **DISTRIBUTION** E. and S.W. Australia.

blunt, heavy bill

dark eye stripe

blue-tipped wing coverts

MALE

small feet used mainly for perching

white tips of outer tail feathers

FEMALE

DISTRIBUTION

| Plumage Sexes differ | Habitat | Migration Non-migrant |

| Family ALCEDINIDAE | Species *Dacelo tyro* | Length 13 in (33 cm) |

SPANGLED KOOKABURRA

This is a large, thicket-dwelling kingfisher
with spectacular plumage. It is common within
its range, occurring in monsoon forest, at the fringes
of swamps, and in thickets in savanna (tropical
grassland). Usually it perches low in a bush
or tree, scanning the ground for food. It feeds
on a variety of invertebrates, including beetles,
ants, and stick insects. This bird is sometimes
seen in small flocks, and it is possible
that, like its Australian relatives, the
Spangled Kookaburra has a complex
social system that includes "helpers" at the
nest. The call is a gurgling noise, followed
by a rattling, even pitched laughing sound.
Birds also utter a single, loud "kurk" note.

*spangled
pattern made
by white
• feather tips*

*bright blue
wing
• coverts*

• **NEST** A hole in the
side of a tree-termite
nest, often as much as 16½ ft
(5 m) above the ground.
• **DISTRIBUTION**
Lowlands in S. New
Guinea and the Aru Islands
(off S.W. New Guinea).

*• short
legs used
mainly for
perching*

DISTRIBUTION

| Plumage Sexes alike | Habitat 🌳🌳 ▬ ✈ | Migration Non-migrant |

| Family ALCEDINIDAE | Species *Halcyon malimbica* | Length 11 in (28 cm) |

BLUE-BREASTED KINGFISHER

Typical of thicket-dwelling kingfishers, this bird is stoutly
built, with a shorter and blunter bill than those of plunge-
diving species. It lives in forests bordering open country,
also occurring in mature secondary forest (where trees
have regrown after forest clearance) and in mangrove
swamps. Watching from a perch, it swoops down
to take insects and other small creatures. It will
occasionally dive for fish. The usual call is
a far-carrying series of 7–10 slow, plaintive
whistling notes, falling in pitch and volume.
• **NEST** An unlined cavity, bored in the
side of a tree-termite nest.
• **DISTRIBUTION**
Tropical W. Africa.

*stout bill •
with upwardly
curved lower
mandible*

*bright blue
wing patch •*

*• two toes are partly
joined, giving a broader
base for perching*

DISTRIBUTION

| Plumage Sexes alike | Habitat 🌳🌳 🌳🌳 ▬ | Migration Non-migrant |

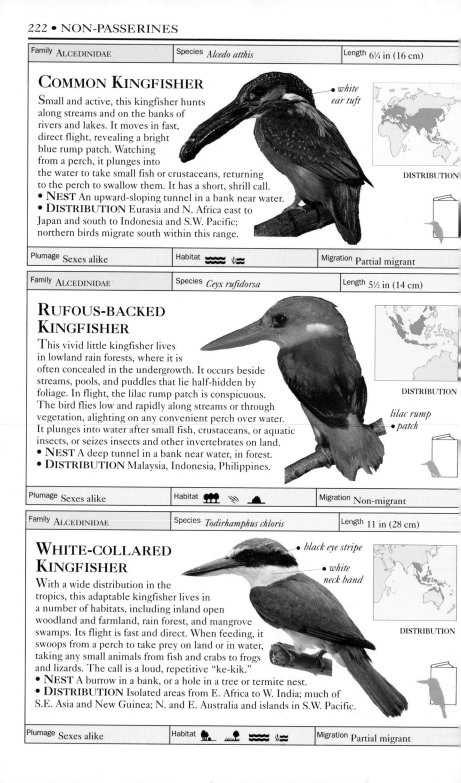

Family ALCEDINIDAE	Species *Alcedo atthis*	Length 6¼ in (16 cm)

COMMON KINGFISHER

Small and active, this kingfisher hunts
along streams and on the banks of
rivers and lakes. It moves in fast,
direct flight, revealing a bright
blue rump patch. Watching
from a perch, it plunges into
the water to take small fish or crustaceans, returning
to the perch to swallow them. It has a short, shrill call.
• **NEST** An upward-sloping tunnel in a bank near water.
• **DISTRIBUTION** Eurasia and N. Africa east to
Japan and south to Indonesia and S.W. Pacific;
northern birds migrate south within this range.

white
ear tuft

DISTRIBUTION

Plumage Sexes alike	Habitat 〰〰 ⩊	Migration Partial migrant

Family ALCEDINIDAE	Species *Ceyx rufidorsa*	Length 5½ in (14 cm)

RUFOUS-BACKED KINGFISHER

This vivid little kingfisher lives
in lowland rain forests, where it is
often concealed in the undergrowth. It occurs beside
streams, pools, and puddles that lie half-hidden by
foliage. In flight, the lilac rump patch is conspicuous.
The bird flies low and rapidly along streams or through
vegetation, alighting on any convenient perch over water.
It plunges into water after small fish, crustaceans, or aquatic
insects, or seizes insects and other invertebrates on land.
• **NEST** A deep tunnel in a bank near water, in forest.
• **DISTRIBUTION** Malaysia, Indonesia, Philippines.

DISTRIBUTION

lilac rump
• patch

Plumage Sexes alike	Habitat 🌲🌲 〰 ⛰	Migration Non-migrant

Family ALCEDINIDAE	Species *Todirhamphus chloris*	Length 11 in (28 cm)

WHITE-COLLARED KINGFISHER

With a wide distribution in the
tropics, this adaptable kingfisher lives in
a number of habitats, including inland open
woodland and farmland, rain forest, and mangrove
swamps. Its flight is fast and direct. When feeding, it
swoops from a perch to take prey on land or in water,
taking any small animals from fish and crabs to frogs
and lizards. The call is a loud, repetitive "ke-kik."
• **NEST** A burrow in a bank, or a hole in a tree or termite nest.
• **DISTRIBUTION** Isolated areas from E. Africa to W. India; much of
S.E. Asia and New Guinea; N. and E. Australia and islands in S.W. Pacific.

black eye stripe

white
neck band

DISTRIBUTION

Plumage Sexes alike	Habitat 🌳 🌲 〰〰 ⩊	Migration Partial migrant

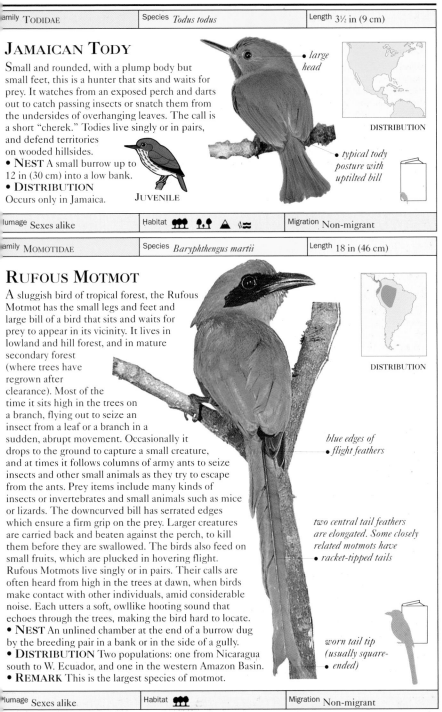

Family TODIDAE	Species *Todus todus*	Length 3½ in (9 cm)

JAMAICAN TODY

Small and rounded, with a plump body but small feet, this is a hunter that sits and waits for prey. It watches from an exposed perch and darts out to catch passing insects or snatch them from the undersides of overhanging leaves. The call is a short "cherek." Todies live singly or in pairs, and defend territories on wooded hillsides.
• **NEST** A small burrow up to 12 in (30 cm) into a low bank.
• **DISTRIBUTION** Occurs only in Jamaica.

• *large head*

DISTRIBUTION

• *typical tody posture with uptilted bill*

JUVENILE

Plumage Sexes alike	Habitat	Migration Non-migrant

Family MOMOTIDAE	Species *Baryphthengus martii*	Length 18 in (46 cm)

RUFOUS MOTMOT

A sluggish bird of tropical forest, the Rufous Motmot has the small legs and feet and large bill of a bird that sits and waits for prey to appear in its vicinity. It lives in lowland and hill forest, and in mature secondary forest (where trees have regrown after clearance). Most of the time it sits high in the trees on a branch, flying out to seize an insect from a leaf or a branch in a sudden, abrupt movement. Occasionally it drops to the ground to capture a small creature, and at times it follows columns of army ants to seize insects and other small animals as they try to escape from the ants. Prey items include many kinds of insects or invertebrates and small animals such as mice or lizards. The downcurved bill has serrated edges which ensure a firm grip on the prey. Larger creatures are carried back and beaten against the perch, to kill them before they are swallowed. The birds also feed on small fruits, which are plucked in hovering flight. Rufous Motmots live singly or in pairs. Their calls are often heard from high in the trees at dawn, when birds make contact with other individuals, amid considerable noise. Each utters a soft, owllike hooting sound that echoes through the trees, making the bird hard to locate.
• **NEST** An unlined chamber at the end of a burrow dug by the breeding pair in a bank or in the side of a gully.
• **DISTRIBUTION** Two populations: one from Nicaragua south to W. Ecuador, and one in the western Amazon Basin.
• **REMARK** This is the largest species of motmot.

DISTRIBUTION

blue edges of • *flight feathers*

two central tail feathers are elongated. Some closely related motmots have • *racket-tipped tails*

worn tail tip (usually square- • *ended)*

Plumage Sexes alike	Habitat	Migration Non-migrant

Family MEROPIDAE	Species *Nyctyornis amictus*	Length 12½ in (32 cm)

RED-BEARDED BEE-EATER

This forest-dwelling bee-eater has a downcurved bill, rounded wings, and loose, shaggy-looking, red feathers on its throat and forehead. It occurs singly or in pairs in the upper and middle foliage of forest and at the forest edge. Here it hunts insects from a perch. It has a chuckling call.
• **NEST** A burrow in a sand or earth bank beside a forest stream.
• **DISTRIBUTION** S. Thailand, Malay Peninsula, Sumatra, and Borneo.

DISTRIBUTION

large head

short, rounded wings

JUVENILE

square-tipped tail

Plumage Sexes alike	Habitat	Migration Non-migrant

Family MEROPIDAE	Species *Merops albicollis*	Length 9 in (23 cm)

WHITE-THROATED BEE-EATER

A typical bee-eater of open country, this species has a thin, downcurved bill, long, narrow wings, and two thin tail streamers which are made up of the elongated central tail feathers. A useful identification feature is the combination of a white brow, a white throat, and a pale breast below a black neck band. This is a migrant species, alternating between two habitats. It breeds in dry, very open country with some thorn scrub, and winters in moister savanna (tropical grassland) and forest borders and clearings. Flight is light and fast, with frequent glides, either straight or in circling patterns. The bee-eater usually hunts from a low perch, taking flying insects, particularly bees and wasps. It recognizes ones that are venomous and holds them carefully in the tip of its bill, rubbing the sting of the insect against a perch or the ground to discharge the poison, after which the prey can be swallowed safely. Flying termites are taken avidly when they swarm. Insects are also captured on open ground, as well as spiders and small lizards. This bird is highly sociable and often occurs in parties and flocks. In cooler weather, and when roosting, birds are seen huddling together in tightly packed rows on perches. When breeding, however, birds roost in their nest burrows. Breeding usually takes place in large colonies. The flock selects a site and then all the pairs excavate their nest burrows simultaneously, apparently stimulated by the activity of the group as a whole. The pairs show few signs of territorial behavior and limit themselves to guarding a small area around the entrances to their burrows. In this species, a majority of pairs in a colony are likely to have at least one additional individual helping in nesting tasks, and up to six "helpers" have been recorded at a single nest.
• **NEST** A tunnel dug in flat or sloping sand, ending in an unlined nest chamber.
• **DISTRIBUTION** Breeds in a narrow band south of the Sahara. Winters further south in W. and C. Africa.

DISTRIBUTION

black-and-white striped head and throat

JUVENILE

long, narrow wings

two elongated central tail feathers

Plumage Sexes alike	Habitat	Migration Migrant

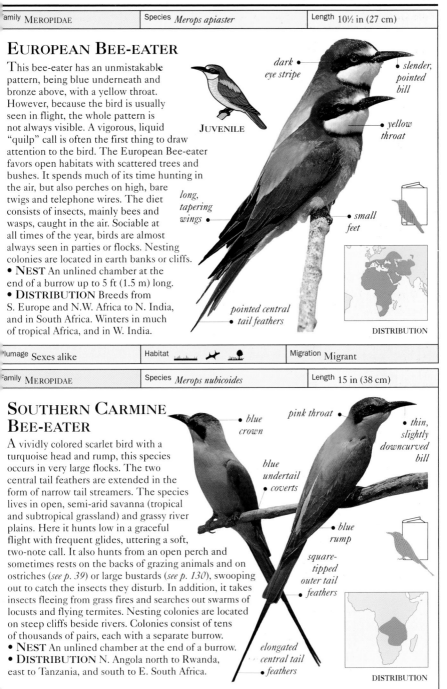

| Family MEROPIDAE | Species *Merops apiaster* | Length 10½ in (27 cm) |

EUROPEAN BEE-EATER

This bee-eater has an unmistakable pattern, being blue underneath and bronze above, with a yellow throat. However, because the bird is usually seen in flight, the whole pattern is not always visible. A vigorous, liquid "quilp" call is often the first thing to draw attention to the bird. The European Bee-eater favors open habitats with scattered trees and bushes. It spends much of its time hunting in the air, but also perches on high, bare twigs and telephone wires. The diet consists of insects, mainly bees and wasps, caught in the air. Sociable at all times of the year, birds are almost always seen in parties or flocks. Nesting colonies are located in earth banks or cliffs.
• **NEST** An unlined chamber at the end of a burrow up to 5 ft (1.5 m) long.
• **DISTRIBUTION** Breeds from S. Europe and N.W. Africa to N. India, and in South Africa. Winters in much of tropical Africa, and in W. India.

dark eye stripe
slender, pointed bill
yellow throat
JUVENILE
long, tapering wings
small feet
pointed central tail feathers

DISTRIBUTION

| Plumage Sexes alike | Habitat | Migration Migrant |

| Family MEROPIDAE | Species *Merops nubicoides* | Length 15 in (38 cm) |

SOUTHERN CARMINE BEE-EATER

A vividly colored scarlet bird with a turquoise head and rump, this species occurs in very large flocks. The two central tail feathers are extended in the form of narrow tail streamers. The species lives in open, semi-arid savanna (tropical and subtropical grassland) and grassy river plains. Here it hunts low in a graceful flight with frequent glides, uttering a soft, two-note call. It also hunts from an open perch and sometimes rests on the backs of grazing animals and on ostriches (*see p. 39*) or large bustards (*see p. 130*), swooping out to catch the insects they disturb. In addition, it takes insects fleeing from grass fires and searches out swarms of locusts and flying termites. Nesting colonies are located on steep cliffs beside rivers. Colonies consist of tens of thousands of pairs, each with a separate burrow.
• **NEST** An unlined chamber at the end of a burrow.
• **DISTRIBUTION** N. Angola north to Rwanda, east to Tanzania, and south to E. South Africa.

blue crown
pink throat
thin, slightly downcurved bill
blue undertail coverts
blue rump
square-tipped outer tail feathers
elongated central tail feathers

DISTRIBUTION

| Plumage Sexes alike | Habitat | Migration Partial migrant |

Family CORACIIDAE	Species *Coracias garrulus*	Length 12 in (30 cm)

EUROPEAN ROLLER

A heavily built, blue bird with a chestnut back, this roller is usually seen hunched on a commanding lookout perch in a tree, on a post, or on a telephone wire. It watches for large insects on the ground, suddenly exposing its long, broad wings as it swoops to seize them, then returns to the perch. Insects are also caught in midair. In the breeding season, the displaying male flies high in the air and performs steep ascents followed by wild, twisting dives that show off his wing colors. The display is accompanied by croaking and rattling calls. Breeding pairs defend territories, but flocks form before migration.
• NEST An unlined cavity in a tree, or exceptionally in a bank or cliff.
• DISTRIBUTION Breeds in parts of Europe and N. Africa. Winters as far south as South Africa.

• *vivid blue wing patch shows in flight*

• *square-tipped blue tail*

JUVENILE

DISTRIBUTION

Plumage Sexes alike	Habitat	Migration Migrant

Family CORACIIDAE	Species *Coracias caudata*	Length 16 in (40 cm)

LILAC-BREASTED ROLLER

Identified by its lilac-colored breast and forked, swallow-like tail, this roller lives in dry, open places ranging from open grassland with a few bushes and trees to thornbush savanna (grassland) and dry, open woodland. It watches from an exposed perch, then swoops down on its large, blue wings to seize prey from the ground, taking large insects, spiders, and sometimes small reptiles and birds. During the midday heat it abandons its exposed perch and seeks shade. It is aggressive and noisy, with loud, squawking calls. Similar wild, raucous calling is heard during the male's aerial display, which apparently serves to advertise the pair's presence as well as impress the female. The displaying male repeatedly climbs steeply then dives in rolling and twisting flight.
• NEST A cavity in a dead tree or termite mound, some 10–16½ ft (3–5 m) above the ground.
• DISTRIBUTION From Ethiopia through E. Africa and Angola into N. South Africa.

• *white streaks on the throat*

• *vivid blue wing patch*

two elongated outer tail feathers form the • *point*

JUVENILE

DISTRIBUTION

Plumage Sexes alike	Habitat	Migration Partial migrant

Family CORACIIDAE	Species *Coracias spatulata*	Length 16 in (40 cm)

RACKET-TAILED ROLLER

The tail of this roller has an elongated pair of outer feathers ending in expanded tips which give this species its name. A subtly colored bird of open woodland, it is sparsely distributed within its range. It occurs singly or in pairs or family parties, individuals feeding separately but within sight of each other. Swooping from a perch, it takes prey mainly from the ground, but also from the air. It eats insects such as flying ants and termites, as well as grasshoppers, crickets, centipedes, and scorpions.
• **NEST** An unlined cavity in a branch or tree trunk.
• **DISTRIBUTION** S. Angola, S.E. Zaire, and through Zimbabwe to N.E. South Africa.

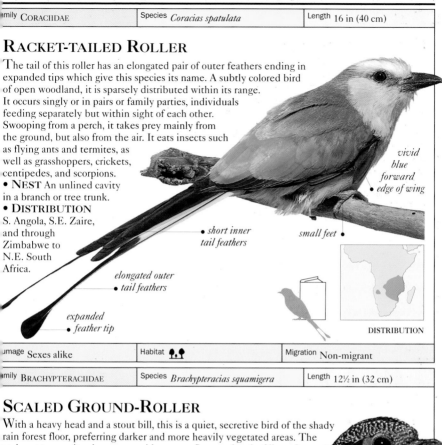

vivid blue forward edge of wing

short inner tail feathers

small feet

elongated outer tail feathers

expanded feather tip

DISTRIBUTION

Plumage Sexes alike	Habitat	Migration Non-migrant

Family BRACHYPTERACIIDAE	Species *Brachypteracias squamigera*	Length 12½ in (32 cm)

SCALED GROUND-ROLLER

With a heavy head and a stout bill, this is a quiet, secretive bird of the shady rain forest floor, preferring darker and more heavily vegetated areas. The scaly pattern on its plumage provides camouflage against leaf litter. In spite of having long legs, usually associated with rapid movement on the ground, this is a sluggish bird. It takes a few steps or makes a short run before pausing and remaining still. Prey items include earthworms, insects, spiders, and snails. The short, rounded wings are used only for brief flights to low perches, with rapid, whirring wingbeats.
• **NEST** A cavity lined with dead leaves at the end of a burrow up to 3¼ ft (1 m) long in the ground or in a low bank.
• **DISTRIBUTION** N.E. Madagascar.

short, rounded wings

long legs of a ground feeder

DISTRIBUTION

Plumage Sexes alike	Habitat	Migration Non-migrant

| Family LEPTOSOMATIDAE | Species *Leptosomus discolor* | Length 20 in (50 cm) |

CUCKOO-ROLLER

This species has the short legs, heavy bill, and large head of a roller (*see pp. 226–227*), but with its long wings and tail it has a slight resemblance to a cuckoo (*see pp. 188–191*). A bird of tropical forest and open woodland, it feeds on insects, particularly hairy caterpillars, and also takes chameleons. Liquid, whistling notes are uttered from a perch, or in circling flight over the territory.
• **NEST** A hole in a tree.
• **DISTRIBUTION** Madagascar.

feathers ruffled and raised as bird turns its head

MALE

DISTRIBUTION

pale, spotted underside of female bird

| Plumage Sexes differ | Habitat | Migration Non-migrant |

| Family UPUPIDAE | Species *Upupa epops* | Length 11½ in (29 cm) |

HOOPOE

Unmistakable with its bold coloring and crest, the Hoopoe has stripes that, like those of a zebra, merge into the background when seen at a distance. It feeds mostly on the ground, probing for insects and small lizards. The call is a soft, repeated "hoop" sound.
• **NEST** A hole in a tree, termite mound, or wall.
• **DISTRIBUTION** Eurasia, Africa, and Madagascar. Northern populations winter in tropical Africa, India, and S.E. Asia.
• **REMARK** Hoopoes breeding south of the Sahara are sometimes regarded as a separate species.

crest is almost lowered

slender bill for probing

SPREAD WING

DISTRIBUTION

barred wing pattern

black tail with white band revealed in flight

| Plumage Sexes alike | Habitat | Migration Partial migrant |

| Family PHOENICULIDAE | Species *Phoeniculus purpureus* | Length 16 in (40 cm) |

GREEN WOOD-HOOPOE

Adapted for clambering on tree trunks and branches, this species has short, strong legs and sharp claws for gripping bark firmly. The long, graduated tail with a white bar near the feather tips is used, either closed or spread, as a support. In flight a white wing bar is revealed. This bird occurs wherever there are large trees except in thick rain forest, individuals following each other in single file in short flights from one tree to another. Green Wood-Hoopoes probe into crevices and holes with their long, slender, slightly curved bills, feeding on insects and other invertebrates, together with some fruit such as berries. This species is sociable and lives in small parties of up to 16 individuals, which are noisy with loud, cackling calls. These are frequently used in social display in which several birds perform a rapid, exaggerated bowing movement, vigorously flexing the tail up and down. Other members of the party help a dominant pair by feeding the incubating female and the nestlings when hatched.
• **NEST** A natural cavity in a tree, or an old woodpecker hole, up to 72 ft (22 m) above the ground.
• **DISTRIBUTION** Africa south of the Sahara.

JUVENILE

• *white wing patch*

DISTRIBUTION

• *white bars on outer tail feathers*

long, tapering • *tail*

| Plumage Sexes alike | Habitat | Migration Non-migrant |

| Family PHOENICULIDAE | Species *Rhinopomastus cyanomelas* | Length 11 in (28 cm) |

COMMON SCIMITARBILL

A slender bird, the Scimitarbill is adapted for foraging and clambering among trees. The legs are short and the feet strong, with sharp claws for maintaining a strong grip on the bark. It is agile and acrobatic and often feeds while hanging upside down. The plumage is dark, glossed with violet-blue in the male. Scimitarbills probe holes and crevices with their long, slender, curved bills in search of beetles and spiders, and also catch large insects such as preying mantises. They use their long tails to support themselves while feeding. They have rounded wings, and this species has a white wingbar that is revealed in flight. It lives in trees in woodland and dry, open scrub, usually occurring singly or in pairs, and nesting in isolated pairs. However, it often joins parties of mixed bird species feeding in woodland. The call is a series of plaintive whistles.
• **NEST** A narrow hollow in a tree trunk.
• **DISTRIBUTION** From Somalia and Kenya through E. Africa to Angola and southern Africa.

• *thin, curved bill for probing*

DISTRIBUTION

FEMALE

• *long, tapering tail*

| Plumage Sexes differ slightly | Habitat | Migration Non-migrant |

| Family BUCEROTIDAE | Species *Tockus erythrorhynchus* | Length 17½ in (45 cm) |

RED-BILLED HORNBILL

This is a small, slender hornbill with a narrow, downcurved bill. Usually occurring in pairs or small parties, it gathers into flocks at an abundant food source. Red-billed Hornbills feed by hopping on the ground, searching the surface and probing holes for insects. They follow the paths of game animals in order to hunt for dung beetles.

JUVENILE

• **NEST** A hole in a tree, sparsely lined with plants. The female inside the nest, helped by the male outside, plasters the entrance with mud and droppings, leaving only a narrow slit. The male brings food which is passed through the slit, and droppings are squirted out. The female leaves when the young are half-grown, and they reseal the nest until ready to leave.

• **DISTRIBUTION** From the S. Sahara through E. Africa to South Africa.

bare skin around the eye

white underside

long tail

DISTRIBUTION

| Plumage Sexes alike | Habitat | Migration Non-migrant |

| Family BUCEROTIDAE | Species *Ceratogymna bucinator* | L. 26 in (65 cm)/23 in (58 cm) |

TRUMPETER HORNBILL

A heavily built hornbill of forest and woodland, this species has a long, curved casque on the top of its bill. It feeds mainly on fruit and insects found in the trees, and normally occurs in small flocks.

JUVENILE

large casque (shorter in the female)

• **NEST** A natural hole in a tree. The female seals herself in by plastering the entrance with a mixture of mud and droppings, leaving only a narrow, vertical slit. The male brings all the food for the female and the young. All birds leave the nest at the same time.

• **DISTRIBUTION** E. and C. Africa.

bare skin around the eye

DISTRIBUTION

| Plumage Sexes alike | Habitat | Migration Non-migrant |

Family BUCEROTIDAE	Species *Buceros rhinoceros*	L. 49 in (125 cm)/35 in (90 cm)

RHINOCEROS HORNBILL

One of the larger hornbills, this species has a huge casque extending along most of the bill and curving upward at the end. A bird of lowland and foothill forest, it prefers the tops of high trees in areas of mature growth. In spite of its size, it moves easily among the branches with large, springy hops. It flies strongly above the trees with noisy, flapping wingbeats, frequently uttering its resonant, trumpeting call. The wings are broad and black, and in flight the white rump and white tail with a black band are revealed. Usually occurring singly or in pairs, it gathers in small parties where fruiting trees offer an abundant food source. Although fruit forms the main part of its diet, small birds and nestlings are sometimes taken, and also other small creatures.
• **NEST** A hole in a tree, the entrance plastered over to leave only a narrow slit for feeding.
• **DISTRIBUTION** S.E. Asia in Malay Peninsula, Sumatra, Borneo, and Java.

massive casque

DISTRIBUTION

broad, rounded wings

white tail

Plumage Sexes alike	Habitat	Migration Non-migrant

Family BUCORVIDAE	Species *Bucorvus cafer*	Length 42 in (107 cm)

SOUTHERN GROUND-HORNBILL

A large, dark hornbill, this bird walks and forages on the ground most of the time, although it roosts in trees. It lives in groups of up to eight birds, that share and defend a territory. Groups patrol their territories, probing, pecking, and digging at the ground, and eating small animals including insects, snakes, tortoises, and rodents. Some members of the group act as "helpers" for the dominant pair when they nest.
• **NEST** A hole in a tree, lined with dry leaves.
• **DISTRIBUTION** Parts of Africa south of the Sahara.
• **REMARK** This is the largest species of hornbill.

red throat wattle

JUVENILE   **FEMALE**

white wing patch revealed in flight

DISTRIBUTION

Plumage Sexes alike	Habitat	Migration Non-migrant

Family GALBULIDAE	Species *Galbula ruficauda*	Length 8 in (20 cm)

RUFOUS-TAILED JACAMAR

Slenderly built with a long, thin bill, a long tail, and short, weak legs, this is one of the birds that sits and waits to snatch its prey. It lives in lower vegetation whether this be at forest edges, in clearings, or in cleared areas where trees have begun to regrow. It is often seen along streams. Alert and nervously active, the Rufous-tailed Jacamar sits on an open perch with bill uptilted, moving its head frequently. It flies out to catch passing insects before returning to the same perch, or to one nearby. Food is swallowed whole, but big butterflies are first beaten against the perch to remove the wings. Other prey includes dragonflies, bees, wasps, and flying beetles. This species lives in pairs, and the two birds frequently perch and hunt close to one another. They utter frequent, sharp, high pitched calls that merge into a trill at times of agitation.
• **NEST** An unlined burrow up to 20 in (50 cm) long, in a bank, an upturned tree root, or a chamber in a termite nest.
• **DISTRIBUTION** Two populations; one from Mexico to N. Brazil, the other from C. Brazil south to N.E. Argentina.

FEMALE

DISTRIBUTION

• *two toes forward, two back (outer toes are reversed)*

• *tail is glossy green above, with pale orange outer feathers below*

Plumage Sexes differ	Habitat 🏞 🌳 🌿 ✈	Migration Non-migrant

Family BUCCONIDAE	Species *Bucco macrodactylus*	Length 5½ in (14 cm)

CHESTNUT-CAPPED PUFFBIRD

A squat bird with a large head, this species has lax, fluffy-looking plumage from which its name is derived. The bill is stout, with bristles surrounding the base to help in trapping insects, and the legs and feet are small and weak. The species is found in forest, along river banks within forest, and in low woodland that grows up in clearings. It sits on a low perch that may be either exposed or partly hidden in foliage, and makes short flights to take insects from nearby vegetation. Usually quiet, it utters a rising sequence of short notes, dying away to a twitter.
• **NEST** A burrow excavated in the ground, or cut into a tree-termite nest.
• **DISTRIBUTION** From Colombia and Venezuela south to Bolivia and W. Brazil.

DISTRIBUTION

• *loose, fluffy plumage*

short, rounded wings •

• *squat, heavy posture*

Plumage Sexes alike	Habitat 🌿 🌳 〰	Migration Non-migrant

| Family BUCCONIDAE | Species *Monasa nigrifrons* | Length 11½ in (29 cm) |

BLACK-FRONTED NUNBIRD

A sleek and alert-looking puffbird, this species watches for prey at all levels within the vegetation. It sits quietly, then swoops to snatch an insect as it flies past, or takes insects and other invertebrates from the foliage or from the ground. Moving frequently, it flies from perch to perch with a few, rapid wingbeats followed by a glide. At times it follows troops of monkeys for the insects they disturb. It occurs singly, in pairs, or in small groups and is seen at riversides, in swampy forest, and in secondary forest (areas where the trees have regrown after clearance). The birds call frequently, and at times whole groups chorus for several minutes. Some members of groups act as nesting "helpers."
• **NEST** A burrow cut in a bank or at an angle into the ground.
• **DISTRIBUTION** South America east of the Andes in Colombia, Peru, N. Bolivia, and Brazil.

curved bill

JUVENILE

two toes forward, two back

short, rounded wings

reversed outer toe

broad tail with rounded tip

DISTRIBUTION

| Plumage Sexes alike | Habitat | Migration Non-migrant |

| Family INDICATORIDAE | Species *Indicator indicator* | Length 8 in (20 cm) |

GREATER HONEYGUIDE

Although unspectacular in appearance, with dull plumage, the honeyguides are unique among birds in their ability to digest wax. This species occurs in open forest or mixed trees and bushes. Resembling a songbird in size and shape, it feeds mainly on insects but also adopts a specialized strategy to procure wax. When it has located a bees' nest it leads a human, honeybadger, baboon, or mongoose to the nest with chattering calls and short flights, waits for it to be opened, and later feeds on the wax and brood. It does not rear its own young but lays an egg in the nest of another bird species. The newly hatched honeyguide has temporary, sharp hooks on the tip of its bill for killing the nestlings of the host.
• **NEST** This bird parasitizes other species' nests. A single egg is laid in the nest of an insect-eating bird.
• **DISTRIBUTION** Parts of Africa, from Senegal to the Cape.

DISTRIBUTION

white ear patch

white-edged wing coverts

JUVENILE

long wings

tail is normally square-tipped

| Plumage Sexes differ slightly | Habitat | Migration Non-migrant |

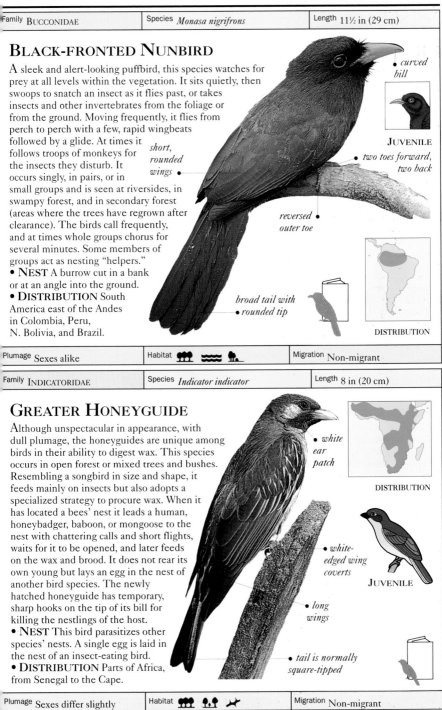

Family CAPITONIDAE	Species *Eubucco bourcierii*	Length 6 in (15 cm)

RED-HEADED BARBET

This small barbet feeds deliberately in the middle and lower branches of mountain forest, probing into dead leaf clusters and sometimes hanging upside down to feed on insects and fruit. Unlike most barbets, it is usually silent.
- **NEST** A cavity in a rotten tree.
  - **DISTRIBUTION** From Costa Rica south to N. Peru.

glossy red head •

reversed outer toe •

DISTRIBUTION

FEMALE

Plumage Sexes differ	Habitat 🌳🌳🌳 🌿 ⛰	Migration Non-migrant

Family CAPITONIDAE	Species *Semnornis ramphastinus*	Length 7½ in (19 cm)

TOUCAN BARBET

A mountain barbet inhabiting the permanently misty, high-altitude "cloud forests" of the Andes, this species has a long-bodied look. It often hops along branches in a forward-leaning attitude, raising its tail for balance as it turns quickly. Single birds or pairs join mixed-species flocks that feed at all levels in the forest. Toucan Barbets feed mainly on fruit, also taking insects, other invertebrates, and small creatures such as lizards. The call is a loud honk, and pairs often perform duets.
- **NEST** An unlined cavity in a tree hole.
- **DISTRIBUTION** S.W. Colombia, W. Ecuador.

DISTRIBUTION

• *heavy bill with irregular edges used for gripping fruit*

• *flame-colored underside*

Plumage Sexes alike	Habitat 🌳🌳🌳 🌿 ⛰	Migration Non-migrant

Family CAPITONIDAE	Species *Psilopogon pyrolophus*	Length 11 in (28 cm)

FIRE-TUFTED BARBET

Inconspicuously colored except for the reddish tuft on its forehead, this is a bird of mountain forest. Usually occurring in small parties in tall trees, it clambers about among vines and foliage, looking more like a parrot (*see pp. 169–185*) than a typical barbet. It feeds greedily on small fruits, at times staining its plumage. Birds are quiet but keep in contact by uttering soft whistles and buzzing notes like the noise of a cicada.
- **NEST** Unknown; probably a cavity in a tree.
- **DISTRIBUTION** Mountains in Malay Peninsula and Sumatra.

DISTRIBUTION

two toes • *forward, two back (outer toe reversed)*

Plumage Sexes alike	Habitat 🌳🌳🌳 ⛰	Migration Non-migrant

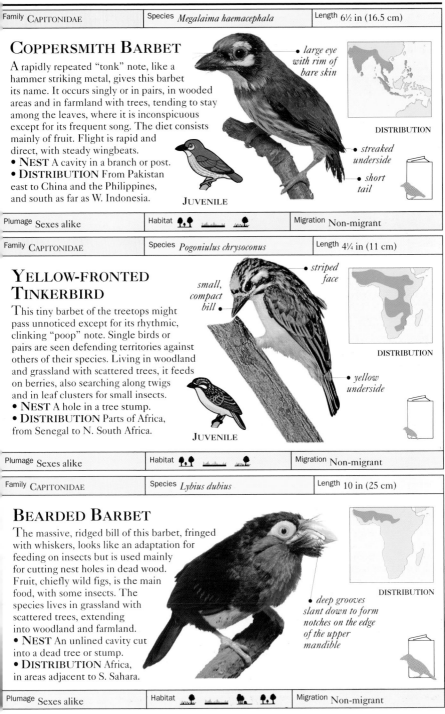

| Family CAPITONIDAE | Species *Megalaima haemacephala* | Length 6½ in (16.5 cm) |

COPPERSMITH BARBET

A rapidly repeated "tonk" note, like a
hammer striking metal, gives this barbet
its name. It occurs singly or in pairs, in wooded
areas and in farmland with trees, tending to stay
among the leaves, where it is inconspicuous
except for its frequent song. The diet consists
mainly of fruit. Flight is rapid and
direct, with steady wingbeats.
• **NEST** A cavity in a branch or post.
• **DISTRIBUTION** From Pakistan
east to China and the Philippines,
and south as far as W. Indonesia.

• *large eye
with rim of
bare skin*

DISTRIBUTION

• *streaked
underside*

• *short
tail*

JUVENILE

| Plumage Sexes alike | Habitat | Migration Non-migrant |

| Family CAPITONIDAE | Species *Pogoniulus chrysoconus* | Length 4¼ in (11 cm) |

YELLOW-FRONTED TINKERBIRD

This tiny barbet of the treetops might
pass unnoticed except for its rhythmic,
clinking "poop" note. Single birds or
pairs are seen defending territories against
others of their species. Living in woodland
and grassland with scattered trees, it feeds
on berries, also searching along twigs
and in leaf clusters for small insects.
• **NEST** A hole in a tree stump.
• **DISTRIBUTION** Parts of Africa,
from Senegal to N. South Africa.

*small,
compact
bill* •

• *striped
face*

DISTRIBUTION

• *yellow
underside*

JUVENILE

| Plumage Sexes alike | Habitat | Migration Non-migrant |

| Family CAPITONIDAE | Species *Lybius dubius* | Length 10 in (25 cm) |

BEARDED BARBET

The massive, ridged bill of this barbet, fringed
with whiskers, looks like an adaptation for
feeding on insects but is used mainly
for cutting nest holes in dead wood.
Fruit, chiefly wild figs, is the main
food, with some insects. The
species lives in grassland with
scattered trees, extending
into woodland and farmland.
• **NEST** An unlined cavity cut
into a dead tree or stump.
• **DISTRIBUTION** Africa,
in areas adjacent to S. Sahara.

DISTRIBUTION

• *deep grooves
slant down to form
notches on the edge
of the upper
mandible*

| Plumage Sexes alike | Habitat | Migration Non-migrant |

Family RAMPHASTIDAE	Species *Pteroglossus castanotis*	Length 14½ in (37 cm)

CHESTNUT-EARED ARACARI

The long, slim, gently curved bill of this species, with its distinctly serrated edges, is typical of the aracaris. Living in forest and forest edge, this slenderly built bird is active and sociable. It usually occurs in small parties that hunt together, moving in single file in short flights through the trees, and roosting huddled in a cavity such as an old woodpecker's hole. The diet consists of fruit such as figs, tree catkins, insects, and a variety of small animals.

• **NEST** An unlined cavity in a tree or an old woodpecker hole.

• **DISTRIBUTION** From E. Colombia and Ecuador south to Bolivia and N.E. Argentina.

bare blue skin around the eye •

DISTRIBUTION

dull chestnut • ear patch revealed at certain angles to the light

red band • across the belly

serrated • edges on both mandibles

slender • tongue

• long tail tapering at the tip

Plumage Sexes alike	Habitat 🌳 🌿	Migration Non-migrant

Family RAMPHASTIDAE	Species *Andigena laminirostris*	Length 20 in (50 cm)

PLATE-BILLED MOUNTAIN-TOUCAN

The most obvious feature of toucans is the brightly colored and massive bill. In this species there is an additional bright yellow horny plate on the outside of the upper mandible, the purpose of which is unknown. The long bill is used to help the bird reach for food, which consists mainly of fruit, with some insects and other small creatures. This species has the typical coloring of a mountain-toucan, with dark upperparts and mainly blue-gray underside, and the plumage is fine, with a hairy texture. It is a bird of mountain forest, occurring in pairs or small groups. At times these groups join flocks of mixed species to move through the forest looking for fruit and eating the insects that they disturb in the process. The usual call is a rising series of querulous, whining notes, uttered while the bird is hidden in foliage. The species also has a loud, rattling call.

• **NEST** A natural hole in a tree.

• **DISTRIBUTION** W. Andes in S.W. Colombia and W. Ecuador.

• flat yellow plate on side of bill

• yellow flank patch

• red undertail coverts

reddish tail • tip

DISTRIBUTION

Plumage Sexes alike	Habitat 🌳 ⛰	Migration Non-migrant

| Family RAMPHASTIDAE | Species *Ramphastos tucanus* | Length 21 in (53 cm) |

RED-BILLED TOUCAN

This large toucan inhabits tall rain forest and forest edges, usually staying in the higher branches and foliage canopy of mature trees. Like other toucans, it roosts by squatting with its head turned backward, resting its bill on its back, with the tail turned forward and resting on the bill. It usually lives singly or in pairs, but at times it may gather in larger groups since five birds have been reported roosting huddled together on a branch. Seen in flight it appears top-heavy with its large bill; it makes a few quick wingflaps, then glides along on set wings. Red-billed Toucans feed on fruit, tree catkins, insects, spiders, other animals such as lizards, snakes, and eggs and nestlings of small birds. The call is a loud series of rhythmic yelps, often accompanied by upward jerks of the bill and tail.
• NEST A natural cavity in a tree, sometimes lined unintentionally with regurgitated fruit stones.
• DISTRIBUTION N. Amazonia from E. Colombia and E. Venezuela to the Guianas and N. Brazil.

• *bare blue skin around eye*

DISTRIBUTION

• *short wings*

yellow rump •

red undertail coverts •

square tipped tail •

| Plumage Sexes alike | Habitat | Migration Non-migrant |

| Family RAMPHASTIDAE | Species *Ramphastos toco* | Length 24 in (60 cm) |

TOCO TOUCAN

The huge, unwieldy bill of this toucan gives the bird an unbalanced look, but the bill is light and hollow in structure. It is very conspicuous when the bird is seen in flight, which is undulating, with alternating flaps and glides. The white rump and red undertail coverts are also noticeable in flight. The Toco Toucan lives in woodland, secondary forest (areas where the trees have regrown after forest clearance), and coconut and other palm plantations. It is seen moving along branches with heavy, bounding hops, taking mainly fruit and insects, but also other small creatures and the eggs and nestlings of small birds. The large bill enables the bird to reach food on the end of thin twigs that cannot support its weight.

• *bare yellow skin around eye*

• *white throat*

DISTRIBUTION

Food is seized in the bill tip and the head is tossed back, opening the bill. This throws the food to the back of the throat where the long, bristly tongue may help catch it. Toco Toucans utter deep, croaking calls in a deliberate manner, often from a high twig.
• NEST A hollow in a dead or living tree.
• DISTRIBUTION From Venezuela south through Brazil to N.W. Argentina.

red undertail • *coverts*

| Plumage Sexes alike | Habitat | Migration Non-migrant |

| Family PICIDAE | Species *Jynx torquilla* | Length 6¼ in (16 cm) |

EURASIAN WRYNECK

This bird's name refers to its neck-stretching and head-twisting movements, used to threaten an enemy. It feeds on ants, extending its sticky tongue into their burrows to extract them.
• **NEST** A hole in a tree, wall, or bank.
  • **DISTRIBUTION** Eurasia and N.W. Africa. Winters in Africa, India, and S.E. Asia.

small, thin bill

DISTRIBUTION

finely patterned plumage for camouflage

JUVENILE

| Plumage Sexes alike | Habitat | Migration Migrant |

| Family PICIDAE | Species *Sasia abnormis* | Length 4 in (10 cm) |

RUFOUS PICULET

Tiny and active, this woodpecker sometimes looks more like a small passerine when seen feeding and foraging. It lives in undergrowth in forests, clambering and hopping among branches, leaves, and twigs, and searching the ground litter, taking ants and other small insects. When feeding in bamboo and small trees, it taps the surface and probes the bark in more usual woodpecker fashion.
• **NEST** A hole excavated in a branch.
• **DISTRIBUTION** S.E. Asia in Malay Peninsula, Sumatra, Java, and Borneo.

DISTRIBUTION

FEMALE

strong feet with a wide grasp for clambering

very short tail

| Plumage Sexes differ | Habitat | Migration Non-migrant |

| Family PICIDAE | Species *Melanerpes formicivorus* | Length 9 in (23 cm) |

ACORN WOODPECKER

This sociable woodpecker has a close association with oak trees. It lives in groups of up to 12 birds that defend a shared territory and nest communally. In late summer, the birds bore rows of holes into trees, fences, and wooden buildings, fixing an acorn in each hole to be stored as a future food supply for the group. Insects are also eaten in the summer, and some other nuts and fruits in winter. The call is a raucous double note.
• **NEST** A hole cut in a trunk.
• **DISTRIBUTION** From W. North America to Colombia.

staring eye

white facial markings

FEMALE

streaked breast pattern

DISTRIBUTION

| Plumage Sexes differ | Habitat | Migration Non-migrant |

amily PICIDAE	Species *Melanerpes candidus*	Length 9½ in (24 cm)

WHITE WOODPECKER

The vividly pied plumage of this species, combined with the fact that it is often seen in open country, make the bird very conspicuous. The male bird (not illustrated) has yellow patches on the nape and belly. Habitats range from semi-open forest and forest edges to open grassland with trees. For a woodpecker, this species has unusually direct, strong flight (*see p. 16*). When crossing open country, it tends to pause and rest periodically in the tops of dead trees. White Woodpeckers usually occur in small parties, but it is not known whether these are families. The birds are often seen climbing up trees, tapping and searching for insects, but their main food is fruit, and the species has become a pest at orange groves. White Woodpeckers also eat seeds such as grain. Captive specimens show a fondness for honey, which suggests that wild birds may take nectar from flowers.
• **NEST** A hole excavated in a tree.
• **DISTRIBUTION** E. South America from Surinam south through Brazil to N. Argentina.

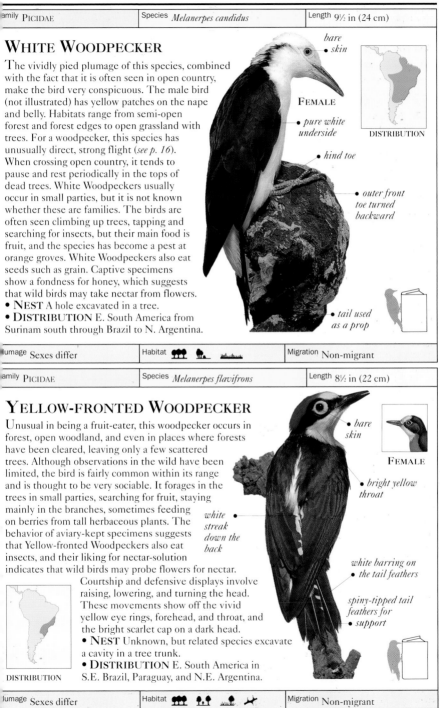

bare skin

FEMALE

pure white underside

DISTRIBUTION

hind toe

outer front toe turned backward

tail used as a prop

lumage Sexes differ	Habitat	Migration Non-migrant

amily PICIDAE	Species *Melanerpes flavifrons*	Length 8½ in (22 cm)

YELLOW-FRONTED WOODPECKER

Unusual in being a fruit-eater, this woodpecker occurs in forest, open woodland, and even in places where forests have been cleared, leaving only a few scattered trees. Although observations in the wild have been limited, the bird is fairly common within its range and is thought to be very sociable. It forages in the trees in small parties, searching for fruit, staying mainly in the branches, sometimes feeding on berries from tall herbaceous plants. The behavior of aviary-kept specimens suggests that Yellow-fronted Woodpeckers also eat insects, and their liking for nectar-solution indicates that wild birds may probe flowers for nectar.
Courtship and defensive displays involve raising, lowering, and turning the head. These movements show off the vivid yellow eye rings, forehead, and throat, and the bright scarlet cap on a dark head.
• **NEST** Unknown, but related species excavate a cavity in a tree trunk.
• **DISTRIBUTION** E. South America in S.E. Brazil, Paraguay, and N.E. Argentina.

bare skin

FEMALE

bright yellow throat

white streak down the back

white barring on the tail feathers

spiny-tipped tail feathers for support

DISTRIBUTION

lumage Sexes differ	Habitat	Migration Non-migrant

Family PICIDAE	Species *Melanerpes carolinus*	Length 9½ in (24 cm)

RED-BELLIED WOODPECKER

This species is one of the "ladder-backed" woodpeckers, which have black-and-white barring across the back. It has a large area of red on the head and nape, which is an easier identification mark than the more limited red flush on the belly. In flight, a white rump and a short, white wingbar are revealed. The species is widespread in open woodland and also occurs in parks and suburbs. It is usually seen in pairs, but family groups remain together for a short period after breeding. The diet consists of insects, obtained by hacking at dead and dying wood, and birds visit garden birdfeeders in winter. Feeding in this way, birds make good use of the tail, with its stiffened feather shafts, as a support. The splayed, sharp-clawed feet help the birds to cling firmly to where they feed. The call is a rolling "churr."
• **NEST** An unlined hole, excavated in a tree.
• **DISTRIBUTION** E. North America. Northern populations winter south within this range.

• *male's red cap extends to forehead*

FEMALE

• *transverse barring on the back, typical of the "ladder-backed" woodpeckers*

• *barring on the tail*

• *tapering, spiny feather tips*

DISTRIBUTION

Plumage Sexes differ	Habitat 🌳🌿	Migration Partial migrant

Family PICIDAE	Species *Sphyrapicus varius*	Length 8½ in (22 cm)

YELLOW-BELLIED SAPSUCKER

Tapping into a tree produces more than just burrowing insects, and this species of woodpecker makes holes in the bark in order to feed on the sugary sap. The bird drills grid-like rows of holes into any suitable tree and renews them each year. Broadleaved trees such as maples, fruit trees, birches, and poplars are used, but other tree species are also tested, including conifers. A series of small holes is chiseled into the tree, and after a short while the bird returns to drink the oozing sap. The sapsucker also eats many of the insects attracted by the sap. Other animals also take the opportunity to drink the sap, including squirrels, warblers, and hummingbirds. This bird is mainly silent but has a mewing call note, and advertises possession of its territory in spring by a rapid drumming on a resonant, dead branch. Possibly because it must rely on sap rising in spring, this is a migrant species.
• **NEST** An unlined hole, which is excavated by the bird, in a tree.
• **DISTRIBUTION** Breeds in Canada and N. and E. USA. Winters in S. USA south to C. Panama, and the Caribbean.

• *striped face pattern*

• *black upper breast patch*

FEMALE

DISTRIBUTION

Plumage Sexes differ	Habitat 🌳🌳 🌿🌿	Migration Migrant

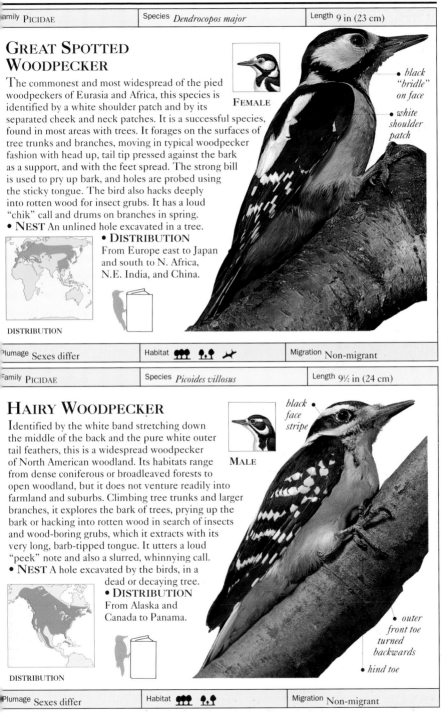

| Family PICIDAE | Species *Dendrocopos major* | Length 9 in (23 cm) |

GREAT SPOTTED WOODPECKER

The commonest and most widespread of the pied woodpeckers of Eurasia and Africa, this species is identified by a white shoulder patch and by its separated cheek and neck patches. It is a successful species, found in most areas with trees. It forages on the surfaces of tree trunks and branches, moving in typical woodpecker fashion with head up, tail tip pressed against the bark as a support, and with the feet spread. The strong bill is used to pry up bark, and holes are probed using the sticky tongue. The bird also hacks deeply into rotten wood for insect grubs. It has a loud "chik" call and drums on branches in spring.

• **NEST** An unlined hole excavated in a tree.

FEMALE

• black "bridle" on face

• white shoulder patch

• **DISTRIBUTION**
From Europe east to Japan and south to N. Africa, N.E. India, and China.

DISTRIBUTION

| Plumage Sexes differ | Habitat 🌳🌳🌳 🌳🌳 ✈ | Migration Non-migrant |

| Family PICIDAE | Species *Picoides villosus* | Length 9½ in (24 cm) |

HAIRY WOODPECKER

Identified by the white band stretching down the middle of the back and the pure white outer tail feathers, this is a widespread woodpecker of North American woodland. Its habitats range from dense coniferous or broadleaved forests to open woodland, but it does not venture readily into farmland and suburbs. Climbing tree trunks and larger branches, it explores the bark of trees, prying up the bark or hacking into rotten wood in search of insects and wood-boring grubs, which it extracts with its very long, barb-tipped tongue. It utters a loud "peek" note and also a slurred, whinnying call.

• **NEST** A hole excavated by the birds, in a dead or decaying tree.

black face stripe •

MALE

• **DISTRIBUTION**
From Alaska and Canada to Panama.

• outer front toe turned backwards

• hind toe

DISTRIBUTION

| Plumage Sexes differ | Habitat 🌳🌳🌳 🌳🌳 | Migration Non-migrant |

Family PICIDAE	Species *Colaptes auratus*	Length 12½ in (32 cm)

NORTHERN FLICKER

Adapted to feeding mainly on the ground, this woodpecker spends most of its time on a level surface, in a posture more like that of a passerine, although its undulating flight is typical of a woodpecker (*see p. 16*). In flight a vivid color is revealed on the underside of the wings: this is yellow in eastern birds and red in western birds; also revealed is the white rump. The Northern Flicker feeds mainly on ants, crouching and probing into the ground with its long, sticky tongue. The calls include loud, repeated "wick," or "wick-ker" notes.
• **NEST** A cavity excavated in a dead tree or branch.
• **DISTRIBUTION** North America, the West Indies, and Central America as far south as Nicaragua. Northern populations winter in the south of this range.

• *red patch on nape*

MALE

• *black crescent*

• *spotted underside*

DISTRIBUTION

Plumage Sexes differ	Habitat 🌳 🐦 ✈	Migration Partial migrant

Family PICIDAE	Species *Celeus flavus*	Length 11 in (28 cm)

CREAM-COLORED WOODPECKER

This species is unmistakable for its pale, creamy-yellow color and its short, tapering, bushy crest, which is permanently raised and makes the bird seem large-headed. It is a rather uncommon bird. Habitats include moist forests of four main types: seasonally flooded forests; swampy forests; swampy secondary forests (where trees have regrown after clearance); and riverside forests in grassland regions. It specializes in feeding on tree ants, breaking open their thin, papery nests, and leaving the hard, mud nests of tree-termites. Feeding mainly in the middle levels of forest vegetation, it also takes other insects from trees and branches, and some fruit. Several birds call in a group, uttering a loud "wheyah" call, usually repeated several times. There is also a "pueer" call which is repeated four times, the final two notes being shorter and falling in pitch.
• **NEST** Unknown; probably a hole in a tree, excavated by the birds.
• **DISTRIBUTION** South America east of the Andes, from Colombia and the Guianas south to Peru, Bolivia, and E. Brazil.

• *male's dark eye ring*

FEMALE

• *tail used as a support*

DISTRIBUTION

Plumage Sexes differ	Habitat 🐦 ▂▂ 〰	Migration Non-migrant

Family PICIDAE	Species *Dryocopus pileatus*	Length 16½ in (42 cm)

PILEATED WOODPECKER

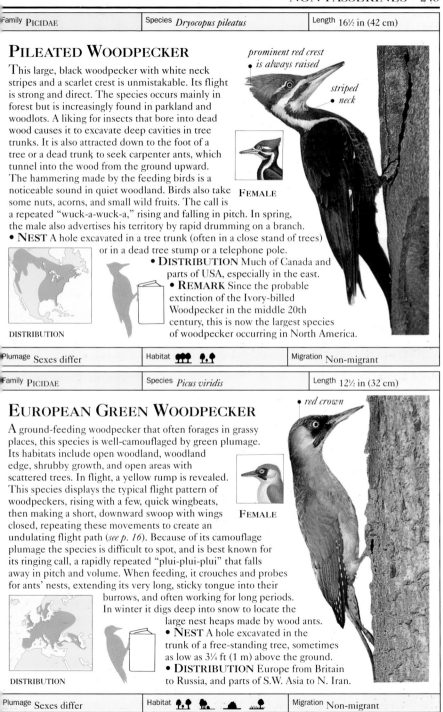

prominent red crest is always raised

striped neck

This large, black woodpecker with white neck stripes and a scarlet crest is unmistakable. Its flight is strong and direct. The species occurs mainly in forest but is increasingly found in parkland and woodlots. A liking for insects that bore into dead wood causes it to excavate deep cavities in tree trunks. It is also attracted down to the foot of a tree or a dead trunk to seek carpenter ants, which tunnel into the wood from the ground upward. The hammering made by the feeding birds is a noticeable sound in quiet woodland. Birds also take some nuts, acorns, and small wild fruits. The call is a repeated "wuck-a-wuck-a," rising and falling in pitch. In spring, the male also advertises his territory by rapid drumming on a branch.

FEMALE

• **NEST** A hole excavated in a tree trunk (often in a close stand of trees) or in a dead tree stump or a telephone pole.

• **DISTRIBUTION** Much of Canada and parts of USA, especially in the east.

• **REMARK** Since the probable extinction of the Ivory-billed Woodpecker in the middle 20th century, this is now the largest species of woodpecker occurring in North America.

DISTRIBUTION

Plumage Sexes differ	Habitat 🌳🌳🌳 🌳🌳	Migration Non-migrant

Family PICIDAE	Species *Picus viridis*	Length 12½ in (32 cm)

EUROPEAN GREEN WOODPECKER

• *red crown*

A ground-feeding woodpecker that often forages in grassy places, this species is well-camouflaged by green plumage. Its habitats include open woodland, woodland edge, shrubby growth, and open areas with scattered trees. In flight, a yellow rump is revealed. This species displays the typical flight pattern of woodpeckers, rising with a few, quick wingbeats, then making a short, downward swoop with wings closed, repeating these movements to create an undulating flight path (*see p. 16*). Because of its camouflage plumage the species is difficult to spot, and is best known for its ringing call, a rapidly repeated "plui-plui-plui" that falls away in pitch and volume. When feeding, it crouches and probes for ants' nests, extending its very long, sticky tongue into their burrows, and often working for long periods. In winter it digs deep into snow to locate the large nest heaps made by wood ants.

FEMALE

• **NEST** A hole excavated in the trunk of a free-standing tree, sometimes as low as 3¼ ft (1 m) above the ground.

• **DISTRIBUTION** Europe from Britain to Russia, and parts of S.W. Asia to N. Iran.

DISTRIBUTION

Plumage Sexes differ	Habitat 🌳🌳 ⛰️ 🌿	Migration Non-migrant

PASSERINES

T HE 74 PASSERINE FAMILIES contain more than half the world's bird species. The precise meaning of the word passerine is "sparrowlike," and a common, though possibly misleading, alternative is "perching birds" (many non-passerines perch). A third name, not always deserved, is "songbirds." Most passerines are relatively small, and there is a basic similarity of shape throughout the group. Identification may depend on minor details. Leg vary according to life-style, fo instance, whether the bird forages o the ground or perches in foliage. Bi shapes vary with the food eaten – mos commonly insects, fruit, or seeds. The shape of body, wings, and tail help too and song can often be decisive i identifying a passerine species.

Family EURYLAIMIDAE	Species *Psarisomus dalhousiae*	Length 11 in (28 cm)

LONG-TAILED BROADBILL

A big-headed bird with a short, heavy bill, this species is found in mountain rain forests, sub-tropical forests, and bamboo thickets. It also occurs in secondary forests (where trees have regrown after clearance). Small flocks feed in the middle height of the trees, taking insects in flight or probing for them on mossy branches and creepers.
• **NEST** A pear-shaped structure with a porched entrance hole at the side, hanging from a branch.
• **DISTRIBUTION** N. India and S. China to Sumatra and Borneo.

broad-based bill •

short legs •

DISTRIBUTION

long tail is unique to this species of broadbill   **JUVENILE**

Plumage Sexes alike	Habitat	Migration Non-migrant

Family EURYLAIMIDAE	Species *Calyptomena viridis*	Length 7½ in (19 cm)

GREEN BROADBILL

The wide mouth and bill of this broadbill are concealed under the feathers of its oversize-looking head. Small groups feed in the lower branches on soft fruit, buds, and occasionally insects.
• **NEST** A pear-shaped structure with a porched entrance hole at the side, hanging from a branch.
• **DISTRIBUTION** Malay Peninsula, Sumatra (including small islands), and Borneo.

crest on the front of the face •

bill hidden • under the crest

typical broadbill tail •

DISTRIBUTION

Plumage Sexes alike	Habitat	Migration Non-migrant

| Family DENDROCOLAPTIDAE | Species *Xiphocolaptes promeropirhynchus* | Length 12 in (30 cm) |

STRONG-BILLED WOODCREEPER

This stoutly built bird, resembling a woodpecker, lives in tropical and mountain forests. Often solitary, it is usually seen climbing up tree trunks and larger branches. It feeds by probing for insects in crevices on tree trunks and branches, as well as hunting them in the foliage. Strong-billed Woodcreepers also descend to feed on or near the rain forest floor. Here they sit and watch army ant swarms from a perch, swooping to the ground to prey on the insects disturbed by the ants.
• **NEST** Unknown.
• **DISTRIBUTION** From Mexico through Central America, south to South America. From Colombia east to Guyana, and south through the Andes as far as Bolivia.

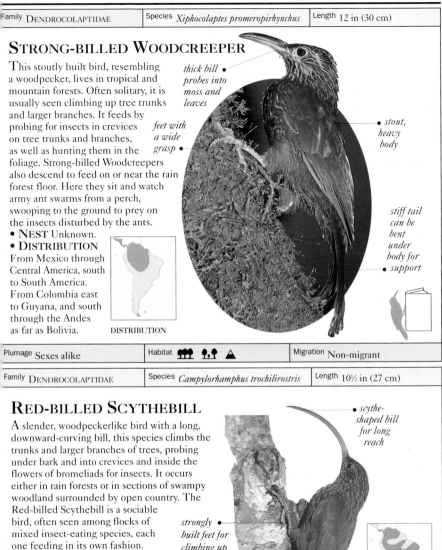

thick bill probes into moss and leaves

feet with a wide grasp

stout, heavy body

stiff tail can be bent under body for support

DISTRIBUTION

| Plumage Sexes alike | Habitat [icons] | Migration Non-migrant |

| Family DENDROCOLAPTIDAE | Species *Campylorhamphus trochilirostris* | Length 10½ in (27 cm) |

RED-BILLED SCYTHEBILL

A slender, woodpeckerlike bird with a long, downward-curving bill, this species climbs the trunks and larger branches of trees, probing under bark and into crevices and inside the flowers of bromeliads for insects. It occurs either in rain forests or in sections of swampy woodland surrounded by open country. The Red-billed Scythebill is a sociable bird, often seen among flocks of mixed insect-eating species, each one feeding in its own fashion.
• **NEST** A cup nest made of plant materials, usually built in the hollow of a broken-open stump.
• **DISTRIBUTION** From Panama through lowland South America to N. Argentina and Paraguay.
• **REMARK** The five species of scythebill all belong to the woodcreeper family, most of whose members have long, sicklelike bills for probing into crevices and pulling out prey. Scythebills have the advantage of a very long reach to search deep inside large flowers and capture insects that hide there.

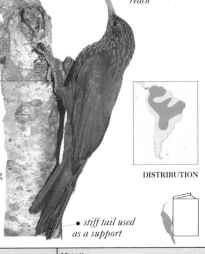

scythe-shaped bill for long reach

strongly built feet for climbing up tree trunks

DISTRIBUTION

stiff tail used as a support

| Plumage Sexes alike | Habitat [icons] | Migration Non-migrant |

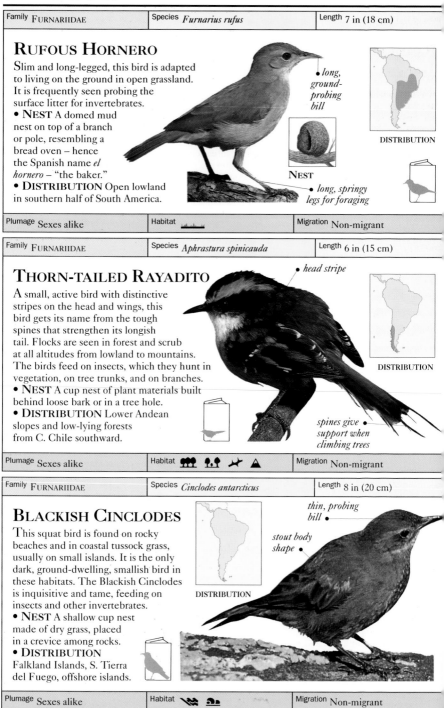

Family FURNARIIDAE	Species *Furnarius rufus*	Length 7 in (18 cm)

RUFOUS HORNERO

Slim and long-legged, this bird is adapted
to living on the ground in open grassland.
It is frequently seen probing the
surface litter for invertebrates.
• **NEST** A domed mud
nest on top of a branch
or pole, resembling a
bread oven – hence
the Spanish name *el
hornero* – "the baker."
• **DISTRIBUTION** Open lowland
in southern half of South America.

• *long,
ground-
probing
bill*

NEST

DISTRIBUTION

• *long, springy
legs for foraging*

Plumage Sexes alike	Habitat	Migration Non-migrant

Family FURNARIIDAE	Species *Aphrastura spinicauda*	Length 6 in (15 cm)

THORN-TAILED RAYADITO

A small, active bird with distinctive
stripes on the head and wings, this
bird gets its name from the tough
spines that strengthen its longish
tail. Flocks are seen in forest and scrub
at all altitudes from lowland to mountains.
The birds feed on insects, which they hunt in
vegetation, on tree trunks, and on branches.
• **NEST** A cup nest of plant materials built
behind loose bark or in a tree hole.
• **DISTRIBUTION** Lower Andean
slopes and low-lying forests
from C. Chile southward.

• *head stripe*

DISTRIBUTION

*spines give •
support when
climbing trees*

Plumage Sexes alike	Habitat	Migration Non-migrant

Family FURNARIIDAE	Species *Cinclodes antarcticus*	Length 8 in (20 cm)

BLACKISH CINCLODES

This squat bird is found on rocky
beaches and in coastal tussock grass,
usually on small islands. It is the only
dark, ground-dwelling, smallish bird in
these habitats. The Blackish Cinclodes
is inquisitive and tame, feeding on
insects and other invertebrates.
• **NEST** A shallow cup nest
made of dry grass, placed
in a crevice among rocks.
• **DISTRIBUTION**
Falkland Islands, S. Tierra
del Fuego, offshore islands.

*thin, probing
bill •*

*stout body
shape •*

DISTRIBUTION

Plumage Sexes alike	Habitat	Migration Non-migrant

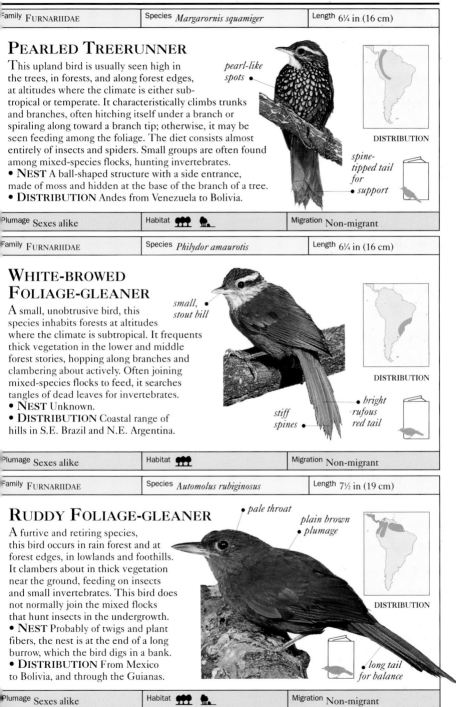

| Family FURNARIIDAE | Species *Margarornis squamiger* | Length 6¼ in (16 cm) |

PEARLED TREERUNNER

This upland bird is usually seen high in the trees, in forests, and along forest edges, at altitudes where the climate is either sub-tropical or temperate. It characteristically climbs trunks and branches, often hitching itself under a branch or spiraling along toward a branch tip; otherwise, it may be seen feeding among the foliage. The diet consists almost entirely of insects and spiders. Small groups are often found among mixed-species flocks, hunting invertebrates.
• **NEST** A ball-shaped structure with a side entrance, made of moss and hidden at the base of the branch of a tree.
• **DISTRIBUTION** Andes from Venezuela to Bolivia.

pearl-like spots

spine-tipped tail for support

DISTRIBUTION

| Plumage Sexes alike | Habitat | Migration Non-migrant |

| Family FURNARIIDAE | Species *Philydor amaurotis* | Length 6¼ in (16 cm) |

WHITE-BROWED FOLIAGE-GLEANER

A small, unobtrusive bird, this species inhabits forests at altitudes where the climate is subtropical. It frequents thick vegetation in the lower and middle forest stories, hopping along branches and clambering about actively. Often joining mixed-species flocks to feed, it searches tangles of dead leaves for invertebrates.
• **NEST** Unknown.
• **DISTRIBUTION** Coastal range of hills in S.E. Brazil and N.E. Argentina.

small, stout bill

stiff spines

bright rufous red tail

DISTRIBUTION

| Plumage Sexes alike | Habitat | Migration Non-migrant |

| Family FURNARIIDAE | Species *Automolus rubiginosus* | Length 7½ in (19 cm) |

RUDDY FOLIAGE-GLEANER

A furtive and retiring species, this bird occurs in rain forest and at forest edges, in lowlands and foothills. It clambers about in thick vegetation near the ground, feeding on insects and small invertebrates. This bird does not normally join the mixed flocks that hunt insects in the undergrowth.
• **NEST** Probably of twigs and plant fibers, the nest is at the end of a long burrow, which the bird digs in a bank.
• **DISTRIBUTION** From Mexico to Bolivia, and through the Guianas.

pale throat

plain brown plumage

DISTRIBUTION

long tail for balance

| Plumage Sexes alike | Habitat | Migration Non-migrant |

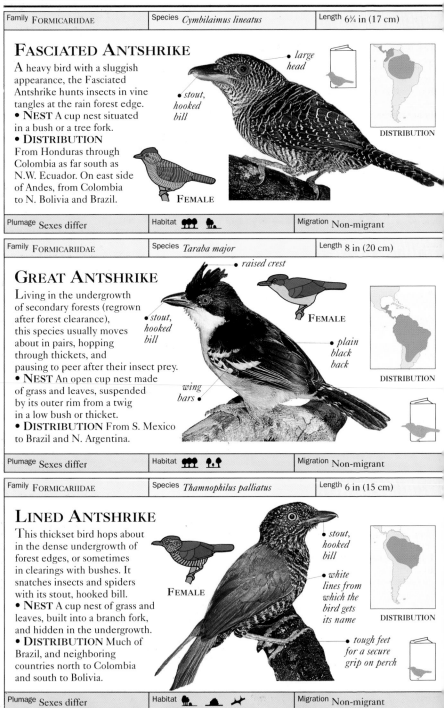

Family FORMICARIIDAE	Species *Cymbilaimus lineatus*	Length 6¾ in (17 cm)

FASCIATED ANTSHRIKE

A heavy bird with a sluggish appearance, the Fasciated Antshrike hunts insects in vine tangles at the rain forest edge.
• **NEST** A cup nest situated in a bush or a tree fork.
• **DISTRIBUTION** From Honduras through Colombia as far south as N.W. Ecuador. On east side of Andes, from Colombia to N. Bolivia and Brazil.

• *large head*

• *stout, hooked bill*

FEMALE

DISTRIBUTION

Plumage Sexes differ	Habitat	Migration Non-migrant

Family FORMICARIIDAE	Species *Taraba major*	Length 8 in (20 cm)

GREAT ANTSHRIKE

Living in the undergrowth of secondary forests (regrown after forest clearance), this species usually moves about in pairs, hopping through thickets, and pausing to peer after their insect prey.
• **NEST** An open cup nest made of grass and leaves, suspended by its outer rim from a twig in a low bush or thicket.
• **DISTRIBUTION** From S. Mexico to Brazil and N. Argentina.

• *raised crest*

• *stout, hooked bill*

FEMALE

• *plain black back*

wing bars •

DISTRIBUTION

Plumage Sexes differ	Habitat	Migration Non-migrant

Family FORMICARIIDAE	Species *Thamnophilus palliatus*	Length 6 in (15 cm)

LINED ANTSHRIKE

This thickset bird hops about in the dense undergrowth of forest edges, or sometimes in clearings with bushes. It snatches insects and spiders with its stout, hooked bill.
• **NEST** A cup nest of grass and leaves, built into a branch fork, and hidden in the undergrowth.
• **DISTRIBUTION** Much of Brazil, and neighboring countries north to Colombia and south to Bolivia.

FEMALE

• *stout, hooked bill*

• *white lines from which the bird gets its name*

DISTRIBUTION

• *tough feet for a secure grip on perch*

Plumage Sexes differ	Habitat	Migration Non-migrant

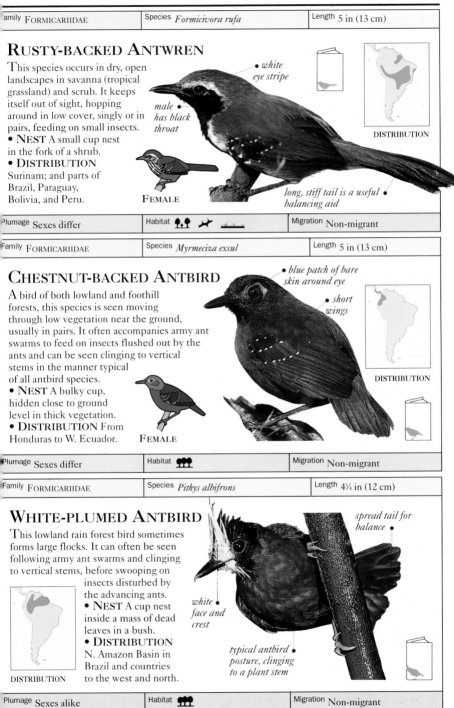

| Family FORMICARIIDAE | Species *Formicivora rufa* | Length 5 in (13 cm) |

RUSTY-BACKED ANTWREN

This species occurs in dry, open
landscapes in savanna (tropical
grassland) and scrub. It keeps
itself out of sight, hopping
around in low cover, singly or in
pairs, feeding on small insects.
• **NEST** A small cup nest
in the fork of a shrub.
• **DISTRIBUTION**
Surinam; and parts of
Brazil, Paraguay,
Bolivia, and Peru.

white eye stripe

male has black throat

DISTRIBUTION

long, stiff tail is a useful balancing aid

FEMALE

| Plumage Sexes differ | Habitat | Migration Non-migrant |

| Family FORMICARIIDAE | Species *Myrmeciza exsul* | Length 5 in (13 cm) |

CHESTNUT-BACKED ANTBIRD

A bird of both lowland and foothill
forests, this species is seen moving
through low vegetation near the ground,
usually in pairs. It often accompanies army ant
swarms to feed on insects flushed out by the
ants and can be seen clinging to vertical
stems in the manner typical
of all antbird species.
• **NEST** A bulky cup,
hidden close to ground
level in thick vegetation.
• **DISTRIBUTION** From
Honduras to W. Ecuador.

blue patch of bare skin around eye

short wings

DISTRIBUTION

FEMALE

| Plumage Sexes differ | Habitat | Migration Non-migrant |

| Family FORMICARIIDAE | Species *Pithys albifrons* | Length 4¾ in (12 cm) |

WHITE-PLUMED ANTBIRD

This lowland rain forest bird sometimes
forms large flocks. It can often be seen
following army ant swarms and clinging
to vertical stems, before swooping on
insects disturbed by
the advancing ants.
• **NEST** A cup nest
inside a mass of dead
leaves in a bush.
• **DISTRIBUTION**
N. Amazon Basin in
Brazil and countries
to the west and north.

DISTRIBUTION

spread tail for balance

white face and crest

typical antbird posture, clinging to a plant stem

| Plumage Sexes alike | Habitat | Migration Non-migrant |

Family FORMICARIIDAE	Species *Phlegopsis nigromaculata*	Length 7 in (18 cm)

BLACK-SPOTTED BARE-EYE

This large antbird inhabits rain forest undergrowth, moving about in flocks. It regularly follows army ant swarms to prey on other insects fleeing from the ants.
• **NEST** An unlined cup nest, usually in the hollow top of a palm stump.
• **DISTRIBUTION** Amazon basin.
• **REMARK** Several antbird species have bare skin around the eye.

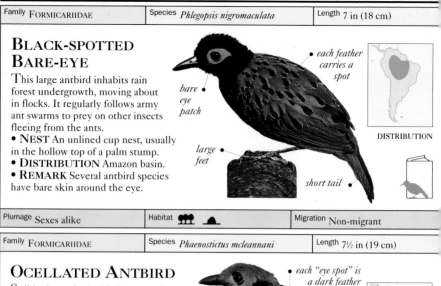

each feather carries a spot

bare eye patch

large feet

short tail

DISTRIBUTION

Plumage Sexes alike	Habitat	Migration Non-migrant

Family FORMICARIIDAE	Species *Phaenostictus mcleannani*	Length 7½ in (19 cm)

OCELLATED ANTBIRD

Strikingly marked with "eye spots" (ocellated), this is a large antbird of lowland rain forest. Like other birds of the antbird family, it characteristically feeds by watching the ground for army ant swarms and pouncing on insects flushed out of their hiding places by the ants. It dominates the smaller antbirds, claiming the lowest perches, so as to have first choice of the insects as they make their escape from the ants.
• **NEST** Unknown.
• **DISTRIBUTION** Central and South America from Honduras to W. Ecuador.

each "eye spot" is a dark feather with a light edge

bare eye patch

DISTRIBUTION

Plumage Sexes alike	Habitat	Migration Non-migrant

Family FORMICARIIDAE	Species *Pittasoma rufopileatum*	Length 6½ in (16.5 cm)

RUFOUS-CROWNED ANTPITTA

This bird lives in tropical rain forest, also occurring in mature secondary forest (regrown after rain forest clearance). It feeds mainly by bounding along on the forest floor, catching insects as it goes; it also watches over army ant swarms to prey on insects flushed from cover by the ants.
• **NEST** Unknown.
• **DISTRIBUTION** Lowlands and foothills west of the Andes in Colombia and Ecuador.

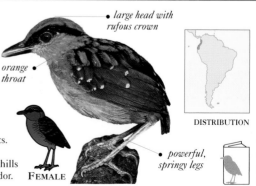

large head with rufous crown

orange throat

FEMALE

powerful, springy legs

DISTRIBUTION

Plumage Sexes differ	Habitat	Migration Non-migrant

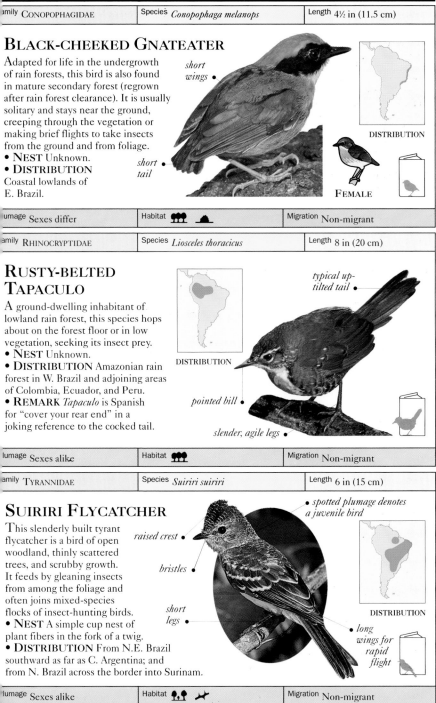

Family CONOPOPHAGIDAE	Species *Conopophaga melanops*	Length 4½ in (11.5 cm)

BLACK-CHEEKED GNATEATER

Adapted for life in the undergrowth of rain forests, this bird is also found in mature secondary forest (regrown after rain forest clearance). It is usually solitary and stays near the ground, creeping through the vegetation or making brief flights to take insects from the ground and from foliage.
• **NEST** Unknown.
• **DISTRIBUTION** Coastal lowlands of E. Brazil.

short wings

short tail

DISTRIBUTION

FEMALE

Plumage Sexes differ	Habitat	Migration Non-migrant

Family RHINOCRYPTIDAE	Species *Liosceles thoracicus*	Length 8 in (20 cm)

RUSTY-BELTED TAPACULO

A ground-dwelling inhabitant of lowland rain forest, this species hops about on the forest floor or in low vegetation, seeking its insect prey.
• **NEST** Unknown.
• **DISTRIBUTION** Amazonian rain forest in W. Brazil and adjoining areas of Colombia, Ecuador, and Peru.
• **REMARK** *Tapaculo* is Spanish for "cover your rear end" in a joking reference to the cocked tail.

typical up-tilted tail

DISTRIBUTION

pointed bill

slender, agile legs

Plumage Sexes alike	Habitat	Migration Non-migrant

Family TYRANNIDAE	Species *Suiriri suiriri*	Length 6 in (15 cm)

SUIRIRI FLYCATCHER

This slenderly built tyrant flycatcher is a bird of open woodland, thinly scattered trees, and scrubby growth. It feeds by gleaning insects from among the foliage and often joins mixed-species flocks of insect-hunting birds.
• **NEST** A simple cup nest of plant fibers in the fork of a twig.
• **DISTRIBUTION** From N.E. Brazil southward as far as C. Argentina; and from N. Brazil across the border into Surinam.

raised crest

bristles

short legs

• *spotted plumage denotes a juvenile bird*

DISTRIBUTION

long wings for rapid flight

Plumage Sexes alike	Habitat	Migration Non-migrant

| Family TYRANNIDAE | Species *Stigmatura budytoides* | Length 6 in (15 cm) |

GREATER WAGTAIL-TYRANT

Like the Old World wagtails, this is a slender bird with a long tail, which it bobs up and down and does not "wag" from side to side. This species normally holds its tail cocked and frequents trees rather than water. It is usually seen in pairs, gleaning insects in open woodland and scrub.
• **NEST** A shallow cup, close to the ground.
• **DISTRIBUTION** S. Bolivia, part of Argentina, and E. Brazil.

striped pattern on wing •

DISTRIBUTION

long, narrow tail •

• long legs

| Plumage Sexes alike | Habitat | Migration Non-migrant |

| Family TYRANNIDAE | Species *Pseudotriccus ruficeps* | Length 4¼ in (11 cm) |

RUFOUS-HEADED PYGMY-TYRANT

This is a plump, wren-size bird with a tiny bill, found on forested mountain slopes, at altitudes where the climate is either subtropical or temperate. Inconspicuous and often solitary, it creeps about hunting insects in the undergrowth. It occasionally makes short, abrupt flights, accompanied by an audible whirr of wings.
• **NEST** Unknown.
• **DISTRIBUTION** The Andes in a series of areas in Colombia, Ecuador, Peru, and Bolivia.

thin • bill

rounded • wings

DISTRIBUTION

• short tail

| Plumage Sexes alike | Habitat | Migration Non-migrant |

| Family TYRANNIDAE | Species *Onychorhynchus coronatus* | Length 6¾ in (17 cm) |

ROYAL FLYCATCHER

A slender tyrant flycatcher, this species inhabits the lower levels of rain forest and subtropical open forest. Its typical way of feeding is to watch from a perch and fly out, either to seize an insect in the air or to take it from the foliage. The vivid, transverse crest is normally folded away and sometimes protrudes behind the head, resulting in a "hammerhead" look. The male's crest is red, the female's yellow.
• **NEST** A slender bag up to 6½ ft (2 m) long, suspended from a branch, often over a stream.
• **DISTRIBUTION** Mexico to Bolivia and S.E. Brazil.

hook-tipped bill •

MALE

DISTRIBUTION

• short legs

| Plumage Sexes differ slightly | Habitat | Migration Non-migrant |

| Family TYRANNIDAE | Species *Contopus sordidulus* | Length 6½ in (16.5 cm) |

WESTERN WOOD-PEWEE

This medium-size flycatcher of open
forest or forest edge is often seen
perching on an open branch or bare
snag, from which it flies out
to catch insects in midair.
• **NEST** An open cup nest fixed
on a horizontal branch, often high.
• **DISTRIBUTION** Breeds in
forests of W. North America
and mountain forests of Central
America. Winters in South America
as far south as Peru and Bolivia.

large
eye

upright,
watchful
posture

short legs

long tail

DISTRIBUTION

| Plumage Sexes alike | Habitat | Migration Migrant |

| Family TYRANNIDAE | Species *Empidonax difficilis* | Length 5¼ in (13.5 cm) |

PACIFIC-SLOPE FLYCATCHER

A small, inconspicuous flycatcher,
this bird perches in an upright posture,
occasionally waving its fanned tail up and
down ("flirting"), and swooping to
seize insects in the air or on foliage.
It frequents woodland on mountain
slopes, as well as wooded canyons.
• **NEST** A cup nest formed from
plant materials, built in a hollow or cavity.
• **DISTRIBUTION** Breeds in W. Canada and
USA. Migrates as far south as W. Mexico in winter.

broad-
based
bill

large eye

short
legs

long
wings

long tail

DISTRIBUTION

| Plumage Sexes alike | Habitat | Migration Migrant |

| Family TYRANNIDAE | Species *Sayornis phoebe* | Length 6¾ in (17 cm) |

EASTERN PHOEBE

Named in imitation of its "fee-
bee" call, the Eastern Phoebe lives
in open woodland and farmland,
hunting insects from an open perch,
usually near water. It has also
adapted successfully to urban habitats,
where it nests readily on buildings. While
perched, it frequently bobs its tail up and down.
• **NEST** A stout cup nest made of mud
and plant materials, on a sheltered ledge. New
nests are sometimes built on top of old ones.
• **DISTRIBUTION** Breeds in C. and E. North
America. Winters in S.E. USA and Mexico.

broad,
flat bill

long
wings

long,
balancing
tail

DISTRIBUTION

| Plumage Sexes alike | Habitat | Migration Migrant |

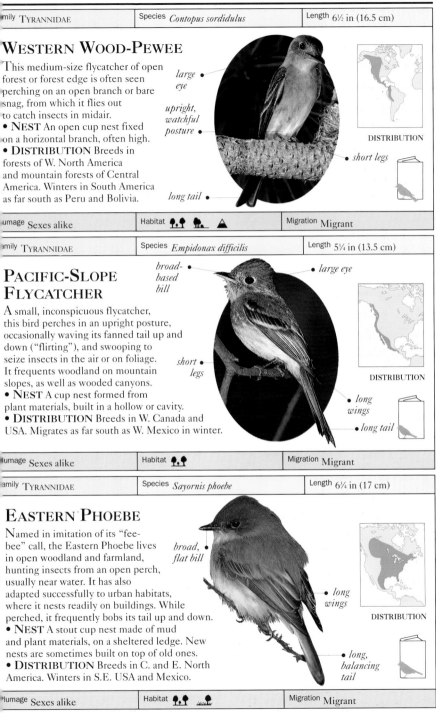

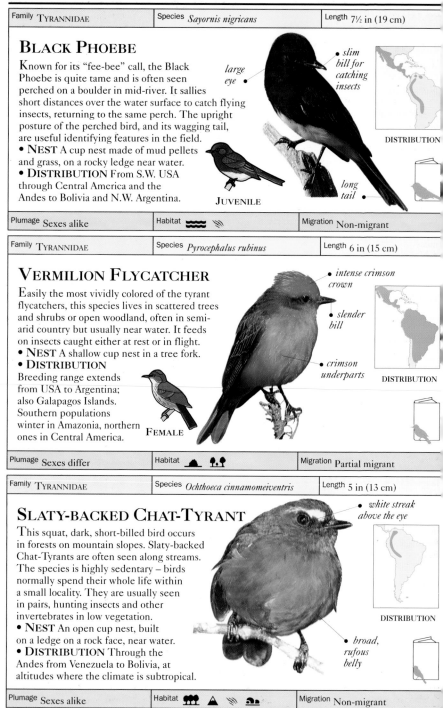

Family TYRANNIDAE	Species *Sayornis nigricans*	Length 7½ in (19 cm)

BLACK PHOEBE

Known for its "fee-bee" call, the Black
Phoebe is quite tame and is often seen
perched on a boulder in mid-river. It sallies
short distances over the water surface to catch flying
insects, returning to the same perch. The upright
posture of the perched bird, and its wagging tail,
are useful identifying features in the field.
• NEST A cup nest made of mud pellets
and grass, on a rocky ledge near water.
• DISTRIBUTION From S.W. USA
through Central America and the
Andes to Bolivia and N.W. Argentina.

large eye

slim bill for catching insects

DISTRIBUTION

long tail

JUVENILE

Plumage Sexes alike	Habitat	Migration Non-migrant

Family TYRANNIDAE	Species *Pyrocephalus rubinus*	Length 6 in (15 cm)

VERMILION FLYCATCHER

Easily the most vividly colored of the tyrant
flycatchers, this species lives in scattered trees
and shrubs or open woodland, often in semi-
arid country but usually near water. It feeds
on insects caught either at rest or in flight.
• NEST A shallow cup nest in a tree fork.
• DISTRIBUTION
Breeding range extends
from USA to Argentina;
also Galapagos Islands.
Southern populations
winter in Amazonia, northern
ones in Central America.

intense crimson crown

slender bill

crimson underparts

DISTRIBUTION

FEMALE

Plumage Sexes differ	Habitat	Migration Partial migrant

Family TYRANNIDAE	Species *Ochthoeca cinnamomeiventris*	Length 5 in (13 cm)

SLATY-BACKED CHAT-TYRANT

This squat, dark, short-billed bird occurs
in forests on mountain slopes. Slaty-backed
Chat-Tyrants are often seen along streams.
The species is highly sedentary – birds
normally spend their whole life within
a small locality. They are usually seen
in pairs, hunting insects and other
invertebrates in low vegetation.
• NEST An open cup nest, built
on a ledge on a rock face, near water.
• DISTRIBUTION Through the
Andes from Venezuela to Bolivia, at
altitudes where the climate is subtropical.

white streak above the eye

DISTRIBUTION

broad, rufous belly

Plumage Sexes alike	Habitat	Migration Non-migrant

amily TYRANNIDAE	Species *Colonia colonus*	Length 9 in (23 cm)

LONG-TAILED TYRANT

Two long tail feathers make this bird conspicuous in flight or in the prominent places where it tends to perch. It spends much of the day on an exposed vantage point in the tree canopy at the outer fringes of lowland rain forest or isolated woodlands. Favored perches are on dead or dying trees, bare branches, and snags. Long-tailed Flycatchers nearly always perch in pairs, and each pair tends to use a particular perch or series of perches habitually. They watch for flying insects and make quick outward flights to seize them, usually returning faithfully to the same perch. Stingless bees are among the most common prey items.
• **NEST** A loose nest of plant materials is placed in a hole in a dead branch.
• **DISTRIBUTION** From Honduras to Colombia; S. Brazil and N.E. Argentina; and the Guianas.

large, watchful eye

• white head stripe

• elongated central tail feathers

DISTRIBUTION

lumage Sexes alike	Habitat	Migration Non-migrant

amily TYRANNIDAE	Species *Fluvicola nengeta*	Length 5 in (13 cm)

MASKED WATER TYRANT

A distinctively pied tyrant, this bird is usually seen on or near the ground, often on vegetation or rocks close to water. Its diet consists of insects, which it gleans from the foliage.
• **NEST** An oval construction with a side entrance, made of grass and plant down, lined with feathers, and placed on a branch tip, low over water.
• **DISTRIBUTION** Two populations: one in W. Ecuador and Peru, and one in E. Brazil.

• black eye stripe

DISTRIBUTION

• vivid, black-and-white tail is often turned up at a jaunty angle

lumage Sexes alike	Habitat	Migration Non-migrant

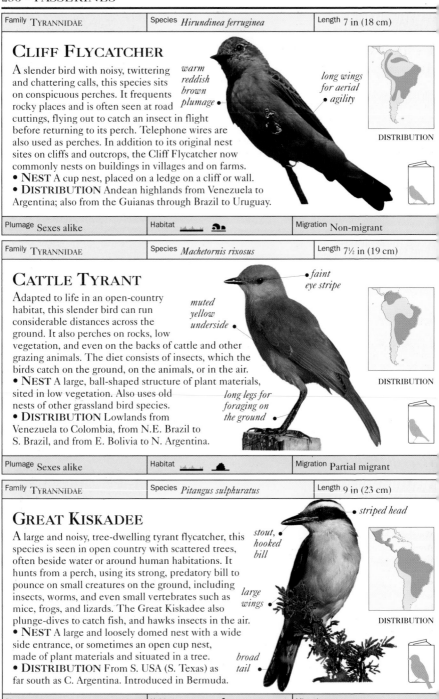

| Family TYRANNIDAE | Species *Hirundinea ferruginea* | Length 7 in (18 cm) |

CLIFF FLYCATCHER

A slender bird with noisy, twittering and chattering calls, this species sits on conspicuous perches. It frequents rocky places and is often seen at road cuttings, flying out to catch an insect in flight before returning to its perch. Telephone wires are also used as perches. In addition to its original nest sites on cliffs and outcrops, the Cliff Flycatcher now commonly nests on buildings in villages and on farms.
• **NEST** A cup nest, placed on a ledge on a cliff or wall.
• **DISTRIBUTION** Andean highlands from Venezuela to Argentina; also from the Guianas through Brazil to Uruguay.

warm reddish brown plumage

long wings for aerial agility

DISTRIBUTION

| Plumage Sexes alike | Habitat | Migration Non-migrant |

| Family TYRANNIDAE | Species *Machetornis rixosus* | Length 7½ in (19 cm) |

CATTLE TYRANT

Adapted to life in an open-country habitat, this slender bird can run considerable distances across the ground. It also perches on rocks, low vegetation, and even on the backs of cattle and other grazing animals. The diet consists of insects, which the birds catch on the ground, on the animals, or in the air.
• **NEST** A large, ball-shaped structure of plant materials, sited in low vegetation. Also uses old nests of other grassland bird species.
• **DISTRIBUTION** Lowlands from Venezuela to Colombia, from N.E. Brazil to S. Brazil, and from E. Bolivia to N. Argentina.

faint eye stripe

muted yellow underside

long legs for foraging on the ground

DISTRIBUTION

| Plumage Sexes alike | Habitat | Migration Partial migrant |

| Family TYRANNIDAE | Species *Pitangus sulphuratus* | Length 9 in (23 cm) |

GREAT KISKADEE

A large and noisy, tree-dwelling tyrant flycatcher, this species is seen in open country with scattered trees, often beside water or around human habitations. It hunts from a perch, using its strong, predatory bill to pounce on small creatures on the ground, including insects, worms, and even small vertebrates such as mice, frogs, and lizards. The Great Kiskadee also plunge-dives to catch fish, and hawks insects in the air.
• **NEST** A large and loosely domed nest with a wide side entrance, or sometimes an open cup nest, made of plant materials and situated in a tree.
• **DISTRIBUTION** From S. USA (S. Texas) as far south as C. Argentina. Introduced in Bermuda.

striped head

stout, hooked bill

large wings

broad tail

DISTRIBUTION

| Plumage Sexes alike | Habitat | Migration Non-migrant |

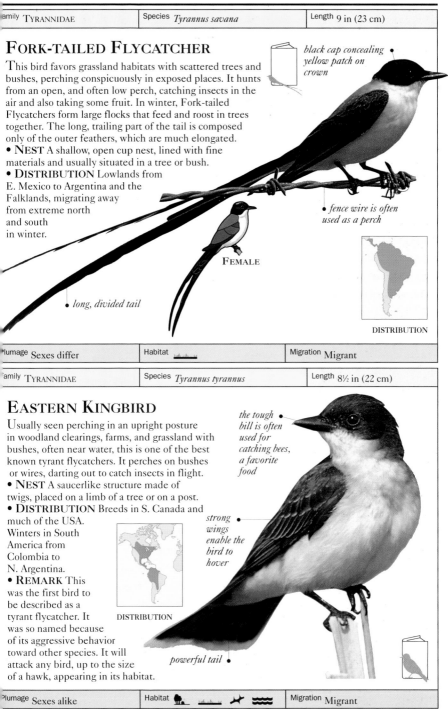

| Family TYRANNIDAE | Species *Tyrannus savana* | Length 9 in (23 cm) |

FORK-TAILED FLYCATCHER

This bird favors grassland habitats with scattered trees and bushes, perching conspicuously in exposed places. It hunts from an open, and often low perch, catching insects in the air and also taking some fruit. In winter, Fork-tailed Flycatchers form large flocks that feed and roost in trees together. The long, trailing part of the tail is composed only of the outer feathers, which are much elongated.
• **NEST** A shallow, open cup nest, lined with fine materials and usually situated in a tree or bush.
• **DISTRIBUTION** Lowlands from E. Mexico to Argentina and the Falklands, migrating away from extreme north and south in winter.

black cap concealing yellow patch on crown

fence wire is often used as a perch

FEMALE

long, divided tail

DISTRIBUTION

| Plumage Sexes differ | Habitat | Migration Migrant |

| Family TYRANNIDAE | Species *Tyrannus tyrannus* | Length 8½ in (22 cm) |

EASTERN KINGBIRD

Usually seen perching in an upright posture in woodland clearings, farms, and grassland with bushes, often near water, this is one of the best known tyrant flycatchers. It perches on bushes or wires, darting out to catch insects in flight.
• **NEST** A saucerlike structure made of twigs, placed on a limb of a tree or on a post.
• **DISTRIBUTION** Breeds in S. Canada and much of the USA. Winters in South America from Colombia to N. Argentina.
• **REMARK** This was the first bird to be described as a tyrant flycatcher. It was so named because of its aggressive behavior toward other species. It will attack any bird, up to the size of a hawk, appearing in its habitat.

the tough bill is often used for catching bees, a favorite food

strong wings enable the bird to hover

DISTRIBUTION

powerful tail

| Plumage Sexes alike | Habitat | Migration Migrant |

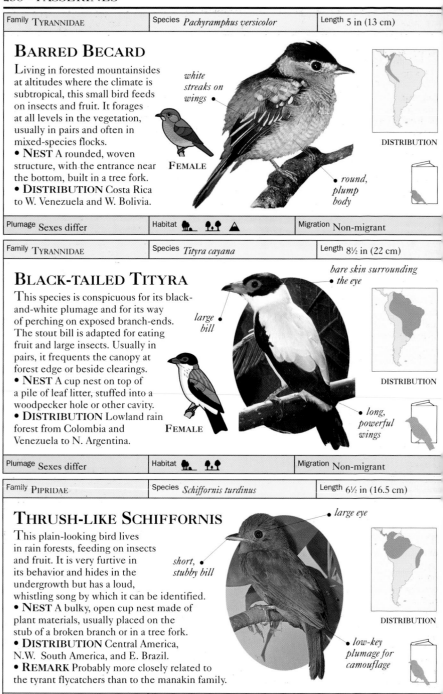

| Family TYRANNIDAE | Species *Pachyramphus versicolor* | Length 5 in (13 cm) |

BARRED BECARD

Living in forested mountainsides at altitudes where the climate is subtropical, this small bird feeds on insects and fruit. It forages at all levels in the vegetation, usually in pairs and often in mixed-species flocks.
• **NEST** A rounded, woven structure, with the entrance near the bottom, built in a tree fork.
• **DISTRIBUTION** Costa Rica to W. Venezuela and W. Bolivia.

white streaks on wings •

FEMALE

DISTRIBUTION

• round, plump body

| Plumage Sexes differ | Habitat | Migration Non-migrant |

| Family TYRANNIDAE | Species *Tityra cayana* | Length 8½ in (22 cm) |

BLACK-TAILED TITYRA

This species is conspicuous for its black-and-white plumage and for its way of perching on exposed branch-ends. The stout bill is adapted for eating fruit and large insects. Usually in pairs, it frequents the canopy at forest edge or beside clearings.
• **NEST** A cup nest on top of a pile of leaf litter, stuffed into a woodpecker hole or other cavity.
• **DISTRIBUTION** Lowland rain forest from Colombia and Venezuela to N. Argentina.

bare skin surrounding • the eye

large • bill

FEMALE

DISTRIBUTION

• long, powerful wings

| Plumage Sexes differ | Habitat | Migration Non-migrant |

| Family PIPRIDAE | Species *Schiffornis turdinus* | Length 6½ in (16.5 cm) |

THRUSH-LIKE SCHIFFORNIS

This plain-looking bird lives in rain forests, feeding on insects and fruit. It is very furtive in its behavior and hides in the undergrowth but has a loud, whistling song by which it can be identified.
• **NEST** A bulky, open cup nest made of plant materials, usually placed on the stub of a broken branch or in a tree fork.
• **DISTRIBUTION** Central America, N.W. South America, and E. Brazil.
• **REMARK** Probably more closely related to the tyrant flycatchers than to the manakin family.

• large eye

short, stubby bill •

DISTRIBUTION

• low-key plumage for camouflage

| Plumage Sexes alike | Habitat | Migration Non-migrant |

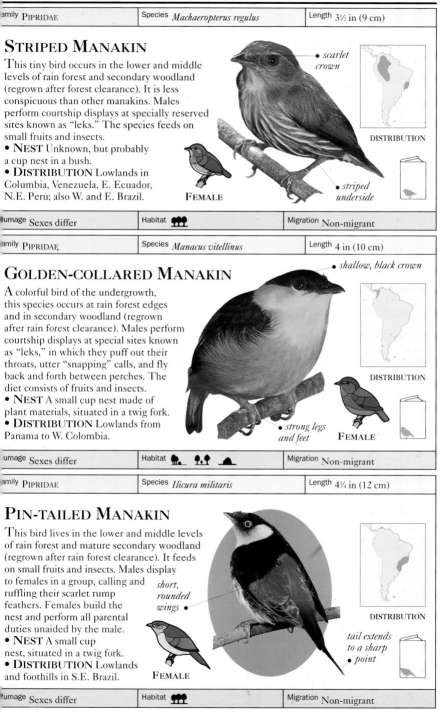

| Family PIPRIDAE | Species *Machaeropterus regulus* | Length 3½ in (9 cm) |

STRIPED MANAKIN

This tiny bird occurs in the lower and middle levels of rain forest and secondary woodland (regrown after forest clearance). It is less conspicuous than other manakins. Males perform courtship displays at specially reserved sites known as "leks." The species feeds on small fruits and insects.
• **NEST** Unknown, but probably a cup nest in a bush.
• **DISTRIBUTION** Lowlands in Columbia, Venezuela, E. Ecuador, N.E. Peru; also W. and E. Brazil.

• *scarlet crown*

DISTRIBUTION

• *striped underside*

FEMALE

| Plumage Sexes differ | Habitat | Migration Non-migrant |

| Family PIPRIDAE | Species *Manacus vitellinus* | Length 4 in (10 cm) |

GOLDEN-COLLARED MANAKIN

A colorful bird of the undergrowth, this species occurs at rain forest edges and in secondary woodland (regrown after rain forest clearance). Males perform courtship displays at special sites known as "leks," in which they puff out their throats, utter "snapping" calls, and fly back and forth between perches. The diet consists of fruits and insects.
• **NEST** A small cup nest made of plant materials, situated in a twig fork.
• **DISTRIBUTION** Lowlands from Panama to W. Colombia.

• *shallow, black crown*

DISTRIBUTION

• *strong legs and feet*

FEMALE

| Plumage Sexes differ | Habitat | Migration Non-migrant |

| Family PIPRIDAE | Species *Ilicura militaris* | Length 4¾ in (12 cm) |

PIN-TAILED MANAKIN

This bird lives in the lower and middle levels of rain forest and mature secondary woodland (regrown after rain forest clearance). It feeds on small fruits and insects. Males display to females in a group, calling and ruffling their scarlet rump feathers. Females build the nest and perform all parental duties unaided by the male.
• **NEST** A small cup nest, situated in a twig fork.
• **DISTRIBUTION** Lowlands and foothills in S.E. Brazil.

short, rounded wings •

DISTRIBUTION

tail extends to a sharp • *point*

FEMALE

| Plumage Sexes differ | Habitat | Migration Non-migrant |

| Family PIPRIDAE | Species *Chiroxiphia caudata* | Length 6 in (15 cm) |

SWALLOW-TAILED MANAKIN

This manakin is a brilliantly colored inhabitant of the undergrowth in rain forest and secondary woodland (where trees have regrown after rain forest clearance). Although Swallow-tailed Manakins usually hide themselves away, males are noticeable when they gather together to perform collective displays to attract females. These displays, at specially reserved sites known as "leks," are characteristic behavior of the manakin family and are usually accompanied by a variety of rasping, buzzing, and rattling sounds. The diet consists mainly of small fruits, with some insects.
• **NEST** A small cup nest of grass and plant fibers, placed in the fork of a bush.
• **DISTRIBUTION** Lowland and subtropical zones of S.E. Brazil, E. Paraguay, and N.E. Argentina.

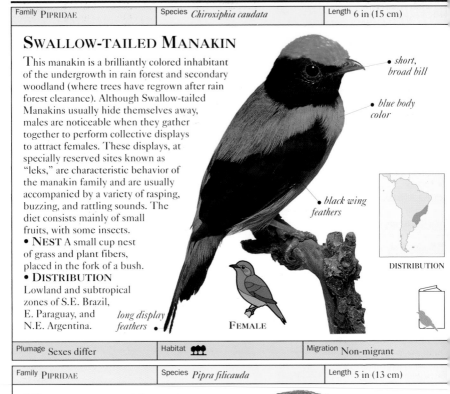

• *short, broad bill*

• *blue body color*

• *black wing feathers*

long display feathers •

FEMALE

DISTRIBUTION

| Plumage Sexes differ | Habitat | Migration Non-migrant |

| Family PIPRIDAE | Species *Pipra filicauda* | Length 5 in (13 cm) |

WIRE-TAILED MANAKIN

Although gaudily marked, Wire-tailed Manakins are easily overlooked in the dense foliage of their rain forest habitat. Males take part in communal displays, at special sites called "leks," in which they perform side jumps, brief flights, and various calls, using their tail filaments to tickle the faces and throats of the females. Calls are simple, but unusual noises are made by rapid vibration of feathers. The Wire-tailed Manakin's short, broad bill is suited to its mixed diet of fruits and insects.
• **NEST** A cup-shaped nest, made of various types of plant fibers, with excess material hanging below, located in a small tree.
• **DISTRIBUTION** N. South America, east of the Andes.
• **REMARK** As in most manakins, the brightly colored male contrasts with the green female.

• *white iris around black pupil*

• *yellow underparts*

filamentous tail feathers •

FEMALE

DISTRIBUTION

| Plumage Sexes differ | Habitat | Migration Non-migrant |

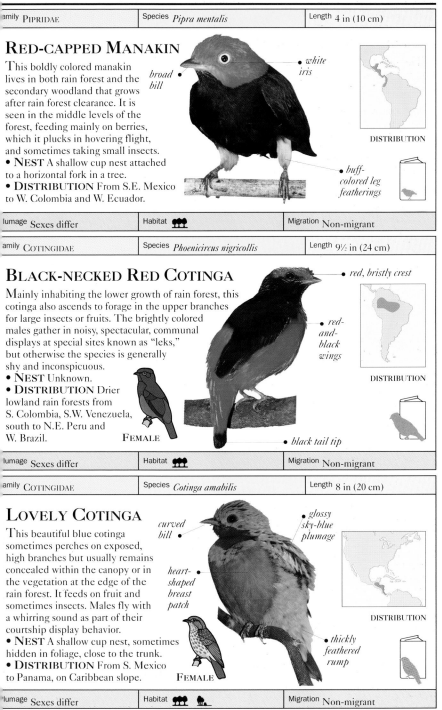

Family PIPRIDAE	Species *Pipra mentalis*	Length 4 in (10 cm)

RED-CAPPED MANAKIN

This boldly colored manakin lives in both rain forest and the secondary woodland that grows after rain forest clearance. It is seen in the middle levels of the forest, feeding mainly on berries, which it plucks in hovering flight, and sometimes taking small insects.
• **NEST** A shallow cup nest attached to a horizontal fork in a tree.
• **DISTRIBUTION** From S.E. Mexico to W. Colombia and W. Ecuador.

broad bill

white iris

buff-colored leg featherings

DISTRIBUTION

Plumage Sexes differ	Habitat	Migration Non-migrant

Family COTINGIDAE	Species *Phoenicircus nigricollis*	Length 9½ in (24 cm)

BLACK-NECKED RED COTINGA

Mainly inhabiting the lower growth of rain forest, this cotinga also ascends to forage in the upper branches for large insects or fruits. The brightly colored males gather in noisy, spectacular, communal displays at special sites known as "leks," but otherwise the species is generally shy and inconspicuous.
• **NEST** Unknown.
• **DISTRIBUTION** Drier lowland rain forests from S. Colombia, S.W. Venezuela, south to N.E. Peru and W. Brazil.

FEMALE

red, bristly crest

red-and-black wings

black tail tip

DISTRIBUTION

Plumage Sexes differ	Habitat	Migration Non-migrant

Family COTINGIDAE	Species *Cotinga amabilis*	Length 8 in (20 cm)

LOVELY COTINGA

This beautiful blue cotinga sometimes perches on exposed, high branches but usually remains concealed within the canopy or in the vegetation at the edge of the rain forest. It feeds on fruit and sometimes insects. Males fly with a whirring sound as part of their courtship display behavior.
• **NEST** A shallow cup nest, sometimes hidden in foliage, close to the trunk.
• **DISTRIBUTION** From S. Mexico to Panama, on Caribbean slope.

curved bill

glossy sky-blue plumage

heart-shaped breast patch

thickly feathered rump

FEMALE

DISTRIBUTION

Plumage Sexes differ	Habitat	Migration Non-migrant

| Family COTINGIDAE | Species *Querula purpurata* | Length 11 in (28 cm) |

PURPLE-THROATED FRUITCROW

A large cotinga with dark
plumage, this species inhabits
the middle and upper levels of
the rain forest, where it feeds on
insects as well as on fruit. Purple-
throated Fruitcrows live in small
social groups. The members of
each of these communities feed
and rest together and care
jointly for the young in the nest.
In courtship, the male displays by puffing
out his ruff of purple throat feathers.
• **NEST** A shallow cup nest made
of twigs, located high in a tree.
• **DISTRIBUTION** Lowlands
from Costa Rica through much
of South America as far south as
N. Bolivia and Amazonian Brazil.
• **REMARK** Fruitcrows are
the only cotingas that live in
social groups. There are three other
species: the Red-ruffed, Crimson,
and Bare-necked Fruitcrows,
all living in South America.

DISTRIBUTION

• broad-
based bill

• throat ruff
swells out in
display

short, •
strong
legs

• long, slender
wings for
rapid flight

FEMALE

| Plumage Sexes differ | Habitat | Migration Non-migrant |

| Family COTINGIDAE | Species *Rupicola peruviana* | Length 12 in (30 cm) |

ANDEAN COCK-OF-THE-ROCK

This vivid bird occurs in forest by
streams and in wooded gorges of the
Andes, feeding on fruit. The highly
colored males perform noisy,
communal courtship displays, at
special sites known as "leks," on bare
branches in middle and upper vegetation.
During display, males extend the crest
forward, completely covering the bill. The
shape of the eye also changes from round
to narrowly elliptical. The females are
cinnamon brown all over and have smaller
crests than the males. They visit the lek and
watch the displaying males, and eventually
each female selects a mate. After
mating, they perform all nesting duties
and parental care, unaided by the males.
• **NEST** A cup-shaped nest made of mud
and stuck to a rock face in a sheltered hollow.
• **DISTRIBUTION** Andes from Venezuela to
Bolivia at altitudes where the climate is subtropical.

semicircular •
crest opens out
further in full
display

round,
staring
• eye

enlarged wing •
coverts

FEMALE

DISTRIBUTION

| Plumage Sexes differ | Habitat | Migration Non-migrant |

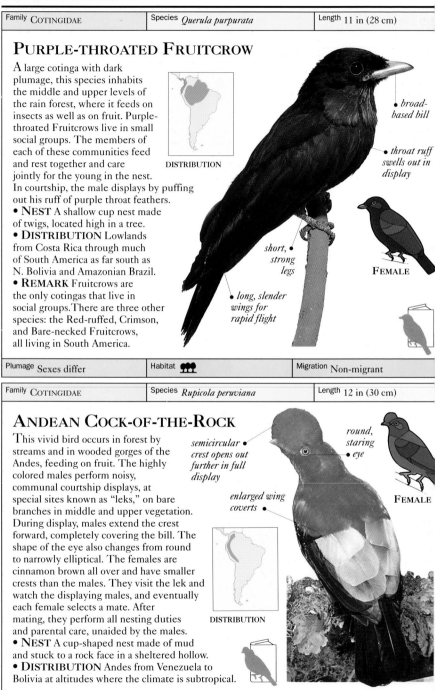

| Family COTINGIDAE | Species *Procnias nudicollis* | Length 11 in (28 cm) |

BARE-THROATED BELLBIRD

Living in the canopy of tropical mountain forests, this bird is more often heard than seen. It is sluggish and rarely leaves the treetops, but can be identified by its calls, which ring out like the clanging of a bell. The Bare-throated Bellbird feeds on fruit. Females seek out males to mate, then nest unaided.
• **NEST** A flimsy cup nest made of twigs, placed in the fork of a bough.
• **DISTRIBUTION** Forested mountains from E. Brazil to S.E. Paraguay.

bare skin on face and throat

white bird stands out against foliage

DISTRIBUTION

FEMALE

| Plumage Sexes differ | Habitat | Migration Non-migrant |

| Family OXYRUNCIDAE | Species *Oxyruncus cristatus* | Length 6¼ in (16 cm) |

SHARPBILL

The Sharpbill is a rain forest bird living among the branches of the canopy or at the forest edge. It feeds on insects and small fruits, clinging with acrobatic skill to the branches. Males gather to perform collective displays at special sites called "leks."
• **NEST** A shallow cup nest in the fork of a tree.
• **DISTRIBUTION** Patchily distributed from Costa Rica as far south as E. Peru and Paraguay.

color of crest not seen when lowered

HEAD AND CREST

strong feet grip firmly

DISTRIBUTION

| Plumage Sexes alike | Habitat | Migration Non-migrant |

| Family PHYTOTOMIDAE | Species *Phytotoma rara* | Length 8 in (20 cm) |

RUFOUS-TAILED PLANTCUTTER

This superficially finchlike bird occurs in dry, open country with shrubs and trees and also in river valleys, orchards, and farmland. It is seen in pairs or small parties. Quiet and unobtrusive in behavior, it feeds mainly on fruit and buds, which it cuts with its serrated bill, and sometimes on insects.
• **NEST** A cup nest in the fork of a shrub or small tree.
• **DISTRIBUTION** C. and S. Chile and adjacent parts of Argentina.

rufous brown undertail coverts

DISTRIBUTION

FEMALE

| Plumage Sexes differ | Habitat | Migration Non-migrant |

Family PITTIDAE	Species *Pitta erythrogaster*	Length 6¼ in (16 cm)

RED-BELLIED PITTA

This pitta is usually seen on the rain forest floor, hopping from place to place and also making short flights. It feeds on small invertebrates (hammering snails on stones) and small fruits. It sometimes ascends the trees to sing and may roost in the branches as well.
• **NEST** Dome with a side entrance, on the ground, on a tree stump, or in a vine tangle.
• **DISTRIBUTION** Philippines, E. Indonesia, New Guinea, and N. Australia. Some limited migration.

large eye

squat, hunched pose

DISTRIBUTION

long legs for ground-feeding

Plumage Sexes alike	Habitat	Migration Partial migrant

Family PITTIDAE	Species *Pitta guajana*	Length 8½ in (22 cm)

BANDED PITTA

Shady rain forests are the main habitat of this pitta, but it can also be found in secondary woodland (regrown after rain forest has been cleared). It can be seen hopping along the ground in search of snails, worms, beetles, and other large insects. Its call is loud and penetrating.
• **NEST** A ball-shaped, hollow structure made of vegetation and placed in a bush.
• **DISTRIBUTION** Malay Peninsula, Sumatra, Borneo, Java, and Bali.

big eyes for vision in poor light

white wing patch

DISTRIBUTION

FEMALE

Plumage Sexes differ	Habitat	Migration Non-migrant

Family PITTIDAE	Species *Pitta brachyura*	Length 8 in (20 cm)

INDIAN PITTA

The habitat of this pitta extends from tropical into subtropical forests and thick scrub. Its flight is limited, although it ascends trees to roost and sing. It travels in springy hops, looking for fruit, insects, and seeds.
• **NEST** A large, domed nest at ground level, with a side entrance.
• **DISTRIBUTION** Indian subcontinent. Migrant populations winter in S. India and Sri Lanka.

large head and eye

powerful bill for digging

agile, bounding legs

DISTRIBUTION

BLUE WING PATCH

Plumage Sexes alike	Habitat	Migration Partial migrant

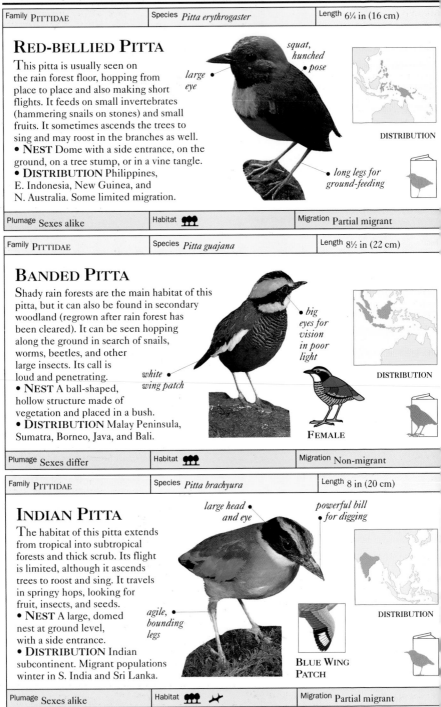

Family PITTIDAE	Species *Pitta caerulea*	Length 11½ in (29 cm)

GIANT PITTA

This shy bird is rarely seen, but its distinctive calls are easily heard. It is at its most common in the lowland rain forests, but it has also been recorded in mountain rain forests. The diet consists mainly of land snails and earthworms.
• **NEST** A domed structure of dead leaves and twigs, hidden in undergrowth, with a side entrance.
• **DISTRIBUTION** Malay Peninsula, Sumatra, and Borneo.

• *large head*

rounded body •

DISTRIBUTION

• *short tail*

FEMALE

Plumage Sexes differ	Habitat 🌳🌳	Migration Non-migrant

Family ACANTHISITTIDAE	Species *Acanthisitta chloris*	Length 3¼ in (8 cm)

RIFLEMAN

Also known as the Titipounamou, this tiny forest bird uses its sharp bill to search crevices in bark and probe mosses and lichens for insects. It has a high pitched call.
• **NEST** A loosely woven, domed nest with a side entrance, in a tree hollow, or sometimes in a bank.
• **DISTRIBUTION** New Zealand.
• **REMARK** A threatened species due to forest destruction.

broad head •

• *short, rounded wings*

DISTRIBUTION

Plumage Sexes alike	Habitat 🌳🌳	Migration Non-migrant

Family PHILEPITTIDAE	Species *Neodrepanis coruscans*	Length 4 in (10 cm)

WATTLED ASITY

Found in dense rain forest, this species feeds at all levels from ground to canopy, taking insects and probing flowers, possibly for nectar. It can adapt to secondary forest (regrown after rain forest clearance). This quiet, rather sluggish bird is usually solitary, or lives in small family groups. After breeding, males molt to resemble the females.
• **NEST** A spherical nest covered with moss and lined with leaves, generally suspended from the end of a branch.
• **DISTRIBUTION** E. Madagascar.

decorative eye wattle •

long, probing bill •

DISTRIBUTION

FEMALE

Plumage Sexes differ	Habitat 🌳🌳🌳	Migration Non-migrant

| Family MENURIDAE | Species *Menura novaehollandiae* | L. 35 in (90 cm)/32 in (80 cm) |

SUPERB LYREBIRD

Resembling a pheasant both in size and life-style, the Superb Lyrebird is a ground-dwelling species living in moist eucalyptus forests. It scratches the ground with its long, strong legs to reveal insects and other invertebrates. The male develops a unique, lyre-shaped tail that features in courtship dances performed on a special display mound, which he scrapes together out of damp soil. The dancing male vibrates his spread tail above his back; the display also includes a highly developed song, with elements of astonishingly clever mimicry.

tail arched over body in display

• **NEST** A large, domed nest with a side entrance, made of sticks, bark, fern fronds, and moss, and lined with rootlets. The nest may be located on the ground or on a stump, tree fern, or rock.

• **DISTRIBUTION** S.E. Australia.

• **REMARKS** The lyre-shaped tail of the adult male accounts for the 4 in (10 cm) length difference between the sexes.

FEMALE

DISTRIBUTION

| Plumage Sexes differ | Habitat | Migration Non-migrant |

| Family ATRICHORNITHIDAE | Species *Atrichornis clamosus* | Length 8 in (20 cm) |

NOISY SCRUB-BIRD

brown plumage for camouflage against • bare ground

This shy, secretive, and almost flightless bird lives in eucalyptus scrub. It seeks its food among dead leaves and ground litter, taking mainly small invertebrates and occasionally small lizards and frogs. Males sing loudly to proclaim their territories.

short, weak • wings

• **NEST** A domed nest in thick vegetation, placed a little above the ground.

• **DISTRIBUTION** S.W. Australia.

• **REMARK** Endangered species.

strong legs •

DISTRIBUTION

FEMALE

| Plumage Sexes differ | Habitat | Migration Non-migrant |

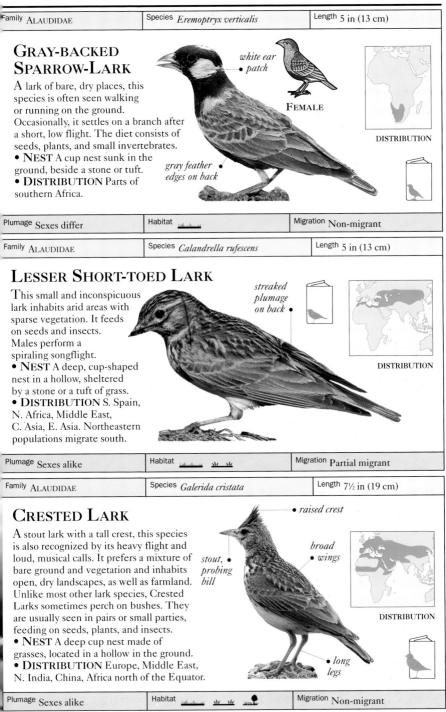

Family ALAUDIDAE	Species *Eremoptryx verticalis*	Length 5 in (13 cm)

GRAY-BACKED SPARROW-LARK

A lark of bare, dry places, this species is often seen walking or running on the ground. Occasionally, it settles on a branch after a short, low flight. The diet consists of seeds, plants, and small invertebrates.
• **NEST** A cup nest sunk in the ground, beside a stone or tuft.
• **DISTRIBUTION** Parts of southern Africa.

white ear patch

FEMALE

gray feather edges on back

DISTRIBUTION

Plumage Sexes differ	Habitat	Migration Non-migrant

Family ALAUDIDAE	Species *Calandrella rufescens*	Length 5 in (13 cm)

LESSER SHORT-TOED LARK

This small and inconspicuous lark inhabits arid areas with sparse vegetation. It feeds on seeds and insects. Males perform a spiraling songflight.
• **NEST** A deep, cup-shaped nest in a hollow, sheltered by a stone or a tuft of grass.
• **DISTRIBUTION** S. Spain, N. Africa, Middle East, C. Asia, E. Asia. Northeastern populations migrate south.

streaked plumage on back

DISTRIBUTION

Plumage Sexes alike	Habitat	Migration Partial migrant

Family ALAUDIDAE	Species *Galerida cristata*	Length 7½ in (19 cm)

CRESTED LARK

A stout lark with a tall crest, this species is also recognized by its heavy flight and loud, musical calls. It prefers a mixture of bare ground and vegetation and inhabits open, dry landscapes, as well as farmland. Unlike most other lark species, Crested Larks sometimes perch on bushes. They are usually seen in pairs or small parties, feeding on seeds, plants, and insects.
• **NEST** A deep cup nest made of grasses, located in a hollow in the ground.
• **DISTRIBUTION** Europe, Middle East, N. India, China, Africa north of the Equator.

raised crest

broad wings

stout, probing bill

DISTRIBUTION

long legs

Plumage Sexes alike	Habitat	Migration Non-migrant

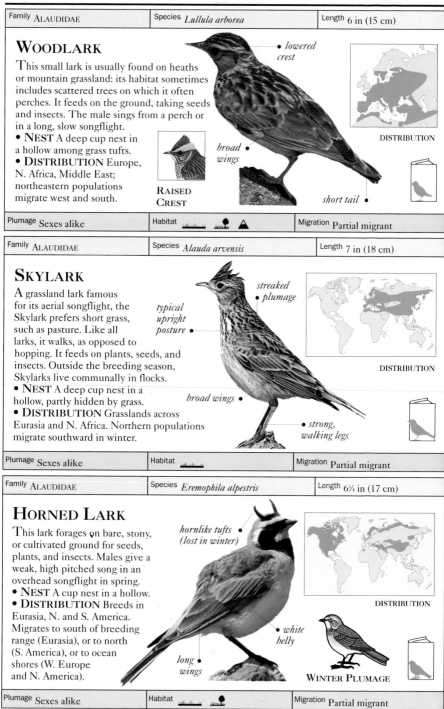

| Family ALAUDIDAE | Species *Lullula arborea* | Length 6 in (15 cm) |

WOODLARK

This small lark is usually found on heaths or mountain grassland: its habitat sometimes includes scattered trees on which it often perches. It feeds on the ground, taking seeds and insects. The male sings from a perch or in a long, slow songflight.
• **NEST** A deep cup nest in a hollow among grass tufts.
• **DISTRIBUTION** Europe, N. Africa, Middle East; northeastern populations migrate west and south.

lowered crest

broad wings

RAISED CREST

short tail

DISTRIBUTION

| Plumage Sexes alike | Habitat | Migration Partial migrant |

| Family ALAUDIDAE | Species *Alauda arvensis* | Length 7 in (18 cm) |

SKYLARK

A grassland lark famous for its aerial songflight, the Skylark prefers short grass, such as pasture. Like all larks, it walks, as opposed to hopping. It feeds on plants, seeds, and insects. Outside the breeding season, Skylarks live communally in flocks.
• **NEST** A deep cup nest in a hollow, partly hidden by grass.
• **DISTRIBUTION** Grasslands across Eurasia and N. Africa. Northern populations migrate southward in winter.

typical upright posture

streaked plumage

broad wings

strong, walking legs

DISTRIBUTION

| Plumage Sexes alike | Habitat | Migration Partial migrant |

| Family ALAUDIDAE | Species *Eremophila alpestris* | Length 6¾ in (17 cm) |

HORNED LARK

This lark forages on bare, stony, or cultivated ground for seeds, plants, and insects. Males give a weak, high pitched song in an overhead songflight in spring.
• **NEST** A cup nest in a hollow.
• **DISTRIBUTION** Breeds in Eurasia, N. and S. America. Migrates to south of breeding range (Eurasia), or to north (S. America), or to ocean shores (W. Europe and N. America).

hornlike tufts (lost in winter)

white belly

long wings

WINTER PLUMAGE

DISTRIBUTION

| Plumage Sexes alike | Habitat | Migration Partial migrant |

Family HIRUNDINIDAE	Species *Tachycineta bicolor*	Length 6 in (15 cm)

TREE SWALLOW

A hole-nesting swallow, this bird is common in thinly wooded habitats near water, where it forages over open country catching small insects in flight. Large flocks gather to migrate.
• **NEST** A lining of plant materials in a cavity, in a tree, post, or building.
• **DISTRIBUTION** Breeds in North America. Winter range extends as far south as Colombia.

large eye

long, slender wing

DISTRIBUTION

JUVENILE

Plumage Sexes alike	Habitat	Migration Migrant

Family HIRUNDINIDAE	Species *Progne subis*	Length 7½ in (19 cm)

PURPLE MARTIN

This dark swallow flies over a variety of open habitats, hunting insects in the air by gliding in circles, with periods of flapping flight.
• **NEST** Tree holes lined with mud and sticks, often in nest boxes in east of range.
• **DISTRIBUTION** Breeds in USA. Winters in S.E. Brazil.

large eye

blue sheen on upper body

short, forked tail

DISTRIBUTION

FEMALE

Plumage Sexes differ	Habitat	Migration Migrant

Family HIRUNDINIDAE	Species *Riparia riparia*	Length 4¾ in (12 cm)

BANK SWALLOW

A small, drab, swallow, this species hunts insects by rivers, lakes, and sand pits near its nesting colonies.
• **NEST** A cup nest is built of plant materials and feathers in a tunnel in a bank or cliff.

powerful, slender wings for long-distance flight

short, blunt tail

• **DISTRIBUTION** Breeds in North America and Eurasia. Winters in South America, Africa, N. India, and S.E. Asia.

DISTRIBUTION

Plumage Sexes alike	Habitat	Migration Migrant

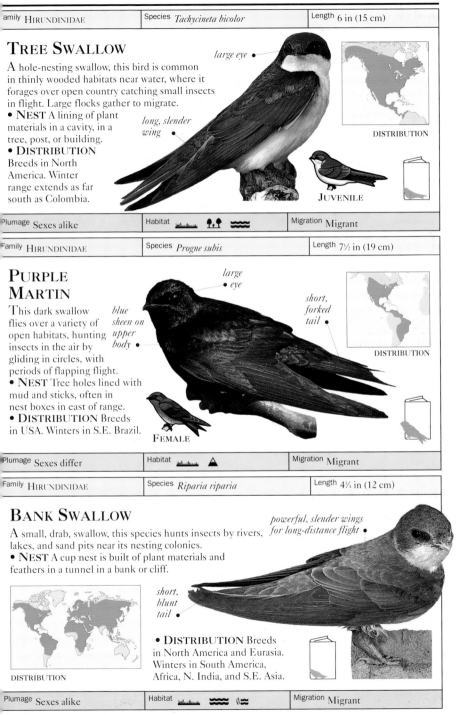

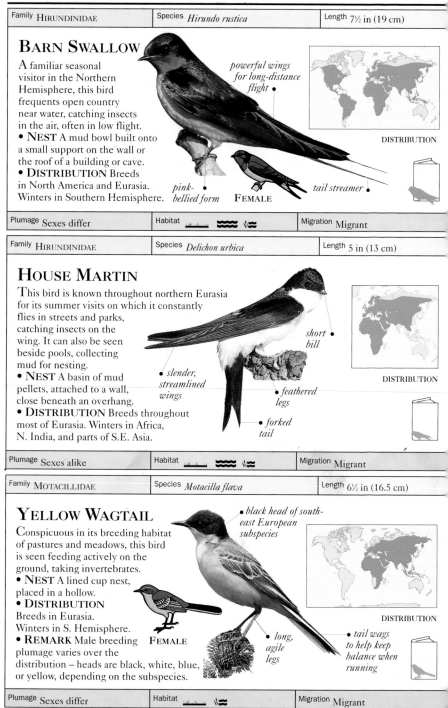

| Family HIRUNDINIDAE | Species *Hirundo rustica* | Length 7½ in (19 cm) |

BARN SWALLOW

A familiar seasonal
visitor in the Northern
Hemisphere, this bird
frequents open country
near water, catching insects
in the air, often in low flight.
• **NEST** A mud bowl built onto
a small support on the wall or
the roof of a building or cave.
• **DISTRIBUTION** Breeds
in North America and Eurasia.
Winters in Southern Hemisphere.

*powerful wings
for long-distance
flight •*

*pink-
bellied form* **FEMALE**

tail streamer •

DISTRIBUTION

| Plumage Sexes differ | Habitat | Migration Migrant |

| Family HIRUNDINIDAE | Species *Delichon urbica* | Length 5 in (13 cm) |

HOUSE MARTIN

This bird is known throughout northern Eurasia
for its summer visits on which it constantly
flies in streets and parks,
catching insects on the
wing. It can also be seen
beside pools, collecting
mud for nesting.
• **NEST** A basin of mud
pellets, attached to a wall,
close beneath an overhang.
• **DISTRIBUTION** Breeds throughout
most of Eurasia. Winters in Africa,
N. India, and parts of S.E. Asia.

*short
bill •*

*• slender,
streamlined
wings*

*• feathered
legs*

*• forked
tail*

DISTRIBUTION

| Plumage Sexes alike | Habitat | Migration Migrant |

| Family MOTACILLIDAE | Species *Motacilla flava* | Length 6½ in (16.5 cm) |

YELLOW WAGTAIL

Conspicuous in its breeding habitat
of pastures and meadows, this bird
is seen feeding actively on the
ground, taking invertebrates.
• **NEST** A lined cup nest,
placed in a hollow.
• **DISTRIBUTION**
Breeds in Eurasia.
Winters in S. Hemisphere.
• **REMARK** Male breeding
plumage varies over the
distribution – heads are black, white, blue,
or yellow, depending on the subspecies.

*• black head of south-
east European
subspecies*

FEMALE

*• long,
agile
legs*

*• tail wags
to help keep
balance when
running*

DISTRIBUTION

| Plumage Sexes differ | Habitat | Migration Migrant |

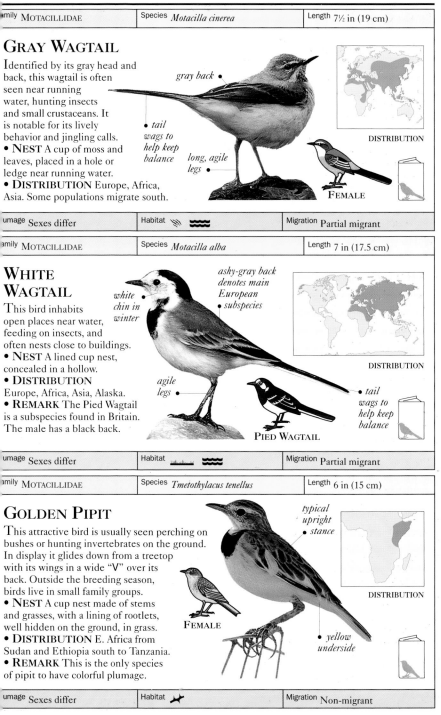

| Family MOTACILLIDAE | Species *Motacilla cinerea* | Length 7½ in (19 cm) |

GRAY WAGTAIL

Identified by its gray head and
back, this wagtail is often
seen near running
water, hunting insects
and small crustaceans. It
is notable for its lively
behavior and jingling calls.
• **NEST** A cup of moss and
leaves, placed in a hole or
ledge near running water.
• **DISTRIBUTION** Europe, Africa,
Asia. Some populations migrate south.

gray back •

• tail
wags to
help keep
balance

long, agile
legs •

DISTRIBUTION

FEMALE

| Plumage Sexes differ | Habitat | Migration Partial migrant |

| Family MOTACILLIDAE | Species *Motacilla alba* | Length 7 in (17.5 cm) |

WHITE WAGTAIL

This bird inhabits
open places near water,
feeding on insects, and
often nests close to buildings.
• **NEST** A lined cup nest,
concealed in a hollow.
• **DISTRIBUTION**
Europe, Africa, Asia, Alaska.
• **REMARK** The Pied Wagtail
is a subspecies found in Britain.
The male has a black back.

white
chin in
winter

ashy-gray back
denotes main
European
• subspecies

DISTRIBUTION

agile
legs •

• tail
wags to
help keep
balance

PIED WAGTAIL

| Plumage Sexes differ | Habitat | Migration Partial migrant |

| Family MOTACILLIDAE | Species *Tmetothylacus tenellus* | Length 6 in (15 cm) |

GOLDEN PIPIT

This attractive bird is usually seen perching on
bushes or hunting invertebrates on the ground.
In display it glides down from a treetop
with its wings in a wide "V" over its
back. Outside the breeding season,
birds live in small family groups.
• **NEST** A cup nest made of stems
and grasses, with a lining of rootlets,
well hidden on the ground, in grass.
• **DISTRIBUTION** E. Africa from
Sudan and Ethiopia south to Tanzania.
• **REMARK** This is the only species
of pipit to have colorful plumage.

typical
upright
• stance

DISTRIBUTION

FEMALE

• yellow
underside

| Plumage Sexes differ | Habitat | Migration Non-migrant |

| Family MOTACILLIDAE | Species *Anthus pratensis* | Length 5¼ in (14.5 cm) |

MEADOW PIPIT

A streaked, brown bird of grassland and
moors, the Meadow Pipit has a weak,
jerky flight and squeaky calls. It runs
and walks on open ground, taking
insects, worms, and seeds.
It performs a songflight
with a parachuting fall.
• **NEST** A cup nest made
of grass stems and blades, lined and
tucked into a hollow in the ground.
• **DISTRIBUTION** From Greenland
to C. Asia. Some birds migrate to N. Africa.

*• slender, insect-
eater's bill*

*• streaked
plumage*

DISTRIBUTION

| Plumage Sexes alike | Habitat | Migration Partial migrant |

| Family CAMPEPHAGIDAE | Species *Lalage sueurii* | Length 7 in (18 cm) |

WHITE-WINGED TRILLER

Normally an inconspicuous brown bird with streaky
wings, this species gets its name from the male's
dashing, pied breeding plumage and loud, trilling
song. Pairs often nest close to one another in a
semi-colonial arrangement. White-winged
Trillers feed on insects, taken either from
foliage or while walking on the ground.
• **NEST** A shallow, saucer-shaped
nest made of roots and grass, bound
to a tree fork with spiderwebs.
• **DISTRIBUTION** Australia.
Winters in N. Australia, New Guinea,
and the island of Timor in Indonesia.

*white
wing
• bar*

DISTRIBUTION

*• long wings for
rapid flight*

FEMALE

| Plumage Sexes differ | Habitat | Migration Migrant |

| Family CAMPEPHAGIDAE | Species *Pericrocotus flammeus* | Length 9 in (23 cm) |

SCARLET MINIVET

This slender, vivid bird flits restlessly in the
rain forest canopy, making short, quick chases
after insects. This species is usually seen in
flocks of up to 20 or more, often associating
with mixed-species hunting parties.
• **NEST** A cup nest made of lichens,
bound with spiderwebs and ornamented
with bark flakes. Usually high in the trees.
• **DISTRIBUTION** Indian subcontinent,
S. China, and much of S.E. Asia.
• **REMARK** The scarlet plumage of the
males is replaced by orange in the Indian
subcontinent south of the Himalayas.

*• orange
plumage of
Sri Lanka
form*

DISTRIBUTION

*• tail often
opens out
during
flight*

FEMALE

| Plumage Sexes differ | Habitat | Migration Non-migrant |

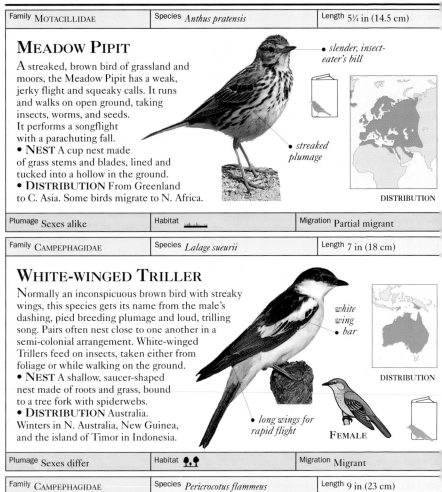
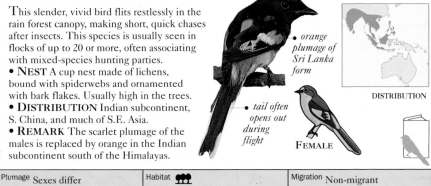

Family CAMPEPHAGIDAE	Species *Coracina novaehollandiae*	Length 13 in (33 cm)

BLACK-FACED CUCKOO-SHRIKE

A slender, tree-dwelling bird of thinly spaced woodland,
this species has an undulating style of flight and a habit
of shuffling its wings just after alighting. The "cuckoo"
in its name refers to the long, slender body shape.
The "shrike" refers to its style of feeding, taking large
insects and their larvae from foliage or the ground,
and sometimes eating berries. The call is either
a grating "kaark" or a gentler, whistling sound.
• **NEST** A small, saucer-shaped nest made of
dry twigs and bark, fixed together with spiderwebs, and built in the fork of a tree branch.
• **DISTRIBUTION** Australia; migrant populations
winter in northern states and New Guinea.
• **REMARK** Migration varies
between local populations. Some
travel to New Guinea, some a
shorter distance, while others
merely roam nomadically within
Australia. These birds settle
in places where recent rain has
resulted in fresh growth of plants,
flowers, and insects. If conditions
are suitable, the birds breed.

DISTRIBUTION

slender wings for •
long-distance flight

Plumage Sexes alike	Habitat 🌳 🌿	Migration Partial migrant/nomadic

Family PYCNONOTIDAE	Species *Pycnonotus zeylanicus*	Length 11 in (28 cm)

STRAW-HEADED BULBUL

The largest of all the bulbuls, this
bird is usually found in trees and
bushes. It occurs at the rain forest edge
and in secondary growth (areas where trees
have regrown after forest clearance). Its diet
consists chiefly of fruit, buds, and berries, which
it supplements with some insects. The song is
loud and strong, consisting of a clear, melodious
warbling. This species is shy and inconspicuous,
more often heard than seen. Among its own
flocks, which usually consist of half-a-dozen
birds, it behaves in a quarrelsome manner, constantly
uttering a harsh and noisy chatter. When excited, the
birds raise the short, bristly feathers on the front of
their crowns to form a small, straw-colored crest.
• **NEST** A shallow, cup-shaped nest of rootlets,
grass, and leaves, placed in a bush or low tree.
• **DISTRIBUTION** Malay Peninsula,
Borneo, Sumatra, and Java.
• **REMARK** This bird has become
rare in much of its range as a result
of trapping for the local cagebird trade.

• lowered crest

black •
mustache

• large, heavily
built body for
a bulbul

DISTRIBUTION

Plumage Sexes alike	Habitat 🌳 🪨	Migration Non-migrant

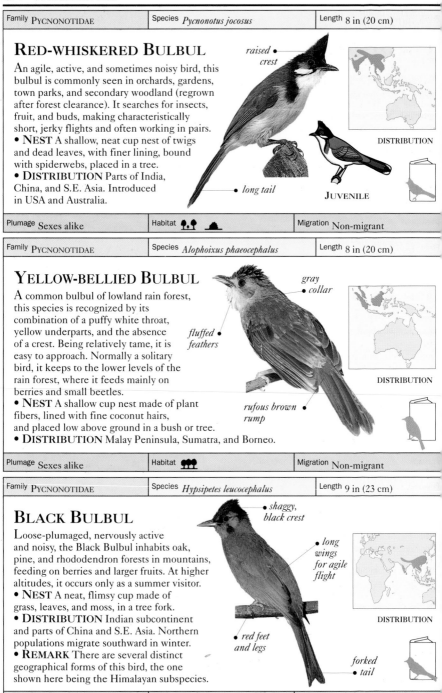

Family PYCNONOTIDAE	Species *Pycnonotus jocosus*	Length 8 in (20 cm)

RED-WHISKERED BULBUL

An agile, active, and sometimes noisy bird, this
bulbul is commonly seen in orchards, gardens,
town parks, and secondary woodland (regrown
after forest clearance). It searches for insects,
fruit, and buds, making characteristically
short, jerky flights and often working in pairs.
• **NEST** A shallow, neat cup nest of twigs
and dead leaves, with finer lining, bound
with spiderwebs, placed in a tree.
• **DISTRIBUTION** Parts of India,
China, and S.E. Asia. Introduced
in USA and Australia.

*raised
crest*

DISTRIBUTION

long tail

JUVENILE

Plumage Sexes alike	Habitat 🌳🌳 🏠	Migration Non-migrant

Family PYCNONOTIDAE	Species *Alophoixus phaeocephalus*	Length 8 in (20 cm)

YELLOW-BELLIED BULBUL

A common bulbul of lowland rain forest,
this species is recognized by its
combination of a puffy white throat,
yellow underparts, and the absence
of a crest. Being relatively tame, it is
easy to approach. Normally a solitary
bird, it keeps to the lower levels of the
rain forest, where it feeds mainly on
berries and small beetles.
• **NEST** A shallow cup nest made of plant
fibers, lined with fine coconut hairs,
and placed low above ground in a bush or tree.
• **DISTRIBUTION** Malay Peninsula, Sumatra, and Borneo.

*gray
collar*

*fluffed
feathers*

DISTRIBUTION

*rufous brown
rump*

Plumage Sexes alike	Habitat 🌳🌳🌳	Migration Non-migrant

Family PYCNONOTIDAE	Species *Hypsipetes leucocephalus*	Length 9 in (23 cm)

BLACK BULBUL

Loose-plumaged, nervously active
and noisy, the Black Bulbul inhabits oak,
pine, and rhododendron forests in mountains,
feeding on berries and larger fruits. At higher
altitudes, it occurs only as a summer visitor.
• **NEST** A neat, flimsy cup made of
grass, leaves, and moss, in a tree fork.
• **DISTRIBUTION** Indian subcontinent
and parts of China and S.E. Asia. Northern
populations migrate southward in winter.
• **REMARK** There are several distinct
geographical forms of this bird, the one
shown here being the Himalayan subspecies.

*shaggy,
black crest*

*long
wings
for agile
flight*

DISTRIBUTION

*red feet
and legs*

*forked
tail*

Plumage Sexes alike	Habitat 🌳🌳🌳 ⛰️	Migration Partial migrant

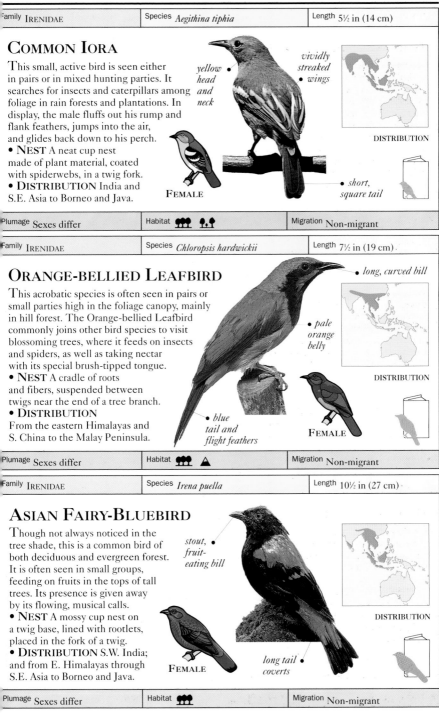

Family IRENIDAE	Species *Aegithina tiphia*	Length 5½ in (14 cm)

COMMON IORA

This small, active bird is seen either in pairs or in mixed hunting parties. It searches for insects and caterpillars among foliage in rain forests and plantations. In display, the male fluffs out his rump and flank feathers, jumps into the air, and glides back down to his perch.
• **NEST** A neat cup nest made of plant material, coated with spiderwebs, in a twig fork.
• **DISTRIBUTION** India and S.E. Asia to Borneo and Java.

yellow head and neck

vividly streaked wings

DISTRIBUTION

short, square tail

FEMALE

Plumage Sexes differ	Habitat	Migration Non-migrant

Family IRENIDAE	Species *Chloropsis hardwickii*	Length 7½ in (19 cm)

ORANGE-BELLIED LEAFBIRD

This acrobatic species is often seen in pairs or small parties high in the foliage canopy, mainly in hill forest. The Orange-bellied Leafbird commonly joins other bird species to visit blossoming trees, where it feeds on insects and spiders, as well as taking nectar with its special brush-tipped tongue.
• **NEST** A cradle of roots and fibers, suspended between twigs near the end of a tree branch.
• **DISTRIBUTION** From the eastern Himalayas and S. China to the Malay Peninsula.

long, curved bill

pale orange belly

DISTRIBUTION

blue tail and flight feathers

FEMALE

Plumage Sexes differ	Habitat	Migration Non-migrant

Family IRENIDAE	Species *Irena puella*	Length 10½ in (27 cm)

ASIAN FAIRY-BLUEBIRD

Though not always noticed in the tree shade, this is a common bird of both deciduous and evergreen forest. It is often seen in small groups, feeding on fruits in the tops of tall trees. Its presence is given away by its flowing, musical calls.
• **NEST** A mossy cup nest on a twig base, lined with rootlets, placed in the fork of a twig.
• **DISTRIBUTION** S.W. India; and from E. Himalayas through S.E. Asia to Borneo and Java.

stout, fruit-eating bill

DISTRIBUTION

FEMALE

long tail coverts

Plumage Sexes differ	Habitat	Migration Non-migrant

| Family LANIIDAE | Species *Eurocephalus anguitimens* | Length 9½ in (24 cm) |

SOUTHERN WHITE-CROWNED SHRIKE

An unusually sociable shrike, this species is usually seen in pairs or small parties. It perches conspicuously on top, or on the outer branches of trees in woodlands or savanna (tropical or subtropical grassland). Like other shrikes it forages for insects and other prey by dropping from a perch to the ground, as well as feeding on berries. Its flight is strong and direct, with shallow, quick wingbeats.
• **NEST** A thick-walled cup nest, made of plant fibers and bound with spiderwebs, located in a tree.
• **DISTRIBUTION** Parts of southern Africa.

• *broad, white crown*

• *hook-tipped bill for seizing large insects*

DISTRIBUTION

• *alert, watchful posture*

• *typical view of the bird – high up on a prominent perch*

| Plumage Sexes alike | Habitat | Migration Non-migrant |

| Family LANIIDAE | Species *Corvinella melanoleuca* | Length 17½ in (45 cm) |

MAGPIE SHRIKE

Unmistakable with its long, black tail, this species inhabits open, semi-arid woodland, often of acacia trees, and scrub. Unusually sociable for a shrike, it is generally seen in noisy groups of up to a dozen individuals. The Magpie Shrike perches on the tops of trees and bushes, dropping down to seize its prey, which consists of insects and small reptiles.
• **NEST** A bulky, cup-shaped nest made of twigs, grass stems, and roots, lined with finer rootlets and the stems and tendrils of creepers, and placed in a tree.
• **DISTRIBUTION** Eastern and southern Africa from Kenya to Mozambique.
• **REMARKS** This bird is also known as the Long-tailed Shrike. It is one of a range of open-country birds that use a long tail as a display feature.

DISTRIBUTION

• *broad, domed head*

• *bold white bars (often concealed)*

• *stout body*

• *long tail impresses females, as well as warning other males to stay off the territory*

| Plumage Sexes alike | Habitat | Migration Non-migrant |

| Family LANIIDAE | Species *Prionops plumatus* | Length 8 in (20 cm) |

WHITE HELMET SHRIKE

Unlike many shrikes, this species
is exceptionally gregarious at all times,
forming groups of up to 20 birds, usually
consisting of siblings from several broods. It
forages at all levels, from the forest canopy to
the ground, taking insects and spiders. Groups
roost together on branches in huddled rows.
• **NEST** A compact cup nest made of
bark shreds, bound on the outside with
spiderswebs, and placed in a tree fork.
• **DISTRIBUTION** Parts of
Africa south of the Sahara.

crest •
projects
over bill

• *yellow
wattle
around
the eye*

DISTRIBUTION

• *short,
rounded
wings*

| Plumage Sexes alike | Habitat | Migration Non-migrant |

| Family LANIIDAE | Species *Tchagra senegala* | Length 8½ in (22 cm) |

BLACK-CROWNED TCHAGRA

Like most shrikes, this bird is usually solitary
or seen in pairs. It forages for invertebrates and
other small animals on or near the ground,
and flies low between bushes in
fluttering flight. In its display
flight it rises from a bush,
calling, then glides down.
• **NEST** A shallow cup nest
of fine twigs and roots, lined
with finer rootlets, in a bush.
• **DISTRIBUTION** N.W. Africa;
parts of Africa south of the
Sahara; S.W. Arabian Peninsula.

*rufous
plumage on
back and
• wings*

DISTRIBUTION

| Plumage Sexes alike | Habitat | Migration Non-migrant |

| Family LANIIDAE | Species *Laniarius atrococcineus* | Length 9 in (23 cm) |

CRIMSON-BREASTED GONOLEK

This vividly colored shrike is
secretive in behavior. It lives in open
woodland, foraging for insects on
the ground or in trees. Calls
are loud and bell-like, and
mating pairs often sing
together in "duets."
• **NEST** A bark
bowl, secured with spiderwebs
and lined with fibers, in a tree.
• **DISTRIBUTION** Parts of southern Africa.

JUVENILE

• *hooked bill*

DISTRIBUTION

• *white
wing stripe*

| Plumage Sexes alike | Habitat | Migration Non-migrant |

Family LANIIDAE	Species *Telephorus zeylonus*	Length 9 in (23 cm)

BOKMAKIERIE

This shrike perches in conspicuous places on bushy hillsides with rocks, in river-valley scrub, and in gardens. It hunts low in the undergrowth for insects and small animals. Pairs sing "duetting" calls all year round.
• **NEST** A bulky bowl made of twigs and stems, usually in a dense bush.
• **DISTRIBUTION** Parts of southern Africa.

pairs sing from the tops of bushes

typical "duetting" posture

DISTRIBUTION

JUVENILE

Plumage Sexes alike	Habitat	Migration Non-migrant

Family LANIIDAE	Species *Lanius collurio*	Length 7 in (18 cm)

RED-BACKED SHRIKE

This predatorlike songbird is seen in bushes and scrub, watching from a vantage point, and swooping on prey. It feeds mainly on insects, sometimes on birds and other small animals.
• **NEST** A deep cup nest of grass and rootlets, placed in a dense bush.
• **DISTRIBUTION** Breeds in Eurasia from S.E. Britain to W. Siberia. Migrates southward, some birds reaching South Africa.

black eye stripe

rich rufous back

alert, upright pose

FEMALE

DISTRIBUTION

Plumage Sexes differ	Habitat	Migration Migrant

Family LANIIDAE	Species *Lanius ludovicianus*	Length 8½ in (22 cm)

LOGGERHEAD SHRIKE

Thinly wooded, open country is the main habitat of this shrike. It moves about in short flights from one lookout perch to another, feeding by swooping to the ground to seize prey, mainly insects.
• **NEST** A well-lined, bulky cup nest made of twigs, weed stems, and rootlets, placed in a thick shrub or low tree.
• **DISTRIBUTION** From S. Canada to Mexico. Northern populations migrate southward.

black eye stripe

hooked bill

JUVENILE

DISTRIBUTION

black wings

Plumage Sexes alike	Habitat	Migration Migrant

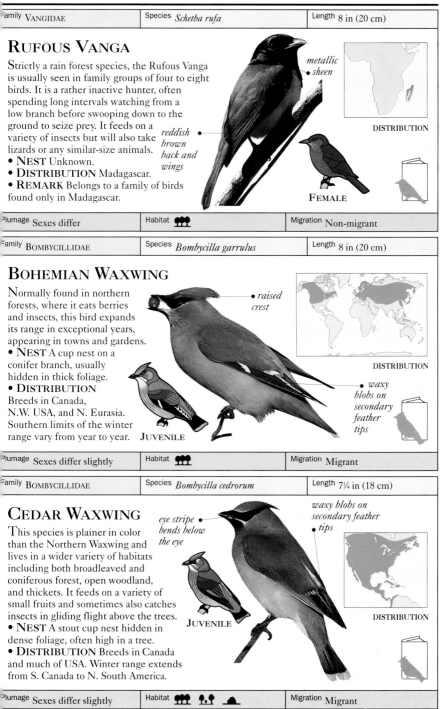

| Family VANGIDAE | Species *Schetba rufa* | Length 8 in (20 cm) |

RUFOUS VANGA

Strictly a rain forest species, the Rufous Vanga is usually seen in family groups of four to eight birds. It is a rather inactive hunter, often spending long intervals watching from a low branch before swooping down to the ground to seize prey. It feeds on a variety of insects but will also take lizards or any similar-size animals.
• **NEST** Unknown.
• **DISTRIBUTION** Madagascar.
• **REMARK** Belongs to a family of birds found only in Madagascar.

metallic sheen

reddish brown back and wings

FEMALE

DISTRIBUTION

| Plumage Sexes differ | Habitat | Migration Non-migrant |

| Family BOMBYCILLIDAE | Species *Bombycilla garrulus* | Length 8 in (20 cm) |

BOHEMIAN WAXWING

Normally found in northern forests, where it eats berries and insects, this bird expands its range in exceptional years, appearing in towns and gardens.
• **NEST** A cup nest on a conifer branch, usually hidden in thick foliage.
• **DISTRIBUTION** Breeds in Canada, N.W. USA, and N. Eurasia. Southern limits of the winter range vary from year to year.

raised crest

waxy blobs on secondary feather tips

JUVENILE

DISTRIBUTION

| Plumage Sexes differ slightly | Habitat | Migration Migrant |

| Family BOMBYCILLIDAE | Species *Bombycilla cedrorum* | Length 7¼ in (18 cm) |

CEDAR WAXWING

This species is plainer in color than the Northern Waxwing and lives in a wider variety of habitats including both broadleaved and coniferous forest, open woodland, and thickets. It feeds on a variety of small fruits and sometimes also catches insects in gliding flight above the trees.
• **NEST** A stout cup nest hidden in dense foliage, often high in a tree.
• **DISTRIBUTION** Breeds in Canada and much of USA. Winter range extends from S. Canada to N. South America.

waxy blobs on secondary feather tips

eye stripe bends below the eye

JUVENILE

DISTRIBUTION

| Plumage Sexes differ slightly | Habitat | Migration Migrant |

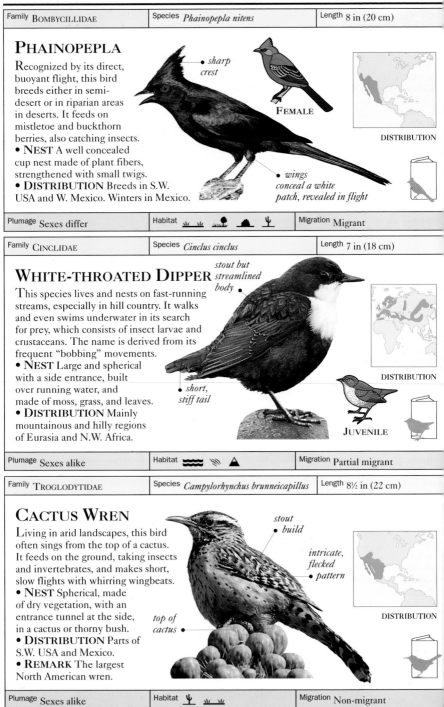

Family BOMBYCILLIDAE	Species *Phainopepla nitens*	Length 8 in (20 cm)

PHAINOPEPLA

Recognized by its direct,
buoyant flight, this bird
breeds either in semi-
desert or in riparian areas
in deserts. It feeds on
mistletoe and buckthorn
berries, also catching insects.
• **NEST** A well concealed
cup nest made of plant fibers,
strengthened with small twigs.
• **DISTRIBUTION** Breeds in S.W.
USA and W. Mexico. Winters in Mexico.

sharp
crest •

FEMALE

DISTRIBUTION

• *wings
conceal a white
patch, revealed in flight*

Plumage Sexes differ	Habitat	Migration Migrant

Family CINCLIDAE	Species *Cinclus cinclus*	Length 7 in (18 cm)

WHITE-THROATED DIPPER

*stout but
streamlined
body* •

This species lives and nests on fast-running
streams, especially in hill country. It walks
and even swims underwater in its search
for prey, which consists of insect larvae and
crustaceans. The name is derived from its
frequent "bobbing" movements.
• **NEST** Large and spherical
with a side entrance, built
over running water, and
made of moss, grass, and leaves.
• **DISTRIBUTION** Mainly
mountainous and hilly regions
of Eurasia and N.W. Africa.

• *short,
stiff tail*

DISTRIBUTION

JUVENILE

Plumage Sexes alike	Habitat	Migration Partial migrant

Family TROGLODYTIDAE	Species *Campylorhynchus brunneicapillus*	Length 8½ in (22 cm)

CACTUS WREN

Living in arid landscapes, this bird
often sings from the top of a cactus.
It feeds on the ground, taking insects
and invertebrates, and makes short,
slow flights with whirring wingbeats.
• **NEST** Spherical, made
of dry vegetation, with an
entrance tunnel at the side,
in a cactus or thorny bush.
• **DISTRIBUTION** Parts of
S.W. USA and Mexico.
• **REMARK** The largest
North American wren.

*stout
• build*

*intricate,
flecked
• pattern*

*top of
cactus* •

DISTRIBUTION

Plumage Sexes alike	Habitat	Migration Non-migrant

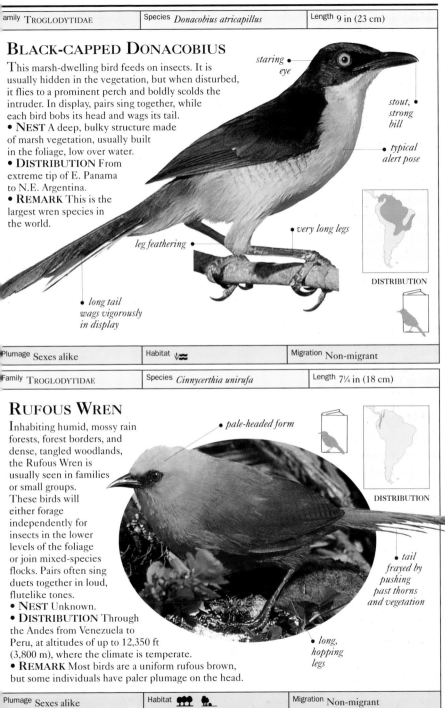

| amily TROGLODYTIDAE | Species _Donacobius atricapillus_ | Length 9 in (23 cm) |

BLACK-CAPPED DONACOBIUS

This marsh-dwelling bird feeds on insects. It is
usually hidden in the vegetation, but when disturbed,
it flies to a prominent perch and boldly scolds the
intruder. In display, pairs sing together, while
each bird bobs its head and wags its tail.
• **NEST** A deep, bulky structure made
of marsh vegetation, usually built
in the foliage, low over water.
• **DISTRIBUTION** From
extreme tip of E. Panama
to N.E. Argentina.
• **REMARK** This is the
largest wren species in
the world.

staring •
eye

stout, •
strong
bill

• typical
alert pose

• very long legs

leg feathering •

DISTRIBUTION

• long tail
wags vigorously
in display

| Plumage Sexes alike | Habitat | Migration Non-migrant |

| Family TROGLODYTIDAE | Species _Cinnycerthia unirufa_ | Length 7¼ in (18 cm) |

RUFOUS WREN

Inhabiting humid, mossy rain
forests, forest borders, and
dense, tangled woodlands,
the Rufous Wren is
usually seen in families
or small groups.
These birds will
either forage
independently for
insects in the lower
levels of the foliage
or join mixed-species
flocks. Pairs often sing
duets together in loud,
flutelike tones.
• **NEST** Unknown.
• **DISTRIBUTION** Through
the Andes from Venezuela to
Peru, at altitudes of up to 12,350 ft
(3,800 m), where the climate is temperate.
• **REMARK** Most birds are a uniform rufous brown,
but some individuals have paler plumage on the head.

• pale-headed form

DISTRIBUTION

• tail
frayed by
pushing
past thorns
and vegetation

• long,
hopping
legs

| Plumage Sexes alike | Habitat | Migration Non-migrant |

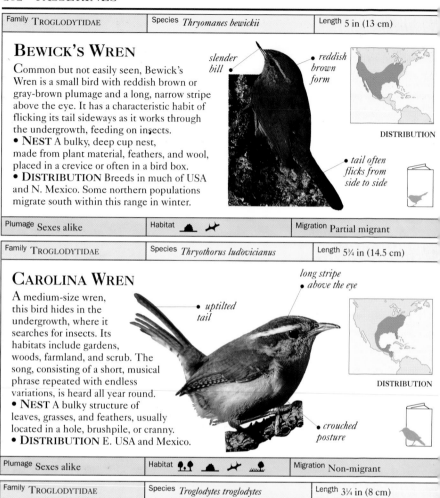

Family TROGLODYTIDAE	Species *Thryomanes bewickii*	Length 5 in (13 cm)

BEWICK'S WREN

Common but not easily seen, Bewick's
Wren is a small bird with reddish brown or
gray-brown plumage and a long, narrow stripe
above the eye. It has a characteristic habit of
flicking its tail sideways as it works through
the undergrowth, feeding on insects.
• **NEST** A bulky, deep cup nest,
made from plant material, feathers, and wool,
placed in a crevice or often in a bird box.
• **DISTRIBUTION** Breeds in much of USA
and N. Mexico. Some northern populations
migrate south within this range in winter.

slender bill

reddish brown form

DISTRIBUTION

tail often flicks from side to side

Plumage Sexes alike	Habitat	Migration Partial migrant

Family TROGLODYTIDAE	Species *Thryothorus ludovicianus*	Length 5¾ in (14.5 cm)

CAROLINA WREN

A medium-size wren,
this bird hides in the
undergrowth, where it
searches for insects. Its
habitats include gardens,
woods, farmland, and scrub. The
song, consisting of a short, musical
phrase repeated with endless
variations, is heard all year round.
• **NEST** A bulky structure of
leaves, grasses, and feathers, usually
located in a hole, brushpile, or cranny.
• **DISTRIBUTION** E. USA and Mexico.

long stripe above the eye

uptilted tail

DISTRIBUTION

crouched posture

Plumage Sexes alike	Habitat	Migration Non-migrant

Family TROGLODYTIDAE	Species *Troglodytes troglodytes*	Length 3¼ in (8 cm)

WINTER WREN

This tiny bird, with its slender bill
and secretive manner, is found in
forests, woods, farmlands, grassland,
and gardens. It is usually seen singly
as it busily seeks insects in tangled
cover. The explosive song is loud
for a bird of this diminutive size.
• **NEST** A dome made of leaves, grass,
and moss, with a side entrance, and
placed in a crevice or sheltered site.
• **DISTRIBUTION** A widespread
species in the temperate zone
of the northern hemisphere.

large head

DISTRIBUTION

short tail

Plumage Sexes alike	Habitat	Migration Non-migrant

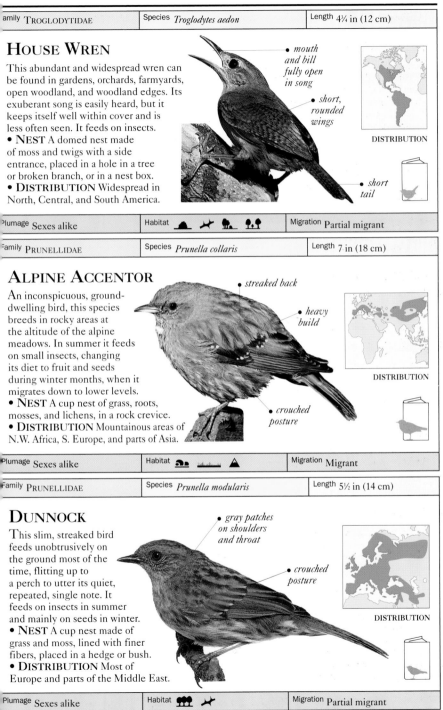

| Family TROGLODYTIDAE | Species *Troglodytes aedon* | Length 4¾ in (12 cm) |

HOUSE WREN

This abundant and widespread wren can be found in gardens, orchards, farmyards, open woodland, and woodland edges. Its exuberant song is easily heard, but it keeps itself well within cover and is less often seen. It feeds on insects.
• **NEST** A domed nest made of moss and twigs with a side entrance, placed in a hole in a tree or broken branch, or in a nest box.
• **DISTRIBUTION** Widespread in North, Central, and South America.

• *mouth and bill fully open in song*

• *short, rounded wings*

DISTRIBUTION

• *short tail*

| Plumage Sexes alike | Habitat | Migration Partial migrant |

| Family PRUNELLIDAE | Species *Prunella collaris* | Length 7 in (18 cm) |

ALPINE ACCENTOR

An inconspicuous, ground-dwelling bird, this species breeds in rocky areas at the altitude of the alpine meadows. In summer it feeds on small insects, changing its diet to fruit and seeds during winter months, when it migrates down to lower levels.
• **NEST** A cup nest of grass, roots, mosses, and lichens, in a rock crevice.
• **DISTRIBUTION** Mountainous areas of N.W. Africa, S. Europe, and parts of Asia.

• *streaked back*

• *heavy build*

DISTRIBUTION

• *crouched posture*

| Plumage Sexes alike | Habitat | Migration Migrant |

| Family PRUNELLIDAE | Species *Prunella modularis* | Length 5½ in (14 cm) |

DUNNOCK

This slim, streaked bird feeds unobtrusively on the ground most of the time, flitting up to a perch to utter its quiet, repeated, single note. It feeds on insects in summer and mainly on seeds in winter.
• **NEST** A cup nest made of grass and moss, lined with finer fibers, placed in a hedge or bush.
• **DISTRIBUTION** Most of Europe and parts of the Middle East.

• *gray patches on shoulders and throat*

• *crouched posture*

DISTRIBUTION

| Plumage Sexes alike | Habitat | Migration Partial migrant |

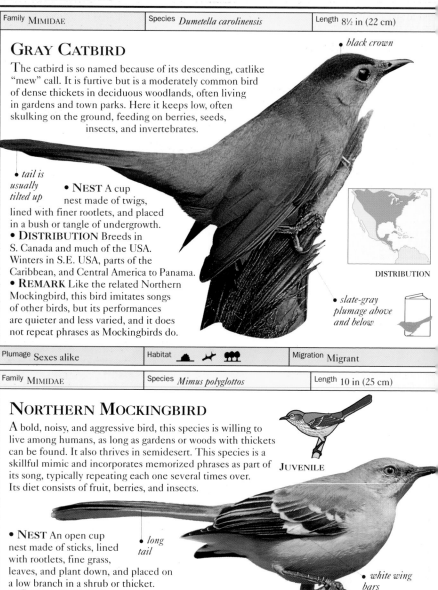

Family MIMIDAE	Species *Dumetella carolinensis*	Length 8½ in (22 cm)

GRAY CATBIRD

The catbird is so named because of its descending, catlike "mew" call. It is furtive but is a moderately common bird of dense thickets in deciduous woodlands, often living in gardens and town parks. Here it keeps low, often skulking on the ground, feeding on berries, seeds, insects, and invertebrates.

• *black crown*

• *tail is usually tilted up*

• **NEST** A cup nest made of twigs, lined with finer rootlets, and placed in a bush or tangle of undergrowth.
• **DISTRIBUTION** Breeds in S. Canada and much of the USA. Winters in S.E. USA, parts of the Caribbean, and Central America to Panama.
• **REMARK** Like the related Northern Mockingbird, this bird imitates songs of other birds, but its performances are quieter and less varied, and it does not repeat phrases as Mockingbirds do.

DISTRIBUTION

• *slate-gray plumage above and below*

Plumage Sexes alike	Habitat	Migration Migrant

Family MIMIDAE	Species *Mimus polyglottos*	Length 10 in (25 cm)

NORTHERN MOCKINGBIRD

A bold, noisy, and aggressive bird, this species is willing to live among humans, as long as gardens or woods with thickets can be found. It also thrives in semidesert. This species is a skillful mimic and incorporates memorized phrases as part of its song, typically repeating each one several times over. Its diet consists of fruit, berries, and insects.

JUVENILE

• **NEST** An open cup nest made of sticks, lined with rootlets, fine grass, leaves, and plant down, and placed on a low branch in a shrub or thicket.
• **DISTRIBUTION** Parts of USA and most of Mexico. Northern populations migrate south within this range in winter.
• **REMARK** The bird's name is a reference to its mimicry of other birds.

• *long tail*

• *white wing bars*

long legs for foraging on the ground •

DISTRIBUTION

Plumage Sexes alike	Habitat	Migration Partial migrant

| Family MIMIDAE | Species *Toxostoma rufum* | Length 11½ in (29 cm) |

BROWN THRASHER

Large compared with other birds that live in the undergrowth, the Brown Thrasher is a shy inhabitant of dense thickets and woodland edges. It feeds by flicking back ("thrashing") leaves with its strong bill to disturb and expose its insect prey.
• **NEST** A cup nest made of twigs and lined with finer material, placed in a bush or tangle of thick undergrowth.
• **DISTRIBUTION** Breeds in S. Canada and C. and E. USA. Spends the winter in S.E. USA.
• **REMARK** Often sings from cover, uttering each phrase only twice.

• *yellow eye distinguishes this species from thrushes, which are dark-eyed*

strong legs for running and hopping on the ground

round-tipped • tail

DISTRIBUTION

| Plumage Sexes alike | Habitat | Migration Migrant |

| Family MIMIDAE | Species *Toxostoma curvirostre* | Length 11 in (28 cm) |

CURVE-BILLED THRASHER

This thrushlike bird lives in arid brush and desert scrub, along streamsides and canyons. It has a bold appearance and is usually alone or in pairs, often seen watching from a prominent perch or searching for food on the ground. Birds keep in contact with short, sharp calls. The fine, curved bill is well adapted for probing and inspecting the ground litter. The Curve-billed Thrasher feeds mainly on insects but sometimes also takes fruit.
• **NEST** A cup nest of twigs, lined with hair, placed in a cactus or bush.
• **DISTRIBUTION** Parts of inland S.W. USA and much of Mexico.
• **REMARK** Thrashers are wilder birds than mockingbirds and catbirds, avoiding human habitation. They are loud singers having an elaborate, musical song, but do not mimic the songs of other birds.

• *bright, orange-red eye*

short, rounded • wings

• *strong legs for running and hopping on the ground*

DISTRIBUTION

| Plumage Sexes alike | Habitat | Migration Non-migrant |

Family TURDIDAE	Species *Chaetops frenatus*	Length 9½ in (24 cm)

RUFOUS ROCK-JUMPER

Found exclusively on rocky mountain slopes, this bird is designed for life among the boulders, running quickly over rock surfaces and seeking insects and lizards. It has a piping call.
• **NEST** A cup nest made of coarse grass, rushes, lichens, and sticks, lined with roots and hairs, on the ground near a rock.
• **DISTRIBUTION** Part of South Africa.

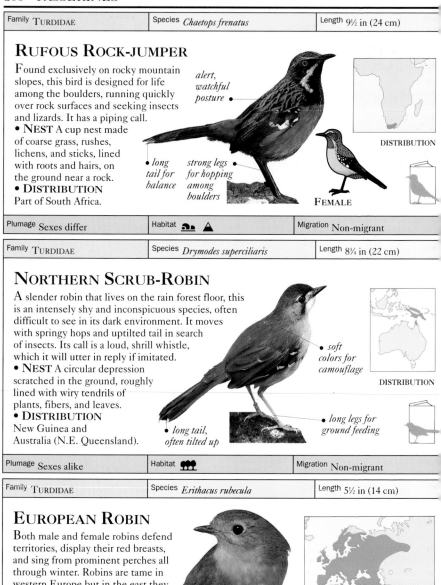

alert, watchful posture •

• long tail for balance

strong legs • for hopping among boulders

DISTRIBUTION

FEMALE

Plumage Sexes differ	Habitat	Migration Non-migrant

Family TURDIDAE	Species *Drymodes superciliaris*	Length 8¾ in (22 cm)

NORTHERN SCRUB-ROBIN

A slender robin that lives on the rain forest floor, this is an intensely shy and inconspicuous species, often difficult to see in its dark environment. It moves with springy hops and uptilted tail in search of insects. Its call is a loud, shrill whistle, which it will utter in reply if imitated.
• **NEST** A circular depression scratched in the ground, roughly lined with wiry tendrils of plants, fibers, and leaves.
• **DISTRIBUTION** New Guinea and Australia (N.E. Queensland).

• soft colors for camouflage

DISTRIBUTION

• long tail, often tilted up

• long legs for ground feeding

Plumage Sexes alike	Habitat	Migration Non-migrant

Family TURDIDAE	Species *Erithacus rubecula*	Length 5½ in (14 cm)

EUROPEAN ROBIN

Both male and female robins defend territories, display their red breasts, and sing from prominent perches all through winter. Robins are tame in western Europe but in the east they are shy, woodland birds. The diet consists of worms and insects, taken mainly from the ground.
• **NEST** A bulky nest of moss and leaves, lined with hair, in a crevice.
• **DISTRIBUTION** Eurasia to W. Siberia, N. Africa, and the Middle East. Eastern populations migrate south in winter.

DISTRIBUTION

• alert posture

JUVENILE

Plumage Sexes alike	Habitat	Migration Partial migrant

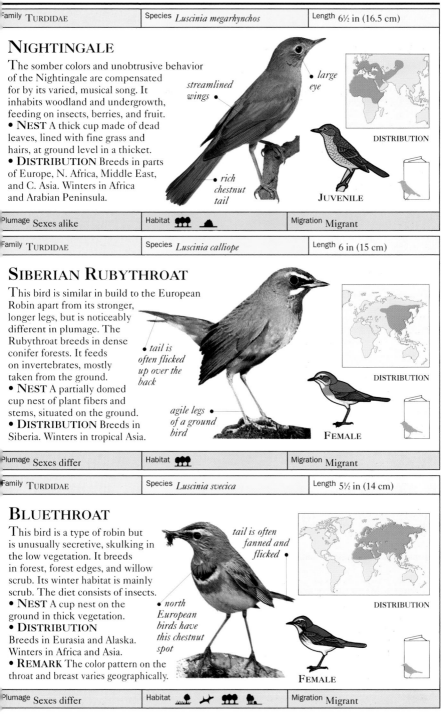

| Family TURDIDAE | Species *Luscinia megarhynchos* | Length 6½ in (16.5 cm) |

NIGHTINGALE

The somber colors and unobtrusive behavior of the Nightingale are compensated for by its varied, musical song. It inhabits woodland and undergrowth, feeding on insects, berries, and fruit.
• **NEST** A thick cup made of dead leaves, lined with fine grass and hairs, at ground level in a thicket.
• **DISTRIBUTION** Breeds in parts of Europe, N. Africa, Middle East, and C. Asia. Winters in Africa and Arabian Peninsula.

streamlined wings •

• large eye

• rich chestnut tail

DISTRIBUTION

JUVENILE

| Plumage Sexes alike | Habitat | Migration Migrant |

| Family TURDIDAE | Species *Luscinia calliope* | Length 6 in (15 cm) |

SIBERIAN RUBYTHROAT

This bird is similar in build to the European Robin apart from its stronger, longer legs, but is noticeably different in plumage. The Rubythroat breeds in dense conifer forests. It feeds on invertebrates, mostly taken from the ground.
• **NEST** A partially domed cup nest of plant fibers and stems, situated on the ground.
• **DISTRIBUTION** Breeds in Siberia. Winters in tropical Asia.

• tail is often flicked up over the back

agile legs • of a ground bird

DISTRIBUTION

FEMALE

| Plumage Sexes differ | Habitat | Migration Migrant |

| Family TURDIDAE | Species *Luscinia svecica* | Length 5½ in (14 cm) |

BLUETHROAT

This bird is a type of robin but is unusually secretive, skulking in the low vegetation. It breeds in forest, forest edges, and willow scrub. Its winter habitat is mainly scrub. The diet consists of insects.
• **NEST** A cup nest on the ground in thick vegetation.
• **DISTRIBUTION** Breeds in Eurasia and Alaska. Winters in Africa and Asia.
• **REMARK** The color pattern on the throat and breast varies geographically.

tail is often fanned and flicked •

• north European birds have this chestnut spot

DISTRIBUTION

FEMALE

| Plumage Sexes differ | Habitat | Migration Migrant |

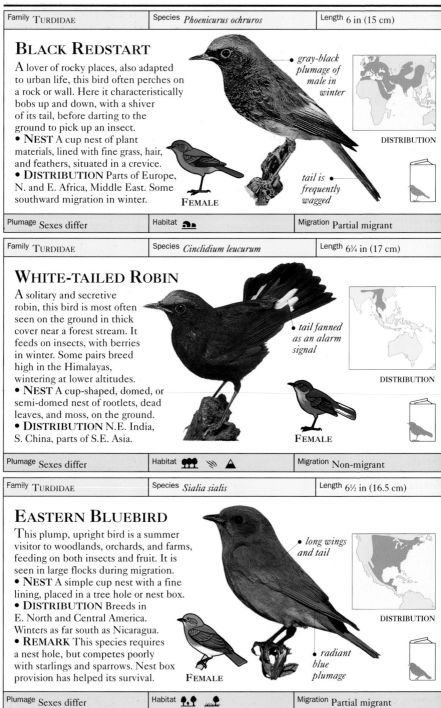

| Family TURDIDAE | Species *Phoenicurus ochruros* | Length 6 in (15 cm) |

BLACK REDSTART

A lover of rocky places, also adapted
to urban life, this bird often perches on
a rock or wall. Here it characteristically
bobs up and down, with a shiver
of its tail, before darting to the
ground to pick up an insect.
• NEST A cup nest of plant
materials, lined with fine grass, hair,
and feathers, situated in a crevice.
• DISTRIBUTION Parts of Europe,
N. and E. Africa, Middle East. Some
southward migration in winter.

gray-black plumage of male in winter

tail is frequently wagged

FEMALE

DISTRIBUTION

| Plumage Sexes differ | Habitat | Migration Partial migrant |

| Family TURDIDAE | Species *Cinclidium leucurum* | Length 6¾ in (17 cm) |

WHITE-TAILED ROBIN

A solitary and secretive
robin, this bird is most often
seen on the ground in thick
cover near a forest stream. It
feeds on insects, with berries
in winter. Some pairs breed
high in the Himalayas,
wintering at lower altitudes.
• NEST A cup-shaped, domed, or
semi-domed nest of rootlets, dead
leaves, and moss, on the ground.
• DISTRIBUTION N.E. India,
S. China, parts of S.E. Asia.

tail fanned as an alarm signal

FEMALE

DISTRIBUTION

| Plumage Sexes differ | Habitat | Migration Non-migrant |

| Family TURDIDAE | Species *Sialia sialis* | Length 6½ in (16.5 cm) |

EASTERN BLUEBIRD

This plump, upright bird is a summer
visitor to woodlands, orchards, and farms,
feeding on both insects and fruit. It is
seen in large flocks during migration.
• NEST A simple cup nest with a fine
lining, placed in a tree hole or nest box.
• DISTRIBUTION Breeds in
E. North and Central America.
Winters as far south as Nicaragua.
• REMARK This species requires
a nest hole, but competes poorly
with starlings and sparrows. Nest box
provision has helped its survival.

long wings and tail

radiant blue plumage

FEMALE

DISTRIBUTION

| Plumage Sexes differ | Habitat | Migration Partial migrant |

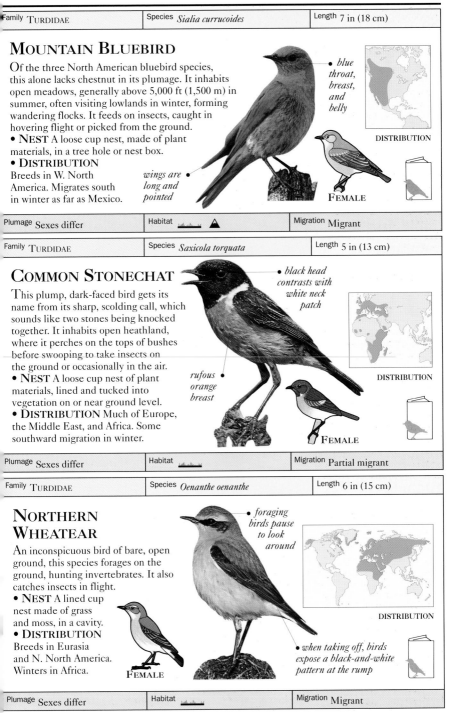

| Family TURDIDAE | Species *Sialia currucoides* | Length 7 in (18 cm) |

MOUNTAIN BLUEBIRD

Of the three North American bluebird species, this alone lacks chestnut in its plumage. It inhabits open meadows, generally above 5,000 ft (1,500 m) in summer, often visiting lowlands in winter, forming wandering flocks. It feeds on insects, caught in hovering flight or picked from the ground.
• **NEST** A loose cup nest, made of plant materials, in a tree hole or nest box.
• **DISTRIBUTION** Breeds in W. North America. Migrates south in winter as far as Mexico.

blue throat, breast, and belly

DISTRIBUTION

wings are long and pointed

FEMALE

| Plumage Sexes differ | Habitat ▲ | Migration Migrant |

| Family TURDIDAE | Species *Saxicola torquata* | Length 5 in (13 cm) |

COMMON STONECHAT

This plump, dark-faced bird gets its name from its sharp, scolding call, which sounds like two stones being knocked together. It inhabits open heathland, where it perches on the tops of bushes before swooping to take insects on the ground or occasionally in the air.
• **NEST** A loose cup nest of plant materials, lined and tucked into vegetation on or near ground level.
• **DISTRIBUTION** Much of Europe, the Middle East, and Africa. Some southward migration in winter.

black head contrasts with white neck patch

rufous orange breast

DISTRIBUTION

FEMALE

| Plumage Sexes differ | Habitat | Migration Partial migrant |

| Family TURDIDAE | Species *Oenanthe oenanthe* | Length 6 in (15 cm) |

NORTHERN WHEATEAR

An inconspicuous bird of bare, open ground, this species forages on the ground, hunting invertebrates. It also catches insects in flight.
• **NEST** A lined cup nest made of grass and moss, in a cavity.
• **DISTRIBUTION** Breeds in Eurasia and N. North America. Winters in Africa.

foraging birds pause to look around

DISTRIBUTION

when taking off, birds expose a black-and-white pattern at the rump

FEMALE

| Plumage Sexes differ | Habitat | Migration Migrant |

Family TURDIDAE	Species *Enicurus ruficapillus*	Length 7 in (18 cm)

CHESTNUT-NAPED FORKTAIL

This species lives beside clear-water streams flowing through rain forest. Here it perches on rocks in mid-stream, running after insects on the rock or darting after them in the air. It is a wary bird, always following the stream-bed when disturbed.

• **NEST** A deep cup nest, lined with plant fibers, and plastered with a layer of mud to an overhanging surface.

• **DISTRIBUTION** Malay Peninsula, Sumatra, and Borneo.

• **REMARK** There are seven species of forktail. All are thrushes of fast-flowing mountain streams, living in different parts of Asia. They are all colorfully marked birds with smartly forked tails and are very sure footed on the rocks and in water.

"scaly" plumage on the breast

DISTRIBUTION

forked tail

strong, agile legs

FEMALE

Plumage Sexes differ	Habitat 🌳 〰 ⛰	Migration Non-migrant

Family TURDIDAE	Species *Myiophonus caeruleus*	Length 12½ in (32 cm)

BLUE WHISTLING-THRUSH

Pale feather tips give the violet blue plumage of this bird a vivid, spangled effect when seen in motion. Its shy behavior, however, and the shaded habitat, make it hard to see. It lives in forests alongside mountain streams, many of them running through ravines and gorges, overshadowed by rock walls. It is sure footed enough to wade through fast-running water and leap from boulder to boulder. Pairs stay on territory all year. The diet consists of invertebrates and fruit.

• **NEST** A cup-shaped nest made mainly of moss, often placed on a ledge in a small cave.

• **DISTRIBUTION** Forests in Himalayan region, and mountain ranges of E. and S.E. Asia as far as Java.

silver-blue feather tips sparkle as the bird turns in the light

DISTRIBUTION

the tail is often fanned out, raised, and swayed from side to side

long wings with black-tipped flight feathers

Plumage Sexes alike	Habitat ⛰ 🌳 〰	Migration Non-migrant

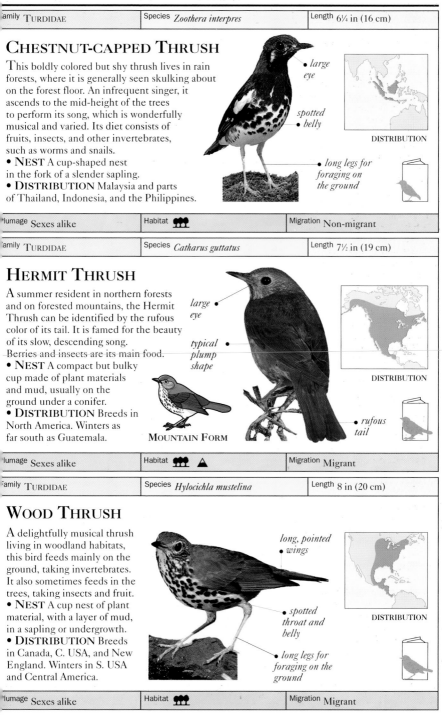

Family TURDIDAE	Species *Zoothera interpres*	Length 6¼ in (16 cm)

CHESTNUT-CAPPED THRUSH

This boldly colored but shy thrush lives in rain forests, where it is generally seen skulking about on the forest floor. An infrequent singer, it ascends to the mid-height of the trees to perform its song, which is wonderfully musical and varied. Its diet consists of fruits, insects, and other invertebrates, such as worms and snails.
• **NEST** A cup-shaped nest in the fork of a slender sapling.
• **DISTRIBUTION** Malaysia and parts of Thailand, Indonesia, and the Philippines.

• *large eye*

• *spotted belly*

DISTRIBUTION

• *long legs for foraging on the ground*

Plumage Sexes alike	Habitat	Migration Non-migrant

Family TURDIDAE	Species *Catharus guttatus*	Length 7½ in (19 cm)

HERMIT THRUSH

A summer resident in northern forests and on forested mountains, the Hermit Thrush can be identified by the rufous color of its tail. It is famed for the beauty of its slow, descending song. Berries and insects are its main food.
• **NEST** A compact but bulky cup made of plant materials and mud, usually on the ground under a conifer.
• **DISTRIBUTION** Breeds in North America. Winters as far south as Guatemala.

large eye

typical plump shape

DISTRIBUTION

MOUNTAIN FORM

• *rufous tail*

Plumage Sexes alike	Habitat	Migration Migrant

Family TURDIDAE	Species *Hylocichla mustelina*	Length 8 in (20 cm)

WOOD THRUSH

A delightfully musical thrush living in woodland habitats, this bird feeds mainly on the ground, taking invertebrates. It also sometimes feeds in the trees, taking insects and fruit.
• **NEST** A cup nest of plant material, with a layer of mud, in a sapling or undergrowth.
• **DISTRIBUTION** Breeds in Canada, C. USA, and New England. Winters in S. USA and Central America.

long, pointed wings

• *spotted throat and belly*

DISTRIBUTION

• *long legs for foraging on the ground*

Plumage Sexes alike	Habitat	Migration Migrant

Family TURDIDAE	Species *Turdus merula*	Length 9½ in (24 cm)

EURASIAN BLACKBIRD

The bold, pure black plumage of the male – made all the more vivid by his contrasting orange bill and eye ring – make this bird a very familiar garden species. In the European part of its range, it frequently feeds on lawns. In the east, it is a bird of forest borders and scrub. Everywhere, it feeds chiefly on the ground, scratching and turning leaves to find invertebrates, sometimes taking fruit. The male utters his musical and varied song from a high vantage point.

• **NEST** A bulky cup nest made of plant materials and mud, in a tree or bush.
• **DISTRIBUTION** Much of Europe, and parts of N. Africa and Asia. Some southward migration in winter. Introduced in Australia and New Zealand.

• *bluntish bill, used for eating fruit as well as probing the ground*

DISTRIBUTION

• *athletic legs can run or make rapid, bounding hops*

FEMALE

Plumage Sexes differ	Habitat	Migration Partial migrant

Family TURDIDAE	Species *Turdus pilaris*	Length 10 in (25 cm)

FIELDFARE

A self-assertive and noisy thrush with a loud, chuckling call, the Fieldfare lives in woodland in small colonies during the breeding season. In winter, roaming flocks often feed and roost in open grassland. Invertebrates form much of the diet; in autumn and winter, birds also eat berries, such as rowan and hawthorn, and fallen fruits such as apples.

• **NEST** A stout cup nest of plant material and mud, with a finer inner lining of grass, placed in a tree or bush.
• **DISTRIBUTION** Breeds across N. Eurasia. Winters in Europe and S.W. Asia.
• **REMARK** Birds will aggressively threaten any observer entering their colony.

• *gray head, nape, and cheeks*

heavy build •

• *strong legs for bounding and hopping*

DISTRIBUTION

Plumage Sexes alike	Habitat	Migration Migrant

Family TURDIDAE	Species *Turdus philomelos*	Length 9 in (23 cm)

SONG THRUSH

With its boldly spotted underside and upright stance, the Song Thrush is a familiar bird in well planted parks and gardens throughout northwest Europe. In the rest of its range, it is purely a woodland bird. It feeds on invertebrates, commonly snails. To eat these, Song Thrushes are seen making regular visits to a chosen stone used as an "anvil" for breaking the shells open. Berries are another important food.
• **NEST** A cup made of plant material, lined with a smooth cup of mud, wood pulp, or clay, in a tree or bush.
• **DISTRIBUTION** Europe, N. Africa, Middle East, and C. Asia. Introduced in Australia and New Zealand.

• slender bill

upright • posture

spotted breast • and belly

long, • slender legs

DISTRIBUTION

numbered band indicates that this captive • bird is aviary-bred – not caught in the wild

Plumage Sexes alike	Habitat 🌳	Migration Partial migrant

Family TURDIDAE	Species *Turdus viscivorus*	Length 11 in (28 cm)

MISTLE THRUSH

This large, pale thrush, with a bold pattern of spots on its underside, is most often seen on the ground, though it sometimes perches in trees. It feeds in pairs or family parties, taking invertebrates on open ground and berries from trees and bushes. Pairs or individual birds can be seen vigorously defending a source of food, such as a fruit tree in winter, from other thrushes. The flight call is a harsh, grating chatter, while the song, which is loud and clear, consists of short, musical phrases.
• **NEST** A cup nest made of grass and moss, usually in the fork of a tree, often higher than nests of other thrushes.
• **DISTRIBUTION** Europe, N.W. Africa, Middle East, and C. Asia. Some populations in east of range migrate.
• **REMARK** Sometimes known as the "storm cock" because of its habit of singing from a treetop in rough weather, early in the year.

• strong bill

upright, self-assertive • stance

DISTRIBUTION

• long, powerful legs

Plumage Sexes alike	Habitat 🌳	Migration Partial migrant

Family TURDIDAE	Species *Turdus migratorius*	Length 10 in (25 cm)

AMERICAN ROBIN

In its original wild state, this bird lived purely in woodland, but it has now become a familiar sight in town parks and suburban gardens. It is primarily a ground-feeding bird and is seen pulling up worms, scratching among leaves, and eating insects and snails. Fruit is taken from orchards. The short, melodious song is heard from early spring.

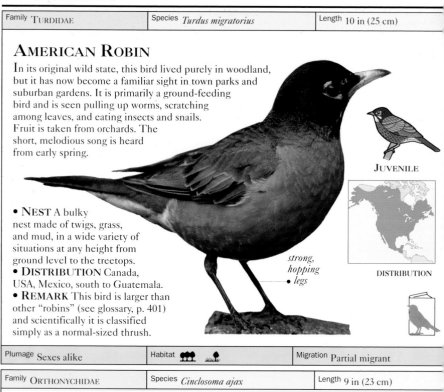

JUVENILE

DISTRIBUTION

• **NEST** A bulky nest made of twigs, grass, and mud, in a wide variety of situations at any height from ground level to the treetops.
• **DISTRIBUTION** Canada, USA, Mexico, south to Guatemala.
• **REMARK** This bird is larger than other "robins" (see glossary, p. 401) and scientifically it is classified simply as a normal-sized thrush.

strong, hopping legs

Plumage Sexes alike	Habitat	Migration Partial migrant

Family ORTHONYCHIDAE	Species *Cinclosoma ajax*	Length 9 in (23 cm)

PAINTED QUAIL-THRUSH

This thrushlike bird rarely leaves the ground and is normally difficult to see in lowland rain forest. Its presence may be more easily detected by its distinctive, thin, whistling call notes. Pairs or small parties walk unhurriedly in the deep shade, searching for insects.
• **NEST** Unknown, but closely related birds build open, cup-shaped nests in a depression on the ground.

• *short, little-used wings*

• **DISTRIBUTION** Lowlands of S. New Guinea.

DISTRIBUTION

• *dull brown upper plumage for camouflage against the ground*

FEMALE

Plumage Sexes differ	Habitat	Migration Non-migrant

| Family ORTHONYCHIDAE | Species *Ptilorrhoa castanonota* | Length 9 in (23 cm) |

CHESTNUT-BACKED JEWEL-BABBLER

This species lives in rain forests, where pairs or small groups forage on the ground for insects and other invertebrates.
• NEST A deep cup in a hollow, against a tree.
• DISTRIBUTION New Guinea.

colors often obscured by forest shadows

broad tail

DISTRIBUTION

short wings

FEMALE

| Plumage Sexes differ | Habitat | Migration Non-migrant |

| Family TIMALIIDAE | Species *Malacocincla malaccensis* | Length 5 in (13 cm) |

SHORT-TAILED BABBLER

A sure footed babbler, this species keeps close to the ground in forest undergrowth. It feeds on beetles and other insects. The call is a metallic whistle, followed by a churring and chattering sound.
• NEST A cup nest on the ground, sheltered, and partly enclosed by a large, fallen leaf.
• DISTRIBUTION Malay Peninsula, Sumatra, and Borneo.

short, rounded wing

DISTRIBUTION

large feet grip the perch firmly

short tail

| Plumage Sexes alike | Habitat | Migration Non-migrant |

| Family TIMALIIDAE | Species *Chamaea fasciata* | Length 6¼ in (16 cm) |

WRENTIT

More often heard than seen, this perky little bird with a cocked tail lives in the chaparral, a semi-arid scrubland terrain. It is a hardy, insect-eating species. Wrentits occupy very small territories, where many remain throughout their lives. Males proclaim their presence with loud singing.
• NEST A compact, cup-shaped nest made of plant fibers, hairs, and spiderwebs, placed in a low bush.
• DISTRIBUTION W. USA from Oregon to California, and part of Mexico (Baja California).

typical up-tilted tail

slender build

DISTRIBUTION

pale yellow iris

| Plumage Sexes alike | Habitat | Migration Non-migrant |

Family TIMALIIDAE	Species *Pomatostomus ruficeps*	Length 8½ in (22 cm)

CHESTNUT-CROWNED BABBLER

This is a slim bird with a long tail and a slender, downcurved bill, living in open scrub, semidesert, and the scrubby woodland formed by mulga trees. It moves about in small flocks, feeding on insects, which the birds take either from low vegetation or from the ground. Flocks are shy of humans. The birds are lively and active. They keep up a constant chattering, louder when they are excited, of the type that gives babblers their name.
• **NEST** A large, domed nest with a side entrance, composed of twigs, lined with grass or wool, and situated in a tree.
• **DISTRIBUTION** Interior of S.E. Australia.

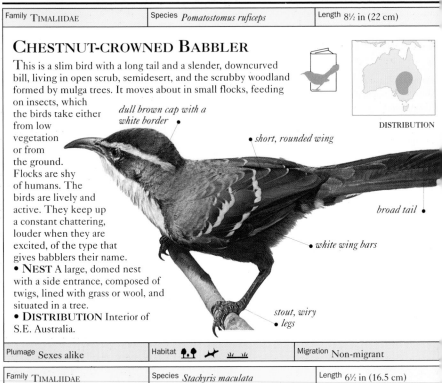

dull brown cap with a white border •

• short, rounded wing

DISTRIBUTION

broad tail •

• white wing bars

stout, wiry • legs

Plumage Sexes alike	Habitat	Migration Non-migrant

Family TIMALIIDAE	Species *Stachyris maculata*	Length 6½ in (16.5 cm)

CHESTNUT-RUMPED BABBLER

With its strong feet and powerful legs, this babbler is well adapted to a life of clambering about in the undergrowth of lowland rain forests. Small, active parties sometimes leave the cover of the undergrowth to forage in the middle height of the trees. The principal diet of this species is insects, but it also takes small fruits, when available. Although small, it is a rather noisy bird. Its song consists of a series of strident phrases, often followed by a long, trilling note. The calling bird puffs out its throat, exposing the two hidden patches of bright blue, bare skin situated on the sides of the neck.

• patch of blue skin

• typical crouching posture

DISTRIBUTION

• large, powerful feet

• **NEST** A loosely constructed globe of dead leaves, placed a little above ground level, in a thick tangle of dead leaves and creepers. Only one example of this bird's nest has ever been reliably recorded.
• **DISTRIBUTION** Malay Peninsula, Sumatra, and Borneo.

Plumage Sexes alike	Habitat	Migration Non-migrant

Family TIMALIIDAE	Species *Garrulax pectoralis*	Length 11 in (28 cm)

GREATER NECKLACED LAUGHING THRUSH

An assertive and inquisitive babbler, this bird goes about in groups, often with other laughing thrushes. Flocks are seen crossing an open space, gliding one after another. The birds feed mainly on the forest floor, moving with large hops, taking insects, fruit, and seeds. They frequently call to each other with piping and grating notes.
• **NEST** A broad, saucer-shaped nest of plant materials, in a tree or bush.
• **DISTRIBUTION** From E. Himalayas across into S. China and N. Vietnam. Introduced in the Hawaiian Islands.

black "mustache" • streak

rufous • collar

• short, rounded wings

black • "necklace"

DISTRIBUTION

• thick legs and large feet

Plumage Sexes alike	Habitat 🌳🌳 ⛰	Migration Non-migrant

Family TIMALIIDAE	Species *Garrulax ocellatus*	Length 13 in (33 cm)

SPOTTED LAUGHING THRUSH

This large babbler of mountain woodlands and scrub is easy to see, less on account of its speckled plumage than because of its bold and inquisitive behavior. It moves around in parties and joins large, mixed-species bird flocks, often calling noisily. These flocks work their way through the bushes and hop around on the ground in search of insects, seeds, and fruit. Like other laughing thrushes, this species is equipped with powerful legs and large feet, adapted for hopping on the ground, as well as perching.
• **NEST** A large, loose cup nest made of twigs and dry leaves, including bamboo leaves, lined with rootlets, suspended within a twig fork in a bush or tree.
• **DISTRIBUTION** E. Himalayas, E. Tibet, N. Burma, S. and W. China.

buff feather tips • on back

white feather • tips on wing

DISTRIBUTION

• rufous tail with black tip

• highly developed legs and feet

Plumage Sexes alike	Habitat 🌳🌳 ✈ ⛰	Migration Non-migrant

| Family TIMALIIDAE | Species *Leiothrix argentauris* | Length 5 in (13 cm) |

SILVER-EARED MESIA

This small babbler occurs in scrub and secondary scrub (new growth after clearance) in mountains. Flocks of about six to 30 birds search actively for insects in the foliage, calling to each other with chattering notes.
• NEST A cup nest of grass, moss, and lichens, lined with rootlets, in a low bush.
• DISTRIBUTION From E. Himalayas and S. China as far south as Sumatra.

blunt bill for fruit and insects

strong legs and feet

DISTRIBUTION

FEMALE

| Plumage Sexes differ | Habitat ✈ ▲ | Migration Non-migrant |

| Family TIMALIIDAE | Species *Minla cyanouroptera* | Length 6 in (15 cm) |

BLUE-WINGED MINLA

Like many babblers, this species often forms groups of about five to 15 birds, which sometimes form part of the large, roving flocks of mixed bird species occurring in hill forests. They are quick and lively feeders and take insects both by gleaning them in the foliage and by catching them in mid-flight.
• NEST A cup nest made of bamboo leaves and rootlets, often wrapped in moss, and hidden in a bush.
• DISTRIBUTION Mountain ranges from E. Himalayas to Malay Peninsula.

blue crown and crest

deep blue flight feathers

DISTRIBUTION

| Plumage Sexes alike | Habitat 🌳🌳 ▲ ✈ | Migration Non-migrant |

| Family TIMALIIDAE | Species *Minla ignotincta* | Length 5½ in (14 cm) |

RED-TAILED MINLA

An insect hunter of the treetops in several types of hill forest, this bird is most common in oak and rhododendron woodland.
• NEST A mossy cup nest, lined and situated in a high fork in a tree.
• DISTRIBUTION Mountain ranges from E. Himalayas to N. Vietnam.

broad, round wing

vivid white stripe above eye

thick black eye stripe

DISTRIBUTION

PERCHED BIRD

| Plumage Sexes alike | Habitat 🌳🌳 🌿🌿 ▲ | Migration Non-migrant |

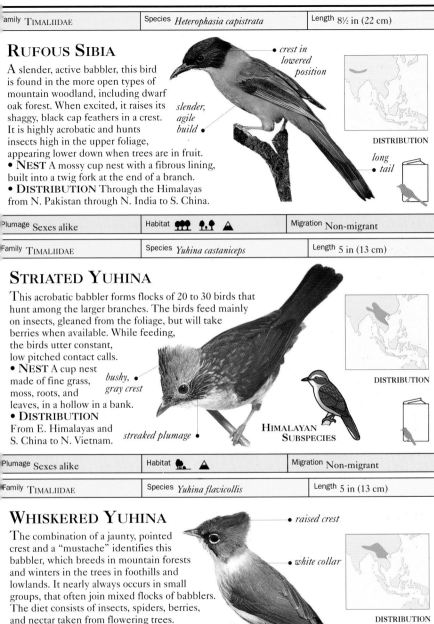

| Family TIMALIIDAE | Species *Heterophasia capistrata* | Length 8½ in (22 cm) |

RUFOUS SIBIA

A slender, active babbler, this bird is found in the more open types of mountain woodland, including dwarf oak forest. When excited, it raises its shaggy, black cap feathers in a crest. It is highly acrobatic and hunts insects high in the upper foliage, appearing lower down when trees are in fruit.
• **NEST** A mossy cup nest with a fibrous lining, built into a twig fork at the end of a branch.
• **DISTRIBUTION** Through the Himalayas from N. Pakistan through N. India to S. China.

crest in lowered position

slender, agile build

long tail

DISTRIBUTION

| Plumage Sexes alike | Habitat | Migration Non-migrant |

| Family TIMALIIDAE | Species *Yuhina castaniceps* | Length 5 in (13 cm) |

STRIATED YUHINA

This acrobatic babbler forms flocks of 20 to 30 birds that hunt among the larger branches. The birds feed mainly on insects, gleaned from the foliage, but will take berries when available. While feeding, the birds utter constant, low pitched contact calls.
• **NEST** A cup nest made of fine grass, moss, roots, and leaves, in a hollow in a bank.
• **DISTRIBUTION** From E. Himalayas and S. China to N. Vietnam.

bushy, gray crest

streaked plumage

HIMALAYAN SUBSPECIES

DISTRIBUTION

| Plumage Sexes alike | Habitat | Migration Non-migrant |

| Family TIMALIIDAE | Species *Yuhina flavicollis* | Length 5 in (13 cm) |

WHISKERED YUHINA

The combination of a jaunty, pointed crest and a "mustache" identifies this babbler, which breeds in mountain forests and winters in the trees in foothills and lowlands. It nearly always occurs in small groups, that often join mixed flocks of babblers. The diet consists of insects, spiders, berries, and nectar taken from flowering trees.
• **NEST** Either domed or cup-shaped, made of moss and lined with roots, and suspended from the fork of a twig in a tree.
• **DISTRIBUTION** From E. Himalayas and S. China to N. Vietnam.

raised crest

white collar

square tip of tail

DISTRIBUTION

| Plumage Sexes alike | Habitat | Migration Non-migrant |

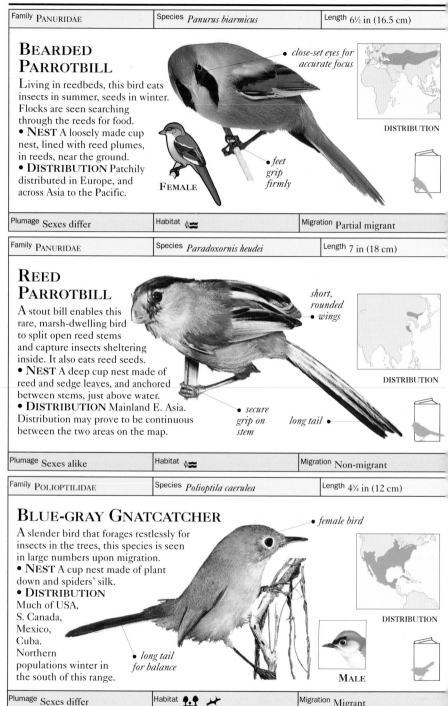

Family PANURIDAE	Species *Panurus biarmicus*	Length 6½ in (16.5 cm)

BEARDED PARROTBILL

Living in reedbeds, this bird eats insects in summer, seeds in winter. Flocks are seen searching through the reeds for food.
• **NEST** A loosely made cup nest, lined with reed plumes, in reeds, near the ground.
• **DISTRIBUTION** Patchily distributed in Europe, and across Asia to the Pacific.

close-set eyes for accurate focus

DISTRIBUTION

feet grip firmly

FEMALE

Plumage Sexes differ	Habitat	Migration Partial migrant

Family PANURIDAE	Species *Paradoxornis heudei*	Length 7 in (18 cm)

REED PARROTBILL

A stout bill enables this rare, marsh-dwelling bird to split open reed stems and capture insects sheltering inside. It also eats reed seeds.
• **NEST** A deep cup nest made of reed and sedge leaves, and anchored between stems, just above water.
• **DISTRIBUTION** Mainland E. Asia. Distribution may prove to be continuous between the two areas on the map.

short, rounded wings

DISTRIBUTION

secure grip on stem

long tail

Plumage Sexes alike	Habitat	Migration Non-migrant

Family POLIOPTILIDAE	Species *Polioptila caerulea*	Length 4¾ in (12 cm)

BLUE-GRAY GNATCATCHER

A slender bird that forages restlessly for insects in the trees, this species is seen in large numbers upon migration.
• **NEST** A cup nest made of plant down and spiders' silk.
• **DISTRIBUTION** Much of USA, S. Canada, Mexico, Cuba. Northern populations winter in the south of this range.

female bird

DISTRIBUTION

long tail for balance

MALE

Plumage Sexes differ	Habitat	Migration Migrant

Family SYLVIIDAE	Species *Cettia cetti*	Length 5½ in (14 cm)

CETTI'S WARBLER

A small, squat warbler, this species usually keeps out of sight in reedbeds and waterside thickets, where it feeds on insects. The song is brief and explosive.
• **NEST** A bulky, deep cup nest, made of grass, situated low in waterside vegetation.
• **DISTRIBUTION** Parts of Europe, N. Africa, Middle East, and C. Asia. Middle Eastern and C. Asian populations migrate to N.W. India.

• *short, wrenlike tail*

squat build •

strongly made feet •

DISTRIBUTION

Plumage Sexes alike	Habitat	Migration Partial migrant

Family SYLVIIDAE	Species *Sphenoeacus afer*	Length 8½ in (22 cm)

CAPE GRASS-WARBLER

A large warbler, the Cape Grass-Warbler has a streaked pattern of chestnut, black, and buff for camouflage in its scrubland and savanna habitat. Usually solitary or in pairs, it is shy and secretive, creeping into tangled vegetation when disturbed. It feeds in cover, taking insects and spiders, but often mounts a prominent perch in the early morning, to sun itself or to sing.
• **NEST** A cup nest made of coarse grass, lined with fine grass, hidden in a grassy tuft.
• **DISTRIBUTION** Parts of Zimbabwe, Mozambique, and South Africa.

strongly streaked • *back*

wiry legs and feet •

DISTRIBUTION

tail worn thin by • *thorns*

Plumage Sexes alike	Habitat	Migration Non-migrant

Family SYLVIIDAE	Species *Locustella naevia*	Length 5 in (13 cm)

GRASSHOPPER WARBLER

The male's prolonged, trilling song, uttered from the top of a bush in the nesting season, sounds like a grasshopper. For the most part, this bird remains in the undergrowth, on heaths or in marshy places, feeding on small insects.
• **NEST** A lined cup nest made of grass and leaves, hidden in a depression in thick vegetation.
• **DISTRIBUTION** Breeds from Europe to W. China. Winters as far south as N. Africa and N. India.

• *slim, streamlined build*

• *faint streaking*

DISTRIBUTION

• *rounded tail*

Plumage Sexes alike	Habitat	Migration Migrant

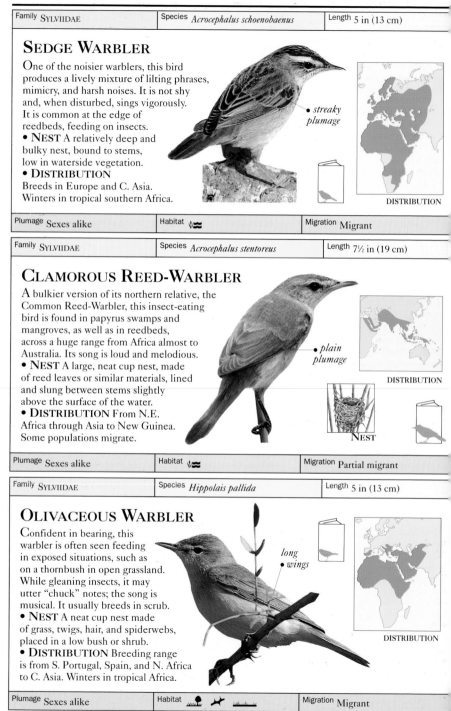

| Family SYLVIIDAE | Species *Acrocephalus schoenobaenus* | Length 5 in (13 cm) |

SEDGE WARBLER

One of the noisier warblers, this bird
produces a lively mixture of lilting phrases,
mimicry, and harsh noises. It is not shy
and, when disturbed, sings vigorously.
It is common at the edge of
reedbeds, feeding on insects.
• **NEST** A relatively deep and
bulky nest, bound to stems,
low in waterside vegetation.
• **DISTRIBUTION**
Breeds in Europe and C. Asia.
Winters in tropical southern Africa.

• streaky plumage

DISTRIBUTION

| Plumage Sexes alike | Habitat | Migration Migrant |

| Family SYLVIIDAE | Species *Acrocephalus stentoreus* | Length 7½ in (19 cm) |

CLAMOROUS REED-WARBLER

A bulkier version of its northern relative, the
Common Reed-Warbler, this insect-eating
bird is found in papyrus swamps and
mangroves, as well as in reedbeds,
across a huge range from Africa almost to
Australia. Its song is loud and melodious.
• **NEST** A large, neat cup nest, made
of reed leaves or similar materials, lined
and slung between stems slightly
above the surface of the water.
• **DISTRIBUTION** From N.E.
Africa through Asia to New Guinea.
Some populations migrate.

• plain plumage

DISTRIBUTION

NEST

| Plumage Sexes alike | Habitat | Migration Partial migrant |

| Family SYLVIIDAE | Species *Hippolais pallida* | Length 5 in (13 cm) |

OLIVACEOUS WARBLER

Confident in bearing, this
warbler is often seen feeding
in exposed situations, such as
on a thornbush in open grassland.
While gleaning insects, it may
utter "chuck" notes; the song is
musical. It usually breeds in scrub.
• **NEST** A neat cup nest made
of grass, twigs, hair, and spiderwebs,
placed in a low bush or shrub.
• **DISTRIBUTION** Breeding range
is from S. Portugal, Spain, and N. Africa
to C. Asia. Winters in tropical Africa.

long • wings

DISTRIBUTION

| Plumage Sexes alike | Habitat | Migration Migrant |

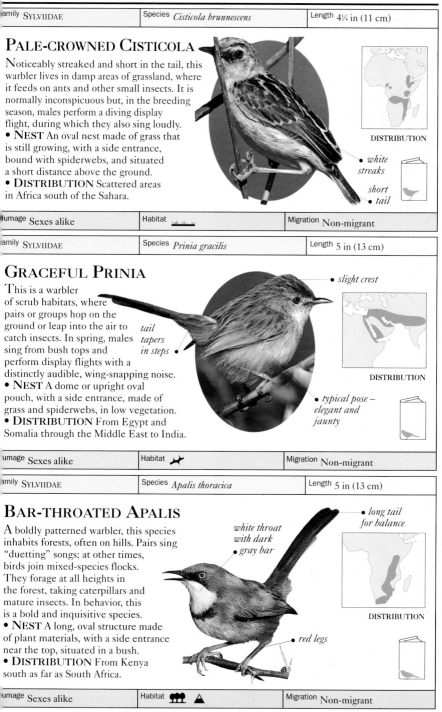

| Family SYLVIIDAE | Species *Cisticola brunnescens* | Length 4¼ in (11 cm) |

PALE-CROWNED CISTICOLA

Noticeably streaked and short in the tail, this
warbler lives in damp areas of grassland, where
it feeds on ants and other small insects. It is
normally inconspicuous but, in the breeding
season, males perform a diving display
flight, during which they also sing loudly.
• **NEST** An oval nest made of grass that
is still growing, with a side entrance,
bound with spiderwebs, and situated
a short distance above the ground.
• **DISTRIBUTION** Scattered areas
in Africa south of the Sahara.

DISTRIBUTION

white streaks

short tail

| Plumage Sexes alike | Habitat | Migration Non-migrant |

| Family SYLVIIDAE | Species *Prinia gracilis* | Length 5 in (13 cm) |

GRACEFUL PRINIA

This is a warbler
of scrub habitats, where
pairs or groups hop on the
ground or leap into the air to
catch insects. In spring, males
sing from bush tops and
perform display flights with a
distinctly audible, wing-snapping noise.
• **NEST** A dome or upright oval
pouch, with a side entrance, made of
grass and spiderwebs, in low vegetation.
• **DISTRIBUTION** From Egypt and
Somalia through the Middle East to India.

slight crest

tail tapers in steps

DISTRIBUTION

*typical pose –
elegant and
jaunty*

| Plumage Sexes alike | Habitat | Migration Non-migrant |

| Family SYLVIIDAE | Species *Apalis thoracica* | Length 5 in (13 cm) |

BAR-THROATED APALIS

A boldly patterned warbler, this species
inhabits forests, often on hills. Pairs sing
"duetting" songs; at other times,
birds join mixed-species flocks.
They forage at all heights in
the forest, taking caterpillars and
mature insects. In behavior, this
is a bold and inquisitive species.
• **NEST** A long, oval structure made
of plant materials, with a side entrance
near the top, situated in a bush.
• **DISTRIBUTION** From Kenya
south as far as South Africa.

*long tail
for balance*

*white throat
with dark
gray bar*

DISTRIBUTION

red legs

| Plumage Sexes alike | Habitat | Migration Non-migrant |

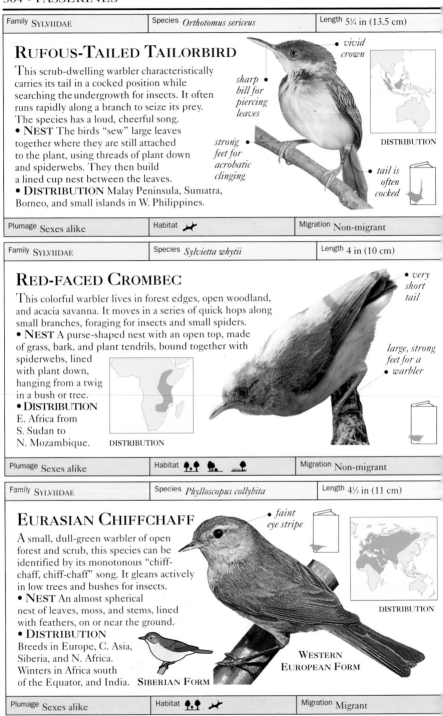

Family SYLVIIDAE	Species *Orthotomus sericeus*	Length 5¼ in (13.5 cm)

RUFOUS-TAILED TAILORBIRD

This scrub-dwelling warbler characteristically carries its tail in a cocked position while searching the undergrowth for insects. It often runs rapidly along a branch to seize its prey. The species has a loud, cheerful song.
• **NEST** The birds "sew" large leaves together where they are still attached to the plant, using threads of plant down and spiderwebs. They then build a lined cup nest between the leaves.
• **DISTRIBUTION** Malay Peninsula, Sumatra, Borneo, and small islands in W. Philippines.

vivid crown

sharp bill for piercing leaves

strong feet for acrobatic clinging

DISTRIBUTION

tail is often cocked

Plumage Sexes alike	Habitat	Migration Non-migrant

Family SYLVIIDAE	Species *Sylvietta whytii*	Length 4 in (10 cm)

RED-FACED CROMBEC

This colorful warbler lives in forest edges, open woodland, and acacia savanna. It moves in a series of quick hops along small branches, foraging for insects and small spiders.
• **NEST** A purse-shaped nest with an open top, made of grass, bark, and plant tendrils, bound together with spiderwebs, lined with plant down, hanging from a twig in a bush or tree.
• **DISTRIBUTION** E. Africa from S. Sudan to N. Mozambique.

very short tail

large, strong feet for a warbler

DISTRIBUTION

Plumage Sexes alike	Habitat	Migration Non-migrant

Family SYLVIIDAE	Species *Phylloscopus collybita*	Length 4¼ in (11 cm)

EURASIAN CHIFFCHAFF

A small, dull-green warbler of open forest and scrub, this species can be identified by its monotonous "chiff-chaff, chiff-chaff" song. It gleans actively in low trees and bushes for insects.
• **NEST** An almost spherical nest of leaves, moss, and stems, lined with feathers, on or near the ground.
• **DISTRIBUTION** Breeds in Europe, C. Asia, Siberia, and N. Africa. Winters in Africa south of the Equator, and India.

faint eye stripe

DISTRIBUTION

SIBERIAN FORM

WESTERN EUROPEAN FORM

Plumage Sexes alike	Habitat	Migration Migrant

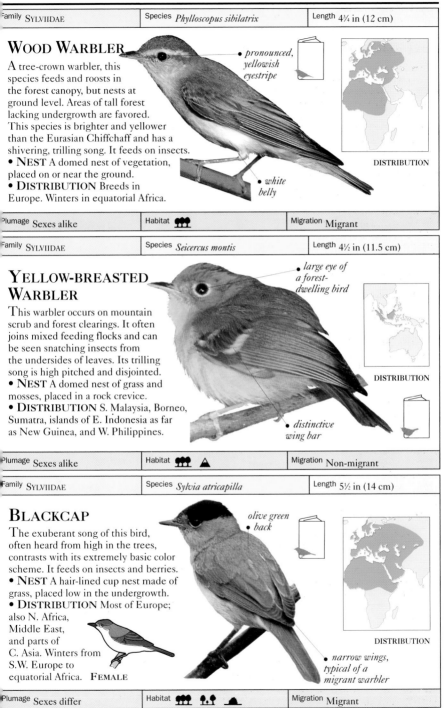

Family SYLVIIDAE	Species *Phylloscopus sibilatrix*	Length 4¼ in (12 cm)

WOOD WARBLER

A tree-crown warbler, this
species feeds and roosts in
the forest canopy, but nests at
ground level. Areas of tall forest
lacking undergrowth are favored.
This species is brighter and yellower
than the Eurasian Chiffchaff and has a
shivering, trilling song. It feeds on insects.
• NEST A domed nest of vegetation,
placed on or near the ground.
• DISTRIBUTION Breeds in
Europe. Winters in equatorial Africa.

• *pronounced,
yellowish
eyestripe*

• *white
belly*

DISTRIBUTION

Plumage Sexes alike	Habitat	Migration Migrant

Family SYLVIIDAE	Species *Seicercus montis*	Length 4½ in (11.5 cm)

YELLOW-BREASTED WARBLER

This warbler occurs on mountain
scrub and forest clearings. It often
joins mixed feeding flocks and can
be seen snatching insects from
the undersides of leaves. Its trilling
song is high pitched and disjointed.
• NEST A domed nest of grass and
mosses, placed in a rock crevice.
• DISTRIBUTION S. Malaysia, Borneo,
Sumatra, islands of E. Indonesia as far
as New Guinea, and W. Philippines.

• *large eye of
a forest-
dwelling bird*

• *distinctive
wing bar*

DISTRIBUTION

Plumage Sexes alike	Habitat	Migration Non-migrant

Family SYLVIIDAE	Species *Sylvia atricapilla*	Length 5½ in (14 cm)

BLACKCAP

The exuberant song of this bird,
often heard from high in the trees,
contrasts with its extremely basic color
scheme. It feeds on insects and berries.
• NEST A hair-lined cup nest made of
grass, placed low in the undergrowth.
• DISTRIBUTION Most of Europe;
also N. Africa,
Middle East,
and parts of
C. Asia. Winters from
S.W. Europe to
equatorial Africa. FEMALE

*olive green
• back*

• *narrow wings,
typical of a
migrant warbler*

DISTRIBUTION

Plumage Sexes differ	Habitat	Migration Migrant

| Family SYLVIIDAE | Species *Sylvia communis* | Length 5½ in (14 cm) |

WHITETHROAT

A warbler of shrubby growth and steppe, this bird feeds on insects and berries. It can be seen and identified easily when singing – with its white throat puffed out conspicuously – or when performing its dancing songflight.
• **NEST** A lined cup nest, made of grass and hidden in a bush.
• **DISTRIBUTION** Breeds in Europe and also N. Africa, Middle East, and parts of C. Asia. Winters in India and tropical Africa.

rufous-tinted wing feathers

DISTRIBUTION

| Plumage Sexes differ slightly | Habitat | Migration Migrant |

| Family SYLVIIDAE | Species *Sylvia rueppelli* | Length 5½ in (14 cm) |

RUEPPELL'S WARBLER

Hunting insects in thick scrub, often on rocky slopes, this bird is hard to see. It is more often detected by its short, musical song, broken with buzzing, rattling notes.
• **NEST** A cup nest of grass and stalks, in a bush.
• **DISTRIBUTION** Breeds from Greece to S. Israel. Winters in N.E. Africa.

black head and throat patch

heavy, solid build

DISTRIBUTION

FEMALE

| Plumage Sexes differ | Habitat | Migration Migrant |

| Family SYLVIIDAE | Species *Sylvia cantillans* | Length 4¼ in (12 cm) |

SUBALPINE WARBLER

This bird is secretive and difficult to observe, hiding in thorny scrub and thick undergrowth in open woodland.
Nonetheless, it is a common species throughout the Mediterranean. Its diet consists of insects and their larvae, and berries.
• **NEST** A cup nest of stems and grass, lined with grass or hairs, placed low in a bush.
• **DISTRIBUTION**

reddish eye ring

FEMALE

white outer tail feathers

DISTRIBUTION

| Plumage Sexes differ | Habitat | Migration Migrant |

| Family SYLVIIDAE | Species *Sylvia undata* | Length 5 in (13 cm) |

DARTFORD WARBLER

A resident (non-migrant) bird in much of its range, the colorful Dartford Warbler survives winter frosts by sheltering low in dense gorse thickets. It sings very musically during the course of its spring display flight. Its diet consists of insects and spiders.
• **NEST** A cup nest made of grass, lined with finer materials, placed low down in a thick, thorny bush.
• **DISTRIBUTION** Parts of W. and S. Europe; N.W. Africa. Some migration within this range.

shaggy crown feathers

long tail

slim, elegant build of a thicket dweller

DISTRIBUTION

| Plumage Sexes differ slightly | Habitat | Migration Partial migrant |

| Family SYLVIIDAE | Species *Regulus regulus* | Length 3½ in (9 cm) |

GOLDCREST

Usually secretive, this species becomes more tame and inquisitive under winter conditions. Inhabiting mixed and coniferous forests, it feeds on insects and spiders. The voice is thin and high pitched.
• **NEST** A hammocklike nest of moss and grass, under a conifer bough.
• **DISTRIBUTION** Europe, parts of N. Africa, and C. Asia to Japan. Northern populations winter in the south of this range.

RAISED CREST

rounded body

DISTRIBUTION

| Plumage | Habitat Sexes differ | Migration Partial migrant |

| Family SYLVIIDAE | Species *Regulus satrapa* | Length 3½ in (9 cm) |

GOLDEN-CROWNED KINGLET

This tiny bird is difficult to observe, as it tends to stay high in coniferous trees, often the only clue being its almost inaudible, high pitched song. In the fall, northern populations migrate south, and the birds are more easily seen, hunting insects in lower cover.
• **NEST** A deep, feather-lined cup nest of moss and grass, slung below a branch, usually in a conifer.
• **DISTRIBUTION** Parts of Canada, much of USA, parts of Mexico and Guatemala. Some migration within this range.

vivid, white stripe above the eye

FEMALE

pale wing bar

DISTRIBUTION

| Plumage Sexes differ | Habitat | Migration Partial migrant |

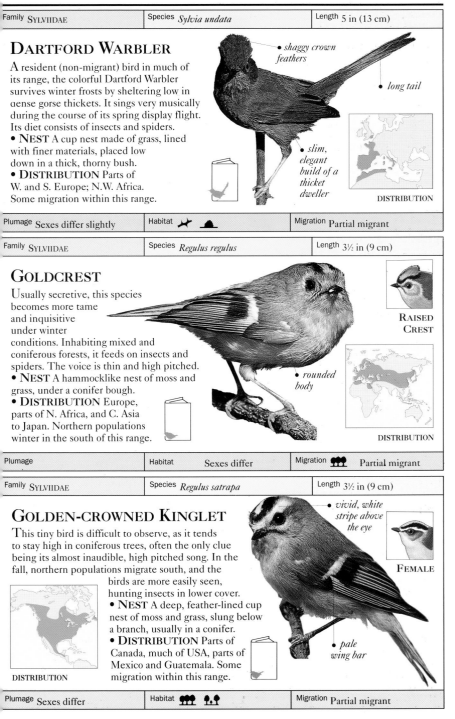

| Family SYLVIIDAE | Species *Regulus calendula* | Length 4¼ in (11 cm) |

RUBY-CROWNED KINGLET

Constantly on the move, this bird searches the trees for insects. Birds are nervously active, flicking their wings and uttering their high pitched calls while hunting.
• **NEST** A mossy ball in a tree.
• **DISTRIBUTION** Breeds in much of Canada and in W. USA. Winters in S. USA, Mexico, and Guatemala.

• *narrow, scarlet crest*

FEMALE

DISTRIBUTION

short, square tail

• *pale wing bar*

| Plumage Sexes differ | Habitat | Migration Migrant |

| Family SYLVIIDAE | Species *Leptopoecile sophiae* | Length 4 in (10 cm) |

WHITE-BROWED TIT-WARBLER

A tiny bird with unusual tints of blue and pink in its plumage, this species occurs in dwarf juniper scrub in mountains and river valley thickets. It is seen in pairs in summer and in small, restless parties in winter, gleaning insects in the undergrowth.
• **NEST** A domed nest of moss and animal hairs, lined with feathers, situated in a bush.
• **DISTRIBUTION** Himalayas from N. India to Tibet, and parts of S.W. China.

• *pronounced white stripe*

• *pink and blue tints on plumage*

DISTRIBUTION   **FEMALE**

| Plumage Sexes differ slightly | Habitat | Migration Non-migrant |

| Family MUSCICAPIDAE | Species *Muscicapa striata* | Length 5½ in (14 cm) |

SPOTTED FLYCATCHER

This small, brown bird is found as a spring migrant in woodland fringes. Its typical behavior is to watch from a tree, then sally out to catch an insect in the air before returning to its perch.
• **NEST** A slight cup made of moss, fibers, and spiderwebs, behind the stem of a creeper or in a crevice, or on a wall or tree trunk.
• **DISTRIBUTION** Breeds in Europe, N. Africa, the Middle East, and C. Asia. Winters in Africa, Middle East, and N.W. India.

• *large eye*

DISTRIBUTION   **JUVENILE**

| Plumage Sexes alike | Habitat | Migration Migrant |

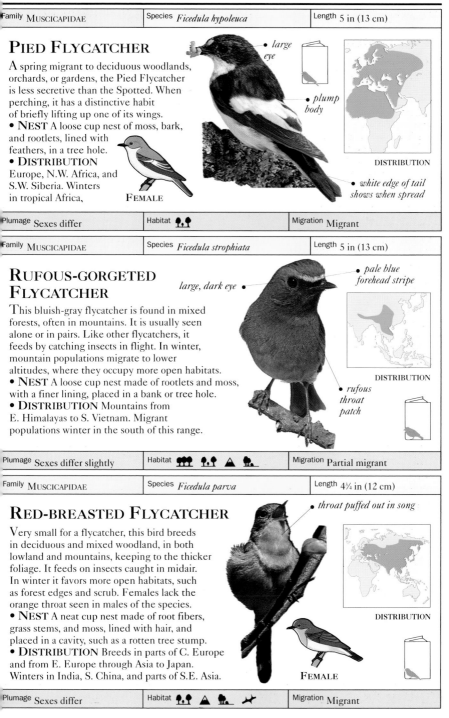

| Family MUSCICAPIDAE | Species *Ficedula hypoleuca* | Length 5 in (13 cm) |

PIED FLYCATCHER

A spring migrant to deciduous woodlands, orchards, or gardens, the Pied Flycatcher is less secretive than the Spotted. When perching, it has a distinctive habit of briefly lifting up one of its wings.
• **NEST** A loose cup nest of moss, bark, and rootlets, lined with feathers, in a tree hole.
• **DISTRIBUTION** Europe, N.W. Africa, and S.W. Siberia. Winters in tropical Africa,

• *large eye*

• *plump body*

DISTRIBUTION

• *white edge of tail shows when spread*

FEMALE

| Plumage Sexes differ | Habitat | Migration Migrant |

| Family MUSCICAPIDAE | Species *Ficedula strophiata* | Length 5 in (13 cm) |

RUFOUS-GORGETED FLYCATCHER

This bluish-gray flycatcher is found in mixed forests, often in mountains. It is usually seen alone or in pairs. Like other flycatchers, it feeds by catching insects in flight. In winter, mountain populations migrate to lower altitudes, where they occupy more open habitats.
• **NEST** A loose cup nest made of rootlets and moss, with a finer lining, placed in a bank or tree hole.
• **DISTRIBUTION** Mountains from E. Himalayas to S. Vietnam. Migrant populations winter in the south of this range.

large, dark eye •

• *pale blue forehead stripe*

DISTRIBUTION

• *rufous throat patch*

| Plumage Sexes differ slightly | Habitat | Migration Partial migrant |

| Family MUSCICAPIDAE | Species *Ficedula parva* | Length 4¾ in (12 cm) |

RED-BREASTED FLYCATCHER

Very small for a flycatcher, this bird breeds in deciduous and mixed woodland, in both lowland and mountains, keeping to the thicker foliage. It feeds on insects caught in midair. In winter it favors more open habitats, such as forest edges and scrub. Females lack the orange throat seen in males of the species.
• **NEST** A neat cup nest made of root fibers, grass stems, and moss, lined with hair, and placed in a cavity, such as a rotten tree stump.
• **DISTRIBUTION** Breeds in parts of C. Europe and from E. Europe through Asia to Japan. Winters in India, S. China, and parts of S.E. Asia.

• *throat puffed out in song*

DISTRIBUTION

FEMALE

| Plumage Sexes differ | Habitat | Migration Migrant |

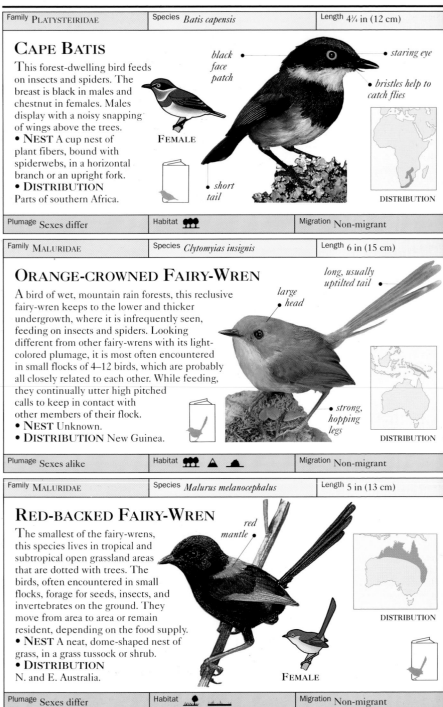

Family PLATYSTEIRIDAE	Species *Batis capensis*	Length 4¾ in (12 cm)

CAPE BATIS

This forest-dwelling bird feeds on insects and spiders. The breast is black in males and chestnut in females. Males display with a noisy snapping of wings above the trees.
• **NEST** A cup nest of plant fibers, bound with spiderwebs, in a horizontal branch or an upright fork.
• **DISTRIBUTION** Parts of southern Africa.

black face patch
staring eye
bristles help to catch flies
FEMALE
short tail
DISTRIBUTION

Plumage Sexes differ	Habitat 🌳🌳	Migration Non-migrant

Family MALURIDAE	Species *Clytomyias insignis*	Length 6 in (15 cm)

ORANGE-CROWNED FAIRY-WREN

A bird of wet, mountain rain forests, this reclusive fairy-wren keeps to the lower and thicker undergrowth, where it is infrequently seen, feeding on insects and spiders. Looking different from other fairy-wrens with its light-colored plumage, it is most often encountered in small flocks of 4–12 birds, which are probably all closely related to each other. While feeding, they continually utter high pitched calls to keep in contact with other members of their flock.
• **NEST** Unknown.
• **DISTRIBUTION** New Guinea.

long, usually uptilted tail
large head
strong, hopping legs
DISTRIBUTION

Plumage Sexes alike	Habitat 🌳🌳 ▲ 🏔	Migration Non-migrant

Family MALURIDAE	Species *Malurus melanocephalus*	Length 5 in (13 cm)

RED-BACKED FAIRY-WREN

The smallest of the fairy-wrens, this species lives in tropical and subtropical open grassland areas that are dotted with trees. The birds, often encountered in small flocks, forage for seeds, insects, and invertebrates on the ground. They move from area to area or remain resident, depending on the food supply.
• **NEST** A neat, dome-shaped nest of grass, in a grass tussock or shrub.
• **DISTRIBUTION** N. and E. Australia.

red mantle
DISTRIBUTION
FEMALE

Plumage Sexes differ	Habitat 🌿🔹	Migration Non-migrant

Family MALURIDAE	Species *Malurus leucopterus*	Length 4¾ in (12 cm)

WHITE-WINGED FAIRY-WREN

This bird of arid country is seen in parties comprising a colorful male and his partner, with a retinue of females and subordinate males. They forage for insects on the ground.
• **NEST** A dome of grass and bark, with a side entrance, on the ground under cover.
• **DISTRIBUTION** W. and interior Australia.

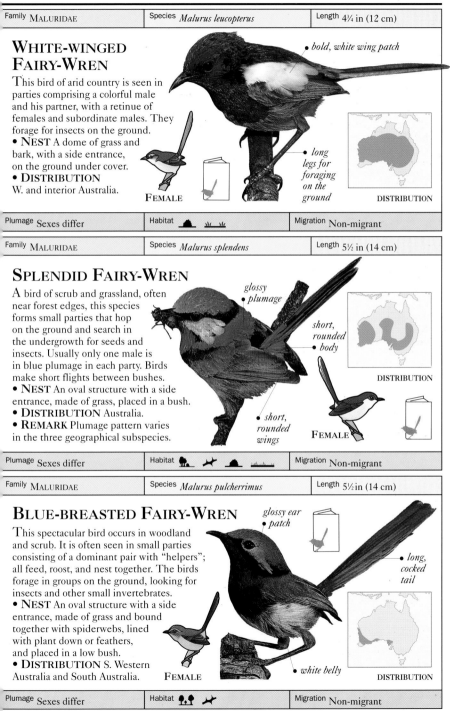

• *bold, white wing patch*

• *long legs for foraging on the ground*

FEMALE

DISTRIBUTION

Plumage Sexes differ	Habitat	Migration Non-migrant

Family MALURIDAE	Species *Malurus splendens*	Length 5½ in (14 cm)

SPLENDID FAIRY-WREN

A bird of scrub and grassland, often near forest edges, this species forms small parties that hop on the ground and search in the undergrowth for seeds and insects. Usually only one male is in blue plumage in each party. Birds make short flights between bushes.
• **NEST** An oval structure with a side entrance, made of grass, placed in a bush.
• **DISTRIBUTION** Australia.
• **REMARK** Plumage pattern varies in the three geographical subspecies.

glossy • plumage

short, rounded • body

DISTRIBUTION

short, rounded wings

FEMALE

Plumage Sexes differ	Habitat	Migration Non-migrant

Family MALURIDAE	Species *Malurus pulcherrimus*	Length 5½ in (14 cm)

BLUE-BREASTED FAIRY-WREN

This spectacular bird occurs in woodland and scrub. It is often seen in small parties consisting of a dominant pair with "helpers"; all feed, roost, and nest together. The birds forage in groups on the ground, looking for insects and other small invertebrates.
• **NEST** An oval structure with a side entrance, made of grass and bound together with spiderwebs, lined with plant down or feathers, and placed in a low bush.
• **DISTRIBUTION** S. Western Australia and South Australia.

glossy ear • patch

• *long, cocked tail*

FEMALE

• *white belly*

DISTRIBUTION

Plumage Sexes differ	Habitat	Migration Non-migrant

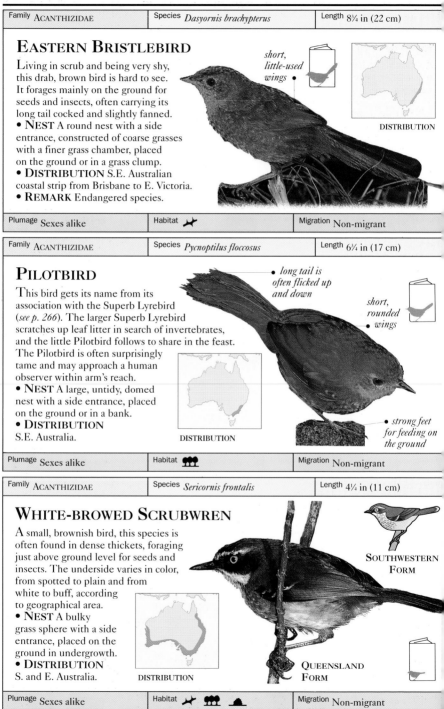

| Family ACANTHIZIDAE | Species *Dasyornis brachypterus* | Length 8¾ in (22 cm) |

EASTERN BRISTLEBIRD

Living in scrub and being very shy, this drab, brown bird is hard to see. It forages mainly on the ground for seeds and insects, often carrying its long tail cocked and slightly fanned.
• **NEST** A round nest with a side entrance, constructed of coarse grasses with a finer grass chamber, placed on the ground or in a grass clump.
• **DISTRIBUTION** S.E. Australian coastal strip from Brisbane to E. Victoria.
• **REMARK** Endangered species.

short, little-used wings

DISTRIBUTION

| Plumage Sexes alike | Habitat | Migration Non-migrant |

| Family ACANTHIZIDAE | Species *Pycnoptilus floccosus* | Length 6¾ in (17 cm) |

PILOTBIRD

This bird gets its name from its association with the Superb Lyrebird (*see p. 266*). The larger Superb Lyrebird scratches up leaf litter in search of invertebrates, and the little Pilotbird follows to share in the feast. The Pilotbird is often surprisingly tame and may approach a human observer within arm's reach.
• **NEST** A large, untidy, domed nest with a side entrance, placed on the ground or in a bank.
• **DISTRIBUTION** S.E. Australia.

long tail is often flicked up and down

short, rounded wings

strong feet for feeding on the ground

DISTRIBUTION

| Plumage Sexes alike | Habitat | Migration Non-migrant |

| Family ACANTHIZIDAE | Species *Sericornis frontalis* | Length 4¼ in (11 cm) |

WHITE-BROWED SCRUBWREN

A small, brownish bird, this species is often found in dense thickets, foraging just above ground level for seeds and insects. The underside varies in color, from spotted to plain and from white to buff, according to geographical area.
• **NEST** A bulky grass sphere with a side entrance, placed on the ground in undergrowth.
• **DISTRIBUTION** S. and E. Australia.

SOUTHWESTERN FORM

QUEENSLAND FORM

DISTRIBUTION

| Plumage Sexes alike | Habitat | Migration Non-migrant |

Family ACANTHIZIDAE	Species *Acanthiza pusilla*	Length 4 in (10 cm)

BROWN THORNBILL

A small, insect-hunting bird with red eyes, this
species is found in almost all types of woodland,
usually in pairs or small parties. It forages in the
undergrowth, rarely on the ground.
• **NEST** An untidy,
bulky, oval nest with a
side entrance, made of
grass, and placed on
or near the ground.
• **DISTRIBUTION**
Australia, mostly south
of Tropic of Capricorn.

chestnut rump •

• *fine
streaking*

• *scaly
forehead
pattern*

DISTRIBUTION

Plumage Sexes alike	Habitat	Migration Non-migrant

Family ACANTHIZIDAE	Species *Smicrornis brevirostris*	Length 3½ in (9 cm)

WEEBILL

This tiny, stubby-billed bird of the trees is tame
and inquisitive but usually stays hidden
in the outer foliage. It hovers amid the
leaves, gleaning and snatching insects
from leaf surfaces. For such a small
bird, the Weebill has a loud song.
• **NEST** A neat, dome-shaped
nest with a spoutlike entrance,
constructed of plant
down, twigs, and grasses,
lined with feathers, and placed
high in the outer foliage of a tree.
• **DISTRIBUTION** Most of Australia.

• *short
tail*

• *squat
build*

DISTRIBUTION

Plumage Sexes alike	Habitat	Migration Non-migrant

Family ACANTHIZIDAE	Species *Aphelocephala leucopsis*	Length 4¼ in (11 cm)

SOUTHERN WHITEFACE

A mainly ground-dwelling bird with a
white forehead, this species forages
in open spaces on bare, dry ground for
seeds, insects, and other invertebrates. It
is often seen in small parties, which may
suddenly take flight.
• **NEST** A large, untidy
sphere of grass with a
side entrance, in a low
bush or tree hollow.
• **DISTRIBUTION**
Interior of southern
half of Australia.

*pale edges of
• flight feathers*

• *chestnut flank
denotes western
form*

DISTRIBUTION

Plumage Sexes alike	Habitat	Migration Non-migrant

Family ACANTHIZIDAE	Species *Ephthianura tricolor*	Length 4¼ in (11 cm)

CRIMSON CHAT

Living in arid places with sparse, low
plants, the Crimson Chat supplements its
insect diet with nectar from desert flowers.
It is nomadic, appearing anywhere where
rain has produced fresh plant growth.
• **NEST** A compact, deep cup of grass
and twigs, lined with
hair and fine rootlets,
and placed close to
the ground in low cover.
• **DISTRIBUTION**
Arid areas of Australia.

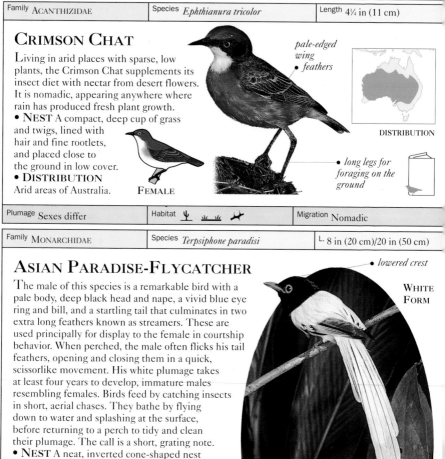

pale-edged wing feathers

DISTRIBUTION

• *long legs for foraging on the ground*

FEMALE

Plumage Sexes differ	Habitat 🌱 〰️ 〰️ 🐾	Migration Nomadic

Family MONARCHIDAE	Species *Terpsiphone paradisi*	L. 8 in (20 cm)/20 in (50 cm)

ASIAN PARADISE-FLYCATCHER

• *lowered crest*

WHITE FORM

The male of this species is a remarkable bird with a
pale body, deep black head and nape, a vivid blue eye
ring and bill, and a startling tail that culminates in two
extra long feathers known as streamers. These are
used principally for display to the female in courtship
behavior. When perched, the male often flicks his tail
feathers, opening and closing them in a quick,
scissorlike movement. His white plumage takes
at least four years to develop, immature males
resembling females. Birds feed by catching insects
in short, aerial chases. They bathe by flying
down to water and splashing at the surface,
before returning to a perch to tidy and clean
their plumage. The call is a short, grating note.
• **NEST** A neat, inverted cone-shaped nest
made of grass and plastered with
spiderwebs on its outer layer.
Inside the structure there is a
nesting cup lined with silky
down. The nest is placed in a
tree, often high above the ground.
• **DISTRIBUTION** Breeds in
Indian subcontinent, C. Asia,
parts of China, and Korea.
Northern populations winter as
far south as S. India, Sri Lanka,
and parts of E. Indonesia.
• **REMARK** The color
of the male's body and
tail plumage varies
geographically, the
Sri Lankan form
never becoming white.

FEMALE

DISTRIBUTION

flexible tail streamers hang in a graceful curve

Plumage Sexes differ	Habitat 🌳🌳 🌿🌿 ✈️	Migration Partial migrant

Family MONARCHIDAE	Species *Chasiempis sandwichensis*	Length 5½ in (14 cm)

ELEPAIO

This forest bird feeds on insects, which it gleans from the foliage or catches in aerial sallies from a perch. Often seen perching with tail cocked up, it is bold and inquisitive.
• **NEST** A small cup nest made of tree fern scales and lichens, bound together with spiderwebs, and placed in a shrub or low tree.
• **DISTRIBUTION** Hawaiian Islands.

• *white-edged tail*

white belly •

DISTRIBUTION

Plumage Sexes alike	Habitat 🌳	Migration Non-migrant

Family MONARCHIDAE	Species *Monarcha trivirgatus*	Length 6 in (15 cm)

SPECTACLED MONARCH

broad-based bill •

This rain forest bird has variously colored underparts, from all white to all orange, in the different parts of its range. It favors the lower levels of the vegetation, where it gleans insects and spiders.
• **NEST** A cup nest made of plant fibers, leaf skeletons, and bark, decorated with moss, and placed in a tree fork.
• **DISTRIBUTION** E. Indonesia, New Guinea, and N.E. and E. Australia.

• *extent of color varies between local forms*

DISTRIBUTION

white-tipped tail •

JUVENILE

Plumage Sexes alike	Habitat 🌳 🌿	Migration Partial migrant

Family MONARCHIDAE	Species *Machaerirhynchus flaviventer*	Length 5 in (13 cm)

YELLOW-BREASTED BOATBILL

The broadened and flattened bill of this species is adapted for catching small insects, mainly gleaned from the foliage but also caught in aerial sallies. The Yellow-breasted Boatbill is usually seen in the canopy of rain forest, where it sometimes joins mixed-species parties of insectivorous birds.
• **NEST** A saucer-shaped nest made of plant stems lined with plant fibers, high in a tree.
• **DISTRIBUTION** New Guinea and N.E. Queensland.

extent of color varies between local forms •

DISTRIBUTION

white-edged tail •

Plumage Sexes differ slightly	Habitat 🌳	Migration Non-migrant

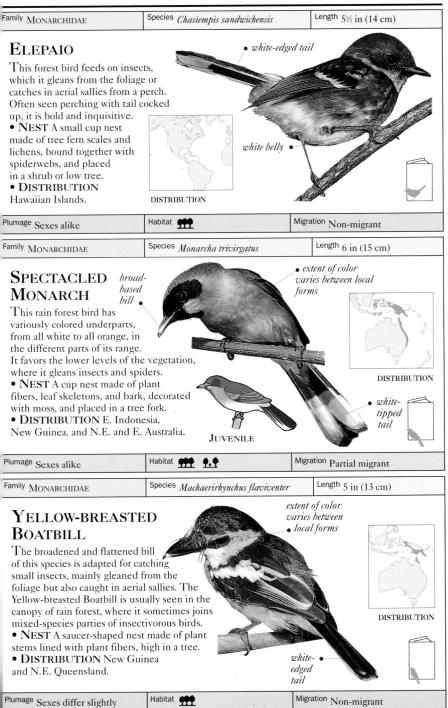

Family MONARCHIDAE	Species *Rhipidura leucophrys*	Length 8 in (20 cm)

WILLIE WAGTAIL

This ground-dwelling fantail is a common, conspicuous, and tame bird, typically seen holding its spread tail at a low angle. It then pivots its body and swings the tail from side to side as it searches the ground for insects and spiders. Insects are also caught on the wing, and in quick, short runs across open ground.
• **NEST** A cup nest made of bark, grass, spiderwebs, and a finer lining, situated in a tree, on a building, or on a post.
• **DISTRIBUTION** Moluccan Islands, New Guinea, Solomon Islands, Australia.

• *waving tail frightens insect prey*

strong legs for • *foraging*

DISTRIBUTION

Plumage Sexes alike	Habitat	Migration Non-migrant

Family MONARCHIDAE	Species *Rhipidura rufifrons*	Length 6¼ in (16 cm)

RUFOUS FANTAIL

This tree-dwelling fantail lives in the middle levels and under-growth of rain forest and scrub. It hunts by holding its fanned tail high, tilting it and jerking it from side to side to disturb resting insects. In doing this, it reveals its rufous tail and rump.
• **NEST** A compact cup nest of grass and spiderwebs, with a pendant "tail," in a tree fork.
• **DISTRIBUTION** Pacific islands, New Guinea, and N. and E. Australia.

• *waving tail frightens insect prey*

DISTRIBUTION

Plumage Sexes alike	Habitat	Migration Partial migrant

Family EOPSALTRIIDAE	Species *Microeca fascinans*	Length 5½ in (14 cm)

JACKY WINTER

A small, gray flycatcher, this species hunts from a perch, often in the cooler parts of the day, such as at dawn and dusk. It flies out to catch insects in the air or swoops to take invertebrates from the ground. Usually in pairs or small parties, the species is unobtrusive, though its "jacky-winter" call is easily heard.
• **NEST** A shallow cup nest constructed of grass and rootlets, bound with spiderwebs, and lined with lichens. This is placed on a horizontal tree branch, often high above the ground.
• **DISTRIBUTION** Woodland and grassland areas in Australia and S.E. New Guinea.

• *pale stripe above eye*

• *upright posture*

white-edged tail •

DISTRIBUTION

Plumage Sexes alike	Habitat	Migration Partial migrant

| Family EOPSALTRIIDAE | Species *Petroica multicolor* | Length 4¾ in (12 cm) |

SCARLET ROBIN

This bird of forest and scrubland feeds by perching on a low branch and watching for invertebrates on the ground, on which it pounces. The male advertises himself to either mate or rival with his scarlet breast.
• **NEST** A cup nest made of grass and bark strips, spiderwebs, and lichens, in a hollow, on a branch, or in a fork.
• **DISTRIBUTION** Australia, Solomon Islands, Vanuatu, Fiji, and Samoa.
• **REMARKS** Fifteen subspecies are recognized.

DISTRIBUTION

• *typical upright posture*

FEMALE

| Plumage Sexes differ | Habitat | Migration Non-migrant |

| Family EOPSALTRIIDAE | Species *Petroica macrocephela* | Length 5 in (13 cm) |

TOMTIT

Small and robinlike, this forest-dwelling bird hunts insects on tree trunks, branches, or the ground. It is aggressive and inquisitive in its behavior, and is not shy of people.
• **NEST** A cup nest of moss and feathers, placed in a tree.
• **DISTRIBUTION** New Zealand.
• **REMARK** Snares Island form is black.

DISTRIBUTION

FEMALE

white wing bar •

yellow throat band •

| Plumage Sexes differ | Habitat | Migration Non-migrant |

| Family EOPSALTRIIDAE | Species *Eopsaltria australis* | Length 6¼ in (16 cm) |

EASTERN YELLOW ROBIN

This robin of forest undergrowth and scrub is so tame and inquisitive that it is likely to approach any people who appear in its territory. It feeds mainly by pouncing from a branch or stem to seize invertebrates on the ground. Despite its name, it is mostly gray, with yellow only on the underside and rump.
• **NEST** A cup nest of bark and grass, bound with spiderwebs, lined with fine grass and leaves, placed in the fork of a sapling.
• **DISTRIBUTION** E. and S.E. Australia.

DISTRIBUTION

• *alert, flycatcher's eye*

• *yellow rump*

| Plumage Sexes alike | Habitat | Migration Non-migrant |

| Family PACHYCEPHALIDAE | Species *Colluricincla harmonica* | Length 9½ in (24 cm) |

GRAY SHRIKE-THRUSH

A heavy, hooked bill and active hunting methods
earn the name "shrike" for this forest bird, which
otherwise resembles a thrush. The species is
unobtrusive but tame and is seen seeking
prey in undergrowth and scrub. It feeds
on invertebrates and small vertebrates,
such as lizards and bird nestlings.
• **NEST** A grass and bark cup nest
placed just above ground in
vegetation or a crevice.
• **DISTRIBUTION**
Australia and parts of
New Guinea.

*brown patch
on back*

NORTHWESTERN
FORM

EASTERN
FORM

• **REMARK** The brown
patch on the back is
variable or absent according
to geographical race. It is
largest in northwestern birds.

DISTRIBUTION

| Plumage Sexes alike | Habitat | Migration Non-migrant |

| Family PACHYCEPHALIDAE | Species *Pitohui dichrous* | Length 9 in (23 cm) |

HOODED PITOHUI

A heavily built, fruit-eating bird, this species lives in tropical rain forest and scrub. Its
most unmistakable feature is its coloration – black hood, wings, and tail, and a body
color between orange and rufous brown. It is usually seen in pairs or small parties, in
the undergrowth or the tree canopy, seeking berries as well as larger fruits.
• **NEST** A cup nest of curly vine tendrils, lined with finer
tendrils, situated close to ground level in a bush.
• **DISTRIBUTION** New Guinea.
• **REMARK** The feathers and skin of this
bird have recently been found to be
toxic and harmful
to humans.

*short,
rounded
wings*

black hood

DISTRIBUTION

*short, springy
legs for hopping
among the twigs*

| Plumage Sexes alike | Habitat | Migration Non-migrant |

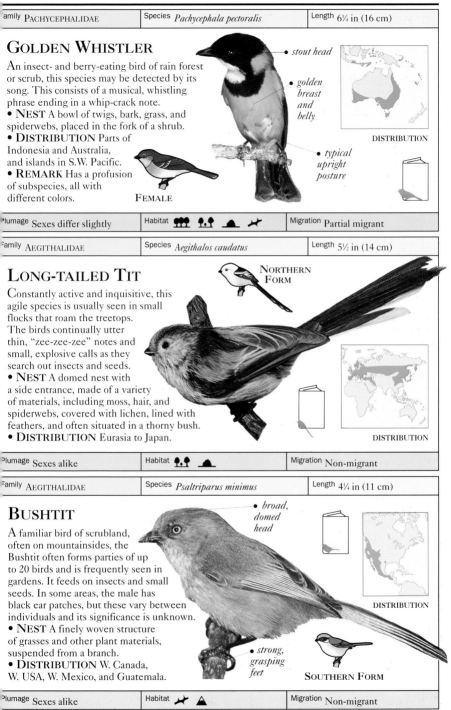

| Family PACHYCEPHALIDAE | Species *Pachycephala pectoralis* | Length 6¼ in (16 cm) |

GOLDEN WHISTLER

An insect- and berry-eating bird of rain forest
or scrub, this species may be detected by its
song. This consists of a musical, whistling
phrase ending in a whip-crack note.
• **NEST** A bowl of twigs, bark, grass, and
spiderwebs, placed in the fork of a shrub.
• **DISTRIBUTION** Parts of
Indonesia and Australia,
and islands in S.W. Pacific.
• **REMARK** Has a profusion
of subspecies, all with
different colors.

stout head

*golden
breast
and
belly*

DISTRIBUTION

*typical
upright
posture*

FEMALE

| Plumage Sexes differ slightly | Habitat | Migration Partial migrant |

| Family AEGITHALIDAE | Species *Aegithalos caudatus* | Length 5½ in (14 cm) |

LONG-TAILED TIT

Constantly active and inquisitive, this
agile species is usually seen in small
flocks that roam the treetops.
The birds continually utter
thin, "zee-zee-zee" notes and
small, explosive calls as they
search out insects and seeds.
• **NEST** A domed nest with
a side entrance, made of a variety
of materials, including moss, hair, and
spiderwebs, covered with lichen, lined with
feathers, and often situated in a thorny bush.
• **DISTRIBUTION** Eurasia to Japan.

**NORTHERN
FORM**

DISTRIBUTION

| Plumage Sexes alike | Habitat | Migration Non-migrant |

| Family AEGITHALIDAE | Species *Psaltriparus minimus* | Length 4¼ in (11 cm) |

BUSHTIT

A familiar bird of scrubland,
often on mountainsides, the
Bushtit often forms parties of up
to 20 birds and is frequently seen in
gardens. It feeds on insects and small
seeds. In some areas, the male has
black ear patches, but these vary between
individuals and its significance is unknown.
• **NEST** A finely woven structure
of grasses and other plant materials,
suspended from a branch.
• **DISTRIBUTION** W. Canada,
W. USA, W. Mexico, and Guatemala.

*broad,
domed
head*

DISTRIBUTION

*strong,
grasping
feet*

SOUTHERN FORM

| Plumage Sexes alike | Habitat | Migration Non-migrant |

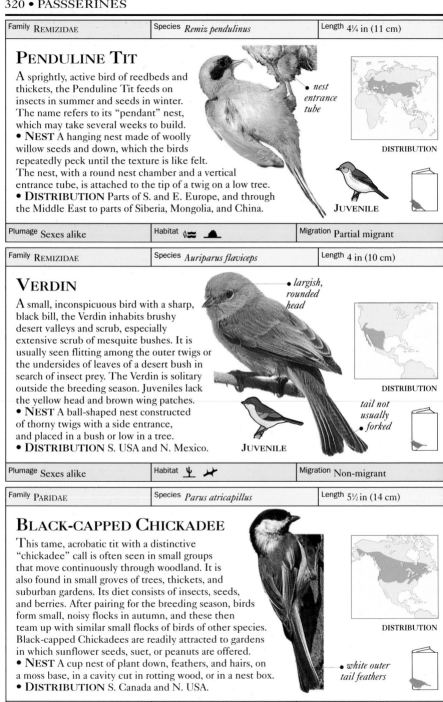

Family REMIZIDAE	Species *Remiz pendulinus*	Length 4¼ in (11 cm)

PENDULINE TIT

A sprightly, active bird of reedbeds and
thickets, the Penduline Tit feeds on
insects in summer and seeds in winter.
The name refers to its "pendant" nest,
which may take several weeks to build.
• **NEST** A hanging nest made of woolly
willow seeds and down, which the birds
repeatedly peck until the texture is like felt.
The nest, with a round nest chamber and a vertical
entrance tube, is attached to the tip of a twig on a low tree.
• **DISTRIBUTION** Parts of S. and E. Europe, and through
the Middle East to parts of Siberia, Mongolia, and China.

• *nest entrance tube*

DISTRIBUTION

JUVENILE

Plumage Sexes alike	Habitat	Migration Partial migrant

Family REMIZIDAE	Species *Auriparus flaviceps*	Length 4 in (10 cm)

VERDIN

A small, inconspicuous bird with a sharp,
black bill, the Verdin inhabits brushy
desert valleys and scrub, especially
extensive scrub of mesquite bushes. It is
usually seen flitting among the outer twigs or
the undersides of leaves of a desert bush in
search of insect prey. The Verdin is solitary
outside the breeding season. Juveniles lack
the yellow head and brown wing patches.
• **NEST** A ball-shaped nest constructed
of thorny twigs with a side entrance,
and placed in a bush or low in a tree.
• **DISTRIBUTION** S. USA and N. Mexico.

• *largish, rounded head*

DISTRIBUTION

tail not usually • forked

JUVENILE

Plumage Sexes alike	Habitat	Migration Non-migrant

Family PARIDAE	Species *Parus atricapillus*	Length 5½ in (14 cm)

BLACK-CAPPED CHICKADEE

This tame, acrobatic tit with a distinctive
"chickadee" call is often seen in small groups
that move continuously through woodland. It is
also found in small groves of trees, thickets, and
suburban gardens. Its diet consists of insects, seeds,
and berries. After pairing for the breeding season, birds
form small, noisy flocks in autumn, and these then
team up with similar small flocks of birds of other species.
Black-capped Chickadees are readily attracted to gardens
in which sunflower seeds, suet, or peanuts are offered.
• **NEST** A cup nest of plant down, feathers, and hairs, on
a moss base, in a cavity cut in rotting wood, or in a nest box.
• **DISTRIBUTION** S. Canada and N. USA.

DISTRIBUTION

• *white outer tail feathers*

Plumage Sexes alike	Habitat	Migration Non-migrant

Family PARIDAE	Species *Parus ater*	Length 4¼ in (11 cm)

COAL TIT

Found in all types of woodland in its range, this insect-eating bird feeds in the treetops, but often comes to ground level to nest.
• **NEST** A cup nest made of moss, in a hole in a tree, stump, or bank.
• **DISTRIBUTION** Most of Europe with parts of N.W. Africa, Middle East, Siberia, C. and E. Asia.

DISTRIBUTION

• *white cheek and nape*

EUROPEAN FORM

NORTH AFRICAN FORM

Plumage Sexes alike	Habitat	Migration Non-migrant

Family PARIDAE	Species *Parus cristatus*	Length 4½ in (11.5 cm)

CRESTED TIT

Identified by its spiky crest and soft, trilling song, the Crested Tit is almost wholly a bird of coniferous woodland. For most of the year it feeds in pine foliage, often high in the crowns of trees, where it is difficult to see. It feeds on insects, seeds, and berries.
• **NEST** A cup nest in a hole in a rotten tree, which the bird excavates itself.
• **DISTRIBUTION** From Spain through most of Europe to C. Asia.

• *spiky crest*

• *patterned face*

DISTRIBUTION

• *short legs with strong, grasping feet*

Plumage Sexes alike	Habitat	Migration Non-migrant

Family PARIDAE	Species *Parus major*	Length 5½ in (14 cm)

GREAT TIT

Bigger and bolder than most other tits, this bird lives in deciduous or mixed woodland, farmland, parks, and semi-open areas. It advertises its presence with loud, repetitive singing. Its diet includes insects and fruit. Plumage varies geographically, some of the populations in Asia lacking green or yellow plumage.
• **NEST** A cup nest lined with fine grass, placed in a hole in a tree or wall, or in a nest box.
• **DISTRIBUTION** Most of Europe with N.W. Africa; parts of Siberia and E. Asia; parts of C. Asia, Indian subcontinent, and S.E. Asia.

• *powerful head and bill*

DISTRIBUTION

• *yellow underside*

Plumage Sexes alike	Habitat	Migration Non-migrant

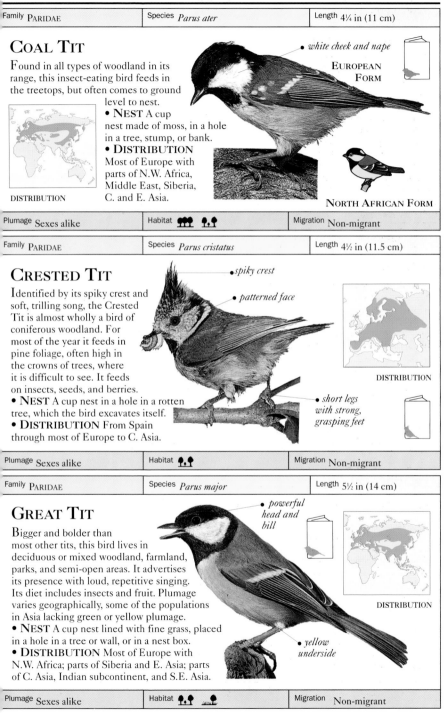

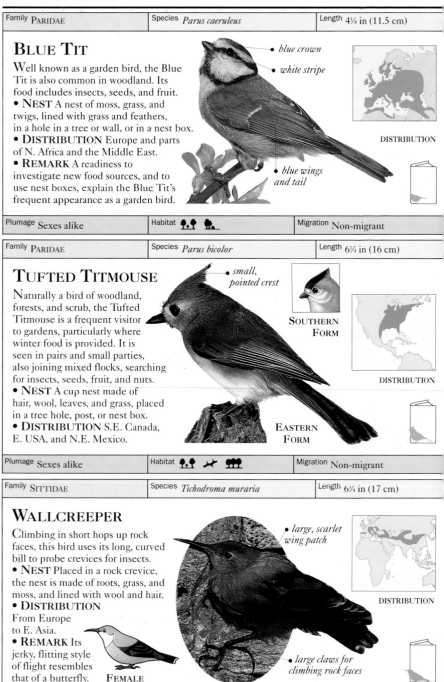

Family PARIDAE	Species *Parus caeruleus*	Length 4¼ in (11.5 cm)

BLUE TIT

Well known as a garden bird, the Blue Tit is also common in woodland. Its food includes insects, seeds, and fruit.
• **NEST** A nest of moss, grass, and twigs, lined with grass and feathers, in a hole in a tree or wall, or in a nest box.
• **DISTRIBUTION** Europe and parts of N. Africa and the Middle East.
• **REMARK** A readiness to investigate new food sources, and to use nest boxes, explain the Blue Tit's frequent appearance as a garden bird.

• *blue crown*

• *white stripe*

DISTRIBUTION

• *blue wings and tail*

Plumage Sexes alike	Habitat	Migration Non-migrant

Family PARIDAE	Species *Parus bicolor*	Length 6¼ in (16 cm)

TUFTED TITMOUSE

Naturally a bird of woodland, forests, and scrub, the Tufted Titmouse is a frequent visitor to gardens, particularly where winter food is provided. It is seen in pairs and small parties, also joining mixed flocks, searching for insects, seeds, fruit, and nuts.
• **NEST** A cup nest made of hair, wool, leaves, and grass, placed in a tree hole, post, or nest box.
• **DISTRIBUTION** S.E. Canada, E. USA, and N.E. Mexico.

• *small, pointed crest*

SOUTHERN FORM

DISTRIBUTION

EASTERN FORM

Plumage Sexes alike	Habitat	Migration Non-migrant

Family SITTIDAE	Species *Tichodroma muraria*	Length 6¾ in (17 cm)

WALLCREEPER

Climbing in short hops up rock faces, this bird uses its long, curved bill to probe crevices for insects.
• **NEST** Placed in a rock crevice, the nest is made of roots, grass, and moss, and lined with wool and hair.
• **DISTRIBUTION** From Europe to E. Asia.
• **REMARK** Its jerky, flitting style of flight resembles that of a butterfly. **FEMALE**

• *large, scarlet wing patch*

DISTRIBUTION

• *large claws for climbing rock faces*

Plumage Sexes differ	Habitat	Migration Partial migrant

Family SITTIDAE	Species *Sitta europaea*	Length 5½ in (14 cm)

EURASIAN NUTHATCH

Usually seen running along tree branches or up and down the trunk in search of insects, this bird also takes nuts, which it wedges into a crevice and breaks open with blows of its bill.
• **NEST** A cup nest made of bark flakes, in a tree hole. The entrance is often plastered with mud to reduce its size.
• **DISTRIBUTION** Much of Eurasia.

short tail •

DISTRIBUTION

SIBERIAN FORM

Plumage Sexes alike	Habitat 🌳🌳	Migration Non-migrant

Family SITTIDAE	Species *Sitta carolinensis*	Length 5½ in (14 cm)

WHITE-BREASTED NUTHATCH

Common in deciduous woodland and mixed forest areas within its range, the White-breasted Nuthatch characteristically works its way up, down, and across tree trunks in all directions as it forages for small insects. Like other nuthatches, it will also take nuts, which it hammers open with blows from its stout bill. Its song is a series of low, nasal whistles.
• **NEST** A hole in a tree, often lined with bark chippings and softer materials.
• **DISTRIBUTION** Parts of S. Canada, much of USA, and mountains of Mexico.

typical upended • posture

DISTRIBUTION

• strong, hammering bill

Plumage Sexes alike	Habitat 🌳🌳	Migration Non-migrant

Family NEOSITTIDAE	Species *Daphoenositta chrysoptera*	Length 4¾ in (12 cm)

VARIED SITELLA

NORTHWESTERN FORM

This small and gregarious species forages actively among the branches and twigs of trees, feeding on invertebrates. Plumage colors on the head, back, and wing stripe vary with the subspecies.
• **NEST** A cup nest made of insect cocoons, spiderwebs, hair, and wool, camouflaged with bark flakes, and built into an upright fork of a tree.
• **DISTRIBUTION** Much of Australia and Highlands of New Guinea.

DISTRIBUTION

EASTERN FORM

Plumage Sexes differ slightly	Habitat 🌳🌳 🌿 ✈	Migration Non-migrant

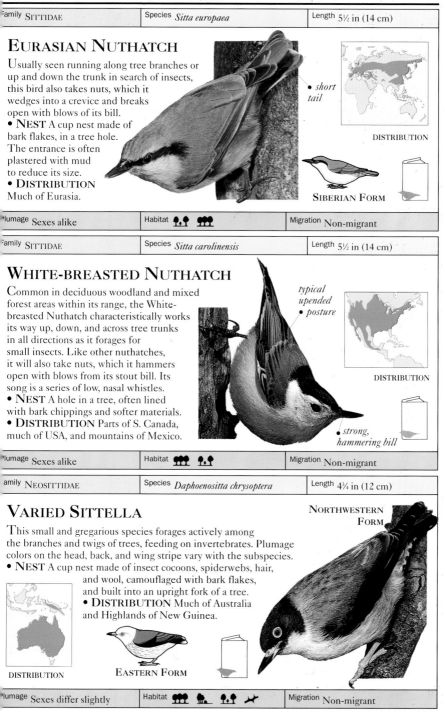

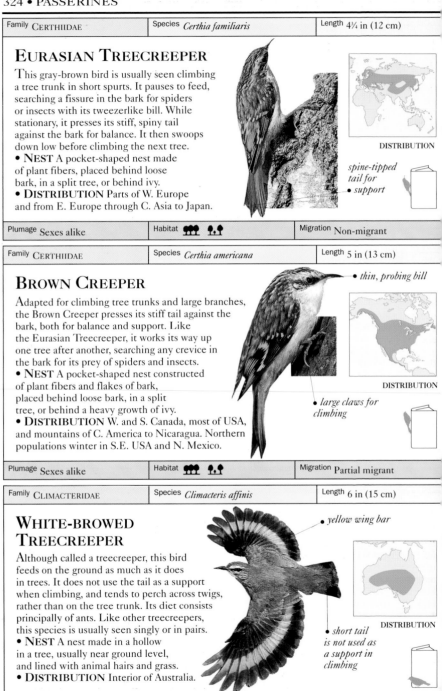

Family CERTHIIDAE	Species *Certhia familiaris*	Length 4¾ in (12 cm)

EURASIAN TREECREEPER

This gray-brown bird is usually seen climbing a tree trunk in short spurts. It pauses to feed, searching a fissure in the bark for spiders or insects with its tweezerlike bill. While stationary, it presses its stiff, spiny tail against the bark for balance. It then swoops down low before climbing the next tree.
• **NEST** A pocket-shaped nest made of plant fibers, placed behind loose bark, in a split tree, or behind ivy.
• **DISTRIBUTION** Parts of W. Europe and from E. Europe through C. Asia to Japan.

DISTRIBUTION

spine-tipped tail for support

Plumage Sexes alike	Habitat	Migration Non-migrant

Family CERTHIIDAE	Species *Certhia americana*	Length 5 in (13 cm)

BROWN CREEPER

thin, probing bill

Adapted for climbing tree trunks and large branches, the Brown Creeper presses its stiff tail against the bark, both for balance and support. Like the Eurasian Treecreeper, it works its way up one tree after another, searching any crevice in the bark for its prey of spiders and insects.
• **NEST** A pocket-shaped nest constructed of plant fibers and flakes of bark, placed behind loose bark, in a split tree, or behind a heavy growth of ivy.
• **DISTRIBUTION** W. and S. Canada, most of USA, and mountains of C. America to Nicaragua. Northern populations winter in S.E. USA and N. Mexico.

DISTRIBUTION

large claws for climbing

Plumage Sexes alike	Habitat	Migration Partial migrant

Family CLIMACTERIDAE	Species *Climacteris affinis*	Length 6 in (15 cm)

WHITE-BROWED TREECREEPER

yellow wing bar

Although called a treecreeper, this bird feeds on the ground as much as it does in trees. It does not use the tail as a support when climbing, and tends to perch across twigs, rather than on the tree trunk. Its diet consists principally of ants. Like other treecreepers, this species is usually seen singly or in pairs.
• **NEST** A nest made in a hollow in a tree, usually near ground level, and lined with animal hairs and grass.
• **DISTRIBUTION** Interior of Australia.

DISTRIBUTION

short tail is not used as a support in climbing

Plumage Sexes alike	Habitat	Migration Non-migrant

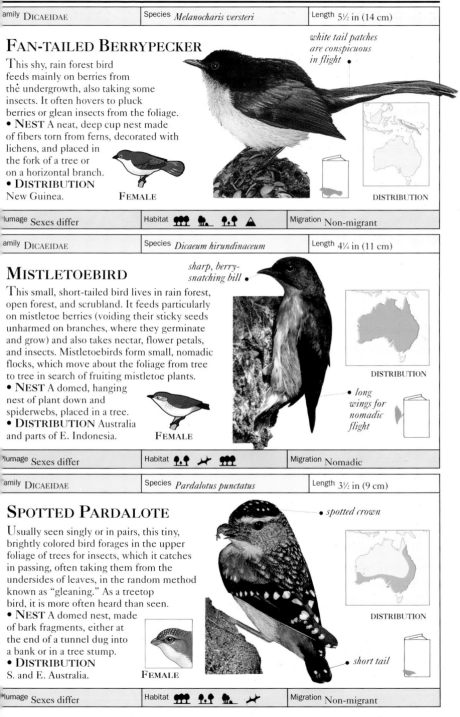

Family DICAEIDAE	Species *Melanocharis versteri*	Length 5½ in (14 cm)

FAN-TAILED BERRYPECKER

white tail patches are conspicuous in flight •

This shy, rain forest bird feeds mainly on berries from the undergrowth, also taking some insects. It often hovers to pluck berries or glean insects from the foliage.
• **NEST** A neat, deep cup nest made of fibers torn from ferns, decorated with lichens, and placed in the fork of a tree or on a horizontal branch.
• **DISTRIBUTION** New Guinea.

FEMALE

DISTRIBUTION

Plumage Sexes differ	Habitat	Migration Non-migrant

Family DICAEIDAE	Species *Dicaeum hirundinaceum*	Length 4¼ in (11 cm)

MISTLETOEBIRD

sharp, berry-snatching bill •

This small, short-tailed bird lives in rain forest, open forest, and scrubland. It feeds particularly on mistletoe berries (voiding their sticky seeds unharmed on branches, where they germinate and grow) and also takes nectar, flower petals, and insects. Mistletoebirds form small, nomadic flocks, which move about the foliage from tree to tree in search of fruiting mistletoe plants.
• **NEST** A domed, hanging nest of plant down and spiderwebs, placed in a tree.
• **DISTRIBUTION** Australia and parts of E. Indonesia.

FEMALE

DISTRIBUTION

• *long wings for nomadic flight*

Plumage Sexes differ	Habitat	Migration Nomadic

Family DICAEIDAE	Species *Pardalotus punctatus*	Length 3½ in (9 cm)

SPOTTED PARDALOTE

• *spotted crown*

Usually seen singly or in pairs, this tiny, brightly colored bird forages in the upper foliage of trees for insects, which it catches in passing, often taking them from the undersides of leaves, in the random method known as "gleaning." As a treetop bird, it is more often heard than seen.
• **NEST** A domed nest, made of bark fragments, either at the end of a tunnel dug into a bank or in a tree stump.
• **DISTRIBUTION** S. and E. Australia.

FEMALE

DISTRIBUTION

• *short tail*

Plumage Sexes differ	Habitat	Migration Non-migrant

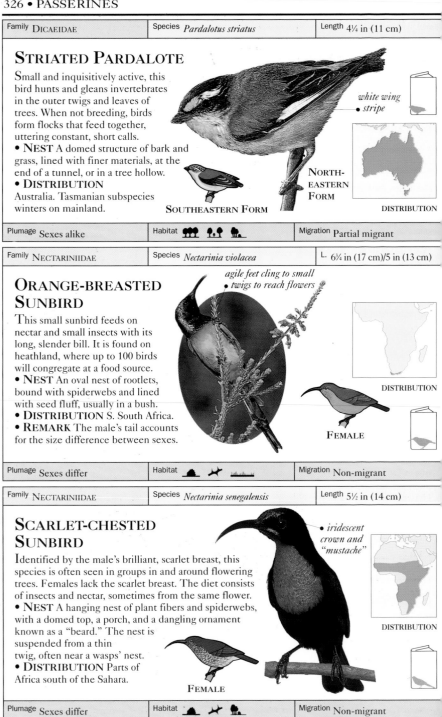

| Family DICAEIDAE | Species *Pardalotus striatus* | Length 4¼ in (11 cm) |

STRIATED PARDALOTE

Small and inquisitively active, this bird hunts and gleans invertebrates in the outer twigs and leaves of trees. When not breeding, birds form flocks that feed together, uttering constant, short calls.
• **NEST** A domed structure of bark and grass, lined with finer materials, at the end of a tunnel, or in a tree hollow.
• **DISTRIBUTION**
Australia. Tasmanian subspecies winters on mainland.

white wing stripe

NORTH-EASTERN FORM

SOUTHEASTERN FORM

DISTRIBUTION

| Plumage Sexes alike | Habitat | Migration Partial migrant |

| Family NECTARINIIDAE | Species *Nectarinia violacea* | L. 6¾ in (17 cm)/5 in (13 cm) |

ORANGE-BREASTED SUNBIRD

This small sunbird feeds on nectar and small insects with its long, slender bill. It is found on heathland, where up to 100 birds will congregate at a food source.
• **NEST** An oval nest of rootlets, bound with spiderwebs and lined with seed fluff, usually in a bush.
• **DISTRIBUTION** S. South Africa.
• **REMARK** The male's tail accounts for the size difference between sexes.

agile feet cling to small twigs to reach flowers

DISTRIBUTION

FEMALE

| Plumage Sexes differ | Habitat | Migration Non-migrant |

| Family NECTARINIIDAE | Species *Nectarinia senegalensis* | Length 5½ in (14 cm) |

SCARLET-CHESTED SUNBIRD

Identified by the male's brilliant, scarlet breast, this species is often seen in groups in and around flowering trees. Females lack the scarlet breast. The diet consists of insects and nectar, sometimes from the same flower.
• **NEST** A hanging nest of plant fibers and spiderwebs, with a domed top, a porch, and a dangling ornament known as a "beard." The nest is suspended from a thin twig, often near a wasps' nest.
• **DISTRIBUTION** Parts of Africa south of the Sahara.

iridescent crown and "mustache"

DISTRIBUTION

FEMALE

| Plumage Sexes differ | Habitat | Migration Non-migrant |

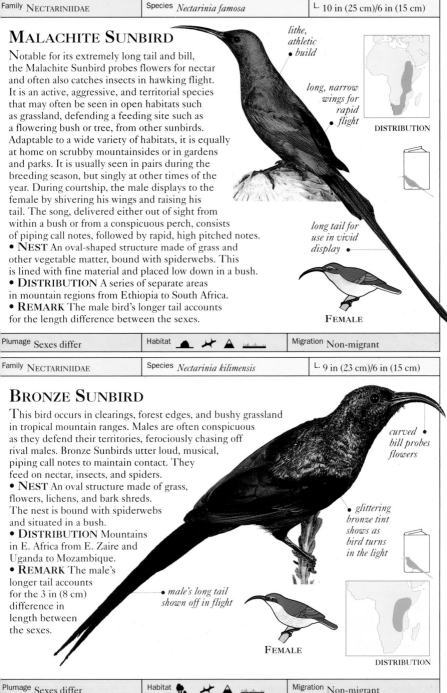

Family NECTARINIIDAE	Species *Nectarinia famosa*	L. 10 in (25 cm)/6 in (15 cm)

MALACHITE SUNBIRD

Notable for its extremely long tail and bill, the Malachite Sunbird probes flowers for nectar and often also catches insects in hawking flight. It is an active, aggressive, and territorial species that may often be seen in open habitats such as grassland, defending a feeding site such as a flowering bush or tree, from other sunbirds. Adaptable to a wide variety of habitats, it is equally at home on scrubby mountainsides or in gardens and parks. It is usually seen in pairs during the breeding season, but singly at other times of the year. During courtship, the male displays to the female by shivering his wings and raising his tail. The song, delivered either out of sight from within a bush or from a conspicuous perch, consists of piping call notes, followed by rapid, high pitched notes.
• **NEST** An oval-shaped structure made of grass and other vegetable matter, bound with spiderwebs. This is lined with fine material and placed low down in a bush.
• **DISTRIBUTION** A series of separate areas in mountain regions from Ethiopia to South Africa.
• **REMARK** The male bird's longer tail accounts for the length difference between the sexes.

lithe, athletic build

long, narrow wings for rapid flight

DISTRIBUTION

long tail for use in vivid display

FEMALE

Plumage Sexes differ	Habitat	Migration Non-migrant

Family NECTARINIIDAE	Species *Nectarinia kilimensis*	L. 9 in (23 cm)/6 in (15 cm)

BRONZE SUNBIRD

This bird occurs in clearings, forest edges, and bushy grassland in tropical mountain ranges. Males are often conspicuous as they defend their territories, ferociously chasing off rival males. Bronze Sunbirds utter loud, musical, piping call notes to maintain contact. They feed on nectar, insects, and spiders.
• **NEST** An oval structure made of grass, flowers, lichens, and bark shreds. The nest is bound with spiderwebs and situated in a bush.
• **DISTRIBUTION** Mountains in E. Africa from E. Zaire and Uganda to Mozambique.
• **REMARK** The male's longer tail accounts for the 3 in (8 cm) difference in length between the sexes.

curved bill probes flowers

glittering bronze tint shows as bird turns in the light

male's long tail shown off in flight

FEMALE

DISTRIBUTION

Plumage Sexes differ	Habitat	Migration Non-migrant

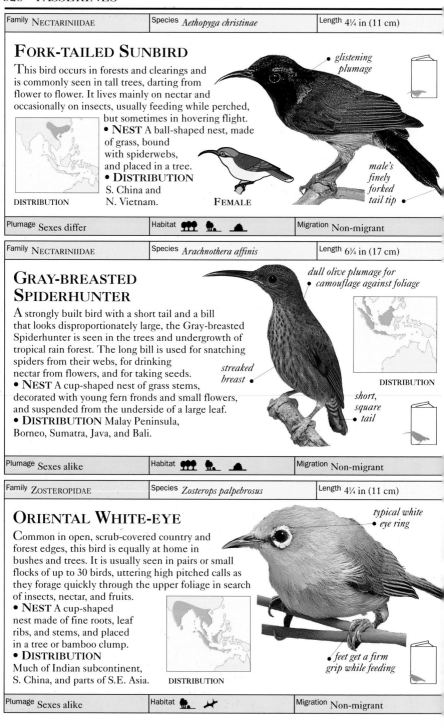

| Family NECTARINIIDAE | Species *Aethopyga christinae* | Length 4¼ in (11 cm) |

FORK-TAILED SUNBIRD

This bird occurs in forests and clearings and is commonly seen in tall trees, darting from flower to flower. It lives mainly on nectar and occasionally on insects, usually feeding while perched, but sometimes in hovering flight.
• **NEST** A ball-shaped nest, made of grass, bound with spiderwebs, and placed in a tree.
• **DISTRIBUTION** S. China and N. Vietnam.

glistening plumage

male's finely forked tail tip

DISTRIBUTION

FEMALE

| Plumage Sexes differ | Habitat | Migration Non-migrant |

| Family NECTARINIIDAE | Species *Arachnothera affinis* | Length 6¾ in (17 cm) |

GRAY-BREASTED SPIDERHUNTER

A strongly built bird with a short tail and a bill that looks disproportionately large, the Gray-breasted Spiderhunter is seen in the trees and undergrowth of tropical rain forest. The long bill is used for snatching spiders from their webs, for drinking nectar from flowers, and for taking seeds.
• **NEST** A cup-shaped nest of grass stems, decorated with young fern fronds and small flowers, and suspended from the underside of a large leaf.
• **DISTRIBUTION** Malay Peninsula, Borneo, Sumatra, Java, and Bali.

dull olive plumage for camouflage against foliage

streaked breast

short, square tail

DISTRIBUTION

| Plumage Sexes alike | Habitat | Migration Non-migrant |

| Family ZOSTEROPIDAE | Species *Zosterops palpebrosus* | Length 4¼ in (11 cm) |

ORIENTAL WHITE-EYE

Common in open, scrub-covered country and forest edges, this bird is equally at home in bushes and trees. It is usually seen in pairs or small flocks of up to 30 birds, uttering high pitched calls as they forage quickly through the upper foliage in search of insects, nectar, and fruits.
• **NEST** A cup-shaped nest made of fine roots, leaf ribs, and stems, and placed in a tree or bamboo clump.
• **DISTRIBUTION** Much of Indian subcontinent, S. China, and parts of S.E. Asia.

typical white eye ring

feet get a firm grip while feeding

DISTRIBUTION

| Plumage Sexes alike | Habitat | Migration Non-migrant |

| Family ZOSTEROPIDAE | Species *Zosterops poliogaster* | Length 4¼ in (11 cm) |

BROAD-RINGED WHITE-EYE

Fairly commonly found in mountain rain forests, this bird occurs in large, noisy flocks that move about in search of food. Its diet consists of a mixture of insects and berries.
• NEST A deep cup nest of plant fibers or lichens, lined with finer fibers, and attached to bushes or small trees, sometimes suspended from a twig.
• DISTRIBUTION N.E. Africa.

• *large, white eye ring*

tapering • *wings*

DISTRIBUTION

strong feet for • *acrobatic perching*

| Plumage Sexes alike | Habitat 🌳 ⛰ | Migration Non-migrant |

| Family MELIPHAGIDAE | Species *Toxorhamphus poliopterus* | Length 5 in (13 cm) |

GREY-WINGED LONGBILL

This bird is found at the edge of mountain rain forests and in secondary growth (bushes or trees regrown after forest clearance). It feeds on insects and nectar, flitting among the foliage in a nervous manner.
• NEST A deep, pouchlike nest of greenish plant material and spiderwebs, decorated with the white cases of spiders' eggs, and placed on the branch of a slender sapling.
• DISTRIBUTION New Guinea.

DISTRIBUTION

bill is • *shaped for snatching insects and for probing flowers*

| Plumage Sexes alike | Habitat 🌿 ⛰ | Migration Non-migrant |

| Family MELIPHAGIDAE | Species *Certhionyx pectoralis* | Length 5½ in (14 cm) |

BANDED HONEYEATER

This species inhabits woodland and waterside foliage, traveling nomadically in search of nectar, insects, and flowers. Flocks of noisy, aggressive birds are seen feeding in blossoming trees.
• NEST A cup nest made of grass and bark, bound with spiderwebs, and suspended in the outer foliage of a tree or bush.
•DISTRIBUTION N. Australia.

JUVENILE

DISTRIBUTION

| Plumage Sexes alike | Habitat 🌳 🌿 🌿 〰 | Migration Nomadic |

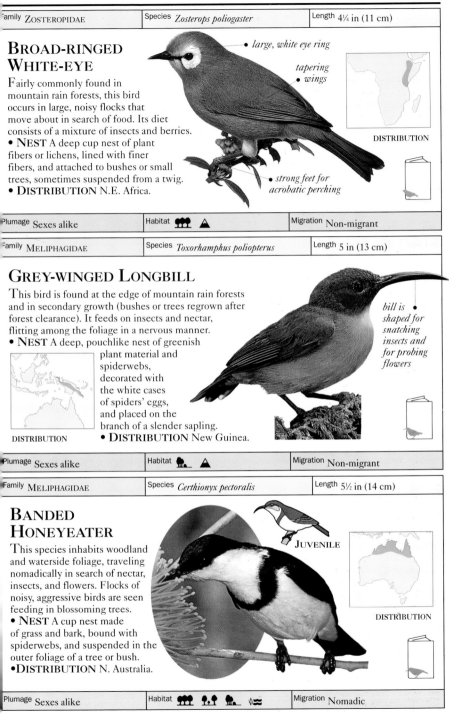

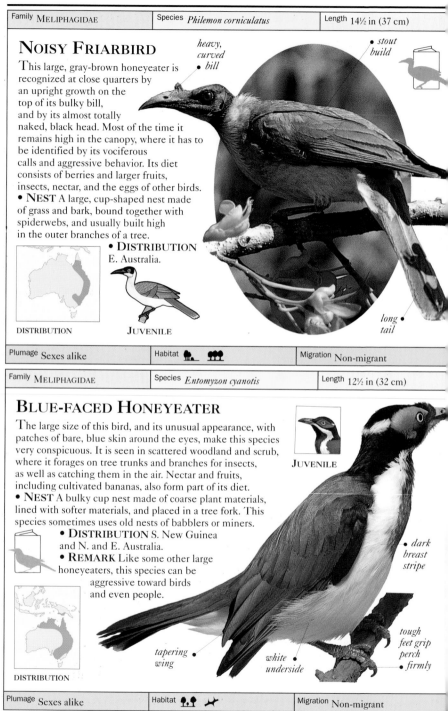

| Family MELIPHAGIDAE | Species *Philemon corniculatus* | Length 14½ in (37 cm) |

NOISY FRIARBIRD

This large, gray-brown honeyeater is
recognized at close quarters by
an upright growth on the
top of its bulky bill,
and by its almost totally
naked, black head. Most of the time it
remains high in the canopy, where it has to
be identified by its vociferous
calls and aggressive behavior. Its diet
consists of berries and larger fruits,
insects, nectar, and the eggs of other birds.
• **NEST** A large, cup-shaped nest made
of grass and bark, bound together with
spiderwebs, and usually built high
in the outer branches of a tree.
• **DISTRIBUTION**
E. Australia.

*heavy,
curved
• bill*

*• stout
build*

*long •
tail*

DISTRIBUTION

JUVENILE

| Plumage Sexes alike | Habitat | Migration Non-migrant |

| Family MELIPHAGIDAE | Species *Entomyzon cyanotis* | Length 12½ in (32 cm) |

BLUE-FACED HONEYEATER

The large size of this bird, and its unusual appearance, with
patches of bare, blue skin around the eyes, make this species
very conspicuous. It is seen in scattered woodland and scrub,
where it forages on tree trunks and branches for insects,
as well as catching them in the air. Nectar and fruits,
including cultivated bananas, also form part of its diet.
• **NEST** A bulky cup nest made of coarse plant materials,
lined with softer materials, and placed in a tree fork. This
species sometimes uses old nests of babblers or miners.
• **DISTRIBUTION** S. New Guinea
and N. and E. Australia.
• **REMARK** Like some other large
honeyeaters, this species can be
aggressive toward birds
and even people.

JUVENILE

*• dark
breast
stripe*

*tapering •
wing*

*white •
underside*

*tough
feet grip
perch
• firmly*

DISTRIBUTION

| Plumage Sexes alike | Habitat | Migration Non-migrant |

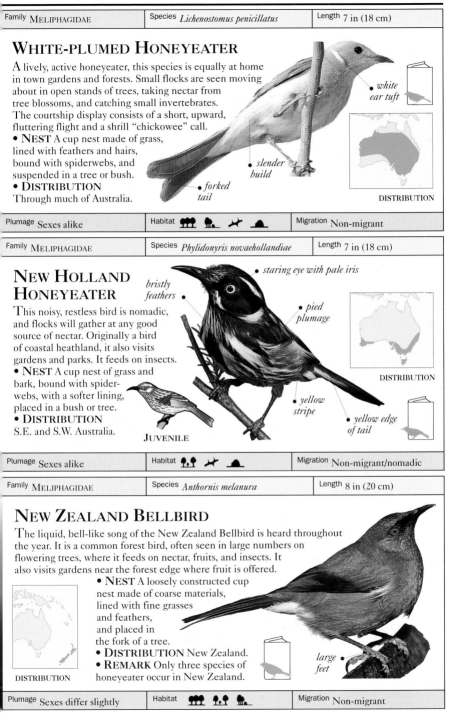

Family MELIPHAGIDAE	Species *Lichenostomus penicillatus*	Length 7 in (18 cm)

WHITE-PLUMED HONEYEATER

A lively, active honeyeater, this species is equally at home
in town gardens and forests. Small flocks are seen moving
about in open stands of trees, taking nectar from
tree blossoms, and catching small invertebrates.
The courtship display consists of a short, upward,
fluttering flight and a shrill "chickowee" call.
• **NEST** A cup nest made of grass,
lined with feathers and hairs,
bound with spiderwebs, and
suspended in a tree or bush.
• **DISTRIBUTION**
Through much of Australia.

*white
ear tuft*

*slender
build*

*forked
tail*

DISTRIBUTION

Plumage Sexes alike	Habitat	Migration Non-migrant

Family MELIPHAGIDAE	Species *Phylidonyris novaehollandiae*	Length 7 in (18 cm)

NEW HOLLAND HONEYEATER

This noisy, restless bird is nomadic,
and flocks will gather at any good
source of nectar. Originally a bird
of coastal heathland, it also visits
gardens and parks. It feeds on insects.
• **NEST** A cup nest of grass and
bark, bound with spider-
webs, with a softer lining,
placed in a bush or tree.
• **DISTRIBUTION**
S.E. and S.W. Australia.

*bristly
feathers*

staring eye with pale iris

*pied
plumage*

*yellow
stripe*

*yellow edge
of tail*

DISTRIBUTION

JUVENILE

Plumage Sexes alike	Habitat	Migration Non-migrant/nomadic

Family MELIPHAGIDAE	Species *Anthornis melanura*	Length 8 in (20 cm)

NEW ZEALAND BELLBIRD

The liquid, bell-like song of the New Zealand Bellbird is heard throughout
the year. It is a common forest bird, often seen in large numbers on
flowering trees, where it feeds on nectar, fruits, and insects. It
also visits gardens near the forest edge where fruit is offered.
• **NEST** A loosely constructed cup
nest made of coarse materials,
lined with fine grasses
and feathers,
and placed in
the fork of a tree.
• **DISTRIBUTION** New Zealand.
• **REMARK** Only three species of
honeyeater occur in New Zealand.

*large
feet*

DISTRIBUTION

Plumage Sexes differ slightly	Habitat	Migration Non-migrant

Family MELIPHAGIDAE	Species *Melipotes ater*	Length 12½ in (32 cm)

SPANGLED HONEYEATER

Although conspicuous because of its large size and colorful appearance, this honeyeater is rather quiet and unobtrusive. Sluggish in general behavior, it occurs in the upper branches of the higher mountain rain forests, usually singly or in pairs, feeding on fruit such as berries, with occasional insects. Presumably because of this diet it has a short, heavy bill and lacks the brush tongue of nectar-feeding species. The typical call is "chut, chut." The yellow face wattle appears capable of becoming red during sexual displays. Because of its isolated range and retiring habits in a difficult habitat for field work, little is known about it.
• **NEST** A bulky, cup-shaped nest, loosely made out of moss, leaves, and other plant material, hanging from the end of a branch.
• **DISTRIBUTION** Mountains of the Huon Peninsula of W. New Guinea, from 3,900 ft (1,200 m) to 11,000 ft (3,300 m).

• *yellow face wattle*

• *dark plumage*

DISTRIBUTION

• *large, powerful feet*

long tail •

Plumage Sexes alike	Habitat 🌳🌳 🌿 ▲	Migration Non-migrant

Family MELIPHAGIDAE	Species *Manorina flavigula*	Length 11 in (28 cm)

YELLOW-THROATED MINER

This heavily built, generally gray-brown honeyeater is a sociable and attractive bird, with a strong, yellow-colored wash on its breast and forehead. It lives in small colonies, often in scattered groups of trees in otherwise open country. Birds probably travel nomadically between such feeding and roosting sites. They feed predominantly on the ground, taking insects and seeds, but they also ascend the trees to take berries, fruit, and sometimes nectar from flowers. Yellow-throated Miners are aggressive birds, with much quarreling within the colony as well as vigorous defense against birds of other species. Often this defensive behavior involves the entire flock, taking wing and chasing a marauding bird of prey out of its territory, mobbing, and even physically attacking the intruder in flight. There is cooperative care of nestlings within the colony.
• **NEST** A loose cup nest made of grass and twigs, lined with wool and feathers, and placed in a tree fork up to 20 ft (6 m) from the ground.
• **DISTRIBUTION** Much of Australia.

DISTRIBUTION

• *yellow throat patch*

• *strong wings for vigorous flight*

• *strong legs for feeding on the ground*

Plumage Sexes alike	Habitat 🌲🌲 🌿	Migration Non-migrant

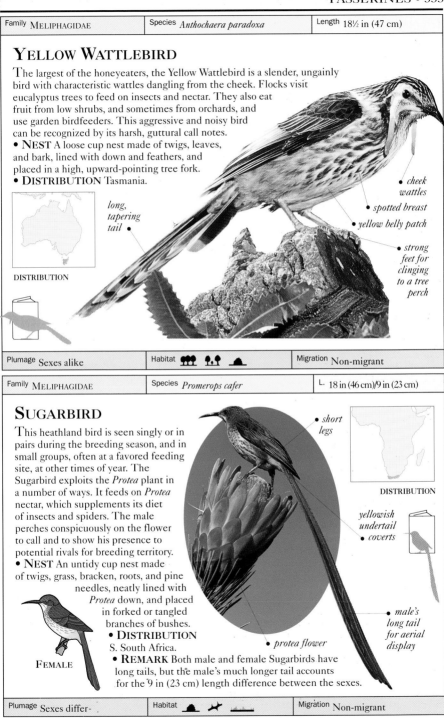

Family MELIPHAGIDAE	Species *Anthochaera paradoxa*	Length 18½ in (47 cm)

YELLOW WATTLEBIRD

The largest of the honeyeaters, the Yellow Wattlebird is a slender, ungainly bird with characteristic wattles dangling from the cheek. Flocks visit eucalyptus trees to feed on insects and nectar. They also eat fruit from low shrubs, and sometimes from orchards, and use garden birdfeeders. This aggressive and noisy bird can be recognized by its harsh, guttural call notes.
• **NEST** A loose cup nest made of twigs, leaves, and bark, lined with down and feathers, and placed in a high, upward-pointing tree fork.
• **DISTRIBUTION** Tasmania.

long, tapering tail •

DISTRIBUTION

• *cheek wattles*
• *spotted breast*
• *yellow belly patch*

• *strong feet for clinging to a tree perch*

Plumage Sexes alike	Habitat	Migration Non-migrant

Family MELIPHAGIDAE	Species *Promerops cafer*	L. 18 in (46 cm)/9 in (23 cm)

SUGARBIRD

This heathland bird is seen singly or in pairs during the breeding season, and in small groups, often at a favored feeding site, at other times of year. The Sugarbird exploits the *Protea* plant in a number of ways. It feeds on *Protea* nectar, which supplements its diet of insects and spiders. The male perches conspicuously on the flower to call and to show his presence to potential rivals for breeding territory.
• **NEST** An untidy cup nest made of twigs, grass, bracken, roots, and pine needles, neatly lined with *Protea* down, and placed in forked or tangled branches of bushes.
• **DISTRIBUTION** S. South Africa.
• **REMARK** Both male and female Sugarbirds have long tails, but the male's much longer tail accounts for the 9 in (23 cm) length difference between the sexes.

• *short legs*

DISTRIBUTION

yellowish undertail • *coverts*

FEMALE

• *protea flower*

• *male's long tail for aerial display*

Plumage Sexes differ	Habitat	Migration Non-migrant

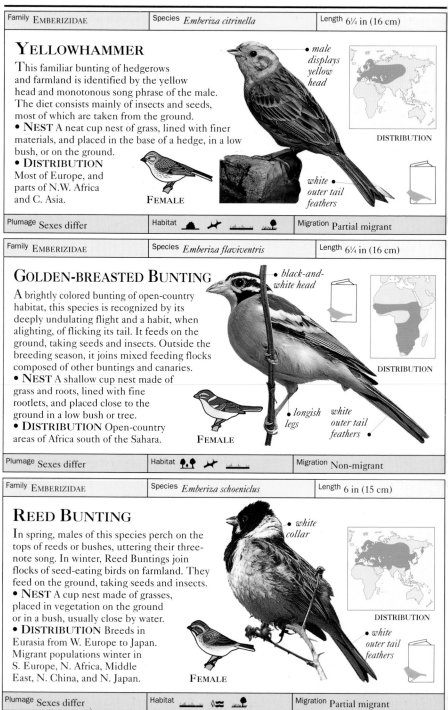

Family EMBERIZIDAE	Species *Emberiza citrinella*	Length 6¼ in (16 cm)

YELLOWHAMMER

This familiar bunting of hedgerows and farmland is identified by the yellow head and monotonous song phrase of the male. The diet consists mainly of insects and seeds, most of which are taken from the ground.
• **NEST** A neat cup nest of grass, lined with finer materials, and placed in the base of a hedge, in a low bush, or on the ground.
• **DISTRIBUTION** Most of Europe, and parts of N.W. Africa and C. Asia.

• *male displays yellow head*

DISTRIBUTION

white outer tail feathers

FEMALE

Plumage Sexes differ	Habitat	Migration Partial migrant

Family EMBERIZIDAE	Species *Emberiza flaviventris*	Length 6¼ in (16 cm)

GOLDEN-BREASTED BUNTING

A brightly colored bunting of open-country habitat, this species is recognized by its deeply undulating flight and a habit, when alighting, of flicking its tail. It feeds on the ground, taking seeds and insects. Outside the breeding season, it joins mixed feeding flocks composed of other buntings and canaries.
• **NEST** A shallow cup nest made of grass and roots, lined with fine rootlets, and placed close to the ground in a low bush or tree.
• **DISTRIBUTION** Open-country areas of Africa south of the Sahara.

• *black-and-white head*

DISTRIBUTION

• *longish legs* *white outer tail feathers* •

FEMALE

Plumage Sexes differ	Habitat	Migration Non-migrant

Family EMBERIZIDAE	Species *Emberiza schoeniclus*	Length 6 in (15 cm)

REED BUNTING

In spring, males of this species perch on the tops of reeds or bushes, uttering their three-note song. In winter, Reed Buntings join flocks of seed-eating birds on farmland. They feed on the ground, taking seeds and insects.
• **NEST** A cup nest made of grasses, placed in vegetation on the ground or in a bush, usually close by water.
• **DISTRIBUTION** Breeds in Eurasia from W. Europe to Japan. Migrant populations winter in S. Europe, N. Africa, Middle East, N. China, and N. Japan.

• *white collar*

DISTRIBUTION

• *white outer tail feathers*

FEMALE

Plumage Sexes differ	Habitat	Migration Partial migrant

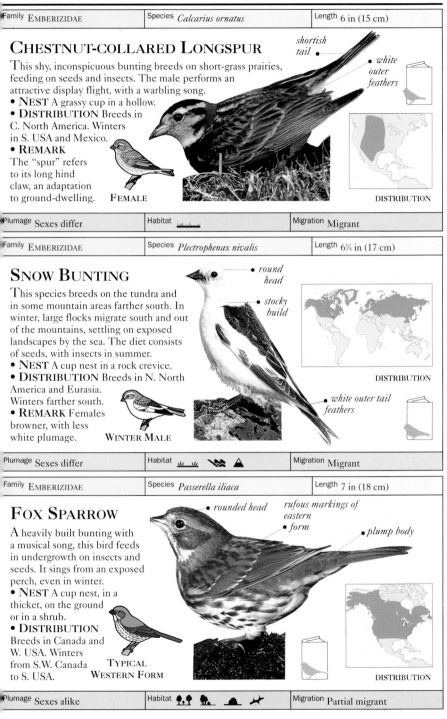

Family EMBERIZIDAE	Species *Calcarius ornatus*	Length 6 in (15 cm)

CHESTNUT-COLLARED LONGSPUR

This shy, inconspicuous bunting breeds on short-grass prairies, feeding on seeds and insects. The male performs an attractive display flight, with a warbling song.
• **NEST** A grassy cup in a hollow.
• **DISTRIBUTION** Breeds in C. North America. Winters in S. USA and Mexico.
• **REMARK**
The "spur" refers to its long hind claw, an adaptation to ground-dwelling.

shortish tail
white outer feathers

FEMALE

DISTRIBUTION

Plumage Sexes differ	Habitat	Migration Migrant

Family EMBERIZIDAE	Species *Plectrophenax nivalis*	Length 6¾ in (17 cm)

SNOW BUNTING

This species breeds on the tundra and in some mountain areas farther south. In winter, large flocks migrate south and out of the mountains, settling on exposed landscapes by the sea. The diet consists of seeds, with insects in summer.
• **NEST** A cup nest in a rock crevice.
• **DISTRIBUTION** Breeds in N. North America and Eurasia. Winters farther south.
• **REMARK** Females browner, with less white plumage.

round head
stocky build

WINTER MALE

DISTRIBUTION

white outer tail feathers

Plumage Sexes differ	Habitat	Migration Migrant

Family EMBERIZIDAE	Species *Passerella iliaca*	Length 7 in (18 cm)

FOX SPARROW

A heavily built bunting with a musical song, this bird feeds in undergrowth on insects and seeds. It sings from an exposed perch, even in winter.
• **NEST** A cup nest, in a thicket, on the ground or in a shrub.
• **DISTRIBUTION** Breeds in Canada and W. USA. Winters from S.W. Canada to S. USA.

rounded head
rufous markings of eastern form
plump body

TYPICAL WESTERN FORM

DISTRIBUTION

Plumage Sexes alike	Habitat	Migration Partial migrant

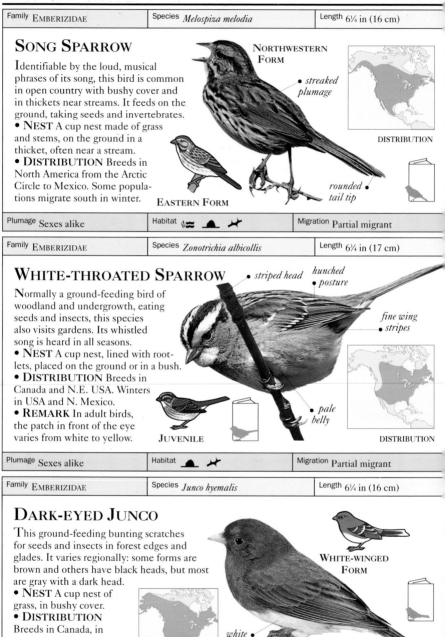

Family EMBERIZIDAE	Species *Melospiza melodia*	Length 6¼ in (16 cm)

SONG SPARROW

Identifiable by the loud, musical phrases of its song, this bird is common in open country with bushy cover and in thickets near streams. It feeds on the ground, taking seeds and invertebrates.
• **NEST** A cup nest made of grass and stems, on the ground in a thicket, often near a stream.
• **DISTRIBUTION** Breeds in North America from the Arctic Circle to Mexico. Some populations migrate south in winter.

NORTHWESTERN FORM

• *streaked plumage*

DISTRIBUTION

EASTERN FORM

rounded tail tip •

Plumage Sexes alike	Habitat	Migration Partial migrant

Family EMBERIZIDAE	Species *Zonotrichia albicollis*	Length 6¼ in (17 cm)

WHITE-THROATED SPARROW

Normally a ground-feeding bird of woodland and undergrowth, eating seeds and insects, this species also visits gardens. Its whistled song is heard in all seasons.
• **NEST** A cup nest, lined with rootlets, placed on the ground or in a bush.
• **DISTRIBUTION** Breeds in Canada and N.E. USA. Winters in USA and N. Mexico.
• **REMARK** In adult birds, the patch in front of the eye varies from white to yellow.

• *striped head*   *hunched* • *posture*

fine wing • *stripes*

pale • *belly*

JUVENILE

DISTRIBUTION

Plumage Sexes alike	Habitat	Migration Partial migrant

Family EMBERIZIDAE	Species *Junco hyemalis*	Length 6¼ in (16 cm)

DARK-EYED JUNCO

This ground-feeding bunting scratches for seeds and insects in forest edges and glades. It varies regionally: some forms are brown and others have black heads, but most are gray with a dark head.
• **NEST** A cup nest of grass, in bushy cover.
• **DISTRIBUTION** Breeds in Canada, in northerly and mountainous parts of USA, and in N. Mexico. Northern birds migrate south.

WHITE-WINGED FORM

white • *belly*

FEMALE OF SLATE-GRAY FORM

DISTRIBUTION

Plumage Sexes differ slightly	Habitat	Migration Partial migrant

Family EMBERIZIDAE	Species *Spizella arborea*	Length 6¼ in (16 cm)

AMERICAN TREE SPARROW

A bird of open country with bushy cover, this bunting is identified by the dark spot on its gray breast. In winter it joins mixed flocks of ground-feeding birds, taking seeds and invertebrates.

- **NEST** A shallow cup nest of grasses and other coarse vegetable materials, lined with feathers, and placed in a low bush or on the ground.
- **DISTRIBUTION** Breeds in Alaska and N. Canada. Winters in USA as far south as Texas.

• chestnut crown
white bars •

fluffed plumage • for winter warmth

DISTRIBUTION

Plumage Sexes alike	Habitat	Migration Migrant

Family EMBERIZIDAE	Species *Poospiza nigrorufa*	Length 6 in (15 cm)

BLACK-AND-RUFOUS WARBLING FINCH

A small and active seed-eater with a short bill, this species inhabits areas of extensive shrubs, sometimes with scattered trees, and is a common bird in this habitat. It is usually found in pairs, which forage on or near the ground for seeds and insects. Males commonly proclaim their territory by singing from an exposed perch and displaying the chestnut breast in the breeding season.

- **NEST** Unknown.
- **DISTRIBUTION** River Plate basin in N.E. Brazil, E. Paraguay, Uruguay, and N.E. Argentina.

• white stripe over eye
• black back
• chestnut breast

DISTRIBUTION

Plumage Sexes alike	Habitat	Migration Non-migrant

Family EMBERIZIDAE	Species *Sicalis flaveola*	Length 5½ in (14 cm)

SAFFRON FINCH

This scrub and grassland bird is easily identified by the intense yellow plumage of the male, with a darker yellow, almost orange, patch at the front of the crown. Flocks are commonly seen feeding quietly on the ground, taking small seeds.

- **NEST** In cavities or abandoned nests of other scrub and grassland birds.
- **DISTRIBUTION** Scattered areas in South America. Also Trinidad. Introduced in Panama, Jamaica, and Puerto Rico.
- **REMARK** A popular cage bird.

JUVENILE

• strong legs
slightly forked tail •

DISTRIBUTION

Plumage Sexes differ slightly	Habitat	Migration Non-migrant

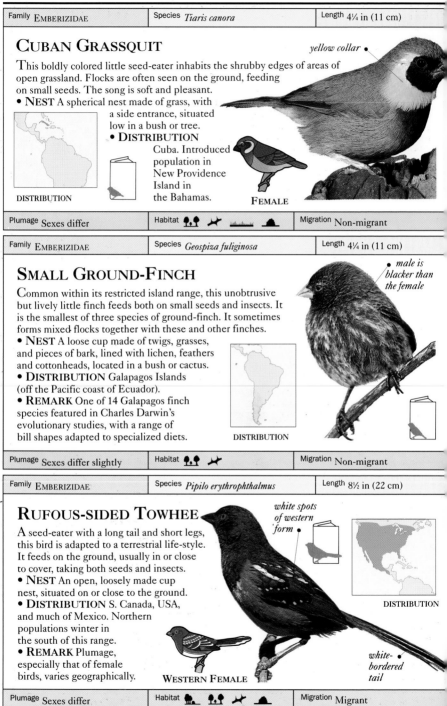

| Family EMBERIZIDAE | Species *Tiaris canora* | Length 4¼ in (11 cm) |

CUBAN GRASSQUIT

yellow collar •

This boldly colored little seed-eater inhabits the shrubby edges of areas of open grassland. Flocks are often seen on the ground, feeding on small seeds. The song is soft and pleasant.
• **NEST** A spherical nest made of grass, with a side entrance, situated low in a bush or tree.
• **DISTRIBUTION** Cuba. Introduced population in New Providence Island in the Bahamas.

DISTRIBUTION

FEMALE

| Plumage Sexes differ | Habitat | Migration Non-migrant |

| Family EMBERIZIDAE | Species *Geospiza fuliginosa* | Length 4¼ in (11 cm) |

SMALL GROUND-FINCH

• *male is blacker than the female*

Common within its restricted island range, this unobtrusive but lively little finch feeds both on small seeds and insects. It is the smallest of three species of ground-finch. It sometimes forms mixed flocks together with these and other finches.
• **NEST** A loose cup made of twigs, grasses, and pieces of bark, lined with lichen, feathers and cottonheads, located in a bush or cactus.
• **DISTRIBUTION** Galapagos Islands (off the Pacific coast of Ecuador).
• **REMARK** One of 14 Galapagos finch species featured in Charles Darwin's evolutionary studies, with a range of bill shapes adapted to specialized diets.

DISTRIBUTION

| Plumage Sexes differ slightly | Habitat | Migration Non-migrant |

| Family EMBERIZIDAE | Species *Pipilo erythrophthalmus* | Length 8½ in (22 cm) |

RUFOUS-SIDED TOWHEE

white spots of western form •

A seed-eater with a long tail and short legs, this bird is adapted to a terrestrial life-style. It feeds on the ground, usually in or close to cover, taking both seeds and insects.
• **NEST** An open, loosely made cup nest, situated on or close to the ground.
• **DISTRIBUTION** S. Canada, USA, and much of Mexico. Northern populations winter in the south of this range.
• **REMARK** Plumage, especially that of female birds, varies geographically.

DISTRIBUTION

white-bordered tail

WESTERN FEMALE

| Plumage Sexes differ | Habitat | Migration Migrant |

Family EMBERIZIDAE	Species *Paroaria coronata*	Length 7½ in (19 cm)

RED-CRESTED CARDINAL

A lively bird with an expressive crest, this species combines strong coloring with a bold, assertive manner. It is common in areas of grassland mixed with scattered trees and shrubbery, often near water. It is usually seen in pairs or small groups, feeding on a variety of seeds on the ground. Its rich, melodious song makes it a popular cage bird.
• **NEST** A neat, cup-shaped nest made of rootlets and grass, placed low in a bush or a small tree.
• **DISTRIBUTION** E. Bolivia, Paraguay, Uruguay, S. Brazil, and N. Argentina. Introduced population in Hawaiian Islands.

white collar •

gray back •

DISTRIBUTION

long, ground-feeder's legs •

Plumage Sexes alike	Habitat	Migration Non-migrant

Family EMBERIZIDAE	Species *Catamblyrhynchus diadema*	Length 5½ in (14 cm)

PLUSH-CAPPED FINCH

The stiff, gold-colored feathers on the front of this bird's crown give the species its name. It is usually seen in pairs or in mixed feeding flocks, taking insects and some plant material. Feeding in the lower and middle levels of the forest, Plush-capped Finches use their strong, stubby bills to probe into the leaf-tufts of South American bamboos in search of food.
• **NEST** Unknown.
• **DISTRIBUTION** Andes from N. Venezuela to N. Argentina.

velvet texture •

short legs •

DISTRIBUTION

Plumage Sexes alike	Habitat	Migration Non-migrant

Family EMBERIZIDAE	Species *Spiza americana*	Length 6¼ in (16 cm)

DICKCISSEL

Named after the sound of its song, the Dickcissel is a sparrowlike seed-eater of open grassland. It is gregarious, especially on migration, when enormous flocks are seen. Dickcissels feed on the ground on a variety of seeds and insects.
• **NEST** A bulky cup of plant materials situated in a shrub or a grass clump.
• **DISTRIBUTION** Breeds in C. Canada and in interior and E. USA. Winters from S. Mexico to N. South America.

yellowish eyebrow •

black bib •

FEMALE

chestnut • coverts

DISTRIBUTION

Plumage Sexes differ	Habitat	Migration Migrant

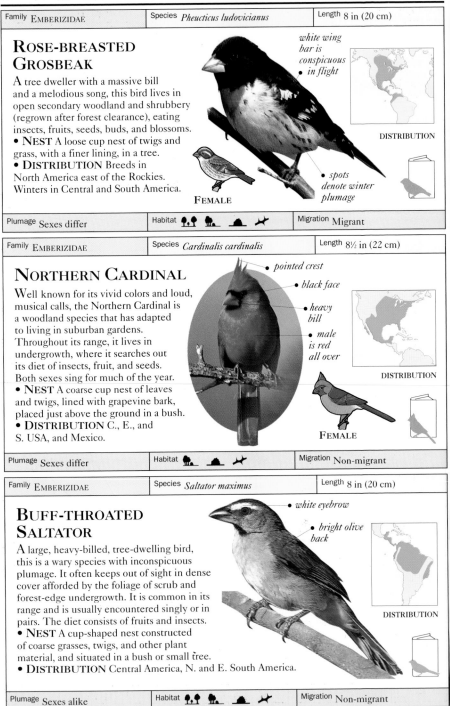

| Family EMBERIZIDAE | Species *Pheucticus ludovicianus* | Length 8 in (20 cm) |

ROSE-BREASTED GROSBEAK

A tree dweller with a massive bill and a melodious song, this bird lives in open secondary woodland and shrubbery (regrown after forest clearance), eating insects, fruits, seeds, buds, and blossoms.
• **NEST** A loose cup nest of twigs and grass, with a finer lining, in a tree.
• **DISTRIBUTION** Breeds in North America east of the Rockies. Winters in Central and South America.

white wing bar is conspicuous in flight

DISTRIBUTION

spots denote winter plumage

FEMALE

| Plumage Sexes differ | Habitat | Migration Migrant |

| Family EMBERIZIDAE | Species *Cardinalis cardinalis* | Length 8½ in (22 cm) |

NORTHERN CARDINAL

Well known for its vivid colors and loud, musical calls, the Northern Cardinal is a woodland species that has adapted to living in suburban gardens. Throughout its range, it lives in undergrowth, where it searches out its diet of insects, fruit, and seeds. Both sexes sing for much of the year.
• **NEST** A coarse cup nest of leaves and twigs, lined with grapevine bark, placed just above the ground in a bush.
• **DISTRIBUTION** C., E., and S. USA, and Mexico.

pointed crest
black face
heavy bill
male is red all over

DISTRIBUTION

FEMALE

| Plumage Sexes differ | Habitat | Migration Non-migrant |

| Family EMBERIZIDAE | Species *Saltator maximus* | Length 8 in (20 cm) |

BUFF-THROATED SALTATOR

A large, heavy-billed, tree-dwelling bird, this is a wary species with inconspicuous plumage. It often keeps out of sight in dense cover afforded by the foliage of scrub and forest-edge undergrowth. It is common in its range and is usually encountered singly or in pairs. The diet consists of fruits and insects.
• **NEST** A cup-shaped nest constructed of coarse grasses, twigs, and other plant material, and situated in a bush or small tree.
• **DISTRIBUTION** Central America, N. and E. South America.

white eyebrow
bright olive back

DISTRIBUTION

| Plumage Sexes alike | Habitat | Migration Non-migrant |

| Family EMBERIZIDAE | Species *Passerina leclancherii* | Length 5 in (13 cm) |

ORANGE-BREASTED BUNTING

This colorful but shy bunting is more often heard than seen. It lives in semi-arid countryside on hillsides covered with scrub and bushes. The diet consists of seeds and insects. These are taken from low branches or the foliage of bushes, from the ground underneath vegetation, or from open ground. However, foraging birds rarely move any distance away from the safety of cover. The male sings with a varied series of clear, warbled phrases from the top of a bush.
• **NEST** Unknown. Closely related species are known to make a neat cup nest of grass, lined with finer grasses and animal hairs, and placed in a bush or a low tree.
• **DISTRIBUTION** Foothills and Pacific slope of W. Mexico.

DISTRIBUTION

FEMALE

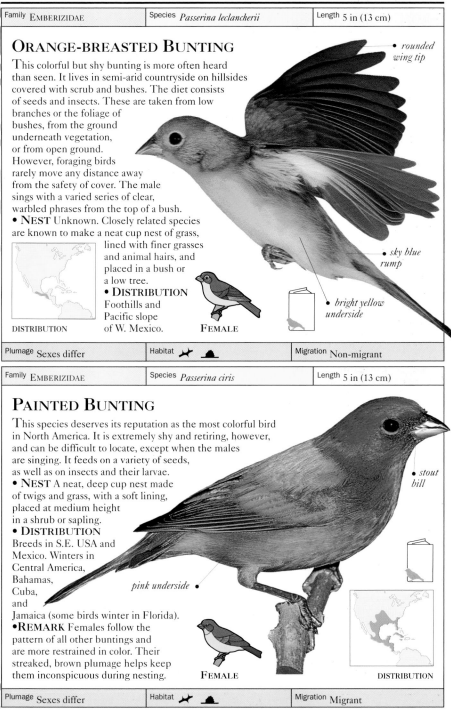

• *rounded wing tip*

• *sky blue rump*

• *bright yellow underside*

| Plumage Sexes differ | Habitat | Migration Non-migrant |

| Family EMBERIZIDAE | Species *Passerina ciris* | Length 5 in (13 cm) |

PAINTED BUNTING

This species deserves its reputation as the most colorful bird in North America. It is extremely shy and retiring, however, and can be difficult to locate, except when the males are singing. It feeds on a variety of seeds, as well as on insects and their larvae.
• **NEST** A neat, deep cup nest made of twigs and grass, with a soft lining, placed at medium height in a shrub or sapling.
• **DISTRIBUTION** Breeds in S.E. USA and Mexico. Winters in Central America, Bahamas, Cuba, and Jamaica (some birds winter in Florida).
•**REMARK** Females follow the pattern of all other buntings and are more restrained in color. Their streaked, brown plumage helps keep them inconspicuous during nesting.

pink underside •

FEMALE

• *stout bill*

DISTRIBUTION

| Plumage Sexes differ | Habitat | Migration Migrant |

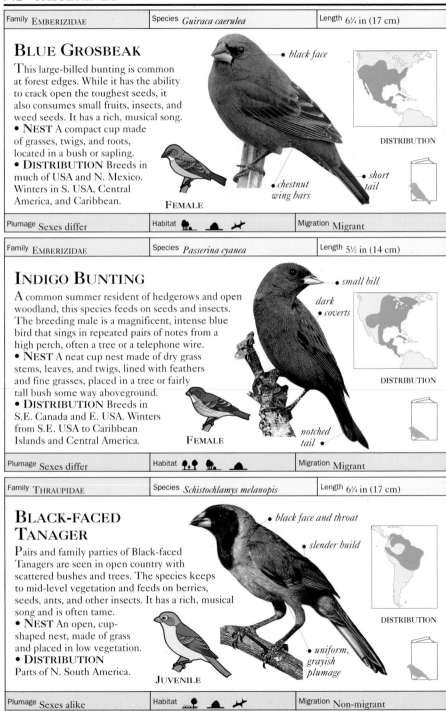

Family EMBERIZIDAE	Species *Guiraca caerulea*	Length 6¾ in (17 cm)

BLUE GROSBEAK

This large-billed bunting is common at forest edges. While it has the ability to crack open the toughest seeds, it also consumes small fruits, insects, and weed seeds. It has a rich, musical song.
• **NEST** A compact cup made of grasses, twigs, and roots, located in a bush or sapling.
• **DISTRIBUTION** Breeds in much of USA and N. Mexico. Winters in S. USA, Central America, and Caribbean.

• *black face*

DISTRIBUTION

• *short tail*

• *chestnut wing bars*

FEMALE

Plumage Sexes differ	Habitat 🌿 🌳 ✈	Migration Migrant

Family EMBERIZIDAE	Species *Passerina cyanea*	Length 5½ in (14 cm)

INDIGO BUNTING

A common summer resident of hedgerows and open woodland, this species feeds on seeds and insects. The breeding male is a magnificent, intense blue bird that sings in repeated pairs of notes from a high perch, often a tree or a telephone wire.
• **NEST** A neat cup nest made of dry grass stems, leaves, and twigs, lined with feathers and fine grasses, placed in a tree or fairly tall bush some way aboveground.
• **DISTRIBUTION** Breeds in S.E. Canada and E. USA. Winters from S.E. USA to Caribbean Islands and Central America.

• *small bill*

dark
• *coverts*

DISTRIBUTION

notched tail •

FEMALE

Plumage Sexes differ	Habitat 🌳 🌿 🌳	Migration Migrant

Family THRAUPIDAE	Species *Schistochlamys melanopis*	Length 6¾ in (17 cm)

BLACK-FACED TANAGER

Pairs and family parties of Black-faced Tanagers are seen in open country with scattered bushes and trees. The species keeps to mid-level vegetation and feeds on berries, seeds, ants, and other insects. It has a rich, musical song and is often tame.
• **NEST** An open, cup-shaped nest, made of grass and placed in low vegetation.
• **DISTRIBUTION** Parts of N. South America.

• *black face and throat*

• *slender build*

DISTRIBUTION

• *uniform, grayish plumage*

JUVENILE

Plumage Sexes alike	Habitat 🌿 🌳 ✈	Migration Non-migrant

Family THRAUPIDAE	Species *Cissopis leveriana*	Length 10½ in (27 cm)

MAGPIE-TANAGER

This bird is easily recognized by its distinctive, black-and-white plumage and long tail. Often in pairs or small groups, it is a noisy and conspicuous species that can usually be located by its loud, metallic calls, or be seen perching in open situations. The Magpie-Tanager is a widespread bird in the lowlands of its range, inhabiting areas of very open woodland, where bushes and trees are interspersed with grassland. Feeding mainly on fruit, it forages at all levels in the foliage, but especially in the tree canopy.
• **NEST** A large, cup-shaped nest, constructed from small twigs and grass, with a finer lining inside made of grass, and well concealed in dense foliage.
• **DISTRIBUTION** Parts of tropical South America.

DISTRIBUTION

dark neck feathers all have pointed tips

short legs

end of tail is rounded with white tips

Plumage Sexes alike	Habitat	Migration Non-migrant

Family THRAUPIDAE	Species *Rhodinocichla rosea*	Length 8 in (20 cm)

ROSE-BREASTED THRUSH-TANAGER

This beautiful tanager is extremely shy and difficult to view in its tangled thicket habitat. Single birds or pairs forage on the ground and flick leaf litter aside in search of invertebrates.
• **NEST** A shallow cup nest, made of twigs and leaves and situated in dense cover.
• **DISTRIBUTION** W. Mexico, and from Costa Rica to Colombia and Venezuela.

narrow stripe above eye

longish bill

FEMALE

pink undertail coverts

pinkish underside

DISTRIBUTION

long tail, usually rounded

strong, ground-feeder's legs

Plumage Sexes differ	Habitat	Migration Non-migrant

Family THRAUPIDAE	Species *Piranga olivacea*	Length 6¼ in (17 cm)

SCARLET TANAGER

As it lives and feeds mostly in the upper foliage of trees, this species is more likely to be heard than seen. It breeds in deciduous forest and winters in the canopy of lowland rain forest. The diet consists of insects and fruit.
• **NEST** A shallow cup nest, lined and placed in a tree.
• **DISTRIBUTION** Breeds in S.E. Canada and E. USA. Winters from Panama as far south as Bolivia.

scarlet body

black wings

DISTRIBUTION

black tail

FEMALE

Plumage Sexes differ	Habitat	Migration Migrant

Family THRAUPIDAE	Species *Piranga ludoviciana*	Length 6¼ in (17 cm)

WESTERN TANAGER

Yellow wing bars, and a vigorous song, draw attention to this bird. Usually solitary, it forms flocks of up to 30 birds or more on migration. It feeds mostly on insects but in late summer it also takes fruit, such as berries.
• **NEST** A cup nest, lined with grass and placed in a fir or pine, often high above the ground.
• **DISTRIBUTION** Breeds in mountains of S.W. Canada and W. USA. Winters in Central America.

FEMALE

orange-red color of head in summer

yellow underside

short legs

DISTRIBUTION

Plumage Sexes differ	Habitat	Migration Migrant

Family THRAUPIDAE	Species *Ramphocelus bresilius*	Length 7 in (18 cm)

BRAZILIAN TANAGER

Chattering groups of this species feed in the shrubby edges of forests, taking fruits, seeds, and insects.
• **NEST** A grass cup nest, placed in a low tree or hidden in marsh grass.
• **DISTRIBUTION** S.E. Brazil, N.E. Argentina.

white bill patch

glossy red plumage

DISTRIBUTION

rounded, black wings

FEMALE

Plumage Sexes differ	Habitat	Migration Non-migrant

| Family THRAUPIDAE | Species *Thraupis sayaca* | Length 6¼ in (17 cm) |

SAYACA TANAGER

A bird of scrub and open woodland, this species favors damp areas with thicker vegetation along watercourses. When perched, it has a habit of turning its body from side to side. It feeds chiefly on fruit. The song is a jumbled but melodious series of notes.
• **NEST** A carefully woven, compact cup nest, well hidden in a low bush or small tree.
• **DISTRIBUTION** Much of Brazil south of the Amazon basin, extending into Bolivia, Paraguay, Uruguay, and N. Argentina.

grayish head and body

pale blue wings and tail

DISTRIBUTION

| Plumage Sexes alike | Habitat | Migration Non-migrant |

| Family THRAUPIDAE | Species *Anisognathus igniventris* | Length 6¼ in (16 cm) |

SCARLET-BELLIED MOUNTAIN-TANAGER

Known for its striking pattern and tinkling song, this mountain bird occurs in woodland and scrub on the Andean uplands, extending upward into high-altitude pasture and farmland. Usually occurring in pairs or small groups, it feeds on fruit pulp, seeds, leaves, and buds.
• **NEST** A cup nest made of coarse grass, lined with finer grass, in a tree or thicket.
• **DISTRIBUTION** Andes from Venezuela to Bolivia.

scarlet cheek patch

blue shoulder patch

blue rump

DISTRIBUTION

typical short legs of a tanager

| Plumage Sexes alike | Habitat | Migration Non-migrant |

| Family THRAUPIDAE | Species *Anisognathus somptuosus* | Length 6¾ in (17 cm) |

BLUE-WINGED MOUNTAIN-TANAGER

This species occurs in mountain forests and secondary growth (regrown after clearance). It hops about in the outer branches and foliage, plucking fruit and searching for insects.
• **NEST** A cup nest made of grass, probably in a bush or small tree.
• **DISTRIBUTION** Andean forests from Venezuela to Bolivia.

yellow cap

blue shoulder

DISTRIBUTION

yellow underside

light blue feather edges

| Plumage Sexes alike | Habitat | Migration Non-migrant |

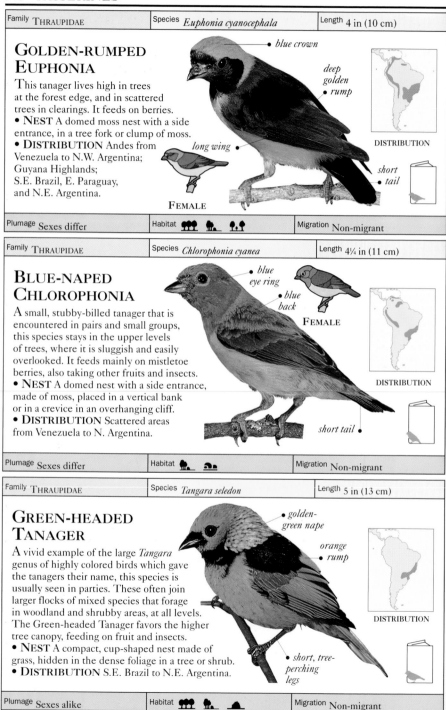

| Family THRAUPIDAE | Species *Euphonia cyanocephala* | Length 4 in (10 cm) |

GOLDEN-RUMPED EUPHONIA

This tanager lives high in trees at the forest edge, and in scattered trees in clearings. It feeds on berries.
• **NEST** A domed moss nest with a side entrance, in a tree fork or clump of moss.
• **DISTRIBUTION** Andes from Venezuela to N.W. Argentina; Guyana Highlands; S.E. Brazil, E. Paraguay, and N.E. Argentina.

• blue crown

deep golden
• rump

long wing

short
• tail

DISTRIBUTION

FEMALE

| Plumage Sexes differ | Habitat | Migration Non-migrant |

| Family THRAUPIDAE | Species *Chlorophonia cyanea* | Length 4¼ in (11 cm) |

BLUE-NAPED CHLOROPHONIA

A small, stubby-billed tanager that is encountered in pairs and small groups, this species stays in the upper levels of trees, where it is sluggish and easily overlooked. It feeds mainly on mistletoe berries, also taking other fruits and insects.
• **NEST** A domed nest with a side entrance, made of moss, placed in a vertical bank or in a crevice in an overhanging cliff.
• **DISTRIBUTION** Scattered areas from Venezuela to N. Argentina.

• blue eye ring

• blue back

FEMALE

DISTRIBUTION

short tail •

| Plumage Sexes differ | Habitat | Migration Non-migrant |

| Family THRAUPIDAE | Species *Tangara seledon* | Length 5 in (13 cm) |

GREEN-HEADED TANAGER

A vivid example of the large *Tangara* genus of highly colored birds which gave the tanagers their name, this species is usually seen in parties. These often join larger flocks of mixed species that forage in woodland and shrubby areas, at all levels. The Green-headed Tanager favors the higher tree canopy, feeding on fruit and insects.
• **NEST** A compact, cup-shaped nest made of grass, hidden in the dense foliage in a tree or shrub.
• **DISTRIBUTION** S.E. Brazil to N.E. Argentina.

• golden-green nape

orange
• rump

DISTRIBUTION

• short, tree-perching legs

| Plumage Sexes alike | Habitat | Migration Non-migrant |

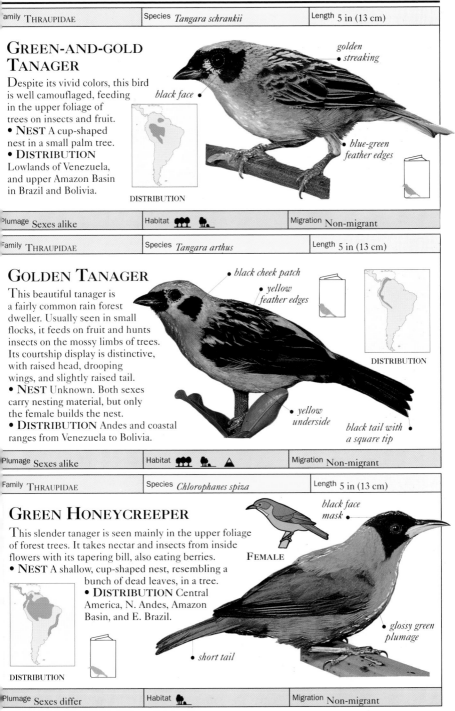

| Family THRAUPIDAE | Species *Tangara schrankii* | Length 5 in (13 cm) |

GREEN-AND-GOLD TANAGER

Despite its vivid colors, this bird is well camouflaged, feeding in the upper foliage of trees on insects and fruit.
• **NEST** A cup-shaped nest in a small palm tree.
• **DISTRIBUTION** Lowlands of Venezuela, and upper Amazon Basin in Brazil and Bolivia.

black face

golden streaking

blue-green feather edges

DISTRIBUTION

| Plumage Sexes alike | Habitat | Migration Non-migrant |

| Family THRAUPIDAE | Species *Tangara arthus* | Length 5 in (13 cm) |

GOLDEN TANAGER

This beautiful tanager is a fairly common rain forest dweller. Usually seen in small flocks, it feeds on fruit and hunts insects on the mossy limbs of trees. Its courtship display is distinctive, with raised head, drooping wings, and slightly raised tail.
• **NEST** Unknown. Both sexes carry nesting material, but only the female builds the nest.
• **DISTRIBUTION** Andes and coastal ranges from Venezuela to Bolivia.

black cheek patch

yellow feather edges

yellow underside

black tail with a square tip

DISTRIBUTION

| Plumage Sexes alike | Habitat | Migration Non-migrant |

| Family THRAUPIDAE | Species *Chlorophanes spiza* | Length 5 in (13 cm) |

GREEN HONEYCREEPER

This slender tanager is seen mainly in the upper foliage of forest trees. It takes nectar and insects from inside flowers with its tapering bill, also eating berries.
• **NEST** A shallow, cup-shaped nest, resembling a bunch of dead leaves, in a tree.
• **DISTRIBUTION** Central America, N. Andes, Amazon Basin, and E. Brazil.

FEMALE

black face mask

glossy green plumage

short tail

DISTRIBUTION

| Plumage Sexes differ | Habitat | Migration Non-migrant |

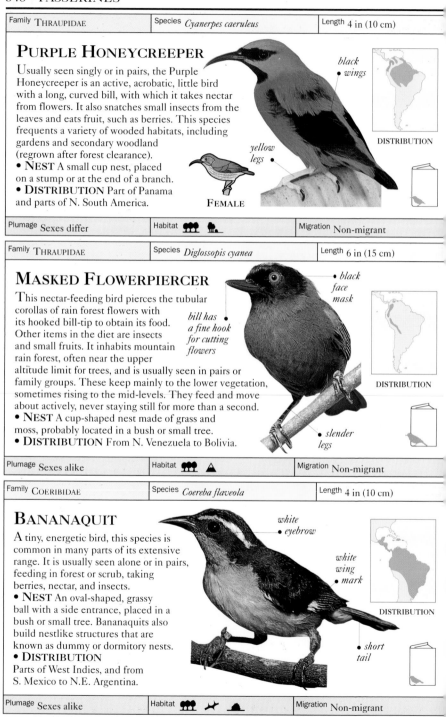

| Family THRAUPIDAE | Species *Cyanerpes caeruleus* | Length 4 in (10 cm) |

PURPLE HONEYCREEPER

Usually seen singly or in pairs, the Purple
Honeycreeper is an active, acrobatic, little bird
with a long, curved bill, with which it takes nectar
from flowers. It also snatches small insects from the
leaves and eats fruit, such as berries. This species
frequents a variety of wooded habitats, including
gardens and secondary woodland
(regrown after forest clearance).
• **NEST** A small cup nest, placed
on a stump or at the end of a branch.
• **DISTRIBUTION** Part of Panama
and parts of N. South America.

black wings

yellow legs

DISTRIBUTION

FEMALE

| Plumage Sexes differ | Habitat | Migration Non-migrant |

| Family THRAUPIDAE | Species *Diglossopis cyanea* | Length 6 in (15 cm) |

MASKED FLOWERPIERCER

This nectar-feeding bird pierces the tubular
corollas of rain forest flowers with
its hooked bill-tip to obtain its food.
Other items in the diet are insects
and small fruits. It inhabits mountain
rain forest, often near the upper
altitude limit for trees, and is usually seen in pairs or
family groups. These keep mainly to the lower vegetation,
sometimes rising to the mid-levels. They feed and move
about actively, never staying still for more than a second.
• **NEST** A cup-shaped nest made of grass and
moss, probably located in a bush or small tree.
• **DISTRIBUTION** From N. Venezuela to Bolivia.

black face mask

bill has a fine hook for cutting flowers

DISTRIBUTION

slender legs

| Plumage Sexes alike | Habitat | Migration Non-migrant |

| Family COERIBIDAE | Species *Coereba flaveola* | Length 4 in (10 cm) |

BANANAQUIT

A tiny, energetic bird, this species is
common in many parts of its extensive
range. It is usually seen alone or in pairs,
feeding in forest or scrub, taking
berries, nectar, and insects.
• **NEST** An oval-shaped, grassy
ball with a side entrance, placed in a
bush or small tree. Bananaquits also
build nestlike structures that are
known as dummy or dormitory nests.
• **DISTRIBUTION**
Parts of West Indies, and from
S. Mexico to N.E. Argentina.

white eyebrow

white wing mark

DISTRIBUTION

short tail

| Plumage Sexes alike | Habitat | Migration Non-migrant |

| Family PARULIDAE | Species *Mniotilta varia* | Length 5 in (13 cm) |

BLACK-AND-WHITE WARBLER

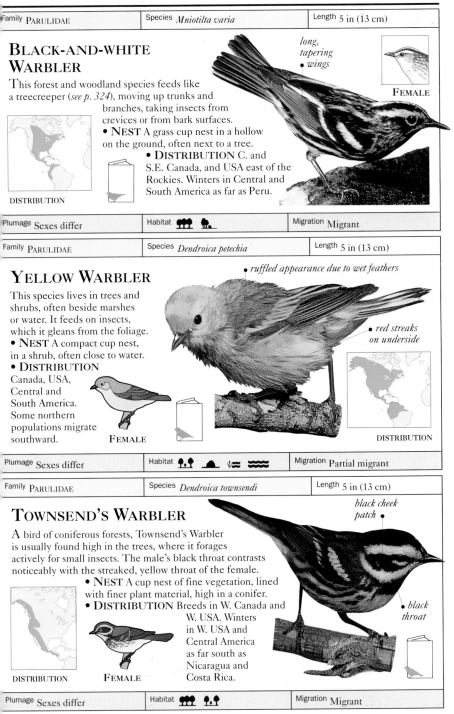

long, tapering • wings

FEMALE

This forest and woodland species feeds like a treecreeper (*see p. 324*), moving up trunks and branches, taking insects from crevices or from bark surfaces.
• **NEST** A grass cup nest in a hollow on the ground, often next to a tree.
• **DISTRIBUTION** C. and S.E. Canada, and USA east of the Rockies. Winters in Central and South America as far as Peru.

DISTRIBUTION

| Plumage Sexes differ | Habitat 🌳 🌳 | Migration Migrant |

| Family PARULIDAE | Species *Dendroica petechia* | Length 5 in (13 cm) |

YELLOW WARBLER

• ruffled appearance due to wet feathers

This species lives in trees and shrubs, often beside marshes or water. It feeds on insects, which it gleans from the foliage.
• **NEST** A compact cup nest, in a shrub, often close to water.
• **DISTRIBUTION** Canada, USA, Central and South America. Some northern populations migrate southward.

FEMALE

• red streaks on underside

DISTRIBUTION

| Plumage Sexes differ | Habitat 🌳🌳 🌿 〰️ 〰️ | Migration Partial migrant |

| Family PARULIDAE | Species *Dendroica townsendi* | Length 5 in (13 cm) |

TOWNSEND'S WARBLER

black cheek patch •

A bird of coniferous forests, Townsend's Warbler is usually found high in the trees, where it forages actively for small insects. The male's black throat contrasts noticeably with the streaked, yellow throat of the female.
• **NEST** A cup nest of fine vegetation, lined with finer plant material, high in a conifer.
• **DISTRIBUTION** Breeds in W. Canada and W. USA. Winters in W. USA and Central America as far south as Nicaragua and Costa Rica.

• black throat

DISTRIBUTION

FEMALE

| Plumage Sexes differ | Habitat 🌳🌳 🌳🌳 | Migration Migrant |

| Family PARULIDAE | Species *Dendroica fusca* | Length 5 in (13 cm) |

BLACKBURNIAN WARBLER

white wing patch •

This bird is usually seen in the treetops, where it feeds on insects. Breeding habitats range from spruce and fir forests to oak woodland. The wintering habitat is tropical forest.
• **NEST** A cup nest of twigs and grasses in a conifer.

reddish throat •

• **DISTRIBUTION**
Breeds in C. and S.E. Canada and E. USA. Winters from Costa Rica as far south as Peru, and in the West Indies.

DISTRIBUTION

FEMALE

| Plumage Sexes differ | Habitat 🌳🌳 | Migration Migrant |

| Family PARULIDAE | Species *Dendroica magnolia* | Length 5 in (13 cm) |

MAGNOLIA WARBLER

• white eyebrow

white feather • edges

A common bird of moist, coniferous forest, the Magnolia Warbler is recognized by its musical "weety-weety-weeteo" song. It feeds in the tree-tops, gleaning insects from the leaves. In winter, the male loses its bold head pattern.
• **NEST** A loose, cup-shaped nest of grasses and twigs, placed on a branch in a small tree.
• **DISTRIBUTION**
Breeds in Canada and N.E. USA. Winters in Central America as far as Panama.

yellow underside with black • streaks

FEMALE

DISTRIBUTION

| Plumage Sexes differ | Habitat 🌳🌳 | Migration Migrant |

| Family PARULIDAE | Species *Dendroica coronata* | Length 5½ in (14 cm) |

YELLOW-RUMPED WARBLER

• yellow crown

yellow rump •

This bird inhabits northern forests, coniferous as well as mixed, feeding on insects. The eastern form (Myrtle Warbler) has a white throat and the western form (Audubon's Warbler) has a yellow throat.
• **NEST** A lined cup nest of grass and small twigs, in a tree.
• **DISTRIBUTION** Breeds in North and Central America. Winters in W. and S. USA, West Indies, and Central America.

DISTRIBUTION

MYRTLE WARBLER

FEMALE

| Plumage Sexes differ | Habitat 🌳🌳 🌳🌳 | Migration Migrant |

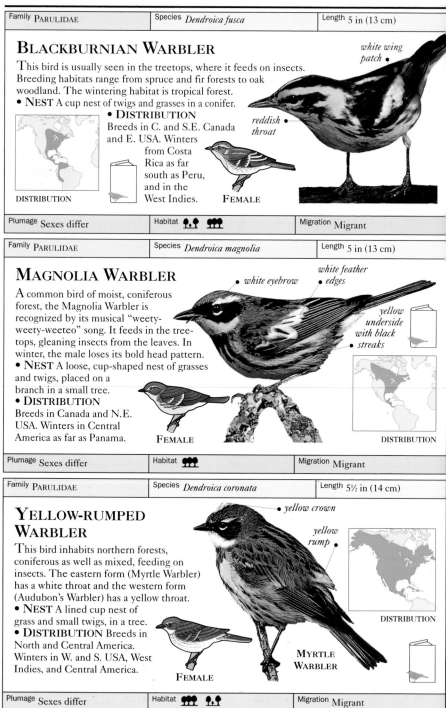

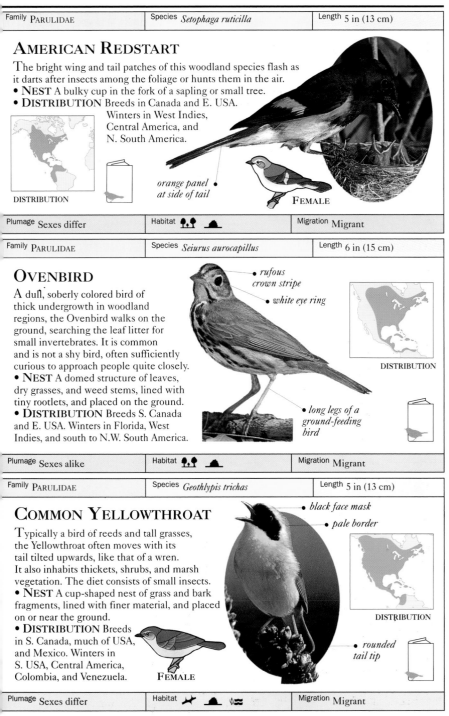

| Family PARULIDAE | Species *Setophaga ruticilla* | Length 5 in (13 cm) |

AMERICAN REDSTART

The bright wing and tail patches of this woodland species flash as it darts after insects among the foliage or hunts them in the air.
• **NEST** A bulky cup in the fork of a sapling or small tree.
• **DISTRIBUTION** Breeds in Canada and E. USA. Winters in West Indies, Central America, and N. South America.

DISTRIBUTION

orange panel at side of tail

FEMALE

| Plumage Sexes differ | Habitat | Migration Migrant |

| Family PARULIDAE | Species *Seiurus aurocapillus* | Length 6 in (15 cm) |

OVENBIRD

A dull, soberly colored bird of thick undergrowth in woodland regions, the Ovenbird walks on the ground, searching the leaf litter for small invertebrates. It is common and is not a shy bird, often sufficiently curious to approach people quite closely.
• **NEST** A domed structure of leaves, dry grasses, and weed stems, lined with tiny rootlets, and placed on the ground.
• **DISTRIBUTION** Breeds S. Canada and E. USA. Winters in Florida, West Indies, and south to N.W. South America.

rufous crown stripe
white eye ring

DISTRIBUTION

long legs of a ground-feeding bird

| Plumage Sexes alike | Habitat | Migration Migrant |

| Family PARULIDAE | Species *Geothlypis trichas* | Length 5 in (13 cm) |

COMMON YELLOWTHROAT

Typically a bird of reeds and tall grasses, the Yellowthroat often moves with its tail tilted upwards, like that of a wren. It also inhabits thickets, shrubs, and marsh vegetation. The diet consists of small insects.
• **NEST** A cup-shaped nest of grass and bark fragments, lined with finer material, and placed on or near the ground.
• **DISTRIBUTION** Breeds in S. Canada, much of USA, and Mexico. Winters in S. USA, Central America, Colombia, and Venezuela.

black face mask
pale border

DISTRIBUTION

rounded tail tip

FEMALE

| Plumage Sexes differ | Habitat | Migration Migrant |

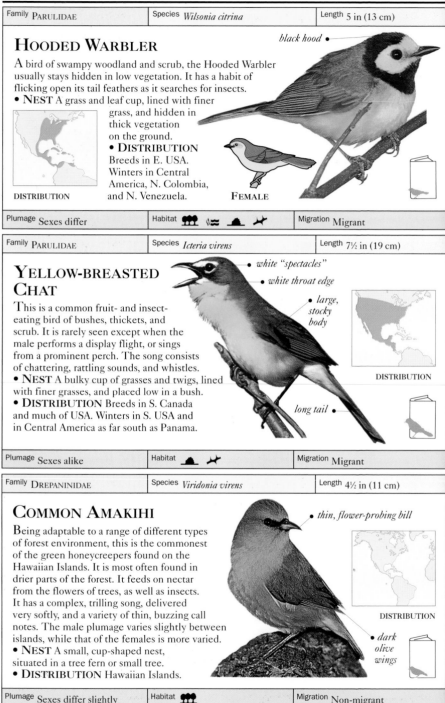

Family PARULIDAE	Species *Wilsonia citrina*	Length 5 in (13 cm)

HOODED WARBLER

black hood •

A bird of swampy woodland and scrub, the Hooded Warbler usually stays hidden in low vegetation. It has a habit of flicking open its tail feathers as it searches for insects.
• **NEST** A grass and leaf cup, lined with finer grass, and hidden in thick vegetation on the ground.
• **DISTRIBUTION** Breeds in E. USA. Winters in Central America, N. Colombia, and N. Venezuela.

DISTRIBUTION

FEMALE

Plumage Sexes differ	Habitat	Migration Migrant

Family PARULIDAE	Species *Icteria virens*	Length 7½ in (19 cm)

YELLOW-BREASTED CHAT

• *white "spectacles"*
• *white throat edge*
• *large, stocky body*

This is a common fruit- and insect-eating bird of bushes, thickets, and scrub. It is rarely seen except when the male performs a display flight, or sings from a prominent perch. The song consists of chattering, rattling sounds, and whistles.
• **NEST** A bulky cup of grasses and twigs, lined with finer grasses, and placed low in a bush.
• **DISTRIBUTION** Breeds in S. Canada and much of USA. Winters in S. USA and in Central America as far south as Panama.

DISTRIBUTION

long tail •

Plumage Sexes alike	Habitat	Migration Migrant

Family DREPANINIDAE	Species *Viridonia virens*	Length 4½ in (11 cm)

COMMON AMAKIHI

• *thin, flower-probing bill*

Being adaptable to a range of different types of forest environment, this is the commonest of the green honeycreepers found on the Hawaiian Islands. It is most often found in drier parts of the forest. It feeds on nectar from the flowers of trees, as well as insects. It has a complex, trilling song, delivered very softly, and a variety of thin, buzzing call notes. The male plumage varies slightly between islands, while that of the females is more varied.
• **NEST** A small, cup-shaped nest, situated in a tree fern or small tree.
• **DISTRIBUTION** Hawaiian Islands.

DISTRIBUTION

• *dark olive wings*

Plumage Sexes differ slightly	Habitat	Migration Non-migrant

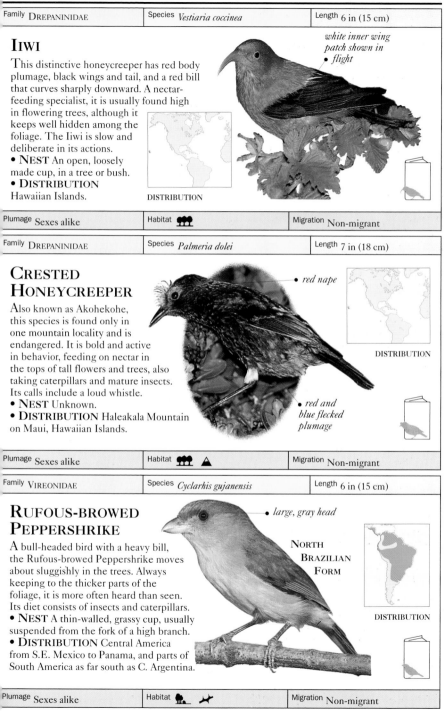

Family DREPANINIDAE	Species *Vestiaria coccinea*	Length 6 in (15 cm)

IIWI

This distinctive honeycreeper has red body plumage, black wings and tail, and a red bill that curves sharply downward. A nectar-feeding specialist, it is usually found high in flowering trees, although it keeps well hidden among the foliage. The Iiwi is slow and deliberate in its actions.
• NEST An open, loosely made cup, in a tree or bush.
• DISTRIBUTION Hawaiian Islands.

white inner wing patch shown in flight

DISTRIBUTION

Plumage Sexes alike	Habitat	Migration Non-migrant

Family DREPANINIDAE	Species *Palmeria dolei*	Length 7 in (18 cm)

CRESTED HONEYCREEPER

Also known as Akohekohe, this species is found only in one mountain locality and is endangered. It is bold and active in behavior, feeding on nectar in the tops of tall flowers and trees, also taking caterpillars and mature insects. Its calls include a loud whistle.
• NEST Unknown.
• DISTRIBUTION Haleakala Mountain on Maui, Hawaiian Islands.

red nape

red and blue flecked plumage

DISTRIBUTION

Plumage Sexes alike	Habitat	Migration Non-migrant

Family VIREONIDAE	Species *Cyclarhis gujanensis*	Length 6 in (15 cm)

RUFOUS-BROWED PEPPERSHRIKE

A bull-headed bird with a heavy bill, the Rufous-browed Peppershrike moves about sluggishly in the trees. Always keeping to the thicker parts of the foliage, it is more often heard than seen. Its diet consists of insects and caterpillars.
• NEST A thin-walled, grassy cup, usually suspended from the fork of a high branch.
• DISTRIBUTION Central America from S.E. Mexico to Panama, and parts of South America as far south as C. Argentina.

large, gray head

NORTH BRAZILIAN FORM

DISTRIBUTION

Plumage Sexes alike	Habitat	Migration Non-migrant

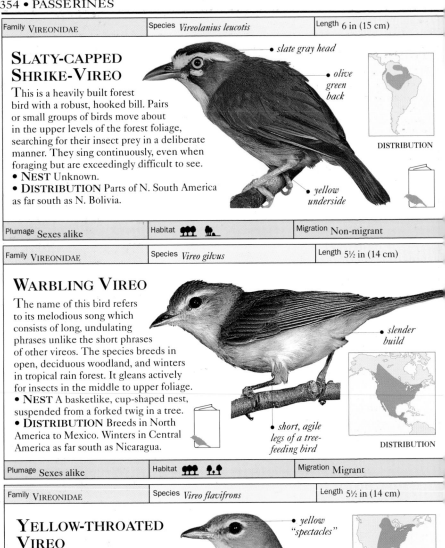

Family VIREONIDAE	Species *Vireolanius leucotis*	Length 6 in (15 cm)

SLATY-CAPPED SHRIKE-VIREO

This is a heavily built forest
bird with a robust, hooked bill. Pairs
or small groups of birds move about
in the upper levels of the forest foliage,
searching for their insect prey in a deliberate
manner. They sing continuously, even when
foraging but are exceedingly difficult to see.
• **NEST** Unknown.
• **DISTRIBUTION** Parts of N. South America
as far south as N. Bolivia.

• *slate gray head*

• *olive green back*

DISTRIBUTION

• *yellow underside*

Plumage Sexes alike	Habitat	Migration Non-migrant

Family VIREONIDAE	Species *Vireo gilvus*	Length 5½ in (14 cm)

WARBLING VIREO

The name of this bird refers
to its melodious song which
consists of long, undulating
phrases unlike the short phrases
of other vireos. The species breeds in
open, deciduous woodland, and winters
in tropical rain forest. It gleans actively
for insects in the middle to upper foliage.
• **NEST** A basketlike, cup-shaped nest,
suspended from a forked twig in a tree.
• **DISTRIBUTION** Breeds in North
America to Mexico. Winters in Central
America as far south as Nicaragua.

• *slender build*

• *short, agile legs of a tree-feeding bird*

DISTRIBUTION

Plumage Sexes alike	Habitat	Migration Migrant

Family VIREONIDAE	Species *Vireo flavifrons*	Length 5½ in (14 cm)

YELLOW-THROATED VIREO

A large vireo with bright yellow
eye patches and throat, this species is
common in woodland edges and thickets,
where it searches carefully for insects at
mid-height in the foliage. It is relatively
tame and will allow an observer to approach.
• **NEST** An intricate cup nest of grass and other
vegetable materials, hung from a branch.
• **DISTRIBUTION** Breeds in
S.E. Canada and E. USA. Winters
in C. America and N. South America.

• *yellow "spectacles"*

DISTRIBUTION

• *gray rump*

white wing bars

• *white outer tail feathers*

Plumage Sexes alike	Habitat	Migration Migrant

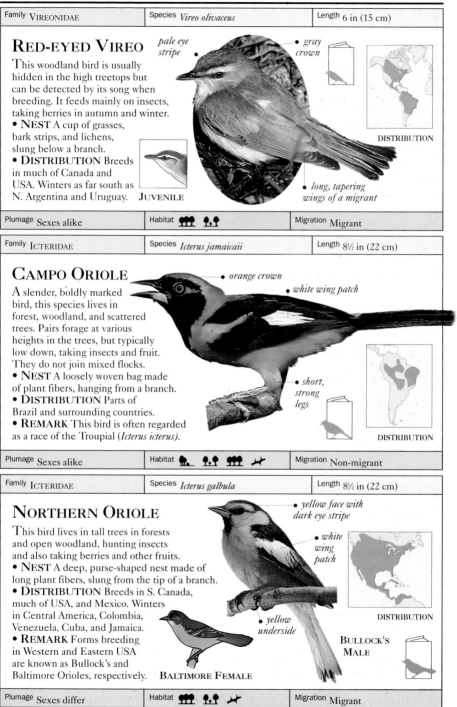

Family VIREONIDAE	Species *Vireo olivaceus*	Length 6 in (15 cm)

RED-EYED VIREO

pale eye stripe

gray crown

This woodland bird is usually hidden in the high treetops but can be detected by its song when breeding. It feeds mainly on insects, taking berries in autumn and winter.
• **NEST** A cup of grasses, bark strips, and lichens, slung below a branch.
• **DISTRIBUTION** Breeds in much of Canada and USA. Winters as far south as N. Argentina and Uruguay.

JUVENILE

DISTRIBUTION

long, tapering wings of a migrant

Plumage Sexes alike	Habitat	Migration Migrant

Family ICTERIDAE	Species *Icterus jamaicaii*	Length 8½ in (22 cm)

CAMPO ORIOLE

orange crown

white wing patch

A slender, boldly marked bird, this species lives in forest, woodland, and scattered trees. Pairs forage at various heights in the trees, but typically low down, taking insects and fruit. They do not join mixed flocks.
• **NEST** A loosely woven bag made of plant fibers, hanging from a branch.
• **DISTRIBUTION** Parts of Brazil and surrounding countries.
• **REMARK** This bird is often regarded as a race of the Troupial (*Icterus icterus*).

short, strong legs

DISTRIBUTION

Plumage Sexes alike	Habitat	Migration Non-migrant

Family ICTERIDAE	Species *Icterus galbula*	Length 8½ in (22 cm)

NORTHERN ORIOLE

yellow face with dark eye stripe

This bird lives in tall trees in forests and open woodland, hunting insects and also taking berries and other fruits.
• **NEST** A deep, purse-shaped nest made of long plant fibers, slung from the tip of a branch.
• **DISTRIBUTION** Breeds in S. Canada, much of USA, and Mexico. Winters in Central America, Colombia, Venezuela, Cuba, and Jamaica.
• **REMARK** Forms breeding in Western and Eastern USA are known as Bullock's and Baltimore Orioles, respectively.

white wing patch

yellow underside

DISTRIBUTION

BULLOCK'S MALE

BALTIMORE FEMALE

Plumage Sexes differ	Habitat	Migration Migrant

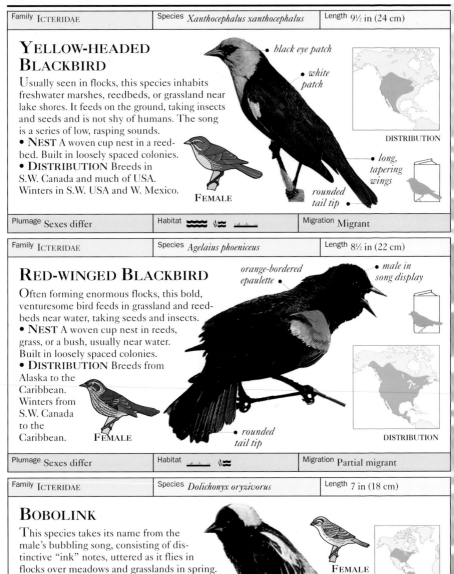

| Family ICTERIDAE | Species *Xanthocephalus xanthocephalus* | Length 9½ in (24 cm) |

YELLOW-HEADED BLACKBIRD

Usually seen in flocks, this species inhabits freshwater marshes, reedbeds, or grassland near lake shores. It feeds on the ground, taking insects and seeds and is not shy of humans. The song is a series of low, rasping sounds.
• **NEST** A woven cup nest in a reed-bed. Built in loosely spaced colonies.
• **DISTRIBUTION** Breeds in S.W. Canada and much of USA. Winters in S.W. USA and W. Mexico.

black eye patch
white patch
long, tapering wings
rounded tail tip

FEMALE

DISTRIBUTION

| Plumage Sexes differ | Habitat 〰 〰 �⌉ | Migration Migrant |

| Family ICTERIDAE | Species *Agelaius phoeniceus* | Length 8½ in (22 cm) |

RED-WINGED BLACKBIRD

Often forming enormous flocks, this bold, venturesome bird feeds in grassland and reed-beds near water, taking seeds and insects.
• **NEST** A woven cup nest in reeds, grass, or a bush, usually near water. Built in loosely spaced colonies.
• **DISTRIBUTION** Breeds from Alaska to the Caribbean. Winters from S.W. Canada to the Caribbean.

orange-bordered epaulette
male in song display
rounded tail tip

FEMALE

DISTRIBUTION

| Plumage Sexes differ | Habitat ⌐industrial⌐ 〰 | Migration Partial migrant |

| Family ICTERIDAE | Species *Dolichonyx oryzivorus* | Length 7 in (18 cm) |

BOBOLINK

This species takes its name from the male's bubbling song, consisting of distinctive "ink" notes, uttered as it flies in flocks over meadows and grasslands in spring. The Bobolink is a bird of grassy areas, feeding mainly on the ground and taking weed seeds, grain, and insects and other invertebrates.
• **NEST** A cup-shaped nest constructed loosely of grasses and rootlets, placed at the foot of a tussock in dense, grassy vegetation.
• **DISTRIBUTION** Breeds in S. Canada and adjoining areas of USA. Winters in South America as far south as Argentina.

FEMALE

DISTRIBUTION

white rump and back
spiky tail tip

| Plumage Sexes differ | Habitat ⌐industrial⌐ ⛰ | Migration Migrant |

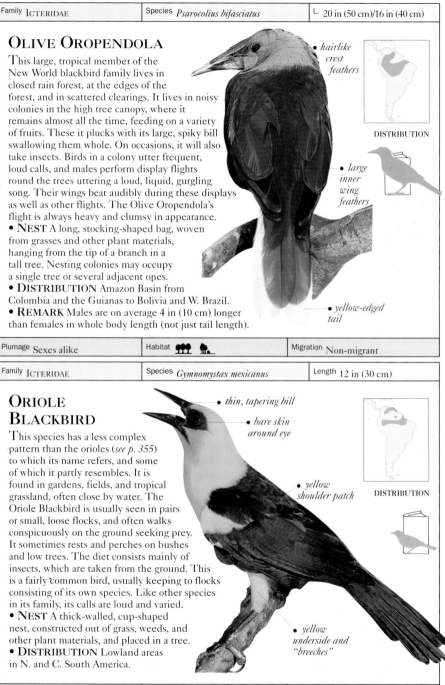

Family ICTERIDAE	Species *Psarocolius bifasciatus*	L. 20 in (50 cm)/16 in (40 cm)

OLIVE OROPENDOLA

This large, tropical member of the
New World blackbird family lives in
closed rain forest, at the edges of the
forest, and in scattered clearings. It lives in noisy
colonies in the high tree canopy, where it
remains almost all the time, feeding on a variety
of fruits. These it plucks with its large, spiky bill
swallowing them whole. On occasions, it will also
take insects. Birds in a colony utter frequent,
loud calls, and males perform display flights
round the trees uttering a loud, liquid, gurgling
song. Their wings beat audibly during these displays
as well as other flights. The Olive Oropendola's
flight is always heavy and clumsy in appearance.
• **NEST** A long, stocking-shaped bag, woven
from grasses and other plant materials,
hanging from the tip of a branch in a
tall tree. Nesting colonies may occupy
a single tree or several adjacent ones.
• **DISTRIBUTION** Amazon Basin from
Colombia and the Guianas to Bolivia and W. Brazil.
• **REMARK** Males are on average 4 in (10 cm) longer
than females in whole body length (not just tail length).

• *hairlike crest feathers*

• *large inner wing feathers*

• *yellow-edged tail*

DISTRIBUTION

Plumage Sexes alike	Habitat	Migration Non-migrant

Family ICTERIDAE	Species *Gymnomystax mexicanus*	Length 12 in (30 cm)

ORIOLE BLACKBIRD

This species has a less complex
pattern than the orioles (*see p. 355*)
to which its name refers, and some
of which it partly resembles. It is
found in gardens, fields, and tropical
grassland, often close by water. The
Oriole Blackbird is usually seen in pairs
or small, loose flocks, and often walks
conspicuously on the ground seeking prey.
It sometimes rests and perches on bushes
and low trees. The diet consists mainly of
insects, which are taken from the ground. This
is a fairly common bird, usually keeping to flocks
consisting of its own species. Like other species
in its family, its calls are loud and varied.
• **NEST** A thick-walled, cup-shaped
nest, constructed out of grass, weeds, and
other plant materials, and placed in a tree.
• **DISTRIBUTION** Lowland areas
in N. and C. South America.

• *thin, tapering bill*

• *bare skin around eye*

• *yellow shoulder patch*

DISTRIBUTION

• *yellow underside and "breeches"*

Plumage Sexes alike	Habitat	Migration Non-migrant

Family ICTERIDAE	Species *Sturnella neglecta*	Length 9½ in (24 cm)

WESTERN MEADOWLARK

With its streaky, brown upperparts and yellow underparts, the Western Meadowlark is a distinctive and familiar bird of grassland and farmland. Small flocks feed on the ground, while single birds are often seen perching on vantage points, such as fence posts. Meadowlarks have powerful, daggerlike beaks, which they use to work over the turf, picking up insects and other invertebrates.
• **NEST** A partially domed nest, made of grass and other plant materials, and placed on the ground in a concealed spot.
• **DISTRIBUTION** Breeds in W. and C. North America from S. Canada to C. Mexico. Winter range extends from S.W. Canada to C. Mexico.
• **REMARK**
The bubbling, fluty song contrasts with the whistling of the Eastern Meadowlark, which is similar in appearance. **WINTER PLUMAGE**

tapering head and bill

dark eye stripe

DISTRIBUTION

streaked back

Plumage Sexes alike	Habitat	Migration Partial migrant

Family ICTERIDAE	Species *Quiscalus quiscula*	Length 12½ in (32 cm)

COMMON GRACKLE

A conspicuous, glossy blackbird, this species occurs in a range of habitats including farmland and suburbs. It lives in flocks throughout the year, joining huge roosts of mixed bird species in winter, and feeds on invertebrates, seeds, fruit, and nuts.
• **NEST** A bulky, loose cup nest of grass and stems, usually placed low in a tree.
• **DISTRIBUTION** Breeds in C. and E. North America from Alberta as far south as Texas and Florida. Winters within the southern half of this range.

sharp, tapering bill

bronze tinge denotes eastern form

large, strong feet

broad, tapering wings

outer feathers of tail curve upward, making a concave upper surface

DISTRIBUTION

JUVENILE

Plumage Sexes alike	Habitat	Migration Partial migrant

Family ICTERIDAE	Species *Euphagus cyanocephalus*	Length 9 in (23 cm)

BREWER'S BLACKBIRD

This is a common, ground-feeding bird of farmland, roadsides, open grassland, and other open habitats. The male is a glossy blackbird with yellow eyes, while the female is dark brown above and lighter brown below. Brewer's Blackbird forages on the ground in large flocks, often in the company of other, similar species. Its diet consists of seeds, insects, and other invertebrates.

• **NEST** A cup-shaped nest made of twigs, lined with grass, and placed on the ground or in a bush or tree. Nests are built in loose colonies.

• **DISTRIBUTION** Breeds in S. Canada west of the Great Lakes, and in W. USA. Winters in N. America from S.W. Canada to Florida and C. Mexico.

• *purple gloss on head*

DISTRIBUTION

• *green gloss on body revealed as bird turns in light*

• *streamlined, slender build*

FEMALE *strong legs for foraging on the ground* •

Plumage Sexes differ	Habitat	Migration Migrant

Family ICTERIDAE	Species *Molothrus ater*	Length 7½ in (19 cm)

BROWN-HEADED COWBIRD

dull brown head •

Originally living in open woodland and natural grassland, this ground-feeding bird with a stout bill has adapted to farmland and suburban gardens. Flocks often form around livestock or wild herbivores such as bison, catching insects disturbed by, or attracted to, the grazing animals.

• **NEST** Parasitizes the nests of other passerines, including Yellow Warbler (*see p. 349*), Red-eyed Vireo (*p. 355*), and Song Sparrow (*p. 336*).

• **DISTRIBUTION** Breeds in most of North America. Winters from C. USA to Mexico.

• *short, conical bill*

• *glossy plumage on body*

DISTRIBUTION

tail is relatively short, with a blunt tip •

strong, tapering wings •

JUVENILE

• *long legs and strong feet of a ground forager*

Plumage Sexes differ	Habitat	Migration Migrant

Family FRINGILLIDAE	Species *Fringilla coelebs*	Length 6 in (15 cm)

CHAFFINCH

A woodland bird that has adapted
to gardens, the Chaffinch feeds
on the ground, often forming flocks in
winter, taking seeds, fruit, and insects.
• **NEST** A cup nest of moss, in the
fork of a tree or shrub.
• **DISTRIBUTION**
Europe, N. Africa,
Middle East, Siberia.
Some populations
winter in N. Africa
and India.

FEMALE

pale wing bars

pink breast

longish legs

DISTRIBUTION

Plumage Sexes differ	Habitat	Migration Partial migrant

Family FRINGILLIDAE	Species *Serinus serinus*	Length 4¾ in (12 cm)

EUROPEAN SERIN

This streaked, green-and-yellow finch is
inconspicuous for most of the year. In spring,
however, the male performs a downward-
spiralling display flight with an exuberant,
fizzing song. European Serins forage
for small seeds on the ground.
• **NEST** A small cup nest made of grass,
roots, and moss, bound with spiderwebs,
lined with hair and vegetable down,
and placed in a tree or shrub.
• **DISTRIBUTION** Much of
continental Europe, Mediterranean
islands, N. Africa, and Turkey.

yellow face pattern

small bill

short legs

yellow tail edge

FEMALE

DISTRIBUTION

Plumage Sexes differ	Habitat	Migration Migrant

Family FRINGILLIDAE	Species *Carduelis pinus*	Length 5 in (13 cm)

PINE SISKIN

A finch of coniferous forests, this active, acrobatic bird can feed upside down,
extracting seeds from cones and also feeding on alder and birch catkins.
Flocks of up to several hundred Pine Siskins feed in trees
and on herbaceous plants, taking buds, tender leaves,
and insects, as well as seeds.
• **NEST** A cup nest made
of grass, twigs, and moss,
lined with down,
fur, and feathers, and
placed in a coniferous tree.
• **DISTRIBUTION** Breeds in North America
and in the mountains of Mexico. In winter, many
populations migrate southward within this range.

DISTRIBUTION

yellow flash on wings

Plumage Sexes alike	Habitat	Migration Partial migrant

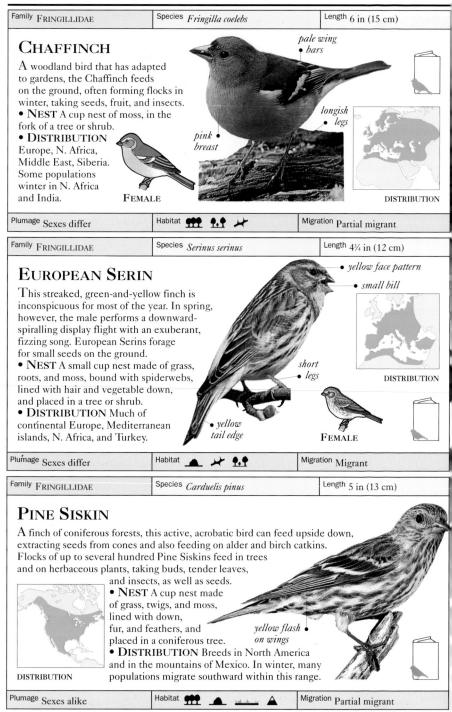

Family FRINGILLIDAE	Species *Carduelis tristis*	Length 5 in (13 cm)

AMERICAN GOLDFINCH

The dashing, black-and-yellow breeding plumage of the male is replaced in winter by drab brown. American Goldfinches form large flocks in winter. Their diet consists of weed seeds, insects, and buds.
• **NEST** An open cup nest of bark, grass, and plant stems, placed in a fork of a tree.
• **DISTRIBUTION** S. Canada and much of USA. Northern populations migrate south as far as N. Mexico in winter.

bright yellow summer plumage

white pattern on wings

DISTRIBUTION

FEMALE

Plumage Sexes differ	Habitat	Migration Partial migrant

Family FRINGILLIDAE	Species *Carduelis chloris*	Length 5½ in (14 cm)

EUROPEAN GREENFINCH

This bird is often seen in gardens and farmland. Males perform a butterflylike display flight above the trees in spring. Their musical song alternates with long, harsh notes. Their diet consists of seeds, berries, and insects.
• **NEST** A bulky cup nest of grass stems and other plant materials, sited in a bush or tree.
• **DISTRIBUTION** From Europe and N. Africa to W. Asia. Some southward migration within this range in winter.

FEMALE

dull olive plumage

yellow wing bar

DISTRIBUTION

yellow tail edge

Plumage Sexes differ	Habitat	Migration Partial migrant

Family FRINGILLIDAE	Species *Carduelis carduelis*	Length 4¾ in (12 cm)

EURASIAN GOLDFINCH

A colorful finch that flocks in autumn, this bird frequents open spaces, taking seeds from thistle heads or the ground.
• **NEST** A cup nest made of plant materials, on a horizontal tree branch.
• **DISTRIBUTION** Europe, N. Africa, Middle East, and across C. Asia.

yellow wing bar

pale rump shows in flight

DISTRIBUTION

JUVENILE

forked tail

Plumage Sexes alike	Habitat	Migration Non-migrant

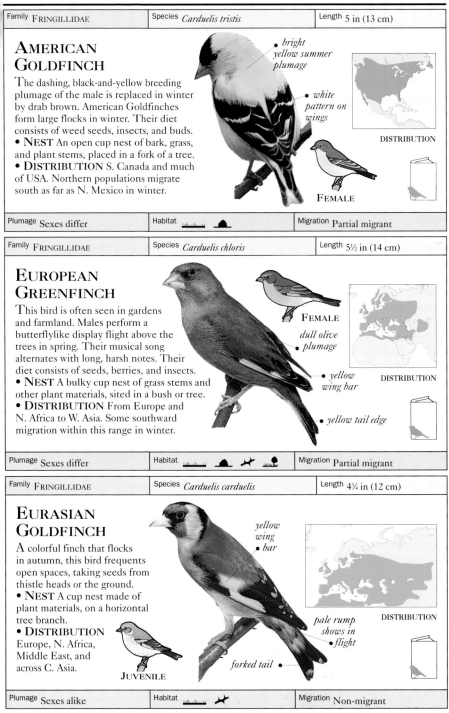

Family FRINGILLIDAE	Species *Carduelis flammea*	Length 4¾ in (12 cm)

COMMON REDPOLL

red cap

A tree-dwelling finch, the Common Redpoll feeds among twigs and leaves, sometimes upside down, and sometimes clinging to catkins of silver birch. The diet consists mainly of seeds and insects.
• **NEST** A cup nest of twigs and grasses, lined with finer materials, placed in a bush or tree.
• **DISTRIBUTION** Breeds in N. Canada and USA, S. Greenland, Iceland, and most of Eurasia. Some southward movement in winter.

strong legs for clinging

DISTRIBUTION

FEMALE

Plumage Sexes differ	Habitat	Migration Partial migrant

Family FRINGILLIDAE	Species *Carduelis cannabina*	Length 5½ in (14 cm)

EURASIAN LINNET

red spot on forehead

gray head

Renowned for its sweet "twangy" song, this species is a finch of open places, particularly gorse-covered heaths. Linnets become sociable in autumn and form huge, wandering flocks, which often move south. They feed mainly on seeds and sometimes on insects.
• **NEST** A cup nest of grass and moss, lined and placed low in a bush or tree.
• **DISTRIBUTION** Most of Europe and N. Africa; parts of the Middle East and C. Asia. Some southward movement in winter.

DISTRIBUTION

white tail edge

FEMALE

Plumage Sexes differ	Habitat	Migration Partial migrant

Family FRINGILLIDAE	Species *Rhodopechys obsoleta*	Length 5½ in (14 cm)

DESERT FINCH

sandy pink plumage

This bird inhabits steppe (arid grassland) and semidesert, its soft, plain colors merging with the bare landscape. Pink, black, and white markings on wing and tail show in flight. Usually seen in pairs, it is not shy and will allow an observer to approach. It feeds on or near the ground, taking seeds and buds.
• **NEST** A cup-shaped nest made of weed stems, grass, and twigs, lined with wool or feathers, and located in a bush or low tree.
• **DISTRIBUTION** Isolated areas in the Middle East, Iran, N.W. Pakistan, C. Asia, and W. China.

DISTRIBUTION

black-and-white tail

Plumage Sexes differ slightly	Habitat	Migration Partial migrant

| Family FRINGILLIDAE | Species *Carpodacus mexicanus* | Length 6 in (15 cm) |

HOUSE FINCH

Having learned to exploit human
dwellings as a source of food and
nest sites, this species is common in
villages and suburbs. Winter flocks
feed on seeds and orchard fruit.
• **NEST** A cup nest of grasses and
other soft materials, in a bush
or on a post or building.
• **DISTRIBUTION**
From S.W. Canada to Mexico.
Introduced populations in
S.E. Canada and E. USA.

• broad,
red eyebrow
stripe

red
rump •

DISTRIBUTION

• short legs

FEMALE

| Plumage Sexes differ | Habitat | Migration Non-migrant |

| Family FRINGILLIDAE | Species *Carpodacus roseus* | Length 6¼ in (16 cm) |

PALLAS' ROSEFINCH

A ground-feeding finch of northern
coniferous forests, this bird is partly
nomadic, moving about in search of
suitable conditions for breeding. In
winter it forms small flocks that
travel about, feeding on seeds
and sometimes on insects.
• **NEST** Unknown.
• **DISTRIBUTION**
E. Siberia and
N. Mongolia. Some
populations migrate into
China, Korea, and Japan.

pale wing
• bars

DISTRIBUTION

pink rump •

shallow •
tail fork

FEMALE

| Plumage Sexes differ | Habitat | Migration Partial migrant/nomadic |

| Family FRINGILLIDAE | Species *Pinicola enucleator* | Length 9 in (23 cm) |

PINE GROSBEAK

A large finch with two wing bars, this bird has a capacious
bill adapted for eating buds. Other foods include seeds,
flowers, insects, and berries. It lives in pairs when breeding,
and flocks roam about in search of food during the winter.

FEMALE

• **NEST** A cup nest of twigs,
moss, and heather, lined and
placed high in a conifer.
• **DISTRIBUTION** Northern
forest zone of North
America, Europe, and
Siberia. Some birds
move south within
this range in winter.

• *white
feather
edges*

DISTRIBUTION

| Plumage Sexes differ | Habitat | Migration Partial migrant |

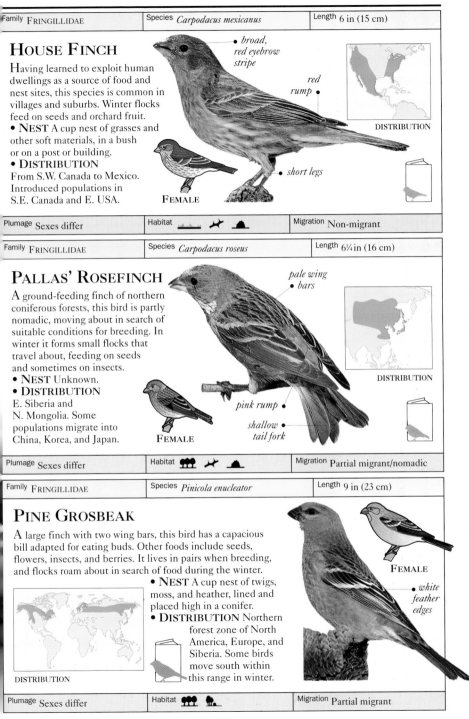

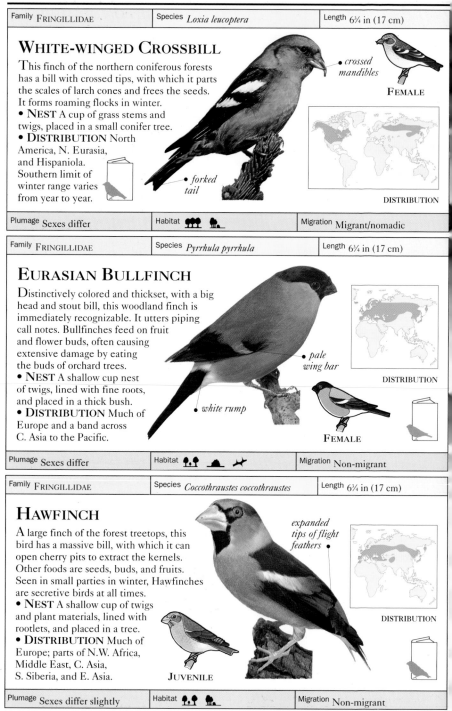

Family FRINGILLIDAE	Species *Loxia leucoptera*	Length 6¾ in (17 cm)

WHITE-WINGED CROSSBILL

This finch of the northern coniferous forests has a bill with crossed tips, with which it parts the scales of larch cones and frees the seeds. It forms roaming flocks in winter.
• **NEST** A cup of grass stems and twigs, placed in a small conifer tree.
• **DISTRIBUTION** North America, N. Eurasia, and Hispaniola. Southern limit of winter range varies from year to year.

crossed mandibles

FEMALE

forked tail

DISTRIBUTION

Plumage Sexes differ	Habitat	Migration Migrant/nomadic

Family FRINGILLIDAE	Species *Pyrrhula pyrrhula*	Length 6¾ in (17 cm)

EURASIAN BULLFINCH

Distinctively colored and thickset, with a big head and stout bill, this woodland finch is immediately recognizable. It utters piping call notes. Bullfinches feed on fruit and flower buds, often causing extensive damage by eating the buds of orchard trees.
• **NEST** A shallow cup nest of twigs, lined with fine roots, and placed in a thick bush.
• **DISTRIBUTION** Much of Europe and a band across C. Asia to the Pacific.

pale wing bar

DISTRIBUTION

white rump

FEMALE

Plumage Sexes differ	Habitat	Migration Non-migrant

Family FRINGILLIDAE	Species *Coccothraustes coccothraustes*	Length 6¾ in (17 cm)

HAWFINCH

A large finch of the forest treetops, this bird has a massive bill, with which it can open cherry pits to extract the kernels. Other foods are seeds, buds, and fruits. Seen in small parties in winter, Hawfinches are secretive birds at all times.
• **NEST** A shallow cup of twigs and plant materials, lined with rootlets, and placed in a tree.
• **DISTRIBUTION** Much of Europe; parts of N.W. Africa, Middle East, C. Asia, S. Siberia, and E. Asia.

expanded tips of flight feathers

DISTRIBUTION

JUVENILE

Plumage Sexes differ slightly	Habitat	Migration Non-migrant

| Family FRINGILLIDAE | Species *Eophona personata* | Length 9 in (23 cm) |

JAPANESE GROSBEAK

This large, migratory finch is common in woodland, where it is seen in pairs in the breeding season and in small flocks in winter. Its diet consists of pine nuts, seeds of berries, and insects.
• **NEST** A shallow cup nest made of twigs and lined with finer material, placed in a tree.
• **DISTRIBUTION** Breeds in S.E. Siberia, N. China, and N. Japan. Winters in S. Japan and C. China.

black mask
massive bill
blue wing patch
white wing bar

DISTRIBUTION

JUVENILE

| Plumage Sexes differ slightly | Habitat | Migration Migrant |

| Family FRINGILLIDAE | Species *Hesperiphona vespertina* | Length 8 in (20 cm) |

EVENING GROSBEAK

The black-and-yellow plumage of the male, and the white wing patches of both sexes, identify this finch. It is a woodland bird that visits birdfeeders in winter. Its diet ranges from insect larvae to seeds.
• **NEST** A cup nest of twigs, placed in a tree fork.
• **DISTRIBUTION** Breeds in coniferous zone of S. Canada, W. USA, and south to Mexico. Some birds winter in E. and C. USA.

yellow brow
massive bill
stocky build
short tail

FEMALE

DISTRIBUTION

| Plumage Sexes differ | Habitat | Migration Partial migrant |

| Family ESTRILDIDAE | Species *Uraeginthus ianthinogaster* | Length 5½ in (14 cm) |

PURPLE GRENADIER

In spite of its gaudy colors, this is a secretive bird, living in arid, tropical scrubland. Small flocks feed on the ground, close to cover, taking seeds and insects. The birds utter quiet, indistinct call notes, often heard as they fly past.
• **NEST** A loose, round nest of grass with a side entrance, lined with feathers, low in a shrub.
• **DISTRIBUTION** E. Africa from Ethiopia and Somalia as far south as Tanzania.

purple rump

FEMALE

long, tapering tail

DISTRIBUTION

| Plumage Sexes differ | Habitat | Migration Non-migrant |

| Family ESTRILDIDAE | Species *Estrilda astrild* | Length 4¼ in (12 cm) |

COMMON WAXBILL

Typically a bird of long grass in open country, sometimes near water, this is one of the commonest species of African finch. Small flocks feed on the ground or on standing grass, taking seeds (mainly of grasses) and sometimes small insects.
• **NEST** An oval structure with a tubular side entrance, made of grass and lined with soft feathers or grass flowers, in a grass clump or low in a bush.
• **DISTRIBUTION** Africa south of the Sahara. Small populations introduced elsewhere in the world.

scarlet • eye stripe

DISTRIBUTION

• *finely barred underside*

• *feet can grip several grass stems at once*

| Plumage Sexes alike | Habitat | Migration Non-migrant |

| Family ESTRILDIDAE | Species *Amandava subflava* | Length 4 in (9 cm) |

ZEBRA WAXBILL

The red rump of this grassland finch is conspicuous as it feeds among grass stems, taking seeds, insects, and soft shoots. Flocks often visit water to drink and bathe in the early afternoon.
• **NEST** An oval nest of grass, at ground level or slightly above. Often uses old nests of other bird species.
• **DISTRIBUTION** Africa south of the Sahara.
• **REMARK** Also known as the Orange-breasted Waxbill.

FEMALE

• *red rump*

• *dark bars on flank*

DISTRIBUTION

| Plumage Sexes differ | Habitat | Migration Non-migrant |

| Family ESTRILDIDAE | Species *Neochmia temporalis* | Length 4¼ in (12 cm) |

RED-BROWED FINCH

conspicuous red stripe •

This bird has a bouncy flight and is common along forest edges, in open, grassy areas with shrubs, and even in town gardens within its range. The Red-browed Finch is seen either in pairs or in small, fussy flocks, feeding among grasses and low plants and taking small seeds.
• **NEST** A horizontal, bottle-shaped nest with an entrance tube, made of grass stems, lined and placed in a tree or bush.
• **DISTRIBUTION** E. Australia. Introduced populations in S.W. Australia and S. Pacific (on Society Islands and Marquesas Islands).

DISTRIBUTION

| Plumage Sexes alike | Habitat | Migration Non-migrant |

Family ESTRILDIDAE	Species *Taeniopygia guttata*	Length 4¾ in (12 cm)

ZEBRA FINCH

So named because of its black-and-white, barred tail, this species lives in semidesert areas near water, feeding on seeds. It is seen in lively flocks which utter short, nasal notes.
• **NEST** A dome of grass with a side entrance, in a bush or hollow branch.
• **DISTRIBUTION** E. Indonesia and much of Australia.

DISTRIBUTION

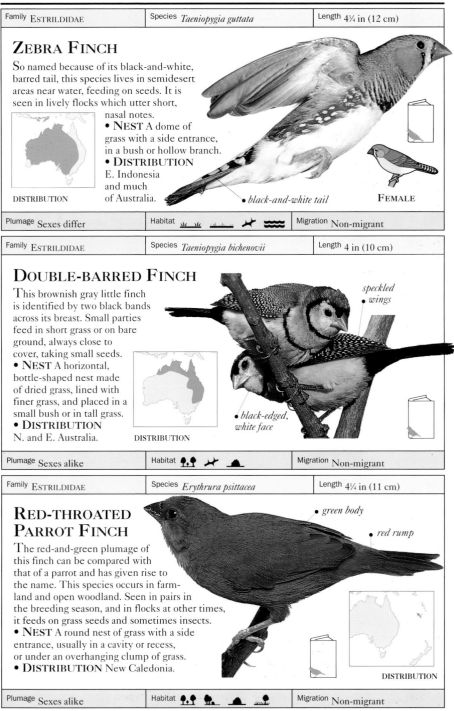

• *black-and-white tail*

FEMALE

Plumage Sexes differ	Habitat	Migration Non-migrant

Family ESTRILDIDAE	Species *Taeniopygia bichenovii*	Length 4 in (10 cm)

DOUBLE-BARRED FINCH

This brownish gray little finch is identified by two black bands across its breast. Small parties feed in short grass or on bare ground, always close to cover, taking small seeds.
• **NEST** A horizontal, bottle-shaped nest made of dried grass, lined with finer grass, and placed in a small bush or in tall grass.
• **DISTRIBUTION** N. and E. Australia.

DISTRIBUTION

speckled • *wings*

• *black-edged, white face*

Plumage Sexes alike	Habitat	Migration Non-migrant

Family ESTRILDIDAE	Species *Erythrura psittacea*	Length 4¼ in (11 cm)

RED-THROATED PARROT FINCH

The red-and-green plumage of this finch can be compared with that of a parrot and has given rise to the name. This species occurs in farmland and open woodland. Seen in pairs in the breeding season, and in flocks at other times, it feeds on grass seeds and sometimes insects.
• **NEST** A round nest of grass with a side entrance, usually in a cavity or recess, or under an overhanging clump of grass.
• **DISTRIBUTION** New Caledonia.

• *green body*

• *red rump*

DISTRIBUTION

Plumage Sexes alike	Habitat	Migration Non-migrant

| Family ESTRILDIDAE | Species *Lonchura griseicapilla* | Length 4¼ in (12 cm) |

GRAY-HEADED SILVERBILL

This common African finch is typically
found in tropical grassland with thornbushes
and in thickets along river valleys. It feeds
on seeds of grasses and other plants. Small
flocks come to waterholes regularly in the
afternoons to drink and bathe. Birds are often
seen perching and roosting in huddled groups.
• **NEST** A large, untidy, domed structure made
of grass heads, lined with feathers, and placed
at the end of a branch in a moderately high tree.
• **DISTRIBUTION** N.E. Africa from Sudan
and Ethiopia to Tanzania.

• *white spots on cheek*

DISTRIBUTION

rounded tail tip •

| Plumage Sexes alike | Habitat | Migration Non-migrant |

| Family ESTRILDIDAE | Species *Padda oryzivora* | Length 6¼ in (16 cm) |

JAVA SPARROW

A heavily built but sleek-looking seed-eater,
the Java Sparrow lives in tropical grassland and
farmland. It feeds on grass seeds and cultivated
cereals, and on occasional insects. Large flocks visit
rice fields in the nonbreeding season.
• **NEST** A bell-shaped, domed
structure, made of woven grass,
usually under the eaves of a building.
• **DISTRIBUTION** Java and Bali.
Introduced in the tropics worldwide.
• **REMARK** This is a popular cage bird, particularly in
Asia. Its highly sociable nature makes it an easy bird to breed
in captive conditions. Escaped populations occur in some countries.

• *white cheek patch*

DISTRIBUTION

• *pale pink flanks*

| Plumage Sexes alike | Habitat | Migration Non-migrant |

| Family ESTRILDIDAE | Species *Amadina fasciata* | Length 4¼ in (12 cm) |

CUT-THROAT

This is a perky little finch
of tropical grassland and drier
woodland regions that feeds
on seeds and insects. Only
the adult males possess the red throat
patch referred to in the name. Cut-
throats form pairs during the breeding
season and associate together in lively,
chirping flocks at other times of the year.
• **NEST** Makes a spherical nest of grass
and feathers. Alternatively, it may take
over an old nest of a sparrow or weaver.
• **DISTRIBUTION** Africa south of the Sahara.

• *"scaly" head pattern*
spotted wings •

FEMALE

DISTRIBUTION

• *chestnut belly patch*

| Plumage Sexes differ | Habitat | Migration Non-migrant |

Family ESTRILDIDAE	Species *Chloebia gouldiae*	Length 5 in (13 cm)

GOULDIAN FINCH

F ew species of bird in the world can rival this bird for sheer splendor of color. It is a seed-eater of tropical open woodland and scrub, feeding in small flocks on the ground.

• **NEST** A loosely built dome of grass, usually in a hollow in the ground.
• **DISTRIBUTION** N. Australia.
• **REMARK** There are three color phases (*see p. 13*): Black-headed, Red-headed, and the rare Yellow-headed phase.

DISTRIBUTION

blue-bordered face

RED-HEADED   YELLOW-HEADED

forked tail
tip

Plumage Sexes differ slightly	Habitat	Migration Non-migrant

Family PLOCEIDAE	Species *Vidua regia*	L. 12 in (30 cm)/5 in (13 cm)

SHAFT-TAILED WHYDAH

An inhabitant of extensive grasslands in the subtropics, this bird forages on the ground for fallen seeds. It does this with an unusual hopping movement, in which it scratches the ground while jumping up with both feet. Early in the breeding season, it is seen in small parties in which males outnumber females. The males have long tails, which they show off in competitive songflights to attract females. Once the males have ceased to display, the long tail is shed and a new plumage is grown, resembling that of the female. When breeding is over, the birds gather and feed in large flocks, which are seen roosting in tall trees.
• **NEST** This bird makes no nest, but fosters out the care of its young by laying eggs, cuckoo fashion, in nests of Violet-eared Waxbills (*Uraeginthus granatina*).The young whydahs resemble young waxbills in mouth markings and in their calls, and the nestlings of both species are reared together by the waxbills.
• **DISTRIBUTION** Parts of southern Africa.

male's elaborate tail is present only during the early stages of breeding

expanded tail tips

golden-buff breast

red legs and feet

four elongated tail shafts

FEMALE

DISTRIBUTION

Plumage Sexes differ	Habitat	Migration Non-migrant

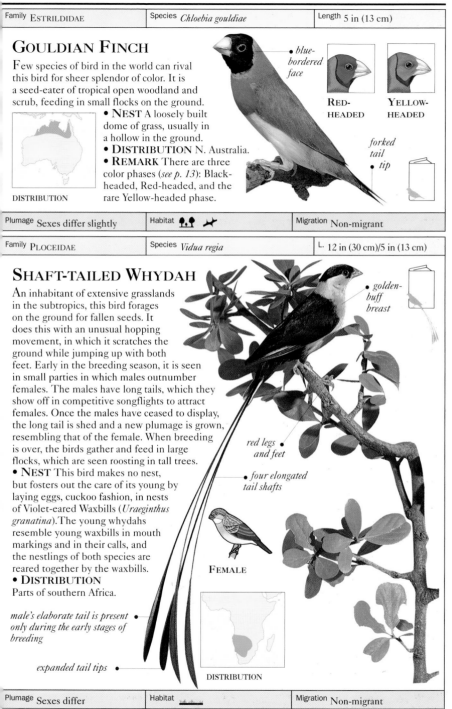

Family PASSERIDAE	Species *Passer domesticus*	Length 6 in (15 cm)

HOUSE SPARROW

This species evolved as a seed-eater but now lives in close association with man. Its ability to feed on anything from worms and fruit to kitchen scraps has enabled it to flourish in countries far beyond its original range.

• **NEST** An untidy nest of grass and other materials, often on buildings.

• **DISTRIBUTION** Originally Eurasia, N. Africa, Middle East. Introduced in many other countries.

gray crown

DISTRIBUTION

FEMALE

Plumage Sexes differ	Habitat	Migration Partial migrant

Family PASSERIDAE	Species *Montifringilla nivalis*	Length 6¾ in (17 cm)

WHITE-WINGED SNOWFINCH

Inhabiting alpine meadows and barren, rocky crags and screes up as high as the snow line, the Snow Finch feeds mainly on seeds.

• **NEST** A bulky cup nest made of grasses, leaves, hairs, and feathers, and situated in a rock crevice or wall.

• **DISTRIBUTION** Isolated areas in mountain ranges in S. Europe, Turkey, Iran, W. Mongolia, C. Asia, and Himalayan region.

gray head

WING PATCH

DISTRIBUTION

black-and-white tail

Plumage Sexes alike	Habitat	Migration Non-migrant

Family PLOCEIDAE	Species *Sporopipes frontalis*	Length 4½ in (11 cm)

SPECKLE-FRONTED WEAVER

Tame and confiding, this grassland bird is seen in small flocks that feed on the ground, mainly eating grass seeds. At dusk, groups of three or four birds gather to roost, packed closely together on tree branches, or sometimes in thin-roofed "nests," constructed only for roosting. In flight, birds utter a pleasant contact call. The song is rolling and musical and is interspersed with chirping notes, uttered particularly when taking flight, to alert other birds.

• **NEST** A hollow ball woven out of dry grass, with an entrance tube at the side, placed in a tree.

• **DISTRIBUTION** Tropical Africa, from the southern Sahara through Ethiopia to Kenya.

speckled forehead

rufous nape

DISTRIBUTION

pale feather edges

Plumage Sexes alike	Habitat	Migration Non-migrant

| Family PLOCEIDAE | Species *Ploceus ocularis* | Length 6¼ in (16 cm) |

SPECTACLED WEAVER

Living in scrub, thickets, and riverside forests, and
spreading into farms and suburban gardens, this shy
species rarely emerges from cover. Pairs creep up and
down stems, foraging for their prey of insects, spiders,
and millipedes, and also taking nectar, seeds, and fruit.
Males hang upside down from the nest in their display.
• **NEST** A rounded, finely woven
nest, suspended from a twig over
water, with a long entrance
tube hanging down below.
• **DISTRIBUTION** Parts of
Africa south of the Sahara.

pale eye in black streak

olive green back

DISTRIBUTION

FEMALE

| Plumage Sexes differ | Habitat | Migration Non-migrant |

| Family PLOCEIDAE | Species *Ploceus cucullatus* | Length 6¾ in (17 cm) |

VILLAGE WEAVER

black face mask

Africa's commonest weaver, this
bird forms colonies in trees, often
near villages. It feeds on insects
and seeds. Males display by hanging
below the nest, fluttering their wings.
• **NEST** An oval nest of reeds, sedges,
and grasses, with a nest chamber on one side
and an entrance chamber on the other, with
a vertical entrance tube hanging below.
• **DISTRIBUTION** Much of Africa
south of the Sahara, except in desert areas.

FEMALE

yellow feather edges

golden yellow underside

DISTRIBUTION

| Plumage Sexes differ | Habitat | Migration Non-migrant |

| Family PLOCEIDAE | Species *Quelea cardinalis* | Length 4¼ in (11 cm) |

CARDINAL QUELEA

This bird is gregarious, sometimes
forming nomadic flocks. It breeds in large
colonies in dense stands of grass and
swamps and feeds on small seeds. The
male sings from the top of a tall reed,
fluffing out his plumage, quivering
his wings, and jerking his fanned tail.
• **NEST** A compactly woven nest made
of grass, with an entrance at the top on
one side, tied between upright grass stems.
• **DISTRIBUTION** Kenya to Mozambique.
• **REMARK** A relative of the Common
Quelea, which occurs in million-strong flocks.

DISTRIBUTION

FEMALE

| Plumage Sexes differ | Habitat | Migration Partial migrant/nomadic |

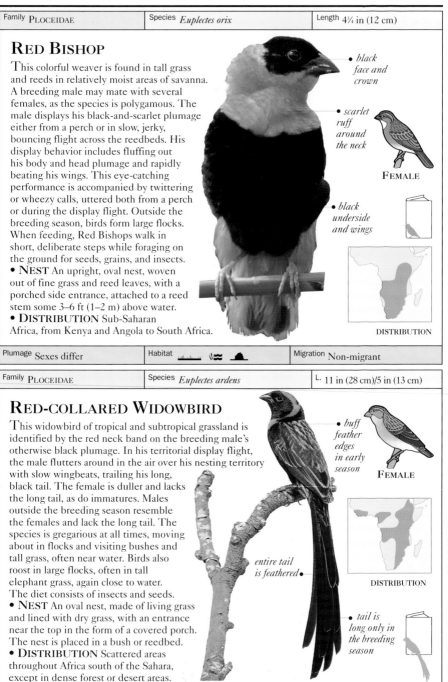

Family PLOCEIDAE	Species *Euplectes orix*	Length 4¼ in (12 cm)

RED BISHOP

This colorful weaver is found in tall grass and reeds in relatively moist areas of savanna. A breeding male may mate with several females, as the species is polygamous. The male displays his black-and-scarlet plumage either from a perch or in slow, jerky, bouncing flight across the reedbeds. His display behavior includes fluffing out his body and head plumage and rapidly beating his wings. This eye-catching performance is accompanied by twittering or wheezy calls, uttered both from a perch or during the display flight. Outside the breeding season, birds form large flocks. When feeding, Red Bishops walk in short, deliberate steps while foraging on the ground for seeds, grains, and insects.
• NEST An upright, oval nest, woven out of fine grass and reed leaves, with a porched side entrance, attached to a reed stem some 3–6 ft (1–2 m) above water.
• DISTRIBUTION Sub-Saharan Africa, from Kenya and Angola to South Africa.

• *black face and crown*

• *scarlet ruff around the neck*

FEMALE

• *black underside and wings*

DISTRIBUTION

Plumage Sexes differ	Habitat	Migration Non-migrant

Family PLOCEIDAE	Species *Euplectes ardens*	L. 11 in (28 cm)/5 in (13 cm)

RED-COLLARED WIDOWBIRD

This widowbird of tropical and subtropical grassland is identified by the red neck band on the breeding male's otherwise black plumage. In his territorial display flight, the male flutters around in the air over his nesting territory with slow wingbeats, trailing his long, black tail. The female is duller and lacks the long tail, as do immatures. Males outside the breeding season resemble the females and lack the long tail. The species is gregarious at all times, moving about in flocks and visiting bushes and tall grass, often near water. Birds also roost in large flocks, often in tall elephant grass, again close to water. The diet consists of insects and seeds.
• NEST An oval nest, made of living grass and lined with dry grass, with an entrance near the top in the form of a covered porch. The nest is placed in a bush or reedbed.
• DISTRIBUTION Scattered areas throughout Africa south of the Sahara, except in dense forest or desert areas.

• *buff feather edges in early season*

FEMALE

entire tail is feathered •

DISTRIBUTION

• *tail is long only in the breeding season*

Plumage Sexes differ	Habitat	Migration Non-migrant

| Family PLOCEIDAE | Species *Euplectes jacksoni* | L. 13 in (33 cm)/5 in (13 cm) |

JACKSON'S WIDOWBIRD

This is a common and lively species, living in open, tropical grassland at high altitude. During the breeding season, it is easy to see, since the male performs a wild display dance around his own selected tuft of grass, leaping high into the air and arching his long tail over his back. Flocks gather in the post-breeding period and visit farmland, where they feed on seeds and insects, either on the ground or in high grass.

• **NEST** A flimsy nest made of grass and lined with seedheads, with a side entrance. It is placed low in a tuft of grass, with growing blades woven into the structure.

• **DISTRIBUTION** From S.W. Kenya to N. Tanzania.

• **REMARK** The male's long tail accounts for the 8 in (20 cm) length difference between the sexes.

• *neck arched in display*

• *buff edges of newly grown feathers*

DISTRIBUTION

• *whole tail is elongated in breeding plumage*

FEMALE

| Plumage Sexes differ | Habitat | Migration Non-migrant |

| Family PLOCEIDAE | Species *Anomalospiza imberbis* | Length 5 in (13 cm) |

PARASITIC WEAVER

A grassland bird with a short tail and stubby bill, this species is usually found near water. It feeds almost exclusively on seeds. During the breeding season, it is seen singly or in pairs, or more rarely in small groups; males perform a "swizzling" song when displaying. Outside the breeding season, larger flocks gather together. In flight, flocks utter warbling contact notes.

• **NEST** This bird builds no nest of its own but lays eggs in nests of some *Cisticola* and *Prinia* warblers, which foster the young.

• **DISTRIBUTION** Scattered areas throughout Africa south of the Sahara.

• **REMARK** Also popularly known as the Cuckoo-Finch. Its inconspicuous coloration may help it visit the nests of host birds without being detected.

• *round, heavy head*

streaked back

DISTRIBUTION

• *short, squat build*

small, short tail

FEMALE

| Plumage Sexes differ | Habitat | Migration Non-migrant |

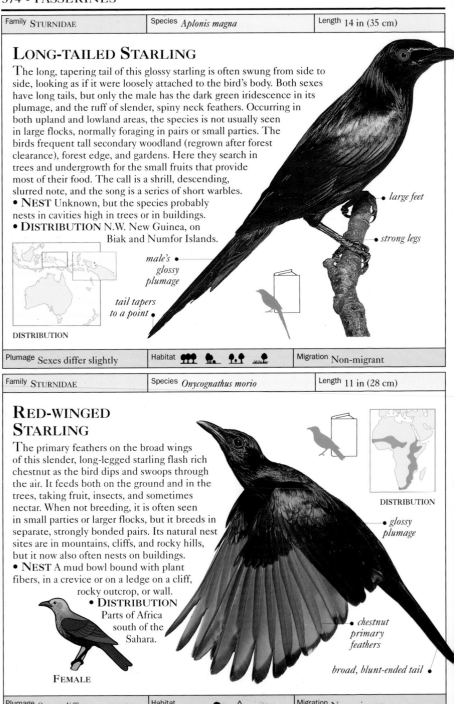

Family STURNIDAE	Species *Aplonis magna*	Length 14 in (35 cm)

LONG-TAILED STARLING

The long, tapering tail of this glossy starling is often swung from side to side, looking as if it were loosely attached to the bird's body. Both sexes have long tails, but only the male has the dark green iridescence in its plumage, and the ruff of slender, spiny neck feathers. Occurring in both upland and lowland areas, the species is not usually seen in large flocks, normally foraging in pairs or small parties. The birds frequent tall secondary woodland (regrown after forest clearance), forest edge, and gardens. Here they search in trees and undergrowth for the small fruits that provide most of their food. The call is a shrill, descending, slurred note, and the song is a series of short warbles.
• **NEST** Unknown, but the species probably nests in cavities high in trees or in buildings.
• **DISTRIBUTION** N.W. New Guinea, on Biak and Numfor Islands.

• *large feet*

• *strong legs*

male's glossy plumage •

tail tapers to a point •

DISTRIBUTION

Plumage Sexes differ slightly	Habitat 🌳 🏚 🌲 🌿	Migration Non-migrant

Family STURNIDAE	Species *Onycognathus morio*	Length 11 in (28 cm)

RED-WINGED STARLING

The primary feathers on the broad wings of this slender, long-legged starling flash rich chestnut as the bird dips and swoops through the air. It feeds both on the ground and in the trees, taking fruit, insects, and sometimes nectar. When not breeding, it is often seen in small parties or larger flocks, but it breeds in separate, strongly bonded pairs. Its natural nest sites are in mountains, cliffs, and rocky hills, but it now also often nests on buildings.
• **NEST** A mud bowl bound with plant fibers, in a crevice or on a ledge on a cliff, rocky outcrop, or wall.
• **DISTRIBUTION** Parts of Africa south of the Sahara.

DISTRIBUTION

• *glossy plumage*

• *chestnut primary feathers*

broad, blunt-ended tail •

FEMALE

Plumage Sexes differ	Habitat 🏞 🐚 ⛰	Migration Non-migrant

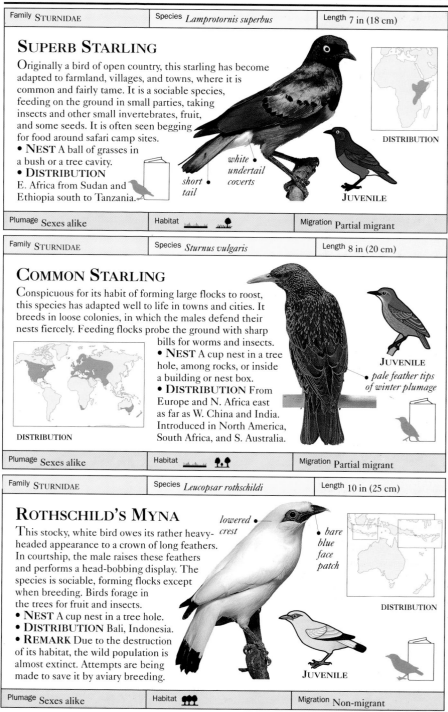

| Family STURNIDAE | Species *Lamprotornis superbus* | Length 7 in (18 cm) |

SUPERB STARLING

Originally a bird of open country, this starling has become adapted to farmland, villages, and towns, where it is common and fairly tame. It is a sociable species, feeding on the ground in small parties, taking insects and other small invertebrates, fruit, and some seeds. It is often seen begging for food around safari camp sites.
• **NEST** A ball of grasses in a bush or a tree cavity.
• **DISTRIBUTION** E. Africa from Sudan and Ethiopia south to Tanzania.

short • tail

white undertail coverts

DISTRIBUTION

JUVENILE

| Plumage Sexes alike | Habitat | Migration Partial migrant |

| Family STURNIDAE | Species *Sturnus vulgaris* | Length 8 in (20 cm) |

COMMON STARLING

Conspicuous for its habit of forming large flocks to roost, this species has adapted well to life in towns and cities. It breeds in loose colonies, in which the males defend their nests fiercely. Feeding flocks probe the ground with sharp bills for worms and insects.
• **NEST** A cup nest in a tree hole, among rocks, or inside a building or nest box.
• **DISTRIBUTION** From Europe and N. Africa east as far as W. China and India. Introduced in North America, South Africa, and S. Australia.

DISTRIBUTION

JUVENILE

• pale feather tips of winter plumage

| Plumage Sexes alike | Habitat | Migration Partial migrant |

| Family STURNIDAE | Species *Leucopsar rothschildi* | Length 10 in (25 cm) |

ROTHSCHILD'S MYNA

lowered • crest

• bare blue face patch

This stocky, white bird owes its rather heavy-headed appearance to a crown of long feathers. In courtship, the male raises these feathers and performs a head-bobbing display. The species is sociable, forming flocks except when breeding. Birds forage in the trees for fruit and insects.
• **NEST** A cup nest in a tree hole.
• **DISTRIBUTION** Bali, Indonesia.
• **REMARK** Due to the destruction of its habitat, the wild population is almost extinct. Attempts are being made to save it by aviary breeding.

DISTRIBUTION

JUVENILE

| Plumage Sexes alike | Habitat | Migration Non-migrant |

Family STURNIDAE	Species *Lamprotornis splendidus*	Length 12 in (30 cm)

SPLENDID GLOSSY STARLING

Flocks of this sociable, noisy species often travel nomadically through open woodland or along the galleries of tall trees beside tropical rivers, searching for ripe fruit and insects in the upper foliage. The Splendid Glossy Starling is particularly fond of wild figs, and a fruiting fig tree may attract large numbers of feeding birds. Being up in the tree canopy for so much of the time, the species is difficult to spot, but when flying between trees it can often be recognized by its distinctive, hunched posture. Its beating wings make a noticeable swishing sound. Calls include shrill whistles, rasping sounds, and deep, throaty noises. These are heard particularly in the evening as the birds gather in their hundreds to roost.

• **NEST** A tree hole, lined with dry grasses, often high above the ground.
• **DISTRIBUTION** Forest zone of W. and C. Africa.

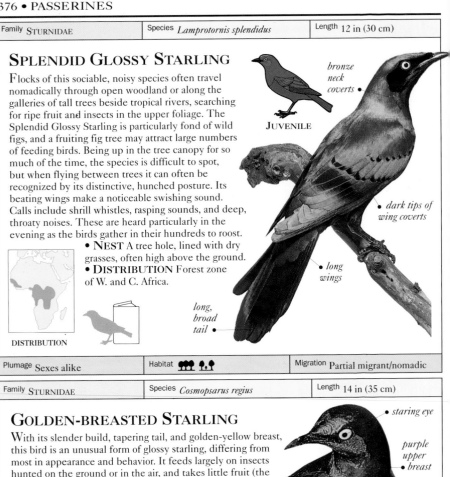

JUVENILE

bronze neck coverts

dark tips of wing coverts

long wings

long, broad tail

DISTRIBUTION

Plumage Sexes alike	Habitat	Migration Partial migrant/nomadic

Family STURNIDAE	Species *Cosmopsarus regius*	Length 14 in (35 cm)

GOLDEN-BREASTED STARLING

With its slender build, tapering tail, and golden-yellow breast, this bird is an unusual form of glossy starling, differing from most in appearance and behavior. It feeds largely on insects hunted on the ground or in the air, and takes little fruit (the usual diet of glossy starlings). Small flocks feed together in tropical grassland with scattered trees, or in dry scrub. Nervous in manner, birds raise the alarm with a whistling chatter when disturbed.

• **NEST** A tree hole lined with plant materials.

• **DISTRIBUTION** E. Africa from Somalia to Tanzania.

staring eye

purple upper breast

golden-yellow underside

long legs

DISTRIBUTION   **JUVENILE**

Plumage Sexes alike	Habitat	Migration Non-migrant

Family STURNIDAE	Species *Acridotheres tristis*	Length 9 in (23 cm)

COMMON MYNA

This grassland starling has adapted well to living in towns and villages. It is a robust bird with a fearless manner, identified by a white wing patch that shows when the wings open in flight. Outside the breeding season it is often seen in small parties or larger flocks, foraging in open places, gardens, or streets. Fruit, seeds, insects, worms, and household scraps are all eaten. At dusk the birds gather in large roosts in the trees, calling noisily with a range of gurgling, squawking, and clicking sounds. When breeding, males perform head-bowing displays to their partners, raising the bristly feathers on their foreheads.
• **NEST** A rough, bowl-shaped structure of grass, roots, and twigs, built in a tree hole or in a building.
• **DISTRIBUTION** From Iran to S.E. Asia. Introduced in Arabia, Africa, Australasia, and some Pacific islands.
• **REMARK** In some of the areas where it has been introduced, the Common Myna has harmed local native species by overcompetition for food and nest sites.

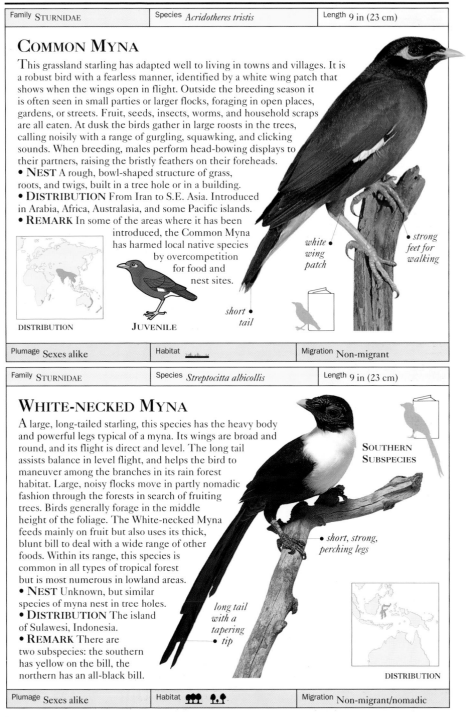

white wing patch

strong feet for walking

short tail

DISTRIBUTION

JUVENILE

Plumage Sexes alike	Habitat	Migration Non-migrant

Family STURNIDAE	Species *Streptocitta albicollis*	Length 9 in (23 cm)

WHITE-NECKED MYNA

A large, long-tailed starling, this species has the heavy body and powerful legs typical of a myna. Its wings are broad and round, and its flight is direct and level. The long tail assists balance in level flight, and helps the bird to maneuver among the branches in its rain forest habitat. Large, noisy flocks move in partly nomadic fashion through the forests in search of fruiting trees. Birds generally forage in the middle height of the foliage. The White-necked Myna feeds mainly on fruit but also uses its thick, blunt bill to deal with a wide range of other foods. Within its range, this species is common in all types of tropical forest but is most numerous in lowland areas.
• **NEST** Unknown, but similar species of myna nest in tree holes.
• **DISTRIBUTION** The island of Sulawesi, Indonesia.
• **REMARK** There are two subspecies: the southern has yellow on the bill, the northern has an all-black bill.

SOUTHERN SUBSPECIES

short, strong, perching legs

long tail with a tapering tip

DISTRIBUTION

Plumage Sexes alike	Habitat	Migration Non-migrant/nomadic

Family STURNIDAE	Species *Mino dumontii*	Length 10 in (25 cm)

YELLOW-FACED MYNA

When this bird is perched, its bare face patches are its most distinctive feature. In flight, the white rump, tail coverts, and wing patches become more conspicuous. The species lives in trees, favoring those with open space around them. These include tall trees rising above the surrounding rain forest, trees at the forest edge, and single trees on open ground. The Yellow-faced Myna occurs in pairs or small parties by day but often gathers in flocks at dusk to roost. The birds feed mainly on forest fruits, but occasionally fly out from the branches to snatch swarming insects in midair. Perched birds utter frequent, croaking calls. When breeding, pairs are often assisted at the nest by a "helper," typically one of the previous season's brood.
• **NEST** A bowl-shaped nest of twigs, leaves, and dry stems, built in a tree cavity well aboveground.
• **DISTRIBUTION** New Guinea, the Bismarck Archipelago, and the Solomon Islands.

bare skin around eye

short, bristly feathers

DISTRIBUTION

white wing patch

WING PATTERN

white rump and tail coverts

Plumage Sexes alike	Habitat	Migration Non-migrant

Family STURNIDAE	Species *Gracula religiosa*	Length 11½ in (29 cm)

HILL MYNA

Known in captivity for its ability to mimic human speech, the Hill Myna also chatters constantly in the wild. Its calls are very varied and can be musical, harsh, or wheezy. The species occurs in tropical forests and plantations. It lives in the forest canopy, foraging for food in small parties; if it has to visit the ground it hops slowly and heavily. The birds feed mainly on fruit and berries, also gleaning insects, catching winged termites, and visiting flowering trees to sip nectar.
• **NEST** A cup nest placed deep in a hole in a tall tree.
• **DISTRIBUTION** Scattered areas in the Indian subcontinent, and from the Himalayas east into S. China and much of S.E. Asia.
• **REMARK** Aviary-bred birds reared in isolation from their parents become good mimics of human speech.

bare yellow wattle

short tail

DISTRIBUTION

JUVENILE

short, strong, perching legs

Plumage Sexes alike	Habitat	Migration Non-migrant

Family STURNIDAE	Species *Buphagus africanus*	Length 8½ in (22 cm)

YELLOW-BILLED OXPECKER

This grassland bird finds its food on the bodies of large grazing mammals such as giraffes, rhinoceroses, zebras, and cattle. It clambers about with its sharp claws, using its tail as a prop, and removes ticks and other skin parasites with its bill, which is flattened sideways, with a blunt tip for dislodging the prey. The oxpecker also probes into skin wounds and sometimes feeds on wound tissue. If alarmed, the bird dodges around the host's body to hide. Oxpeckers take the opportunity to drink when their host visits water. At night they roost in flocks in trees, in reedbeds, or among rocks.
• **NEST** A pad of feathers, grass, and hair, placed in a natural hole in a tree.
• **DISTRIBUTION** Africa south of the Sahara.

JUVENILE

• *red eye*

short tail used as a prop

strong claws for clambering on animals

DISTRIBUTION

Plumage Sexes alike	Habitat	Migration Non-migrant

Family ORIOLIDAE	Species *Oriolus oriolus*	Length 8½ in (22 cm)

GOLDEN ORIOLE

This species occurs in deciduous woodland, preferring trees with high, open canopies. Females are well camouflaged, but even the vivid male is often hard to see as he searches the treetop foliage for fruit and insects. The birds can be detected by their loud, fluting, three-note calls. They fly swiftly, often in shallow swoops. Uneasy on the ground, they stay in the air even to bathe, splashing into water momentarily before returning to the safety of the trees.
• **NEST** A cup nest slung in a horizontal twig fork, made of grasses, wool, and strips of bark, finely lined, and situated high in the outer twigs of a tree.
• **DISTRIBUTION** Breeds in much of Europe, C. Asia, and N. India. Winters in Africa and India.

• *black eye streak*

long, narrow wing

short tail

yellow side panels

short legs of a tree dweller

DISTRIBUTION

FEMALE

Plumage Sexes differ	Habitat	Migration Migrant

Family ORIOLIDAE	Species *Sphecotheres viridis*	Length 11 in (28 cm)

GREEN FIGBIRD

A strong, slender oriole with a powerful bill, the Green Figbird has a distinctive patch of bare skin around the eye. In the female, this patch is dark purplish gray and easily overlooked, but in the male it is a pale pinkish red and flushes a deeper, brighter red in moments of agitation or excitement. The bird is usually seen at the forest edge or in clearings. Here it searches for wild fruits with a dipping flight on long, slender wings, in which the white outer edges of its tail are revealed. It also occurs among the scattered trees of towns and suburbs, where it feeds on cultivated fruit such as bananas and pawpaws. Adults normally forage singly or in pairs, but immature birds tend to form noisy flocks that squabble among themselves in harsh, high pitched notes.
• **NEST** A shallow cup nest made of vine tendrils, reinforced with thin twigs, and suspended in a horizontal twig fork high in a tree.
• **DISTRIBUTION** E. Indonesia (islands of Roti and Timor), S.E. New Guinea, and N. and E. Australia.

• bare skin around eye

DISTRIBUTION

white outer • edge of tail

FEMALE

Plumage Sexes differ	Habitat	Migration Non-migrant

Family DICRURIDAE	Species *Dicrurus forficatus*	Length 10½ in (27 cm)

CRESTED DRONGO

Often conspicuous as it perches upright on a tree, post, or rock, watching for food, this bird makes little attempt to conceal itself from potential enemies. It sometimes harries passing birds of prey with aggressive mock attacks. Its name refers to the tuft of feathers that springs from its forehead. The species often hunts in open woodland, where it watches vigilantly from a perch, then darts out to intercept a passing insect in midair. The long, outward-curving, forked tail provides great agility in the air, and the bird frequently twists and tumbles in pursuit of its prey, finally snatching it up in a short, stout bill that is slightly hooked to ensure a grip on the victim. The Crested Drongo also frequents more open grassland, where it hunts for insects that have been disturbed by grazing cattle, which it uses as mobile perches. The bird also benefits from brush or grass fires, picking off insects as they escape from the heat. Crested Drongos hunt alone or in pairs, uttering twanging, metallic call notes.
• **NEST** A light cup nest of interwoven plant fibers, suspended between two twigs forming a horizontal fork at the end of a branch in a tree.
• **DISTRIBUTION** Madagascar and Comoro Islands (northwest of Madagascar).

• small, erect crest

• typical upright posture

• long, forked tail

DISTRIBUTION

Plumage Sexes alike	Habitat	Migration Non-migrant

Family DICRURIDAE	Species *Dicrurus paradiseus*	Length 25 in (63 cm)

GREATER RACKET-TAILED DRONGO

This large drongo can be recognized by its two long tail feathers. Each of these is composed of a long, wirelike shaft with a broad vane, known as a racket, at its tip. In flight, the rackets ripple and bounce as they trail behind the bird. Another recognition feature is the loose, backward-drooping crest on the crown of the head. The species is common in rain forest and bamboo jungle and feeds almost exclusively on insects, caught on the wing or picked from twigs and foliage. It can use its versatile feet to clamp a large insect to the perch, or to grasp and raise the prey to its bill. Greater Racket-tailed Drongos hunt by flying out repeatedly from the same perch, or by moving from tree to tree, either alone or in small parties. Such parties often associate with birds of other species, to form large hunting flocks. These flocks flush insects out of the vegetation as they pass, making them easy to catch. Like other drongos, the Greater Racket-tail is boldly aggressive towards predators. It utters metallic calls, as well as a song that includes musical, whistling sounds and skillful mimicry of other birds.

• **NEST** A deep, loose cup nest made of fine twigs, bark strips, grass stems, and spiderwebs, bound by its outer rim to a horizontally forked twig, and situated high in a tree.
• **DISTRIBUTION** Much of India and through the Himalayan region to S. China, and south as far as Borneo, Java, and Bali.
• **REMARK** This bird is the largest species of drongo, not only on account of tail length but in overall body size too.

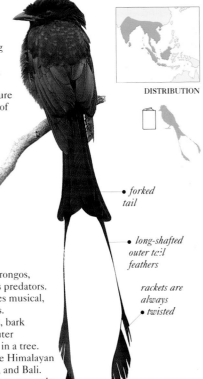

DISTRIBUTION

• *forked tail*

• *long-shafted outer tail feathers*

rackets are always • *twisted*

Plumage Sexes alike	Habitat 🌲🌲	Migration Non-migrant

Family CALLAEATIDAE	Species *Creadion carunculatus*	Length 10 in (25 cm)

SADDLEBACK

chestnut "saddle" • *on the back*

Identified by its fleshy wattles, this forest bird lives mainly in the trees, probing bark for insects and taking fruit and nectar. It makes only brief flights. Pairs remain together.
• **NEST** A cup nest in a tree hole or dense foliage.
• **DISTRIBUTION** New Zealand; once widespread, now only on a few small islands.

DISTRIBUTION

SOUTH ISLAND
JUVENILE

Plumage Sexes alike	Habitat 🦅 🌲🌲	Migration Non-migrant

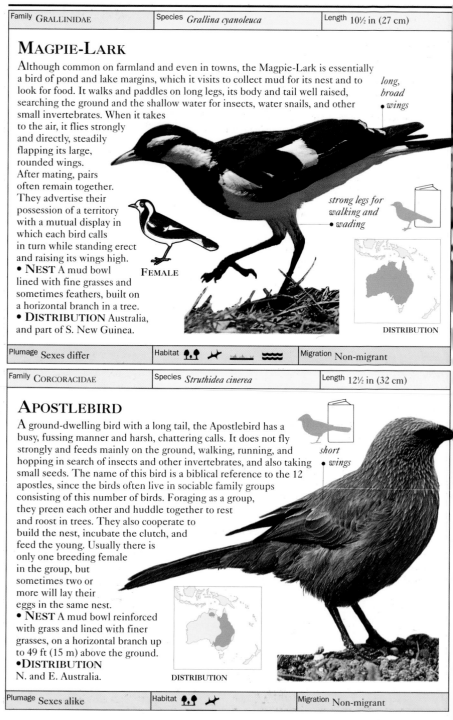

Family GRALLINIDAE	Species *Grallina cyanoleuca*	Length 10½ in (27 cm)

MAGPIE-LARK

Although common on farmland and even in towns, the Magpie-Lark is essentially
a bird of pond and lake margins, which it visits to collect mud for its nest and to
look for food. It walks and paddles on long legs, its body and tail well raised,
searching the ground and the shallow water for insects, water snails, and other
small invertebrates. When it takes
to the air, it flies strongly
and directly, steadily
flapping its large,
rounded wings.
After mating, pairs
often remain together.
They advertise their
possession of a territory
with a mutual display in
which each bird calls
in turn while standing erect
and raising its wings high.
• **NEST** A mud bowl
lined with fine grasses and
sometimes feathers, built on
a horizontal branch in a tree.
• **DISTRIBUTION** Australia,
and part of S. New Guinea.

long, broad wings

strong legs for walking and wading

FEMALE

DISTRIBUTION

Plumage Sexes differ	Habitat	Migration Non-migrant

Family CORCORACIDAE	Species *Struthidea cinerea*	Length 12½ in (32 cm)

APOSTLEBIRD

A ground-dwelling bird with a long tail, the Apostlebird has a
busy, fussing manner and harsh, chattering calls. It does not fly
strongly and feeds mainly on the ground, walking, running, and
hopping in search of insects and other invertebrates, and also taking
small seeds. The name of this bird is a biblical reference to the 12
apostles, since the birds often live in sociable family groups
consisting of this number of birds. Foraging as a group,
they preen each other and huddle together to rest
and roost in trees. They also cooperate to
build the nest, incubate the clutch, and
feed the young. Usually there is
only one breeding female
in the group, but
sometimes two or
more will lay their
eggs in the same nest.
• **NEST** A mud bowl reinforced
with grass and lined with finer
grasses, on a horizontal branch up
to 49 ft (15 m) above the ground.
•**DISTRIBUTION**
N. and E. Australia.

short wings

DISTRIBUTION

Plumage Sexes alike	Habitat	Migration Non-migrant

Family ARTAMIDAE	Species *Artamus cinereus*	Length 7 in (18 cm)

BLACK-FACED WOODSWALLOW

Despite its stout, heavy-headed appearance, the Black-faced Woodswallow is very agile in the air, flying easily on long, tapering wings in pursuit of its insect prey. Found in open country with scattered trees, it watches alertly from a high, bare branch, darting out to ambush passing insects. At other times it circles or glides in prolonged aerial hunts, catching insects in its broad-based bill. It usually occurs in pairs or small flocks, which huddle together to roost. The birds are sociable when breeding and the nesting pair can often rely on help from other family members.

EASTERN FORM

• **NEST** A cup nest made of twigs and rootlets, built inside a shrub or a hollow stump.

• **DISTRIBUTION** Timor, S. New Guinea, and Australia.

DISTRIBUTION

• *black undertail coverts of western form*

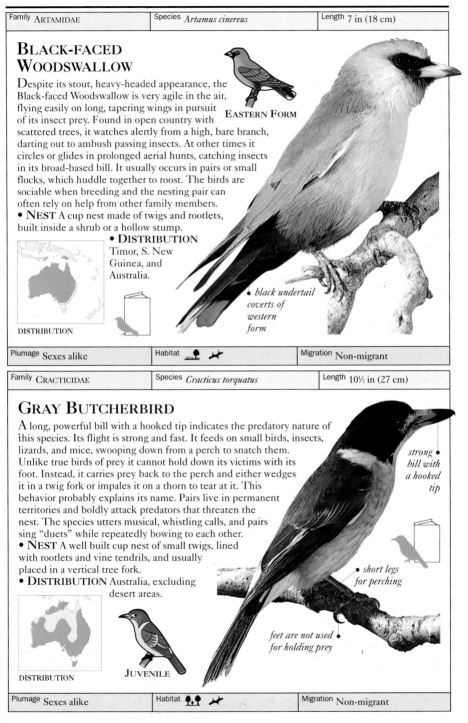

Plumage Sexes alike	Habitat	Migration Non-migrant

Family CRACTICIDAE	Species *Cracticus torquatus*	Length 10½ in (27 cm)

GRAY BUTCHERBIRD

A long, powerful bill with a hooked tip indicates the predatory nature of this species. Its flight is strong and fast. It feeds on small birds, insects, lizards, and mice, swooping down from a perch to snatch them. Unlike true birds of prey it cannot hold down its victims with its foot. Instead, it carries prey back to the perch and either wedges it in a twig fork or impales it on a thorn to tear at it. This behavior probably explains its name. Pairs live in permanent territories and boldly attack predators that threaten the nest. The species utters musical, whistling calls, and pairs sing "duets" while repeatedly bowing to each other.

strong • bill with a hooked tip

• **NEST** A well built cup nest of small twigs, lined with rootlets and vine tendrils, and usually placed in a vertical tree fork.

• **DISTRIBUTION** Australia, excluding desert areas.

• short legs for perching

DISTRIBUTION

JUVENILE

feet are not used • for holding prey

Plumage Sexes alike	Habitat	Migration Non-migrant

| Family CRACTICIDAE | Species *Gymnorhina tibicen* | Length 16 in (40 cm) |

AUSTRALASIAN MAGPIE

The chorus of musical call notes uttered by a
perched group of males of this species is a familiar sound
throughout much of Australia. The species is most common
in farmland with scattered trees, and in open woodland. The
birds feed in groups on the ground, digging out insect larvae
and other invertebrates with their powerful bills. Each group
has a complex social structure, in which all the females mate
with a single, dominant male and then nest separately. Younger
males in the group may mate with the females if they get the
opportunity, but unlike the dominant male they take
no part in feeding the young. Each group defends its
breeding territory against neighboring groups.
• **NEST** A shallow bowl, lined and placed in a tree.
• **DISTRIBUTION** S.C. New Guinea and throughout
Australia; introduced
in Fiji and New Zealand.

white nape patch

DISTRIBUTION   **FEMALE**

| Plumage Sexes differ | Habitat | Migration Non-migrant |

| Family CRACTICIDAE | Species *Strepera graculina* | Length 20 in (50 cm) |

PIED CURRAWONG

With its slender build, powerful bill, staring eyes, and
slightly furtive manner, the Pied Currawong appears intent
on mischief. Indeed it is a nest robber during the breeding
season, when it frequently feeds in the forest, taking eggs and
nestlings as well as insects (particularly stick insects). It also eats
berries and carrion, and feeds on the ground, probing for insects
in open, grassy places. In winter, large flocks roam nomadically,
roosting communally and visiting towns and parks.
The name is derived from the "curra-wong" call.
• **NEST** A large cup nest, lined,
in a forked branch of a tree.
• **DISTRIBUTION**
Forest regions of
E. Australia.

staring eye •

heavy bill

long wing •
• white base of tail
• long legs for walking

DISTRIBUTION   **JUVENILE**

| Plumage Sexes alike | Habitat | Migration Partial migrant/nomadic |

Family PTILONORHYNCHIDAE	Species *Ailuroedus crassirostris*	Length 13 in (33 cm)

GREEN CATBIRD

This rain forest species belongs to the bowerbird family, although it does not build a bower. It feeds mainly on fruit and tender young leaves in the middle levels of the forest, but occasionally descends to ground level, moving in bounding hops interspersed with short, heavy flights. Although normally quiet, the male bird becomes demonstrative when breeding. Calling with a catlike, wailing note and bobbing his head and body, he chases after females.
• **NEST** A cup nest, located in a tree fork, a tree fern top, or a vine tangle.
• **DISTRIBUTION** E. Australia.
• **REMARK** Unlike the true bowerbirds, the male mates with only one female. He defends the nest and helps to rear the young.

stout bill

pale streaks on underside

bands for study and recognition of individuals in the wild

green plumage is inconspicuous in forest foliage

DISTRIBUTION

Plumage Sexes alike	Habitat	Migration Non-migrant

Family PTILONORHYNCHIDAE	Species *Ptilonorhynchus violaceus*	Length 12 in (30 cm)

SATIN BOWERBIRD

While the females and young males of this species wander in small flocks through the forest in search of fruit, young leaves, and insects, the adult male spends much of his time at the "bower." Working near other males, he claims a small area of the forest floor and erects a narrow avenue of twigs, staining them black with a mixture of charcoal and saliva. He decorates the area with feathers, flowers, and stones, preferably bright blue ones. When a female visits, he woos her with fizzing and chirring notes while exhibiting his brightest objects in his bill. After mating, the female leaves to nest and rear the young alone.
• **NEST** A shallow cup nest of twigs and dry leaves, built in a twig fork or mistletoe clump, in a tree.
• **DISTRIBUTION** E. Australia.

glossy plumage

rounded wings

short, broad tail

DISTRIBUTION

FEMALE

Plumage Sexes differ	Habitat	Migration Non-migrant

Family PTILONORHYNCHIDAE	Species *Chlamydera maculata*	Length 11 in (28 cm)

SPOTTED BOWERBIRD

This bird occurs in dense, dry forest, both in foothills and alongside creeks, feeding on insects, seeds, and berries. Its name refers to the bowers built by the males to court the females. In this species the bower is a short avenue of interwoven stems, tinted red with a mixture of grass juice and saliva. Each end is ornamented with white or green objects – bones, stones, snail shells, and even glass. Males are polygamous, and the builder attracts females by a display of his bright magenta nape patch, accompanied by a variety of hissing and chirring sounds.

• **NEST** A loose saucer of twigs and stems, on a horizontal branch or among mistletoe in a tree.
• **DISTRIBUTION** Interior and some coastal areas of E. Australia.

FEMALE

DISTRIBUTION

• *magenta nape patch*

bower • *decorations*

"spotted" plumage • *consisting of feathers with pale tips*

Plumage Sexes alike	Habitat	Migration Non-migrant

Family PARADISAEIDAE	Species *Cicinnurus regius*	L. 11 in (28 cm)/6¾ in (17 cm)

KING BIRD-OF-PARADISE

Though vividly colored, the male of this species is inconspicuous for much of the time, hiding in lowland rain forest. When active, he hops through the branches in search of insects, berries, and other small fruits. To court females, he selects a suitable tree for his display, puffs out his plumage, raises his tail plumes, and utters repeated screams. After mating, females nest alone.
• **NEST** A thick cup nest of palm fibers, in a tree hole.
• **DISTRIBUTION** Lowland areas of New Guinea.
• **REMARK** The male's tail accounts for the length difference between sexes.

• *coiled feather vane*

black • *mark above eye*

bright orange-red plumage •

DISTRIBUTION

FEMALE

Plumage Sexes differ	Habitat	Migration Non-migrant

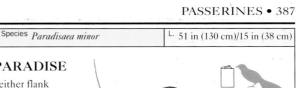

Family PARADISAEIDAE	Species *Paradisaea minor*	L. 51 in (130 cm)/15 in (38 cm)

LESSER BIRD-OF-PARADISE

Spectacular tufts of plumes on either flank of the male help to identify this rain forest bird. In contrast with males of most other bird-of-paradise species, he does not display alone but with other males. Groups of males gather on bare branches high in the forest trees, to call and arch their plumes invitingly, advertising their presence with loud, staccato notes. Females visit displaying males to mate. After mating, the female nests and rears the young alone. Mature males are solitary, while females and young males forage in small groups. Both sexes feed on fruit and insects.
• **NEST** A cup of twigs, tendrils, and leaves, in a small tree.
• **DISTRIBUTION** N.W. New Guinea; the islands of Misool and Yapen; and along N. New Guinea extending as far west as Huon Peninsula.
• **REMARK** The male's tail streamers account for the length difference between the sexes.

flank feathers

tail streamer

DISTRIBUTION

FEMALE

Plumage Sexes differ	Habitat 🌳	Migration Non-migrant

Family PARADISAEIDAE	Species *Paradisaea rudolphi*	L. 25 in (63 cm)/11½ in (29 cm)

BLUE BIRD-OF-PARADISE

This rain forest bird inhabits the foothills of mountainous regions and feeds on tree fruits and insects. Females and young males often forage in small parties, while the mature male usually feeds alone. He also performs his courtship display alone, choosing an open perch as a display site, and uttering a series of plaintive call notes. Then, fanning out his blue belly and flank feathers, he drops upside down and vibrates his body. He also rhythmically expands and contracts a special patch of rust-red and black plumage. While doing this he utters a throbbing, machinelike sound. The female moves along the branch to perch between his feet, looking down on the display, until he swings back upright to stand beside her.
• **NEST** A shallow cup nest, in a low tree.
• **DISTRIBUTION** E. New Guinea.
• **REMARK** The male's long tail streamers account for the 13½ in (34 cm) length difference between the sexes.

finely divided flank feathers

FEMALE

elongated tail filaments

DISTRIBUTION

Plumage Sexes differ	Habitat 🌳	Migration Non-migrant

| Family CORVIDAE | Species *Platylophus galericulatus* | Length 13 in (33 cm) |

CRESTED JAY

The long crest of this jay is composed mainly of two large feathers with their flat surfaces facing forward. The crest is often flicked up and down as the jay utters its calls, which include whistles and harsh, rattling cries. Like other birds of the crow family, it lacks a loud advertising song. Inhabiting lowland rain forest and mountain forest up to 2,500 ft (800 m), it usually forages in pairs or small parties. Uncommon and little studied despite its wide distribution, the Crested Jay seems to take only live food, including large insects such as cockroaches and wasps, and other invertebrates such as millipedes. When approached, it is often surprisingly tame, possibly because in its remote habitat it is isolated from human contact. On occasion, however, Crested Jays have been known to "mob" a human in the same way that small birds will mob a bird of prey. This may serve to alert other birds as well as to drive the intruder away.

• **NEST** A solid twig nest placed in a tree or tall sapling.

• **DISTRIBUTION** S.E. Asia from S.W. Thailand to Borneo and Java.

flat-fronted crest

JUVENILE

white neck patch

broad tail

DISTRIBUTION

| Plumage Sexes alike | Habitat | Migration Non-migrant |

| Family CORVIDAE | Species *Cyanocitta cristata* | Length 11 in (28 cm) |

BLUE JAY

A harsh screech and a flash of bright blue wing and tail feathers in flight usually announce the presence of this bold and inquisitive bird. Originally inhabiting broadleaved woodland, the Blue Jay has now become common in farmland, towns, parks, and suburbs. It forages in vegetation and on the ground, taking nuts, seeds, berries, and other fruits, as well as insects and other small animals. It has a reputation as a nest robber. Although many individuals are migrants, Blue Jays very often store quantities of nuts by burying them in the ground or in crevices in trees. Migrating Blue Jays often travel in flocks, but the birds are more usually seen in pairs or family groups.

• **NEST** A cup nest made of twigs, grass, and stems, lined and placed in a tree or bush.

• **DISTRIBUTION** E. and C. North America.

short crest

barred wing pattern

DISTRIBUTION

| Plumage Sexes alike | Habitat | Migration Partial migrant |

Family CORVIDAE	Species *Cyanocitta stelleri*	Length 11½ in (29 cm)

STELLER'S JAY

This shy, slender-crested jay inhabits wooded hillsides, preferring open woodland, either coniferous or mixed, and areas of scattered trees. Agile on the wing, it is adept at moving through branches and foliage, and crosses open spaces with rapid, level flight. It usually occurs in pairs and families, although larger groups gather at a good food source, calling with a range of screeches and softer, low notes. The song is soft and sweet. In common with all other birds of the crow family, Steller's Jay can clamp food to the perch with its foot and can hold an acorn and hammer it open with its bill. The bill is also used for digging, and for stripping loose bark. The birds feed mainly on nuts, seeds, and fruits, and they bury acorns and seeds for winter. Insects and other invertebrates are taken, as well as the occasional egg or nestling.
• **NEST** A bowl made of twigs, lined with fine rootlets, and placed in a tree.
• **DISTRIBUTION** W. North America from Alaska to Nicaragua.

DARK SUBSPECIES

• *blue wings*

blue tail

DISTRIBUTION

Plumage Sexes alike	Habitat	Migration Non-migrant

Family CORVIDAE	Species *Aphelocoma californica*	Length 11½ in (29 cm)

SCRUB JAY

Although slow in flight, this bird is active and agile on the ground. Originally a bird of dry lowland, occurring in arid scrub, forest edge, and broken woodland near water, it has spread to cultivated areas and city suburbs. It forages in trees and on the ground or among low bushes, hopping on long legs and taking a wide range of food. Its diet includes nuts, seeds, and small fruits, insects and other small invertebrates, small reptiles, frogs, toads, eggs, nestlings, and mice. Noisy and excitable, Scrub Jays often gang together to drive off predators.
• **NEST** A cup nest in a bush or low tree.
• **DISTRIBUTION** W. USA to S. Mexico.
• **REMARK** The Florida Scrub Jay, one of a number of jays that nest communally, often with related birds assisting the breeding pair, is a separate species.

white eyebrow •

strong, grasping foot holds down • *food*

DISTRIBUTION

JUVENILE

Plumage Sexes alike	Habitat	Migration Non-migrant

Family CORVIDAE	Species *Calocitta colliei*	Length 28 in (70 cm)

BLACK-THROATED MAGPIE-JAY

With its flamboyant, forward-arching crest and long, tapering tail, this species is exceptionally ornate for a jay. When the bird is excited, its crest rises up and extends forward until the tip hangs over the front of the bill. Typically found in open woodland on lower hill slopes and along rivers, it feeds mainly among the trees, taking insects and fruit such as berries. The birds forage in small parties, communicating with a variety of calls and noisily mobbing potential predators. Reports of more than one individual feeding an incubating female suggest that the parties may stay together throughout the year.
• **NEST** A structure made of twigs and lined with rootlets and plant fibers, built in a tree up to 100 ft (30 m) above the ground.
      • **DISTRIBUTION** Pacific region of N.W. Mexico.

DISTRIBUTION

black throat patch

Plumage Sexes alike	Habitat 🌳🌳 〰️	Migration Non-migrant

Family CORVIDAE	Species *Garrulus glandarius*	Length 14 in (35 cm)

EURASIAN JAY

Often cautious and suspicious in its behavior, the Eurasian Jay is better known for its harsh cries than for its colorful plumage. It is a bird of deciduous and mixed woodland, where it lives in pairs or small groups, foraging for a variety of foods including nuts, seeds, fruits, insects, and small mammals. In the fall, it collects acorns to last it through the winter, burying them in open ground and finding them months later without difficulty.
• **NEST** A coarse nest of twigs and woody stems, placed in a tall tree.
• **DISTRIBUTION** From Europe and N.W. Africa through C. Asia to E. and S.E. Asia.

DISTRIBUTION

barred, blue
• *wing patch*

INDIAN SUBSPECIES

• *white rump revealed in flight*

Plumage Sexes alike	Habitat 🌳🌳🌳 🌳🌳 ✈️	Migration Partial migrant

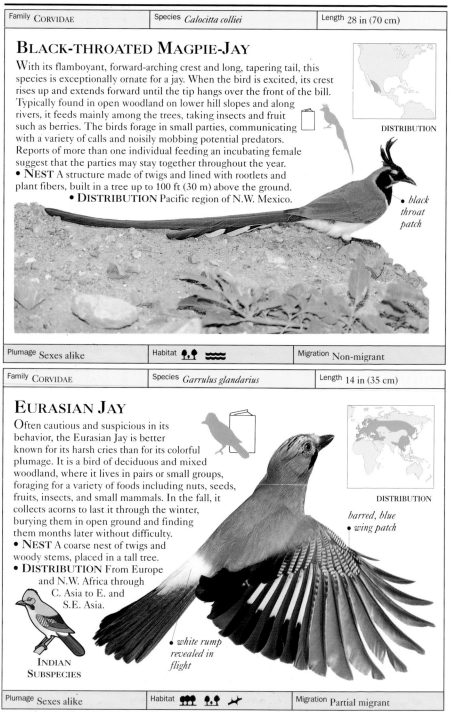

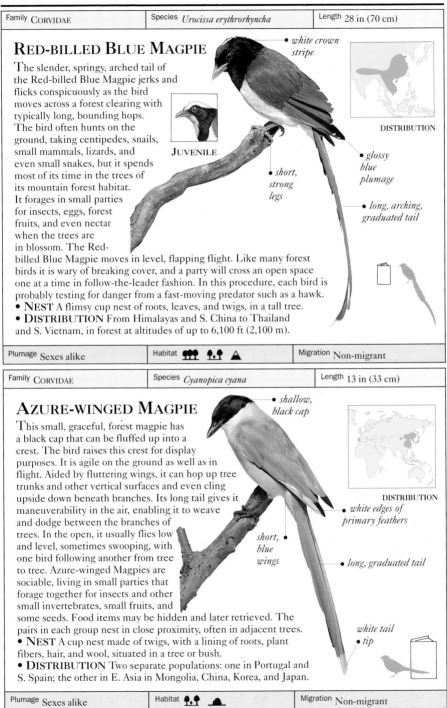

Family CORVIDAE	Species *Urocissa erythrorhyncha*	Length 28 in (70 cm)

RED-BILLED BLUE MAGPIE

The slender, springy, arched tail of the Red-billed Blue Magpie jerks and flicks conspicuously as the bird moves across a forest clearing with typically long, bounding hops. The bird often hunts on the ground, taking centipedes, snails, small mammals, lizards, and even small snakes, but it spends most of its time in the trees of its mountain forest habitat. It forages in small parties for insects, eggs, forest fruits, and even nectar when the trees are in blossom. The Red-billed Blue Magpie moves in level, flapping flight. Like many forest birds it is wary of breaking cover, and a party will cross an open space one at a time in follow-the-leader fashion. In this procedure, each bird is probably testing for danger from a fast-moving predator such as a hawk.

• **NEST** A flimsy cup nest of roots, leaves, and twigs, in a tall tree.
• **DISTRIBUTION** From Himalayas and S. China to Thailand and S. Vietnam, in forest at altitudes of up to 6,100 ft (2,100 m).

• *white crown stripe*

DISTRIBUTION

• *glossy blue plumage*

JUVENILE

• *short, strong legs*

• *long, arching, graduated tail*

Plumage Sexes alike	Habitat	Migration Non-migrant

Family CORVIDAE	Species *Cyanopica cyana*	Length 13 in (33 cm)

AZURE-WINGED MAGPIE

This small, graceful, forest magpie has a black cap that can be fluffed up into a crest. The bird raises this crest for display purposes. It is agile on the ground as well as in flight. Aided by fluttering wings, it can hop up tree trunks and other vertical surfaces and even cling upside down beneath branches. Its long tail gives it maneuverability in the air, enabling it to weave and dodge between the branches of trees. In the open, it usually flies low and level, sometimes swooping, with one bird following another from tree to tree. Azure-winged Magpies are sociable, living in small parties that forage together for insects and other small invertebrates, small fruits, and some seeds. Food items may be hidden and later retrieved. The pairs in each group nest in close proximity, often in adjacent trees.

• **NEST** A cup nest made of twigs, with a lining of roots, plant fibers, hair, and wool, situated in a tree or bush.
• **DISTRIBUTION** Two separate populations: one in Portugal and S. Spain; the other in E. Asia in Mongolia, China, Korea, and Japan.

• *shallow, black cap*

DISTRIBUTION

• *white edges of primary feathers*

short, blue wings

• *long, graduated tail*

white tail tip

Plumage Sexes alike	Habitat	Migration Non-migrant

Family CORVIDAE	Species *Pica pica*	Length 19 in (48 cm)

BLACK-BILLED MAGPIE

Active and inquisitive, with a swaggering walk and a harsh, chattering call, the Black-billed Magpie originally inhabited scrub or trees with dense foliage, but has now adapted to cultivated and urban areas. Feeding on almost anything it can find, it mainly takes insects and other invertebrates, as well as other small animals, carrion, fruits, and seeds. Its reputation as a nest robber is greatly exaggerated. Despite its weak flight it can be quite agile in the air, its long tail enabling it to make sudden attacking or evading movements.

• **NEST** A bowl made of twigs and lined with fine rootlets and some mud, roofed with a loose dome of twigs, built in a bush or tree.

• **DISTRIBUTION** N.W. North America, Europe, N.W. Africa, parts of the Middle East, and much of C. and E. Asia.

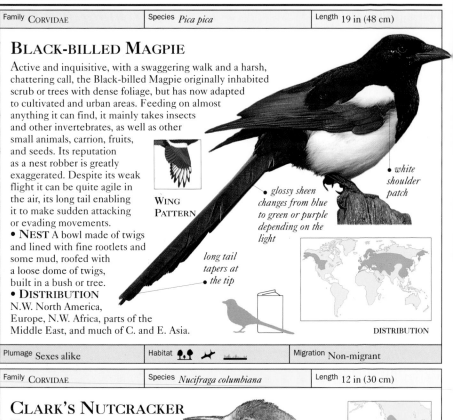

WING PATTERN

• *glossy sheen changes from blue to green or purple depending on the light*

• *white shoulder patch*

long tail tapers at • *the tip*

DISTRIBUTION

Plumage Sexes alike	Habitat	Migration Non-migrant

Family CORVIDAE	Species *Nucifraga columbiana*	Length 12 in (30 cm)

CLARK'S NUTCRACKER

The slender, slightly downcurved bill of this species is adapted for probing into pine cones and extracting the seeds. The bird either breaks into the cone on the tree, or pulls the whole cone off and delves into it while holding it down with its foot. It also eats other seeds and fruits when available, as well as robbing nests and probing rotten wood for insects. Pine seeds are the most important food item in its native mountain conifer forests. After collecting seeds in its throat pouch, it carries them to special hoarding sites to ensure a food supply throughout the snowbound winter. If the seed crop fails, the nutcrackers may be forced to make an irruptive migration, appearing in large numbers in lowland forest. Each pair normally lives within its own territory, but also searches outside it for food. The birds communicate with a variety of calls, the commonest being a single, loud note.

• **NEST** A cup nest of twigs, usually at the end of a conifer branch.

• **DISTRIBUTION** W. North America from S. Canada to N. Mexico.

DISTRIBUTION

long, broad • *wings*

Plumage Sexes alike	Habitat	Migration Non-migrant/nomadic

Family CORVIDAE	Species *Pyrrhocorax graculus*	Length 15 in (38 cm)

ALPINE CHOUGH

The broad wings of the Alpine Chough, with their splayed, fingerlike tips, enable it to fly strongly and skillfully in turbulent mountain winds. Here it soars and glides on air currents and performs aerobatic flights. With its small head, slender bill, and high pitched, trilling whistle, it is unlike most other members of the crow family. On the ground it walks and runs actively on short legs, probing in rock crevices and open pastures. Although it feeds mainly on insects, snails, and fruit, it will also scavenge on small animal carcasses and search for scraps at garbage dumps and picnic sites. The Alpine Chough inhabits high mountains in summer, descending to lowlands in winter. A highly sociable species, it lives in flocks composed mainly of strongly bonded pairs. Flocks roost communally in caves and large crevices, and the pairs often nest in the same sites, though some distance apart.
• **NEST** A mass of sticks and dry roots, either in a large crevice or on a cave ledge.
• **DISTRIBUTION** Spain and N.W. Africa through S. Europe and Middle East to Asia.

• *small, slender bill*

DISTRIBUTION

long, broad wings

• *short legs*

Plumage Sexes alike	Habitat	Migration Non-migrant

Family CORVIDAE	Species *Corvus monedula*	Length 13 in (33 cm)

EURASIAN JACKDAW

Sociable, noisy, and confident, this small, bright-eyed crow is a grassland feeder that probes for insects and worms as well as taking fruit and carrion. It has adapted well to farmland, and also uses buildings as nest sites, forming colonies made up of long-term pairs. The name is derived from its explosive "jack" call.
• **NEST** A lined cup nest made of sticks and stems, placed in a cavity in a tree, cliff, or building.
• **DISTRIBUTION** Eurasia, south to N.W. Africa; northern populations are migratory.

JUVENILE

DISTRIBUTION

• *gray nape*

• *grayish black plumage*

strong, gripping feet •

Plumage Sexes alike	Habitat	Migration Partial migrant

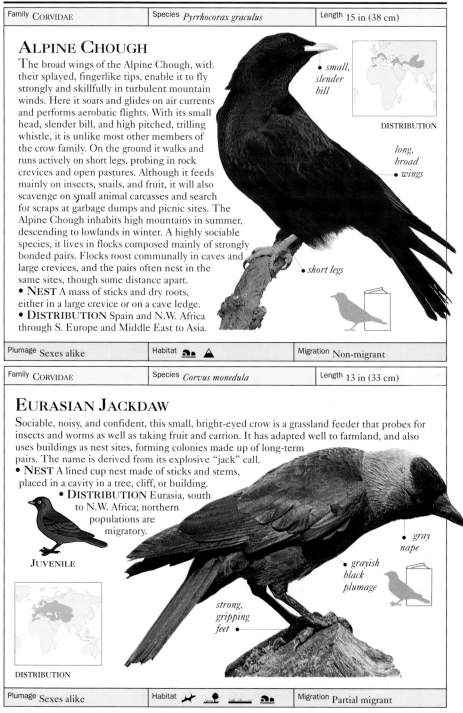

| Family CORVIDAE | Species *Corvus frugilegus* | Length 18½ in (47 cm) |

ROOK

The tapering bill and bare face of this heavy-bodied crow are adapted to its feeding technique of probing deep into the soil. It takes insect larvae and worms, carrying them back to the nest in a prominent throat pouch. In the fall, the Rook tends to turn to nuts and seeds, including grain, and it benefits from mixed farming methods in which fields of grain are grown alongside grassy meadows and pastures. Like most other crows it will take a wide range of alternative foods, including kitchen scraps and carrion. It is highly sociable, feeding and roosting in large flocks and nesting in conspicuous, noisy colonies.
• **NEST** An untidy structure of sticks, lined with finer material, in the top of a tall tree.
• **DISTRIBUTION** Much of Europe, the Middle East, C. and E. Asia. Siberian populations winter as far south as S. Iran, N. India, S. China. Introduced in New Zealand.

• *high forehead*
• *bare, white skin*

DISTRIBUTION

• *glossy plumage*

JUVENILE

| Plumage Sexes alike | Habitat | Migration Partial migrant |

| Family CORVIDAE | Species *Corvus brachyrhynchos* | Length 17½ in (45 cm) |

AMERICAN CROW

This glossy black bird with its rounded tail and steady, flapping flight is a familiar sight in open country throughout North America. In farming areas its habit of feeding in flocks on corn and pea crops has earned the American Crow a bad reputation. The diet also includes nuts and fruit, insects, and small animals such as young birds and mice, and sometimes carrion. During the breeding season, the birds nest either in separate pairs, or sometimes in small colonies. At other times of the year, they congregate in large communal roosts for the night, dispersing during the day to search for food. The usual call is a harsh "caw," but as in other birds there are other call notes, each one used to convey a particular meaning.
• **NEST** A large, cup-shaped nest of sticks, with a soft lining of finer plant material, in a tree or a bush, or on top of a telephone pole.
• **DISTRIBUTION** Much of North America.

• *light build*
• *glossy plumage*
• *long wings*
rounded tail tip

DISTRIBUTION

| Plumage Sexes alike | Habitat | Migration Partial migrant |

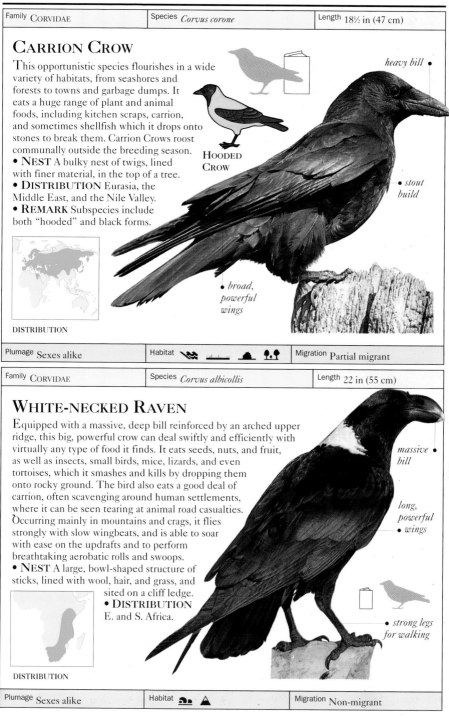

Family CORVIDAE	Species *Corvus corone*	Length 18½ in (47 cm)

CARRION CROW

This opportunistic species flourishes in a wide
variety of habitats, from seashores and
forests to towns and garbage dumps. It
eats a huge range of plant and animal
foods, including kitchen scraps, carrion,
and sometimes shellfish which it drops onto
stones to break them. Carrion Crows roost
communally outside the breeding season.
• **NEST** A bulky nest of twigs, lined
with finer material, in the top of a tree.
• **DISTRIBUTION** Eurasia, the
Middle East, and the Nile Valley.
• **REMARK** Subspecies include
both "hooded" and black forms.

HOODED
CROW

heavy bill

*stout
build*

*broad,
powerful
wings*

DISTRIBUTION

Plumage Sexes alike	Habitat	Migration Partial migrant

Family CORVIDAE	Species *Corvus albicollis*	Length 22 in (55 cm)

WHITE-NECKED RAVEN

Equipped with a massive, deep bill reinforced by an arched upper
ridge, this big, powerful crow can deal swiftly and efficiently with
virtually any type of food it finds. It eats seeds, nuts, and fruit,
as well as insects, small birds, mice, lizards, and even
tortoises, which it smashes and kills by dropping them
onto rocky ground. The bird also eats a good deal of
carrion, often scavenging around human settlements,
where it can be seen tearing at animal road casualties.
Occurring mainly in mountains and crags, it flies
strongly with slow wingbeats, and is able to soar
with ease on the updrafts and to perform
breathtaking aerobatic rolls and swoops.
• **NEST** A large, bowl-shaped structure of
sticks, lined with wool, hair, and grass, and
sited on a cliff ledge.
• **DISTRIBUTION**
E. and S. Africa.

*massive
bill*

*long,
powerful
wings*

*strong legs
for walking*

DISTRIBUTION

Plumage Sexes alike	Habitat	Migration Non-migrant

GLOSSARY

A NUMBER OF the words used in this book may be unfamiliar to some readers. This glossary explains specialist terms both clearly and concisely. Most words defined in the glossary are the names of types of birds. Some of these types are bird families, and the scientific name of the family is given in brackets, with an equals sign,

e.g. "(= family Anatidae)." Other types are only "parts" of families. In these cases, the family is mentioned either in English in the course of the definition, in bold type, e.g. "a type of **falcon**," or in brackets at the end, e.g. "(part of family Laridae)." All words that appear in **bold** type are defined elsewhere in the glossary.

• **ACCENTOR**
A type of sparrowlike bird with a thin, finely pointed bill (= family Prunellidae).

• **ADAPTATION**
Any aspect of a bird's structure or behavior that has evolved to suit its present environment.

• **ADVERTISEMENT**
Display behavior by which a bird signals its presence to other birds.

• **ALBATROSS**
A type of oceangoing seabird that glides for great distances on long, narrow wings, nesting on islands (= family Diomedeidae).

• **ANHINGA**
Name for the North American species of **darter**; alternatively used as a name for all three darter species in the world.

• **ANTBIRD**
A type of rain forest passerine that feeds on the insects and other invertebrates that become easy to catch when fleeing from army ants (= family Formicariidae).

• **AUK**
A type of **penguin**like seabird that is able to fly and typically hunts under water, propelling itself with its wings rather than its feet (= family Alcidae).

• **BABBLER**
A type of short-winged, strong-footed passerine of forest or scrub, often occurring in small, noisy groups (= family Timaliidae).

• **BARBET**
A type of small, sturdy, perching non-passerine with a stout bill, living in trees or bushes (= family Megalaimidae).

• **BARN OWL**
A type of long-legged **owl** in which the **facial disks** form a heart shape (= family Tytonidae).

• **BELLBIRD**
A type of forest-dwelling bird with loud, bell-like calls; refers to a number of species in the **cotinga** and **honeyeater** families.

• **BIRD-OF-PARADISE**
A type of forest-dwelling passerine in which the male has strikingly ornate and sometimes extraordinary display plumage (= family Paradisaeidae).

• **BIRD OF PREY**
A hunting bird; most commonly refers to the day-flying **raptors**, but sometimes refers to all birds hunting land prey of any size larger than insects, thus including **owls**, **skuas**, and **shrikes**. This phrase generally tends not to be used to describe insect-eating and fish-eating birds.

• **BLACKBIRD**
A type of medium-size passerine which is either all black or mostly black; refers to a few species of Old World **thrushes** and several **New World blackbirds**.

• **BOWERBIRD**
A type of forest-dwelling passerine in which males build elaborate twig bowers to which they attract females for mating (= family Ptilonorhynchidae).

• **BROADBILL**
A type of forest-dwelling passerine with a sturdy body, a wide mouth, and a wide bill (= family Eurylaimidae).

• **BULBUL**
A type of passerine that feeds mainly on fruit, and has musical calls (= family Pycnonotidae).

• **BUNTING**
A type of sparrowlike bird with a short, sturdy bill for cracking open husks to feed on seeds (part of family Emberizidae).

• **BUSTARD**
A type of open-country bird of up to **goose** size with long, strong legs and small feet, and a long neck (= family Otididae).

• **BUTCHERBIRD**
A type of passerine bird of trees and shrubs that hunts prey with a strong, hooked bill, and either impales it on thorns or wedges it between twigs to feed (= family Cracticidae). Previously also referred to some typical **shrikes**.

• **BUTTON-QUAIL**
A type of ground bird the size and shape of a **quail** , but with a slender bill (= family Turnicidae).

• **BUZZARD**
A type of broad-winged **bird of prey** that hunts animals and scavenges for **carrion** (part of family Accipitridae).

• **CALL**
A short sound used by a bird purely to convey information, as distinct from **song**.

• **CARACARA**
A type of **falcon** that feeds on helpless or slow-moving prey, or scavenges for **carrion**.

• **CARDINAL**
A type of finchlike bird, often brightly colored, with a heavy, seed-eating type of bill (part of family Emberizidae).

• **CARRION**
Carcasses or parts of dead animals eaten by birds (or other carrion-eaters) that have not killed them.

• **CASQUE**
A hard, hornlike feature that projects upward from the head or bill of a bird.

• **CATBIRD**
This name is given to birds of various different families that utter sounds like the mew of a cat,

e.g. Gray Catbird (part of family Mimidae), Green Catbird (part of family Ptilonorhynchidae).

• **CHANTING-GOSHAWK**
A slenderly built **bird of prey** of open country, not particularly resembling a **goshawk**.

• **CHAT**
(i) A type of small **thrush** that typically watches from a low perch or from the ground before swooping on small invertebrates (part of family Turdidae). (ii) A species of American **warbler** (part of family Parulidae).

• **CHICKADEE**
Alternative word for **tit**.

• **CLUTCH**
The total quantity of eggs incubated by one parent or pair of birds at a time.

• **COCKATOO**
A large and usually crested type of Australasian **parrot**.

• **COLONY**
A group of pairs of birds that nest in close proximity to each other, or the place in which this occurs.

• **COLOR PHASE**
A type of plumage color that distinguishes a bird from others of the same **species**, is not related to sex, age, or **subspecies**, and is not a genetic abnormality (mutation).

• **CONDOR**
A type of **New World vulture**.

• **CONURE**
A popular name sometimes used to refer to some species of South American **parrot**.

• **CONTOUR FEATHER**
A small feather that provides protective cover to the body or wing of a bird.

• **CORMORANT**
A type of slenderly built, web-footed **waterbird** that swims and chases fish under water (= family Phalacrocoracidae).

• **COTINGA**
A type of rain forest passerine, often with display ornaments including **wattles**, bare skin patches, and vividly colored or unusually shaped feathers (= family Cotingidae).

• **COUCAL**
A type of slim-built, nonparasitic **cuckoo** with weak flight, that **skulks** in vegetation and runs on the ground.

• **COURSER**
A type of fast-running **shorebird** with long legs and small feet,

living in dry, open landscapes (part of family Glareolidae).

• **COVERTS**
Contour feathers of the wings and above and below the base of the tail, some overlapping the bases of larger **flight feathers**.

• **COVEY**
A small group of **gamebirds**.

• **CRAKE**
A type of small **rail**, usually living in swamp or grassland vegetation.

• **CRANE**
A type of tall non-passerine with long neck and legs, and a sharp but relatively short bill, occurring in open landscapes, often by water (= family Gruidae).

• **CREEPER**
A type of passerine that hunts insects by climbing up the trunks and branches of trees (= families Certhiidae, Rhabdornithidae, Climacteridae).

• **CROW**
A type of large passerine, typically black, that often feeds on the ground; alternatively refers to all the birds of the crow family (part or whole of family Corvidae).

• **CUCKOO**
A type of slenderly built, insect-eating non-passerine, living in trees or bushes, or on the ground; many species of cuckoo are nest parasites (= Cuculidae).

• **CURASSOW**
A type of large, long-tailed, long-legged forest bird resembling a **gamebird**, often perching in trees (part of family Cracidae).

• **CURRAWONG**
A type of large-billed, **crow**like passerine (part of Cracticidae).

• **DABBLING DUCK**
A type of **duck** that feeds by filtering food particles from the water with its bill.

• **DARTER**
A type of **waterbird** with a long, snakelike neck, a thin, dagger-like bill, and webbed feet, that swims underwater to catch fish (= family Anhingidae).

• **DISPLAY**
Conspicuous behavior by which a bird indicates feelings, such as sexual or aggressive excitement.

• **DISTRIBUTION**
The total area in which a bird is regularly seen. In this book, distribution maps include areas where the bird has been introduced by humans.

• **DIVER**
A type of fish-eating **waterbird** with legs positioned well back on the body for underwater pursuit of prey; known as **loons** in North America (= family Gaviidae).

• **DIVING DUCK**
A type of **duck** that finds food by swimming underwater, propelling itself with webbed feet.

• **DIVING-PETREL**
A type of seabird like a **petrel** that feeds on **plankton** by diving, often plunging through waves (= family Pelecanoididae).

• **DOMESTICATED**
A bird bred in captive or farm conditions to produce a type that is useful, decorative, or otherwise desirable to humans.

• **DOVE**
Alternative name for some (often smaller) species of **pigeon**.

• **DOWN**
A loose-textured feather structure, occurring either as whole feathers or as parts of feathers, that helps insulate the body and retain heat.

• **DRONGO**
A type of strong-billed, long-tailed, alert passerine, usually black, that hunts insects from a perch (= family Dicruridae).

• **DUCK**
A type of **waterfowl** that spends most of its time on water rather than on land and typically has a broad, flattened bill for extracting food from water or mud.

• **EAGLE**
A type of large, strong **bird of prey** that actively hunts other animals (part of family Accipitridae).

• **ECLIPSE PLUMAGE**
A camouflage plumage briefly assumed by a male after molting out of its vivid breeding plumage.

• **EGRET**
A slenderly built type of **heron** that is often pure white and often has fine, loose-textured display plumes when breeding.

• **EURASIA**
The landmass comprising the continents of Europe and Asia and adjacent islands.

• **EYE RING**
A narrow and distinctively colored ring, either of feathers or bare skin, around the eye.

• **EYE STRIPE**
A distinctly colored stripe that passes across the side of the head including the area of the eye.

• FACIAL DISKS
The two prominent, roughly semicircular shapes made by the feathers on either side of the eyes of most **owl** species.

• FAIRY-WREN
A type of small passerine of Australasia with a long tail that is usually carried upright (= family Maluridae).

• FALCON
A stoutly built **bird of prey** with tapering wings and a short, strongly-curved bill (= family Falconidae).

• FANTAIL
A type of flycatcher of forest or scrub, often hunting insects in foliage, fanning and raising its tail (part of family Monarchidae).

• FINCH
A type of sparrowlike bird with a short, stout bill used for cracking seeds (= family Fringillidae); alternatively refers to similar birds of other families, e.g. **waxbills.**

• FLAMINGO
A type of wading bird of saline waters with very long legs, wings, and neck, and a short, broad, angled bill used for filtering fine food particles (= family Phoenicopteridae).

• FLIGHT FEATHERS
Large, long feathers of wings and tail, used in flight.

• FLOCK
A group of birds remaining together for social reasons.

• FLYCATCHER
A type of passerine that typically catches aerial prey by flying out from a perch, to which it then returns (= families Monarchidae, Muscicapidae, and Tyrannidae).

• FORAGE
To search for food of any kind by hunting over an area.

• FORM
A variant of a **species.** This word can refer to (i) a type clearly identifiable as a **subspecies;** (ii) a broader regional type comprising two or more **subspecies;** or (iii) a **color phase.**

• FRANCOLIN
A type of **gamebird** resembling a **partridge,** usually feeding on the ground and living in open country (part of family Phasianidae).

• FROGMOUTH
A type of nocturnal, perching non-passerine with a short, wide bill and huge gape, swooping down to the ground to snatch prey (= family Podargidae).

• FRUIT-DOVE
Another name for a **fruit-pigeon.**

• FRUIT-PIGEON
A type of **pigeon** living in trees or shrubs and feeding mainly on fruit taken from the branches.

• FRUITCROW
A type of crowlike, fruit-eating **cotinga** showing patches of bright plumage color.

• GAMEBIRD
Any bird of the **pheasant** family; these are often hunted for food or sport (= family Phasianidae).

• GENUS
A group of closely related **species** that have all evolved from the same ancestor (plural is "genera").

• GLEANING
Randomly searching for and picking up food items.

• GLOSSY STARLING
A type of **starling** with shiny and often brightly colored feathers.

• GNATCATCHER
A type of small, slender passerine with a thin bill and long tail, that hunts insects in trees and bushes (= family Polioptilidae).

• GODWIT
A type of **shorebird** with a long, thin bill, which may be either straight or slightly upcurved (part of family Scolopacidae).

• GOOSE
A type of **waterfowl** with relatively long legs and a short, strong bill, adapted for walking, grazing, and digging for roots.

• GOSHAWK
A type of large, forest-dwelling **hawk** with broad, rounded wings and a long tail.

• GRACKLE
(i) A type of glossy-plumaged **New World** blackbird with a slim, tapering bill and a long tail. (ii) Also describes certain species of **myna** and **starling.**

• GRASSLAND
Open areas where vegetation is dominated by short or tall grasses.

• GREBE
A type of thin-necked, fine-billed **waterbird** that is almost tailless and feeds by pursuing underwater prey, propelled by feet with lobed toes (= family Podicipedidae).

• GREEN-PIGEON
A type of fruit-eating **pigeon** with green plumage for camouflage, living among trees and shrubs.

• GROSBEAK
A finchlike bird with a very stout, seed-cracking bill. Refers to some birds in the **finch** family (Fringillidae) and some **cardinals** (part of family Emberizidae).

• GROUSE
A type of stout, mainly ground-dwelling **gamebird** with dense feathering.

• GUAN
A type of tree-dwelling bird that resembles a **gamebird,** with long, strong legs and often with bare **wattles** (part of Cracidae).

• GUINEAFOWL
A type of compactly built **gamebird** with a short tail, living mainly on dry, open ground.

• GULL
A type of web-footed **waterbird,** often coastal, with a strong bill; scavenging or partly predatory (part of family Laridae).

• HABITAT
The part of the environment in which a species normally occurs.

• HARRIER
A type of **bird of prey** with long, narrow wings used in low, gliding flight, and with long legs and tail (part of family Accipitridae).

• HAWK
A type of **bird of prey** that actively hunts live animals (part of family Accipitridae).

• HAWK-OWL
(i) A type of **owl** with a hawklike shape. (ii) Alternatively a type of Australasian **owl** with small **facial disks** and a relatively prominent bill (parts of family Strigidae).

• HELPER
A bird other than the parents that assists in some stages of nesting.

• HEMIPODE
An old name for a **button-quail,** meaning "half-foot" in reference to the absence of a hind toe (= family Turnicidae).

• HERMIT
A type of **hummingbird** living solitarily among forest vegetation.

• HERON
A type of wading bird with long legs, long neck, broad wings, and a dagger bill, usually wading to catch fish (= family Ardeidae).

• HONEYCREEPER
(i) A type of **tanager** with a slender bill for extracting nectar from flowers (part of family Thraupidae). (ii) A type of finch-like bird belonging to an island

group with varied bill shapes
(= family Drepanidae).

• **HONEYEATER**
A type of small to moderate-size
passerine with a brush-tipped
tongue, feeding mostly on nectar
from flowers, sometimes also on
insects (= family Meliphagidae).

• **HONEYGUIDE**
A type of small, perching non-
passerine that feeds by catching
insects in the foliage and eating
wax, brood, and honey from bees'
nests (= family Indicatoridae).

• **HOOD**
An area of a single plumage color
extending over the head.

• **HORNBILL**
A type of non-passerine with long
tail and enormous, downcurved
bill that is usually surmounted by
a casque. Some hornbills are tree
dwellers (= family Bucerotidae);
others feed only on the ground
(= family Bucorvidae).

• **HUMMINGBIRD**
A type of tiny, often brightly
colored non-passerine with a thin
bill used for feeding on flower
nectar, often while hovering
(= family Trochilidae).

• **IBIS**
A type of goose-size wading bird
with long legs and neck and a
long, downcurved bill (part of
family Threskiornithidae).

• **IMMATURE**
Alternative word for a juvenile.

• **IMPERIAL PIGEON**
A large and often dull-colored
type of fruit-pigeon.

• **INCUBATE**
To provide constant warmth for an
egg, allowing the embryo inside it
to develop.

• **INTRODUCED**
Describes a bird species that has
been brought by humans to an
area where it would not naturally
occur, and is now established.

• **INVERTEBRATE**
A type of small animal having no
backbone, such as a worm, insect,
spider, snail, shrimp, or crab.

• **IRIDESCENT**
A term describing the glittering
appearance of a feather that has a
structure that causes it to reflect
different colors according to the
direction of the light.

• **JACAMAR**
A type of slender, long-tailed,
perching non-passerine with a
long, thin bill, that flies out from a

perch after insects (= family
Galbulidae).

• **JACANA**
A type of small **waterbird** with
long legs, toes and claws, that
walks on floating waterplants
(= family Jacanidae).

• **JAY**
A type of perching passerine of
the **crow** family, usually noisy
and brightly colored and often
sociable in behavior.

• **JUVENILE**
(i) A young bird that is not yet
mature enough to breed, often
having a plumage differing in
color and pattern from adults. (ii)
Alternatively (but not in this
book) used to describe a young
bird that is not yet independent
from its parents, and is usually
less than three months old.

• **KESTREL**
A type of sturdily built **falcon**
that usually hovers when hunting
and takes small, weak prey.

• **KINGBIRD**
A type of **tyrant flycatcher**,
often aggressive enough to harry
predators.

• **KINGFISHER**
A type of large-headed, dagger-
billed, perching non-passerine that
plunge-dives into water in
pursuit of insects or fish, some
species taking prey from the
ground (= family Alcedinidae).

• **KITE**
A type of lightly built **bird of
prey** with long wings and often
forked tail, and with agile flight,
that typically takes weak prey or
scavenges for **carrion** (part of
family Accipitridae).

• **KOOKABURRA**
A type of large **kingfisher** with
noisy calls and a heavy, blunt bill,
often living far away from water.

• **LARK**
A type of inconspicuous, ground-
dwelling passerine, the male bird
usually advertising itself with
prolonged aerial songflights
(= family Alaudidae).

• **LAUGHING THRUSH**
A type of **babbler** that utters
laughing calls, often in chorus.

• **LEK**
A communal display site used by
certain bird species. A number of
males display simultaneously and
females visit the site in order to
mate with a male. The lek may be
on the ground or in a tree.

• **LOON**
The North American and
Scandinavian name for a **diver**.

• **LORIKEET**
A type of Australasian **parrot**
feeding on nectar and pollen.

• **LORY**
A heavily built type of **lorikeet**.

• **LOVEBIRD**
A type of small, slender-billed,
short-tailed African **parrot**,
usually seen in pairs that keep in
close contact with one another.

• **MACAW**
A type of South or Central
American **parrot** with a long tail
and heavy bill, the best known
species being distinctively large.

• **MALLEE**
Low-growing eucalyptus woodland
of semi-arid areas, in which trees
are multi-trunked.

• **MANAKIN**
A type of small, brightly colored,
fruit-eating passerine of forest and
scrub (= family Pipridae).

• **MANGROVE SWAMP**
A forest habitat in tropical
estuaries and lagoons, in which the
trees are supported on roots raised
above the mud.

• **MARTIN**
Alternative name for some species
of **swallow**.

• **MEGAPODE**
A type of chicken-size ground-bird
that builds a mound in which its
eggs are incubated, or digs a hole
in warm ground for this purpose (=
family Megapodiidae).

• **MIGRANT**
A bird that makes regular seasonal
movements between breeding and
nonbreeding areas.

• **MIMICRY**
The ability of a bird to imitate
sounds it hears, such as the songs
and calls of other bird species, or
occasionally other sounds,
including the human voice.

• **MINER**
A type of moderate-size, sociable
honeyeater.

• **MOBBING**
Noisy calling and mock attacks
carried out by a group of birds
against a predator, making the
presence of the predator known to
other birds in the area.

• **MONARCH FLYCATCHER**
A type of **flycatcher**, often with
bright colors, occurring in Africa,
Asia, or Australasia, often in the
tropics (= family Monarchidae).

• **MOTMOT**
A type of tropical forest non-passerine with a long, often racket-shaped tail and a long, strong bill, that perches and swoops on small prey (= family Momotidae).

• **MOUSEBIRD**
A type of small, plump, mouse-colored non-passerine with a long tail, mainly eating leaves and buds (= family Coliidae).

• **MUDFLATS**
Level areas of mud created by tidal movements on coasts, in bays, and bordering large rivers.

• **MYNA**
A type of **starling** with a heavy build and a stout bill.

• **NECTAR**
A sugar solution found in small amounts inside flowers.

• **NESTLING**
A very young bird that needs to remain in a nest and to be tended by adults.

• **NEW WORLD BLACKBIRD**
Refers to the varied passerine family to which the American blackbirds belong; the family is also sometimes known as the **troupials** and sometimes as the icterids (= family Icteridae).

• **NEW WORLD VULTURE**
A type of large, bare-headed scavenging bird of the Americas (= family Cathartidae).

• **NIGHTHAWK**
An American type of **nightjar** often flying in daylight. Like other nightjars, it resembles a **hawk** or **falcon** in outline.

• **NIGHTJAR**
A type of non-passerine, usually night-flying, with long wings and tail and a very wide mouth, feeding on insects caught in flight (= family Caprimulgidae).

• **NODDY**
A type of dark sea **tern** with a pale forehead that paired birds show to one another in mutual nodding displays at the nest.

• **NOMADIC**
Having a tendency to wander unpredictably.

• **NON-PASSERINE**
A bird species other than those that constitute the passerine order of mainly perching songbirds (see also p. 38).

• **NUNBIRD**
A type of dark, sluggish non-passerine living in forests, that

perches and flies out after insects (part of family Galbulidae).

• **NUTHATCH**
A type of strong-footed, small passerine with a short, strong bill that climbs tree trunks and branches for food and hammers open nuts (= family Sittidae).

• **OLD WORLD FLYCATCHER**
A small **flycatcher** of Eurasia or Africa (= family Muscicapidae).

• **OPEN FOREST**
Forest in which trees and undergrowth are well spread, with spaces between allowing visibility and movement.

• **ORIOLE**
A type of agile, slender-billed passerine of the higher foliage of trees and scrub, feeding on fruit and insects. Refers both to Old World orioles (= family Oriolidae) and New World orioles (part of family Icteridae).

• **OROPENDOLA**
A type of large passerine of tropical forests with a strong, tapering bill, that weaves a long, bag-shaped nest and suspends it from branches of tall trees in colonies (part of family Icteridae).

• **OVENBIRD**
A bird that makes a domed nest with a side entrance resembling an old-fashioned bread oven. Only one species is known as the Ovenbird (part of family Parulidae). Seven species make ovenlike mud nests, and the family to which they belong is known as the ovenbird family (= Furnariidae), although these seven species are themselves known as horneros, rather than ovenbirds.

• **OWL**
A type of predatory bird, usually flying at night, with large eyes set in **facial disks**, strong, grasping feet and claws, and usually silent flight (= families Tytonidae and Strigidae).

• **OWLET-NIGHTJAR**
A type of soft-plumaged non-passerine with a large head, large eyes, and a small bill but a very broad mouth, swooping down onto prey from a perch (= family Aegothelidae).

• **PARADISE-FLYCATCHER**
A type of **monarch flycatcher** in which the male has a very long, slender, forked tail.

• **PARAKEET**
Alternative name for a small, long-tailed **parrot**.

• **PARDALOTE**
A type of small, stubby-billed passerine that hunts insects in tree foliage (part of Dicaeidae).

• **PARROT**
A type of non-passerine bird with strong feet for grasping and holding, and with a strong, short, deep bill with a hooked tip, that can manipulate and split open food items (= family Psittacidae).

• **PARROTBILL**
A type of small passerine with a short, stout bill for extracting insects from reed or bamboo stems (= family Panuridae).

• **PARROTLET**
A type of very small, short-tailed **parrot** of South American forests.

• **PARTRIDGE**
A type of stoutly built, ground-dwelling **gamebird** with a short tail and rounded wings.

• **PARTY**
A small group of individual birds.

• **PASSERINE**
A bird belonging to the passerine order of usually perching songbirds (see also p. 244).

• **PELICAN**
A type of heavily built **waterbird** with a long bill and an expandable skin pouch hanging from the bill and throat (= family Pelecanidae).

• **PENGUIN**
A type of flightless seabird with short legs set well back on the body, hunting underwater by swimming with narrow, flipper-like wings, and walking upright when on land (= family Spheniscidae).

• **PEPPERSHRIKE**
A type of heavily built **vireo** with a stout, hook-tipped bill.

• **PERCHING BIRD**
A bird with feet adapted for grasping the more level twigs and branches in order to stand or rest, usually living mainly in trees or shrubs. A perching bird is not necessarily a **passerine**.

• **PETREL**
A type of oceanic seabird with nostrils in the form of tubes lying along the top of the bill, with long, narrow wings and fast flight, usually feeding by taking small creatures from or just under the sea surface (part of family Procellariidae).

● **PEWEE**
A type of small, drab-looking **tyrant flycatcher** named after the sound of its usual song.

● **PHASE**
Another word for **color phase**.

● **PHOEBE**
A type of **tyrant flycatcher** named after its "fee-bee" call.

● **PICULET**
A type of tiny **woodpecker**.

● **PIGEON**
A type of non-passerine with thick, soft plumage, a small, rounded head, fleshy nostrils, and cooing calls. Some are perching birds and others are ground birds, usually walking with rapid steps (= family Columbidae).

● **PILEATED**
Refers to a bird in which the feathers of the whole top of the head form a crest.

● **PIPIT**
A type of small, inconspicuously colored, mainly ground-dwelling passerine with a slender, insect-eating bill, usually walking and running but not hopping (part of family Motacillidae).

● **PITTA**
A type of forest-floor passerine with a large head, round body, very short tail, and long legs (= family Pittidae).

● **PLANKTON**
A varied community of animals and plants, mostly microscopically small, swimming or suspended in seawater or lakes.

● **PLOVER**
A type of **shorebird** with a rounded head and relatively short bill. Plovers typically feed in open places by making short runs and snatching up small prey that is visible on the ground surface (= family Charadriidae).

● **PRATINCOLE**
A type of **shorebird** with a short, broad bill, large eyes, and often a forked tail, that catches insects in flight (part of family Glareolidae).

● **PREENING**
Actions by which a bird grooms its plumage and maintains it in good condition by use of bill and claws.

● **PRIMARY FEATHERS**
Long flight feathers on the outer half of the wing.

● **PUFFBIRD**
A type of stout, loose-plumaged, perching non-passerine with a short, stout bill, that flies out from a perch to seize prey in nearby vegetation (part of Bucconidae).

● **QUAIL**
A type of small, plump, ground-living **gamebird** with a short tail.

● **RACE**
Alternative word for **subspecies**.

● **RACKET**
The expanded and usually rounded tip of a long feather.

● **RAIL**
A type of compact, long-toed non-passerine of low vegetation, marsh, and waterside (= family Rallidae).

● **RAIN FOREST**
Evergreen tropical forest that depends on constant rainfall throughout the year.

● **RAPTOR**
Alternative word for **bird of prey**.

● **RATITE**
Typically a type of large, flightless, running bird such as an Ostrich, which lacks the projecting keel of the breastbone found in all other birds. The group also includes **tinamous**.

● **REDSTART**
A type of **chat** with a rufous tail and rump (part of family Turdidae); also refers to certain species of American **warbler** (part of family Parulidae).

● **RESIDENT**
A bird that normally spends all of its life within a limited area.

● **ROBIN**
Name often given to a number of passerine species, mostly small; most have a conspicuously orange, red, or pink breast (part of families Turdidae and Eopsaltriidae).

● **ROLLER**
A type of stout, colorful, big-headed non-passerine with long wings, that typically watches from a perch and swoops to catch prey on the ground. The name describes its acrobatic display flight (= family Coracidae).

● **ROOST**
(i) To rest or sleep. (ii) A place where birds do this. (iii) A site where many birds roost. Day-flying birds roost by night, nocturnal birds by day.

● **RUMP**
The lower part of a bird's back, above the tail and underneath the wings when these are closed.

● **SALTMARSH**
Level areas of coastal marsh where the water is salty.

● **SANDGROUSE**
A type of short-billed, long-winged non-passerine with feathered legs, that lives on the ground in dry, open landscapes and looks like a **gamebird** (= family Pteroclididae).

● **SANDPIPER**
A type of gray or brown **shorebird** that usually travels in large flocks. May be large or small (part of family Scolopacidae).

● **SAPSUCKER**
A type of **woodpecker** that feeds on the sap oozing from rows of holes that it makes in tree trunks, and the insects attracted to it.

● **SCALY PATTERN**
A plumage pattern produced by the overlapping effect of rounded feathers that have distinct edges, either dark or light.

● **SCRAPE**
A nest hollow on the ground which a bird makes by pressing its body to the ground, rotating its body, and kicking backward with its feet while doing so.

● **SCREAMER**
A type of large, South American **waterbird** with big and long-toed but unwebbed feet, a small, curved bill, and loud, far-carrying calls (= family Anhimidae).

● **SCRUB**
A type of vegetation made up of shrubs or low trees or a mixture of the two, often thickly grown, and frequently including thorns.

● **SECONDARY FEATHERS**
Medium-length flight feathers situated on the inner wing.

● **SECONDARY FOREST**
Forest that has recently regrown after the original forest has been cleared; the trees are usually less tall and more uniform in height, and with less variety of species, thus offering a different selection of bird habitats from those in the original (primary) forest.

● **SEED-EATER**
A type of bird that relies mainly on seed for its diet and usually has a short, stout bill adapted for cracking and removing the husk, to eat the seed inside.

● **SHELDUCK**
A type of long-legged **duck** that frequently walks on land and feeds typically by dabbling on the surface of mudflats or in shallow water. It is sometimes more like a **goose** in its general behavior.

• **SHOREBIRD**
A type of non-passerine that often walks or runs on the ground, typically with long legs, wings, and neck, and usually lives at the edge of water. Includes **plovers**, **sandpipers**, and similar birds.

• **SHRIKE**
A type of small, fierce passerine with a largish head and short, stout, hook-tipped bill that hunts small animals (= family Laniidae).

• **SKULKING**
Tending to choose to hide in vegetation or other cover whenever the opportunity arises.

• **SNAKEBIRD**
Alternative word for **darter**.

• **SNIPE**
A type of **shorebird** of marshy places with a very long, slender bill for probing deeply for food in mud or soft ground.

• **SOLITARY**
Usually remaining as an isolated individual or pair, rather than joining other birds of its species.

• **SONG**
A usually elaborate sound that a bird utters for the purpose of advertising itself or in display.

• **SONGBIRDS**
Used by many writers to refer to passerines.

• **SPANGLED**
Refers to birds whose plumage is scattered over with conspicuous light marks, usually made up of pale feather tips.

• **SPARROW**
A type of small, dull-colored passerine with a short, blunt bill for cracking seeds (= family Passeridae, and part of family Emberizidae).

• **SPARROWHAWK**
A type of small, Old World **hawk** with short, rounded wings, long tail, and long claws, adapted for hunting and eating small birds.

• **SPECIES**
A group of individuals that are related through a common origin and are capable of freely interbreeding and perpetuating the identity of the group.

• **SPINETAIL**
A type of small passerine with stiff, spiny tips to the shafts of the tail feathers, that perches; in contrast with the **treecreepers**, spinetails do not use their tails as a support for climbing (part of family Furnariidae).

• **SPOONBILL**
A type of large wading bird of shallow waters with long legs and a long neck, and a long bill whose tip is broad, flat, and rounded, for filtering food from the water (part of family Threskiornithidae).

• **STARLING**
A type of slender passerine, usually with a sharp, tapering bill for eating insects and fruit (= family Sturnidae).

• **STORK**
A type of large bird with long legs and neck and a long, tapering bill. Storks walk on land and wade in shallow water in rivers, lakes, and marshes (= family Ciconiidae).

• **STORM-PETREL**
A type of small **petrel** with low, fluttering flight (= family Hydrobatidae).

• **SUBSPECIES**
A geographical subdivision of a **species** in which all birds show certain features that distinguish them from other subspecies.

• **SUNBIRD**
A type of passerine, usually small and brightly colored, that perches to feed on nectar from flowers, taken with a very slender bill and a fine, tubular tongue (= family Nectariniidae).

• **SWALLOW**
A type of small passerine with a small bill, a broad mouth, narrow wings, and usually a forked tail, that sits on a perch when resting and feeds by pursuing insects in the air (= family Hirundinidae).

• **SWAN**
A type of large, usually white, mainly swimming **waterfowl** with a long body, short legs, and a long, slender neck for reaching underwater to pull up waterplants for food.

• **SWIFT**
A type of aerial non-passerine with long, narrow wings and with a short and very wide mouth, that feeds by catching insects in the air. Swifts have small feet and can only cling to surfaces rather than perching (= family Apodidae).

• **TANAGER**
A type of passerine, often brightly colored, of trees and bushes, mostly in the tropics. Most have a seed-cracking type of bill, but use it mainly to feed on fruits (part of family Emberizidae).

• **TEAL**
A type of small, surface-feeding **dabbling duck**.

• **TERN**
A type of seagoing or inland **waterbird** with narrow, tapering wings, a tapering bill, and usually a forked tail, that swoops down or plunge-dives to seize prey in the water (= family Laridae).

• **TERRITORY**
An area defended by a bird, pair, or small social group against others, for feeding and often also for nesting, varying in size from the immediate surroundings of an individual bird to several square miles.

• **THICK-KNEE**
A type of **shorebird**, usually nocturnal, with a large head and large eyes, occurring in open spaces (= family Burhinidae).

• **THORNBILL**
A type of small, insect-eating passerine, usually with a short, thin bill (= family Acanthizidae).

• **THRASHER**
A type of thrushlike passerine of low vegetation with a slender bill which it uses to probe among leaves and toss leaf litter aside in search of food (part of family Mimidae).

• **THRUSH**
A type of small to moderate-size passerine, often ground-dwelling, with a slender bill and often with a melodious song (= family Turdidae).

• **TINAMOU**
A type of ground-living non-passerine with limited powers of flight, a long neck with a small head, and long, strong legs (= family Tinamidae).

• **TIT**
A type of small passerine of trees and shrubs, with a small, strong bill and strong feet for acrobatic feeding. Tits are known as **chickadees** in North America (= family Paridae).

• **TITMOUSE**
Alternative word for **tit**.

• **TODY**
A type of small, green, rounded, perching non-passerine with a long bill, that flies out from a perch to take insects from the air or foliage (= family Todidae).

• **TOUCAN**
A type of fruit-eating, perching, forest-dwelling non-passerine

with an enlarged, blunt-tipped bill (= family Rhamphastidae).

• **TREE-DUCK**
An alternative name for **whistling-duck**.

TREE-SWIFT
A type of aerial non-passerine with a short, very wide mouth, and long wings and tail, feeding on insects caught in the air, and able to perch, rest, and nest in trees (= family Hemiprocnidae).

• **TREECREEPER**
A type of small passerine with a slender, slightly downcurved bill, that climbs tree trunks and branches, some species using the tail as a support (= families Certhiidae and Climacteridae).

• **TROGON**
A type of tree-dwelling non-passerine with a compact body, long tail, and round head with a short, wide bill; it flies out from a perch to snatch insects in midair, or to take fruit while hovering (= family Trogonidae).

• **TROUPIAL**
An alternative name referring either to the **New World blackbirds** in general (= family Icteridae) or to a common species of South American **oriole** that belongs to this family.

• **TRUMPETER**
A type of forest-dwelling non-passerine, living mainly on the ground, with a longish neck and round head, long, strong legs, and deep calls (= family Psophiidae).

• **TUNDRA**
A **habitat** consisting of short vegetation, often waterlogged, bordering the polar regions; the underlying soil is frozen in winter, but the surface thaws in summer, allowing some low plant growth.

• **TURACO**
A type of slender, soft-plumaged non-passerine of trees and shrubs with a long tail, rounded wings, and a short, blunt bill for eating fruit (= family Musophagidae).

• **TURKEY-VULTURE**
The most common species of **New World vulture**; this name is sometimes used for the family (Cathartidae) as a whole.

• **TYRANT FLYCATCHER**
A type of **flycatcher** of the Americas (= family Tyrannidae).

• **VIREO**
A type of small, slender passerine with a short, sturdy bill. Vireos

typically hunt insects among the foliage (= family Vireonidae).

• **VULTURE**
A type of scavenging **bird of prey** feeding on **carrion** and lacking or partly lacking feathers on head and neck (= family Cathartidae and part of family Accipitridae).

• **WADER**
(i) A British term, in common use until the 1970s, now generally replaced by the North American term **shorebird**. (ii) A North American term for a large, long-legged wading bird such as a **stork, heron**, or **spoonbill**.

• **WAGTAIL**
A type of slender, ground-dwelling passerine with a long tail that is flexed up and down when the bird is active (part of family Motacillidae); also refers to certain similar-looking species of **tyrant** and **monarch flycatcher**.

• **WARBLER**
A type of insect-eating passerine, often with a frequently used, musical song (families Sylviidae, Parulidae). Also refers to certain species in the **thornbill** family (Acanthizidae).

• **WATERBIRD**
A bird that is usually found in, on, or near water. This term covers a broad range of bird families.

• **WATERFOWL**
A type of web-footed **waterbird** of the **duck, goose**, and **swan** family (= Anatidae).

• **WATTLE**
A prominent or pendant patch of bare skin on the head or neck, usually brightly colored and often capable of being enlarged in display.

• **WAXBILL**
A type of small or very small passerine with a seed-cracking bill that is often bright red or orange (= family Estrildidae).

• **WEAVER**
A type of small passerine with a seed-cracking bill. Most species weave their nests with strips of fresh plant material (= family Ploceidae).

• **WHEATEAR**
A type of small, thrushlike bird that lives mainly on the ground and has a conspicuous white **rump** (part of family Turdidae).

• **WHISTLER**
A type of passerine with a rounded head and strong or hook-

tipped bill, and often a loud, musical song (= family Pachycephalidae).

• **WHISTLING-DUCK**
A type of long-legged and long-necked **duck**, usually gregarious and having noisy, whistling calls, some species resting and nesting in trees.

• **WHITE-EYE**
A type of tiny passerine living in trees and shrubs, with a small, thin bill and with a white ring of feathers around each eye (= family Zosteropidae).

• **WHYDAH**
A type of long-tailed **weaver** parasitizing nests of **waxbills**.

• **WIDOWBIRD**
A type of long-tailed **weaver** that is not a nest parasite. The long, black tail gave rise to the "widow" part of this name.

• **WILDFOWL**
Another name for **waterfowl**.

• **WING BAR**
A short, brightly colored or white band on the wing.

• **WING STRIPE**
A brightly colored band along the extended wing.

• **WOODCREEPER**
A type of slender-bodied passerine that climbs tree trunks and branches, often supported by its tail; bills vary between species, from slender to strong and from long to short (= family Dendrocolaptidae).

• **WOODPECKER**
A type of non-passerine that clambers up tree trunks and branches, partly propped up by its tail, with a strong, tapering bill that can make holes in wood (= family Picidae).

• **WOODSWALLOW**
A type of perching passerine with a large head, short, broad bill, and long wings, that feeds in flocks by chasing insects in the air (= family Artamidae).

• **WREN**
A type of passerine of low vegetation, often small, normally thin-billed, and usually with an upright tail (= family Troglodytidae); or a similar-looking bird of another family (Acanthisittidae, Maluridae, Acanthizidae).

INDEX

ACKNOWLEDGMENTS

Dorling Kindersley, Inc. would like to thank Frank Gill, David Wiedner, and Keith Russell of the Academy of Natural Sciences of Philadelphia for their invaluable help in preparing the US edition of the book.

PICTURE CREDITS
Illustrations: endpapers and pages 6–243, 304–395 by Simone End, pages 244–303 by Linden Artists/Steve Lings. Computer map origination: Alastair Wardle. Abbreviations: *b* = bottom, *t* = top, *c* = center, *l* = left, *r* = right. Photographs not listed here are copyright Dorling Kindersley, supplied by Cyril Laubscher, Dennis Avon, and Maslowski Photo. Jacket photographs: Front: Jim Battles *bl*; Bruce Coleman/Wayne Lankinen *bc*; Sharon Cummings *tl*; Nature Photographers/Roger Tidman *cl*; John Snyder *c*. Back: Oxford Scientific Films/C.W. Helliwell. Front flap: Paul Doherty. Back flap: Jim Battles. Spine: VIREO/J. Dunning. Inside photographs: Aquila/Hans Gebuis *56b*; Conrad Greaves *145t*, *195t*; Brian Hawkes *153t*; Stuart Horton *189b*; Wayne Lankinen *46b*, *140c*, *200t* , *200b*, *216t*, *216c*, *257b*, *279b*, *280t*, *350b*, *356t*; T. Leach *191t*; Robert Maier *73b*; J. Mills *52b*; M. Mockler *289c*; A .T . Moffett *392t*; B. Speake *269b*; C. & T. Stuart *64*; M.C. Wilkes *11tl*, *39*, *56t*, *65b*, *150t*, *152b*, *155b*, *186b*,

393b; Gary Weber *41*. Ardea/Peter Alden *204b*; Dennis Avon *166b*, *176c*, *221b*, *239t*, *275b*, *278c*, *348c*, *366b*; J. A. Bailey *67*, *293b*; L.R. Beames *128b*, *376b*; Hans and Judy Beste *99t*, *136b*, *154b*, *205b*, *311c*, *313b*; J.B. & S. Bottomley *161t*; G.K. Brown *137t*; Graeme Chapman *325b*; John Daniels *280c*; Hans Dossenbach *63t*; J.S. Dunning *190t*, *247t*, *258b*, *259t*, *259b*, *261t*, *285t*, *352t*; M.D. England *210t*, *274b*, *283t*, *348b*; Jean-Paul Ferrero *49t*; K.W. Fink *42t*, *87*, *98t*, *107b*, *111b*, *113b*, *117t*, *143b*, *157t*, *192b*, *194b*, *199b*, *231t*, *289t*; François Gohier *43t*, *120*, *129b*, *215t*, *244t*; A. Greensmith *51b*, *57t*, *124t*, *228t*, *331b*, *338c*; Joanna van Grulsen *209b*; Clem Haagner *276t*; J.L. Mason *244c*; E. McNamara *272c*, *312t*, *312c*; P. Morris *193t*, *322b*, *387t*; Don Hadden *140b*; Irene Neufeldt *308c*; S. Roberts *217t*, *254t*; Peter Steyn *6t*, *91b*, *246b*, *286t*, *303b*; W.R. Taylor *314t*;

A.D. Trounson & M.C. Clampett *296t, 331t, 332b, 383t, 383b*; Peter Vaughn *52c*; Alan Weaving *190b, 276b*; Wardene Weisser *114b, 282t, 291c, 381t, 390t*. **Jim Battles** *288b, 339b, 361t*. **Steve Bentsen** *205c*. **Frank Blackburn** *94t, 94b, 144t, 207t, 222t, 241t, 268t, 270c, 282b, 304b, 306t, 307t, 307c, 309t, 319c, 321t, 324t, 334b*; Kevin Carlson *287b, 304c, 254c, 321c, 372t*; Melvin Grey *80b, 93b, 108b, 139b, 143c, 147b*. **BIOS/D.** Halleux *118t, 227b*; C. Seitre *384b*. **Alan Bovee** *294t, 323c, 351t*. **David Broadbent** *55t, 149b*. **Mike Buxton** *323t*. **Bruce Coleman Ltd** *165t, 209t, 266t, 268b, 320t, 325c, 334c*; Jen & Des Bartlett *58t, 130b, 141t*; N.G. Blake *15cr*; B. & C. Calhoun *219b, 238b, 253t, 280t, 354c, 358t, 360b, 363t*; Brian J. Coates *294b*; Raymond Cramm *130t*; Gerald Cubitt *115b*; Peter Davey *112t*; Ernest Duscher *158b*; Inigo Everson *50b*; John Fennell *148t*; C.B. & D.W Frith *167t, 386t*; Jose Luis Gonzales Grande *188t, 379b*; Pekka Heto *202t*; Udo Hirsch *146t*; Stephen Kraseman *83t, 125b*; O. Langrand *265b, 279t, 380b*; Gordon Langsbury *7b, 15cl, 15bl, 149t, 271b, 279c*; Wayne Lankinen *336c, 340t, 341b, 363b*; Werner Layer *231b, 287c, 288t*; Dr Rocco Longo *283c*; L.C Marigo *42b, 70b, 97b, 180t, 256t,256b*; Rinnie van Meurs *156t, 309b*; Dr Scott Nielson *85t, 110b*; M.R. Phicton *105b, 164t*; Dieter & Mary Plage *109t, 131t*; Dr Eckart Potts *121t*; Mike Price *257t, 275t*; Hans Reinhard *44, 98b, 113t, 165b, 197b, 272b, 295c, 363c*; Norbert Rosing *138b*; John Shaw *127b*; Norman Tomalin *264c, 265t*; Joseph van Wormer *212t, 338b*; Uwe Walz *133t*; Paul R. Wilkinson *203t*; Rod Williams *257t*; Konrad Wothe *53t, 301t, 305b, 360c*; Günter Zeisler *191b, 218b*. **Brian J. Coates** *166t, 315b, 380t*. **Bill Coster** *50t, 86b, 201b*. **Sharon Cummings** *78b, 81b, 108t, 240b, 242t, 320b, 356c, 388b*. **Rob Curtis** *269c, 270t, 351c*. **R.S. Daniell** *135t, 163t, 277t, 303t, 379t*. **Peter Davey** *61b, 66b, 99b*. **Paul Doherty** *11t, 70t, 74t, 89t, 97t, 103t, 122t, 126t, 132b, 142b, 148b, 151b, 159t, 160t, 160b, 162t, 208t, 220t, 271c, 302t, 303c, 334t, 336t, 362c*. **Brian Gadsby** *82t, 85b*. **Peter Ginn** *128t, 229b, 373b*. **Robert Harding Picture Library** *6tr*. S.C. Hendricks *118b, 225t, 368b, 371c, 377t*. **Jack Jeffery** *315t, 352b, 353t, 353c*. **Zig Koch** *6bc, 107t, 122b, 252c*. **Frank Lane Picture Agency/R.** Austing *95t*; A. R. Hamblin *188b*; T. & P. Gardener *310b*; M. Gore *235c*; John Hawkins *395t*; E. & D. Hosking *101b, 183t, 186t, 208b, 217b, 224t, 394b*; F.W. Lane *180b, 261b*; G. Moon *51t, 185b, 381b*; R. van Nostrand *146b, 187b*; L. Lee Rue *96b*; L. West *337t*; E. Wilmhurst *75b*; M. B. Withers *60*; W. Wisniewski *68t*. **Cyril Laubscher** *11tcl, 47b, 164c, 168t, 170b, 171t, 175t, 176t, 177c, 179b, 195b, 234c, 264b, 278t, 298c, 299t, 299b, 326c, 327t, 327b, 331c, 338t, 341t, 347c, 362b, 364b, 369t, 369b, 370b, 385t*. **Nico Myburgh** *76b, 124b, 267t, 301c, 310t, 333b, 371t*. **National Photographic Index of Australian Wildlife**/L.F. Schick *382b*; T.A. Waite *333t*; J.D. Waterhouse *385b*; H. Webster *266c*; Babs & Bert Wells *329b*. **Nature Photographers**/Kevin Carlson *270b, 382t*; Andrew Cleave *126b*; P Craig-Cooper *65t, 138t*; Michael Gore *207t*; James Hancock *256c*; M. P. Harris *48*; Hugh Miles *114t*; Paul Sterry *54b, 115t, 123t, 125t, 359t*; Don Smith *145b*; Roger Tidman *144b, 284t, 355t*. **Natural Elements**/Greg Homel *88b, 131b, 133t, 253c, 300b, 392b*. **NHPA**/Henry Ausloos *59t,198b*; A.P. Barnes *321b*; George Bernard *102b*; L Campbell *289b*; Stephen Dalton *301b*; Nigel Dennis *233b, 395b*; Robert Erwin *285b*;

Melvin Grey *134b, 267b*; Helio and Van Ingen *79t, 89b*; A. Janes *104t*; E.A. Jones *77t*; Rich Kirchner *40*; Stephen J. Kraseman *269t*; Lacz Lemoine *91t*; Michael Morcombe *311b*; Haraldo Palo *88t, 233t, 242b, 248c, 255b*; Jany Sauvanet *164b*; Philippa Scott *74b*; John Shaw *47t, 61t*; Morton Strange *132t, 219t*; Phillip Wayne *119b*; Alan Williams *152t, 268c*; David Woodfall *193b*. **NHPA/ANT** *45t*/R.J. Allingham *330t*; Anthony Howard *52t*; B. Chudleigh *317c*; I.R. McCann *177t, 323b*; Frank Park *313c*; Otto Rogge *45b*; M. F. Soper *265c*; Cyril Webster *106t*. **Oxford Scientific Films**/Mike Brown *302b*; Roger Brown *316t*; Ray Coombes *147t*; Michael Fogden *261c*; Jim Frazier & Mantis Wildlife Films *72t*; Max Gibbs *116t*; C.W. Helliwell *157b*; Ben Osborne *49b*; Richard Packwood *58t*; Stan Osolinski *216b*; Tony Tilford *328t, 328b*; Babs & Bert Wells *324b*; Graham J. Wren *335c*. **OSF/Animals Animals**/Patti Murray *284b*. **OSF/Okapia**/Hans Reinhard *370c*. **William Peckover** *123b, 155t, 162b, 167b, 170t, 173b, 204t, 273t, 286c, 310c, 317t, 329c, 332t, 378t, 384t, 387b*. **J. F. Reynolds** *68b, 117b, 121b, 141b, 143t, 224b, 226t, 226b, 228b, 371b, 373t*. **T. Robinson** *308b*. **Swan Photographic Agency**/John Buckingham *84b, 137b, 153b, 243b, 272t*; David M. Cottridge *306c*; Grant Demar *267t, 292b, 305t*; Bill Moorcroft *271t, 360t*; Andrew Ruck *11cc, 80t*; R. Thomas *201t*; Don Withey *84t*. **John Snyder** *90b, 106b, 192t, 282c, 340c*. **Roger Steele** *79b*. **Peter Steyn** *277c*. **Swift Picture Library**/Thomas Dressler *230t*. **Roger Tidman** *82b, 83b, 86t, 92b, 135b, 142t, 150b, 156b, 238t, 394t*. **R.E. Viljoen** *9c, 311t, 312b, 313t, 315c, 316c, 316b, 317b, 318t, 326t, 367c*. **VIREO**/A. Carey *102t, 112b*; R. & N. Bowers *206b*; R.J. Chandler *136t*; B. Chudleigh *168b*; H. Clarke *295b, 349b*; H. Cruikshank *335t*; J. Dunning *43b, 63b, 206t, 212b, 218t, 232b, 234t, 245b, 246t, 246c, 247t, 247b, 248t, 248b, 249t, 249c, 250t, 250c, 250b, 251t, 251b, 252t, 252c, 255t, 258t, 258c, 259c, 263c, 263b, 281t, 281b, 337c, 337b, 339c, 340b, 342b, 343t, 343b, 345t, 345c, 345b, 346b, 347t, 347b, 348t, 353b, 354t, 354b, 355c, 357b*; W. Green *78t, 243t*; C.H. Greenwalt *161b, 211t, 211c, 212c, 213b, 214t, 215c, 215b, 223t, 260b, 263t, 295t, 319t, 344b, 346t, 346c, 386b*; B. Henry *364t*; D.R. Herr *95b*; J. Hoffman *320c*; Stephen Holt *57b, 278b*; M.P. Kahl *66t, 69b, 71*; A.J. Knystautas *300c*; H.C. Kyllingstad *139t*; P. La Tourrette *319b*; S.J. Lang *356b*; J. Larsen *119t*; A. Morris *253b, 351b, 362c*; R. Mellon *151t*; T. Parker *203b*; B. Schorre *342c, 349t, 349c, 350t, 350c*; William Peckover *103b, 205t, 221t, 222b, 264t, 302c, 318b, 325t*; B. Randall *389b*; M.J. Rauzon *59b*; T.J. Ulrich *127t*; *344c*; D. Wechsler *210c, 222c,223b, 232t, 236b, 238c, 245t, 249b, 251c, 254b, 262b, 273b, 274c, 290t, 296b, 304t, 305c, 314b*; J.R. Woodward *291b, 322c, 335b*; D. & M. Zimmerman *55b, 158t, 308t, 389t*. **Alan Weaving** *100, 225b*. **Alan Wilson** *104b, 230b*.